AF883586

CBSE CLASS 11

CHAPTER-WISE

QUESTION BANK

MATHEMATICS

NEW SYLLABUS & COMPETENCY PATTERN

2022-23

आत्मनिर्भर भारत

COMPLETE SELF-PREP BOOK

AGRAWAL GROUP OF PUBLICATIONS

EduCart | Agrawal Publications | AGRAWAL EXAMCART

Book Name | Educart CBSE Class 11 Math Question Bank 2022 - 2023

Editor Name | Sonali Khosla

Edition | Latest

Published by | Agrawal Group Of Publications (AGP)

ADDRESS (Head office) | 28/115 Jyoti Block, Sanjay Place, Agra, U.P. 282002

CONTACT | quickreply@agpgroup.in
We reply super fast

BUY BOOK | www.educart.co
Cash on delivery available

WHATSAPP (Head office) | 8937099777

PRINTED BY | Schoolcart

DESKTOP PUBLISHING | Agrawal Group Of Publications (AGP)

ISBN | 978-93-5561-164-2

WHY
THIS BOOK
is a must for Chapter-wise study?

Class 11
(2022-23)

NEW PAPER PATTERN

COMPETENCY BASED LEARNING

Conceptual Learning

Full Practice of NCERT & CBSE

TOPIC NOTES

- ✔ Simplified NCERT Chapters
- ✔ Pictorial Concepts
- ✔ Case-based Examples
- ✔ Important NCERT Solutions

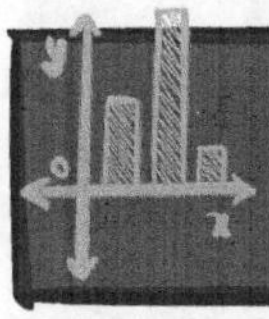

QUESTIONS

- ✔ New Pattern Questions
- ✔ Detailed Explanations
- ✔ Caution Points
- ✔ All CBSE Sources Covered*

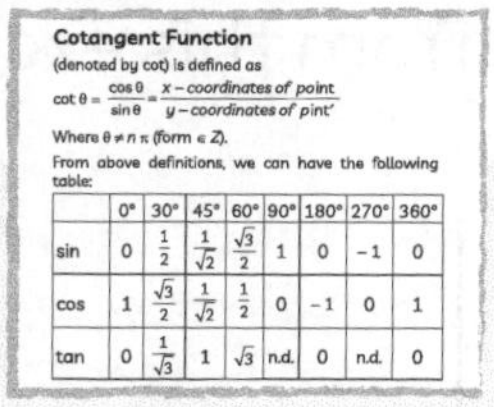
Cotangent Function

(denoted by cot) is defined as

$\cot\theta = \frac{\cos\theta}{\sin\theta} = \frac{x\text{-coordinates of point}}{y\text{-coordinates of pint}}$

Where $\theta \neq n\pi$ (form $\in Z$).

From above definitions, we can have the following table:

	0°	30°	45°	60°	90°	180°	270°	360°
sin	0	$\frac{1}{2}$	$\frac{1}{\sqrt{2}}$	$\frac{\sqrt{3}}{2}$	1	0	−1	0
cos	1	$\frac{\sqrt{3}}{2}$	$\frac{1}{\sqrt{2}}$	$\frac{1}{2}$	0	−1	0	1
tan	0	$\frac{1}{\sqrt{3}}$	1	$\sqrt{3}$	n.d.	0	n.d.	0

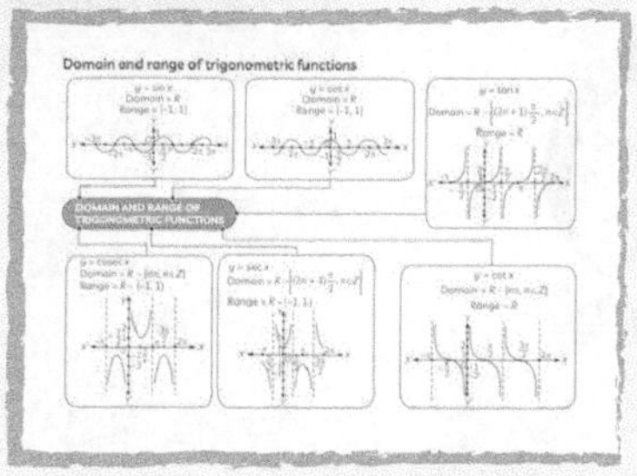

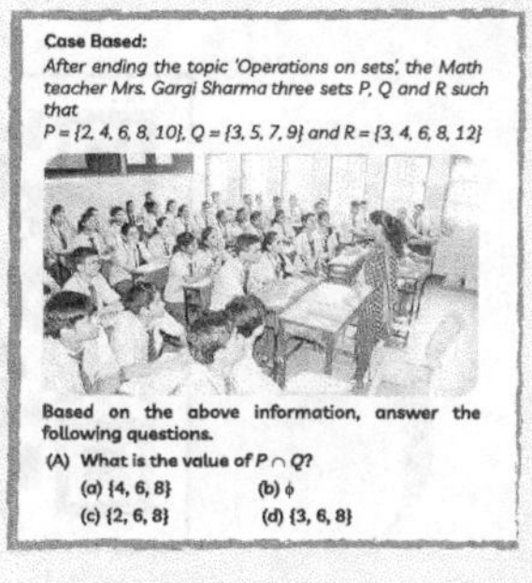
Case Based:

After ending the topic 'Operations on sets', the Math teacher Mrs. Gargi Sharma three sets P, Q and R such that

$P = \{2, 4, 6, 8, 10\}$, $Q = \{3, 5, 7, 9\}$ and $R = \{3, 4, 6, 8, 12\}$

Based on the above information, answer the following questions.

(A) What is the value of $P \cap Q$?

(a) {4, 6, 8} (b) ϕ
(c) {2, 6, 8} (d) {3, 6, 8}

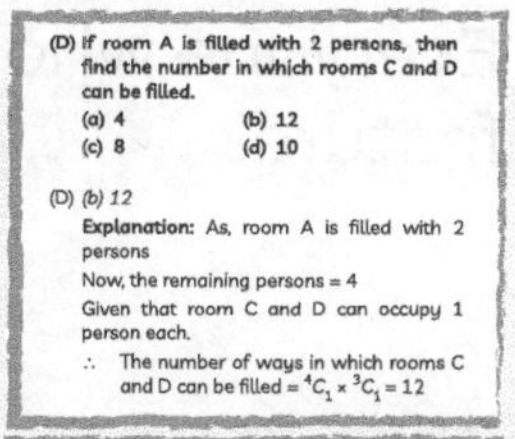
(D) If room A is filled with 2 persons, then find the number in which rooms C and D can be filled.

(a) 4 (b) 12
(c) 8 (d) 10

(D) (b) 12

Explanation: As, room A is filled with 2 persons

Now, the remaining persons = 4

Given that room C and D can occupy 1 person each.

∴ The number of ways in which rooms C and D can be filled = ${}^4C_1 \times {}^3C_1 = 12$

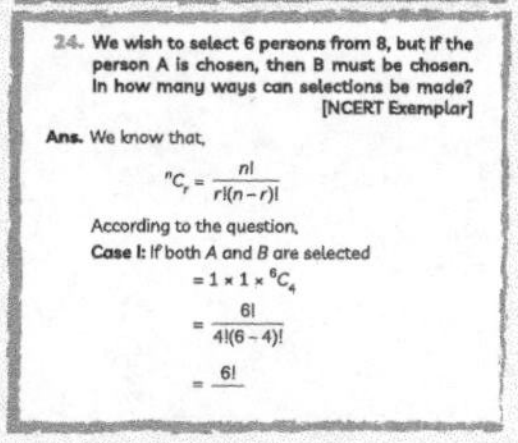
24. We wish to select 6 persons from 8, but if the person A is chosen, then B must be chosen. In how many ways can selections be made? [NCERT Exemplar]

Ans. We know that,

${}^nC_r = \frac{n!}{r!(n-r)!}$

According to the question,

Case I: If both A and B are selected

$= 1 \times 1 \times {}^6C_4$

$= \frac{6!}{4!(6-4)!}$

$= \frac{6!}{...}$

*NCERT Exemplar, DIKSHA

INDEX

CHAPTER-WISE

TOPIC NOTES

FOR BEST LEARNING OUTCOMES

Pictorial Concepts

Diagrams and visual elements are used to explain NCERT concepts wherever possible.

Diagrammatic Representation of Cartesian Product of two Sets

To represent $A \times B$ by an arrow diagram, we first draw Venn diagrams representing sets A and B one opposite to the other as shown in given figure. Now, we draw line segments starting from each element of set A and terminating with each element of set B.

If $A = \{1, 3, 5\}$ and $B = \{a, b\}$, then the following figure gives the arrow diagram of $A \times B$.

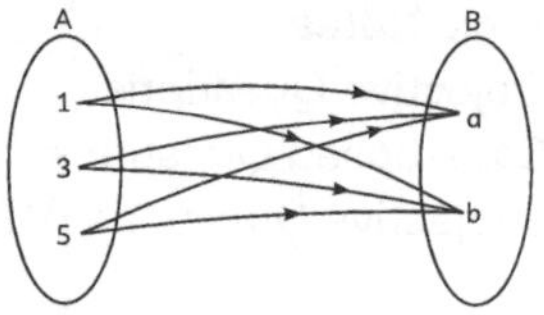

Illustrations:

(A) The set Q of rational numbers is a subset of the set R of real numbers, and we write $Q \subset R$.

(B) If A is the set of all divisors of 56 and B the set of all prime divisors of 56, then B is a subset of A and we write $B \subset A$.

(C) Let $A = \{1, 3, 5\}$ and $B = \{x: x \text{ is an odd natural number less than } 6\}$. Then $A \subset B$ and $B \subset A$ and hence $A = B$.

Illustrations

Topics in several chapters are explained in a simple language to understand NCERT line-by-line.

Important + Caution Points

Critical examinable points are added in between the theory to cover useful concepts for tricky questions.
Caution Points will help you avoid making silly mistakes and lose marks.

Important

➡ *The notation $n!$ represent the product of first n natural numbers.*

Caution

➡ *Students should know that factorial of fractions or negative integers are not defined. $n!$ is defined only for whole, i.e., for non-negative integers.*

NEW PATTERN

QUESTIONS

COMPLETELY REFRESHED, FROM ALL CBSE SOURCES

New Pattern Questions

Our Subject Experts have prepared new types of Competency-based questions on the latest CBSE pattern.

Read the following passages questions that follow:

17. *Function as a Relation from a non-empty set A to a non-empty set B is said to be a function if every element of set A has one and only one function from a set A to a set B, then we write $f: A \to B$ and it is read as f is a function from A to B or f maps A to B.*

(A) The given curve is *a*:

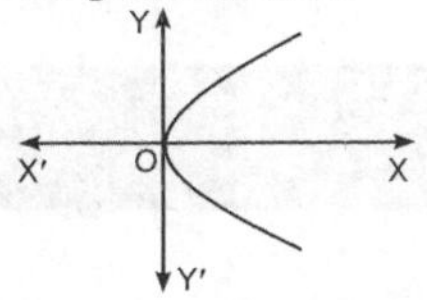

(a) Function **(c) Can't say anything**
(b) Relation **(d) Data not suffcient**

Example 1: If ${}^nC_8 = {}^nC_6$, find ${}^nC_2$:

Ans. If ${}^nC_x = {}^nC_y$ and $x + y = n$.

$\therefore \quad {}^nC_8 = {}^nC_6$

$\Rightarrow \quad n = (8 + 6) = 14$

Now, ${}^nC_2 = {}^{14}C_2$

$= \frac{14}{2} \times \frac{13}{1} \times {}^{12}C_0$

$\left[\because {}^nC_r = \frac{n}{r} \cdot {}^{n-1}C_{r-1}\right]$

$= \frac{14}{2} \times \frac{13}{1} \times 1 = 91.$

Examples for Practice

For self assessment, lots of unsolved questions are given in between solved questions.

Detailed Explanations

NCERT excerpts also added for detailed information regarding the solutions of the questions.

7. Find value of *x* such that $\frac{{}^xP_4}{{}^{x-1}P_4} = \frac{5}{3}, x > 4$.

(a) 11 **(b) 15**
(c) 12 **(d) 10**

Ans. *(d) 10*

Explanation: Given that $\frac{{}^xP_4}{{}^{x-1}P_4} = \frac{5}{3}$

$3x(x-1)(x-2)(x-3) = 5(x-1)(x-2)(x-3)(x-4)$

$3x = 5(x-4)$ as $((x-1)(x-2)(x-3) \neq 0, x > 4)$

$x = 10$

Hence, option (d) is correct.

Syllabus

Units	Unit Name	Marks
I	Sets and Functions	23
II	Algebra	25
III	Coordinate Geometry	12
IV	Calculus	08
V	Statistics and Probability	12
	INTERNAL ASSESSMENT Periodic Test (10) + Activities (10)	**20**
	Total	**80 + 20**

UNIT I: SETS AND FUNCTIONS

Chapter 1: Sets

Sets and their representations, Empty set, Finite and Infinite sets, Equal sets, Subsets,. Subsets of a set of real numbers, especially intervals (with notations). Power set. Universal set. Venn diagrams. Union and Intersection of sets. Difference of sets. Complement of a set. Properties of Complement.

Chapter 2: Relations & Functions

Ordered pairs. Cartesian product of sets. Number of elements in the Cartesian product of two finite sets. Cartesian product of the set of reals with itself (upto R x R x R). Definition of relation, pictorial diagrams, domain, co-domain and range of a relation. Function as a special type of relation.

Pictorial representation of a function, domain, co-domain and range of a function. Real valued functions, domain and range of these functions, constant, identity, polynomial, rational, modulus, signum, exponential, logarithmic and greatest integer functions, with their graphs. Sum, difference, product and quotients of functions.

Chapter 3: Trigonometric Functions

Positive and negative angles. Measuring angles in radians and in degrees and conversion from one measure to another. Definition of trigonometric functions with the help of unit

Text in red are topics/ chapters deleted from 2022-23 syllabus

Text in green are topics/ chapters added in 2022-23 syllabus

circle. Truth of the identity sin2x + cos2x = 1, for all x.

Signs of trigonometric functions. Domain and range of trigonometric functions and their graphs. Expressing sin (x±y) and cos (x±y) in terms of sinx, siny, cosx & cosy and their simple applications. Deducing identities like the following:

$\tan(x \pm y) = \tan x \pm \tan y / (1 \pm \tan x \tan y)$, $\cot(x \pm y) = \cot x \cot y \pm 1 / (\cot y \pm \cot x)$

$\sin\alpha \pm \sin\beta = 2\sin \frac{1}{2} (\alpha \pm \beta) \cos \frac{1}{2} (\alpha \pm \beta)$

$\cos\alpha + \cos\beta = 2\cos \frac{1}{2} (\alpha + \beta) \cos \frac{1}{2} (\alpha - \beta)$

$\cos\alpha - \cos\beta = -2\sin \frac{1}{2} (\alpha + \beta) \sin \frac{1}{2} (\alpha - \beta)$

Identities related to sin2x, cos2x, tan2x, sin3x, cos3x and tan3x.

General solution of trigonometric equations of the type sin y = sin a, cos y = cos a and tan y = tan a.

UNIT II: ALGEBRA

Chapter 4: Principle of Mathematical Induction (Deleted)

Chapter 5: Complex Numbers and Quadratic Equations

Need for complex numbers, especially $\sqrt{-1}$, to be motivated by inability to solve some of the quadratic equations. Algebraic properties of complex numbers. Argand plane and polar representation of complex numbers.Statement of Fundamental Theorem of Algebra, solution of quadratic equations (with real coefficients) in the complex number system. Square root of a complex number.

Chapter 6: Linear Inequalities

Linear inequalities. Algebraic solutions of linear inequalities in one variable and their representation on the number line. Graphical solution of linear inequalities in two variables. Graphical method of finding a solution of a system of linear inequalities in two variables.

Chapter 7: Permutations and Combinations

Fundamental principle of counting. Factorial *n*. (n!) Permutations and combinations, derivation of Formulae for ^nP_r and ^nC_r and their connections, simple applications.

Chapter 8: Binomial Theorem

Historical perspective, statement and proof of the binomial theorem for positive integral indices. Pascal's triangle, General and middle term in binomial expansion, simple applications.

Chapter 9: Sequence and Series

Sequence and Series. Arithmetic Progression (A.P.). Arithmetic Mean (A.M.) Geometric Progression (G.P.), general term of a G.P., sum of n terms of a G.P., infinite G.P. and its sum, geometric mean (G.M.), relation between A.M. and G.M. Formulae for the following special sums.

$\sum_{k=1}^{n} k$, $\sum_{k=1}^{n} k^2$ and $\sum_{k=1}^{n} k^3$

UNIT III: COORDINATE GEOMETRY

Chapter 10: Straight Lines

Brief recall of two dimensional geometry from earlier classes. Shifting of origin. Slope of a line and angle between two lines. Various forms of equations of a line: parallel to axis, point-slope form, slope-intercept form, two-point form, intercept form and normal form. General equation of a line. Equation of family of lines passing through the point of intersection of two lines. Distance of a point from a line.

Chapter 11: Conic Sections

Sections of a cone: circles, ellipse, parabola, hyperbola, a point, a straight line and a pair of intersecting lines as a degenerate case of a conic section. Standard equations and simple properties of parabola, ellipse and hyperbola. Standard equation of a circle.

Chapter 12: Introduction to Three-dimensional Geometry

Coordinate axes and coordinate planes in three dimensions. Coordinates of a point. Distance between two points and section formula.

UNIT IV: CALCULUS

Chapter 13: Limits and Derivatives

Derivative introduced as rate of change both as that of distance function and geometrically. Intuitive idea of limit. Limits of polynomials and rational functions trigonometric, exponential and logarithmic functions. Definition of derivative, relate it to scope of tangent of the curve, derivative of sum, difference, product and quotient of functions. Derivatives of polynomial and trigonometric functions.

Chapter 14: Mathematical Reasoning (Deleted)

UNIT VI: STATISTICS AND PROBABILITY

Chapter 15: Statistics

Measures of Dispersion: Range, Mean deviation, variance and standard deviation of ungrouped/ grouped data.

Chapter 16: Probability

Random experiments; outcomes, sample spaces (set representation). Events; occurrence of events, 'not', 'and' and 'or' events, exhaustive events, mutually exclusive events, Axiomatic (set theoretic) probability, connections with other theories of earlier classes. Probability of an event, probability of 'not', 'and' and 'or' events.

1

Sets

Parliament house is example of sets. Here the people belonging to various departments have to sit separately from other departments. For example, the legal department and finance department don't sit intermixed with each other.

Topic Notes

- *Sets and their Representation*

SETS AND THEIR REPRESENTATION

TOPIC 1

REPRESENTATION OF SETS

Sets and Their Representation

In our day-to-day life, we come across collections of objects of a particular type, such as days in a week, months in a year, playing cards in a pack, vowels in the English alphabet, etc. In mathematics also, we come across collections, for example, collections of natural numbers, prime numbers, etc.

There are a few collections given below:

A collection of whole numbers less than 10.

A collection of all river in Uttar Pradesh.

A collection of prime factors of 64.

A collection of prime factors of 64.

A collection of prime ministers of India independence.

We can see these are collections of well-defined objects in the sense that we can definitely decide whether a given particular object belongs to a given collection or not. However, it may not always be the case. For instance, the collection of the five most renowned mathematicians of the world, is not well-defined, because the criterion for determining a mathematician as most renowned may vary from person to person. Thus, it is not a well-defined collection, and hence not a set, as defined in mathematics. Any type of object can be collected into a set, but the set theory is applied more often to objects that are relevant to Mathematics.

Hence, we can say that **a set is a well-defined collection of objects.**

Any type of object can be collected into a set, but the set theory is applied more often to objects that are relevant to Mathematics.

Set theory plays a foundation role in modern mathematics. **Georg Cantor,** a German mathematician, is the founder of set theory.

Illustration: The collection of the first five prime natural numbers is a set containing the elements 2, 3, 5, 7, 11.

Illustration: The solution of the equation: $x^2 - 5x + 6 = 0$, *viz*, 2 and 3 is a set of solutions.

Illustration: The collection of all states including all union territories in the Indian Union is a set.

Illustration: The collection of cricketers in the world who were out for 99 runs in a test match is a set.

We give below a few more examples of sets used particularly in mathematics, viz.

N : Set of all-natural number

Z : Set of all integers

Z^+ : Set of all positive integers

Q : Set of all rational numbers

Q^+ : Set of all the positive rational numbers

R^+: Set of all positive real numbers

C: Set of all complex numbers.

The following points may be noted:

(i) Objects, elements and members of a set are synonymous terms.

(ii) Sets are usually denoted by capital letters A, B, C, X, Y, Z, etc.

(iii) The elements of a set are represented by small letters *a, b, c, x, y, z*, etc.

(iv) If a is an element of set A. we say that "a belongs to A" and we write '$a \in A$'. Here '$\in$' (Epsilon) is a Greek symbol that is used to denote the phrase 'belongs to'. If *b* is not an element of set A. We say that '*b* does not belong to A' and we write '$b \notin A$'.

Caution

➥ *In sets, $\in$ means 'belongs to' and '$\notin$' means "does not belong to".*

Methods of Representation of Sets

A set can be represented in two ways:

Roster Form or Tabular Form

In roster or tabular form all the elements of a set are listed, separated by commas and are enclosed within curly braces { }.

Illustration: Let A be the set of all letters in the word 'MATH'. Then, set A can be written in roster form as

$$A = \{M, A, T, H, S\}.$$

Illustration: Let *A* be the set of all vowels in the English alphabet, then $A = \{a, e, i, o, u\}$

Important

➥ *In roster form, the order in which the elements are listed is immaterial.*

Set-Builder Form

In set-builder form, all the elements of a set possess a single common property that is not possessed by any element outside the set. In this form the descriptions of the elements of the set by using a symbol *x* which is followed by a colon ':' or a vertical bar '|' (read as such that) and then enclosing the whole description within braces { }.

Illustration: If B is the set of all even integers then B can be written in set-builder form as

$$B = \{x : x = 2x, x \in Z\}$$

Or

$$B = \{x \mid x = 2x, x \in Z\}$$

Illustration: Let A be a set of squares of natural numbers is written is set-builder form as

$A = \{x: x \text{ is the square of natural number}\}$

Or $A = \{x: x = n^2, \text{ where } n \in N\}$

Example 1.1: Write the following sets in roster form:

(A) $A = \{x : x$ is an integer and $-3 \leq x \leq 7\}$.

(B) $B = \{x : x$ is a natural number less than 6$\}$.

(C) $C = \{x : x$ is a two-digit natural number such that the sum of its digits is 8$\}$.

(D) $D = \{x : x$ is a prime number which is a divisor of 60$\}$.

(E) E = The set of all letters in the word TRIGONOMETRY.

(F) F = The set of all letters in the word BETTER. **[NCERT]**

Ans. (A) $A = \{x : x$ is an integer and $-3 \leq x < 7\}$.

The elements of set A are $-3, -2, -1, 0, 1, 2, 3, 4, 5$ and 6 only.

Therefore, the roster form of set

$A = \{-3, -2, -1, 0, 1, 2, 3, 4, 5, 6\}$

(B) $A = \{x : x$ is a natural number less than 6$\}$.

The elements of set B are 1, 2, 3, 4 and 5 only.

Therefore, the roster form of set

$B = \{1, 2, 3, 4, 5\}$

(C) $C = \{x : x$ is a two-digit natural number such that the sum of its digits is 8$\}$.

The elements of set C are 17, 26, 35, 44, 53, 62 and 71 only.

Therefore, the roster form of set

$C = \{17, 26, 35, 44, 53, 62, 71\}$

(D) $D = \{x : x$ is a prime number which is divisor of 60$\}$.

Prime number which are divisor of 60 are:

$60 \div 2 = 30$, $60 \div 3 = 20$, and $60 \div 5 = 12$

Therefore, the elements of the set D are 2, 3, and 5.

Hence, the roster form of set $D = \{2, 3, 5\}$

(E) E = The set of all letters in the word TRIGONOMETRY

There are 12 letters in the word TRIGONOMETRY.

Out of which letters T, R, and O are repeated.

Therefore, the roster form of set

$E = \{T, R, I, G, O, N, M, E, Y\}$

(F) F = The set of all letters in the word BETTER.

There are 6 letters in the word BETTER, out of which letters E and T are repeated.

Therefore, the roster form of set $F = \{B, E, T, R\}$

Example 1.2: Write the following sets in the set-builder form:

(A) (3, 6, 9, 12} **(B) {2, 4, 8, 16, 32}**

(C) {5, 25, 125, 625} **(D) {2, 4, 6, ...}**

(E) {1, 4, 9, ... , 100} **[NCERT]**

Ans. (A) Let $A = \{3, 6, 9, 12\}$

All elements of the set A are natural numbers that are multiples of 3 having value less than or equal to 12.

$\therefore$ The set-builder form of set $A = \{x : x = 3n, n \in N \text{ and } 1 \leq n \leq 4\}$.

(B) Let $B = \{2, 4, 8, 16, 32\}$

All elements of the set B are natural numbers that are powers of 2.

$\therefore$ The set-builder form of set $B = \{x : x = 2^n, n \in N \text{ and } 1 \leq n \leq 5\}$.

(C) Let $C = \{5, 25, 125, 625\}$

All the elements of the set C are natural numbers that are powers of 5.

$\therefore$ The set-builder form of set $C = \{x : x = 5^n, n \in N \text{ and } 1 \leq n \leq 4\}$.

(D) Let $D = \{2, 4, 6, ...\}$

All the elements of the set D are even natural numbers.

$\therefore$ The set-builder form of set $D = \{x : x$ is an even natural number$\}$.

(E) Let $E = \{1, 4, 9, ... , 100\}$

All the elements of the set E are perfect square numbers.

$\therefore$ The set-builder form of set $E = \{x: x = n^2 \text{ and } 1 \leq n \leq 10\}$.

Example 1.3: Let A {1, 2, 3, 4, 5, 6}. Insert the appropriate symbol $\in$ or $\notin$ in the blank spaces:

(A) 5 ... A **(B) 8 ... A**

(C) 0 ... A **(D) 4 ... A**

(E) 2 ... A **(F) 10 ... A**

Ans. Given $A = \{1, 2, 3, 4, 5, 6\}$, Therefore,

(A) Here, 5 is in set A. Therefore, $5 \in A$

(B) Since, 8 is not in set A. Therefore, $8 \notin A$

(C) Since, 0 is not in set A Therefore, $0 \notin A$

(D) Since, 4 is in set A. Therefore, $4 \in A$

(E) Since, 2 is in set A. Therefore, $2 \in A$

(F) Since, 10 is not in set A. Therefore, $10 \notin A$

TOPIC 2

TYPES OF SETS

Different types of sets are classified according to the number of elements they have. Let's now learn the types of sets in this article.

Empty Set/Null Set/Void Set

A set that does not contain any element is called the empty set or the null set or the void set. It is denoted by the symbol ϕ (phi) or { }.

E.g, $A = \{x: x$ is a natural number less than 1}, there is no natural possibility that it is less than 1. Hence, Set A is an empty or null set, i.e., $A = \phi$ or { }.

Example 1.4. Which of the following are examples of the null set?

(A) Set of odd natural numbers divisible by 2

(B) Set of even prime numbers

(C) $\{x : x$ is a natural numbers, $x < 5$ and $x > 7\}$

(D) $\{y : y$ is a point common to any two parallel lines} [NCERT]

Ans. (A) A set of odd natural numbers divisible by 2 is a null set because no odd number is divisible by 2.

(B) Let A be a set of even prime numbers.

Since, 2 is only even prime number, i.e., $A = \{2\}$.Hence, it is not an empty or null set.

(C) Let $A = \{x : x$ is a natural number, $x < 5$ and $x > 7\}$.

There is no natural number possible which is less than 5 and greater than 7. Hence, A is a null set, i.e., $A = \{ \}$.

(D) $\{y : y$ is a point common to any two parallel lines} is a null set because parallel lines do not intersect. Hence, they have no common point.

Singleton Set

A set that contains only one element is called a singleton set.

Illustration : Let $A = \{x : x + 5 = 0, x \in Z\}$ is a singleton set as set A contains only one integer –5.

Caution

➥ *{0} is a singleton set not an empty set.*

Finite and Infinite Set

A set which is empty or consists of a definite number of elements, is called a finite set otherwise is called an infinite set.

Example 1.5. State which of the following sets are finite or infinite:

(A) $\{x : x \in N$ and $(x - 1) (x - 2) = 0\}$

(B) $\{x : x \in N$ and $2x - 1 = 0\}$

(C) $\{x: x \in N$ and x is prime}

(D) $\{x : x$ $N \in$ and x is odd}

Ans. (A) Given set = {1, 2}. Hence, it is finite.

(B) Given set = $\{\phi\}$. Hence, it is finite.

(C) The given set is the set of all prime numbers and since the set of prime numbers is infinite. Hence, the given set is infinite.

(D) Since there are infinite numbers of odd numbers, hence, the given set is infinite.

Equal Sets

Two sets A and B are said to be equal sets if they have the **same elements**, and we write $A = B$, otherwise two sets are said to be unequal sets, i.e., $A \neq B$.

Equivalent Set

Two finite sets A and B are said to be equivalent sets, if they have the **same number of elements**, *i.e.*, $n(A) = n(B)$ we can write $A \equiv B$ or $A \leftrightarrow B$.

Illustration : If $A = \{1, 2, 3, 4, 5\}$ and $B = \{a, e, i, o, u\}$

Since, $n(A) = n(B) = 5$, so A and B are equivalent sets.

Important

➥ *The number of distinct elements in a finite set is called the cardinal number of the set and it is denoted by n (A). E.g., if A = {1, 2, 3, 4, 5}, then n (A) = 5.*

Example 1.6: In the following, state whether $A = B$ or not:

(A) $A = \{2, 4, 6, 8, 10\}$, $B = \{x : x$ is positive even integer and $x \leq 10\}$

(B) $A = \{x : x$ is a multiple of 10};

$B = \{10, 15, 20, 25, 30, \ldots\}$

Ans. (A) $A = \{2, 4, 6, 8, 10\}$

$B = \{x : x$ is a positive even integer and $x \leq 10\}$.

Positive even integers less than equal to 10 = 2, 4, 6, 8, 10.

Hence, $B = \{2, 4, 6, 8, 10\}$

Elements of set A = 2, 4, 6, 8, 10

Elements of set B = 2, 4, 6, 8, 10

Since, all elements of set A are B are the same. Hence, $A = B$

(B) $B = \{10, 15, 20, 25, 30 \ldots\}$

And $A = \{x : x$ is a multiple of 10}.

Multiples of 10 are = 10, 20, 30, 40 50, . . .

Therefore, $A = \{10, 20, 30, 40, 50, \ldots\}$

Here, 15 is in set B but not in set A, i.e., $15 \in B$ but $15 \notin A$.

Hence, $\therefore A \neq B$

Example 1.7: From the sets given below, select equal sets:

$A = \{2, 4, 8, 12\}$, $B = \{1, 2, 3, 4,\}$, $C = \{4, 8, 12, 14\}$, $D = \{3, 1, 4, 2\}$, $E = \{-1, 1\}$, $F = \{0, a\}$, $G = \{1, -1\}$, $H = \{0, 1\}$. **[NCERT]**

Ans. $A = \{2, 4, 8, 12\}, n(A) = 4$

$B = \{1, 2, 3, 4\}, n(B) = 4$

$C = \{4, 8, 12, 14\}, n(C) = 4$

$D = \{3, 1, 4, 2\}, n(D) = 4$

$E = \{-1, 1\}, n(E) = 2$

$F = \{0, a\}, n(F) = 2$

$G = \{1, -1\}, n(G) = 2$

$H = \{0, 1\}, n(H) = 2$

Number of elements in A, B, C, D are the same, i.e., all have 4 elements. So they are comparable.

Now, we see that B and D have the same elements.

So, B and D are equal sets.

Similarly, E, F, G, H are comparable as they all have the same number of elements i.e. 2.

Clearly, E and G have the same elements.

So, E and G are equal sets.

TOPIC 3

SUBSET, POWER SET AND UNIVERSAL SET

Subset

Let A and B two sets. If every element of set A is an element of set B, then we can say that 'A is called a subset of B' or 'A is contained in B', i.e., A set A is said to be a subset of a set B if every element of A is also an element of B and we denote it by writing $A \subseteq B$.

The symbol '$\subseteq$' is used to denote the phrase 'is a subset of' or 'it is contained in'.

In notational form, we can write the following as:

$A \subseteq B$ if $a \in A \Rightarrow a \in B$.

The symbol '$\Rightarrow$' is used to denote the word 'implies that'.

So we read the above statement as "A is a subset of B, if a belongs to A implies that a also belongs to B".

If there exists at least one element of A which is not an element of B, then we say that, 'A is not a subset of B' or 'A is not contained in B' and we denote it by writing $A \not\subset B$.

We may note that for A to be a subset of B all that is needed is that every element of A is also in B. It is possible that every element of B may or may not be in A. If it so happens that every element of B is also in A, then we shall also have $B \subseteq A$. In this case, A and B are the same sets so that we have $A \subset B$ and $B \subset A \Leftrightarrow A = B$, where "$\Leftrightarrow$" is a symbol for two way implications, and is usually read as if and only if (briefly written as "iff").

Illustrations:

(A) The set Q of rational numbers is a subset of the set R of real numbers, and we write $Q \subset R$.

(B) If A is the set of all divisors of 56 and B the set of all prime divisors of 56, then B is a subset of A and we write $B \subset A$.

(C) Let $A = \{1, 3, 5\}$ and $B = \{x: x$ is an odd natural number less than 6$\}$. Then $A \subset B$ and $B \subset A$ and hence $A = B$.

Let A and B be two sets. If $A \subseteq B$ and $A \neq B$, then A, is called a proper subset of B and B is called a superset of A. For example, $A = \{1, 2, 3\}$ is a proper subset of $B = \{1, 2, 3, 4\}$. It is denoted by $A \subset B$.

A subset of a set A can be equal to set A but a proper subset of a set A can never be equal to set A. A proper subset of a set A is a subset of A that cannot be equal to A. In other words, if B is a proper subset of A, then all elements of B are in A but A contains at least one element that is not in B.

Important

- *Every set is a subset of itself, i.e., $A \subset A$.*
- *ϕ is a subset of every set.*
- *The total number of subsets of a set is 2^n, where n is the number of elements contained in a set.*

  E.g. Let $A = \{a, b, c\}$, $n(A) = 3$, then total number of subsets of set $A = 2^3 = 8$. The subsets as follows:

  $\phi, \{a\}, \{b\}, \{c\}, \{a, b\}, \{b, c\}, \{a, c\}, \{a, b, c\}$
- *The number of proper subsets of A is one less than the number of elements in the power the set i.e $2^n - 1$ set itself will not be counted in the proper subset.*

Example. 1.8: Let $A = \{1, 2, \{3, 4,\}, 5\}$. Which of the following statements are incorrect and why?

(A) $\{3, 4\} \subset A$	**(B)** $\{\{3, 4\}\} \subset A$
(C) $1 \subset A$	**(D)** $\{1, 2, 5\} \subset A$
(E) $\{1, 2, 3\} \subset A$	**(F)** $\Phi \in A$
(G) $\Phi \subset A$	**(H)** $\{\Phi\} \subset A$ **[NCERT]**

Ans. Given, set $A = \{1, 2, \{3, 4\}, 5\}$

(A) The statement $\{3, 4\} \subset A$ is incorrect because $3 \in \{3, 4\}$; however, $3 \notin A$.

(B) The statement $\{\{3, 4\}\} \subset A$ is correct because $\{3, 4\} \in \{\{3, 4\}\}$ and $\{3, 4\} \in A$.

(C) The statement $1 \subset A$ is incorrect because an element of a set can never be a subset of itself.

(D) The statement $\{1, 2, 5\} \subset A$ is correct because each element of $\{1, 2, 5\}$ is also an element of A.

(E) The statement $\{1, 2, 3\} \subset A$ is incorrect because $3 \in \{1, 2, 3\}$; however, $3 \notin A$.

(F) The statement $\Phi \in A$ is incorrect because Φ is not an element of A.

(G) The statement $\Phi \subset A$ is correct because Φ is a subset of every set.

(H) The statement $\{\Phi\} \subset A$ is incorrect because $\Phi \in \{\Phi\}$; however, $\Phi \in A$

Example 1.9: Write down all the subsets of the following sets:

(A) $\{a\}$ **(B) $\{1, 2, 3\}$**

(C) $\{-1, 0, 1\}$ **(D) Φ**

Ans. (A) Subsets of $\{a\}$ are Φ, $\{a\}$

(B) Subsets of $\{1, 2, 3\}$ are $\Phi, \{1\}, \{2\}, \{3\}, \{1,2\}, \{2, 3\}, \{3,1\}, \{1, 2, 3\}$.

(C) Subsets of $\{-1, 0, 1\}$ are Φ, $\{-1\}$, $\{0\}$, $\{1\}$, $\{-1, 0\}$, $\{0,1\}$, $\{-1,1\}$, $\{-1, 0, 1\}$.

(D) Since, Φ is a subset of every set, hence, the subset of Φ is Φ itself.

Subsets of Set of Real Numbers

Some important subsets of real numbers are as under:

(i) The set of natural numbers $N = \{1, 2, 3,...\}$.

(ii) The set of integers $Z - \{\ldots -3, -2, -1, 0, 1, 2,. 3,...\}$.

(iii) The set of a rational number

$$Q = \left\{x : x = \frac{p}{q}, \text{where } p, q \in Z \text{ and } q \neq 0\right\}$$

(iv) The set of irrational numbers $T = \{x : x \in R \text{ and } x \notin Q\}$, i.e., all real numbers that are not rationals.

Thus, the obvious relations among these subsets are:

$N \subseteq Z \subseteq Q \subseteq R$,

Intervals as Subsets of R

Let us now discuss the various types of intervals which are subsets of the set R of all real numbers. There are four types of intervals:

Open Interval

Let $a, b \in R$ such that $a < b$. Then, the set of all real numbers between a and b excluding both a and b is called an open interval from a to b. It is denoted by} (a, b).

$$(a, b) = [x : x \in R \text{ and } a < x < b\}.$$

Closed Interval

Let $a, b \in R$ such that $a < b$. Then, the set of all real numbers between a and b including both a and b is called a closed interval from a to b. In other words, the interval which contains the end points is also called a closed interval. It is denoted by $[a, b]$.

$$[a, b] = [x : x \in R \text{ and } a \leq x \leq b\}.$$

Semi-Closed Interval

Let $a, b \in R$ such that $a < b$, then, the set of all real numbers between a and b, including a but excluding b, is called semi-closed interval (left closed-right open) from a to b. It is denoted by $[a, b)$.

$$[a, b) = \{x : x \in R \text{ and } a \leq x < b\}.$$

Semi-Open Interval

Let $a, b \in R$ such that $a < b$, then, the set of all real numbers between a and b, excluding a but including b, is called semi-open interval (left open-right closed) from a to b. It is denoted by $(a, b]$.

$$(a, b] = [x : x \in R \text{ and } a < x \leq b\}.$$

On a real number line, various types of intervals described above as subsets of R, are shown in the figure below.

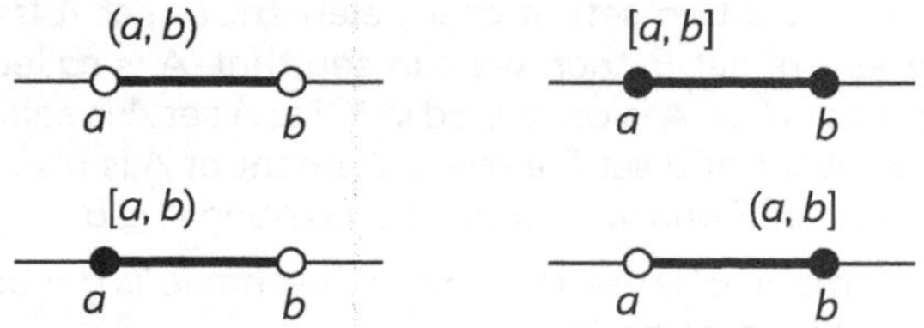

Important

- *The set $[0, \infty)$ defines the set of non-negative real numbers.*
- *The set $(-\infty, 0)$ defines the set of negative real numbers.*
- *The set $(-\infty, \infty)$ describes the set of real numbers.*

Example 1.10: Write the following as intervals:

(A) $\{x : x \in R, -4 < x \leq 6\}$

(B) $\{x : x \in R, -12 < x < -10\}$

(C) $\{x : x \in R, 0 \leq x < 7\}$

(D) $\{x : x \in R, 3 \leq x \leq 4\}$ **[NCERT]**

Ans. (A) $\{x : x \in R, -4 < x \leq 6\}$

This set excludes -4 and includes 6, so, this set can be written as a semi-open interval, as $(-4, 6]$.

Hence, $\{x: x \in R, -4 < x \leq 6\} = (-4, 6]$.

(B) $\{x : x \in R, -12 < x < -10\}$

This set excludes -12 and -10, so, this set can be written as an open interval, as $(-12, -10)$.

Hence, $\{x : x \in R, -12 < x < -10\} = (-12, -10)$.

(C) $\{x : x \in R, 0 \leq x < 7\}$.

This set includes 0 and excludes 7, so, this set can be written as a semi-closed interval, as $[0, 7)$.

Hence, $\{x: x \in R, 0 \leq x < 7\} = [0, 7)$.

(D) $\{x: x \in R, 3 \le x \le 4\}$

This set includes both 3 and 4, so, this set can be written as a closed interval, as [3, 4].

Hence, $\{x: x \in R, 3 \le x \le 4\} = [3, 4]$.

Example 1.11: Write the following intervals in set-builder form:

(A) (–3, 0) **(B) [6, 12]**

(C) (6, 12] **(D) [–23, 5)** **[NCERT]**

Ans. (A) (–3, 0)

Here, it shows an open interval that is both –3 and 2 are also excluded in the set. Hence,

$(-3, 0) = \{x : x \in R, -3 < x < 0\}$

(B) [6, 12]

Here, it shows a closed intervals that is both 6 and 12 are also included in the set. Hence,

$[6, 12] = \{12\} = \{x : x \in R, 6 \le x \le 12\}$

(C) (6, 12]

Here, it shows a semi-open intervals that is 6 excluded but 12 included in the set. Hence,

$(6, 12] = \{x : x \in R, 6 < x \le 12\}$

(D) [–23, 5)

Here, it shows a semi-closed interval that is –23 included but 5 excluded in the set. Hence,

$[-23, 5) = \{x : x \in R, -23 \le x < 5\}$

Universal Set

A set that contains elements of all sets under consideration is called a universal set. It is denoted by U. For example, for the set of all integers, the universal set can be the set of rational numbers or, for that matter, the set R of real numbers.

Illustration: Let $A = \{1, 2, 3, 4\}$, $B = \{2, 4, 6\}$, $C = \{1, 3, 5, 7\}$, the universal set for these set can be $U = \{1, 2, 3, 4, 5, 6, 7, 8, 9\}$

Example 1.12: Given the sets $A = \{1, 3, 5\}$ $B = \{2, 4, 6\}$ and $C = \{0, 2, 4, 6, 8\}$ which of the following may be considered as universal set (s) for all the three sets *A*, *B* and *C*.

(A) {0, 1, 2, 3, 4, 5, 6}

(B) ϕ

(C) {0, 1, 2, 3, 4, 5, 6, 7, 8, 9, 10}

(D) {1, 2, 3, 4, 5, 6, 7, 8}. **[NCERT]**

Ans. Given sets are $A = \{1, 3, 5\}$, $B = \{2, 4, 6\}$, and $C = \{0, 2, 4, 6, 8\}$

(A) {0, 1, 2, 3, 4, 5, 6}

Elements of *A*, *B* and *C* together = {1, 3, 5, 2, 4, 6, 0, 8}

The given set does not contain 8, so it cannot be a universal set for *A*, *B* and *C*.

(B) ϕ

Elements of *A*, *B* and *C* together = {1, 3, 5, 2, 4, 6, 0, 8}

Since, ϕ does not contain any element,so, it cannot be a universal set for *A*, *B* and *C*.

(C) {0, 1, 2, 3, 4, 5, 6, 7, 8, 9, 10}

Elements of A, B and C together = {1, 3, 5, 2, 4, 6, 0, 8}

Since, the given set contains all the elements of set *A*, *B* and *C*, so it is a universal set for *A*, *B* and *C*.

(D) {1, 2, 3, 4, 5, 6, 7, 8}

Elements of A, B and C together = {1, 3, 5, 2, 4, 6, 0, 8}

Since, the given set does not contain 0, so, it cannot be a universal set for *A*, *B* and *C*.

TOPIC 4

VENN DIAGRAM AND OPERATIONS ON SETS

Venn Diagram

Most of the relationships between sets can be represented by means of diagrams which are known as Venn diagrams. First of all a Swiss mathematician, Euler gave an idea to represent a set by the points in a closed curve. Later on, British mathematician John-Venn (1834- 1883) brought this idea to practice. That is why the diagrams drawn to represent sets are called Venn-Euler diagrams or simply Venn diagrams. These diagrams consist of rectangles and closed curves, usually circles. The universal set is represented usually by a rectangle and its subsets by circles. In Venn diagrams, the elements of the sets are written in their respective circles. Sometimes pictures are very helpful in our thinking.

In Venn diagrams, the universal set *U* is represented by points within a rectangle and its subsets are represented by points in closed curves (usually circles) within the rectangle and the elements of the sets are written in their respective circles. Also, the elements of a set are within the circle of the set and represented by a point.

Illustration: Let $U = \{1, 2, 3, ..., 10\}$ is an universal set of which $A = \{2, 4, 6, 8, 10\}$ is a subset, the its Venn diagram is shown follows:

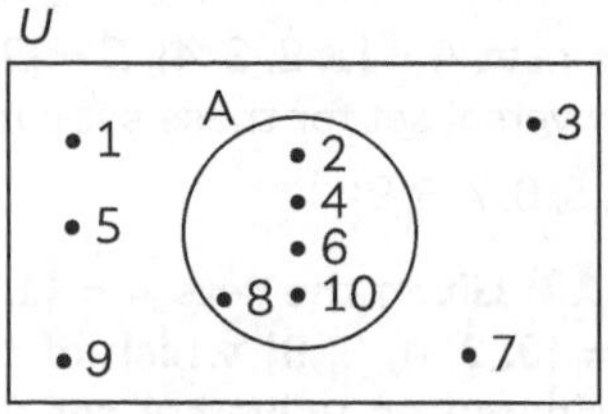

If $B = \{4, 6\}$ is another set such that $B \subset A$, then its Venn diagram can also be drawn as

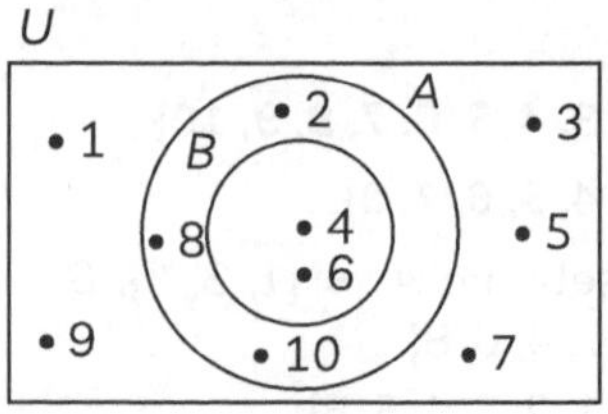

Operations on Sets

We are already familiar with the fundamental operations (addition, subtraction, multiplication, and division) on numbers. Each one of these operations was performed on a pair of numbers to get another number. Similarly, there are some operations that when performed on two sets give rise to another set. We will now define certain operations on sets and examine their properties. Henceforth, we will refer to all our sets as subsets of some universal set.

For example, suppose you live in a hostel. You, with your new roommate, decide to have a party in your hostel room, and you both invite your friends. At this party, two sets are being combined, though it might turn out that there are some friends that were in both sets.

Union of Sets

Let A and B be any two sets. Then, the set which consists of all the elements of A and all the elements of B, the common elements being taken only once. is known as union of A and B. The symbol '$\cup$' is used to denote the union.

Symbolically, we write the union of A and B as $\boldsymbol{A \cup B}$ and reads as 'A union B', also, we can write $A \cup B$ as $\{x : x \in A \text{ or } x \in B\}$

The union of two sets can be represented by a Venn diagram as

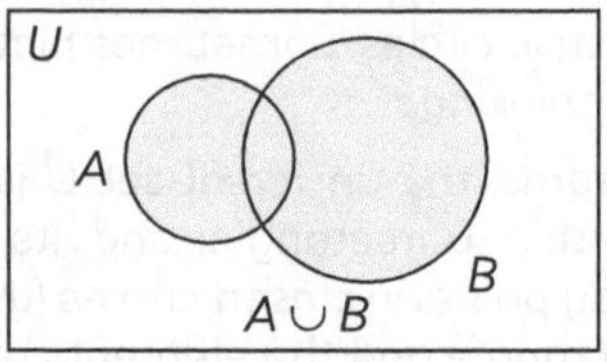

In the above Venn diagram, the shaded portion represents $A \cup B$.

Some important properties of the union operations are

(i) $A \cup B = B \cup A$ (Commutative law)

(ii) $(A \cup B) \cup C = A \cup (B \cup C)$ (Associative law)

(iii) $A \cup \phi = A$ (Law of identity element, ϕ is the identity of $\cup$)

(iv) $A \cup A = A$ (Idempotent law)

(v) $U \cup A = U$ (Law of U)

Intersection of Sets

Let A and B be any two sets. Then, the intersection of sets A and B is the set of all elements that are common to both A and B. The symbol '$\cap$' is used to denote the intersection.

We write the intersection of sets A and B as $A \cap B$ and read as 'A intersection B', also we can write $A \cap B$ as $\{x : x \in A \text{ and } x \in B\}$

The intersection of two sets can be represented by a Venn diagram as

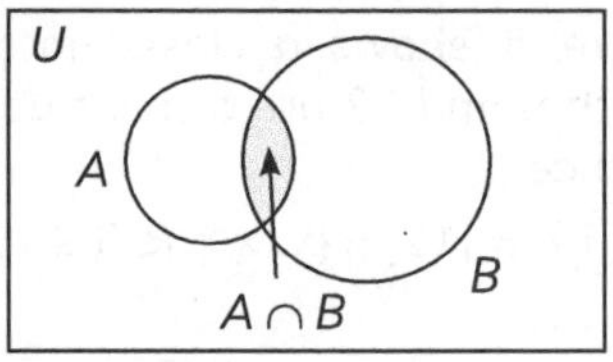

The shaded portion in the above diagram represents $A \cap B$.

If A and B are two sets such that $A \cap B = \phi$, then A and B are called disjoint sets.

For example, let $A = \{2, 4, 6, 8\}$ and $B = \{1, 3, 5, 7\}$.

Clearly, there are no common elements in both sets A and B, which means $A \cap B = \phi$

Then sets A and B are disjoint sets, because there are no elements. Disjoint sets are represented in the Venn diagram as shown in diagram below.

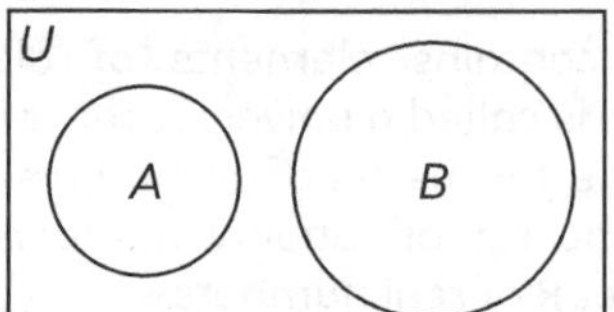

Let A, B and C be the three sets, then some important properties of intersection are:

(i) $A \cap B = B \cap A$ (Commutative law).

(ii) $(A \cap B) \cap C = A \cap (B \cap C)$ (Associative law).

(iii) $\phi \cap A = \phi$, $U \cap A = A$ (Law of ϕ and U).

(iv) $A \cap A = A$ (Idempotent law)

(v) $A \cap (B \cup C) = (A \cap B) \cup (A \cap C)$ (Distributive law) i.e., $\cap$ distributes over $\cup$

These intersection properties can be represented in Venn diagram as follows:

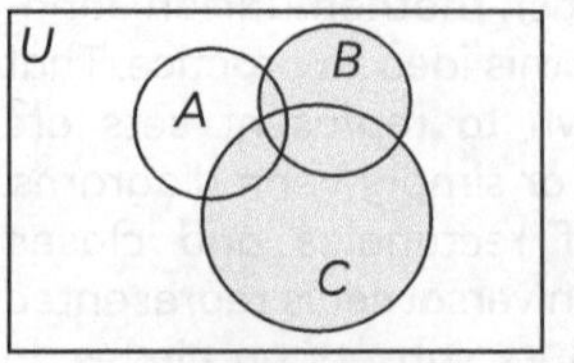

(i) $(B \cup C)$

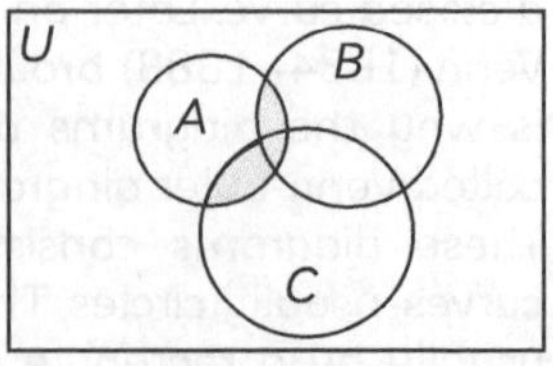

(ii) $A \cap (B \cup C)$

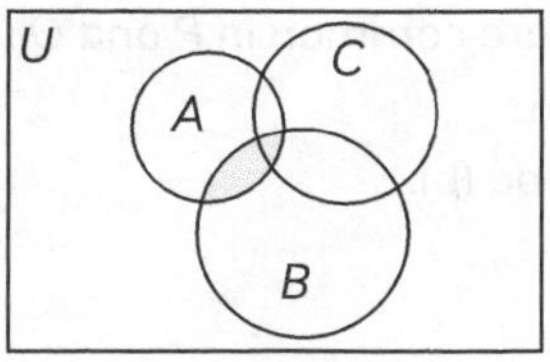

(iii) $(A \cap B)$

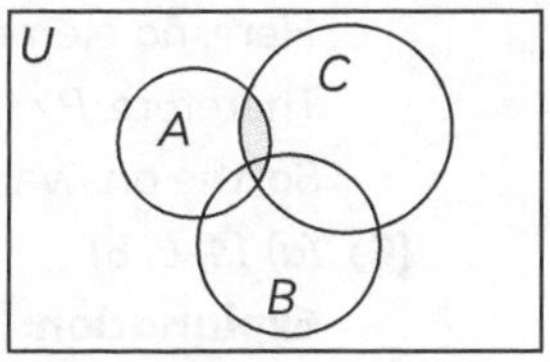

(iv) $(A \cap C)$

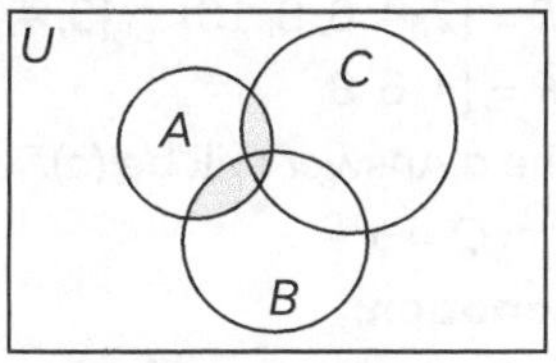

(v) $(A \cup B) \cup (A \cup C)$

Difference of Sets

Let A and B be any two sets. Then, the set of all those elements of set A that are not in set B, is called the difference of the sets A and B.

Symbolically, we write the difference of A and B as $A - B$ and read as 'A minus B', also, we can write $A - B = \{x : x \in A \text{ and } x \notin B\}$

Important

- *For any two sets A and B, we have* $A - B = A \cap B'$.
- *For any two sets A and B, we have* $B - A = B \cap A'$.

Example 1.13: If $A = \{1, 2, 3, 4\}$ $B = \{3, 4, 5, 6\}$, $C = \{5, 6, 7, 8\}$ and $D = \{7, 8, 9, 10\}$. and Find

(A) $A \cup B$ **(B)** $A \cup C$
(C) $B \cup C$ **(D)** $B \cup D$
(E) $A \cup B \cup C$ **(F)** $A \cup B \cup D$
(G) $B \cup C \cup D$ **[NCERT]**

Ans. (A) $A \cup B = \{1, 2, 3, 4\} \cup \{3, 4, 5, 6\}$
$= \{1, 2, 3, 4, 5, 6\}$

(B) $A \cup C = \{1, 2, 3, 4\} \cup \{5, 6, 7, 8\}$
$= \{1, 2, 3, 4, 5, 6, 7, 8\}$

(C) $B \cup C = \{3, 4, 5, 6\} \cup \{5, 6, 7, 8\}$
$= \{3, 4, 5, 6, 7, 8\}$

(D) $B \cup D = \{3, 4, 5, 6\} \cup \{7, 8, 9, 10\}$
$= \{3, 4, 5, 6, 7, 8, 9, 10\}$

(E) $A \cup B \cup C = \{1, 2, 3, 4\} \cup \{3, 4, 5, 6\} \cup \{5, 6, 7, 8\}$
$= \{1, 2, 3, 4, 5, 6, 7, 8\}$

(F) $A \cup B \cup D = \{1, 2, 3, 4\} \cup \{3, 4, 5, 6\} \cup \{7, 8, 9, 10\}$
$= \{1, 2, 3, 4, 5, 6, 7, 8, 9, 10\}$

(G) $B \cup C \cup D = \{3, 4, 5, 6\} \cup \{5, 6, 7, 8\} \cup \{7, 8, 9, 10\}$
$= \{3, 4, 5, 6, 7, 8, 9, 10\}$

Example 1.14: Find the intersection of each pair of sets:

(A) $X = \{1, 3, 5\}$ $Y = \{1, 2, 3\}$

(B) $A = \{a, e, i, o, u\}$ $B = \{a, b, c\}$

(C) $A = \{x : x$ **is a natural number and multiple of 3}** $B = \{x : x$ **is a natural number less than 6}**

(D) $A = \{x : x$ **is a natural number and** $1 < x \le 6\}$. $B = \{x : x$ **is a natural number and** $6 < x < 10\}$

(E) $A = \{1, 2, 3\}$, $B = \phi$ **[NCERT]**

Ans. (A) $X = \{1, 3, 5\}$, $Y = \{1, 2, 3\}$
$X \cap Y = \{1, 3, 5\} \cap \{1, 2, 3\}$
$= \{1, 3\}$

(B) $A = \{a, e, i, o, u\}$, $B = \{a, b, c\}$
$A \cap B = \{a, e, i, o, u\}, \cap \{a, b, c\}$
$= \{a\}$

(C) $A = \{x : x$ is a natural number and multiple of 3$\} = \{3, 6, 9...\}$
$B = \{x : x$ is a natural number less than 6$\}$
$= \{1, 2, 3, 4, 5\}$
$A \cap B = \{3, 6, 9...\} \cap \{1, 2,3, 4, 5\}$
$= \{3\}$

(D) $A = \{x : x$ is a natural number and $1 < x \le 6\}$
$= \{2, 3, 4, 5, 6\}$
$B = \{x : x$ is a natural number and $6 < x < 10\}$
$= \{7, 8, 9\}$
$A \cap B = \{2, 3, 4, 5, 6\} \cap \{7, 8, 9\}$
$= \{\ \}$ or ϕ

(E) $A = \{1, 2, 3\}$, $B = \phi$
$A \cap B = \{1, 2, 3\} \cap \{\ \}$
$= \phi$

Since, there is no common item between both sets.

Example 1.15: Which of the following pairs of sets are disjoint?

(A) $\{1, 2, 3, 4\}$ **and** $\{x : x$ **is a natural number and** $4 \le x \le 6\}$

(B) $\{a, e, i, o, u\}$ **and** $\{c, d, e, f\}$

(C) $\{x : x$ **is an even integer} and** $\{x : x$ **is an odd integer}**

Ans. (A) Let $A = \{1, 2, 3, 4\}$ and $B = \{x : x$ is a natural number and $4 \le x \le 6\} = \{4, 5, 6\}$

We know that two sets are disjoint if they have no common element.

Here, $A \cap B = \{1, 2, 3, 4\} \cap \{4, 5, 6\} = \{4\} \ne \phi$

Since, there is a common element in both sets.

Hence, the given pair of sets is not disjoint.

(B) Let $A = \{a, e, i, o, u\}$ and $B = \{c, d, e, f\}$

We know that have two sets that are disjoint if they have no common element.

Here, $A \cap B = \{a, e, i, o, u\} \cap \{c, d, e, f\}$
$= \{e\} \ne \phi$

Since there is a common element in both sets.

Hence, the given sets are not disjoint.

(C) Let $A = \{x : x \text{ is an even integer}\} = \{\ldots, -4, -2, 0, 2, 4, \ldots\}$ and $B = \{x : x \text{ is an odd integer}\} = \{\ldots, -5, -3, -1, 1, 3, 5, \ldots\}$

We know that have two sets that are disjoint if they have no common element.

Here, $A \cap B = \phi$

Hence, the given pair of sets are disjoint.

Example 1.16: If A and B are two sets such that $A \subset B$, then what is $A \cup B$?

Ans. Let $A = \{1, 2\}$ and $B = \{1, 2, 3\}$

Here, every element of set A is in set B. So, A is a subset of B, i.e., $A \subset B$

$A \cup B = \{1, 2\} \cup \{1, 2, 3\}$

$= \{1, 2, 3\}$

Thus, $A \cup B = B$

Example 1.17: Case Based:

After ending the topic 'Operations on sets', the Math teacher Mrs. Gargi Sharma of class XI wants to check student's understandings about the topic that she taught, so she writes three sets P, Q and R such that $P = \{2, 4, 6, 8, 10\}$, $Q = \{3, 5, 7, 9\}$ and $R = \{3, 4, 6, 8, 12\}$ on the blackboard and ask the students of the class observe these sets written on the blackboard and to answer the questions.

Based on the above information, answer the following questions.

(A) What is the value of $P \cap Q$?

(a) $\{4, 6, 8\}$ **(b) ϕ**

(c) $\{2, 6, 8\}$ **(d) $\{3, 6, 8\}$**

(B) What is the value of $P \cap R$?

(a) $\{4, 6, 8\}$ **(b) ϕ**

(c) $\{2, 6, 8\}$ **(d) $\{4, 5, 8\}$**

(C) Which of the following is correct for two sets P and Q to be disjoint?

(a) $P \cap Q = \phi$ **(b) $P \cap Q \neq \phi$**

(c) $P \cup Q = \phi$ **(d) $P \cup Q \neq \phi$**

(D) Which of the following is correct for two sets P and R to be intersecting?

(E) Find $P \cup Q \cup R$.

Ans. (A) *(b)* ϕ

Explanation:

$P = \{2, 4, 6, 8, 10\}$, $Q = \{3, 5, 7, 9\}$

$P \cap Q = \{2, 4, 6, 8, 10\} \cap \{3, 5, 7, 9\}$

Here, no elements are common in P and Q.

Therefore, $P \cap Q = \phi$

So, the answer will be (b).

(B) *(a) {4, 6, 8}*

Explanation:

$P = \{2, 4, 6, 8, 10\}$ and $R = \{3, 4, 6, 8, 12\}$

$P \cap R = \{2, 4, 6, 8, 10\} \cap \{3, 4, 6, 8, 12\}$

$P \cap R = \{4, 6, 8$

So, the a Answer will be (a).

(C) *(a)* $P \cap Q = \phi$

Explanation:

There is no common element in P and Q.

Also, we know that two sets are disjoint, if they have no common elements.

Hence, $P \cap Q = \phi$ represent disjoint sets.

(D) If P and R are intersecting, that means there are some elements common in P and R,

But $P \cap R = \{4, 6, 8\}$ (From B)

So, $P \cap R \neq \phi$

(E) Given, $P = \{2, 4, 6, 8, 10\}$, $Q = \{3, 5, 7, 9\}$ and $R = \{3, 4, 6, 8, 12\}$

$P \cup Q \cup R = \{2, 4, 6, 8, 10\} \cup \{3, 5, 7, 9\} \cup \{3, 4, 6, 8, 12\}$

So, $P \cup Q \cup R = \{2, 3, 4, 5, 6, 7, 8, 9, 10, 12\}$

Complement of a Set

Let U be the universal set and A be any subset. Then the complement of A is the set of all elements which are in U but not in A.

We can write

$A' = \{x : x \in \cup$ and $x \notin A$ or $A' = U - A$

Illustration: Let $U = \{1, 2, 3, 4, 5, 6, 7, 8, 9, 10\}$ and $A = \{1, 3, 5, 7, 9\}$, then $A' = U - A = \{2, 4, 6, 8, 10\}$

De Morgan's Laws

If A and B are any two subsets of the universal set U, then the complement of the union of two sets is the intersection of their complements and the complement of the intersection of two sets is the union of their complements. $(A \cup B)' = A' \cap B'$ and $(A \cap B)' = A' \cup B'$

These are called De Morgan's laws. These are named after the mathematician De Morgan.

Illustration: Let $U = \{1, 2, 3, 4, 5, 6\}$, $A = \{2, 3\}$ and $B = \{3, 4, 5\}$, then $A' = U - A = \{1, 4, 5, 6\}$, $B' = U - B = \{1, 2, 6\}$, $A \cup B = \{2, 3, 4, 5\}$, $A' \cap B' = \{1, 6\}$ and $(A \cup B)' = U - (A \cup B) = \{1, 6\}$. Hence, $(A \cup B)' = A' \cap B'$

Important Properties

(i) Complement Law: $A \cup A = U$ and $A \cap A' = \phi$.

(ii) Law of double complementation: $(A')' = A$.

(iii) Laws of empty set and universal set: $\phi' = U$ and $' = \phi$.

(iv) De Morgan's Law: $(A \cup B)' = A' \cap B'$ and $(A \cap B)' = A' \cup B'$.

Important

➥ *If A is a subset of the universal set U, then its complement A′ is also a subset of U.*

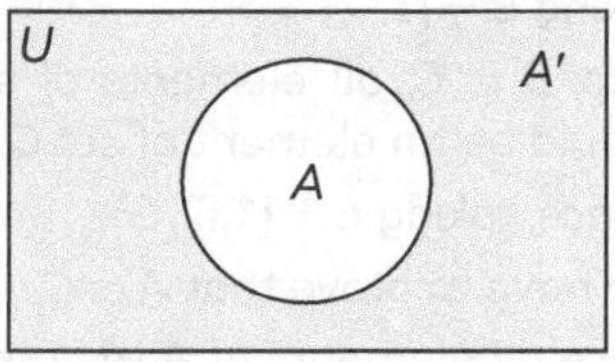

➥ *The shaded portion represents the complement of set A.*

Example 1.18: Fill in the blanks to make each of the following a true statement:

(A) $A \cup A' = \ldots$ **(B)** $\phi' \cap A = \ldots$

(C) $A \cup A' = \ldots$ **(D)** $U' \cap A = \ldots$

Ans.

(A)	$A \cup A' = U$	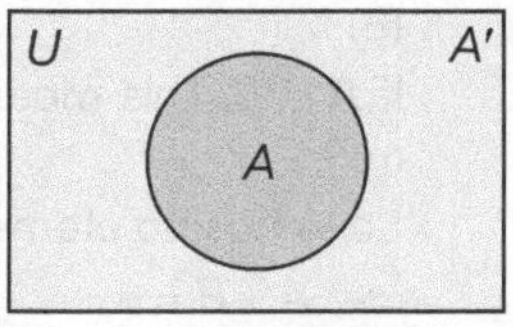
(B)	$\phi' = U - \{\ \} = U$ So, $\phi' = U$ Now, $\phi' \cap A = U \cap A = A$	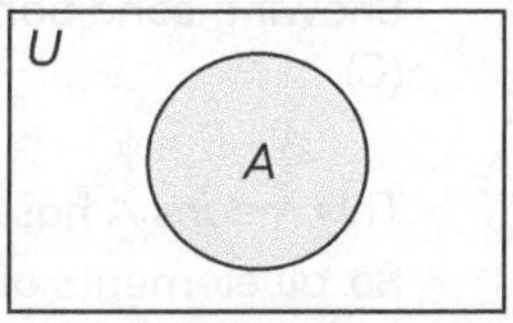
(C)	$A \cap A' = \phi$	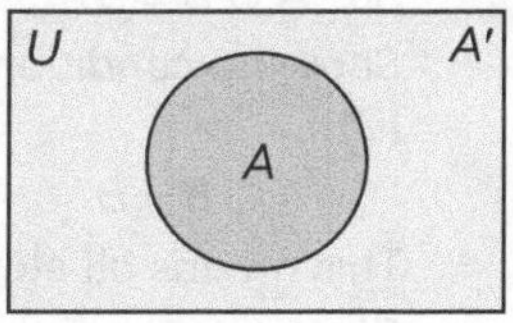
(D)	$U' \cap A = U' = U - U$ $= \{\} = \phi$ So, $U' = \phi$ Thus, $U' = A = \phi \cap A = \phi$	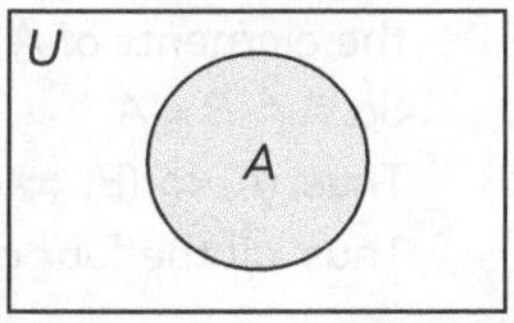

Example 1.19: If $U = \{1, 3, 3, 4, 5, 6, 7, 8, 9\}$ $A = \{2, 4, 6, 8\}$ and $B = \{2, 3, 5, 7\}$. Verify that

(A) $(A \cup B)' = A' \cap B'$

(B) $(A \cap B)' = A' \cup B'$ **[NCERT]**

Ans. (A) To verify that $(A \cup B)' = A' \cap B'$

$A \cup B = \{2, 4, 6, 8\} \cup \{2, 3, 5, 7\}$

LHS $= (A \cup B)' = U - (A \cup B)$

$= \{1, 2, 3, 4, 5, 6, 7, 8, 9\} - \{2, 3, 4, 5, 6, 7, 8\}$

Also, $A' = U - A$

$= \{1, 2, 3, 4, 5, 6, 7, 8, 9\} - \{2, 4, 6, 8\}$

$= \{1, 3, 5, 7, 9\}$

and $B' = U - B$

$= \{1, 2, 3, 4, 5, 6, 7, 8, 9\} - \{2, 3, 5, 7\}$

$= \{1, 4, 6, 8, 9\}$

Thus, RHS $= A' \cap B' = \{1, 3, 5, 7, 9\} \cap \{1, 4, 6, 8, 9\}$

$= \{1, 9\}$

Clearly, $(A \cup B)' = A' \cap B'$ Hence verified.

(B) We have to verify that $(A \cup B)' = A' \cap B'$

$A \cap B = \{2, 4, 6, 8\} \cap \{2, 3, 5, 7\} = \{2\}$

Thus, LHS $= (A \cup B)' = U - (A \cap B)$

$= \{1, 2, 3, 4, 5, 6, 7, 8, 9\} - \{2\}$

$= \{1, 3, 4, 5, 6, 7, 8, 9\}$

$A' = U - A = \{1, 2, 3, 4, 5, 6, 7, 8, 9\} - \{2, 4, 6, 8\}$

$= \{1, 3, 5, 7, 9\}$

$B' = U - B = \{1, 2, 3, 4, 5, 6, 7, 8, 9\} - \{2, 3, 5, 7\}$

$= \{1, 4, 6, 8, 9\}$

And so, RHS $= A' \cup B' = \{1, 3, 5, 7, 9\} \cup \{1, 4, 6, 8, 9\}$

$= \{1, 3, 4, 5, 6, 7, 8, 9\}$

$(A \cap B)' = A' \cup B'$ Hence verified.

Example 1.20: Taking the set of natural numbers as the universal set, write down the complements of the following sets:

(A) $\{x : x$ is a prime number$\}$

(B) $\{x : 2x + 5 = 9\}$

(C) $\{x : x \in N$ and $2x + 1 > 10\}$ **[NCERT]**

Ans. (A) We have to find complements of $\{x : x$ is a prime number$\}$

Natural Number

Prime numbers	Composite numbers	Neither prime nor composite
Eg. 2, 3, 7, 11, 13	Eg. 4, 6, 8, 9, 10, 12	Eq. 1

U is set of natural numbers

$\{x : x$ is a prime number$\}' = \{x : x \in N$ and x is a composite number or $x = 1\}$

(B) we have to find complements of $\{x : 2x + 5 = 9\} = \{x : 2x + 5 = 9\}$

$U = \{1, 2, 3, 4, 5, \ldots\}$

$2x + 5 = 9$

$2x = 9 - 5$

$2x = 4$

$x = \dfrac{4}{2}$

$x = 2$

$\{x : 2x + = 9\}' = \{x : x = 2\}'$

$= \{x : x \in N$ and $x \neq 2\}$

(C) we have to find complements of $\{x : x \in N$ and $2x + 1 > 10\} = \{x : x \in N$ and $2x + 1 > 10\}'$

$U = \{1, 2, 3, 4, 5, \ldots\}$

$2x + 1 > 10$

$2x > 10 - 1$

$2x > 9$

$x > \frac{9}{2}$

$x > 4.5$

i.e. $\{x : x \in N \text{ and } 2x + 1 > 10 = \{x : x \in N \text{ and } x > 4.5\}$

Thus, $\{x : x \in \text{N and } 2x + 1 > 10 = \{x : x \in N \text{ and } x > 4.5\}'$

$= \{x : x \in N \text{ and } x \leq 4.5\}$

Example 1.21: Show that for any sets A and B,

$A = (A \cap B) \cup (A - B)$ and

$A \cup (B - A) = (A \cup B)$

Ans. Let $U = \{1, 2, 3, 4, 5\}$, $A \{1, 2\}$ and $B = \{2, 3, 4\}$

We have, $B' = U - B$

$= \{1, 2, 3, 4, 5\} - \{2, 3, 4\} = \{1, 5\}$

Also, $A - B = A - (A \cap B) = \{1, 2\} - \{2\} = \{1\}$

$A - B = A \cap B' = \{1, 2\} \cap \{1, 5\} = \{1\}$

Hence, $A - B = A \cap B'$

Example 1.22: In each of the following, determine whether the statement is true or false. If it is true, prove it. If it is false, give an example.

(A) If $A \subset B$ and $B \in C$, then $A \in C$

(B) If $A \subset B$ and $B \subset C$, then $A \subset C$ [NCERT]

Ans. (A) If $A \subset B$ and $B \in C$, then $A \in C$

Let $A = \{2\}$,

Since, $A \subset B$, element of set A i.e., 2 should be an element of set B aking $B = \{0, 2\}$

Also, since $B \in C$, i.e., whole set B is an element of set C

Taking $C = \{1, \{0, 2\}, 3\}$

We have to prove that $A \in C$

But, $\{2\} \notin C$ as $\{2\}$ is not element of C

$\Rightarrow$ Hence, $A \notin C$

So, the given statement is False.

(B) If $A \subset B$ and $B \subset C$, then $A \subset C$

Let $A = \{1\}$,

Since, $A \subset B$, all elements of set A i.e., 1 should be an element of set B

Taking $B = \{1, 2\}$

Also, $B \subset C$, all elements of set B i.e., 1, 2 should be an element of set C

Hence, taking $C = \{1, 2, 3\}$

We have to prove that $A \subset C$

Since all elements of A i.e., 1 is in set C, A is a subset of C

So, the given statement is true.

Example 1.23: Show that the following four conditions are equivalent:

(A) $A \subset B$ **(B) $A - B = \phi$**

(C) $A \cup B = B$ **(D) $A \cap B = A$**

Ans. Showing condition (A) is equivalent to condition (B)

If $A \subset B$, This means that all elements of A are in B,

So, A has no element different from B

$\Rightarrow A - B = \phi$

Showing condition (B) is equivalent to condition (C)

$A - B = \phi$

This means A has no elements different from B

So, all elements of A are in B

So, $A \cup B = B$

Showing condition (C) is equivalent to condition (D)

$A \cup B = B$

This means all elements of A are in B,

So, the common elements of A and B must be the elements of A

So, $A \cap B = A$

Thus, (A) $\Leftrightarrow$ (B) $\Leftrightarrow$ (C) $\Leftrightarrow$ (D)

Thus, all the four conditions are equivalent.

TOPIC 5

APPLICATIONS OF SETS

If A and B are two finite sets, then there are two cases that may arise.

Case I: If A and B are disjoint sets then, there will no common element in A and B, i.e., $A \cap B = \phi$

Thus, $n(A \cup B) = n(A) + n(B)$

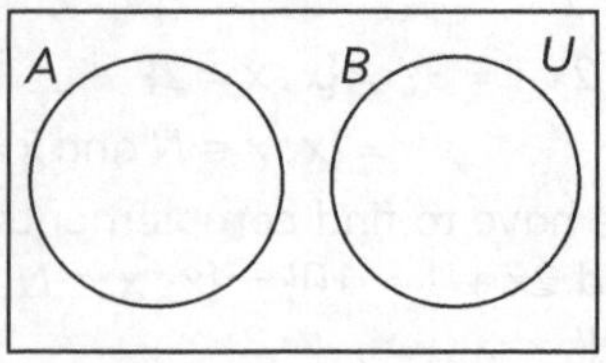

Case II: If A and B are not disjoint sets then, there will be common element in A and B, then

$$n(A \cup B) = n(A) + n(B) - n(A \cap B)$$

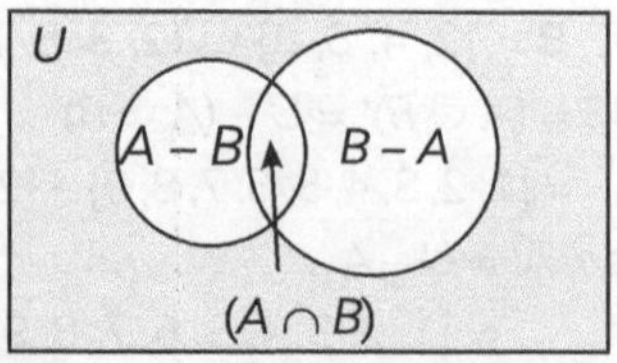

⚠ Caution

↪ *If A and B are disjoint sets, then the formula will be written as*

$n(A \cup B) = n(A) + n(B)$ because for disjoint set $A \cap B = \phi$

Some Important results

(i) If A and B are finite sets and $A \cap B = \phi$, then $n(A \cup B) = n(A) + n(B)$

(ii) If A and B are non-disjoint finite sets, then $n(A \cup B) = n(A) + n(B) - n(A \cap B)$

(iii) We can see from the above Venn diagram that the sets $A - B$, $A \cap B$ and $B - A$ are disjoint and their union is $A \cup B$, therefore we can write,

- $n(A \cup B) = n(A) + n(B) - n(A \cap B)$

we can also write,

- $n(A) = n(A - B) + n(A \cap B)$
- $n(B) = n(B - A) + n(A \cap B)$

(iv) If A, B and C are finite sets, and number of elements of three sets are given, then

$n(A \cup B \cup C) = n(A) + n(B) + n(C) - n(A \cap B) - n(B \cap C) - (A \cap C) + n(A \cap B \cap C)$

In the following table, we give some verbal descriptions with their equivalent set-theoretic notation.

Verbal Description	**Theoretical Notation**
For two sets problems:	
Not *A*	A'
Only *A*	$A \cap B'$
A but not *B*	$A \cap B'$
Only *B*	$A' \cap B$
B but not *A*	$A' \cap B$
Either *A* or *B*	$A \cup B$
At least one of *A* and *B*	$A \cup B$
A and *B*	$A \cap B$
A or *B*	$A \cup B$
Neither *A* nor *B*	$A' \cap B'$
For three sets problems:	
Not *A*	A'
Only *A*	$A \cap B' \cap C'$
Only *B*	$A' \cap B \cap C'$
Only C	$A' \cap B' \cap C$
Only *A* and *B*	$A' \cap B \cap A \cap B \cap C'$
Only *B* and *C*	$A' \cap B \cap C$
Only *A* and *C*	$A \cap B' \cap C$
At least one of *A*, *B*, and *C*	$A \cup B \cup C$
None of *A*, *B*, and *C*	$A' \cap B' \cap C'$

Example 1.24: If X and Y are two sets such that $X \cup Y$ has 18 elements, X has 8 elements and Y has 15 elements; how many elements does $X \cap Y$ have? [NCERT]

Ans. Given, $n(X \cup Y) = 18$

$n(X) = 8$

$n(Y) = 15$

$n(X \cap Y) = ?$

We know that:

$$n(X \cup Y) = n(X) + n(Y) - n(X \cap Y)$$

$$18 = 8 + 15 - n(X \cap Y)$$

$$18 = 23 - n(X \cap Y) =$$

$$n(X \cap Y) = 23 - 18$$

$$n(X \cap Y) = 5$$

Example 1.25: In a group of 65 people, 40 like cricket, 10 like both cricket and tennis. How many like tennis only and not cricket? How many like tennis? [NCERT]

Ans. Let C and T denote the set of people who like cricket & tennis, respectively.

Number of people in the group

= Number of people who like cricket or tennis

$= n(C \cup T) = 65$

Number of people who like cricket $= n(C) = 40$,

Number of people who like both cricket and tennis $= n(C \cap T) = 10$

We know that

$$n(C \cup T) = n(C) + n(T) - n(C \cap T)$$

$$65 = 40 + n(T) - 10$$

$$65 = 40 - 10 + n(T)$$

$$65 = 30 + n(T)$$

$$65 - 30 = n(T)$$

$$35 = n(T)$$

$$n(T) = 35$$

Therefore, 35 People like tennis (i.e who like only tennis and also those who like both tennis and cricket, as depicted below)

People who like tennis

↙ ↘

People who like only tennis | People who like both tennis & cricket

Number of people who like only tennis but not cricket

= Number of people who like tennis – Number of people who like both tennis and cricket

$= n(T - C)$

$= n(T) - n(T \cap C)$

$= 35 - 10$

$= 25$

Thus, 25 People only like tennis.

Example 1.26: If X and Y are two sets such that X has 40 elements, $X \cup Y$ has 60 elements and $X \cap Y$ has 10 elements, how many elements does Y have? [NCERT]

Ans. Given

$n(X) = 40, n(X \cup Y) = 60, n(X \cap Y) = 10$

We know that:

$n(X \cup Y) = n(X) + n(Y) - n(X \cap Y)$

$60 = 40 + n(Y) - 10$

$60 = 40 - 10 + n(Y)$

$60 = 30 + n(Y)$

$\therefore \quad n(Y) = 60 - 30 = 30$

Thus, the set Y has 30 elements.

Example 1.27: In a survey it was found that 21 people liked product *A*, 26 liked product *B* and 29 liked product *C*. If 14 people liked products and *B*, 12 people liked products *C* and *A*, 14 people liked products *B* and *C* and 8 liked all the three products. Find how many liked product *C* only. [NCERT]

Ans. Let *A*, *B*, *C* be the sets of people who like product *A*, product *B* and product *C* respectively.

Number of people who liked product

$A = n(A) = 21,$

Number of people who liked product

$B = n(B) = 26,$

Number of people who liked product

$C = n(C) = 29,$

Number of people who liked product

$A \text{ and } B = n(A \cap B) = 14$

Number of people who liked product

$C \text{ and } A = n(C \cap A) = 12$

Number of people who liked product

$B \text{ and } C = n(B \cap C) = 14$

Number of people who liked all three products

$A, B \text{ and } C = n(A \cap B \cap C) = 8$

We have to find how many people liked product C only.

Let us draw a Venn diagram

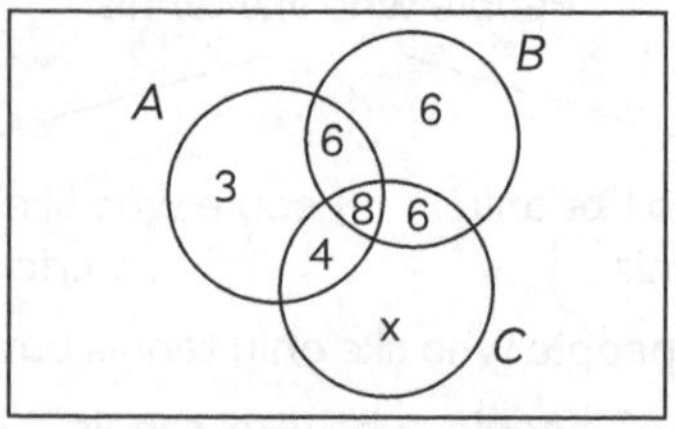

Number of people who liked product *C* only

$= n(C) - n(C \cap A) - n(B \cap C) + n(A \cap B \cap C)$

$= 29 - 12 - 14 + 8 = 11$

Hence, the number of people who like product *C* only is 11.

Example 1.28: Case Based:

In a school, during the new academic session 2021-2022, in all sections of class XI, out of 200 students, 30 students offered English only, 24 students offered Sanskrit only, 16 students offered only Hindi, 80 students offered Hindi and English, 40 students offered Hindi and Sanskrit, 20 students offered English and Sanskrit, 130 students offered Hindi.

Based on the above information answer the following questions:

(A) The number of students who offered all the three subjects is:

(a) 6 (b) 3

(c) 2 (d) 5

(B) The number of students who offered English is:

(a) 130 (b) 120

(c) 124 (d) 100

(C) The number of students who offered Sanskrit is:

(a) 56 (b) 62

(c) 75 (d) 78

(D) Find the number of students who offered English and Sanskrit but not Hindi.

(E) Find the number of students who did not offer any of the above three subjects.

Ans. Let *E*, *S* and *H* be the sets of students who offered English, Sanskrit and Hindi, respectively. Let *x* be the number of students who offered all the three subjects, then the number of members in different regions are shown in the following diagram.

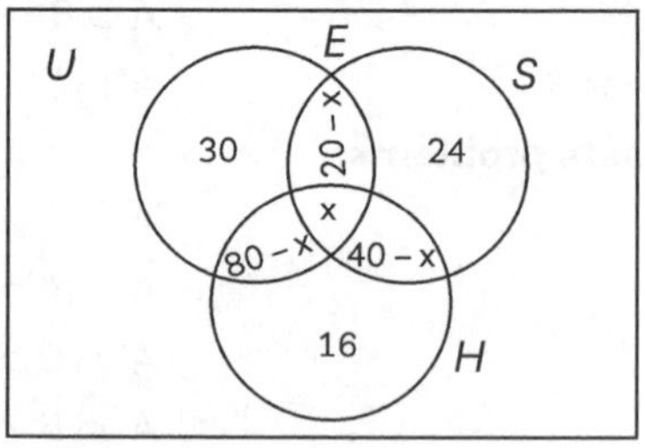

(A) *(a) 6*

Explanation:

From the above Venn diagram,

We have, the number of students who offered Hindi.

$(80 - x) + x + (40 - x) + 16 = 130$ [Given]

$\Rightarrow \quad 136 - x = 130$

$\Rightarrow \quad x = 6$

The number of students who offered all the three subjects are 6.

(B) *(c) 124*

Explanation:

From the above Venn diagram,

The number of students who offered English

$= 30 + (20 - x) + x + (80 - x)$

$= 130 - x$

$= 130 - 6 = 124$

[$\because x = 6$, from question *(A)*]

(C) *(d) 78*

Explanation:

From the above Venn diagram,

The number of students who offered Sanskrit

$= 24 + (20 - x) + x + (40 - x)$

$= 84 - x$

$= 84 - 6 = 78$

[$\because x = 6$, form question *(A)*]

(D) From the above Venn diagram,

The number of students who offered English and Sanskrit but not Hindi

$= 20 - x = 20 - 6 = 14$

[$\because x = 6$, from question *(A)*]

(E) The number of students who offered anyone of the three subjects

$= 30 + 24 + 16 + (20 - x) + (80 - x) + (40 - x) + x$

$= 210 - 2x$

$= 210 - 2 \times 6 = 198$

[$\because x = 6$, from question *(A)*]

The number of students who did not offer any one of the three subjects $= 200 - 198 = 2$

OBJECTIVE Type Questions

[**1** mark]

Multiple Choice Questions

1. **1. If $X = \{8^n - 7n - 1 \mid n \in N\}$ and $Y = \{49n - 49 \mid n \in N\}$, then:**

(a) $X \subset Y$ (b) $Y \subset X$

(c) $X = Y$ (d) $X \cap Y = \phi$

[NCERT Exemplar]

Ans. *(a)* $X \subset Y$

Explanation:

$X = \{8^n - 7n - 1 \mid n \in N\} = \{0, 49, 490, \ldots\}$

$Y = \{49n - 49 \mid n \in N\} = \{0, 49, 98, 147, \ldots 490, \ldots\}$

Clearly, every element of *X* is in *Y* but every element of *Y* is not in *X*.

$\therefore \quad (X \subset Y)$

2. **The roster form of the following set is a set of integers between -5 and 5 is:**

(a) $\{-4, -3, -2, -1, 0, 1, 2, 3, 4\}$

(b) $\{-5, -4 \ldots 4, 5\}$

(c) $\{0, 1, 2, 3, 4, 5\}$

(d) None of these

Ans. *(a)* $\{-4, -3, -2, -1, 0, 1, 2, 3, 4\}$

Explanation: According to questions we have to write the integers that come in between –5, and 5 means –5, 5 are not included, so the correct option will be (a).

3. **Which of the following set is a finite set ?**

(a) Set of concentric circles

(b) Set of letters in English alphabets

(c) $x \in R : a < x > 1\}$

(d) None of these

Ans. *(b) Set of letters in English alphabets*

Explanation: From the above options, only option *B* contains countable elements, as we can count the elements of a set of letters in English alphabets, hence it is a finite set.

4. **If $X = \{1, 2, 3\}$, if *n* represents any member of *x*, then all elements of a set, containing element $n + 6$ is given by:**

(a) $\{6, 7, 8\}$ (b) $\{5, 6, 7\}$

(c) $\{7, 8, 9\}$ (d) $\{8, 9, 10\}$

Ans. *(c)* $\{7, 8, 9\}$

Explanation: The elements in a set containing $n + 6$ elements where $n \in x$ will

$1 + 6, 2 + 6, 3 + 6 = \{7, 8\ 9\}$.

5. **Let S be an infinite set and S1, S2, S3, . . . , Sn be sets such that $S1 \cup S2 \cup S3 \cup Sn = S$ then**

(a) at least one of the sets S_i is a finite set

(b) not more than one of the set S_i can be infinite

(c) At least one of the sets S_i is an infinite set

(d) none of these **[DIKSHA]**

Ans. *(a) at least one of the sets S_j is a finite set*

Explanation: $S1 \cup S2 \cup S3 \cup Sn$. For S to be an infinite set, at least one of sets Si must be infinite, since if all S_i were finite, then *S* will also be finite.

6. **The symmetric difference of *A* and *B* is not equal to**

(a) $(A - B) \cap (B - A)$
(b) $(A - B) \cup (B - A)$
(c) $(A \cup B) - (A \cap B)$
(d) $\{(A \cup B) - A\} \cup \{(A \cap B) - B\}$

Ans. (a) $(A - B) \cap (B - A)$

Explanation: $(A - B) \cap (B - A) = \phi$

Hence, $A \cap B = (A - B) \cup (B - A)$

So, option (a) is correct.

7. The symmetric difference of $A = \{1, 2, 3\}$ and $B = \{3, 4, 5\}$ is:

(a) $\{1, 2\}$ (b) $\{1, 2, 4, 5\}$
(c) $\{4, 3\}$ (d) $\{2, 5, 1, 4, 3\}$

[DIKSHA]

Ans. (b) $\{1, 2, 4, 5\}$

Explanation: $A \Delta B = (A - B) \cup (B - A)$

$A - B = \{1, 2\}$

$B - A = \{4, 5\}$

So, $(A - B) \cup (B - A) = \{1,2,4,5\}$

Option (b) is correct.

8. Let $A = \{x : x \in R, x > 6\}$ and $B = \{x \in R : x < 9\}$. Then, $A \cap B =$

(a) $(7, 8]$ (b) $(7, 8)$
(c) $[7, 8)$ (d) $[7, 8]$

Ans. (b) $(7, 8)$

Explanation:

$A = \{x: x \in R, x > 6\} = A = \{7,8,9,....\},$

$\{ \quad \}$

$B = \{x \in R: x < 9\} = \{8, 7, 6, 5,...\}$

$A \cap B = \{x: x \in R, x > 6\} \cap \{x \in R: x < 9\}$

$= \{x: x \in R, x > 6 \text{ and } x < 9\} =$

$\{x : x \in R, 6 < x < 9\}$ (it shows a closed interval.)

$= (7, 8)$

9. Let $\cup$ be the universal set containing 700 elements. If A, B are subsets of $\cap$ such that $n(A) = 300$, $n(B) = 400$ and $n(A \cap B) = 50$. Then, $n(A' \cap B') =$

(a) 400 (b) 650
(c) 300 (d) None of these

Ans. (d) None of these

Explanation: Given,

$n(A) = 300, n(B) = 400$ and $n(A \cap B) = 50$ and $n(U) = 700$

We have, $n(A' \cap B') = n(A \cup B)'$

$n(A \cup B) = n(A) + n(B) - n(A \cap B)$

$= 300 + 400 - 50$

$= 650$

$n(A \cup B)' = 700 - 650 = 50$

10. Let A and B be two sets such that $n(A) = 20$, $n(B) = 10$, $n(A \cup B) = 15$. Then, $n(A \cap B)$ is equal to:

(a) 30 (b) 40
(c) 15 (d) None of these

Ans. (c) 15

Explanation: Given, A and B are two sets such that

$n(A) = 20, n(B) = 10, n(A \cup B) = 15$

We have,

$n(A) = 20, n(B) = 10, n(A \cup B) = 15$

$n(A \cup B) = n(A) + n(B) - n(A \cap B)$

$15 = 20 + 10 - n(A \cap B)$

$15 = 30 - n(A \cap B)$

$n(A \cap B) = 15$

11. If A and B are two disjoint sets, then $n(A \cap B)$ is equal to:

(a) 0
(b) $n(A) + n(B) - n(A \cap B)$
(c) $n(A) + n(B) + n(A \cap B)$
(d) $n(A)\, n(B)$

Ans. (a) 0

Explanation: If A and B are two disjoint sets, then there will be no common elements set A and B.

thus, $A \cap B = \phi$

Hence, $n(A \cap B) = 0$.

12. If A and B are two sets such that $n(A) = 50$, $n(B) = 20$, $n(A \cap B) = 40$, $n(A \cup B)$ then $n(A \cup B)$ is equal to:

(a) 20 (b) 30
(c) 40 (d) 50

Ans. (b) 30

Explanation: Given, A and B are two sets such that $n(A) = 50$, $n(B) = 20$, $n(A \cap B) = 40$,

We have,

$n(A \cup B) = n(A) + n(B) - n(A \cap B)$

Putting the values,

$n(A \cup B) = 50 + 20 - 40$

$n(A \cup B) = 30$

13. Two finite sets have m and n elements. The number of subsets of the first set is 112 more than that of the second set. The values of m and n are, respectively.

(a) 4, 7 (b) 7, 4
(c) 4, 4 (d) 7, 7

[NCERT Exemplar]

Ans. (b) 7, 4

Explanation: Given that m and n are elements of two finite sets.

Number of subsets of first set $= 2^m$

Number of subsets of first set $= 2^n$

According to question,

$$2^m - 2^n = 112 = 2^4 \times 7$$

$$\Rightarrow \quad 2^n(2^{m-n} - 1) = 2^4(2^3 - 1)$$

On comparing, we get

$$n = 4 \text{ and } m - n = 3$$

$$\Rightarrow \quad n = 4 \text{ and } m = 7$$

14. If $S = \{ x \mid x$ is a positive multiple of 3 less than 100$\}$ and $P = \{ x \mid x$ is a prime number less than 20$\}$. Then, $n(S) + n(P)$ is equal to:

(a) 34 (b) 31

(c) 33 (d) 41

[NCERT Exemplar]

Ans. *(d) 41*

Explanation: $S = \{x: x$ is a positive multiple of 3 less than 100$\}$

$\Rightarrow S = \{3, 6, 9, 12, \ldots, 99\}$

$\Rightarrow n(S) = 33$

$P = \{x: x$ is a prime number less than 20$\}$

$\Rightarrow P = \{2, 3, 5, 7, 11, 13, 17, 19\}$

$n(P) = 8$

$n(S) + n(P) = 33 + 8 = 41$

15. In a town, 840 persons, 450 persons read Hindi, 300 read English and 200 read both. Then the number of persons who read neither is:

(a) 210 (b) 290

(c) 180 (d) 260

[NCERT Exemplar]

Ans. *(b) 290*

Explanation: Let H be the set of persons who read Hindi and E be the set of persons who read English.

Then

$n(U) = 840, n(H) = 540, n(E) = 300$

$n(H \cap E) = 200$

Number of persons who read neither

$= n(H' \cap F')$

$= n(H \cap E)' = n(U) - n(H \cup E)$

$= 840 - [n(H) + n(E) - n(H \cap E)]$

$= 840 - (450 + 300 - 200)$

$= 840 - 550$

$= 290$

16. If $A = \{x : x$ is a multiple of 3$\}$ and, $B = \{x : x$ is a multiple of 5$\}$, then $A \cap B$ is:

(a) $\{x: x$ is a multiple of 3$\}$

(b) $\{x: x$ is a multiple of 5$\}$

(c) $\{x : x$ is a multiple of 15$\}$

(d) None of the above

Ans. *(c) $\{x : x$ is a multiple of 15$\}$*

Explanation:

$A = \{3, 6, 9, 12, 15, 18, 21, \ldots\}$

$B = \{5, 10, 15, 20, 25, 30, \ldots\}$

Then,

$A \cap B = \{3, 6, 9, 12, 15, 18, 21, \ldots\} \cap \{5, 15, 20, 25, 30 \ldots\}$

$= \{15, 30, 45, \ldots\} = \{x : x$ is a multiple of 15$\}$

17. An investigator interviewed 100 students to determine the performance of three drinks: milk, coffee, and tea. The investigator reported that 10 students take all three drinks milk, coffee, and tea; 20 students take milk and coffee; 25 students take milk and tea; 20 students take coffee and tea; 12 students take milk only; 5 students take coffee only and 8 students take tea only. Then the number of students who did not take any of the three drinks is

(a) 10 (b) 20

(c) 25 (d) 30

Ans. *(d) 30*

Explanation: According to the given information, the Venn diagram is:

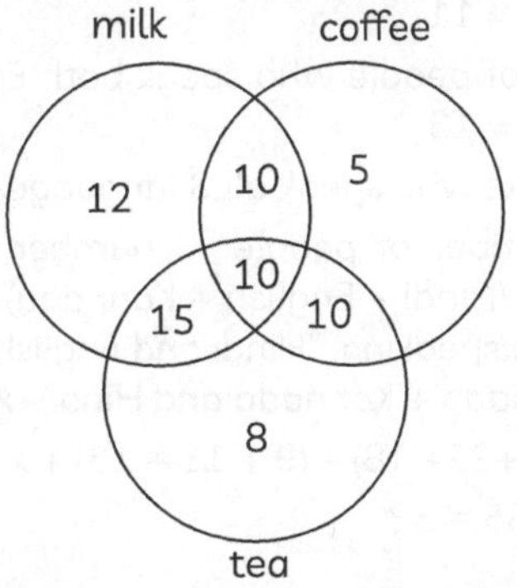

Now, $n(M \cup C \cup T) = 12 + 5 + 8 + 10 + 15 + 10 + 10 = 70$

Now, number of people who did not took any of the drinks is $n(M' \cap C' \cap T') = n(M \cup C \cup T)'$

$\Rightarrow \quad n(M \cup C \cup T)' = N - n(M \cup C \cup T)$

$\Rightarrow \quad n(M \cup C \cup T)' = 100 - 70 = 30$

18. In a class of 175 students, the following data shows the number of students opting for one or more subjects. Mathematics 100; Physics 70; Chemistry 40; Mathematics and Physics 30; Mathematics and chemistry 28; Physics and Chemistry 23; Mathematics, Physics and Chemistry 18. How many students have been offered Mathematics alone?

(a) 35 (b) 48

(c) 60 (d) 22

Ans. *(c) 60*

Explanation: Let M, P and C denote the set of students who opt Mathematics, Physics and Chemistry respectively.

Number of students who opted Mathematics only

$= n(M) - n(M \cap P) - n(M \cap C) + n(M \cap P \cap C)$

$= 100 - 30 - 28 + 18 = 60$

19. **In a room containing 28 people, there are 18 people who speak English, 15 people who speak Hindi and 22 people speak Kannada. 9 people speak English and Hindi, 11 people speak both Hindi and Kannada and 13 people who speak both English and Kannada. Find the number of people who speak all the 3 languages.**

(a) 6 (b) 7

(c) 8 (d) 9 **[DIKSHA]**

Ans. *(a) 6*

Explanation:

Total number of people = 28

Number of people who speak English = 18

Number of people who speak Hindi = 15

Number of people who speak Kannada = 22

Number of people who speak both English and Hindi = 9

Number of people who speak both Hindi and Kannada = 11

Number of people who speak both English and Kannada = 13

Let, people who speak all 3 languages be x

Total number of people = number of people speaking (Hindi + English + Kannada) – number of people speaking (Hindi and English + English and Kannada + Kannada and Hindi)+x

$28 = (15 + 22 + 18) - (9 + 11 + 13) + x$

$x = 28 - 55 + 33$

$x = 6$

Assertion-Reason (A-R)

DIRECTION: In the following questions, a statement of assertion (A) is followed by a statement of the reason (R). Mark the correct choice as:

(a) Both assertion (A) and reason (R) are true, and reason (R) is the correct explanation of assertion (A).

(b) Both assertion (A) and reason (R) are true, but reason (R) is not the correct explanation of assertion (A).

(c) Assertion (A) is true but reason (R) is false.

(d) Assertion (A) is false but reason (R) is true.

20. **Assertion (A):** The set $D = \{x : x$ is even prime number$\}$ in roster form is {2,3}.

Reason (R): The set E = the set of all letters in the word: 'SCHOOL', in the roster form is {S, C, H, O, L}.

Ans. *(d) Assertion (A) is false but reason (R) is true.*

Explanation: We have 2 is only even prime number. So,

$D = \{x: x \text{ is even prime number}\} = \{2\}$

Thus, the given roster form of set D is wrong.

There are 6 letters in the word 'SCHOOL' out of which letters O are repeated.

Hence, set E in the roster form is $\{S, C, H, O, L\}$.

Hence, Assertion (A) is false but reason (R) is true.

21. **Assertion (A): The set {1, 8, 27,. . ., 1000} in the set-builder form is $\{x: x = n^3$, where $n \in N$ and $1 \leq n \leq 10\}$.**

Reason (R): In roster form, the order in which the elements are listed is immaterial.

Ans. *(b) Both assertion (A) and reason (R) are true, but reason (R) is not the correct explanation of assertion (A).*

Explanation: We see that each member in the given set is the cube of a natural number.

Hence, the given set in the set-builder form is $\{x : x = n^3$, where $n \in N$ and $1 \leq n \leq 10\}$.

Also, in roster form, the order in which the elements are listed is immaterial.

Hence, assertion (A) and reason (R) both are true, but the reason is not the correct explanation of assertion (A).

22. **Assertion (A): The set {x : x is a month of a year not having 30 days} in roster form is {January, February, March, May, July, August, October, December}.**

Reason(R): A collection of objects is called set.

Ans. *(c) Assertion (A) is true but reason (R) is false.*

Explanation: The months not containing 30 days are January, February, March, May, July, August, October, and December.

So, the roster form of a given set = {January, February, March, May, July, August, October, December}, which is a well-defined collection of months

R is wrong as mere collection of objects is not a set. the collection should be well defined.

Hence, assertion is true but reason (R) is false .

23. **Assertion (A): The set A = {a, e, i, o, u} is a finite set.**

Reason (R): Finite set has finite number of elements.

Ans. *(a) Both assertion (A) and reason (R) are true, and reason (R) is the correct explanation of assertion (A).*

Explanation: We have a set that is empty or consists of a definite number of elements is called a finite set. Here, set $A = \{a, e, i, o, u\}$

which contains 5 elements. So, it is a finite set. Hence, assertion (R) and reason (R) both are true, and the reason is the correct explanation of assertion (A).

24. **Assertion (A):** **Let $A = \{2, 3, 4\}$ and $B = \{1, 2, 3, 4\}$ Then $A \subset B$**

Reason (R): **If every element of set A is also an element of set B, then A is a subset of B.**

Ans. *(a) Both assertion (A) and Reason (R) are true, and Reason (R) is the correct explanation of assertion (A).*

Explanation: Since every element of A is in B so $A \subset B$.

CASE BASED Questions (CBQs)

[**4** & **5** marks]

Read the following passages and answer the questions that follow:

25. *To check the understanding of sets, a Math teacher writes two sets A and B having finite numbers of elements. The sum of cardinal numbers of two finite sets A and B is 9. The ratio of a cardinal number of the power set of A is to a cardinal number of the power set of B is 8 : 1.*

(A) The cardinal number of set A is:

(a) 2 (b) 3
(c) 6 (d) 8

(B) The cardinal number of set B is:

(a) 2 (b) 3
(c) 6 (d) 8

(C) The maximum value of $n(A \cup B)$ is:

(a) 3 (b) 6
(c) 8 (d) 9

(D) The minimum value of n $(A \cup B)$ is:

(a) 3 (b) 6
(c) 8 (d) 9

(E) If $B \subset A$, then n $A \cap B$ is:

(a) 3 (b) 6
(c) 8 (d) 6

Ans. (A) *(c) 6*

Explanation: Let the cardinal numbers of sets A and B be $n(A)$ and $n(B)$ respectively.

Given $n(A) + n(B) = 9$ ...(i)

Also, the cardinal number of the power set of $A = 2^{n(A)}$

And the cardinal number of the power set of $B = 2^{n(B)}$

Given, $\frac{2^{n(A)}}{2^{n(B)}} = \frac{8}{1}$ $2^{n(A)-n(B)} = 2^3$

$\Rightarrow$ $n(A) - n(B) = 3$ ...(ii)

On adding (i) and (ii) , we get

$2n(A) = 12$

$\Rightarrow$ $n(A) = 6$

Thus, the cardinal number of set A is 6.

(B) *(b) 3*

Explanation: On subtracting (ii) from (i), we get

$2n(B) = 6 \Rightarrow n(B) = 3$

Thus, the cardinal number of set B is 3.

(C) *(d) 9*

Explanation: We have,

$n(A \cup B) = n(A) + n(B) - n(A \cup B)$

The value of $n(A \cup B)$ will be maximum when $n(A \cap B)$ will be minimum.

The minimum value of $n(A \cap B) = 0$.

So, maximum value of

$n(A \cap B) = n(A) + n(B) = 6 + 3 = 9$

(D) *(b) 6*

Explanation: We have, $n(A \cup B) = n(A) + n(B) - n(A \cup B)$

The value of $n(A \cup B)$ will be minimum when $n(A \cap B)$ will be maximum.

The maximum value of $n(A \cap B) = 3$.

So, minimum value of

$n(A \cup B) = n(A) + n(B) = 6 + 3 - 3 = 6$

(E) *(a) 3*

Explanation: Given $B \subset A \Rightarrow A \cap B = B$

$\Rightarrow$ $n(A \cap B) = n(B)$

$\Rightarrow$ $n(A(\cap B) = 3$

26. *In a library, 25 students are reading books on physics, chemistry, and mathematics. It was found that 15 students were reading mathematics, 12 reading physics and 11 reading chemistry, 5 students reading both mathematics and chemistry, 9 students reading physics and mathematics, 4 students reading physics and chemistry, and 3 students reading all three subjects.*

(A) Find the number of students reading only Chemistry and also find the number of students reading only Mathematics.

(B) Find the number of students reading at least one of the subject and also find the numbers.

Ans. Let M denote a set of students who are reading mathematics, P denotes who is reading Physics and C denotes who is reading chemistry.

We have,

$n(U) = 25, n(M) = 15, n(P) = 12, n(C) = 11$

$n(M \cap C) = 5, n(M \cap P) = 9, n(P \cap C) = 4$

$n(M \cap P \cap C) = 3$

(A) The number of students reading only chemistry $= n(M' \cap P' \cap C)$

But, $n(M' \cap P' \cap C) = n((M \cap P)' \cap C)$

$= n(C) - n((M \cup P) \cap C)$

[since, $n(A \cap B') = n(A) - n(A \cap B)$]

$= n(C) - n((M \cap C) \cup (P \cap C))$

$= n(C) - n(M \cap C) + n(P \cap C) - n(M \cap P \cap C))$

$= 11 - (5 + 4 - 3) = 5$

The number of students reading only Mathematics $n(M \cap P' \cap C')$

But, $(M \cap P' \cap C') = n(M \cap (P \cap C)')$

$= n(M) - n(M \cap (P \cap C))$

$= n(M) - n((M \cap P) \cup (M \cap C))$

$= n(M) - (n(M \cap P) + n(M \cap C) - n(M \cap P \cap C))$

$= 15 - (9 + 5 - 3) = 4$

(B) The number of students reading at least one of the subject $= n(M \cup P \cup C)$

$n(M \cup P \cup C)\ n(M) + n(P) + n(C) - n(M \cap P) - n(P \cap C) - n(M \cap C) + n(M \cap P \cap C)$

$15 + 12 + 11 - 9 - 4 - 5 + 3$

$= 41 - 18 = 23$

The number of students reading none of the subjects

$= n(M' \cap P' \cap C') = n\,(M \cup P \cup C)$

But, $n(M \cup P \cup C)'$

$= n(U) - ((M \cup P \cup C) = 25 - 23 = 2$

VERY SHORT ANSWER Type Questions (VSA)

[**1** mark]

27. If $X = \{a, b, c, d\}$ and $Y = \{f, b, d, g\}$, find $X - Y$ and $Y - X$.

Ans. Given $X = \{a, b, c, d\}$ and $Y = \{f, b, d, g\}$.

Then, $X - Y = \{a, b, c, d\} - \{f, b, d, g\} = \{a, c\}$

And $Y - X = \{f. b, d, g\} - \{a, b, c, d\} = \{f, g\}$.

28. For any two sets A and B, prove that:

(A) $(A - B) \cup B = A \cup B$.

(B) $(A - B) \cap B = \phi$

Ans. (A) $(A - B) \cup B = (A \cup B') \cup B$

$= (A \cup B) \cap (B' \cup B)$

[By Distributive Law]

$= (A \cup B) \cup U = A \cup B$

(B) $(A - B) \cap B = (A \cap B') \cap B$

$= A \cap (B' \cap B)$

[By Associative Law]

$= A \cap \phi = \phi$

29. If $U = \{1. 2, \ldots 10\}$, $A = \{1, 2, 3, 5\}$, $B = \{2,4,6,7\}$ and $C = (A \cup B) \cap$, find

(A) $(B \cup C)'$ (B) $(C - A)'$

Ans. Given that $U = \{1. 2, \ldots 10\}$, $A = \{1, 2, 3, 5\}$, $B = \{2,4,6,7\}$ and $C = \{2, 3, 4, 8\}$.

(A) $B \cup C = \{2,4,6,7\} \cup \{2, 3, 4, 8\} = \{2, 3, 4, 6, 7, 8\}$.

Hence, $(B \cup C)' = \{1, 5, 9, 10\}$.

(B) $C - A = \{2, 3, 4, 8\} - \{1, 2, 3, 5\} = \{4, 8\}$.

Hence, $(C - A)' = \{1, 2, 3, 5, 6, 7, 9, 10\}$

30. If R is the set of all real numbers and Q is the set of all rational numbers, then what is $R - Q$?

Ans. Given that R is the set of all numbers and Q is the set of all rational numbers. Then, $R - Q = \{x: x \in R \text{ and } x \notin Q\}$ = set of all irrational numbers.

31. If $a \in N$ such that $aN = \{ax: x \in N\}$. Describe the set $2N \cap 4N$.

Ans. We have, $aN = \{ax: x \in N\}$

$\therefore\ 2N = \{2x: x \in N\} = \{2, 4, 6, 8, \ldots\}$

and, $4N = \{4x: x \in N\} = \{4, 8, 12, 16, \ldots\}$

Hence, $2N \cap 4N = \{4, 8, 12, \ldots\} = \{4x: x \in N\} = 4N$

32. If $A = \{2, 4, 6, 8, 10\ldots\}$, $B = \{1, 3, 5, 7, \ldots\}$ and N is the universal set, then find $A' \cup ((A \cup B) \cap B')$.

Ans. Clearly, $(A \cup B) \cap B' = A$

[$\because$ A, B are disjoint sets]

$\therefore\ A' \cup ((A \cup B) \cap B') = A' \cup A = N$.

(the Universal set.)

33. Fill in the blanks.

(A) $A \cup A' = ...$ **(B) $\phi' \cap A...$**

(C) $A \cap A' ...$ **(D) $\cup' \cap A = ...$**

Ans. (A) $A \cup A' = \cup$ (B) $\phi' \cap A = A$

(C) $A \cap A' = \phi$ (D) $\cup' \cap A = \phi$

34. Which of the following are examples of the empty set?

(A) set of all even natural numbers divisible by 5.

(B) Set of all even prime numbers.

(C) $\{x: x^2 - 2 = 0$ and x is rational$\}$.

(D) $\{x: x$ is a natural number, $x < 8$ and simultaneously $x > 12\}$

(E) $\{x: x$ is a point common to any two parallel lines$\}$.

Ans. (C), (D) and (E) are examples of empty set.

(A) 10, 20, 30. . . are the elements that are even and also divisible by 5. So it is not an empty set.

(B) 2 is the even prime number. So it is not the empty set.

(C) $x^2 - 2 = 0$, $x^2 \Rightarrow 2 = x = \sqrt{2}.\sqrt{2}$ is an irrational number, hence it is the empty set.

(D) No number that is greater than 12 and less than 8, hence it is an empty set.

(E) There is no common point between two parallel lines, hence it is an empty set.

35. Write all the elements of each of the following sets:

(A) Sets of prime number ≤ 11.

(B) $\{x : x \in Z$ and $x > -3$.

Ans. (A) Sets of prime number $\leq 11 = \{2, 3, 5, 7, 11\}$

(B) $\{x: x \in Z$ and $x > -3\} = \{-2, -1, 0, 1, 2, ...\}$

36. List all the proper subsets of the set $\{a, b, c\}$

Ans. Given set is $\{a, b, c\}$.

The proper subsets of the given set are:

$\phi, \{a\}, \{b\}, \{c\}, \{a, b\}, \{a, c\}, \{a, c\}$.

37. If $A = \{1, 2, 3, 4\}$, $B = \{3, 4, 5, 6\}$. Find $A \cap B$ and $A \cup B$

Ans. We have, $A \cap B = \{3, 4\}$

$A \cup B = \{1, 2, 3, 4, 5, 6\}$

38. Let $A\{a, s, d, f\}$, $B = \{a, b, c, d, e\}$ and $\cup = \{a, b, c, d, e, f, s, t\}$. **[DIKSHA]**

(A) $(A \cup B)'$ **(B) $A' \cup B'$**

Ans. Given:

$A\{a, s, d, f\}$, $B\{a, b, c, d, e\}$ and $\cup$ $\{a, b, c, d, e, f, s, t\}$ $A \cup B$ $\{a, b, c, d, e, f, s\}$

(A) $(A \cup B)' = U - (A \cup B)$

$= \{a, b, c, d, e, f, s, t\} - \{a, b, c, d, e, f, s\} = \{t\}$

(B) $A' = U - A = \{b, c, e, s, t\}$

$B' = U - B = \{f, s, t\}$

$A' \cup B' = \{b, c, e, s, t, f\}$

39. In a class of 60 students, 25 students play cricket and 20 students play tennis, and 10 students play both the games. Find the number of students who play neither. **[NCERT Exemplar]**

Ans. Let C be the set of students who play cricket and T be the set of students who play tennis.

$n(U) = 60, n(C) = 25, n(T) = 20$, and $n(C \cap T) = 10$

$n(C \cup T) = n(C) + n(T) - n(C \cap T) = 25 + 20 - 10 = 35$

40. If $\cup = \{7, 8, 9, 10, 11, 12\}$, $A - \{8, 9\}$ and $B = \{9, 10, 11\}$. find $A' \cup B'$

Ans. $A' = \{7, 10, 11, 12, \}$

$B' = \{7, 8, 12\}$

$A' \cup B' = \{7, 8, 10, 11, 12\}$

41. For any to sets A and B, prove that $A \cap (A' \cap B) = A \cap B$.

Ans. $A \cap (A' \cap B) = (A \cap A') \cup (A \cap B)$

[By Distributive Law]

$= \phi \cup (A \cap B) = A \cap B$.

42. For any two sets A and B, prove that $A \cap (A \cap B)' = \phi$

Ans. $A \cap (A \cup B)' = A \cap (A' \cap B')$

[By De Morgan's Law]

$= (A \cap A') \cap B'$

[By Associative Law]

$= \phi \cap B' = \phi$.

43. In a class of 60 students, 25 students play cricket and 20 students play tennis, and 10 students play both the games. Find the number of students who play neither. **[NCERT Exemplar]**

Ans. Explanation: Let C be the set of students who play cricket and T be the set of students who play tennis.

$n(U) = 60, n(C) = 25, n(T) = 20$, and $n(C \cap T) = 10$

$n(C \cup T) = n(C) + n(T) - n(C n T)$

$= 25 + 20 - 10 = 35$

The number of students who play neither Cricket nor Tennis $= n(U) - n(C \cup T)$

$= 60 - 35 = 25$

44. If $U = \{7, 8, 9, 10, 11, 11\}$, $A = \{8, 9\}$ and $B = \{9, 10, 11\}$. find $A' \cup B'$.

Ans.

Explanation: $A' = \cup - A = \{7, 10, 11, 12\}$

$B' = U - B = \{7, 8, 12\}$

$A' \cup B' = \{7, 8, 10, 11, 13\}$

SHORT ANSWER Type-I Questions (SA-I)

[2 marks]

45. If $X = \{5, 6, 7, 8\}$, $Y = \{7, 8, 9, 10\}$, $Z = \{3, 4, 5, 6\}$. Find:

(A) $((X \cap Y) \cup Z)$

(B) $((X \cup Y) \cap Z)$

Ans. Given, $X = \{5, 6, 7, 8\}$, $Y = \{7, 8, 9, 10\}$, $Z = \{3, 4, 5, 6\}$

(A) $X \cap Y = \{5, 6, 7, 8\} \cap \{7, 8, 9, 10\} = \{7, 8\}$

$(X \cap Y) \cup Z = \{7, 8\} \cup \{3, 4, 5, 6\}$
$= \{3, 4, 5, 6, 7, 8\}$

(B) $XY = \{5, 6, 7, 8\} \cup \{7, 8, 9, 10\}$
$= \{5, 6, 7, 8, 9, 10\}$

$(X \cup Y) \cap Z = \{5, 6, 7, 8, 9, 10\} \cap \{3, 4, 5, 6\}$
$= \{5, 6\}$

46. Write the following in roster form.

(A) The set of all even prime numbers.

(B) $\{x : x \in N, x > 2 \text{ and } x < 10\}$

(C) Set all letters in the word BETTER.

(D) $\{x :$ xis a natural number less than 6$\}$.

(E) $\{x : x$ is a positive integer and $x^2 < 40\}$.

Ans. (A) $\{2\}$

(B) $\{3, 4, 5, 6, 7, 8, 9\}$

(C) $\{B, E, T, R\}$

(D) $\{1, 2, 3, 4, 5\}$

(E) $\{1, 2, 3, 4, 5, 6\}$

47. Write the following sets in set-builder form

(A) $\{5, 25, 125, 625\}$

(B) $\{2, 4, 6...\}$

(C) set of all even natural numbers

(D) set of all letters in the word 'TEACHER'.

Ans. (A) $\{x: x = 5^n, x \in N$ and $n \leq 4$

(B) $\{x: x = 2n, n \in N]$

(C) $\{x: x$ is an even natural number$\}$

(D) $\{x: x$ is a letter in word "TEACHER"$\}$

48. Given that $N = \{1, 2, 3,... 100\}$, then

(A) Write the subset A of N, whose elements are odd numbers.

(B) Write the subset B of N, whose elements are represented by $x + 2$, where $x \in N$.

[NCERT Exemplar]

Ans. Given, $N = \{1, 2, 3, \ldots, 100\} = \{x : x = n \text{ and } n \in N\}$

(A) $A = \{x \mid x \in N \text{ and } x \text{ is odd}\} = \{1, 3, 5, 7, \ldots 99\}$

(B) $B = \{y \mid y = x + 2, x \in N\}$

The set whose elements are represented by $x + 2$ where $x \in N$ is

obtained by putting $x=1, 2, 3$ and so on in $y = x + 2$ and we get

$y = x + 2 = 1 + 2 = 3$
$y = x + 2 = 2 + 2 = 4$
$y = x + 2 = 3 + 2 = 5$
$y = x + 2 = 4 + 2 = 6\ldots$
$y = x + 2 = 100 + 2 = 102$

So the required set will be $A = \{3, 4, 5, 6, \ldots 102\}$

49. For any two sets A and B, prove that:

(A) $A \cup (B - A) = A \cup B$.

(B) $(A \cap B) \cup (A - B) = A$

Ans. (A) $A \cup (B - A) = A \cup (B \cap A')$
$= (A \cup B) \cap (A \cup A')$

[By Distributive Law]

$= (A \cup B) \cap U = A \cup B.$

(B) $(A \cap B) \cup (A - B) = (A \cap B) \cup (A \cap B')$
$= A \cap (B \cup B')$

[By Distributive Law]

$= A \cap U = A.$

50. Given $A = \{1, 2, 3, 4, 5\}$, $B = \{2, 4, 6\}$ and $C = \{3, 5, 7\}$.

Find $A - (B \cup C)$ and $A - (B \cap C)$.

Ans. Given

$A = \{1, 2, 3, 4, 5\}$, $B = \{2, 4, 6\}$ and $C = \{3, 5, 7\}$.

Then,

$B \cup C = \{2, 4, 6\} \cup \{3, 5, 7\} = \{2, 3, 4, 5, 6, 7\}$

$B \cap C = \{2, 4, 6\} \cap \{3, 5, 7\} = \phi$

Hence,

$A - (B \cup C) = \{1, 2, 3, 4, 5\} - \{2, 3, 4, 5, 6, 7\} = \{1, 6, 7\}$.

And

$A - (B \cap C) = \{1, 2, 3, 4, 5\} - \phi = \{1, 2, 3, 4, 5\}$

51. Show that if $A \cup B = A \cap B$ it implies that $A = B$

Ans. Given that $A \cup B = A \cap B$ ...(i)

To show $A = B$.

Let $a \in A$ be any element.

$\Rightarrow a \in A \cup B\ [\because A \subseteq A \cup B] \Rightarrow a \in A \cap B$ [Using (1)]

$\Rightarrow a \in A$ and $a \in B \Rightarrow a \in B$

Then, $A \subseteq B$ ....(ii)

Let $a \in B$ be any element

$\Rightarrow a \in A \cup B$ $[\because B \subseteq A \cup B]$

$\Rightarrow a \in A \cap B$ [Using (1)]

$\Rightarrow a \in A$ and $a \in B \Rightarrow a \in A$

Thus, $B \subseteq A$ ...(iii)

From (ii) and (iii), we get

$A = B$.

52. Given that $E = \{2, 4, 6, 8, 10\}$. If n represents any member of E, then write the sets containing all numbers represented by the following:

(A) $2n + 2$ (B) n^3

Ans. (A) Here $E = \{2, 4, 6, 8, 10\}$.

A set containing elements in the form $2n + 2$:

If $n = 2 \Rightarrow 2n + 2 = 2 \times 2 + 2 = 6$

If $n = 4 \Rightarrow 2n + 2 = 2 \times 4 + 2 = 10$

If $n = 6 \Rightarrow 2n + 2 = 2 \times 6 + 2 = 14$

If $n = 8 \Rightarrow 2n + 2 = 2 \times 8 + 2 = 18$

If $n = 10 \Rightarrow 2n + 2 = 2 \times 10 + 2 = 22$

So, the required set is $\{6, 10, 14, 18, 22\}$

(B) A set containing elements in the form of n^3 are

If $n = 2 \Rightarrow n^3 = 2^3 = 8$

If $n = 4 \Rightarrow n^3 = 4^3 = 64$

If $n = 6 \Rightarrow n^3 = 6^3 = 216$

If $n = 8 \Rightarrow n^3 = 8^3 = 512$

If $n = 10 \Rightarrow n^3 = 10^3 = 1000$

So, the set required is $\{8, 64, 216, 512, 1000\}$.

53. If $P(A) = P(B)$, show that $A = B$.

Ans. Given, $P(A) = P(B)\ \forall a \in A$

$\Rightarrow \{a\} \subset A$

$\Rightarrow \{a\} \in P(A)$

$\Rightarrow \{a\} \in P(B)$ $[\because P(A) = P(B)]$

$\Rightarrow \{a\} \in B$

$\Rightarrow a \subset B$

$\Rightarrow a \subset B$

For all $b \in B$

$\Rightarrow \{b\} \subset B$

$\Rightarrow \{b\} \in P(B)$ $[\because P(A) = P(B)]$

$\Rightarrow \{b\} \subset A$

$\Rightarrow \{b\} \in A$

$\Rightarrow B \subset A$

Since, $A \subset B$ and $B \subset A$

$\Rightarrow A = B$

54. Write the following set in the roster form $A = \{x : x$ is a positive integer less than 10 and $2^x - 1$ is an odd number.

Ans. Here in this question, both conditions will be satisfied, which means the element in set A must be a positive integer less than 10 and $2^x - 1$ an odd number

So, here x can have values between 1 and 9 and thus putting the values of x, we get,

$2^x - 1 = 2^1 - 1 = 1$

$2^2 - 1 = 3$

$2^3 - 1 = 7$

$2^4 - 1 = 15$

$2^5 - 1 = 31....$

$2^9 - 1 = 511$

So, $A = \{1, 2, 3, 4, 5, 6, 7, 8, 9\}$.

55. In a class of 60 students, 25 students play cricket and 20 students play tennis, and 10 students play both the games. Find the number of students who play neither.

[NCERT Exemplar]

Ans. Let U denote a set of all students in the class. A denotes the set of students who play cricket and B denotes the set of students who play tennis.

We have, as per the question,

$n(U) = 60, n(A) = 25, n(B) = 20, n(A \cap B) = 10, n(A' \cap B') = ?$

Now,

$n(A' \cap B') = n[(A \cap B)'] = n(U) - n(A \cup B)$

$= n(U) - [n(A) + n(B) - n(A \cap B)]$

$= n(U) - n(A) - n(B) + n(A \cap B)$

$= 60 - 25 - 20 + 10 = 25.$

Hence, the number of students who play neither cricket nor tennis is 25.

56. In a class of 45 students, 25 students like Hindi, 20 like science and 11 like both. Find the no. of students who like

(A) Either Hindi or science

(B) Neither Hindi nor science.

Ans. Let U = all the students of the class, H = students who like Hindi

S = Students who like Science

(A) The no. of student who like either Hindi or science $= n(H \cup S)$

We have, $n(H \cup S) = n(H) + n(S) - n(H \cap S)$

$= 25 + 20 - 11$

$= 34$

(B) $n(H' S') = n(H \cup S)'$

$= \cup - n(H \cup S)$

$= 45 - 34$

$= 11$

SHORT ANSWER Type-II Questions (SA-II)

[**3** marks]

57. Let $A = \{1, 2, 3, 4\}$ $B = \{1, 2, 3\}$ and $C = \{2, 4\}$. Find all sets X satisfying each pair of conditions:

(A) $X \subset B$ and $X \not\subset C$

(B) $X \subset B, X \neq B$ and $X \not\subset C$

(C) $X \subset A, X \subset B$ and $X \subset C$

Ans. (A) We have,

$X \subset B$ and $X \not\subset B$

$\Rightarrow$ X is a subset of B but X is not a subset of C.

$\Rightarrow$ $X \in P(B)$ but $X \notin P(C)$

$\Rightarrow$ $X = \{1\}, \{3\}, \{1, 2\}, \{1, 3\}, \{2, 3\}, \{1, 2, 3\},$

(B) We have,

$X \subset B, X \neq B$ and $X \not\subset B$

$\Rightarrow$ X is a subset of B other than B itself, and X is not a subset of C.

$X \in P(B)$

$\Rightarrow$ $X \in P(B)$, $X \notin P(C)$ but $X \neq B$

$\Rightarrow$ $X = \{1\}, \{3\}, \{1, 2\}, \{1, 3\}, \{2, 3\}$

(C) We have,

$X \subset B, X \subset B$ and $X \subset C$

$\Rightarrow$ $X \in P(A), X \in P(B)$ and $X \in P(C)$

$\Rightarrow$ $X$is a subset of A, B, and C.

$\Rightarrow$ $X = \phi, \{2\}$.

58. In a town of 10000 families it was found that 40% families buy newspaper A, 20% families buy newspaper B, 10% families buy newspaper C, 5% families buy A and B, 3% buy B and C and 4% buy A and C. If 2% families buy all the three newspapers. Find

(A) The number of families which buy newspaper A only.

(B) The number of families which buy none of A, B and C. [DIKSHA]

Ans. Here,

$n(A) = 40\%$

$n(U) = 20\%, n(C) = 10\%, n(A \cap U) = 5\%, n(U \cap C) = 3\%, n(C \cap A) = 4\%, n[A \cap B \cap C] = 2\%$

We can draw a Venn-diagram using the above values

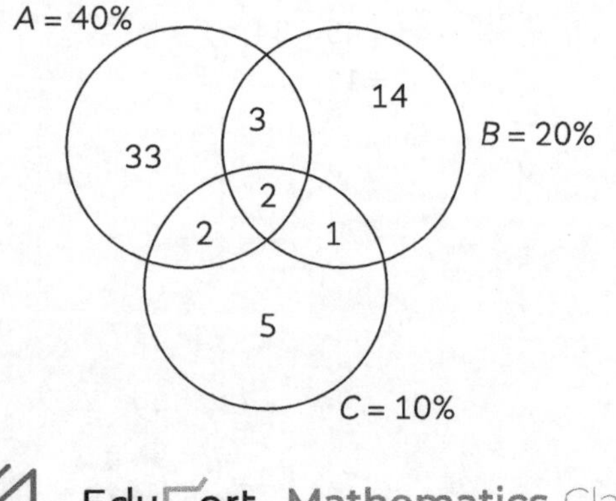

(A) $n(A)$ only $= n(A) - [n(A \cap B) + n(A \cap C)] + n(A \cap B \cap C)$

$= 40\% - [5\% + 4\%] + 2\%$

$= 40\% - [9\%] + 2\%$

$= 33\%$

Thus, the number of families who buy newspaper A only

$= 33\%$ of 100000

$= 3300$

(B) The number of families which buy none of is Total families - those who buy either A, B or C

$= 100\% - [n(A) + n(B) + n(C) - n(A \cap B) - n(B \cap C) - n(C \cap A) + n(A \cap B \cap C)$

$= 100\% - [40\% + 20\% + 10\% - 5\% - 3\% - 4\% - 2\%]$

$= 100\% - [60\%] = 40\%$

$\therefore$ Number of families, who buy none of A, B and C newspapers out of 10000 families are

$= 10000 \times \frac{40}{100}$

$= 4000$ families

59. There are 230 students. 80 play football, 42 play soccer and 12 play rugby. 32 play exactly 2 sports and 4 play all three. How many students play none? [DIKSHA]

Ans. We will calculate the number of students who play none of the sports by the formula which is given below:

Total students = students play football + students play soccer + students play rugby – (students who play exactly 2 sports)– 2^x (students who play all three sports) + students who play none

Putting the values in the above formula, we get,

$230 = 80 + 42 + 12 - 32 - 2 \times 4 +$ students who play none

Students who play none $= 230 - 80 - 42 - 12 + 32 + 8$

Students who play none = 136

Hence, the number of students who play none of the sports is 136.

60. Prove that if $P \cup Q = R$ and $P \cap Q = \phi$ then $P = R - Q$.

Ans. We have, $R - Q$

$RHS = R - Q$

$= (P \cup Q) - Q$

$= (P \cup Q) \cap Q'$

$= Q' \cap (P \cup Q)$

$= (Q' \cap P) \cup (Q' \cap Q)$

$= (Q' \cap P) \cup \phi$

$= Q' \cap P$

$= P \cap Q'$

$= P - Q$

$= P$ [as $P \cap Q = \phi$]

Hence, proved.

61. Let P and Q be sets, if $P \cap X = Q \cap X = \phi$ and $P \cup X = Q \cup X$ for some set X. Show that $P = Q$.

Ans. Given that $P \cap X = Q \cap X = \varnothing$ and $P \cup X = Q \cup X$

To prove $P = Q$

Using $P \cup X = Q \cup X$ (given) we have,

$P \cap (P \cup X) = P \cap (Q \cup X)$

Using distributive property,

$(P \cap P) \cup (P \cap X) = (P \cap Q) \cup (P \cap X)$

$P \cap = (P \cap Q) \cup \Phi$

$P = (P \cap Q)$ ...(i)

Again using, $P \cup X = Q \cup X$

$Q \cap (P \cup X) = Q \cap (Q \cup X)$

Using distributive property,

$(Q \cap P) \cup (Q \cap X) = (Q \cap Q) \cup (Q \cap X)$

$(Q \cap P) \cup \phi = Q \cup \phi$

$Q = (Q \cap P)$

$Q = (P \cap Q)$ ...(ii)

From (i) and (ii), we get

$P = Q$

Hence proved

LONG ANSWER Type Questions (LA)

[**4** & **5** marks]

62. In a competition, a school awarded medals in different categories, 36 medals in dance, 12 medals in dramatics and 18 in music. If these medals went to a total of 45 students and only 4 students got medals in all the three categories, how many did receive medals in exactly two of the categories? [DIKSHA]

Ans. Let A = set of persons who get medals in dance.

B = set of persons who got medals in dramatics.

C = set of persons who got medals in music.

Given,

$n(A) = 36, n(B) = 12, n(C) = 18,$

$n(A \cap B \cap C) = 45\ n(A \cap B \cap C) = 4$

We know that the number of elements belonging to exactly two of the three sets A, B, C

$= n(A \cap B) + n(B \cap C) + n(A \cap C) - 3n(A \cap B \cap C)$

$= n(A \cap B) + n(B \cap C) + n(A \cap C) - 3 \times 4$ ...(i)

Also, $= n(A \cup B \cup C)$

$= n(A) + n(B) + n(c) - n(A \cap B) - n(B \cap C) - n(A \cap B) + n(A \cap B \cap C)$

$= n(B + n(B \cap C) + n(A \cap C)$

$= n(A) + n(B) + n(c) + n(A \cap B \cap C) - n(A \cup B \cup C)$

From (i),

$n(A \cup B \cup C) = n(A) + n(B) + n(c) + n(A \cap B \cap C) - n(A \cup B \cup C) - 12$

$n(A \cup B \cup C) = 36 + 12 + 18 + 4 - 45 - 12$

$n(A \cup B \cup C) = 70 - 57$

$n(A \cup B \cup C) = 13$

63. There are 2000 students in a school. Out of these, 1000 play cricket, 600 play basketball and 550 play football, 120 play cricket and basketball, 80 play basketball and football and 150 play cricket and football and 45 play all three games. How many students play none of the games? [NCERT Exemplar]

Ans. Let U denote a set of all students in the school.

(A) denoted the set of students who play cricket.

(B) denotes the set of students who play basketball and

(C) denotes the set of students who play football.

We have, $n(U) = 2000, n(A) = 1000, n(B) = 600,$ $n(C) = 550, n(A \cap B) = 120$

$n(A \cap C) + 150, n(B \cup C) = 80, n(A \cap B \cap C) = 45,$ $n(A' \cap B' \cap C') = ?$

Now, we know that

$n(A' \cap B' \cap C') = n(U) - n(A \cup B \cup C)$

$= n(U) - [n(A) + n(B) + n(C) - n(A \cap B) - n(A \cap C) - n(B \cap C) - n(A \cap B \cap C)]$

$= 2000 - [1000 + 600 + 500 - 120 - 150 - 80 + 45] = 155$

Hence, the number of students who play none of the games is 155.

64. In a group, 150 students know Hindi and English and 10 know both Hindi and English. If there are 30 students who know neither of the two languages, how many students are there in the group?

Ans. Let U denote a set of all students in the group, A denoted the set of student s who Know Hindi and

B denotes the set of students who Know English.

We have, $n(A) = 150, n(B) = 60, n(A \cap B) = 10, n(A' \cap B') = 30, n(U) = ?$

Now, $n(A' \cap B') = n[(A' \cap B)']$
$= n(U) - n(A \cup B)$
$= n(U) - [n(A) + n(B) - n(A \cap B)]$
$= n(U) - n(A) - n(B) + n(A \cap B)$

$\therefore \quad n(U) = n(A) + n(B) - n(A \cap B) + n(A' \cap B')$
$= 150 + 60 - 10 + 30 = 230$

Hence, the number of students in the group is 230.

65. In a survey of 200 students of a school, it was found that 120 study Mathematics, 90 study Physics and 70 study Chemistry, 40 study Mathematics and Physics, 30 study Physics and Chemistry, 50 study Chemistry and Mathematics and 20 none of these subjects. Find the number of students who study all the three subjects.

Ans. Let M be the set of students who study mathematics, P be the set of students who study E physics and C be the set of students who study chemistry.

Then,

$n(U) = 200, n(M) = 120, n(P) = 90, n(C) = 70,$
$n(M \cap P) = 40, \; n(P \cap C) = 30, n(C \cap M) = 50$

Also, $n(U) - n(M \cup P \cup C) = 20$

Or $n(M \cup P \cup C) = 200 - 20 = 180$

$n(M \cup P \cup C) = n(M) + n(P) + n(C) - n(M \cap P) - n(P \cap C) - n(C \cap M) + n(M \cap P \cap C)$

$\Rightarrow \quad 1180 = 120 + 90 + 70 - 40 - 30 - 50 + n(M \cap P \cap C)$

$\Rightarrow \quad 180 = 160 + n(M \cap P \cap C)$

$\Rightarrow \quad n(M \cap P \cap C) = 180 - 160 = 20$

So, the number of students who study all the three subjects is 20.

66. Let A, B and C be sets. Then show that $A \cup (B \cap C) = (A \cup B) \cap (A \cup C)$.
[NCERT Exemplar]

Ans. We first show that $A \cup (B \cap C) \subset (A \cup B) \cap (A \cup C)$

Let $x \in A \cup (B \cap C)$.

Then $x \in A$ or $x \in B \cap C$

$\Rightarrow \quad x \in A$ or ($x \in B$ and $x \in C$)

$\Rightarrow \quad$ ($x \in A$ or $x \in B$) and ($x \in A$ or $x \in C$)

$\Rightarrow \quad$ ($x \in A \cup B$) and ($x \in A \cup C$)

$\Rightarrow \quad x \in (A \cup B) \cap (A \cup C)$

Thus, $\quad A \cup (B \cup C) \subset (A \cup B) \cap (A \cup C)$ ...(1)

Now we will show that

$(A \cup B) \cap (A \cup C) \subset (A \cup C)$

Let $x \in (A \cup B) \cap (A \cup C)$

$\Rightarrow \quad x \in A \cup B$ and $x \in A \cup C$

$\Rightarrow \quad$ ($x \in A$ or $x \in B$) and ($x \in A$ or $x \in C$)

$\Rightarrow \quad x \in A$ or ($x \in B$ and $x \in C$)

$\Rightarrow \quad x \in A$ or ($x \in B \cap C$)

$\Rightarrow \quad x \in A \cup (B \cap C)$

Thus, $(A \cup B) \cap (A \cup C) \subset A \cup (B \cap C)$ ...(2)

So, from (1) and (2)

We have $A \cap (B \cup C) = (A \cup B) \cap (A \cup C)$

Hence Proved.

67. Let P be the set of prime numbers and let $S = \{t |\ 2^t - 1$ is a prime$\}$. Prove that $S \subset P$.

Ans. Now the equivalent contrapositive statement of $x \in S \Rightarrow x \in P$ is $x \notin P \Rightarrow x \notin S$.

Now, we will prove the above contrapositive statement by contradiction method

Let $x \notin P \Rightarrow x$ is a composite number

Let us now assume that $x \in S$

$\Rightarrow \quad 2^x - 1 = m$ (where m is a prime number)

$\Rightarrow \quad 2^x = m + 1$

Which is not true for all composite numbers, say for $x = 4$ because $2^4 = 16$ which cannot be equal to the sum of any prime number m and 1.

Thus, we arrive at a contradiction $\Rightarrow x \notin S$.

Thus, when $x \notin P$, we arrive at $x \notin S$

So, $S \subset P$

Hence, proved.

2 Relations and Functions

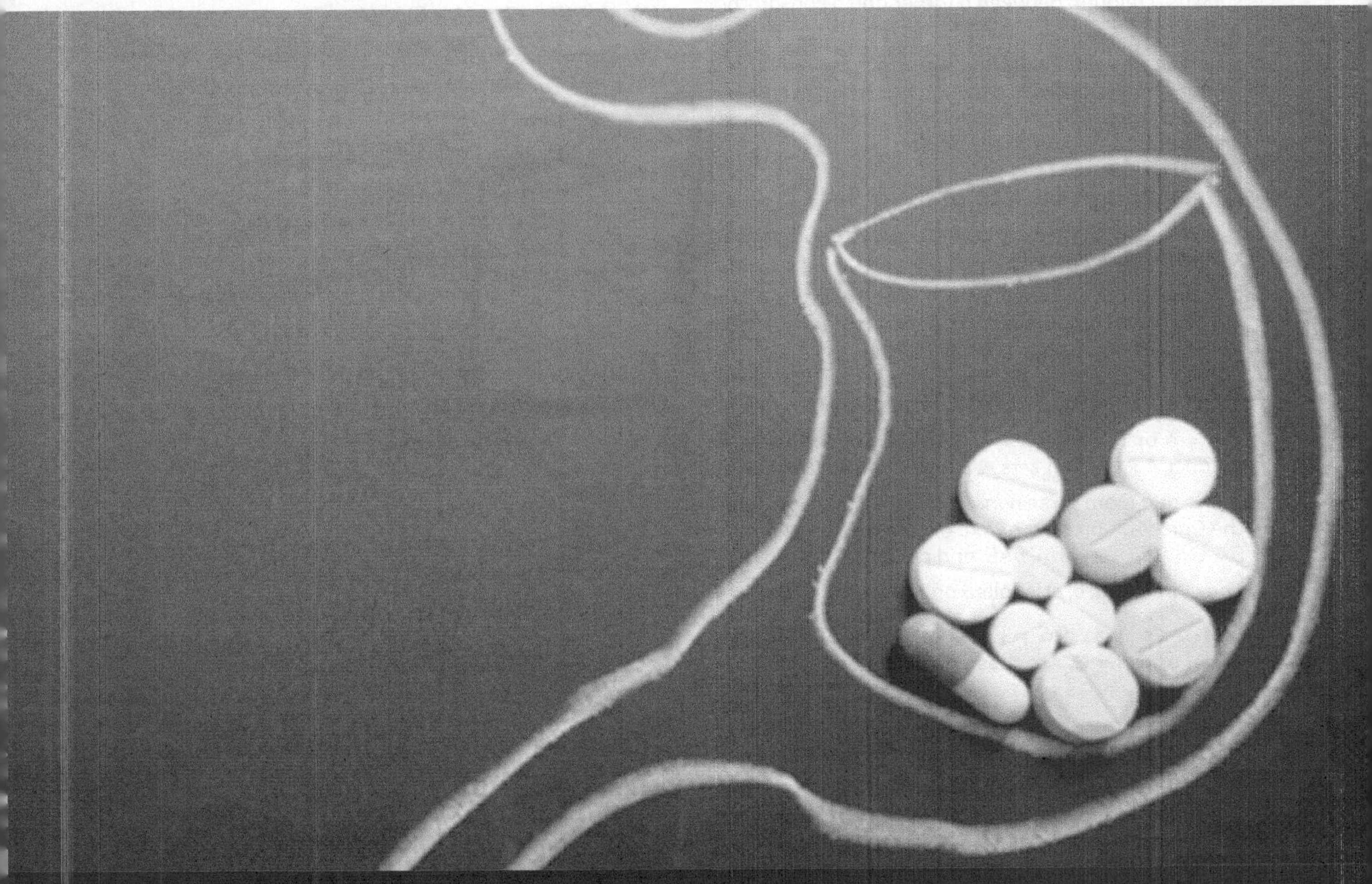

When medicine is given over time a certain amount is going to be absorbed into the body so we need to know the exact amount of the medicine that is existing in that body for a certain Period of time. We will use the relations and functions in determining the concentration of the medicine in the body.

Topic Notes

- *Relations*
- *Functions and it's Types*

RELATIONS 1

TOPIC 1

CARTESIAN PRODUCT OF SETS

Introduction

Relations and Functions give us the link between any two parameters. In our daily lives, we come across many patterns and links that characterise relations, such as a relation between a father and a son, brother and sister, etc.

A person owns one dog, and the dog is owned by one person. In relationships, a person has a partner, who is only partnered with that person. A person owns a car, and the car is owned by the person.

Cartesian Products of Two Sets

If $A = \phi$ or $B = \phi$, then we define the Cartesian product $A \times B$ of sets. A and B as $A \times B = \phi$.

If A and B are two non-empty sets, then we define the Cartesian product $a \times b$ of sets A and B as $A \times B = \{(a, b) \mid a \in A \text{ and } b \in B\}$.

Cartesian Product of Three Sets

If $A = \phi$ or $B = \phi$ or $C = \phi$, then we define Cartesian product $A \times B \times C$ of sets A, B, and C as, $A \times B \times C = \phi$.

If A, B, and C are three non-empty sets, then we define the Cartesian product $a \times b \times c$ of sets A, B, and C as $A \times B \times C = \{(a, b, c) : a \in A, b \in B, \text{ and } c \in C\}$.

The element (a, b, c) is called an **ordered triplet.**

Example 1.1: If $G = \{7, 8\}$ and $H = \{5, 4, 2\}$, find $G \times H$ and $H \times G$. Are these products equal? **[NCERT]**

Ans. Given $G = \{7, 8\}$ and $H = \{5, 4, 2\}$.

Then, $G \times H = \{7, 8\} \times \{5, 4, 2\} = \{(7, 5), (7, 4), (7, 2), (8, 5), (8, 4), (8, 2)\}$

And $H \times G = \{5, 4, 2\} \times \{7, 8\} = \{(5, 7), (5, 8), (4, 7), (4, 8), (2, 7), (2, 8)\}$

Clearly, $G \times H \neq H \times G$.

Example 1.2: If $A = \{-1, 1\}$ then find $A \times A \times A$. **[NCERT]**

Ans. Given $A = \{-1, 1\}$

$A \times A \times A = \{-1, 1\} \times \{-1, 1\} \times \{-1, 1\}$

$A \times A \times A = \{(-1, -1, -1), (-1, -1, 1), (-1, 1, -1), (-1, 1, 1), (1, -1, -1), (1, -1, 1), (1, 1, -1), (1, 1, 1)\}$

Example 1.3: If set A has two elements and set $B = \{0, -1, -2\}$ then find the number of elements in $A \times B$. **[NCERT]**

Ans. No. of elements in $A = 2$

No. of elements in $B = 3$

So, No. of elements in $A \times B = m \times n$

$= 2 \times 3 = 6$

Example 1.4: Let $A = \{1, 2\}$, $B = \{1, 2, 3, 4\}$, $C = \{5, 6\}$ and $D = \{5, 6, 7, 8\}$. Verify that

(A) $A \times (B \cap C) = (A \times B) \cap (A \times C)$

(B) $A \times C$ is a subset of $B \times D$ **[NCERT]**

Ans. (A) To verify: $A \times (B \cap C) = (A \times B) \cap (A \times C)$

L.H.S. $= A \times (B \cap C)$

$B \cap C = \{1, 2, 3, 4\} \cap \{5, 6\} = \phi$

Thus,

$A \times (B \cap C) = \{1, 2\} \times \phi = \phi$

R.H.S. $= (A \times B) \cap (A \times C)$

$A \times B = \{1, 2\} \times \{1, 2, 3, 4\}$

$= \{(1, 1), (1, 2), (1, 3) (1, 4) (2, 1) (2, 2), (2, 3), (2, 4)\}$

$A \times C = \{1, 2\} \times \{5, 6\}$

$= \{(1, 5), (1, 6), (2, 5), (2, 6)\}$

$(A \times B) \cap (A \times C) = \phi$

Therefore, L. H. S. = R. H. S.

Hence, verified.

(B) To verify $A \times C$ is a subset of $B \times D$.

$\subset$ – is a subset

$A \subset B$ if all elements of A are in B.

$A \times C = \{1, 2\} \times \{5, 6\}$

$= \{(1, 5), (1, 6), (2, 5), (2, 6)\}$

$B \times D = \{1, 2, 3, 4\} \times \{5, 6, 7, 8\}$

$= \{(1, 5), (1, 6), (1, 7), (1, 8), (2, 5), (2, 6), (2, 7), (2, 8), (3, 5), (3, 6), (3, 7), (3, 8), (4, 5), (4, 6), (4, 7), (4, 8)\}$

Since all the elements of set $A \times C$ are the elements of set $B \times D$.

$\therefore$ $A \times C$ is a subset of $B \times D$.

Example 1.5: Let A and B be two sets such that $n(A) = 3$ and $n(B) = 2$. If $(x, 1)$, $(y, 2)$, $(z, 1)$ are in $A \times B$, find A and B, where x, y and z are distinct elements. **[NCERT]**

Ans. Given,

$n(A) = 3$ and $n(B) = 2$; and $(x, 1)$, $(y, 2)$, $(z, 1)$ are in $A \times B$.

We know that,

A = Set of first elements of the ordered pair elements of $A \times B$.

B = Set of second elements of the ordered pair elements of $A \times B$.

So, clearly x, y, and z are the elements of A; and 1 and 2 are the elements of B.

As n (A) = 3 and n (B) = 2, it is clear that set A = {x, y, z} and set B = {1, 2}.

TOPIC 2

RELATION

A Relation R between two sets A and B is defined as the subset of the Cartesian product of A and B.

$R \subset A \times B$

Domain, Co-domain and Range of a Relation

Let R be a relation from a non-empty set A to a non-empty set B. Then:

1. The set of all first elements of the ordered pairs in the relation R is called domain of the relation R.
2. The set of all second elements of the ordered pairs in the relation R is called the range of the relation R.
3. The set B is called the co-domain of the relation R.

   For example, consider the relation R defined from A = {2, 3} to B = {6, 9, 12} as R = {(x, y) : x∈A, y∈B, y = 3 x} = {(2, 6), (3, 9)}.

   Then, the domain of R = (2, 3}, co-domain of R ={6, 9, 12}, and the range of R = {6, 9}.

Important

1. *The Domain of R is a subset of A.*
2. *Range of R is a subset of B,*
3. *Co-domain of R is B,*

   i.e., The range is always a subset of the co-domain.
4. *If n (A) = m, n (B) = n; then the n (A × B) = mn and the total number of possible relations from the set A to set B =$2^{m \times n}$.*

Representation of a Relation

A relation can be represented algebraically by roster form or by set-builder form and visually, it can be represented by an arrow diagram.

Roster Form

The relation is represented by the set of all ordered pairs belonging to R.

Set-Builder Form

The relation is represented by, R from set A to set B as R = {(a , b) : a∈A, b∈B and the rule which relate the elements of A and B}.

Example 1.6: If A = {x, y, z} and B = {1, 2}. Find the number of relations from A to B. [NCERT]

Ans. Here, the number of elements in A = 3

And, number of elements in B = 2

So, the number of relation from A to B is

$= 2^{3\times2} = 2^6 = 64$

Diagrammatic Representation of Cartesian Product of two Sets

To represent A × B by an arrow diagram, we first draw Venn diagrams representing sets A and B one opposite to the other as shown in given figure. Now, we draw line segments starting from each element of set A and terminating with each element of set B.

If A = {1, 3, 5} and B = {a, b}, then the following figure gives the arrow diagram of A × B.

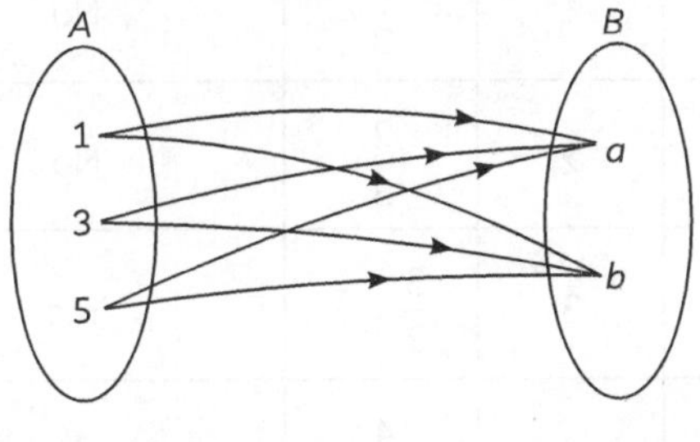

Example 1.7: Let A = {1, 2, 3, 4, 6}. Let R be the relation on A defined by {(a, b) : a, b∈A, b is exactly divisible by a}. [NCERT]

(A) Write R in roaster form

(B) Find the domain of R.

(C) Find the range of R.

Ans. (A) A = {1, 2, 3, 4, 6}

a, b ∈ A

Also, b is exactly divisible by a

Value of a	Value of b	$\frac{b}{a}$	Whether exactly divisible
1	1	$\frac{1}{1} = 1$	Yes
1	2	$\frac{2}{1} = 2$	Yes
1	3	$\frac{3}{1} = 3$	Yes
1	4	$\frac{4}{1} = 4$	Yes
1	6	$\frac{6}{1} = 6$	Yes

A = {1, 2, 3, 4, 6}

Value of a	Value of b	$\frac{b}{a}$	Whether exactly divisible
2	1	$\frac{1}{2}$	No
2	2	$\frac{2}{2}=1$	Yes
2	3	$\frac{3}{2}$	No
2	4	$\frac{4}{2}=2$	Yes
2	6	$\frac{6}{2}=3$	Yes
3	1	$\frac{1}{3}$	No
3	2	$\frac{2}{3}$	No
3	3	$\frac{3}{3}=1$	Yes
3	4	$\frac{4}{3}$	No
3	6	$\frac{6}{3}=2$	Yes

Value of a	Value of b	$\frac{b}{a}$	Whether exactly divisible
4	1	$\frac{1}{4}$	No
4	2	$\frac{2}{4}$	No
4	3	$\frac{3}{4}$	No
4	4	$\frac{4}{4}=1$	Yes
4	6	$\frac{6}{4}$	No
6	1	$\frac{1}{6}$	No
6	2	$\frac{2}{6}$	No
6	3	$\frac{3}{6}$	No
6	4	$\frac{4}{6}$	No
6	6	$\frac{6}{6}=1$	Yes

R = {(1, 1), (1, 2), (1, 3),(1, 4), (1, 6), (2, 2), (2, 4), (2, 6), (3, 3),(3, 6), (4, 4), (6, 6)}

(B) R = {(1, 1), (1, 2), (1, 3), (1, 4), (1, 6), (2, 2), (2, 4), (2, 6), (3, 3), (3, 6), (4, 4), (6, 6)}

Domain of R = Set of first elements of relation
= {1, 2, 3, 4, 6}

(C) R = {(1, 1), (1, 2), (1, 3), (1, 4), (1, 6), (2, 2), (2, 4), (2, 6), (3, 3), (3, 6), (4, 4), (6, 6)}

Range of R = Set of second elements of relation
= {1, 2, 3, 4, 6}

Example 1.8 Let A = {1, 2, 3, . . .14}. Define a relation R from A to A by R = {(x, y) : 3 x − y = 0, where x, y∈A}. Write down its domain, co-domain and range. [NCERT]

Ans. It is given ,

$$3x - y = 0$$
$$3x = y$$
$$y = 3x$$

Value of x	Value of y = 3x	Whether x, y∈A
1	3 × 1 = 3	Yes
2	3 × 2 = 6	Yes
3	3 × 3 = 9	Yes
4	3 × 4 = 12	Yes
5	3 × 5 = 15	Yes
6	3 × 6 = 18	Yes
7	3 × 7 = 21	Yes

Finding relation R

First, we check which values of x, y are in set A.

If both x and y are in set A, then (x, y) ∈R

∴ R = {(1, 3), (2, 6), (3, 9), (4, 12)}

Domain of R = Set of all first elements of the ordered pairs

= {(1, 2, 3, 4}

Range of R = Set of all second elements of the ordered pairs

= {(3, 6, 9, 12}

Codomain

R is defined from A to A

∴ Co-domain of R = A

= {1, 2, 3. . . ,14}

OBJECTIVE Type Questions

[1 mark]

Multiple Choice Questions

1. If $A = \{1, 2, 4\}$, $B = \{2, 4, 5\}$, $C = \{2, 5\}$, then $(A - B) \times (B - C)$ is:

(a) $\{(1, 2), (1, 5), (2, 5)\}$

(b) $\{(1, 4)\}$

(c) $(1, 4)$

(d) None of these

Ans. *(b)* $\{(1, 4)\}$

Explanation: $A - B = \{1\}$

$B - C = \{4\}$

So, $(A - B) \times (B - C) = \{(1, 4)\}$

Hence, option *(b)* is the correct answer.

2. If R is a relation on the set $A = \{1, 2, 3, 4, 6, 7, 8, 9, 11, 12\}$ given by $x R y \Leftrightarrow y = 2x$, then $R =$

(a) $\{(2,1),(4,2),(8,2),(9,3)\}$

(b) $\{(2,1),(4,2),(6,3)\}$

(c) $(5,1),(2,4),(3,6)\}$

(d) None of these

Ans. *(b)* $\{(2, 1), (4, 2), (6, 3)\}$

Explanation: Here $y = 2x$

$y = 2 \times 1 = 2$

if, $x = 1, y = 2$

$x = 2, y = 4$

$x = 3, y = 6$

So, $\{(2, 1), (4, 2), (6, 3)\}$

Hence, option *(b)* is the correct answer.

3. The domain for which the functions defined by $f(x) = 3x^2 - 1$ and $g(x) = 3 + x$ are equal is:

(a) $\left\{-1, \frac{4}{3}\right\}$ **(b) $\left\{-1, \frac{2}{3}\right\}$**

(c) $\left\{-1, \frac{2}{3}\right\}$ **(d) $\left\{-2, \frac{4}{2}\right\}$**

[NCERT Exemplar]

Ans. *(a)* $\left\{-1, \frac{4}{3}\right\}$

Explanation: Given that

$f(x) = 3x^2 - 1$ and $g(x) = 3 + x$

$f(x) = g(x)$

$\Rightarrow \quad 3x^2 - 1 = 3 + x$

$\Rightarrow \quad 3x^2 - x - 4 = 0$

$\Rightarrow \quad 3x^2 - 4x + 3x - 4 = 0$

$\Rightarrow \quad x(3x - 4) + 1(3x - 4) = 0$

$\Rightarrow \quad (x + 1)(3x - 4) = 0$

$\Rightarrow \quad x + 1 = 0$ or $3x - 4 = 0$

$\Rightarrow \quad x = -1,$ or $x = \frac{4}{3}$

$\therefore$ Domain $= \left\{-1, \frac{4}{3}\right\}$

Hence, option *(a)* is the correct answer.

4. Let $A = \{a, b, c\}$, $B = \{1, 3, 5\}$. If relation R from A to B is given by $R = \{(a, 3), (b, 5), (c, 3)\}$. Then, R^{-1} is:

(a) $\{(3, a), (5, b), (3, c)\}$

(b) $\{(1, a), (2, b), (3, c)\}$

(c) $\{(a, 3), (b, 2)\}$

(d) None of these

Ans. *(a)* $\{(3, a), (5, b), (3, c)\}$

Explanation: If $R = \{(a, 3) (b, 5) (c, 3)\}$,

Then

$R^{-1} = \{(3, a), (5, b), (3, c)\}$

Hence, option *(a)* is the correct answer.

5. $R = \{(x, y) | x + 2y = 5\}$ is defined on set $A = \{1, 2, 3, 4, 5\}$ then the domain will be:

(a) $\{1, 2\}$ **(b) $\{1, 2, 3\}$**

(c) $\{1, 2, 3, 4\}$ **(d) $\{1, 2, 3, 4, 5\}$**

[DIKSHA]

Ans. *(d)* $\{1, 2, 3, 4, 5\}$

Explanation: Here, $x + 2y = 5$

For $x = 1, 1 + 2y = 5$

$2y = 4$

$y = 2$

For $x = 2, 2 + 2y = 5$

$2y = 3$

$y = \frac{3}{2} = 1.5$

So, domain $= \{1, 2, 3, 4, 5\}$

Hence, option *(d)* is the correct answer.

6. If $A = \{1, 2, 3\}$, $B = \{1, 4, 6, 9\}$ and R is a relation from A to B defined by x is less than y. The range of R is:

(a) $\{1, 2, 3\}$ **(b) $\{4, 6, 9\}$**

(c) $\{13\}$ **(d) None of these**

Ans. *(b)* $\{4, 6, 9\}$

Explanation: The relation from A to B is x is less than y.

Hence, Range is $\{4, 6, 9\}$

Hence, option *(b)* is the correct answer.

7. Let f and g be two real functions given by

$f = \{(0, 1), (2, 0), (3, -4), (4, 2), (5, 1)\}$

$g = \{(1, 0), (2, 2), (3, -1), (4, 4), (5, 3)\}$

then the domain of f. g is:

(a) {2, 3, 4, 5, 6} (b) {1, 2, 3, 4}

(c) {1, 2, 3, 4, 5} (d) {2, 3, 4, 5}

[NCERT Exemplar]

Ans. *(d) {2, 3, 4, 5}*

Explanation: Given that:

$f(x) = \{(0, 1), (2, 0), (3, -4), (4, 2), (5, 1)\}$

and $g(x) = \{(1, 0), (2, 2), (3, -1), (4, 4), (5, 3)\}$

$\therefore$ domain of $f = \{0, 2, 3, 4, 5\}$ and domain of $g = \{1, 2, 3, 4, 5\}$

So, domain of $f.g$ = Domain of $f \cap$ Domain of g $= \{2, 3, 4, 5\}$

Hence, option (d) is the correct answer.

8. If $R = \{(x, y) : x, y \in Z, x^2 + y^2 \le 16\}$ is a relation on Z, then the domain of R is:

(a) {0, 1, 2, 3, 4}

(b) {0, –1, –2, –3, –4}

(c) {–4, –3, –2, –1, 0, 1, 2, 3, 4}

(d) None of these

Ans *(c) {–4, –3, –2, –1, 0, 1, 2, 3, 4}*

Explanation: $R = \{(x, y) : x, y \in Z, x^2 + y^2 \le 16\}$

then domain

$y^2 = 16 - x^2$

$y = \sqrt{16 - x^2}$

$16 - x^2 \ge 0$

$16 \ge x^2 - 4 \le x \le 4$

So, the domain is {–4, –3, –2, –1, 0, 1, 2, 3, 4}.

Hence, option (c) is the correct answer.

9. A relation R is defined from {2, 3, 4, 5} to {3, 6, 7, 10} by : xRy ⇔ x is factor of y. Then, the domain of R is:

(a) {2, 3, 5} (b) {3,5}

(c) {2,3,4} (d) {2,3,4,5}

Ans. *(a) {2, 3, 5}*

Explanation: Relations x is a factor of y. Here in set {2, 3, 4, 5} the factors of y are {2, 3, 5}.

So,

domain of R = {2, 3, 5}.

Hence, option (a) is the correct answer.

10. How many elements will be there in the Cartesian product of A and B, if number of elements in A and B are respectively 10 and 7 ?

(a) 3 (b) 17

(c) 70 (d) 10^7 [DIKSHA]

Ans. *(c) 70*

Explanation: $n(A) = 10$

$n(B) = 7$

So number of elements in $A \times B = m \times n$

$= 10 \times 7$

$= 70$

Hence, option (c) is the correct answer.

11. The number of relations from an empty set is:

(a) 0 (b) 1

(c) 2 (d) 3

Ans. *(b) 1*

Explanation: Empty set contains no elements means number of relations from empty set is

$2^0 = 1$

Hence, option (c) is the correct answer.

12. Let n (A) = m and n (B) = n, then the total number of non-empty relations that can be defined from A to B is:

(a) m^n (b) $n^m - 1$

(c) $mn - 1$ (d) $2^{mn} - 1$

[NCERT Exemplar]

Ans. *(d) $2^{mn} - 1$*

Explanation: Given that:

$n(A) = m$ and $n(B) = n$

$\therefore n(A \times B) = n(A) . n(B) = mn$

So, the total number of relations from

A to $B = 2^{mn} - 1$.

Hence, option (d) is the correct answer.

13. If A is the finite set and B is an infinite set, then what is A × B?

(a) Infinite set (b) finite set

(c) Undefined (d) A singleton set

Ans. *(a) Infinite set*

Explanation: If A is finite set means elements in A are countable and Set B has an infinite number of elements, which means set B contains uncountable elements so the cartesian product of A and B is Infinite.

Assertion-Reason (A-R)

DIRECTION: In the following questions, a statement of assertion (A) is followed by a statement of the reason (R). Mark the correct choice as:

(a) Both assertion (A) and reason (R) are true and reason (R) is the correct explanation of assertion (A).

(b) Both assertion (A) and reason (R) are true but reason (R) is not the correct explanation of assertion (A).

(c) Assertion (A) is true but reason (R) is false.

(d) Assertion (A) is false but reason (R) is true.

14. Assertion (A): The Domain of the Relation $R = \{x + 2, x + 4 : x \in N, x < 8\}$ is {3, 4, 5, 6, 7, 8, 9}.

Reason (R): The range of the relation $R = \{(x + 2, x + 4 : x \in N, x < 8\}$ is {1, 2, 3, 4, 5, 6, 7}.

Ans. *(c) Assertion (A) is true but reason (R) is false.*

Explanation: The given Relation is R = {(3, 5) (4, 6) (5, 7) (6, 8) (7, 9)(8, 10) (9, 11)}.

Domain = {3, 4, 5, 6, 7, 8, 9}

Range of R = {5, 6, 7, 8, 9, 10, 11}. So, R is false

Thus, assertion is true and reason is false.

Hence, option (c) is the correct answer.

15. Assertion (A): If $(x - 1, y + 2) = (2, 4)$, then $x = 3$ and $y = 2$.

Reason (R): Two ordered pairs (x, y) and (p, q) equal, if their corresponding elements are equal.

Ans. *(a) Both assertion (A) and reason (R) are true and reason (R) is the correct explanation of assertion (A).*

Explanation: Two ordered Pairs are equal, then their corresponding elements are also equal.

So, $x - 1 = 2 \Rightarrow x = 3$, $y + 2 = 4 \Rightarrow y = 2$

Thus, assertion and reason both are true and reason is the correct explanation of assertion.

Hence, option (a) is the correct answer.

16. Assertion (A): If $(x, 1)$, $(y, 1)$ and $(z, 2)$ are in $A \times B$ and $n(A) = 3$, $n(B) = 2$, then $A = (x, y, z)$ and $B = \{1, 2\}$.

Reason (R): If $n(A) = 3$ and $n(B) = 2$ Then $n(A \times B) = 6$.

[NCERT Exemplar]

Ans. *(b) Both assertion (A) and reason (R) are true but reason (R) is not the correct explanation of assertion (A).*

Explanation: $A = \{x, y, z\}$, $B = \{1, 2\}$

$n(A) = 3$, $n(B) = 2$

$n(A \times B) = n(A) \times n(B) = 3 \times 2 = 6$

Thus, both are true but reason is not the correct explanation of assertion.

Hence, option (b) is the correct answer.

17. Assertion (A): Let $A = \{1, 2\}$ and $B = \{3, 4\}$ Then the number of relations from A to B is 16.

Reason (R): If $n(A) = p$ and $n(B) = q$, then number of a relation is 2^{pq}.

[NCERT Exemplar]

Ans. *(a) Both assertion (A) and reason (R) are true and reason (R) is the correct explanation of assertion (A).*

Explanation: Assertion total no of relation $= 2^{mn} = 2^{2\times2} = 2^4 = 16$

Reason total no. of a relation $= 2^{pq}$.

Thus, both are true and reason is the correct explanation of assertion.

Hence, option (a) is the correct answer.

18. Let $A = \{1, 2, 3, 4, 5, 6\}$. If R is the relations on A desired by $\{(a, b) : a, b \in A$ where b is square of $a\}$:

Assertion (A): The relations R in Roster form is $\{(1, 1)(2, 4)\ (3, 9)\ (4, 16)\ (5, 25), (6, 36)\}$.

Reason (R): The domain and range of R is $\{1, 2, 3, 4, 5, 6\}$.

Ans. *(c) Assertion (A) is true but reason (R) is false.*

Explanation: $R = \{(1, 1)\ (2, 4)\ (3, 9)\ (4, 16)\ (5, 25)\ (6, 36)\ (5, 25)\}$

Reason: Domain of $R = \{1, 2, 3, 4, 5, 6\}$

Range of $R = \{1, 4, 9, 16, 25, 36\}$

Hence, assertion is true but reason is false.

CASE BASED Questions (CBQs)

[**4** & **5** marks]

Read the following passages and answer the questions that follow:

19. *The figure shows a relation between the sets P and Q.*

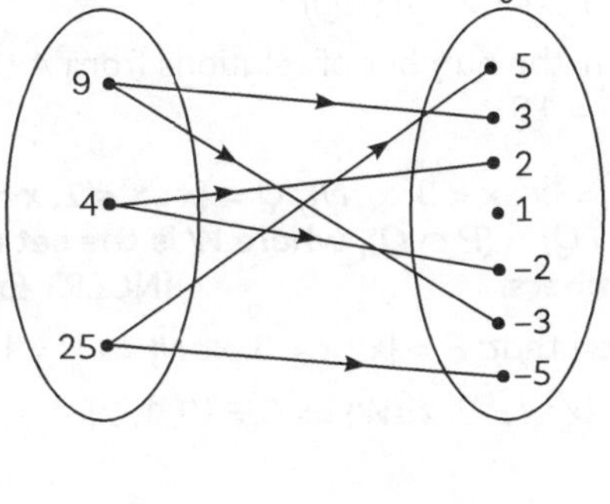

(A) This relation in set builder form is:

(a) $R = \{(x, y) : x$ is square root of y, $x \in P$, $y \in Q\}$

(b) $R = \{(x, y) : y$ is square of x, $x \in P$, $y \in Q\}$

(c) $R = \{(x, y) : x$ is square of y, $x \in P$, $y \in Q\}$

(d) None of these

(B) The domain of relation is:

(a) (1, 2, 3, 4, 5) **(b) {4, 9, 25, 5}**

(c) {4, 9} **(d) {4, 9, 25}**

(C) The range of relation is:

(a) {4, 9, 25}

(b) {1, 2, 3, 4, 5}

(c) {–2, 2, –3, 3, –5, 5}

(d) {–5, –3, –2, 1, 2, 3, 5}

(D) **This relation is roster form is:**

(a) **{(9, 3), (4, 2), (25, 5)}**

(b) **{(9, 3), (9, –3), (4, 2), (4, –2), (25, 5), (25, –5)}**

(c) **{(9, –3), (4, –2), (25, –5)}**

(d) **None of the above**

(E) **The total number of relation from set P to:**

(a) **32** (b) **64**

(c) **128** (d) **None of these**

Ans. (A) (c) $R = \{(x, y) : x$ is square of y, $x\ P, y \in Q\}$

Explanation: Relation R is "x is the square of y".

$\therefore$ In set builder form, $R = \{(x, y) : x$ is the square of $y, x \in P, y \in Q\}$.

(B) (d) $\{4, 9, 25\}$

Explanation: The domain of relation is an element of set P i.e. $\{4, 9, 25\}$.

(C) (c) $\{-2, 2, -3, 3, -5, 5\}$

Explanation: The range of relation is $\{-2, 2, -3, 3, -5, 5\}$.

(D) (b) $\{(9, 3), (9, -3), (4, 2), (4, -2), (25, 5), (25, -5)\}$

Explanation: In roster form $R = \{(9, 3), (9, -3), (4, 2), (4, -2), (25, 5), (25, -5)\}$.

(E) (b) 64

Explanation: Total number of ordered pair in $R = 6$ (note that total no. of ordered pairs possible are $3 \times 7 = 21$)

$\therefore$ Total number of relation $= 2^6 = 64$

20. *Method to find the sets when cartesian product is given.*

For finding these two sets, we write the first element of each ordered pair in first set say A and corresponding second element in second set B (say).

Number of elements in cartesian product of two sets.

If there are p elements in set A and q elements in set B, then there will be pq elements in A × B i.e., if $n(A) = p$ and $n(B) = q$, then $n(A \times B) = pq$.

(A) **If $A \times B = \{(a, 1), (b, 3), (a, 3), (b, 1), (a, 2), (b, 2)\}$. Then, find A and B. If the set A has 3 elements and set B has 4 elements, then find the number of elements in $A \times B$.**

(B) **The Cartesian product $P \times P$ has 16 elements among which are found $(a, 1)$ and $(b, 2)$. Then find the set P.**

Ans. (A) Here, the first element of each ordered pair of $A \times B$ gives the elements of set A and the corresponding second element gives the elements of set B.

$\therefore$ $A = \{a, b\}$ and $B = \{1, 3, 2\}$

Given $n(A) = 3$ and $n(B) = 4$

$\therefore$ The number of elements in $A \times B$ is

$n(A \times B) = n(A) \times n(B) = 3 \times 4 = 12$

(B) Given, $n(P \times P) = 16$

$\Rightarrow$ $n(P).\ n(P) = 16$

$\Rightarrow$ $n(P) = 4$ ...(1)

Now, as $(a, 1) \in P \times P$

$\therefore$ $a \in P$ and $1 \in P$

Again, $(b, 2) \in P \times P$

$\therefore$ $b \in P$ and $2 \in P$

$\Rightarrow$ $a, b, 1, 2 \in P$

VERY SHORT ANSWER Type Questions (VSA)

[1 mark]

21. Is $R = \{(1, 5), (2, 9), (3, 1), (4, 5), (2, 11)\}$ a relation from set A to set B, where $A = \{1, 2, 3, 4\}$ and $B = \{1, 5, 9, 11, 15, 16\}$? Justify your answer.

Ans. Given: $A = \{1, 2, 3, 4\}$, $B = \{1, 5, 9, 11, 15, 16\}$.

Since, $R = \{(1, 5), (2, 9), (3, 1), (4, 5), (2, 11)\} \subseteq A \times B$.

So, R is a relation from A to B.

22. Let $A = \{a, b, c\}$, $B = \{b, c, d\}$ and $C = \{b, d\}$ then find $(A - B) \times (B - C)$. [DIKSHA]

Ans. Here,

$A - B = \{a\}$

And $B - C = \{c\}$

So, $(A - B) \times (B - C) = \{a\} \times \{c\} = \{(a, c)\}$

23. Let $A = \{-1, -2\}$. Find the number of relations from A to A.

Ans. Given $A = \{-1, -2\}$

$n(A) = 2 = n$ (say).

Then, the number of relations from A to $A = 2^{n^2} = 2^4 = 16$

24. If $P = \{x : x < 3, x \in N\}$, $Q = \{x : x \leq 2, x \in W\}$. Find $(P \cup Q) \times (P \cap Q)$, where W is the set of whole numbers. [NCERT Exemplar]

Ans. Given that: $P = \{x : x < 3, x \in N\} \Rightarrow P = \{1, 2\}$

$Q = \{x : x \leq 2, x \in W\} \Rightarrow Q = \{0, 1, 2\}$

Now,$(P \cup Q) = \{0, 1, 2\}$ and $(P \cap Q) = \{1, 2\}$

$\therefore$ $(P \cup Q) \times (P \cap Q) = \{(0, 1), (0, 2), (1, 1), (1, 2), (2, 1), (2, 2)\}$

25. Write the Relation, $R = \{(x, x^4) : x$ is an even number less than 10} in roster form.

Ans. Here 2, 4, 6, 8 are the even numbers less than 10.

So, $(x, x^4) = (2, 16)\ (4, 256)\ (6, 1296)\ (8, 4096)\}$

So, $R = \{(2, 16)\ (4, 256)\ (6, 1296)\ (8,4096)\}$.

26. If $R = \{(1, 8)\ (3, 6)\ (5, 2)\ (1, 4)\}$ then find A and B.

Ans. Given $R = \{(1, 8)\ (3, 6)\ (5, 2)\ (1,4)\}$

$A = \{1, 3, 5,\}$

$B = \{8, 6, 2, 4\}$

27. Determine the Domain and Range of R.

$R = \{(x, x + 5) : x \in \{0, 1, 2, 3, 4, 5\}$

Ans. Domain $= \{0, 1, 2, 3, 4, 5\}$

Range $= \{5, 6, 7, 8, 9, 10\}$

28. If $A = \{x : x \in W, x < 2\}$ $B = \{x : x \in N, 1 < x < 5\}$ $C = \{3, 5\}$ find

(A) $A \times (B \cap C)$ (B) $A \times (B \cup C)$

[NCERT Exemplar]

Ans. Given that: $A = \{x : x \in W, x < 2\} \Rightarrow A = \{0, 1\}$

$B = \{x : x \in N, 1 < x < 5\} \Rightarrow B = \{2, 3, 4\}$

$C = \{3, 5\}$

(A) $A \times (B \cap C) = \{0, 1\} \times \{3\} = \{(0, 3), (1, 3)\}$

(B) $A \times (B \cup C) = \{0, 1\} \times \{2, 3, 4, 5\}$

$= \{(0, 2), (0, 3), (0,4), (0, 5), (1, 2), (1, 3), (1, 4), (1, 5)\}$

29. The cartesian product $A \times A$ has 16 elements among which are found $(-2, 1)$ $(0, 3)$and $(1, 3)$. Find set A.

Ans. $(-2, 1) \in A \times A, (0, 3) \in A \times A$ and $(1, 3) \in A \times A$

Hence,

$-2, 1, 0, 3 \in A$

So, set $= \{-2, 1, 0, 3\}$.

30. If $\left(\frac{x}{4}+1, y-\frac{2}{4}\right) = \left(\frac{3}{4}, \frac{1}{4}\right)$, then find the values of x and y.

Ans. Given that $\left(\frac{x}{4}+1, y-\frac{2}{4}\right) = \left(\frac{3}{4}, \frac{1}{4}\right)$,

$\therefore$ Corresponding elements of above-ordered pairs must be equal.

We have,

$$\frac{x}{4}+1=\frac{3}{4} \quad \Rightarrow x = -1$$

$$y-\frac{2}{4}=\frac{1}{4} \quad \Rightarrow y = 3/4$$

Hence, $x = -1$, $y = \frac{3}{4}$.

31. Given $R = \{(x, y) : x, y \in W, x^2 + y^2 = 64\}$. Where W is the set of all whole numbers. Find the domain and range of R.

Ans. Here $R = \{(x, y) : x, y \in W, x^2 + y^2 = 64\}$

So, $x = \sqrt{64 - y^2}$

So, $-8 \leq y \leq 8$

Hence, Domain $= [-8, 8]$

And Range $= [0, 8]$

32. If $A = \{0, 1, 2\}$ and $B = \{3, 4\}$. Find domain of $A \times B$.

Ans. Given,

$A = \{0, 1, 2\}$ and $B = \{3, 4\}$

$A \times B = \{(0, 3)\ (0, 4)\ (1 ,3)\ (1, 4)\ (2, 3)\ (2, 4)\}$

So, the domain of $A \times B = \{0, 1, 2\}$

Hence, Domain of $A \times B = A$

33. Find the domain and range of the relation $R = \{(x, y) : y = x + \frac{8}{x}$, where $x, y \in N$ and $x < 8\}$

Ans. Given, $R = \{(x, y) : y = x + \frac{8}{x}$,where $x, y \in N$ and $x < 8\} = \{(1, 9), (2, 6), (4, 6), (8, 9)\}$.

Hence, domain of $R = \{1, 2, 4, 8\}$ and range of $R = \{6, 9\}$.

SHORT ANSWER Type-I Questions (SA-I)

[**2** marks]

34. Let $A = \{1, 3, 5, 7\}$ and $B = \{2, 4, 6, 8\}$ be two sets and let R be a relation from A to B defined by the phrase "$(x, y) \in R \Leftrightarrow x > y$".

Ans. Under this relation R, we obtain $3R2$, $5R2$, $5R4$, $7R2$, $7R4$ and $7R6$.

i.e. $R = \{(3, 2), (5, 2), (5, 4), (7, 2), (7, 4), (7, 6)\}$.

$\therefore$ Domain $(R) = \{3, 5, 7\}$ and range $(R) = \{2, 4, 6\}$

35. **In each of the following cases, find *a* and *b*.**

(A) $(2a + b, a - b) = (8, 3)$

(B) $\left(\frac{a}{4}, a - 2b\right) = (0, 6 + b)$

[NCERT Exemplar]

Ans. (A) Given that: $(2a + b, a - b) = (8, 3)$

Comparing the domains and ranges, we get

$2a + b = 8$ ...(i)

$a - b = 3$ ...(ii)

Solving (i) and (ii) we get $a = \frac{11}{3}$ and $b = \frac{2}{3}$

(B) Given that: $\left(\frac{a}{4}, a - 2b\right) = (0, 6 + b)$

Comparing the domains and ranges, we get

$\frac{a}{4} = 0 \Rightarrow a = 0, a - 2b = 6 + b$

$\Rightarrow \quad a - 3b = 6 \Rightarrow 0 - 3b = 6$

$\therefore \quad b = -2$

So, $a = 0$, $b = -2$.

36. **In function $f = \{(1, 1), (0, -2), (3, 0), (2, 4)\}$ be a linear function defined by formula, $f(x) = ax + b$. Then find 'a' and 'b'. [DIKSHA]**

Ans. $f = \{(1, 1)\}$ $(0, -2), (3, 0), (2, 4)\}$

and $f(x) = ax + b$

then, $f(0) = -2$

$-2 = a \times 0 + b$

$-2 = b$

and

$f(1) = 1$

$1 = a \times 1 + b$

$1 = a + b$

$1 = a - 2$

$3 = a$

37. **If R is a relation from set $A = \{2, 4, 5\}$ to set $B = \{1, 2, 3, 4, 6, 8\}$ defined by $x\,R\,y \Leftrightarrow x - y$ is an odd number.**

(A) Write R as a set of ordered pairs.

(B) Find the domain and the range of R.

Ans. Clearly, $2R1$, $2R3$, $4R1$, $4R3$, $5R2$, $5R4$, $5R6$ and $5R8$.

$\therefore \quad R = \{(2, 1), (2, 3), (4, 1), (4, 3), (5, 2), (5, 4), (5, 6), (5, 8)\}$

Clearly, Domain $(R) = \{2, 4, 5\}$ and Range $(R) = \{1, 2, 3, 4, 6, 8\}$

38. **If $f(x) = x^4$ then find the range of the function for $\{x = 1, 2, 3, 4, 5\}$.**

Ans. Here $f(x) = x^4$

For $x = 1$

$f(x) = 1^4 = 1$

For $x = 2$

$f(x) = 2^4 = 16$

For $x = 3$

$f(x) = 3^4 = 81$

For $x = 4$

$f(x) = 4^4 = 256$

For $x = 5$

$f(x) = 5^4 = 625$

Hence, Range of $f(x) = x^4$ for $x = 1, 2, 3, 4, 5$ is $= \{1, 16, 81, 256, 625\}$.

39. **Define a relation R on the set N of natural numbers by**

$R = \{(x, y)\,;\, y = x + 3$, x is a prime number less than $8 : x, y \in N\}$.

Depict this relationship using a roaster form. Write down the domain and the range.

Ans. Given N = Set of all natural numbers and

$R = \{(x, y) : y = x + 3$, x is a prime number less than 8; $x, y \in N\}$

$= \{(x, y) : y = x + 3, x \in \{2, 3, 5, 7\}; x, y \in N\}$.

The given relation in roaster form can be written as

$R = \{(2, 5), (3, 6), (5, 8)\ (7, 10)\}$.

Hence, domain of $R = \{2, 3, 5, 8\}$ and range of $R = \{5, 6, 8, 10\}$.

SHORT ANSWER Type-II Questions (SA-II)

[3 marks]

40. **Let R be a relation from, Q and Q defined by $R = \{(p, q) : p, q \in Q$ and $q + p \in Z\}$. Show that**

(A) $(p, p) \in R$, for all $p \in Q$.

(B) $(p, q) \in R$ implies that $(q, p) \in R$.

(C) $(p, q) \in R$ and $(q, r) \in R$ implies that $(p, r) \in R$.

Ans. Given $R = \{(p, q) : p, q \in Q$ and $p - q \in Z\}$.

(A) Since, $p + p \in Z$, is true, where $p \in Q$.

$\Rightarrow (p, p) \in R$.

(B) Let $(p, q) \in R$, where $p, q \in Q$.

$\Rightarrow p + q \in Z$

$\Rightarrow (p + q) \in Z$

$\Rightarrow q + p \in Z$

$\Rightarrow (q, p) \in R$.

(C) Let $(p, q) \in R$ and $(q, r) \in R$, where $p, q, r \in Z$

$\Rightarrow$ $p + q \in Z$ and $q + r \in Z$

$\Rightarrow$ $p + q = k_1$ and $q + r = k_2$, for some $k_1, k_2 \in Z$

On adding above equations, we get

$p + r = k_1 + k_2 \in Z$

$\Rightarrow$ $(p, r) \in R$.

41. Let R be a relation N to N defined by $R = \{(a, b) : a, b \in N$ and $a = b^3\}$. Are the following true ? Justify your answer in each case.

(A) $(a, a) \in R$, For all $a \in N$

(B) $(a, b) \in R$ implies that $(b, a) \in R$

(C) $(a, b) \in R$ and $(b, c) \in R$ implies $(a, c) \in R$

Ans. Given $R = \{(a, b) : a, b \in N$ and $a = b^3\}$.

(A) Since, $a = a^3$, is not true, for some $a \in N$

For $a = 2$, we have $(a, a) \notin R$

(B) Let $(a, b) \in R$, where $a, b \in N$

$\Rightarrow$ $a = b^3$.

$\Rightarrow$ $b \neq a^3$, for some $a, b \in N$

For $a = 8, b = 2$, we have $(a, b) \in R$ but $(b, a) \in R$.

(C) Let $(a, b) \in R$ and $(b, c) \in R$, where $a, b, c \in N$.

$\Rightarrow$ $a = b^3$ and $b = 3$

$\Rightarrow$ $a \neq c^3$, for some $a, c \in N$

For $a = 64, b = 4$, we have $(a, b) \in R$ and $(b, c) \in R$ but $(a, c) \notin R$.

42. Let $f(x) = \sqrt{x}$ and $g(x) = x$ be two functions defined in the domain $R^+ \cup \{0\}$.

(A) $(f + g)(x)$ (B) $(f - g)(x)$

(C) $(f . g)(x)$ (D) $\left(\frac{f}{g}\right)(x)$

[NCERT Exemplar]

Ans. Given that: $f(x) = \sqrt{x}$ and $g(x) = x$ be two functions defined in the domain $R^+ \cup \{0\}$

(A) $(f + g)(x) = f(x) + g(x) = \sqrt{x} + x$

(B) $(f - g)(x) = f(x) - g(x) = \sqrt{x} - x$

(C) $(f \cdot g)(x) = f(x) . g(x) = \sqrt{x}.x = x^{3/2}$

(D) $\left(\frac{f}{g}\right)(x) = \frac{f(x)}{g(x)} = \frac{\sqrt{x}}{x} = \frac{1}{\sqrt{x}}$

43. Determine the domain and range of the relation R defined by

(A) $R = \{(x, x + 6) : x \in \{0, 1, 2, 3, 4, 5\}$.

(B) $R = \{(x, x^4) : x$ is a prime number less than 20\}.

Ans. (A) $R = \{(x, x + 6) : x \in \{0, 1, 2, 3, 4, 5\}$

Given,

$R = \{(x, x + 6) : x \in \{0, 1, 2, 3, 4, 5\}$

$\therefore$ $R = \{(0, 0 + 6), (1, 1 + 6), (2, 2 + 6), (3, 3 + 6), (4, 4 + 6), (5, 5 + 6)\}$

$R = \{(0, 6), (1, 7), (2, 8), (3, 9), (4, 10), (5, 11)\}$

So,

Domain of relation $R = \{0, 1, 2, 3, 4, 5\}$

Range of relation $R = \{6, 7, 8, 9, 10, 11\}$

(B) $R = \{(x, x^4) : x$ is a prime number less than 20\}

Given,

$R = \{(x, x^4) : x$ is a prime number less than 20\}

Prime numbers less than 20 are 2, 3, 5, 7, 11, 13, 17, 19

$\therefore$ $R = \{(2, 2^4), (3, 3^4), (5, 5^4), (7, 7^4), (11, 11^4), (13, 13^4), (17, 17^4), (19, 19^4)\}$

$R = \{(2, 16), (3, 81), (5, 625), (7, 2401), (11, 14641), (13, 28561), (17, 83521), (19, 130321)\}$

So,

Domain of relation $R = \{2, 3, 5, 7, 11, 13, 17, 19\}$

Range of relation $R = \{16, 81, 625, 2401, 14641, 28561, 83521, 130321\}$

44. Let a the relation R_1 on the set R of all real numbers be defined as $(a, b) \in R_1 \Leftrightarrow 1 + ab > 0$ for all $a, b \in R$.

Show that:

(A) $(a, a) \in R_1$ for all $a \in R$

(B) $(a, b) \in R_1 \Rightarrow (b, a) \in R_1$ for all $a, b \in R$

Ans. (A) For any $a \in R$, we have

$1 + a^2 > 0 \Rightarrow (a, a) \in R_1$

Thus, $(a, a) \in R_1$ for all $a \in R$.

(B) Let $(a, b) \in R_1$. Then,

$(a, b) \in R_1 \Rightarrow 1 + ab > 0$

$\Rightarrow 1 + ba > 0 \Rightarrow (b, a) \in R_1$

Thus, $(a, b) \in R_1$

$\Rightarrow (b, a) \in R_1$ for all $a, b \in R$.

45. Let A = \{1, 2, 3, 4, 5, 6\}. Define a relation R from A to A by $R = \{(x, y) : y = x - 1\}$. Write R in roster form. Write down the domain, co-domain and range of R.

Ans. Given $A = \{1, 2, 3, 4, 5, 6\}$ and

$R = \{(x, y) : y = x - 1\}$.

The given relation in roster form can be written as

$R = \{(1, 0), (2, 1), (3, 2), (4, 3), (5, 4), (6, 5)\}$

The given relation can be represented with the following arrow diagram:

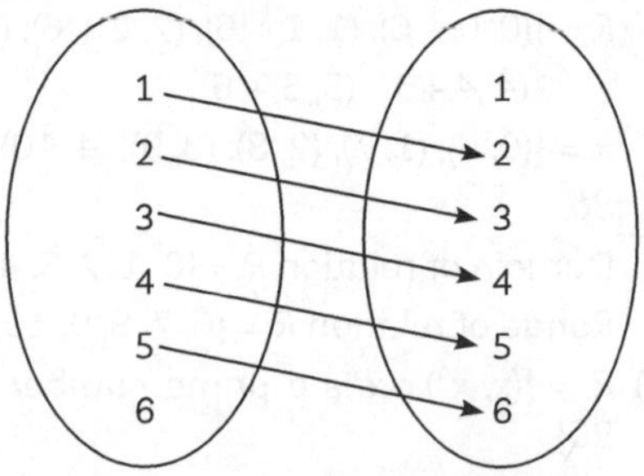

So, domain of $R = \{1, 2, 3, 4, 5, 6\}$, co-domain of $R = \{0, 1, 2, 3, 4, 5\}$ and range of $R = \{2, 3, 4, 5, 6\}$.

46. Is $g = \{(1, 1), (2, 3), (3, 5), (4, 7)\}$ a function? Justify: If this is described by the relation, $g(x) = \alpha x + \beta$, then what values should be assigned to α and β? [NCERT Exemplar]

Ans. Given that: $g = \{(1, 1), (2, 3), (3, 5), (4, 7)\}$

Since every element of the domain in this relations has unique image, so g is a function.

Now, $g(x) = \alpha x + \beta$

For (1, 1), $g(1) = \alpha(1) + \beta = 1 \Rightarrow \alpha + \beta = 1$ ...(i)

For (2, 3), $g(2) = \alpha(2) + \beta = 3 \Rightarrow 2\alpha + \beta = 3$ ...(ii)

Solving eqn. (i) and (ii) we have

$\alpha = 2$ and $\beta = -1$

[Note: We can take any other two ordered pairs]

Hence, the value of $\alpha = 2$ and $\beta = -1$.

LONG ANSWER Type Questions (LA)

[**4** & **5** marks]

47. Let $A = \{-1, 2, 3\}$ and $B = \{1, 3\}$. [NCERT Exemplar]

Determine (A) $A \times B$ (B) $B \times A$ (C) $B \times B$ (D) $A \times A$

Ans. Given, $A = \{-1, 2, 3\}$ and $B = \{1, 3\}$

(A) $A \times B = \{-1, 2, 3\} \times \{1, 3\}$

So, $A \times B = \{(-1, 1), (-1, 3), (2, 1), (2, 3), (3, 1), (3, 3)\}$

Hence, the Cartesian product $= \{(-1, 1), (-1, 3), (2, 1), (2, 3), (3, 1), (3, 3)\}$.

(B) $B \times A = \{1, 3\} \times \{-1, 2, 3\}$

Therefore, $B \times A = \{(1, -1), (1, 2), (1, 3), (3, -1), (3, 2), (3, 3)\}$.

Hence, the Cartesian product $= \{(1, -1), (1, 2), (1, 3), (3, -1), (3, 2), (3, 3)\}$.

(C) $B \times B = \{1, 3\} \times \{1, 3\}$

So, $B \times B = \{(1, 1), (1, 3), (3, 1), (3, 3)\}$

Hence, the Cartesian product $= \{(1, 1), (1, 3), (3, 1), (3, 3)\}$.

(D) $A \times A = \{-1, 2, 3\} \times \{-1, 2, 3\}$

So, $A \times A = \{(-1, -1), (-1, 2), (-1, 3), (2, -1), (2, 2), (2, 3), (3, -1), (3, 2), (3, 3)\}$

Hence, the Cartesian product

$= \{(-1, -1), (-1, 2), (-1, 3), (2, -1), (2, 2), (2, 3), (3, -1), (3, 2), (3, 3)\}$.

48. Let $A = \{-2, -1, 0, 1, 2\}$ and $f : A \to Z$ be given by $f(x) = x^2 - 2x - 3$. Find:

(A) the range of f

(B) pre-images of 6, – 3 and 5.

Ans. (A) We have, $f(x) = x^2 - 2x - 3$,

$\therefore$ $f(-2) = (-2)^2 - 2(-2) - 3 = 5$,

$f(-1) = (-1)^2 - 2(-1) - 3 = 0, f(0) = -3$,

$f(1) = 1^2 - 2 \times 1 - 3 = -4$ and

$f(2) = 2^2 - 2 \times 2 - 3 = -3$.

So, range $(f) = \{f(-2), f(-1), f(0), f(1), f(2)\}$
$= \{5, 0, -3, -4, -3\}$.

(B) Let x be a pre-image of 6. Then,

$f(x) = 6$

$\Rightarrow x^2 - 2x - 3 = 6$

$\Rightarrow x^2 - 2x - 9 = 0$

$\Rightarrow x = 1 \pm \sqrt{10}$

Since $x = 1 \pm \sqrt{10} \notin A$.

So, there is no pre-image of 6.

Let x be a pre-image of –3.

Then,

$f(x) = -3$

$\Rightarrow x^2 - 2x - 3 = -3$

$\Rightarrow x^2 - 2x = 0$

$\Rightarrow x = 0, 2$.

Clearly, $0, 2 \in A$.

So, 0 and 2 are pre-images of –3.

Let x be a pre-image of 5. Then, $f(x) = 5$

$\Rightarrow x^2 - 2x - 3 = 5$

$\Rightarrow x^2 - 2x - 8 = 0$

$\Rightarrow (x - 4)(x + 2) = 0$

$\Rightarrow x = 4, -2$.

Since $-2 \in A$ but $4 \notin A$.

So, –2 is a pre-image of 5.

49. Prove that:

(A) $(P \cup Q) \times R = (P \times R) \cup (Q \times R)$

(B) $(P \cap Q) \times R = (P \times R) \cap (Q \times R)$

Ans. (A) $(P \cup Q) \times R = (P \times R) = (P \times R) \cup (Q \times R)$

Let (x, y)be an arbitrary element of $(P \cup Q) \times R$.

$(x, y) \in (P \cup Q) \times R$

Since, (x, y) are elements of the cartesian product of $(P \cup Q) \times R$.

$x \in (P \cup Q)$ and $y \in R$

$(x \in P$ or $x \in Q)$ and $y \in R$

$(x \in P$ and $y \in R)$ or $(x \in Q$ and $y \in R)$

$(x, y) \in P \times R$ or $(x, y) \in Q \times R$

$(x, y) \in (P \times R) \cup (Q \times R)$ ...(1)

Let (x, y) be an arbitrary element of $(P \times R) \cup (Q \times R)$.

$(x, y) \in (P \times R) \cup (Q \times R)$

$(x, y) \in (P \times R)$ or $(x, y) \in (Q \times R)$

$(x \in P$ and $y \in R)$ or $(x \in Q$ and $y \in R)$

$(x \in P$ or $x \in Q)$ and $y \in R$

$x \in (P \cup Q)$ and $y \in R$

$(x, y) \in (P \cup Q) \times R$ ...(2)

From 1 and 2, we get:

$(P \cup Q) \times R = (P \times R) \cup (Q \times R)$

(B) $(P \cap Q) \times R = (P \times R) \cap (Q \times R)$

Let (x, y) be an arbitrary element of $(P \cap Q) \times R$.

$(x, y) \in (P \cap Q) \times R$

Since, (x, y) are elements of Cartesian product of $(P \cap Q) \times R$

$x \in (P \cap Q)$ and $y \in R$

$(x \in P$ and $x \in Q)$ and $y \in R$

$(x \in P$ and $y \in R)$ and $(x \in Q$ and $y \in R)$

$(x, y) \in P \times R$ and $(x, y) \in Q \times R$

$(x, y) \in (P \times R) \cap (Q \times R)$ ...(1)

Let (x, y) be an arbitrary element of $(P \times R) \cap (Q \times R)$.

$(x, y) \in (P \times R) \cap (Q \times R)$

$(x, y) \in (P \times R)$ and $(x, y) \in (Q \times R)$

$(x \in P$ and $y \in R)$ and $(x \in Q$ and $y \in R)$

$(x \in P$ and $x \in Q)$ and $y \in R$

$x \in (P \cap Q)$ and $y \in R$

$(x, y) \in (P \cap Q) \times R$ ...(2)

From 1 and 2, we get:

$(P \cap Q) \times R = (P \times R) \cap (Q \times R)$

FUNCTIONS AND IT'S TYPES 2

TOPIC 1

FUNCTION

A function *f* from set *A* to *B* defines as a mapping between two sets that satisfy the following two conditions $f: A \rightarrow B$

1. Each every element of Set *A* must be mapped with some elements of Set *B*.
2. No elements of Set *A* must be mapped with more than one element of Set *B*.

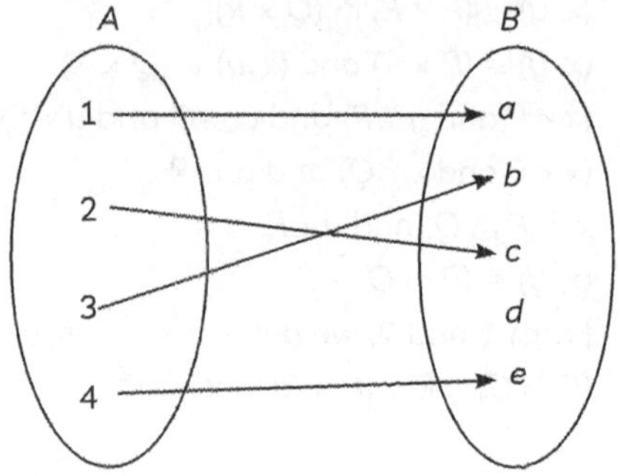

Important

- *Every function is a relation, but every relation is not a function.*
- *If A has m elements and B has n elements, then the number of functions from A to B is n^m. and B to A is m^n.*

Domain and Co-Domain

Let $f: A \rightarrow B$, then set A is known as the domain of , and set *B* is known as the Co-domain of *f*.

If $f: N \rightarrow R$ so, here *N* is the domain and *R* is the co-domain.

Range

The set of elements in set *B* that are mapped with elements of set *A*, is called the Range of the function.

Range of $f \subseteq$ Co-domain of *f*.

Illustration : Let $A = \{-2, -1, 0, 1, 2\}$ and $B = \{0, 1, 2, 3, 4, 5, 6\}$. Consider a rule $f(x) = x^2$. Under this rule, we obtain $f(-2) = (-2)^2 = 4$, $f(-1) = (-1)^2 = 1$, $f(0) = 0^2 = 0$, $f(1) = 1^2 = 1$ and $f(2) = 2^2 = 4$. We observe that each element of *A* is associated to a unique element of *B*. So, $f: A \rightarrow B$ given by $f(x) = x^2$ is a function. Clearly, domain $(f) = A = \{-2, -1, 0, 1, 2\}$ and range $(f) = \{0, 1, 4\}$.

Equal Functions

The two functions *f* and *g* are said to be equal iff.

1. domain of *f* = domain of *g*.
2. domain of *f* = co-domain of *g*.
3. $f(x) = g(x)$ for all *x* belonging to their common domain.

Illustration : Let $A = \{1, 2\}$, $B = \{3, 6\}$ and $f: A \rightarrow B$ given by $f(x) = x^2 + 2$ and $g: A \rightarrow B$ given by $g(x) = 3x$. Then, we observe that *f* and *g* have the same domain and co-domain. Also, we have, $f(1) = 3 = g(1)$ and $f(2) = 6 = g(2)$. Hence, $f = g$.

Example 2.1: Which of the following relations are functions? Give reasons. Also, determine its domain and range.

(A) {(2, 1), (5, 1), (8, 1), (11, 1), (14, 1), (17, 1)}

(B) {(2, 1), (4, 2), (6, 3), (8, 4), (10, 5), (12, 6), (14, 7)}

(C) {(1, 3), (1, 5), (2, 5)}. **[NCERT]**

Ans. (A) Let $R = \{(2, 1), (5, 1), (8, 1), (11, 1), (14, 1), (17, 1)\}$

Then, domain of $R = \{2, 5, 8, 11, 14, 17\}$ and range of $R = \{1\}$.

Since, every element in the domain has only one image.

Hence, *R* is a function.

(B) Let $R = \{(2, 1), (4, 2), (6, 3), (8, 4), (10, 5), (12, 6), (14, 7)\}$

Then, domain of $R = \{2, 4, 6, 8, 10, 12, 14\}$ and range of $R = \{1, 2, 3, 4, 5, 6, 7\}$.

Since every element in the domain has only one image.

Hence, *R* is a function.

(C) Let $R = \{(1, 3), (1, 5), (2, 5)\}$

Then, domain of $R = \{1, 2\}$ and range of $R = \{3, 5\}$.

Since element 1 in the domain does not have only one image. (1 has two images, 3 and 5).

Hence, *R* is not a function.

Example 2.2: Write total number of functions from Set *A* to Set *B*.

(A) $A = \{1, 2, 3\}$, $B = \{a, b, c\}$

(B) $A = \{1, 2, 3\}$, $B = \{a, b, c, d\}$ **[NCERT]**

Ans. (A) In set *A* no. of elements $m = 3$

In set *B* no. of elements $n = 3$

So, total no. of function from *A* to *B* is $= n^m$

$= 3^3 = 27$

(B) In set A, $m = 3$

In set B, $n = 4$

So total no. of function from A to B is $= n^m$

$= 4^3 = 64$

Example 2.3: Find the domain for which the function $f(x) = 2x^2 - 1$ and $g(x) = 1 - 3x$ are equal. **[NCERT]**

Ans. The values of x for which $f(x)$ and $g(x)$ are equal, are given by

$$f(x) = g(x)$$

$$\Rightarrow \quad 2x^2 - 1 = 1 - 3x$$

$$\Rightarrow \quad 2x^2 + 3x - 2 = 0$$

$$\Rightarrow \quad (x + 2)(2x - 1) = 0$$

$$\Rightarrow \quad x = -2, 1/2$$

Thus, $f(x)$ and $g(x)$ are equal on the set $\{-2, 1/2\}$.

Real-Valued Functions

A function $f : A \rightarrow B$ is called a real-valued function if B is a subset of R.

Real Function

A function $f : A \rightarrow B$ is called a real function if both A and B are subsets of R.

Domain of Real Function

The Domain of $f(x)$ is the set of all those real numbers for which $f(x)$ is defined.

Range of Real Function

The range of a real function is the set of all real values taken by $f(x)$ at the points in its domain.

Steps to find Range

(i) Put $y = f(x) \Rightarrow x = g(y)$.

(ii) Find the value of x by solving the equation.

(iii) Find the values of y for which the values of x, obtain from $x = g(y)$, values of x are Real, and in the domain of f.

(iv) The set of values of y obtained is the range of f.

Example 2.4 Find domain of $\sqrt{x-2}$. **[NCERT]**

Ans. $y = f(x)$

$$y = \sqrt{x-2}$$

$$x - 2 \geq 0$$

$$x \geq 2$$

$$x \in [2, \infty)$$

Hence, domain $= [2, \infty)$

Example 2.5 Find the range of $f(x) = \dfrac{x-2}{3-x}$. **[NCERT]**

Ans. Let, $y = f(x)$

$$y = \frac{x-2}{3-x}.$$

$$3y - xy = x - 2$$

$$x(y + 1) = 3y + 2$$

$$x = \frac{3y+2}{y+1}$$

Here, x assumes real values at all points except when

$$y + 1 = 0 \text{ i.e. } y = -1$$

Hence, Range $(f) = R - \{-1\}$.

Some Specific Types of Function & Their graphs

Constant Function

$f(x) = k, \forall x \in R$

Domain $= R$

Range of $f = \{k\}$

Graph of f is a line parallel to x-axis.

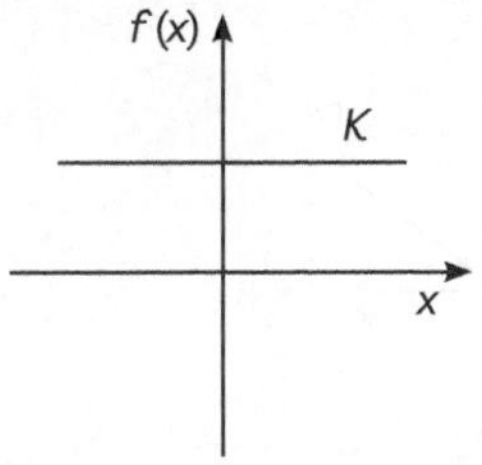

Identity Function

$f(x) = x, \forall x \in R$

Domain of $f = R$

Range of $f = R$

Graph of f is a straight line.

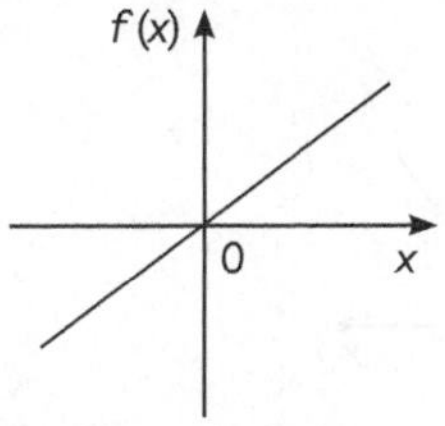

Polynomial Function

$f(x) = a_0 + a_1 x + ... + a_n x^n \ \forall x \in R$

Domain of $f = R$

Range of $f = R$

$f(x) = x^2 + x - 1$

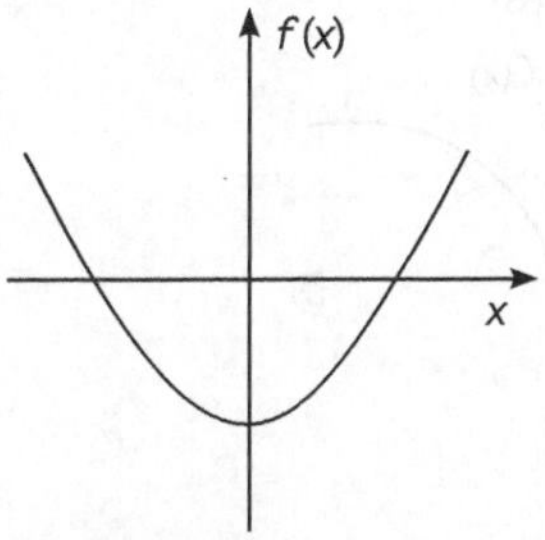

Rational Function

$$f(x) = \frac{g(x)}{h(x)}, \forall x \in R \ h(x) \neq 0$$

Domain of $f \subseteq R$

Range of $f \subseteq R$

$f(x) = \dfrac{x^2}{x+3}$

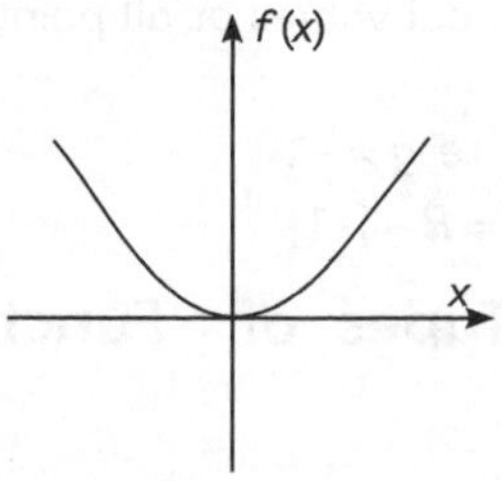

Linear Function

$f(x) = ax + b \ \forall x \in R$, a and b are constant.

Domain of $f = R$

Range of $f = R$

$f(x) = 2x - 1$

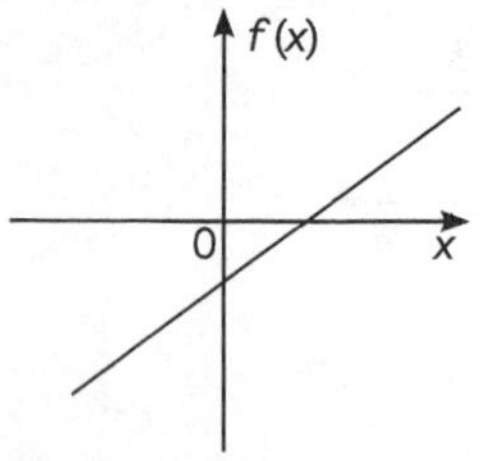

Square function

$f(x) = x^2 \ \ \forall x \in R$

Domain of $f = R$

Range of $f = [0, \infty)$

Graph of parabola

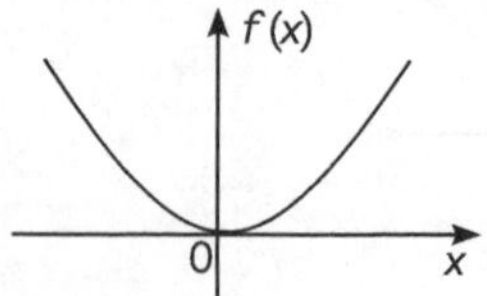

Square root function

$f(x) = \sqrt{x} \ \ \forall \in [0, \infty)$

The domain of $f = [0, \infty)$

Range of $f = [0, \infty)$

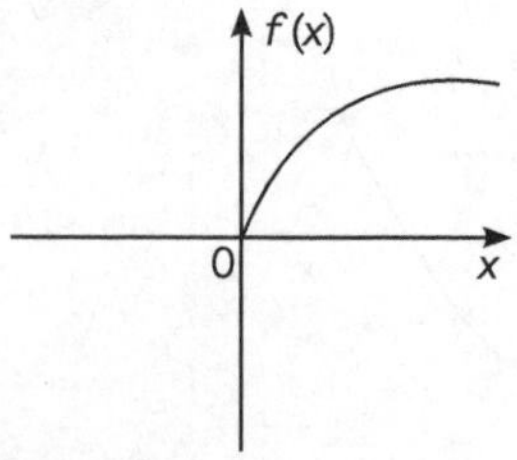

Reciprocal function

$f(x) = \dfrac{1}{x} \ \ \forall x \in R - \{0\}$

Domain of $f = R - \{0\}$

Range of $f = R - \{0\}$

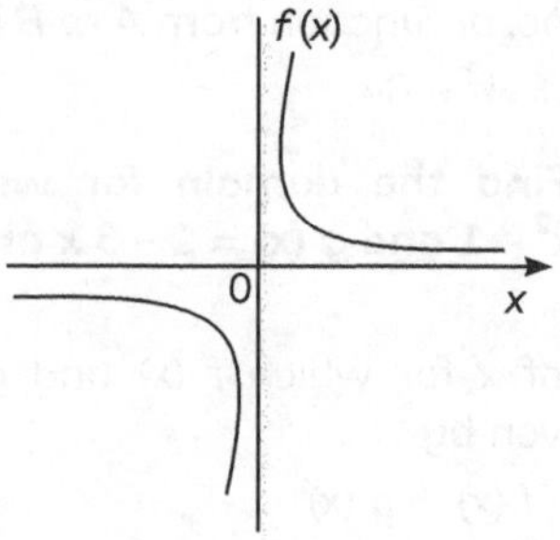

Modulus Function

$f(x) = |x| \ \forall x \in R$

Domain of $f = R$

Range of $f = [0, \infty)$

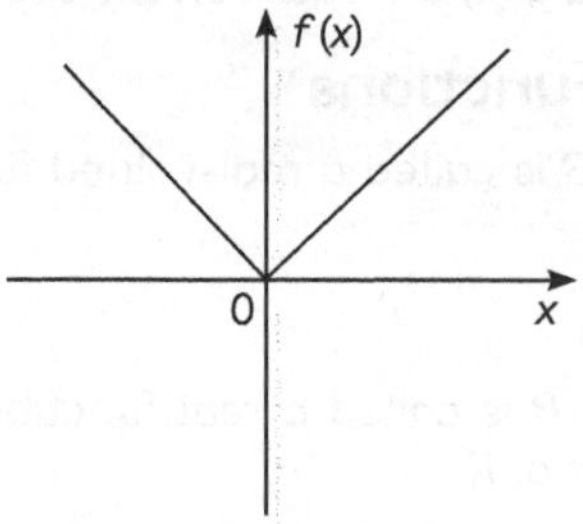

Greatest integer function

$f(x) = [x] \ \forall x \in R$

Domain of $f = R$

Range of $f = Z$

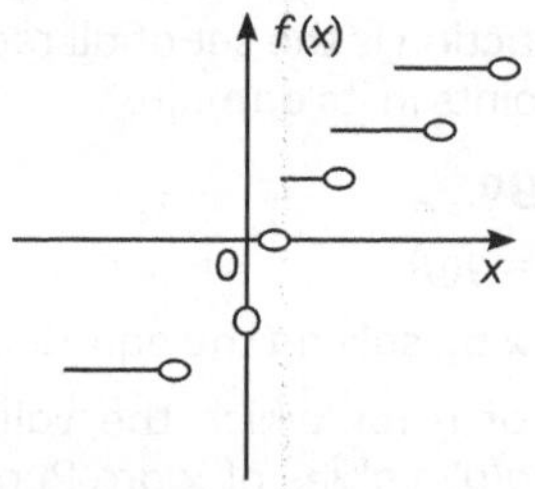

Signum function

$$f(x) = \begin{cases} 1 & x > 0 \\ 0 & > \ = 0 \\ -1 & x < 0 \end{cases} \ \forall x \in R$$

Domain of $f = R$

Range of $f = \{-1, 0, 1\}$

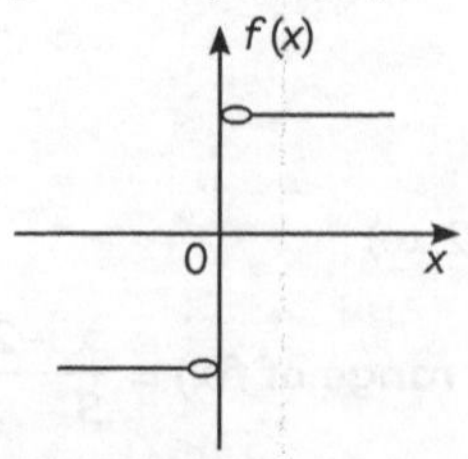

Exponential function

$f(x) = e^{xn} \ \ \forall x \in R$

Domain of $f = R$

Range of $f = (0, \infty)$

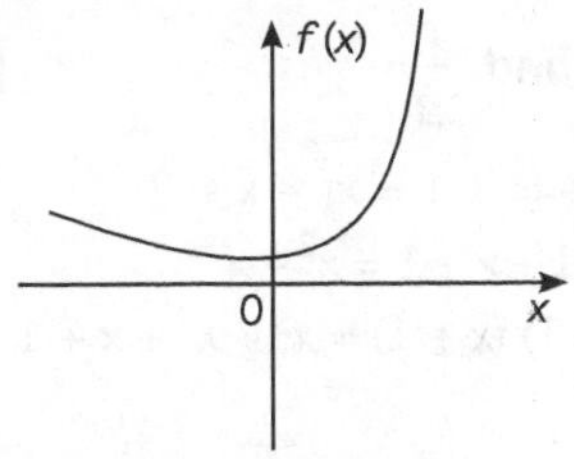

Logarithmic function

$f(x) = \log_b x \ \forall x \in (0, \infty)$

The domain of $f = (0, \infty)$

Range of $f = R$

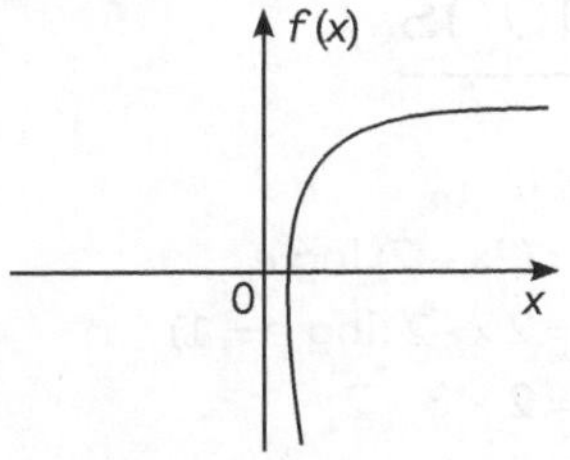

Example 2.6: *A* **function** *f* **is defined by** *f (x)* **= 2*x* – 5 Write values of**

(A) $f(0)$ **(B)** $f(7)$ **(C)** $f(-3)$

[NCERT]

Ans. $f(x) = 2x - 5$

So

(A) $f(0) = 2 \times 0 - 5 = -5$

(B) $f(7) = 2 \times 7 - 5 = 9$

(C) $f(-3) = 2 \times -3 - 5 = -11$

Example 2.7: The function, '*F*' which maps temperature in degree Celsius into temperature in degree Fahrenheit, is defined by $F(C) = \frac{9C}{5} + 32$.

(A) $F(10)$

(B) $F(15)$

(C) $F(-10)$

(D) The value of *C*, when $F(C) = 212$. [NCERT]

Ans. Given $F(C) = \frac{9C}{5} + 32$.

(A) $F(10) = \frac{9}{5}(10) + 32 = 50$

(B) $F(15) = \frac{9}{5}(15) + 32 = 59$

(C) $F(-10) = \frac{9}{5}(-10) + 32 = 14$

(D) We have,

$F(C) = 212$

$\Rightarrow \frac{9C}{5} + 32 = 212$

$\Rightarrow \frac{9C}{5} = 180$

$\Rightarrow C = 100$

Example 2.8: $f(x) = x^2$ **and find** $\frac{f(2.2) - f(2)}{2.2 - 2}$.

[NCERT]

Ans. $f(x) = x^2$

$$\frac{f(2.2) - f(2)}{2.2 - 2} = \frac{(2.2)^2 - (2)^2}{(2.2) - (2)}$$

$$= \frac{(2.2 + 2)(2.2 - 2)}{(2.2 - 2)}$$

$$= 2.2 + 2 = 4.2$$

TOPIC 2

ALGEBRA ON REAL FUNCTION

Let $f: D \to R$ and $g: D \to R$ be any two real functions (where $D \subseteq R$). Then,

1. The Sum of real functions f and g is a function.

   $f + g : D \to R$

   Defined by

   $(f + g)(x) = f(x) + g(x)$, for all $x \in D$.

2. The difference of real functions g from f is a function.

   $f - g : D \to R$

   Defined by

   $(f - g)(x) = f(x) - g(x)$, for all $x \in D$

3. The product (or pointwise multiplication) of real functions f and g is a function.

   $fg : D \to R$

   Defined by

   $(fg)(x) = f(x)\, g(x)$, for all $x \in D$.

4. Multiplication of real functions f by a scalar (i.e., a real number) α is a function $\alpha f: D \to R$.

   Defined by

   $(\alpha f)(x) = \alpha f(x)$, for all $x \in D$

5. The quotient of real functions f by g is a function.

   $\frac{f}{g} : D \to R$

   Defined by

   $\left(\frac{f}{g}\right)(x) = \frac{f(x)}{g(x)}$, for all $x \in D$ where $g(x) \neq 0$.

If the functions f and g have different domains, then we have the following conclusion:

Let f and g be two functions with domains D_1 and D_2 respectively. Let α be a scalar. Then,

1. The domain of $f + g = \{x : x \in D_1 \cap D_2\}$.
2. The domain of $f - g = \{x : x \in D_1 \cap D_2\}$
3. The domain of αf = Domain of f.
4. The domain of $fg = \{x : x \in D_1 \cap D_2\}$.
5. The domain of $\frac{f}{g} = \{x : x \in D_1 \cap D_2, g(x) \neq 0\}$.

Example 2.9: If $f(x) = x^3 + 1$ and $g(x) = x + 1$. Find $f + g$, $f - g$, fg and $\frac{f}{g}$ **[NCERT]**

Ans. $f + g = x^3 + 1 + \propto + 1 = x^3 + x + 2$

$$f - g = x^3 + 1 - x - 1 = x^3 - x$$

$$f.g = (x^3 + 1)(x + 1) = x^4 + x^3 + x + 1$$

$$\frac{f}{g} = \frac{x^3+1}{x+1}$$

OBJECTIVE Type Questions

[**1** mark]

Multiple Choice Questions

1. Let $A = \{a, b, c\}$, $B = \{2, 3, 4\}$, then which of the following is a function from A to B?

(a) $\{(a, 2), (b, 3), (c, 3), (c,3)\}$

(b) $\{(a, 3), (b, 4)\}$

(c) $\{(a, 3), (b, 2), (c, 3)\}$

(d) $\{(a, 2), (b, 3), (c, 2), (c, 4)\}$

Ans. *(c) $\{(a, 3), (b, 2), (c, 3)\}$*

Explanation: Let $A = \{a, b, c\}$

$B = \{2, 3, 4\}$

So, function from A to B is

$\{(a, 3)\ (b, 2)\ (c, 3)\}$

Hence, option (c) is the correct answer.

2. If $f : Q \rightarrow Q$ is defined as $f(x) = x^2$, then $f^1(16)$ is equal to:

(a) 4 **(b) –4**

(c) $\{-4,4\}$ **(d) ϕ**

Ans. *(c) $\{-4, 4\}$*

Explanation:

$$f(x) = x^2$$

$$y = x^2$$

$$\sqrt{y} = x$$

i.e. $f^1(x) = \sqrt{y}$

$$f^1(16) = \sqrt{16} = \{-4, 4\}$$

Hence, option (c) is the correct answer.

3. If $p = e^{2x-2}$ then $\log p$ at $x = 3$ is:

(a) 1 **(b) 2**

(c) 3 **(d) 4**

Ans. *(d) 4*

Explanation: $p = e^{2x-2}$

Taking log both side

$$\log p = \log e^{2x-2}$$

$$= (2x - 2) \log e$$

$$\log p = 2x - 2 \ (\log e = 1)$$

$$\log p = 2 \times 3 - 2$$

$$= 6 - 2$$

$$= 4$$

$$\log p = 4$$

Hence, option (d) is the correct answer.

4. Let $f(x) = |x - 2|$. Then,

(a) $f(x^2) = [f(x)]^2$ **(b) $f(x + y) = f(x) f(y)$**

(c) $f(|x|) = |f(x)|$ **(d) None of these**

Ans. *(d) None of these*

Explanation:

$$f(x) = |x - 2|$$

Here,

$$f(x^2) \neq [f(x)]^2$$

$$f(x + y) \neq f(x).f(y)$$

and

$$f(|x|) \neq |f(x)|$$

Hence, option (*d*) is the correct answer.

5. If $f(x) = 2x^3 - \left(\frac{1}{x}\right)^{1/2}$, then $f(4)$ =

(a) $\frac{255}{2}$ **(b) $\frac{2}{255}$**

(c) 0 **(d) None of these**

Ans. *(a) $\frac{255}{2}$*

Explanation: $f(x) = 2x^3 - \left(\frac{1}{x}\right)^{1/2}$

Put, $x = 4$

$$f(4) = 2 \times 4^3 - \left(\frac{1}{4}\right)^{1/2}$$

$$f(4) = 2 \times 64 - \frac{1}{2}$$

$$f(4) = 128 - \frac{1}{2}$$

$$f(4) = \frac{256-1}{2}$$

$$f(4) = \frac{255}{2}$$

Hence, option (*a*) is the correct answer.

6. Domain of = $\sqrt{a^2 - x^2}$ ($a < 0$) is:

(a) $(-a, a)$ **(b) $[-a, a]$**
(c) $[0, a]$ **(d) $[-a, 0]$**

Ans. (*b*) $[-a, a]$

Explanation: Let, $f(x) = \sqrt{a^2 - x^2}$

For $f(x)$ to be defined $a^2 - x^2 \geq 0$

$$x^2 \leq a^2$$

$$x \leq [-a, a]$$

7. Let $f(x) = \begin{cases} 3 - 2x & x < 1 \\ 3x + 5 & 1 \leq x \leq 2, \\ 5x - 2 & x > 3 \end{cases}$

then $2f(0) + f(3) = ?$

(a) 17 **(b) 19**
(c) 24 **(d) 31** **[DIKSHA]**

Ans. (*b*) 19

Explanation: Here,

$$f(0) = 3 - 2(0) = 3$$

$$f(3) = 5 \times 3 - 2 = 13$$

So,

$$2f(0) + f(3) = 2 \times 3 + 13$$
$$= 6 + 13$$
$$= 19$$

Hence, option (*b*) is the correct answer.

8. If A = {a, b, c} B = {x, y}, then the number of functions that can be defined from A into B is:

(a) 12 **(b) 8**
(c) 6 **(d) 3**

Ans. (*b*) 8

Explanation: Here, $n(A) = 3 = m$

$$n(B) = 2 = m$$

We know that the number of functions from

$A \to B$ is n^m $= 2^3 = 8$

Hence, option (*b*) is the correct answer.

9. Is the given Relation is a function?
R = {(1, 3) (2, 4) (2, 3) (3, 4)}.

(a) Yes **(b) No**
(c) Cannot say **(d) Insufficient**

Ans. (*b*) No

Explanation: Here domain of the relation is repeated.

Hence, it is not a function.

Hence, option (*b*) is the correct answer.

10. If $[x]^2 - 5[x] + 6 = 0$, where [.] denotes the greatest integer function, then

(a) $x \in [3, 4]$ **(b) $x \in (2, 3]$**
(c) $x \in [2, 3]$ **(d) $x \in [2, 4)$**

[NCERT Exemplar]

Ans. (*c*) $x \in [2, 3]$

Explanation: We have

$$[x]^2 - 5[x] + 6 = 0$$
$$\Rightarrow [x]^2 - 3[x] - 2[x] + 6 = 0$$
$$\Rightarrow [x]([x] - 3) - 2([x] - 3) = 0$$
$$\Rightarrow ([x] - 3)([x] - 2) = 0$$
$$\Rightarrow [x] = 2, 3$$

So, $x \in [2, 3]$.

Hence, option (*c*) is the correct answer.

11. Domain of $\sqrt{7 - x^2}$ is:

(a) $[0, \sqrt{7}]$ **(b) $[-\sqrt{7}, \sqrt{7})$**
(c) $[\sqrt{7}, 0]$ **(d) None**

Ans. (*b*) $[-\sqrt{7}, \sqrt{7})$

Explanation: Here $7 - x^2 \geq 0$

$$7 \geq x^2$$

$$\sqrt{7} \geq x > \sqrt{7}$$

Domain is $[-\sqrt{7}, \sqrt{7})$.

Hence, option (*b*) is the correct answer.

12. If $f(x) = \dfrac{1}{2 - \sin 3x}$, then range (*f*) is equal to:

(a) $[-1, 1]$ **(b) $\left[-\frac{1}{3}, \frac{1}{3}\right]$**
(c) $\left[\frac{1}{3}, 1\right]$ **(d) $\left[-1, \frac{-1}{3}\right]$**

Ans. (*c*) $\left[\frac{1}{3}, 1\right]$

Explanation: We know that,

$$-1 \leq -\sin 3x \leq 1$$
$$-1 + 2 \leq 2 - \sin 3x \leq 1 + 2$$
$$1 \leq 2 - \sin 3x \leq 3$$
$$\frac{1}{3} \leq \frac{1}{2 - \sin 3x} \leq 1$$
$$\frac{1}{3} \leq f(x) \leq 1$$

$\therefore$ Range $(f) = \left[\frac{1}{3}, 1\right]$

Assertion-Reason (A-R)

DIRECTION: In the following questions, a statement of assertion (A) is followed by a statement of the reason (R). Mark the correct choice as:

(a) Both assertion (A) and reason (R) are true and reason (R) is the correct explanation of assertion (A).

(b) Both assertion (A) and reason (R) are true but reason (R) is not the correct explanation of assertion (A).

(c) Assertion (A) is true but reason (R) is false.

(d) Assertion (A) is false but reason (R) is true.

13. Assertion (A): The following arrow diagram represents a function.

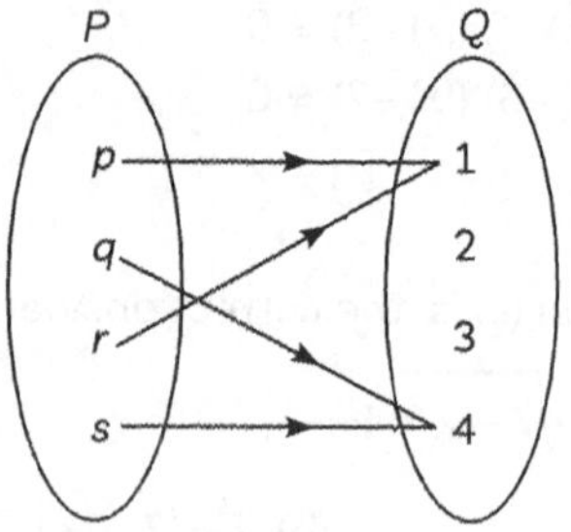

Reason (R): Let $f: R - \{2\} \to R$ be defined by $f(x) = \frac{x^2 - 4}{x - 2}$ and $g: R \to R$ be define by $g(n) = R + 3$. Then $f = g$.

Ans. *(c) Assertion (A) is true but reason (R) is false.*

Explanation: In the arrow diagram, each element of *P* has its unique image in *Q*.

Domain of $f = R - \{2\}$

Domain of $g = R$

$Df \neq Dg$

Hence, option (*c*) is the correct answer.

14. Assertion (A): The range of function $f(x) = 2 - 3x$ is R.

Reason (R): The range of function $f(x) = x^2 + 2$ is $[2, \infty)$.

Ans *(d) Assertion (A) is false but reason (R) is true.*

Explanation: $f(x) = 2 - 3x$

$y = 2 - 3x$

$x = \frac{2-y}{3}$ for $x > 0, y < 2$ hence range $= (-\infty, 2)$.

$f(x) = x^2 + 2$

$y = x^2 + 2$

$\Rightarrow \quad x = \sqrt{y-2}$

Hence, Range $= [2, \infty)$

Thus, assertion (*A*) is false but reason (*R*) is true.

Hence, option (*d*) is the correct answer.

15. Assertion (A): The Domain of the Real function *f* defined by $f(x) = \sqrt{x-1}$ is $R - \{1\}$.

Reason (R): The Range of function $f(x) = \sqrt{x-1}$ is $[0, \infty)$.

Ans. *(d) Assertion (A) is false but reason (R) is true.*

Explanation: $f(x) = \sqrt{x-1}$

$x - 1 \geq 0, x \geq 1$

$D = [1, \infty)$

$y = \sqrt{x-1}$

$x \geq 1$

Range $= [0, \infty)$

Hence, option (*d*) is the correct answer.

16. Assertion (A): Let $A = \{1, 2, 3, 5\}$, $B = \{4, 6, 9\}$ and $f = \{(x, y) : |x - y| \text{ is odd}\}$. Then domain of *f* is $\{1, 2, 3, 5\}$

Reason (R): $|x|$ is always positive $\forall x \in R$

Ans. *(b) Both assertion (A) and reason (R) are true but reason (R) is not the correct explanation of assertion (A).*

Explanation: Given

$R = \{(x, y) : |x - y| \text{ is odd}, x \in A, y \in B\}$

$R = \{(1, 4) (1, 6) (2, 9) (3, 4) (3, 6) (5, 4) (5, 6)\}$

Domain of $R = \{1, 2, 3, 5\}$

$|x|$ is always positive $\forall x \in R$.

Thus, both assertion and Reason are true but reason is not the correct explanation of assertion.

Hence, option (*b*) is the correct answer.

CASE BASED Questions (CBQs)

[**4** & **5** marks]

Read the following passages and answer the questions that follow:

17. *Function as a Relation from a non-empty set A to a non-empty set B is said to be a function if every element of set A has one and only one image in set B. In other words, we can say that a function f is a relation from a non-empty set A to a non-empty set B such that the domain of f is A and no two distinct ordered pairs in f have the same first element or component. If f is a function from a set A to a set B, then we write $f: A \to B$ and it is read as f is a function from A to B or f maps A to B.*

(A) The given curve is *a*:

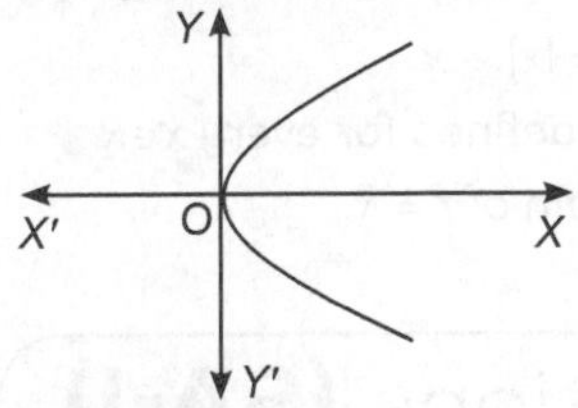

(a) Function
(b) Relation
(c) Can't say anything
(d) Data not sufficient

(B) The given curve is *a*:

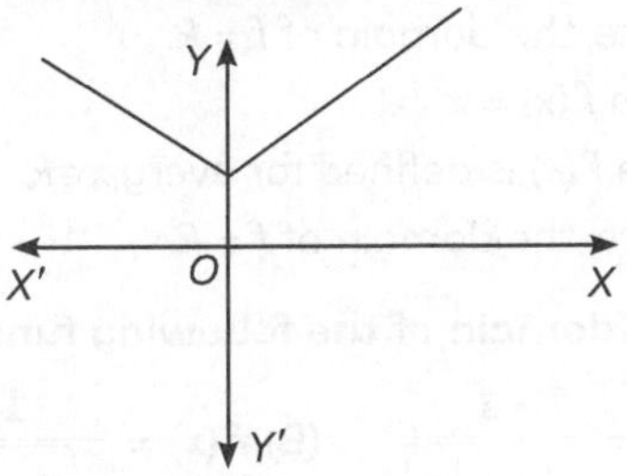

(a) Function
(b) Relation
(c) Can't say anything
(d) Data not suffcient

(C) If $f(x) = x^2 + 2x + 3$, then among $f(1)$, $f(2)$ and $f(3)$, which one gives the maximum value.

(a) $f(1)$ (b) $f(2)$
(c) $f(3)$ (d) $f(1) = f(2) = f(3)$

(D) If $f(1+x) = x^2 + 1$, then $f(2-h)$ is:

(a) $h^2 - 2h - 1$ (b) $h^2 - 2h + 1$
(c) $h^2 - 2h + 2$ (d) $h^2 + 2h + 2$

Ans. (A) *(b) Relation*

Explanation: If we draw a vertical line, then it will intersect the curve at two points. It shows that a given curve is a relation. Hence, option (*b*) is the correct answer.

(B) *(a) Function*

Explanation: If we draw a vertical line, then it will intersect the curve at only one point. It shows that a given curve is a function. Hence, option (*a*) is the correct answer.

(C) *(c) f(3)*

Explanation: $f(1) = 1 + 2 + 3 = 6$, $f(2) = 4 + 4 + 3 = 11$ and $f(3) = 9 + 6 + 3 = 18$. Here 18 is the maximum value. Hence, option (*c*) is the correct answer.

(D) *(c) $h^2 - 2h + 2$*

Explanation: We have, $f(1 + x) = x^2 + 1$ ...(i)

On substituting $x = (1 - h)$ in eq. (i), we get

$f(1 + 1 - h) = (1 - h)^2 + 1$

$f(2 - h) = 1 + h^2 - 2h + 1 = h^2 - 2h + 2$

Hence, option (*c*) is the correct answer.

VERY SHORT ANSWER Type Questions (VSA)

[1 mark]

18. Let $f = \{(2, 2), (3, 4), (0, -2), (-1, -4)\}$ be a function from *Z* to *Z* defined by $f(x) = ax + b$, for some integers *a*, *b*. Determine *a*, *b*.

Ans. Given $f = \{(2, 2), (3, 4), (0, -2), (-1, -4)\}$ be a function from *Z* to *Z* defined by $f(x) = ax + b$.

$\therefore$ we have,

$f(0) = -2 \Rightarrow b = -2$

$f(-1) = -4 \Rightarrow -a + b = -4$

On solving the above equation, we get

$a = 2, b = -2$.

19. If $f(x) = y = \dfrac{ax - b}{cx - a}$, then prove that $f(y) = x$.

Ans. We have, $f(x) = y = \dfrac{ax-b}{cx-a}$, $\therefore f(y) = \dfrac{ax-b}{cx-a}$,

$$= \frac{a\left(\dfrac{ax-b}{cx-a}\right)-b}{c\left(\dfrac{ax-b}{cx-a}\right)-a} = \frac{a(ax-b)-b(cx-a)}{c(ax-b)-a(cx-a)}$$

$$= \frac{a^2x-ab-bcx+ab}{acx-bc-acx+a^2} = \frac{a^2x-bcx}{a^2-bc}$$

$$= \frac{x(a^2-bc)}{(a^2-bc)} = x$$

$\therefore f(y) = x$

Hence proved.

20. Find the domain and range of the real function $f(x) = \sqrt{x-2}$.

Ans. Given $f(x) = \sqrt{x-2}$.

Since, $f(x)$ is defined for every $x \in R$ Such that $x - 2 \geq 0$, i.e., $x \geq 2$.

Hence, the domain of $f = [2, \infty)$.

Let $y = f(x)$

$\Rightarrow y = \sqrt{x-2}$

$\Rightarrow y^2 = x - 2$

$\Rightarrow x = 2 + y^2$,

which is defined for every $y \in R$.

Also, $y = \sqrt{x-2} \geq 0$

Range $= [0, \infty)$.

21. Find the domain of the function $f(x) = [x] + x$

Ans. Given $f(x) = [x] + x$

Since, $f(x)$ is defined for every $x \in R$.

Hence, domain of $f = R$.

SHORT ANSWER Type-I Questions (SA-I)

[**2** marks]

22. Let f and g be real functions defined by $f(x) = 2x + 1$ and $g(x) = 4x - 7$

(A) For what real numbers x, $f(x) = g(x)$?

(B) For what real numbers x, $f(x) < g(x)$?

[NCERT Exemplar]

Ans. Given that:

$f(x) = 2x + 1$ and $g(x) = 4x - 7$

(A) For $f(x) = g(x)$,

we get

$$2x + 1 = 4x - 7$$

$$\Rightarrow \quad 2x - 4x = -7 - 1$$

$$\Rightarrow \quad -2x = -8$$

$$\Rightarrow \quad x = 4$$

Hence, the required real number is 4.

(B) For $f(x) < g(x)$,

We get

$$2x + 1 < 4x - 7$$

$$\Rightarrow \quad 2x - 4x < -1 - 7$$

$$\Rightarrow \quad -2x < -8$$

$$\Rightarrow \quad 2x > 8$$

$$\therefore \quad x > 4$$

Hence, the required real number is $x > 4$.

23. $A = \{1, 2, 3, 4, 5\}$, $S = \{(x, y) : x \in A, y \in A\}$, then find the ordered which satisfy the conditions given below.

(A) $x + y = 5$ (B) $x + y < 5$

Ans. We have,

$A = \{1, 2, 3, 4, 5\}$, $S = \{(x, y) : x \in A, y \in A\}$

(A) The set of ordered pairs satisfying $x + y = 5$ is, $\{(1, 4), (2, 3), (3, 2), (4, 1)\}$.

(B) The set of ordered pairs satisfying $x + y < 5$ is $\{(1, 1), (1, 2), (1, 3), (2, 1), (2, 2), (3, 1)\}$

24. Find the domain of each of the following functions:

(A) $f(x) = -|x - 2|$ (B) $f(x) = x|x|$.

Ans. (A) Given $f(x) = -|x - 2|$.

Since $f(x)$ is defined for every $x \in R$.

Hence, the domain of $f = R$.

(B) Given $f(x) = x\,|x|$.

Since $f(x)$ is defined for every $x \in R$.

Hence, the domain of $f = R$.

25. Find the domain of the following functions:

(A) $f(x) = \dfrac{1}{\sqrt{x-[x]}}$ (B) $f(x) = \dfrac{1}{\sqrt{x+[x]}}$

Ans. (A) Given $f(x) = \dfrac{1}{\sqrt{x-[x]}}$

We have, $x - [x]$: Decimal part of x.

Since $f(x)$ is defined for every $x \in R$ such that

Hence, the domain of $f = R - Z$

(B) Given $f(x) = \dfrac{1}{\sqrt{x+[x]}}$

Since $f(x)$ is defined for every $x \in R$ such that

Hence, the domain of $f = (0, \infty)$.

26. Express the following function as set of ordered pairs and determine their range.

$f: X \rightarrow R$, $f(x) = x^3 + 1$, where $X = \{-1, 0, 3, 9, 7\}$

[NCERT Exemplar]

Ans. Given that: $f: X \rightarrow R$, $f(x) = x^3 + 1$,

Where $X = \{-1, 0, 3, 9, 7\}$

Here $X = \{-1, 0, 3, 9, 7\}$

For $x = -1$, $f(-1) = (-1)^3 + 1 = 0$

For $x = 0$, $f(0) = (0)^3 + 1 = 1$

For $x = 3$, $f(3) = (3)^3 + 1 = 28$

For $x = 9$, $f(9) = (9)^3 + 1 = 730$

For $x = 7$ $f(7) = (7)^3 + 1 = 344$

$\therefore$ The ordered pairs are $(-1, 0)$, $(0, 1)$, $(3, 28)$, $(7, 344)$, $(9, 730)$ and the range $=$ $\{0, 1, 28, 344, 730\}$.

SHORT ANSWER Type-II Questions (SA-II)

[3 marks]

27. Find the domain of $\frac{x^2+2x+7}{x^2-x-6}$.

Ans. We have, $f(x) = \frac{x^2+2x+7}{x^2-x-6}$

Clearly, $f(x)$ is a rational function of x as $\frac{x^2+2x+7}{x^2-x-6}$ is a rational expression in x. We observe that $f(x)$ assumes real values for all x except for all those values of x for which $x^2 - x - 6 = 0$ i.e. $x = 3, -2$. Hence, Domain $(f) = R - \{3, -2\}$.

28. Find the domain of the function $f(x)$ defined by $f(x) = \sqrt{4-x} + \frac{1}{\sqrt{x^2-1}}$.

Ans. Clearly, $f(x)$ is defined for all x satisfying

$4 - x \geq 0$ and $x^2 - 1 > 0$

$\Rightarrow x - 4 \leq 0$ and $(x - 1)(x + 1) > 0$

$\Rightarrow x \leq 4$ and $(x < -1$ or $x > 1)$

$\Rightarrow x \in (-\infty, -1) \cup (1, 4]$.

Hence, Domain $(f) = (-\infty, -1) \cup (1, 4]$.

29. Let f and g be two real functions defined by $f(x) = \frac{1}{x-6}$ and $g(x) = (x-6)^2$.

Find the following:

(A) $f+g$ (B) $f-g$

(C) fg

Ans. We observe that $f(x) = \frac{1}{x-6}$ is defined for all $x = 6$. So, domain $(f) = R - \{6\}$

Clearly, $g(x) = (x-6)^2$ is defined for all $x \in R$. So, domain $(g) = R$.

$\therefore$ Domain $(f) \cap$ Domain $(g) = R - \{6\}$.

(A) $f + g : R - \{6\} \to R$ is given by

$$(f+g)(x) = f(x) + g(x) = \frac{1}{x-6} + (x-6)^2$$

$$= \frac{(x-6)^3+1}{x-6}$$

(B) $f - g : R - \{6\} \to R$ is defined as

$$(f-g)(x) = f(x) - g(x) = \frac{1}{x-6} - (x-6)^2$$

$$= \frac{1-(x-6)^3}{x-6}$$

(C) $fg : R - \{6\} \to R$ is given by

$$(fg)(x) = f(x)\,g(x) = \frac{1}{x-6} \times (x-6)^2 = (x-6)$$

30. Find the range of each of the following functions:

(A) $f(x) = |x - 6|$ (B) $f(x) = 1 - |x - 4|$

(C) $f(x) = \frac{|x-2|}{x-2}$

Ans. (A) We have $f(x) = |x - 6|$

Clearly, $f(x)$ is defined for all $x \in R$. Therefore, Domain $(f) = R$.

$\because$ $|x - 6| > 0$ for all $x \in R$

$\therefore$ $0 \leq |x - 6| < \infty$ for all $x \in R$

$\Rightarrow$ $0 \leq f(x) < \infty$ for all $x \in R$

$\Rightarrow$ $f(x) \in [0, \infty)$ for all $x \in R$

Hence, Range $(f) = [0, \infty)$.

(B) We have, $f(x) = 1 - |x - 4|$.

We observe that $f(x)$ is defined for all $x \in R$. Therefore, Domain $(f) = R$.

$\because$ $0 \leq |x - 4| < \infty$ for all $x \in R$

$\therefore$ $-\infty < -|x - 4| \leq 0$ for all $x \in R$

$\Rightarrow$ $-\infty < 1 - |x - 4| \leq 1$ for all $x \in R$

$\Rightarrow$ $-\infty < f(x) \leq 1$ for all $x \in R$

$\Rightarrow$ $f(x) \in (-\infty, 1]$

Hence, Range $(f) = (-\infty, 1]$

(C) We have $f(x) = \frac{|x-2|}{x-2}$

Clearly, $f(x)$ is defined for all $x \in R$ except at $x = 2$.

Therefore, Domain $(f) = R - \{2\}$

Now,

$$f(x) = \frac{|x-2|}{x-2}$$

Hence, Range $(f) = \{-1, 1\}$

31. If $R_1 = \{(x, y) \mid y = 2x + 7$ where $x \in R$ and $-5 \leq x \leq 5\}$ is a relation. Then find the domain and range. **[NCERT Exemplar]**

Ans. Given that: $R_1 = \{(x, y) \mid y = 2x + 7$ where $x \in R$ and $-5 \leq x \leq 5\}$

Here domain is $-5 \leq x \leq 5 \Rightarrow \{-5, -4, -3, -2, -1, 0, 1, 2, 3, 4, 5\}$ and $y = 2x + 7$.

So, the values of y for the corresponding given values of x are $\{-3, -1, 1, 3, 5, 7, 9, 11, 13, 15, 17\}$

Hence, the domain of $R_1 = [-5, 5]$ and range of $R_1 = [-3, 17]$.

LONG ANSWER Type Questions (LA)

[4 & 5 marks]

32. Find the range of each of the following functions:

(A) $f(x) = \dfrac{1}{\sqrt{x-3}}$ **(B)** $f(x) = \sqrt{36-x^2}$

Ans. (A) We have, $f(x) = \dfrac{1}{\sqrt{x-3}}$

Clearly, $f(x)$ takes real values for all x satisfying $x - 3 > 0 \Rightarrow x > 3 \Rightarrow x \in (3, \infty)$.

$\therefore$ Domain $(f) = (3, \infty)$

For any $x > 3$ we have

$x - 3 > 0 \Rightarrow \sqrt{x-3} > 0 \Rightarrow \dfrac{1}{\sqrt{x-3}} > 0$

$\Rightarrow f(x) > 0$

Thus, $f(x)$ takes all real values greater than zero. Hence, Range $(f) = (0, \infty)$.

(B) We have, $f(x) = \sqrt{36-x^2}$

We observe that $f(x)$ is defined for all x satisfying

$36 - x^2 \geq 0 \Rightarrow x^2 - 36 \leq 0$

$\Rightarrow (x-6)(x+6) \leq 0$

$\Rightarrow -6 \leq x \leq 6 \Rightarrow x \in [-6, 6]$.

$\therefore$ Domain $(f) = [-6, 6]$.

Let $y = f(x)$. Then,

$y = \sqrt{36-x^2} \Rightarrow y^2 = 36 - x^2$

$\Rightarrow x^2 = 36 - y^2 \Rightarrow x = \sqrt{36-y^2}$

Clearly, x will take real values, if

$36 - y^2 \geq 0 \Rightarrow y^2 - 36 \leq 0$

$\Rightarrow (y-6)(y+6) \leq 0 \Rightarrow -6 \leq y \leq 6$

$\Rightarrow y \in [-6, 6]$

Also,

$y = \sqrt{36-x^2} \geq 0$ for all $x \in 0\ [-6, 6]$.

Therefore, $y \in [0, 6]$ for all $x \in [-6, 6]$.

Hence, Range $(f) = [0, 6]$

33. If f and g are real functions defined by $f(x) = x^2 + 7$ and $g(x) = 3x + 5$, find each of the following:

(A) $f(3) + g(-5)$ **(B)** $f\left(\frac{1}{2}\right) \times g(14)$

(C) $f(-2) + g(-1)$ **(D)** $f(t) - f(-2)$

(E) $\dfrac{f(t)-f(5)}{t-5}$ **if $t \neq 5$** **[NCERT Exemplar]**

Ans. Given that: $f(x) = x^2 + 7$ and $g(x) = 3x + 5$

(A) $f(3) + g(-5) = [(3)^2 + 7] + [3(-5) + 5]$

$= (9 + 7) + (-15 + 5) = 16 - 10 = 6$

Hence, $f(3) + g(-5) = 6$

(B) $f\left(\frac{1}{2}\right) \times g(14) = \left[\left(\frac{1}{2}\right)^2 + 7\right] \times [3 \times 14 + 5]$

$= \left(\frac{1}{4} + 7\right) \times (42 + 5) = \frac{29}{4} \times 47 = \frac{1363}{4}$

Hence, $f\left(\frac{1}{2}\right) \times g(14) = \frac{1363}{4}$

(C) $f(-2) + g(-1) = [(-2)^2 + 7] + [3(-1) + 5]$

$= (4 + 7) + (-3 + 5) = 11 + 2 = 13$

Hence, $f(-2) + g(-1) = 13$

(D) $f(t) - f(-2) = (t^2 + 7) - [(-2)^2 + 7] = t^2 + 7 - 11$

$= t^2 - 4$

Hence, $f(t) - f(-2) = t^2 - 4$.

(E) $\dfrac{f(t)-f(5)}{t-5}, t \neq 5 = \dfrac{(t^2+7)-((5)^2+7)}{t-5}$

$= \dfrac{t^2+7-32}{t-5} = \dfrac{t^2-25}{t-5} = t + 5$

Hence, $\dfrac{f(t)-f(5)}{t-5}$ $t \neq 5 = t + 5$.

34. Are the given relations functions? Give reason for your answer.

(A) $h = \{(4, 6), (3, 9), (-11, 6), (3, 11)\}$.

(B) $f = \{(x, x)$ |x is a real number$\}$.

(C) $g = \left\{\left(x, \frac{1}{x}\right) \middle| x \text{ is a positive integer}\right\}$.

(D) $s = \{(x, x^2)$ |x is a positive integer$\}$.

(E) $t = \{(x, 3)$ |x is a real number$\}$.

Ans. (A) We have, $h = \{(4, 6), (3, 9), (-11, 6), (3, 11)\}$.

Since, 3 has two images 9 and 11. So, it is not a function.

(B) We have, $f = \{(x, x) \mid x$ is a real number.

We observe that, every element in the domain has unique image. So, it is a function.

(C) We have, $g = \left\{\left(x, \frac{1}{x}\right) \middle| x \text{ is a positive integer}\right\}$

For every x, it is a positive integer and $\frac{1}{x}$ is unique and distinct.

Therefore, every element in the domain has a unique image.

So, it is a function.

(D) We have, $s = \{(x, x^2) \mid x \text{ is a positive integer}\}$

Since, the square of any positive integer is unique.

So, every element in the domain has a unique image.

Hence, it is a function.

(E) We have, $t = \{(x, 3) \mid x \text{ is a real number}\}$

Since, every element in the domain has the image 3.

So, it is a constant function.

3 Trigonometric Functions

Mario, have you ever played this game? When you see him glide over the roadblocks with such ease. He doesn't actually leap straight along the Y axis; instead, he follows a slightly curved or parabolic path to avoid the obstacles in his way. Mario can leap over these barriers because of trigonometry. Because the gaming business is all about technology and computers, trigonometry is equally important for these engineers

Topic Notes

- *Trigonometric function*
- *Trigonometric Transformation Formulae*

TRIGONOMETRIC FUNCTION 1

TOPIC 1

INTRODUCTION

Trigonometry is a branch of mathematics that studies triangles and the relationships between their sides and angles. The word 'trigonometry' is derived from the Greek words 'trigon' (meaning triangle) and 'metron' (meaning measure) and thus it means 'measuring the sides of a triangle'.

The field evolved during the third century *BC* as a branch of geometry used extensively for astronomical studies. It is also the foundation of the practical art of surveying. Driven by the demands of navigation and the growing need for accurate maps of large areas, trigonometry grew into a major branch of mathematics.

In earlier classes, we have studied the trigonometric ratios of acute angles as the ratio of the sides of a right angled triangle. We have also studied the trigonometric identities and application of trigonometric ratios in solving the problems related to heights and distance. In this chapter, we will generalise the concept of trigonometric ratios to trigonometric functions and study their properties.

TOPIC 2

ANGLES AND THEIR MEASUREMENT

The concept of an angle is one of the most important concepts in geometry. The concept of equality, sums, and differences of angles are important and are used throughout geometry, but the subject of trigonometry is based on the measurement of angles. In this section, we begin with the discussion of angles and their measurement.

Angle

An angle is the figure formed by two rays sharing a common end-point. The two rays are called sides of the angle, and the common end-point is called vertex of the angle.

The word angle is also used to designate the measure of an angle of a rotation. Also, the sides of an angle are called initial sides and terminal sides.

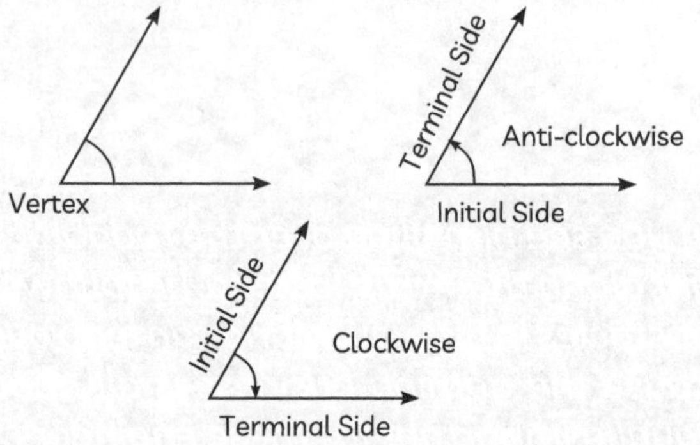

We have the following conventions:

(i) If the direction of rotation is **anti-clockwise**, the angle is taken as **positive**.

(ii) If the direction of rotation is **clockwise**, then the angle is taken as **negative**.

Units for Measurement of Angles

The two most commonly used units for measurement of angles are the following:

Degree

An angle is said to be of 1 degree (denoted by 1°) if it is $\left(\frac{1}{360}\right)^{th}$ part of a revolution.

So, one revolution is of 360°. One advantage of this unit is that many angles common in simple geometry are measured as a whole number of degrees. Fractions of a degree may be written in normal decimal notation (e.g. 7.5° for seven and a half degrees) but the 'degree-minute-second' system is also in use.

Minutes

Each degree is divided into 60 equal parts called minutes. A measure of an angle in minutes is denoted by a single prime (′).

$$1° = 60'$$

So, 7.5° can be called 7 degrees and 30 minutes, written as 7° 30′.

Second

Each minute is further divided into 60 equal parts called seconds. A measure of an angle in seconds is denoted by a double prime (″).

$$1' = 60''$$

So, an angle of 2 degree 5 minutes 30 seconds is written as 2° 5′ 30″.

The division of degrees into minutes and seconds of angle is analogous to the division of hours into minutes and seconds of time.

Radian

An angle is said to be 1 radian (denoted by 1 rad) if the length of arc is equal to the radius of the circle.

But the radian notation is frequently omitted. So, any measure of angle without units means that the angle is in radian.

Relation between Degree and Radian

Consider a circle of radius r. Then, the angle (in radian) subtended by the circle at the centre is given by

$$\theta = \frac{1}{r} = \frac{2\pi r}{r} = 2\pi\theta$$

Also, the angle (in degrees) subtended by the circle at the centre is 360°, which implies.

$$360° = 2\pi \text{ radian}$$

We now list some frequently used angles in degrees and radians.

Degrees	0°	30°	45°	60°	90°	120°	135°
Radians	0	$\frac{\pi}{6}$	$\frac{\pi}{4}$	$\frac{\pi}{3}$	$\frac{\pi}{2}$	$\frac{2\pi}{3}$	$\frac{3\pi}{4}$

Degrees	150°	180°	225°	270°	315°
Radians	$\frac{5\pi}{6}$	π	$\frac{5\pi}{4}$	$\frac{3\pi}{2}$	$\frac{7\pi}{4}$

Important

- *Radian measure =* $\frac{\pi}{180}$ *× Degree measure*
- *Degree measure =* $\frac{180}{\pi}$ *× Radian measure*

Example 1.1: Find the radian measures corresponding to the following degree measures – 47° 30′. [NCERT]

Ans. – 47° 30′

$$= -(47° + 30')$$

$$= -\left(47° + \frac{30°}{60}\right)$$

$$= -\left(47° + \frac{1°}{2}\right)$$

$$= -\left(\frac{94 + 1°}{2}\right)$$

$$= -\left(\frac{95°}{2}\right)$$

$$\text{Radian measure} = \frac{\pi}{180} \times \text{degree measure}$$

$$= \frac{\pi}{180} \times \left(\frac{-95}{2}\right)$$

$$= \pi \times \frac{-19}{72}$$

$$= \frac{-19\pi}{72} \text{ radians}$$

Example 1.2: Find the radian measures corresponding to the following degree measures:

(A) 25° (B) – 47° 30′

(C) 240° (D) 520° [NCERT]

Ans. (A) We know that 180° = π radian

$$\therefore\ 25 = \frac{\pi}{180} \times 25 \text{ radian} = \frac{5\pi}{36} \text{ radian}$$

(B) – 47° 30′

$$-47° 30 = 47\frac{1°}{2}$$

$$= \frac{-95}{2} \text{ degree}$$

Since 180° = π radian

$$\frac{-95}{2} \text{ degree} = \frac{\pi}{180} \times \left(\frac{-95}{2}\right) \text{ radian}$$

$$= \left(\frac{-19}{36 \times 2}\right)\pi \text{ radian}$$

$$= \frac{-19}{72}\pi \text{ radian}$$

$$\therefore -47° 30' = \frac{-95}{72}\pi \text{ radian}$$

(C) 240°

We know that 180° = π radian

$$\therefore\ 240° = \frac{\pi}{180} \times 240 \text{ radian}$$

$$= \frac{4}{3}\pi \text{ radian}$$

(D) 520°

We know that 180° = π radian

$$\therefore\ 520° = \frac{\pi}{180} \times 520$$

$$= \frac{26\pi}{9} \text{ radian}$$

Length of an Arc of a circle

Consider an arc *AB* of length *l* which subtends an angle θ at the centre *O* of a circle of radius *r*.

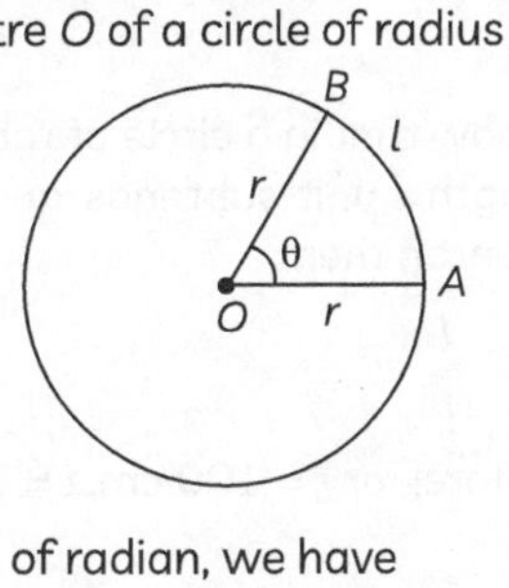

Then, by definition of radian, we have

Angle subtended by an arc of length *r* is 1 radian

⇒ Angle subtended by an arc of length

$$1 \text{ is} = \frac{1}{r} \text{ radian}$$

⇒ Angle subtended by the arc of length

$$l \text{ is } \theta = \frac{l}{r} \text{ radian}$$

So, we conclude the following:

Conclusion: The length of arc, which subtends an angle θ at the center of a circle of radius *r*, is

$l = r\theta$

Example 1.3: If in two circles, arcs of the same length subtend angles 60° and 75° at the centre, find the ratio of their radii. [NCERT]

Ans. We know that $l = r\theta$

There are 2 circles of different radius

So, the radius be denoted by r_1 and r_2.

Length of arc of 1st circle	Length of arc of 2nd circle
$l = r_1\theta$	$l = r_2\theta$
$= r_1 \times 60°$	$= r_2 \times 75°$
$= r_1 \times 60 \times \frac{\pi}{180}$	$= r_2 \times 75° \times \frac{\pi}{180}$
$= r_1 \times \frac{\pi}{3}$	$= r_2 \times \frac{5\pi}{12}$

It is given that arcs are of same length

Hence,

Length of 1st arc = length of 2nd arc

$$r_1 \times \frac{\pi}{3} = r_2 \times \frac{5\pi}{12}$$

$$\frac{r_1}{r_2} = \frac{5\pi}{12} \times \frac{3}{\pi}$$

$$\frac{r_1}{r_2} = \frac{5}{4}$$

Hence, $r_1 : r_2 = 5 : 4$

So, ratio of their radii = 5 : 4

Example 1.4: Find the degree measure of the angle subtended at the center of a circle of radius 100 cm by an arc of length 22 cm. (use $\pi = \frac{22}{7}$) [NCERT]

Ans. We know that in a circle of radius r unit, if an arc of length *l* unit subtends an angle θ radian at the center, then

$$\theta = \frac{l}{r}$$

Therefore, for $r = 100$ cm, $l = 22$ cm, we have

$$\theta = \frac{22}{100}$$

$$\text{radian} = \frac{180}{\pi} \times \frac{22}{100} \text{ degree} = \frac{180 \times 7 \times 22}{22 \times 100} \text{ degree}$$

$$= \frac{126}{10} \text{ degree} = 12\frac{3}{5} \text{ degree} = 12° 36'$$

[1° = 60′]

Thus, the required angle is 12° 36′.

Example 1.5: Find the angle in radian through which a pendulum swings if its radius is 75 cm and the tip describe an arc of length.

(A) 10 cm (B) 15cm (C) 21cm [NCERT]

Ans. We know that in a circle of radius r unit, if an arc of length *l* unit subtends and angle θ radian at the center, then $\theta = \frac{l}{r}$

It is given that $r = 75$cm

(A) Here, $l = 10$cm

$$\theta = \frac{10}{75} \text{ radian} = \frac{2}{15} \text{ radian}$$

(B) Here, $l = 15$cm

$$\theta = \frac{15}{75} \text{ radian} = \frac{1}{5} \text{ radian}$$

(C) Here, $l = 21$cm

$$\theta = \frac{21}{75} \text{ radian} = \frac{7}{25} \text{ radian}$$

Example 1.6: A wheel makes 360 revolutions in one minute. Through how many radians does it turn in one second? [NCERT]

Ans. Number of revolutions made by the wheel in 1 minute = 360

∴ Number of revolutions made by the wheel in 1 second = $\frac{360}{60}$ = 6 revolutions per second

In one complete revolution, the wheel turns an angle of 2π radian.

Hence, in 6 complete revolutions, it will turn an angle of 6 × 2π radian, i.e., 12π radian

Thus, in one second, the wheel turns an angle of 12π radian.

TOPIC 3

TRIGONOMETRIC FUNCTIONS

In earlier classes, we have studied trigonometric ratios (for acute angles) as the ratio of sides of a right-angled triangle. To recall, there are six trigonometric ratios defined as follows:

(i) $\sin\theta = \frac{P}{H}$

(ii) $\text{cosec}\,\theta = \frac{H}{P}$

(iii) $\cos\theta = \frac{B}{H}$

(iv) $\sec\theta = \frac{H}{B}$

(v) $\tan\theta = \frac{P}{B}$

(vi) $\cot\theta = \frac{B}{P}$

Where θ is the acute angle, P is the perpendicular, B is the base and H is the hypotenuse of the right-angled triangle. We will now extend the definition of trigonometric ratios to any angle in terms of radian measure and study them as trigonometric functions.

Consider a system of coordinate axes with origin at O. Also, consider a unit circle with centre at O. For each real number θ, let $P(a, b)$ be the point on the circle such that OP makes an angle θ (measured anticlockwise) with the positive direction of x – axis, as shown in figure.

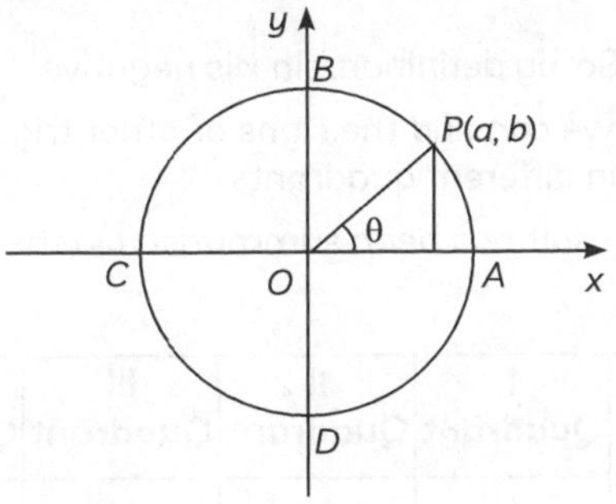

We define,

Sine Function

(denoted by **sin**)as

$\sin\theta = y$ – coordinate of point P.

Cosine Function

(denoted by **cos**) as

$\cos\theta = x$ – coordinates of point P.

From figure, it is clear that the coordinates of the point A, B, C and D are (1, 0), (0, 1), (– 1, 0) and (0, –1).

We observe the following:

$\sin 0 = y$ – coordinate of point $A = 0$

$\cos 0 = x$ – coordinate of point $A = 1$

$\sin\frac{\pi}{2} = y$ – coordinate of point $B = 1$

$\cos\frac{\pi}{2} = x$ – coordinate of point $B = 0$

$\sin\pi = y$ – coordinates of point $C = 0$

$\cos\pi = x$ – coordinate of point $c = -1$

$\sin\frac{3\pi}{2} = y$ – coordinate of point $D = -1$

$\cos\frac{3\pi}{2} = x$ – coordinated of point $D = 0$

We observe that y – coordinates of the points A and C are 0.

So, $\quad \sin\theta = 0.$ for $\theta = 0, \pm\pi, \pm 2\pi, \pm 3\pi, \ldots$

i.e., $\quad \sin\theta = 0$, when θ is an integral multiple of π

Also, we observe that x – coordinates of the points B and D are 0.

So, $\quad \cos\theta = 0$, for $\theta = \pm\frac{\pi}{2}, \pm\frac{3\pi}{3}, \pm\frac{5\pi}{2}, \ldots$

i.e., $\quad \cos\theta = 0$, when θ is an odd multiple of $\frac{\pi}{2}$

$\sin\theta = 0 \Rightarrow \theta = n\pi$, where $n \in Z$

$\cos\theta = 0 \Rightarrow \theta = (2n+1)\frac{\pi}{2}$ where $n \in Z$

We now define other trigonometric functions in terms of sine and cosine functions:

Cosecant Function

(denoted by cosec) defined as

$$\text{cosec}\,\theta = \frac{1}{\sin\theta} = \frac{1}{y - \textit{coordinates of point } P'}$$

Where $\theta \neq n\pi$ (form $\in Z$)

Secant Function

(denoted by sec) is defined as

$$\sec\theta = \frac{1}{\cos\theta} = \frac{1}{x - \textit{coordinate of point } P'}$$

Where $\theta \neq (2n+1)\frac{\pi}{2}$ (form $\in Z$).

Tangent Function

(denoted by tan) is defined as

$$\tan\theta = \frac{\sin\theta}{\cos\theta} = \frac{y - \textit{coordinates of point } P}{x - \textit{coordinates of point } P'}$$

Where $\theta \neq (2n+1)\frac{\pi}{2}$ (form $\in Z$)

Cotangent Function

(denoted by cot) is defined as

$$\cot\theta = \frac{\cos\theta}{\sin\theta} = \frac{x - \textit{coordinates of point}}{y - \textit{coordinates of pint}'}$$

Where $\theta \neq n\pi$ (form $\in Z$).

From above definitions, we can have the following table:

	0°	30°	45°	60°	90°	180°	270°	360°
sin	0	$\frac{1}{2}$	$\frac{1}{\sqrt{2}}$	$\frac{\sqrt{3}}{2}$	1	0	– 1	0
cos	1	$\frac{\sqrt{3}}{2}$	$\frac{1}{\sqrt{2}}$	$\frac{1}{2}$	0	– 1	0	1
tan	0	$\frac{1}{\sqrt{3}}$	1	$\sqrt{3}$	n.d.	0	n.d.	0

cosec	n.d.	2	$\sqrt{2}$	$\frac{2}{\sqrt{3}}$	1	n.d.	– 1	n.d.
sec	1	$\frac{2}{\sqrt{3}}$	$\sqrt{2}$	2	n.d.	– 1	n.d.	1
cot	n.d.	$\sqrt{3}$	1	$\frac{1}{\sqrt{3}}$	0	n.d.	0	n.d.

Here, 'n.d.' means that the trigonometric function is not defined at that value.

We know that one complete revolution subtends an angle of 2π radian at the centre of the circle. If we take one complete revolution from the point *P*, we again come back to the same point *P*. Thus, we observe that if θ increases (or decreases) by an integral multiple of 2π, the value of sine and cosine functions do not change.

Hence, $\sin(2n\pi + \theta) = \sin\theta$, for all $n \in Z$

And $\cos(2n\pi + \theta) = \cos\theta$, for all $n \in Z$

By definition of other four trigonometric functions, we have

$$\text{cosec}\,(2n\pi + \theta) = \frac{1}{\sin(2n\pi+\theta)} = \frac{1}{\sin\theta} = \text{cosec}\,\theta$$

$$\sec\,(2n\pi + \theta) = \frac{1}{\cos(2n\pi+\theta)} = \frac{1}{\cos\theta} = \cot\theta$$

$$\tan\,(2n\pi + \theta) = \frac{\sin(2n\pi+\theta)}{\cos(2n\pi+\theta)} = \frac{\sin\theta}{\cos\theta} = \tan\theta$$

$$\cot\,(2n\pi + \theta) = \frac{\cos(2n\pi+\theta)}{\sin(2n\pi+\theta)} = \frac{\cos\theta}{\sin\theta} = \cot\theta$$

Hence, we can summarise the results as follows:

$\sin(n \times 360° + \theta) = \sin\theta$ for all $n \in Z$

$\cos(n \times 360° + \theta) = \cos\theta$ for all $n \in Z$

$\text{cosec}(n \times 360° + \theta) = \text{cosec}\,\theta$ for all $n \in Z$

$\sec(n \times 360° + \theta) = \sec\theta$ for all $n \in Z$

$\tan(n \times 360° + \theta) = \tan\theta$ for all $n \in Z$

$\cot(n \times 360° + \theta) = \cot\theta$ for all $n \in Z$

Periods of Trigonometric Functions

We shall now understand the meaning of a periodic function. In simple words, a periodic function is a function that repeats its values in regular intervals or periods.

Periodic Function

A function $f: D \to R$ is said to be periodic if there exists a non-zero real number *a* such that $f(x + a) = f(x)$ for all $x \in D$.

Period of a Periodic Function

Let $f: D \to R$ be a periodic function. The least positive real number *p* such that $f(x + a) = f(x)$ for all $x \in D$ is called period of *f*.

From the discussion in the previous subsection, it is clear that all trigonometric functions are periodic functions with period 2π.

Signs of Trigonometric Functions

Let us now find the signs of the trigonometric functions for different values of θ in their respective domains. We observe that the signs of these functions depend on the quadrant in which θ lies.

For example, in I quadrant (i .e .0,< $\frac{\pi}{2}$) and II quadrant (i. e . $\frac{\pi}{2} < \theta < \pi$), the *y*-coordinate of point *P* is positive. So, by definition, sin *x* is positive.

But, in III quadrant (*i. e* .,$\pi < \theta < \frac{3\pi}{2}$) and IV quadrant (*i.e.,* $\frac{3\pi}{2} < \theta < 2\pi$), the *y*-coordinate of point *P* is negative. So, by definition, sin *x* is negative.

Similarly, we can find the signs of other trigonometric functions in different quadrants.

The final result has been summarised in the following table:

	I Quadrant	II Quadrant	III Quadrant	IV Quadrant
sin θ, cosec 2θ	+	+	–	–
tan θ, cot θ	+	+	+	–
cos θ, sec θ	+	–	–	+

One way to remember which functions are positive and which are negative in the various quadrants is to remember a simple four-letter acronym, ASTC.

This acronym can remind you that All are positive in the I quadrant, Since is positive in II quadrant, Tangent is positive in III quadrant and cosine is positive in IV quadrant.

This acronym could stand for After School To College, or(Add Sugar To Coffee) some other four-word expression that will help you remember the relationships.

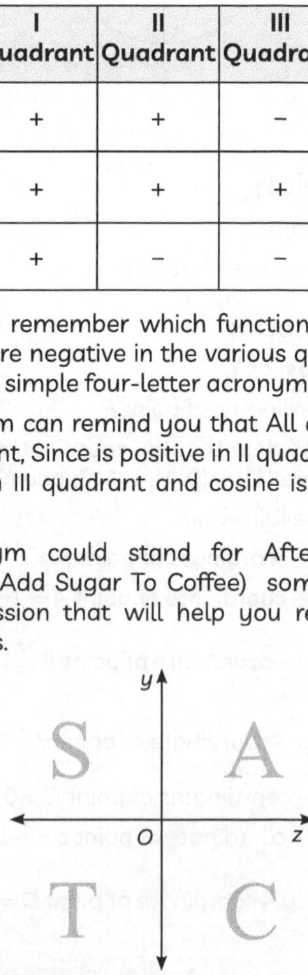

EXAMPLE 1.7: Find the values of other five trigonometric functions if sin $x = \frac{3}{5}$, x lies in the second quadrant. **[NCERT]**

Ans.

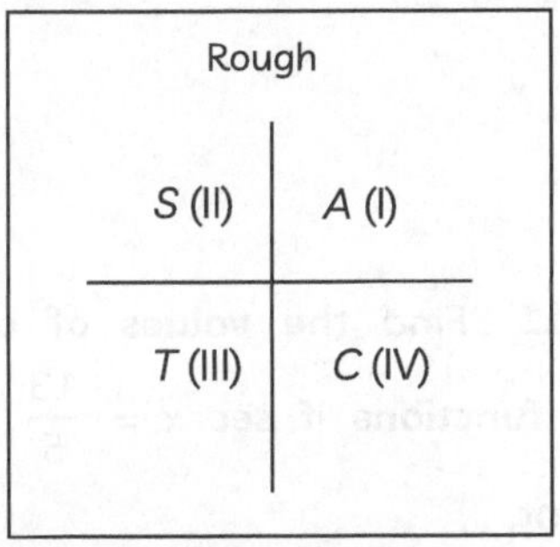

Since, x is in IInd quadrant.

sin will be positive but cos and tan will be negative.

Here, $\sin x = \frac{3}{5}$

We know that

$$\sin^2 x + \cos^2 x = 1$$

$$\left(\frac{3}{5}\right)^2 + \cos^2 x = 1$$

$$\frac{9}{25} + \cos^2 x = 1$$

$$\cos^2 x = 1 - \frac{9}{25}$$

$$\cos^2 x = \frac{25-9}{25}$$

$$\cos^2 x = \frac{16}{25}$$

$$\cos x = \pm\sqrt{\frac{16}{25}}$$

$$\cos x = \pm\frac{4}{5}$$

As x is IInd quadrant and cos x is negative in IInd quadrant.

$$\therefore \quad \cos x = \frac{-4}{5}$$

$$\tan x = \frac{\sin x}{\cos x} = \frac{\frac{3}{5}}{\frac{-4}{5}}$$

$$= \frac{3}{5} \times \frac{5}{-4} = \frac{-3}{4}$$

$$\operatorname{cosec} x = \frac{1}{\sin x} = \frac{1}{\frac{3}{5}}$$

$$= \frac{1 \times 5}{3} = \frac{5}{3}$$

$$\sec x = \frac{1}{\cos x} = \frac{1}{\frac{-4}{5}}$$

$$= \frac{1 \times 5}{-4} = \frac{-5}{4}$$

$$\cot x = \frac{1}{\tan x} = \frac{1}{\frac{-3}{4}}$$

$$= \frac{-4}{3}$$

EXAMPLE 1.8: Find the value of the trigonometric function cosec (– 1410°). **[NCERT]**

Ans. As $\sin(-x) = -\sin x$,

So, $\operatorname{cosec}(-x) = -\operatorname{cosec} x$

$\operatorname{cosec}(-1410°)$

$$= -\operatorname{cosec}(1410°)$$

$$= -\operatorname{cosec}\left(1410 \times \frac{\pi}{180}\right)$$

$$= -\operatorname{cosec}\frac{47\pi}{6}$$

$$= -\operatorname{cosec}\left(7\frac{5}{6}\pi\right)$$

$$= -\operatorname{cosec}\left(8\pi - \frac{1}{6}\pi\right)$$

Values of cosec x repeats after an interval of 2π,
Hence, ignoring $4 \times (2\pi)$ i.e., 8π

$$= -\operatorname{cosec}\left(-\frac{1}{6}\pi\right)$$

$$= -\operatorname{cosec}\left(-\frac{1}{6} \times 180°\right)$$

$$= -\operatorname{cosec}(-30°)$$

$$= -(-\operatorname{cosec} 30°)$$

$$= \operatorname{cosec} 30°$$

$$= \frac{1}{\sin 30°}$$

$$= \frac{1}{\left(\frac{1}{2}\right)}$$

$$= \frac{2}{1}$$

$$= 2$$

Example 1.9 Find the value of the trigonometric function $\tan\frac{19\pi}{3}$. **[NCERT]**

Ans. $\tan\frac{19\pi}{3}$

$$3\overline{)19}\quad 6,\quad 18,\quad 1$$

$= \tan 6\frac{1}{3}\pi$

$= \tan\left(6\pi + \frac{1}{3}\pi\right)$

$= \tan\left(3(2\pi) + \frac{1}{3}\pi\right)$

Values of tan x repeats after an interval of 2π,
Hench ignoring $3 \times (2\pi)$

$= \tan\left(\frac{1}{3}\pi\right)$

$= \tan\left(\frac{1}{3}\times 180°\right)$

$= \tan 60°$

$= \sqrt{3}$

Example 1.10: Find the value of the trigonometric function sub $\left(\frac{11\pi}{3}\right)$. [NCERT]

Ans. $3\overline{)11}\quad 3,\quad 9,\quad 2$

So, $\frac{11}{3} = 3\frac{2}{3}$

$= = 3 \div \frac{2}{3}$ *or* $4 - \frac{1}{3}$

We take $4 - \frac{1}{3}$ as it is even

$\sin\left(-\frac{11\pi}{3}\right)$

$= -\sin\frac{11\pi}{3}$

(As $\sin(-x) = -\sin x$

$= -\sin\left(3\frac{2}{3}\pi\right)$

$= -\sin\left(4\pi - \frac{1}{3}\pi\right)$

Values of sin *x* repeats after an interval of 2π,
Hence ignoring 4π i.e., $2 \times (2\pi)$

$= -\sin\frac{-1}{3}\pi$

$= --\left(-\sin\left(\frac{1}{3}\pi\right)\right)$

(As $\sin(-x) = -\sin x$

$= \sin\left(\frac{1}{3}\pi\right)$

$= \sin 60°$

$= \frac{\sqrt{3}}{2}$

Example 1.11: Find the values of other five trigonometric functions if sec $x = \frac{13}{5}$, x lies in fourth quadrant. [NCERT]

Ans. Since *x* lies in the IVth quadrant, cos will be positive
where,
But sin and tan will be negative
We know that

$1 + \tan^2 x = \sec^2 x$

$1 + \tan^2 x = \left(\frac{13}{5}\right)^2$

$\tan^2 x = \left(\frac{13}{5}\right)^2 - 1$

$\tan^2 x = \frac{169}{25} - 1$

$\tan^2 x = \frac{169 - 25}{25}$

$\tan^2 x = \frac{144}{25}$

$\tan x = \pm\sqrt{\frac{144}{25}}$

$\tan x = \pm\frac{12}{5}$

Since x is in IVth quadrant
tan *x* is negative in IVth quadrant

$\therefore\ \tan x = \frac{-12}{5}$

$\cot x = \frac{1}{\tan x} = \frac{1}{\frac{-12}{5}}$

$= \frac{-5}{12}$

$\tan x = \frac{\sin x}{\cos x}$

$\sin x = (\tan x) \times (\cos x)$

$= \frac{-12}{5} \times \frac{5}{13}$

$$= \frac{-12}{13}$$

$$= \frac{5}{13}$$

$$\cos x = \frac{1}{\sec x} = \frac{1}{\frac{13}{5}}$$

$$\operatorname{cosec} x = \frac{1}{\sin x} = \frac{-13}{12}$$

OBJECTIVE Type Questions

[1 mark]

Multiple Choice Questions

1. A wheel rotates, making 18 revolutions per second. If the radius of the wheel is 49 cm, what linear distance does a point of its rim travel in three minutes? (Take π = 22/7)

(a) 9.97 km **(b) 9.90 km**

(c) 9.80 km **(d) 9.85 km**

Ans. *(a) 9.97 km*

Explanation: Radius of the wheel = 49 cm

∴ Circumference of the wheel

= 2 π × 49 cm = 308 cm

Hence, the linear distance travelled by a point of the rim in one revolution = 308 cm.

Number of revolutions made by the wheel in 3 minutes i.e. 180 seconds == 18 × 3 × 60 = 3240

∴ The linear distance travelled by a point of the rim in 3 minutes

= 308 × 3240 = 997920 cm = 9.97 km.

2. The angle of a triangle are in A.P. and the ratio of angle in degree of the least to the angle in radians of the greatest is 60 : π, find the angles in degrees.

(a) 30°, 60°, 90° **(b) 40°, 60°, 90°**

(c) 30°, 30°, 120° **(d) 20°, 130°, 30°**

Ans. *(a) 30°, 60°, 90°*

Explanation: Let the angles of the triangle be $(a-d)°, a°, (a+d)°$, where $d \geq 0$ (i)

Then $(a-d)+a+(a+d) = 180° \Rightarrow a = 60°$

∴ From (i), the angles are $(60-d)°, 60°, (60+d)°$

Now, the least angle = $(60-d)°$

And the greatest angle = $(60+d)°$

$= (60+d)° \times \frac{\pi}{180}$ radian (∴ 180° = π radian)

By the given condition, we have

$$\frac{60-d}{\frac{\pi}{180}(60+d)} = \frac{60}{\pi} \Rightarrow \frac{180(60-d)}{(60+d)} = 60$$

$\Rightarrow 180 - 3d = 60 + d \quad \Rightarrow 4d = 120 \Rightarrow d = 30$

∴ From (i), the angles are

$(60-30)°, 60°, (60+30)°$ i.e., 30°, 60°, 90°

3. The large hand of a clock is 49 cm long. How much distance does its extremity move in 30 minutes?

(a) 154 cm **(b) 80 cm**

(c) 75 cm **(d) 77 cm**

Ans. *(a) 154 cm*

Explanation:

The large hand of the clock makes a complete revolution in 60 minutes.

∴ Angle traced out by the large hand in 30 minutes (of time)

$$= \frac{360 \times 30}{60} = 180° = \frac{180°}{180} \pi \text{ radian} = \pi \text{ radian}$$

Hence, the distance moved by the extremity of the large hand 49 × π = 49 × 22/7 = 154 *cm*.

4. The radius of the circle whose arc length 15π cm makes an angle of $\frac{3\pi}{4}$ radian at the centre is:

(a) 10 cm **(b) 20 cm**

(c) $11\frac{1}{4}$ **(d) $22\frac{1}{2}$** **[DIKSHA]**

Ans. *(b) 20 cm*

Explanation: Arc of length = 15π cm, angle

$$\theta = \frac{3\pi}{4}$$

We need to calculate the radius of a circle,

Using formula of length

$$l = r \times \theta$$

Where, l = length of arc

r = radius of a circle

θ = angle

Put the value into the formula

$$15\pi = r \times \frac{3\pi}{4}$$

$$r = \frac{15\pi \times 4}{3\pi}$$

$$r = 20 \text{ cm}$$

Hence, the radius of a circle is 20 cm.

5. **Find the radius of the circle in which a central angle of 30° intercepts an arc of length 22 cm. (Use $\pi = \frac{22}{7}$).**

(a) 43 cm (b) 41 cm
(c) 42 cm (d) 40 cm

Ans. *(c) 42 cm*

Explanation: Here $l = 22$ cm and $\theta = 30° = \frac{\pi}{6}$

Hence, by $r = \frac{l}{\theta}$, we have

$$r = \frac{22 \times 6}{\pi} = \frac{22 \times 6 \times 7}{22} = 42 \text{ cm}$$

6. **Find the angle in the radian through which a pendulum swings its length is 80 cm and tip describes an arc of length 20 cm.**

(a) $\frac{1}{4}$ (b) $\frac{2}{25}$
(c) $\frac{3}{25}$ (d) $\frac{4}{25}$

Ans. *(a) $\frac{1}{4}$*

Explanation: Given, length of pendulum = 20 cm
Radius (r) = length of pendulum = 80 cm
Length of arc (l) = 20 cm

Now, $\theta = \frac{l}{r} = \frac{20}{80} = \frac{1}{4}$ radian

7. **The angle between the minute and hour hands of a clock at 8 : 30 is:**

(a) 80° (b) 75°
(c) 60° (d) 105° **[DIKSHA]**

Ans. *(b) 75°*

Explanation: Angle traced by hour hand in

$\frac{17}{2}$ hours $= (360° \div 12) \times \frac{17}{2} = 255°$

Angle traced by minute hand in 30 minute
$= (360° \div 60) \times 30 = 180°$
So, required angle = (255° – 180°) = 75°
Hence, the correct answer is 75°.

8. **If $\sin\theta + \operatorname{cosec}\theta = 2$. then $\sin^2\theta + \operatorname{cosec}^2\theta$ is equal to:**

(a) 1 (b) 4
(c) 2 (d) None of these
[NCERT Exemplar]

Ans. *(c) 2*

Explanation: According to the question,
$\sin\theta + \operatorname{cosec}\theta = 2$
Squaring LHS and RHS,
We get,

$\Rightarrow (\sin\theta + \operatorname{cosec}\theta)^2 = 2^2$
$\Rightarrow \sin^2\theta + \operatorname{cosec}^2\theta + 2\sin\theta\operatorname{cosec}\theta = 4$
$\Rightarrow \sin^2\theta + \operatorname{cosec}^2\theta + 2\sin\theta\left(\frac{1}{\sin\theta}\right) = 4$
$\Rightarrow \sin^2\theta + \operatorname{cosec}^2\theta + 2 = 4$
$\Rightarrow \sin^2\theta + \operatorname{cosec}^2\theta = 2$

Thus, option (c) is the correct answer

9. **If $\tan\theta = 1/2$ and $\tan\phi = 1/3$, then the value of $\theta + \phi$ is:**

(a) $\frac{\pi}{6}$ (b) π
(c) 0 (d) $\frac{\pi}{4}$

[NCERT Exemplar]

Ans. *(d) $\frac{\pi}{4}$*

Explanation: According to the question,

$$\tan\theta = \frac{1}{2} \text{ and } \tan\phi = \frac{1}{3}$$

We know that,

$$\tan(\theta + \phi) = \frac{\tan\theta + \tan\phi}{1 - \tan\theta\tan\phi}$$

$$= \frac{\frac{1}{2} + \frac{1}{3}}{1 - \frac{1}{2} \times \frac{1}{3}} = \frac{\frac{5}{6}}{\frac{5}{6}} = 1$$

$$\Rightarrow \tan(\theta + \phi) = \tan\frac{\pi}{4}$$

$$\Rightarrow \theta + \phi = \frac{\pi}{4}$$

Thus, option(d) is the correct answer.

Assertion-Reason (A-R)

Direction: In the following questions, a statement of assertion (A) is followed by a statement of the reason (R). Mark the correct choice as:

(a) Both assertion (A) and reason (R) are true and reason (R) is the correct explanation of assertion (A).
(b) Both assertion (A) and reason (R) are true but reason (R) is not the correct explanation of assertion (A).
(c) Assertion (A) is true but reason (R) is false.
(d) Assertion (A) is false but reason (R) is true.

10. **Assertion:** Value of sin (– 270)° is 1.
Reason: $\sin(180° + \theta) = -\sin\theta$.

Ans. *(a) Both assertion (A) and reason (R) are true and reason (R) is the correct explanation of assertion (A).*

Explanation: $\sin(-270°) = -\sin(180° + 90°)$
$= \sin 90° = 1$

$\sin(180° + \theta) = -\sin\theta$ as it goes in 3rd quadrant.

So, reason is the correct explanation of assertion.

11. Assertion: Value of $\sin\frac{\pi}{3} = \sin 60° = \frac{\sqrt{3}}{2}$.

Reason: Value of π in degree is $\frac{22}{7}$.

Ans. *(c) Assertion (A) is true but reason (R) is false.*

Explanation: Here $\sin\frac{\pi}{3} = \sin 60° = \frac{\sqrt{3}}{2}$

Value of π in degree is 180°.

So, assertion is true and the reason is false.

12. Assertion: The radius of the circle in which an angle is 60° which intercepts an arc of length 44 cm is 42 cm.

Reason: Formula for a triangle is $r = \frac{l}{\theta}$ where r is radius, l is arc and θ is angle.

Ans. *(a) Both assertion (A) and reason (R) are true and reason (R) is the correct explanation of assertion (A).*

Explanation: $l = 44$ *cm*, $\theta = 60° = \frac{\pi}{3}$

Hence,

$$r = \frac{l}{\theta} = \frac{44 \times 3 \times 7}{22} = 42 \text{ cm}$$

Formula of radius is $r = \frac{l}{\theta}$

Hence, both assertion and reason are true and reason is the correct explanation of assertion.

13. Assertion: The value of $\theta = \frac{\pi}{3}$ or $\frac{2\pi}{3}$, when θ lies between $(0, 2\pi)$ and $\sin^2\theta = \frac{3}{4}$.

Reason: $\sin\theta$ is positive in the first and second quadrant.

Ans. *(d) Assertion (A) is false but reason (R) is true.*

Explanation: Given $\sin^2\theta = \frac{3}{4} \Rightarrow \sin\theta = \frac{\sqrt{3}}{2}$ or $-\frac{\sqrt{3}}{2}$.

Case I: When $\sin\theta = \frac{\sqrt{3}}{2} = \sin\frac{\pi}{3}$

$\Rightarrow \sin\theta = \sin\frac{\pi}{3}$ or $\sin\left(\pi - \frac{\pi}{3}\right)$

$\Rightarrow \theta = \frac{\pi}{3}$ or $\pi - \frac{\pi}{3}$, i.e., $\theta = \frac{\pi}{3}$ or $\frac{2\pi}{3}$

Case II: When $\sin\theta = -\frac{\sqrt{3}}{2}$, then θ lies either in the third or fourth quadrant.

Now, $\sin\theta = -\frac{\sqrt{3}}{2} = -\sin\frac{\pi}{3}$

$= \sin\left(\pi + \frac{\pi}{3}\right)$ or $\sin\left(2\pi - \frac{\pi}{3}\right)$

$\theta = \pi + \frac{\pi}{3}$ or $2\pi - \frac{\pi}{3} \Rightarrow \theta = \frac{4\pi}{3}$ *or* $\frac{5\pi}{3}$,

Hence, $\sin^2\theta = \frac{3}{4}, 0 < \theta < 2\pi$

$\Rightarrow \theta = \frac{\pi}{3}, \frac{2\pi}{3}, \frac{4\pi}{3}, \frac{5\pi}{3}$

CASE BASED Questions (CBQs)

[**4** & **5** marks]

Read the following passages and answer the questions that follow:

14. *Nitish is playing with a Pinwheel toy which he bought from a village fair. He noticed that the pinwheel toy revolves as fast as he blows it. Consider the Pinwheel toy that makes 360 revolutions per minute.*

(A) Find the number of revolutions made by Pinwheel toy in 120 second.

(B) Find the number of revolutions made by Pinwheel toy in 1 sec and angle made by Pinwheel toy (in degree) in 6 revolutions.

Ans. (A) Since the number of revolutions made by Pinwheel toy in 1 minute = 360

And 1 min = 60 seconds

So, the number of revolution made by Pinwheel toy in 60 seconds = 360

$\therefore$ Number of revolutions made by Pinwheel toy in 120 seconds = 720

(B) The number of revolution made by Pinwheel toy in 1 seconds = $\frac{360}{60} = 6$

Since, angle made by Pinwheel toy in 1 revolutions = 360°.

Thus, angle made by Pinwheel toy in 6 revolutions = 360° × 6 = 2160°

15. *Consider a unit circle with centre O. Let A be any point on the circle. Consider O A as the initial side of an angle. Then the length of an arc of the circle will give the radian measure of the angle which the arc will subtend at the centre of the circle.*

A circle subtends an angle at the centre whose radian measure is 2 π and its degree measure is 360°.

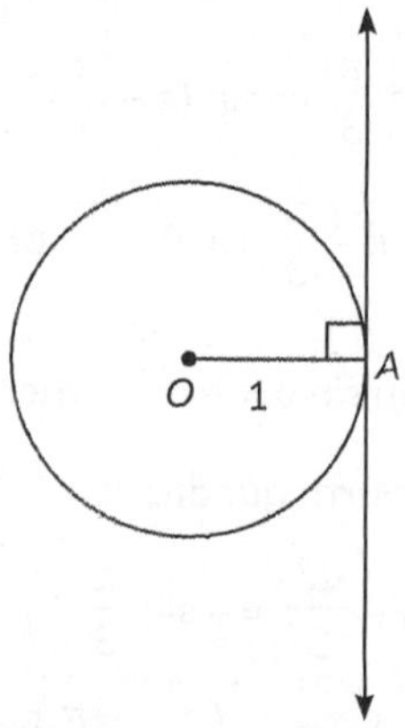

(A) Convert 240° into radian measure.

(a) $\frac{4\pi}{3}$ (b) $\frac{2\pi}{3}$

(c) $\frac{5\pi}{3}$ (d) $\frac{\pi}{3}$

(B) A wheel makes 360 revolutions in one minute. Through how many radians does it turn in one second?

(a) 6π (b) 4π

(c) 3π (d) 12π

(C) Convert (1.2)° into degree measure.

(a) 68° (b) 68°43'37.8"

(c) 68°45'36" (d) 58°46'27"

(D) Find the radius of the circle in which a central angle of 45° intercepts an arc of 132 cm.

(Use π) = $\frac{22}{7}$

(a) 168 cm (b) 50 cm

(c) 160 cm (d) 148 cm

(E) The minute hand of a watch is 35 cm long. How far does it move in 9 minutes?

(a) 15 cm (b) 30 cm

(c) 46 cm (d) 33 cm

Ans. (A) *(a)* $\frac{4\pi}{3}$

Explanation: We have, 240° angle

Its radian measure = $240 \times \frac{\pi}{180} = \frac{4\pi}{3}$

(B) *(d) 12π*

Explanation: In 1 minute i.e., 60 seconds, a wheel makes 360 revolutions.

∴ In one second, a wheel will make $\frac{360}{60}$ = 6 revolutions.

∴ Number of radians = 6 × 2 π = 12 π

(C) *(b) 68°43'37.8"*

Explanation: We have

$$(1.2)^\circ = \left(1.2 \times \frac{180}{\pi}\right) = 1.2 \times \frac{180}{22} \times 7$$

$$= 68.7272^\circ = 68^\circ\ (0.7272 \times 60)'$$

$$= 68^\circ\ 43'(0.63 \times 60)'' = 68^\circ\ 43'\ 37.8''$$

(D) *(a) 168 cm*

Explanation: We have,

$l - 132$ cm, $\theta - 45^\circ - 45 \times \frac{\pi}{180} - \frac{\pi}{4}$

Now, $\theta = \frac{1}{r} = \frac{132}{r}$

$$\frac{\pi}{4} = \frac{132}{r} \Rightarrow r = \frac{132 \times 4}{\pi}$$

$$\Rightarrow \quad r = \frac{132 \times 4}{\frac{22}{7}} = 168 \text{ cm}$$

(E) *(d) 33 cm*

Explanation: The angle made by minute hand in 9 minutes

$$= (9 \times 6)^\circ = 54^\circ = 54 \times \frac{\pi}{180} = \frac{3\pi}{10}$$

$$\therefore \quad \theta = \frac{l}{r}$$

$$\Rightarrow \quad \frac{3\pi}{10} = \frac{l}{35}$$

$$\Rightarrow \quad l = \frac{21\pi}{2}$$

$$\Rightarrow \quad l = \frac{21}{2} \times \frac{22}{7} = 33\text{cm}$$

VERY SHORT ANSWER Type Questions (VSA)

[1 mark]

16. Convert the following decimal-degree to degree minute second measures: 15.5757°

Ans. = 15° + 0.5757°

= 15° + (0.5757 × 60)′

= 15° + 34.542′

= 15° + 34′ + 0.542′

= 15° + 34′ +(0.542 × 60)″

= 15° + 34′ +32.52″

= 15° + 34′ +33″ = 15° 34′ 33″

17. If $a \cos\theta + b \sin\theta = m$ and $a \sin\theta - b \cos\theta = n$ then show that $a^2 + b^2 = m^2 + n^2$

[NCERT Exemplar]

Ans. Given, $a \cos\theta + b \sin\theta = m$ (i)

and $a \sin\theta - b \cos\theta = n$ (ii)

On squaring and adding of eqs (i) and (ii), we get

$m^2 + n^2 = (a \cos\theta + b \sin\theta)^2 + (a \sin\theta - b \cos\theta)^2$

$\Rightarrow m^2 + n^2 = a^2 \cos^2\theta + b^2 \sin\theta^2 + 2ab \cos\theta \sin\theta + a^2 \sin^2\theta + b^2 \cos^2\theta - 2ab \sin\theta \cos\theta$

$\Rightarrow m^2 + n^2 = a^2 (\cos^2\theta + \sin^2\theta) + b^2 (\sin^2\theta + \cos^2\theta)$

$\Rightarrow m^2 + n^2 = a^2 + b^2$

Hence, proved.

18. Find the value of sin(– 240°).

Ans. sin° (– 240°) = – sin 240°

= –sin (180° + 60°)

= – (– sin 60°)

= sin 60°

$= \frac{\sqrt{3}}{2}$

19. Find the value of tan 22° 30′.

[NCERT Exemplar]

Ans. Let, $22° 30' = \frac{\theta}{2}$

$\therefore\ \theta = 45°$

$$\tan 22° 30' = \tan\frac{\theta}{2} = \frac{\sin\frac{\theta}{2}}{\cos\frac{\theta}{2}}$$

$$= \frac{2\sin\frac{\theta}{2}\cos\frac{\theta}{2}}{2\cos^2\frac{\theta}{2}} = \frac{\sin\theta}{1+\cos\theta}$$

$$\therefore\ \frac{\sin\theta}{1+\cos\theta} = \frac{\sin 45°}{1+\cos 45°} = \frac{\frac{1}{\sqrt{2}}}{1+\frac{1}{\sqrt{2}}} = \frac{1}{\sqrt{2}+1}$$

$$= \frac{1\times(\sqrt{2}-1)}{(\sqrt{2}+1)(\sqrt{2}-1)} = \sqrt{2}-1$$

Hence, $\tan 22° 30' = \sqrt{2}-1$

SHORT ANSWER Type-I Questions (SA-I)

[2 marks]

20. Convert following radian measure into degree measures $\frac{-2}{9}$.

Ans. $\frac{-2}{9}$ radian $= \frac{-2}{9}\times\frac{180}{\pi}$

$= -\left(2\times\frac{20}{\pi}\right)$

$= -\left(2\times\frac{20\times 7}{22}\right)$

$= -\left(\frac{20\times 7}{11}\right)$

$= -\left(\frac{140}{11}\right)$

= – 12.7272°

21. Find the radius of the circle in which a central angle of 30° intercepts an arc of length 66 cm. (User $\pi = \frac{22}{7}$)

Ans. Given that length of arc, l = 66 cm and central angle, θ = 60°

Then, θ = 30°

$= \left(30\times\frac{\pi}{180}\right)$ radian $\quad [\therefore\ 1° = \frac{\pi}{180}$ radian$]$

$= \frac{\pi}{6}$ radian

Hence, radius of circle is

$$r = \frac{l}{\theta} = \frac{66\times 6}{\pi} = \frac{66\times 6\times 7}{22} = 126\ cm$$

22. Solve $\tan 4x = -\cot\left[x + \frac{\pi}{4}\right]$.

Ans. $\tan\theta = \cot[90° - \theta]$

$$\tan 4x = -\cot\left[x+\frac{n}{4}\right]$$

$$= \tan\left[\frac{\pi}{2}+x+\frac{\pi}{4}\right]$$

$$\tan 4x = \tan\left[x+\frac{3\pi}{4}\right]$$

$$4x = \left[x+\frac{3\pi}{4}\right]$$

$$4x = n\pi + x + \frac{3\pi}{4}$$

Where $n \in Z$,

$$3x = n\pi + \frac{3\pi}{4}$$

SHORT ANSWER Type-II Questions (SA-II)

[3 marks]

23. Find the value of

$$\sin\frac{\pi}{18}+\sin\frac{\pi}{9}+\sin\frac{2\pi}{9}+\sin\frac{5\pi}{18}.$$

Ans. Given: $\sin\frac{\pi}{18}+\sin\frac{\pi}{9}+\sin\frac{2\pi}{9}+\sin\frac{5\pi}{18}$

$= \sin 10° + \sin 20° + \sin 40° + \sin 50°$

$= \sin 50° + \sin 10° + \sin 40° + \sin 20°$

$= \sin (180° - 130°) + \sin 10° + \sin (180° - 140°) + \sin 20°$

$= \sin 130° + \sin 10° + \sin 140° + \sin 20°$

$[\because \sin(\pi - \theta) = \sin\theta]$

$= 2 \sin 70° \cos 60° + 2 \sin 80° \cos 60°$

$\left[\because \sin x + \sin y = 2\sin\frac{x+y}{2}\cos\frac{x-y}{2}\right]$

$= 2.\frac{1}{2}\sin 70° + 2.\frac{1}{2}\sin 80°$

$= \sin 70° + \sin 80° = \sin\frac{7\pi}{18}+\sin\frac{4\pi}{9}$

24. If $2\sin^2\theta = 3\cos\theta$ where, $0 \le \theta \le 2\theta$, then find the value of θ. [NCERT Exemplar]

Ans. Given, $2\sin^2\theta = 3\cos\theta$

$2(1-\cos^2\theta) = 3\cos\theta$

$2 - 2\cos^2\theta - 3\cos\theta = 0$

$2\cos^2\theta + 3\cos\theta - 2 = 0$

$2\cos^2\theta + 4\cos\theta - \cos\theta - 2 = 0$

$2\cos\theta(\cos\theta + 2) - 1(\cos\theta + 2) = 0$

$(\cos\theta + 2)(2\cos\theta - 1) = 0$

So, either $\cos\theta + 2 = 0$ or $2\cos\theta - 1 = 0$

But, $\cos\theta \ne -2$ $[-1 \le \cos\theta \le 1]$

$2\cos\theta - 1 = 0$

$\cos\theta = \frac{1}{2}$

$\cos\theta = \cos\frac{\pi}{3}$ or $\cos\theta = \cos\left(2\pi - \frac{\pi}{3}\right)$

$\cos\theta = \cos\frac{\pi}{3}$ or $\cos\theta = \cos\frac{5\pi}{3}$

25. Prove that:

$$\cos^4\frac{\pi}{8}+\cos^4\frac{3\pi}{8}+\cos^4\frac{5\pi}{8}+\cos^4\frac{7\pi}{8}=\frac{3}{2}.$$

Ans. L.H.S. $= \cos^4\frac{\pi}{8}+\cos^4\frac{3\pi}{8}+\cos^4\frac{5\pi}{8}+\cos^4\frac{7\pi}{8}$

$= \cos^4\left(\frac{\pi}{8}\right)+\cos^4\left(\frac{3\pi}{8}\right)+\cos^4\left(\pi-\frac{3\pi}{8}\right)+\cos^4\left(\pi-\frac{\pi}{8}\right)$

$= \cos^4\left(\frac{\pi}{8}\right)+\cos^4\left(\frac{3\pi}{8}\right)+\cos^4\left(\frac{3\pi}{8}\right)+\cos^4\left(\frac{\pi}{8}\right)$

$= 2\left[\cos^4\left(\frac{\pi}{8}\right)+\cos^4\left(\frac{3\pi}{8}\right)\right]$

$= 2\left(\left(\frac{1+\cos\frac{\pi}{4}}{2}\right)^2+\left(\frac{1+\cos\frac{3\pi}{4}}{2}\right)^2\right)$

$= \frac{2}{4}\left(\left(1+\frac{1}{\sqrt{2}}\right)^2+\left(1-\frac{1}{\sqrt{2}}\right)^2\right)=\frac{1}{2}(2+1)$

$= \frac{3}{2} =$ R.H.S

26. Find the value of the expression:

$$3\left[\sin^4\left(\frac{3\pi}{2}-\alpha\right)+\sin^4(3\pi+\alpha)\right]$$
$$-2\left[\sin^6\left(\frac{\pi}{2}+\alpha\right)+\sin^6(5\pi-\alpha)\right]$$

[NCERT Exemplar]

Ans. Given,

$$3\left[\sin^4\left(\frac{3\pi}{2}-\alpha\right)+\sin^4(3\pi+\alpha)\right]$$
$$-2\left[\sin^6\left(\frac{\pi}{2}+\alpha\right)+\sin^6(5\pi-\alpha)\right]$$

$= 3[\cos^4 \alpha + \sin^4 (\pi + \alpha)] - 2[\cos^6 \alpha + \sin^6 (\pi - \alpha)]$

$= 3[\cos^4 \alpha + \sin^4 \alpha] - 2[\cos^6 \alpha + \sin^6 \alpha]$

$= 3[(\cos^4 \alpha + \sin^4 \alpha) + 2 \sin^2 \alpha \cos^2 \alpha - 2 \sin^2 \alpha \cos^2 \alpha] - 2[(\cos^2 \alpha + \sin^2 \alpha)^3 - 3 \cos^2 \alpha \sin^2 \alpha (\cos^2 \alpha + \sin^2 \alpha)]$

$= 3[(\cos^2 \alpha + \sin^2 \alpha)^2 - 2\sin^2 \alpha \cos^2 \alpha] - 2[1 - 3 \cos^2 \alpha \sin^2 \alpha]$

$= 3[1 - 2 \sin^2 \alpha \cos^2 \alpha] - 2 + 6 \cos^2 \alpha \sin^2 \alpha$

$= 3 - 6 \sin^2 \alpha \cos^2 \alpha - 2 + 6 \sin^2 \alpha \cos^2 \alpha$

$= 1$

27. The circular measures of two angles of a triangle are 1/2 and 1/3, find the third angle in the English system.

Ans. We know that the sum of three angles of a triangle is 180°,i.e., π radian

$\therefore$ The third angle $= \left(\pi - \frac{1}{2} - \frac{1}{3}\right)$ radian

$$\simeq \left(\frac{22}{7} - \frac{1}{2} - \frac{1}{3}\right)^C = \left(\frac{97}{42} \times \frac{180}{\pi}\right)^\circ \quad (\because \pi^C = 180^\circ)$$

$$= \left(\frac{97 \times 30}{22}\right)^\circ = \frac{1455}{11} \text{ degree}$$

$$= \left(132\frac{3}{11}\right)^\circ = 132^\circ + \left(\frac{3 \times 60}{11}\right)'' \quad (\because 1^\circ = 60')$$

$$= 132^\circ + \left(16\frac{4}{11}\right)' = 132^\circ + 16' + \left(\frac{4}{11} \times 60\right)'' \quad (\because 1' = 60'')$$

$= 132^\circ\ 16'\ 22''$

LONG ANSWER Type Questions (LA)

[**4** & **5** marks]

28. If $\tan\theta = \dfrac{\sin\alpha - \cos\alpha}{\sin\alpha + \cos\alpha}$**, then show that** $\sin\alpha + \cos\alpha = \sqrt{2}\cos\theta$. **[NCERT Exemplar]**

Ans. Given, $\tan\theta = \dfrac{\sin\alpha - \cos\alpha}{\sin\alpha + \cos\alpha}$

Dividing by $\cos\alpha$

$$\Rightarrow \tan\theta = \frac{\tan\alpha - 1}{\tan\alpha + 1}$$

$$\Rightarrow \tan\theta = \frac{\tan\alpha - \tan\frac{\pi}{4}}{1 + \tan\frac{\pi}{4}\tan\alpha} \quad [\therefore \tan\pi/4 = 1]$$

$$\Rightarrow \tan\theta = \tan\left(\alpha - \frac{\pi}{4}\right)$$

$$\Rightarrow \theta = \alpha - \frac{\pi}{4}$$

$$\Rightarrow \alpha = \theta + \frac{\pi}{4}$$

$\therefore$ L.H.S. $= \sin\alpha + \cos\alpha$

$$= \sin\left(\theta + \frac{\pi}{4}\right) + \cos\left(\theta + \frac{\pi}{4}\right)$$

$$= \left(\sin\theta\cos\frac{\pi}{4} + \cos\theta\sin\frac{\pi}{4}\right) + \left(\cos\theta\cos\frac{\pi}{4} - \sin\theta\sin\frac{\pi}{4}\right)$$

$$= \left(\sin\theta\cdot\frac{1}{\sqrt{2}} + \cos\theta\cdot\frac{1}{\sqrt{2}}\right) + \left(\cos\theta\frac{1}{\sqrt{2}} - \sin\theta\frac{1}{\sqrt{2}}\right)$$

$$\left[\because \sin\frac{\pi}{4} = \frac{1}{\sqrt{2}} = \cos\frac{\pi}{4}\right]$$

$$= \frac{1}{\sqrt{2}}[(\sin\theta + \cos\theta) + (\cos\theta - \sin\theta)]$$

$$= \frac{2\cos\theta}{\sqrt{2}}$$

$= \sqrt{2}\cos\theta$ = R.H.S.

29. The moon's distance from the earth is 360,000 km and its diameter subtends an angle of 31' at the eye of the observer. Find the diameter of the moon.

Ans. Let AB be the diameter of the moon and let E be the eye of the observer. Since the distance between the earth and the moon is quite large, so we take diameter AB are arc AB. Let d be the diameter of the moon. Then, d = arc AB.

We have,

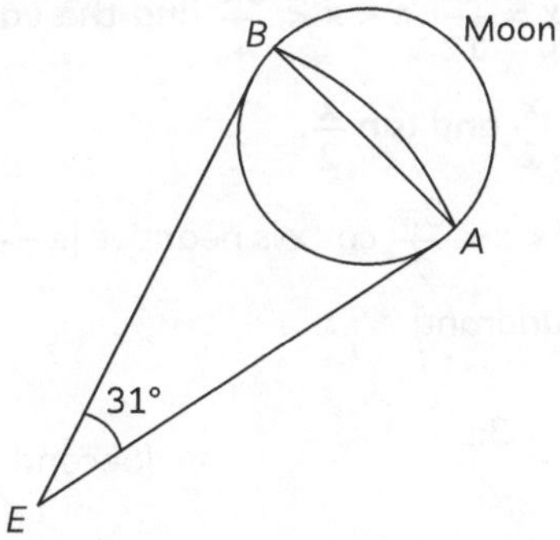

$$\theta = 31' = \left(\frac{31}{60}\right)^{\circ} = \left(\frac{31}{60} \times \frac{\pi}{180}\right)^{c} \text{ and}$$

$r = 360000$ kms

$$\therefore \quad \theta = \frac{\text{arc}}{\text{radius}}$$

$$\Rightarrow \quad \frac{31}{60} \times \frac{\pi}{180} = \frac{d}{360000}$$

$$\Rightarrow \quad d = \left(\frac{31}{60} \times \frac{\pi}{180} \times 360000\right) \text{km}$$

$= 3247.62$ kms

Hence, the diameter of the moon is 3247.62 km.

30. If $x = \sec\phi - \tan\phi$ and $y = \text{cosec}\,\phi + \cot\phi$, then show that $xy + x - y + 1 = 0$.

[NCERT Exemplar]

Ans. Given, $x = \sec\phi - \tan\phi$ and $y = \text{cosec}\,\phi + \cot\phi$

L.H.S. $= xy + x - y + 1$

$= (\sec\phi - \tan\phi)(\text{cosec}\,\phi + \cot\phi) + (\sec\phi - \tan\phi) - (\text{cosec}\,\phi + \cot\phi) + 1$

$$= \left(\frac{1}{\cos\phi} - \frac{\sin\phi}{\cos\phi}\right)\left(\frac{1}{\sin\phi} + \frac{\cos\phi}{\sin\phi}\right) + \left(\frac{1}{\cos\phi} - \frac{\sin\phi}{\cos\phi}\right) - \left(\frac{1}{\sin\phi} + \frac{\cos\phi}{\sin\phi}\right) + 1$$

$$= \left(\frac{1-\sin\phi}{\cos\phi}\right)\left(\frac{1+\cos\phi}{\sin\phi}\right) + \left(\frac{1-\sin\phi}{\cos\phi}\right) - \left(\frac{1+\cos\phi}{\sin\phi}\right) + 1$$

$$= \frac{1 - \sin\phi + \cos\phi - \sin\phi\cos\phi}{\cos\phi\sin\phi} + \frac{\sin\phi - \sin^2\phi - \cos\phi - \cos^2\phi + \sin\phi\cos\phi}{\sin\phi\cos\phi}$$

$$= \frac{1 - \sin^2\phi - \cos^2\phi}{\cos\phi\sin\phi}$$

$$= \frac{1-1}{\cos\phi\sin\phi} = 0$$

= RHS

31. If $\tan x = \frac{5}{12}$, $\pi < x < \frac{3\pi}{4}$ find the value of $\sin\frac{x}{2}$, $\cos\frac{x}{2}$ and $\tan\frac{x}{2}$.

Ans. Since $\pi < x < \frac{3\pi}{2}$, cos x is negative [$\pi - \frac{3\pi}{2}$ shows third quadrant]

Also,

$$\frac{\pi}{2} < \frac{x}{2} < \frac{3\pi}{4} \qquad \text{[Second quadrant]}$$

Therefore, $\sin\frac{x}{2}$ is positive in second quadrants whereas $\cos\frac{x}{2}$ is negative.

Now,

$$\sec^2 x = 1 + \tan^2 x$$

$$\sec^2 x = 1 + \left(\frac{5}{12}\right)^2$$

$$= 1 + \frac{25}{144}$$

$$= \frac{144+25}{144} = \frac{169}{144}$$

$$\therefore \quad \sec^2 x = \frac{169}{144} = \pm\frac{13}{12}$$

And

$$\cos x = \frac{-12}{13}$$

[As in third and second quadrant cos is negative]

Now,

$$2\sin^2\frac{x}{2} = 1 - \cos x$$

$$2\sin^2\frac{x}{2} = 1 - \left[\frac{-12}{13}\right]$$

$$2\sin^2\frac{x}{2} = \frac{25}{13}$$

$$\sin^2\frac{x}{2} = \frac{25}{26}$$

$$\sin\frac{x}{2} = \frac{5}{\sqrt{26}}$$

[In second quadrant sin is positive]

$$2\cos^2\frac{x}{2} = 1 + \cos x$$

$$= 1 - \frac{12}{13} = \frac{1}{13}$$

$$\cos^2\frac{x}{2} = \frac{1}{26}$$

$$\cos\frac{x}{2} = \frac{-1}{\sqrt{26}}$$

$$\text{Hence, } \tan\frac{x}{2} = \frac{\sin\frac{x}{2}}{\cos\frac{x}{2}} = \frac{\frac{5}{\sqrt{26}}}{\frac{-1}{\sqrt{26}}}$$

$$\tan\frac{x}{2} = -5$$

32. Find $\sin\frac{x}{2}$, $\cos\frac{x}{2}$, $\tan\frac{x}{2}$, when $\tan x = \frac{-4}{3}$, x lies in quadrant II. **[DIKSHA]**

Ans. Here, x is in quadrant II

i.e., $\frac{\pi}{2} < x < \pi$

$\Rightarrow \frac{\pi}{4} < \frac{x}{2} < \frac{\pi}{2}$

Therefore, $\sin\frac{x}{2}, \cos\frac{x}{2}$ and $\tan\frac{x}{2}$

all lie in the first quadrant.

It is given that $\tan x = -\frac{4}{3}$.

$\sec^2 x = 1 + \tan^2 x = 1 + \left(\frac{-4}{3}\right)^2 = 1 + \frac{16}{9} = \frac{25}{9}$

$\therefore \sec^2 x = \frac{25}{9} = \pm\frac{5}{3}$

$\Rightarrow \cos x = \pm\frac{3}{5}$

As x is in quadrant II, cos x is negative.

Thus, $\cos x = \frac{-3}{5}$

Now, $\cos x = 2\cos^2\frac{x}{2} - 1$

$\Rightarrow \frac{-3}{5} = 2\cos^2\frac{x}{2} - 1$

$\Rightarrow 2\cos^2\frac{x}{2} = 1 - \frac{3}{5}$

$\Rightarrow 2\cos^2\frac{x}{2} = \frac{2}{5}$

$\Rightarrow \cos^2\frac{x}{2} = \frac{1}{5}$

$\Rightarrow \cos\frac{x}{2} = \frac{1}{\sqrt{5}}$ $\left[\because \cos\frac{x}{2} \text{ is positive}\right]$

$\therefore \cos\frac{x}{2} = \frac{\sqrt{5}}{5}$

$\sin^2\frac{x}{2} + \cos^2\frac{x}{2} = 1$

$\Rightarrow \sin^2\frac{x}{2} + \left(\frac{1}{\sqrt{5}}\right)^2 = 1$

$\Rightarrow \sin^2\frac{x}{2} = 1 - \frac{1}{5} = \frac{4}{5}$

$\Rightarrow \sin\frac{x}{2} = \frac{2}{\sqrt{5}}$ $\left[\because \sin\frac{x}{2} \text{ is positive}\right]$

$\therefore \sin\frac{x}{2} = \frac{2\sqrt{5}}{5}$

$\tan\frac{x}{2} = \frac{\sin\frac{x}{2}}{\cos\frac{x}{2}} = \frac{\left(\frac{2}{\sqrt{5}}\right)}{\left(\frac{1}{\sqrt{5}}\right)} = 2$

Thus, the respective value of $\sin\frac{x}{2}$, $\cos\frac{x}{2}$ and $\tan\frac{x}{2}$ are $\frac{2\sqrt{5}}{5}$, $\frac{\sqrt{5}}{5}$, and 2.

TRIGONOMETRIC TRANSFORMATION FORMULAE 2

TOPIC 1

GRAPH OF TRIGONOMETRIC FUNCTION

Trigonometric Functions of Sum and Difference of Two Angles

Trigonometric Function of Some Allied Angles In Terms of θ

Allied Angles \ T-Ratios	sin	cos	tan	cot	sec	cosec
$-\theta$	$-\sin\theta$	$\cos\theta$	$-\tan\theta$	$-\cot\theta$	$\sec\theta$	$-\text{cosec}\,\theta$
$\left(\frac{\pi}{2}\pm\theta\right)$	$\cos\theta$	$\pm\sin\theta$	$\pm\cot\theta$	$\pm\tan\theta$	$\pm\text{cosec}\,\theta$	$\sec\theta$
$(\pi\pm\theta)$	$\pm\sin\theta$	$-\cos\theta$	$\pm\tan\theta$	$\pm\cot\theta$	$\pm\sec\theta$	$\pm\text{cosec}\,\theta$
$\left(\frac{3\pi}{2}\pm\theta\right)$	$-\cos\theta$	$\pm\sin\theta$	$\mp\cot\theta$	$\mp\tan\theta$	$\mp\text{cosec}\,\theta$	$\mp\sec\theta$
$(2\pi\pm\theta)$	$\pm\sin\theta$	$\cos\theta$	$\pm\tan\theta$	$\pm\cot\theta$	$\sec\theta$	$\pm\text{cosec}\,\theta$

Trigonometric function of Compound Angles

1. $\sin(A+B) = \sin A\cos B + \cos A\sin B$
2. $\sin(A-B) = \sin A\cos B - \cos A\sin B$
3. $\cos(A+B) = \cos A\cos B - \sin A\sin B$
4. $\cos(A-B) = \cos A\cos B + \sin A\sin B$
5. $\tan(A+B) = \dfrac{\tan A+\tan B}{1-\tan A\tan B}$
6. $\tan(A-B) = \dfrac{\tan A-\tan B}{1+\tan A\tan B}$
7. $\cot(A+B) = \dfrac{\cot A\cot B-1}{\cot A+\cot B}$
8. $\cot(A-B) = \dfrac{\cot A\cot B+1}{\cot B-\cot A}$

Transformation Formulae

In this topic, we deal with mainly two types of transformation.

1. Transformation of product into sum or difference.
2. Transformation of sum or difference into product.

Transformation of Product into Sum or Difference

- $2\sin A\cos B = \sin(A+B) + \sin(A-B)$
- $2\cos A\sin B = \sin(A+B) - \sin(A-B)$
- $2\cos A\cos B = \cos(A+B) + \cos(A-B)$
- $2\sin A\sin B = \cos(A-B) - \cos(A+B)$

Transformation of Sum or difference into Product

- $\sin A+\sin B = 2\sin\left(\frac{A+B}{2}\right)\cos\left(\frac{A-B}{2}\right)$
- $\sin A-\sin B = 2\cos\left(\frac{A+B}{2}\right)\sin\left(\frac{A-B}{2}\right)$
- $\cos A+\cos B = 2\cos\left(\frac{A+B}{2}\right)\cos\left(\frac{A-B}{2}\right)$
- $\cos A-\cos B = -2\sin\left(\frac{A+B}{2}\right)\sin\left(\frac{A-B}{2}\right)$

Trigonometric Functions of Multiple Angles

- $\cos 2A = \cos^2 A - \sin^2 A = 1 - 2\sin^2 A$

  $= 2\cos^2 A - 1 = \dfrac{1-\tan^2 A}{1+\tan^2 A}$
- $\sin 2A = 2\sin A\cos A = \dfrac{2\tan A}{1+\tan^2 A}$
- $\tan 2A = \dfrac{2\tan A}{1-\tan^2 A}$
- $\sin 3A = 2\sin A - 4\sin^3 A$
- $\cos 3A = 4\cos^3 A - 3\cos A$
- $\tan 3A = \dfrac{3\tan A-\tan^3 A}{1-3\tan^2 A}$

Trigonometric Functions of Sub-Multiple Angles

1. $\cos x = \cos^2\left(\frac{x}{2}\right) - \sin^2\left(\frac{x}{2}\right) = 2\cos^2\left(\frac{x}{2}\right) - 1$

$$= 1 - 2\sin^2\left(\frac{x}{2}\right)$$

$$\cos x = \frac{1 - \tan^2\left(\frac{x}{2}\right)}{1 + \tan^2\left(\frac{x}{2}\right)}$$

2. $\sin x = 2\sin\frac{x}{2}\cos\frac{x}{2} = \frac{2\tan\frac{x}{2}}{1 + \tan^2\left(\frac{x}{2}\right)}$

3. $\tan x = \frac{2\tan\left(\frac{x}{2}\right)}{1 - \tan^2\left(\frac{x}{2}\right)}$

Trigonometric Ratios of Some Specific Angles

1. $\sin 18° = \cos 72° = \frac{\sqrt{5} - 1}{4}$

2. $\cos 18° = \sin 72° = \frac{\sqrt{10 + 2\sqrt{5}}}{4}$

3. $\cos 36° = \sin 54° = \frac{\sqrt{5} + 1}{4}$

4. $\sin 36° = \cos 54° = \frac{\sqrt{10 - 2\sqrt{5}}}{4}$

Domain and range of trigonometric functions

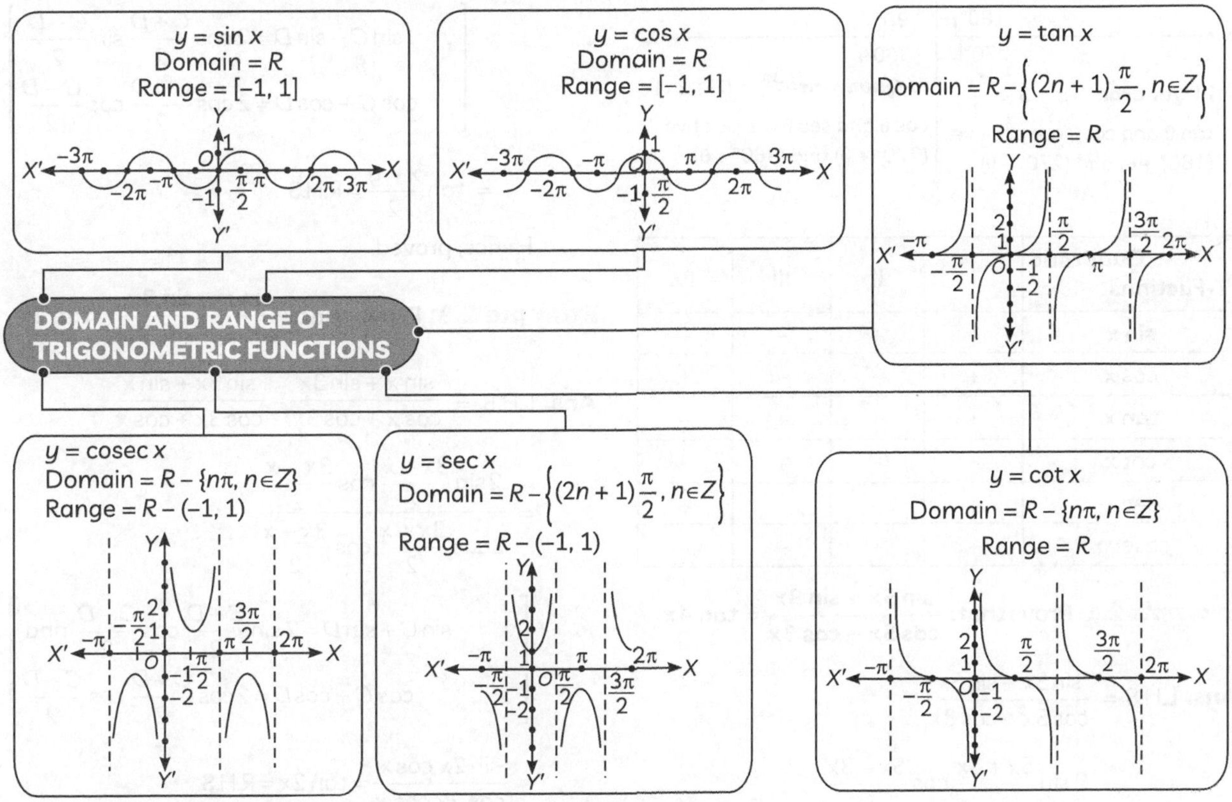

Value of T-Function for some Particular Angles

Angles \ T-Functions	sin	cos	tan	cot	sec	cosec
0	0	1	0	not defined	1	not defined
$\frac{\pi}{12}$	$\frac{\sqrt{3}-1}{2\sqrt{2}}$	$\frac{\sqrt{3}+1}{2\sqrt{2}}$	$2-\sqrt{3}$	$2+\sqrt{3}$	$\sqrt{2}(\sqrt{3}-1)$	$\sqrt{2}(\sqrt{3}+1)$
$\frac{\pi}{6}$	$\frac{1}{2}$	$\frac{\sqrt{3}}{2}$	$\frac{1}{\sqrt{3}}$	$\sqrt{3}$	$\frac{2}{\sqrt{3}}$	2

$\frac{\pi}{4}$	$\frac{1}{\sqrt{2}}$	$\frac{1}{\sqrt{2}}$	1	1	$\sqrt{2}$	$\sqrt{2}$
$\frac{\pi}{3}$	$\frac{\sqrt{3}}{2}$	$\frac{1}{2}$	$\sqrt{3}$	$\frac{1}{\sqrt{3}}$	2	$\frac{2}{\sqrt{3}}$
$\frac{\pi}{2}$	1	0	not defined	0	not defined	1
π	0	–1	0	not defined	–1	not defined
$\frac{3\pi}{2}$	–1	0	not defined	0	not defined	–1
2π	0	1`	0	not defined	1	not defined

Signs of Trigonometric Function in different Quadrants

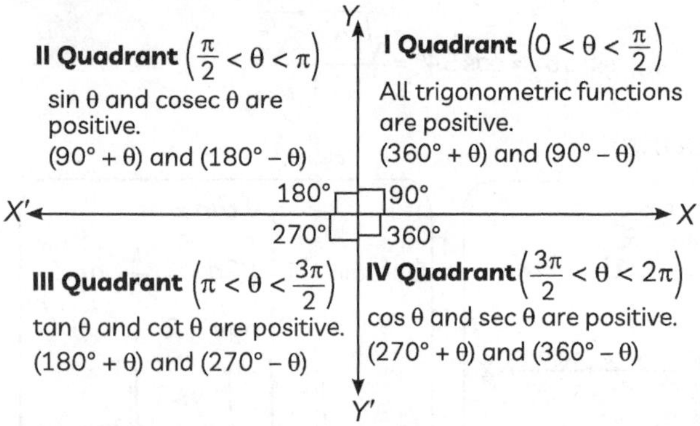

Quadrant / T-Fuctions	I	II	III	IV
sin x	+	+	–	–
cos x	+	–	–	+
tan x	+	–	+	–
cot x	+	–	+	–
sec x	+	–	–	+
cosec x	+	+	–	–

Example 2.1: Prove that: $\frac{\sin 5x + \sin 3x}{\cos 5x + \cos 3x} = \tan 4x.$

Ans. L.H.S $= \frac{\sin 5x + \sin 3x}{\cos 5x + \cos 3x}$

$$= \frac{2\sin\frac{5x+3x}{2}\cos\frac{5x-3x}{2}}{2\cos\frac{5x+3x}{2}\cos\frac{5x-3x}{2}}$$

$$\left[\because \begin{array}{l} \sin C + \sin D = 2\sin\frac{C+D}{2}\cos\frac{C-D}{2} \text{ and} \\ \cos C + \cos D = 2\cos\frac{C+D}{2}\cos\frac{C-D}{2} \end{array}\right]$$

$$= \frac{\sin 4x \cos x}{\cos 4x \cos x} = \tan 4x = \text{R.H.S.}$$

Hence, Proved.

Example 2.2: Prove that: $\frac{\sin x - \sin y}{\cos x + \cos y} = \tan\frac{x-y}{2}$

Ans. L.H.S $\frac{\sin x - \sin y}{\cos x + \cos y} = \frac{2\cos\frac{x+y}{2}\sin\frac{x-y}{2}}{2\cos\frac{x+y}{2}\cos\frac{x-y}{2}}$

$$\left[\because \begin{array}{l} \sin C - \sin D = 2\cos\frac{C+D}{2}\sin\frac{C-D}{2} \\ \cos C + \cos D = 2\cos\frac{C+D}{2}\cos\frac{C-D}{2} \end{array}\right]$$

$$= \tan\frac{x-y}{2} = \text{R.H.S}$$

Hence, proved.

Example 2.3: Prove that: $\frac{\sin x + \sin 3x}{\cos x + \cos 3x} = \tan 2x$

Ans. L.H.S. $= \frac{\sin x + \sin 3x}{\cos x + \cos 3x} = \frac{\sin 3x + \sin x}{\cos 3x + \cos x}$

$$= \frac{2\sin\frac{3x+x}{2}\cos\frac{3x-x}{2}}{2\cos\frac{3x+x}{2}\cos\frac{3x-x}{2}}$$

$$\left[\because \begin{array}{l} \sin C + \sin D = 2\sin\frac{C+D}{2}\cos\frac{C-D}{2} \text{ and} \\ \cos C + \cos D = 2\cos\frac{C+D}{2}\cos\frac{C-D}{2} \end{array}\right]$$

$$= \frac{\sin 2x \cos x}{\cos 2x \cos x} = \tan 2x = \text{R.H.S}$$

Hence, proved.

Example 2.4: Prove that: $\frac{\sin x - \sin 3x}{\sin^2 x - \cos^2 x} = 2\sin x$

Ans. L.H.S. $= \frac{\sin x - \sin 3x}{\sin^2 x - \cos^2 x} = \frac{\sin 3x - \sin x}{\cos^2 - \sin^2 x}$

$$= \frac{2\cos\frac{3x+x}{2}\sin\frac{3x-x}{2}}{\cos 2x}$$

$$\left[\because \quad \sin C - \sin D = 2\cos\frac{C+D}{2}\sin\frac{C-D}{2} \text{ and } \cos^2 x - \sin^2 x = \cos 2x\right]$$

$$= \frac{2\cos 2x \sin x}{\cos 2x} = 2\sin x = \text{R.H.S}$$

Hence Proved.

Example 2.5: **Prove that:**

$$\frac{\cos 4x + \cos 3x + \cos 2x}{\sin 4x + \sin 3x + \sin 2x} = \cot 3x.$$

Ans. L.H.S. $= \dfrac{\cos 4x + \cos 3x + \cos 2x}{\sin 4x + \sin 3x + \sin 2x}$

$$= \frac{(\cos 4x + \cos 2x) + \cos 3x}{(\sin 4x + \sin 2x) + \sin 3x}$$

$$= \frac{2\cos\frac{4x+2x}{2}\cos\frac{4x-2x}{2} + \cos 3x}{2\sin\frac{4x+2x}{2}\cos\frac{4x-2x}{2} + \sin 3x}$$

$$\left[\because \quad \cos C + \cos D = 2\cos\frac{C+D}{2}\cos\frac{C-D}{2} \text{ and } \sin C + \sin D = 2\sin\frac{C+D}{2}\cos\frac{C-D}{2}\right]$$

$$= \frac{2\cos 3x \cos x + \cos 3x}{2\sin 3x \cos x + \sin 3x}$$

$$= \frac{\cos 3x(2\cos x + 1)}{\sin 3x(2\cos x + 1)} = \cot 3x = \text{R.H.S.}$$

Hence Proved.

Example: 2.6: **Prove that: $\cot x \cot 2x - \cot 2x \cot 3x - \cot 3x \cot x = 1$**

Ans. Take, $\cot 3x = \cot(2x + x)$

$$\frac{\cot 3x}{1} = \frac{\cot 2x \cot x - 1}{\cot 2x + \cot x}$$

$$\left[\therefore \quad \cot(A+B) = \frac{\cot A \cot B - 1}{\cot A + \cot B}\right]$$

$\Rightarrow$ $\cot 3x \cot 2x + \cot 3x \cot x = \cot 2x \cot x - 1$

$\Rightarrow$ $\cot x \cot 2x - \cot 2x \cot 3x - \cot 3x \cot x = 1$

$\therefore$ L.H.S. = R.H.S

Example 2.7: **Prove that:**

$$\tan 4x = \frac{4\tan x(1-\tan^2 x)}{1-6\tan^2 x + \tan^2 x}$$

Ans. L.H.S. $= \tan 4x = \tan 2(2x) = \dfrac{2\tan 2x}{1-\tan^2 2x}$

$$\frac{2\dfrac{2\tan x}{1-\tan^2 x}}{1-\left(\dfrac{2\tan x}{1-\tan^2 x}\right)^2} \qquad \left[\therefore \quad \tan 2x = \frac{2\tan x}{1-\tan^2 x}\right]$$

$$= \frac{4\tan x}{1-\tan^2 x} \times \frac{(1-\tan^2 x)^2}{(1-\tan^2 x)^2 - 4\tan^2 x}$$

$$= \frac{4\tan x(1-\tan^2 x)}{1+\tan^4 x - 2\tan^2 x - 4\tan^2 x}$$

$$= \frac{4\tan x(1-\tan^2 x)}{1-6\tan^2 x + \tan^4 x} = \text{R.H.S.}$$

Hence, proved.

Example 2.8: **Prove that:**

$\cos 4x = 1 - 8\sin^2 x \cos^2 x$.

Ans. L.H.S. $= \cos 4x = 1 - 2\sin^2 2x = 1 - 2(\sin 2x)^2$

$[\because \ \cos 2x = 1 - 2\sin^2 2x \cos^2]$

$= 1 - 2(2\sin x \cos x)^2$

$= 1 - 8\sin 2x \cos^2 x$ = R.H.S

$[\because \ \sin 2x = 2\sin x \cos x]$

Hence proved.

Example 2.9: **Prove that: $\cos 6x = 32\cos^6 x - 48\cos^4 x + 18\cos^2 x - 1$**

Ans. L.H.S. $= \cos 6x = \cos 2(3x)$

$= 2\cos^2 3x - 1 = 2(\cos 3x)^2 - 1$

$(\because \ \cos 2\theta = 2\cos^2\theta - 1)$

$= 2(4\cos^3 x - 3\cos x)^2 - 1$

$(\because \ \cos 3\theta = 4\cos^3\theta - 3\cos\theta)$

$= 2(16\cos^6 x + 9\cos^2 x - 24\cos^4 x) - 1$

$= 32\cos^6 x - 48\cos^4 x + 18\cos 2x - 1$

= R.H.S.

Hence proved.

Example 2.10: **If $x\sin^3\theta + y\cos^3\theta = \sin\theta\cos\theta$ and $x\sin\theta = y\cos\theta$ then $x^2 + y^2$ is equal to:**

(a) 2 **(b)** 0

(c) 3 **(d)** 1

Ans. *(d) 1*

Explanation:

$x\sin^3\theta + y\cos^3\theta = \sin\theta\cos\theta$ ...(i)

$x\sin\theta = y\cos\theta \Rightarrow y = x\dfrac{\sin\theta}{\cos\theta}$ ...(ii)

Putting in (i), $x\sin^3\theta + x\dfrac{\sin\theta}{\cos\theta}\cdot\cos^3\theta = \sin\theta\cos\theta$

$\Rightarrow$ $x\sin^3\theta + x\sin\theta\cos^2\theta = \sin\theta\cos\theta$

$\Rightarrow$ $x = \cos\theta$

Putting the value of x in (ii), we get $y = \sin\theta$

$\Rightarrow$ $x^2 + y^2 = \sin^2\theta + \cos^2\theta = 1$

Hence, option(d) is the correct answer.

Example 2.11: **The value of $\sec^2\theta + \text{cosec}^2\theta$ is equal to:**

(a) $\tan^2\theta + \cot^2\theta$ **(b)** $\sec^2\theta\,\text{cosec}^2\theta$

(c) $\sec\theta\,\text{cosec}\,\theta$ **(d)** $\sin^2\theta + \cos^2\theta$

Ans. *(b)* $sec^2 \theta\ cosec^2 \theta$

Explanation:

$$\sec^2\theta + \text{cosec}^2\theta = \frac{1}{\cos^2\theta} + \frac{1}{\sin^2\theta} = \frac{\sin^2\theta + \cos^2\theta}{\sin^2\theta\cos^2\theta}$$

$$= \frac{1}{\sin^2\theta\cos^2\theta} = \text{cosec}^2\theta\sec^2\theta$$

Hence, option(b) is the correct answer.

Example 2.12: If $x \sin\frac{\pi}{4}\cos^2\frac{\pi}{3}$

$$= \frac{\tan^2\left(\frac{\pi}{3}\right)\text{cosec}\left(\frac{\pi}{6}\right)}{\sec\left(\frac{\pi}{4}\right)\cot^2\left(\frac{\pi}{6}\right)}$$ **then x =**

(a) 2 **(b)** 4

(c) 8 **(d)** 16

Ans. *(c)* 8

Explanation:

$$x\sin 45°\cos^2 60° = \frac{\tan^2 60°\ \text{cosec}\ 30°}{\sec 45°\cot^2 30°}$$

$$x\cdot\frac{1}{\sqrt{2}}\cdot\frac{1}{4} = \frac{3.2}{\sqrt{2}.3}$$

$\Rightarrow x = 8$

Hence, option(c) is the correct answer.

OBJECTIVE Type Questions

[1 mark]

Multiple Choice Questions

1. Find the radian measure of 1020°.

(a) $\frac{17\pi}{9}$ **(b)** $\frac{17\pi}{3}$

(c) $\frac{17\pi}{6}$ **(d)** $\frac{6\pi}{9}$

Ans. *(b)* $\frac{15\pi}{6}$

Explanation: Required radian measure

$$= \frac{\pi}{180} \times \text{Degree measure}$$

$$= \frac{\pi}{180}\times 1020 = \frac{17\pi}{3}$$

Hence, option(b) is the correct answer.

2. Value of cot 570° is: [DIKSHA]

(a) $\sqrt{3}$ **(b)** $\frac{1}{\sqrt{3}}$

(c) $-\sqrt{3}$ **(d)** $-\frac{1}{\sqrt{3}}$

Ans. *(a)* $\sqrt{3}$

Explanation: Value of cot 570° is

$= \cot(3\pi + 30°)$

$= \cot 30°$

$= \sqrt{3}$

Hence, option(a) is the correct answer.

3. The value of $\tan\left(\frac{61\pi}{64}\right)$.

(a) $\frac{1}{\sqrt{3}}$ **(b)** $\frac{1}{\sqrt{2}}$

(c) 1 **(d)** 0

Ans. *(a)* $\frac{1}{\sqrt{3}}$

$$\tan\left(\frac{61\pi}{64}\right) = \tan\left(10\pi + \frac{\pi}{6}\right)$$

$$= \tan\left(\frac{\pi}{6}\right) = \frac{1}{\sqrt{3}}$$

Hence, option(a) is the correct answer.

4. If $\cos x = \frac{-1}{2}$ and $0 < x < 2\pi$, then the solutions are: [DIKSHA]

(a) $x = \frac{\pi}{3}, \frac{4\pi}{3}$ **(b)** $x = \frac{2\pi}{3}, \frac{4\pi}{3}$

(c) $x = \frac{2\pi}{3}, \frac{7\pi}{3}$ **(d)** $\theta = \frac{2\pi}{3}, \frac{5\pi}{3}$

Ans. *(b)* $x = \frac{2\pi}{3}, \frac{4\pi}{3}$

Explanation: If $\cos x = -\frac{1}{2}$

Then, $\cos x = -\cos\frac{\pi}{3}$

$$\cos x = \cos\left(\pi - \frac{\pi}{3}\right)$$

$$\cos x = \cos\frac{2\pi}{2}$$

$$x = \frac{2\pi}{3}$$

and $\cos x = \cos\left(\pi + \frac{\pi}{3}\right)$

$$\cos x = \cos\frac{4\pi}{3}$$

$$x = \frac{4\pi}{3}$$

Hence, $x = \frac{2\pi}{3}, \frac{4\pi}{3}$

Hence, option(b) is the correct answer.

5. Find the value of tan (α + β), given that $\cot\alpha = \frac{1}{2}, \alpha \in \left(\pi, \frac{3\pi}{2}\right)$ and $\sec\beta = \frac{-5}{3}, \beta \in \left(\frac{\pi}{2}, \pi\right)$.

(a) $\frac{1}{11}$ **(b)** $\frac{2}{11}$

(c) $\frac{5}{11}$ **(d)** $\frac{3}{11}$

Ans. *(b)* $\frac{2}{11}$

Explanation: Given,

$$\cot\alpha = \frac{1}{2} \Rightarrow \tan\alpha = 2 \text{ and } \sec\beta = \frac{-5}{3}$$

Then, $\tan\beta = \sqrt{\sec^2\beta - 1}$

$$\Rightarrow \tan\beta = \pm\frac{4}{3}$$

But, $\tan\beta = \frac{-4}{3}$ (∵ tan β is –ve in II quadrant)

$$\tan(\alpha+\beta) = \frac{\tan\alpha + \tan\beta}{1 - \tan\alpha \cdot \tan\beta} = \frac{2 + \left(-\frac{4}{3}\right)}{1 - (2)\left(\frac{-4}{3}\right)} = \frac{2}{11}$$

Hence, option(b) is the correct answer.

6. If $\cos x + \sqrt{3}\sin x = 2$, then the value of *x* is:

(a) $\frac{\pi}{3}$ **(b)** $\frac{2\pi}{3}$

(c) $\frac{4\pi}{3}$ **(d)** $\frac{5\pi}{3}$ **[DIKSHA]**

Ans. *(a)* $\frac{\pi}{3}$

Explanation: If $\cos x + \sqrt{3}\sin x = 2$

$$\frac{1}{2}\cos x + \frac{\sqrt{3}}{2}\sin x = 1$$

$$\sin 30° \cos x + \cos 30° \sin x = 1$$

$$\sin(30° + x) = 1$$

$$\sin(30° + x) = \sin 90°$$

$$30° + x = 90°$$

$$x = 60°$$

$$x = \frac{\pi}{3}$$

Hence, option(a) is the correct answer.

7. The value of tan 75° – cot 75° is equal to:

(a) $2\sqrt{3}$ **(b)** $2+\sqrt{3}$

(c) $2-\sqrt{3}$ **(d)** 1

[NCERT Exemplar]

Ans. *(a)* $2\sqrt{3}$

Explanation: We have, tan 75° – cot 75°

$$= \frac{\sin 75°}{\cos 75°} - \frac{\cos 75°}{\sin 75°}$$

$$= \frac{\sin^2 75° - \cos^2 75°}{\cos 75° \sin 75°}$$

$$= \frac{2(\sin^2 75° - \cos^2 75°)}{2\cos 75° \sin 75°}$$

$$= \frac{-2\cos 150°}{\sin 150°}$$

$$= 2\cot 150°$$

$$= -2\cot(180° - 30°)$$

$$= 2\cot 30°$$

$$= 2\sqrt{3}$$

Hence, option(a) is the correct answer. √

8. If tan θ = 3 and θ lies in third quadrant, then the value of sin θ is:

(a) $\frac{1}{\sqrt{10}}$ **(b)** $\frac{-1}{\sqrt{10}}$

(c) $\frac{-3}{\sqrt{10}}$ **(d)** $\frac{3}{\sqrt{10}}$

[NCERT Exemplar]

Ans. *(c)* $\frac{-3}{\sqrt{10}}$

Explanation: According to the question.

Given that, tan θ = 3 and θ lies in third quadrant

⇒ cot θ = 1/3

We know that, $\text{cosec}^2\theta = 1 + \cot^2\theta$

$$= 1 + \left(\frac{1}{3}\right)^2 = 1 + \frac{1}{9} = \frac{10}{9}$$

$\Rightarrow \sin^2\theta = \frac{9}{10}$

$\Rightarrow \sin\theta = \pm\frac{3}{\sqrt{10}}$

$\Rightarrow \sin\theta = -\frac{3}{\sqrt{10}}$,

since θ lies in the third quadrant.

Hence, option(c) is the correct answer.

Assertion-Reason (A-R)

DIRECTION: In the following questions, a statement of assertion (A) is followed by a statement of the reason (R). Mark the correct choice as:

(a) Both assertion (A) and reason (R) are true and reason (R) is the correct explanation of assertion (A).

(b) Both assertion (A) and reason (R) are true but reason (R) is not the correct explanation of assertion (A).

(c) Assertion (A) is true but reason (R) is false.

(d) Assertion (A) is false but reason (R) is true.

9. Let $\sec\theta + \tan\theta = m$, where $0 < m < 1$.

Assertion: $\sec\theta = \frac{m^2+1}{2m}$ **and** $\sin\theta = \frac{m^2-1}{m^2+1}$

Reason: **θ lies in the third quadrant.**

Ans. *(c) Assertion (A) is true but reason (R) is false.*

Explanation: Given $\sec\theta + \tan\theta = m, 0 < m < 1$ ...(i)

Also, $\sec^2\theta - \tan^2\theta = 1$ ...(ii)

Dividing (ii) by (i), we get $\sec\theta - \tan\theta = \frac{1}{m}$ ...(iii)

Note that $\frac{1}{m} > 1$ $(\because 0 < m < 1)$

Adding (i) and (iii), we get $\sec\theta = \frac{m^2+1}{2m} > 0$

And subtracting (iii) from (i), we get $\tan\theta = \frac{m^2-1}{2m} < 0$

As $\sec\theta > 0$ and $\tan\theta < 0$

∴ θ lies in the fourth quadrant.

Also, $\sin\theta = \tan\theta\cos\theta = \frac{\tan\theta}{\sec\theta} = \frac{m^2-1}{m^2+1}$

Hence, option(c) is the correct answer.

10. Let α be a real number lying between 0 and π/2 and n be a positive integer.

Assertion: $\tan\alpha + 2\tan 2\alpha + 2^2\tan 2^2\alpha + \ldots + 2^{n-1}\tan 2^{n-1}\alpha + 2^n\cot 2^n\alpha = \cot\alpha$

Reason: $\cot\alpha - \tan\alpha = 2\cot 2\alpha$.

Ans. *(a) Both assertion (A) and reason (R) are true and reason (R) is the correct explanation of assertion (A).*

Explanation:

Now, $\cot\alpha - \tan\alpha = \frac{1}{\tan\alpha} - \tan\alpha = \frac{1-\tan^2\alpha}{\tan\alpha}$

$= 2\left(\frac{1-\tan^2\alpha}{2\tan\alpha}\right) = 2\cot 2\alpha$

From here, we get $\tan\alpha = \cot\alpha - 2\cot 2\alpha$

Making repeated use of this identify, we shall obtain

$\tan\alpha + 2\tan 2\alpha + 2^2\tan 2^2\alpha + \ldots + 2^{n-1}\tan 2^{n-1}\alpha + 2^n\cot 2^n\alpha$

$= (\cot\alpha - 2\cot 2\alpha) + 2(\cot 2\alpha - 2\cot 2^2\alpha) + 2^2(\cot 2^2\alpha - 2\cot 2^3\alpha) + \ldots + 2^{n-1}(\cot 2^{n-1}\alpha - 2\cot 2^n\alpha) + 2^n\cot 2^n\alpha = \cot\alpha$

Hence, option(a) is the correct answer.

11. Assertion: **The value of $\sin(-690°)\cos(-300°) + \cos(-750°)\sin(-240°) = 1$**

Reason: **The value of sin and cos is negative in the third and fourth quadrant respectively.**

Ans. *(c) Assertion (A) is true but reason (R) is false.*

Explanation: $\sin(-690°) = -\sin 690°$

$= -\sin(2 \times 360° - 30°)$

$= -(-\sin 30°) = \frac{1}{2}$

$\cos(-300°) = \cos 300° = \cos(360° - 60°)$

$= \cos 60° = \frac{1}{2}$

$\cos(-750°) = \cos 750° = \cos(2 \times 360° + 30°)$

$= \cos 30° = \frac{\sqrt{3}}{2}$

$\sin(-240°) = -\sin 240° = -\sin(180° + 60°)$

$= -(-\sin 60°) = \sin 60° = \frac{\sqrt{3}}{2}$

∴ $\sin(-690°)\cos(-300°) + \cos(-750°)\sin(-240°)$

$= \left(\frac{1}{2}\right)\left(\frac{1}{2}\right) + \left(\frac{\sqrt{3}}{2}\right)\left(\frac{\sqrt{3}}{2}\right) = \frac{1}{4} + \frac{3}{4} = 1$

Thus, the assertion is true but the reason is false.

Hence, option(c) is the correct answer.

12. If $A + B + C = 180°$, then

Assertion: $\cos^2\frac{A}{2} + \cos^2\frac{B}{2} - \cos^2\frac{C}{2}$

$$= 2\cos\frac{A}{2}\cos\frac{B}{2}\sin\frac{C}{2}$$

Reason: cos C + cos D

$$= 2\cos\left(\frac{C+D}{2}\right)\cos\left(\frac{C-D}{2}\right)$$

Ans. *(a) Both assertion (A) and reason (R) are true and reason (R) is the correct explanation of assertion (A).*

Explanation: L.H.S. = $\cos^2\frac{A}{2}+\cos^2\frac{B}{2}-\cos^2\frac{C}{2}$

$$= \frac{1+\cos A}{2}+\frac{1+\cos B}{2}-\frac{1+\cos C}{2}$$

$$= \frac{1+(\cos A+\cos B-\cos C)}{2} \quad ...(i)$$

Now $\cos A + \cos B - \cos C$

$$= 2\cos\frac{A+B}{2}\cos\left(\frac{A-B}{2}\right)-\cos\left(2\cdot\frac{C}{2}\right)$$

$$= 2\sin\frac{C}{2}\cos\left(\frac{A-B}{2}\right)-\left(1-2\sin^2\frac{C}{2}\right)$$

$$\left(\because \cos\left(\frac{A+B}{2}\right)=\cos\left(90°-\frac{C}{2}\right)=\sin\left(\frac{C}{2}\right)\right)$$

$$= 2\sin\frac{C}{2}\left\{\cos\left(\frac{A-B}{2}\right)+\sin\left(\frac{C}{2}\right)\right\}-1$$

$$= -1+2\sin\frac{C}{2}\left\{\cos\left(\frac{A-B}{2}\right)+\cos\left(\frac{A+B}{2}\right)\right\}$$

$$= -1+4\sin\left(\frac{C}{2}\right)\cos\left(\frac{A}{2}\right)\cos\left(\frac{B}{2}\right) \quad ...(ii)$$

From (i) and (ii), we get

L.H.S of the given identity

$$= \frac{1+\left(-1+4\cos\left(\frac{A}{2}\right)\cos\left(\frac{B}{2}\right)\sin\left(\frac{C}{2}\right)\right)}{2}$$

$$= 2\cos\left(\frac{A}{2}\right)\cos\left(\frac{B}{2}\right)\sin\left(\frac{C}{2}\right)=\text{R.H.S}$$

Hence, option(a) is the correct answer

CASE BASED Questions (CBQs)

[**4** & **5** marks]

Read the following passages and answer the questions that follow:

13. *Sudhir who is a student of class XI got a Maths assignment from his class teacher. He did all the questions except a few. If the value of $\sin x=\frac{3}{5}$ and $\cos y=-\frac{12}{13}$, where x and y both lie in the second quadrant, then help Sudhir in solving these questions.*

(A) What will be the value of cos x?

(a) $\frac{4}{5}$ (b) $\frac{-3}{5}$

(c) $\frac{-4}{5}$ (d) $\frac{3}{5}$

(B) What will be the value of sin y?

(a) $\frac{5}{12}$ (b) $\frac{-12}{13}$

(c) $\frac{-5}{13}$ (d) $\frac{5}{13}$

(C) Which of the following options is correct?

(a) sin (x – y) = sin x cos y + cos x sin y

(b) sin (x + y) = cos x sin y – sin x cos y

(c) sin (x + y) = sin x cos y + cos x sin y

(d) sin(x – y) = sin x sin y – cos x cos y

(D) The value of sin (x + y) is:

(a) $\frac{-56}{65}$ (b) $\frac{56}{65}$

(c) $\frac{55}{67}$ (d) $\frac{-55}{67}$

(E) Find the value of sin 75°.

(a) $\frac{1-\sqrt{3}}{\sqrt{2}}$ (b) $\frac{1+\sqrt{3}}{2\sqrt{2}}$

(c) $\frac{1-\sqrt{3}}{2\sqrt{2}}$ (d) $\frac{1+\sqrt{3}}{2}$

Ans. (A) *(c)* $\frac{-4}{5}$

Explanation:

$$\cos^2 x=1-\sin^2 x=1-\frac{9}{25}=\frac{16}{25}$$

Thus $\cos x=\pm\frac{4}{5}$

Since x lies in second quadrant

∴ cos x is negative

$$\therefore \cos x=-\frac{4}{5}$$

(B) (d) $\frac{5}{13}$

Explanation: $\sin^2 y = 1 - \cos^2 y$

$$= 1-\frac{144}{169}=\frac{25}{169}=\pm\frac{5}{13}$$

Since y lies in second quadrant

$\therefore$ sin y is positive

$\therefore$ $\sin y = \frac{5}{13}$

(C) (c) $\sin(x + y) = \sin x \cos y + \cos x \sin y$

(D) (a) $\frac{-56}{65}$

Explanation:

$$\sin(x+y)=\left(\frac{3}{5}\right)\times\left(-\frac{12}{13}\right)+\left(-\frac{4}{5}\right)\times\left(\frac{5}{13}\right)$$

$$=-\frac{36}{65}-\frac{20}{65}=-\frac{56}{65}$$

(E) (b) $\frac{1+\sqrt{3}}{2\sqrt{2}}$

Explanation: $\sin 75° = \sin(30° + 45°)$

$= \sin 30° \cos 45° + \cos 30° \sin 45°$

$$=\frac{1}{2}\cdot\frac{1}{\sqrt{2}}+\frac{\sqrt{3}}{2}\cdot\frac{1}{\sqrt{2}}=\frac{1+\sqrt{3}}{2\sqrt{2}}$$

14. *Consider* $\sin A=\frac{4}{5}$ *and* $\cos B=\frac{5}{13}$ *where* $0<A,B<\frac{\pi}{2}$.

(A) Find the value of cos A + sin B.

(B) Find value of cos $(A + B)$ and sin $(A - B)$.

Ans. (A) Given, $\sin A=\frac{4}{5}, 0<A<\frac{\pi}{2}$

$\therefore$ $\cos A=\sqrt{1-\sin^2 A}$ [$\because$ A lies in 1st quadrant]

$$=\sqrt{1-\left(\frac{4}{5}\right)^2}=\sqrt{1-\frac{16}{25}}$$

$\Rightarrow$ $\cos A=\sqrt{\frac{9}{25}}=\frac{3}{5}$

And $\cos B=\frac{5}{13}, 0<B<\frac{\pi}{2}$

$\therefore$ $\sin B=\sqrt{1-\cos^2 B}$ [$\because$ B lies in 1st quadrant]

$$=\sqrt{1-\left(\frac{5}{13}\right)^2}=\sqrt{1-\frac{25}{169}}$$

$\Rightarrow$ $\sin B=\sqrt{\frac{144}{169}}=\frac{12}{13}$

$$\cos A+\sin B=\frac{3}{5}+\frac{12}{13}=\frac{39+60}{65}=\frac{99}{65}$$

(B) $\cos(A + B) = \cos A \cos B - \sin A \sin B$

$$=\frac{3}{5}\times\frac{5}{13}-\frac{4}{5}\times\frac{12}{13}=\frac{15-48}{65}=\frac{-33}{65}$$

$\sin(A - B) = \sin A \cos B - \cos A \sin B$

$$=\frac{4}{5}\times\frac{5}{13}-\frac{3}{5}\times\frac{12}{13}=\frac{20-36}{65}=\frac{-16}{65}$$

VERY SHORT ANSWER Type Questions (VSA)

[1 mark]

15. Find the value of $\cos^2 75° - \cos^2 15°$.

Ans. $\cos^2 75 - \cos^2 15 =$

$= (\cos 75° + \cos 15°) . (\cos 75° - \cos 15°)$

$= (2 \cos 90° . \cos 60°)(2 \sin 90° . \sin 60°)$

$$=2.0.\frac{1}{2}2.1.\frac{\sqrt{3}}{2}$$

$= 0$

16. Find the value of sin (– 240°).

Ans. $\sin(-240°) = -\sin 240°$

$= -\sin(180° + 60°)$

$= \sin 60°$

$$=\frac{\sqrt{3}}{2}$$

17. Find the value of 2 sin 45° . cos 45°.

Ans. We have,

$2 \sin 45° \cos 45°$

$= \sin 2(45°)$

$= \sin 90° = 1$

18. If cos x + sin x = $\sqrt{2}$, then find the value of x.

Ans. $\cos x + \sin x = \sqrt{2}$

$$\frac{1}{\sqrt{2}}\cos x+\frac{1}{\sqrt{2}}\sin x=1$$

$\sin 45° \cos x + \cos 45° \sin x = 1$

$\sin(45° + x) = 1$

$\sin(45° + x) = \sin 90°$

$45° + x = 90°$

$x = 45°$

$$x=\frac{\pi}{4}$$

SHORT ANSWER Type-I Questions (SA-I)

[2 marks]

19. If $m \sin \theta = n \sin (\theta + 2a)$ then prove that $\tan (\theta + a) \cot a = \frac{m+n}{m-n}$ [NCERT Exemplar]

Ans. Given, $m \sin \theta = n \sin (\theta + 2\alpha)$

$$\therefore \quad \frac{\sin(\theta+2\alpha)}{\sin\theta} = \frac{m}{n}$$

Applying componendo and dividendo, we get

$$\frac{\sin(\theta+2\alpha)+\sin\theta}{\sin(\theta+2\alpha)-\sin\theta} = \frac{m+n}{m-n}$$

$$\Rightarrow \frac{2\sin\left(\frac{\theta+2\alpha+\theta}{2}\right)\cdot\cos\left(\frac{\theta+2\alpha-\theta}{2}\right)}{2\cos\left(\frac{\theta+2\alpha+\theta}{2}\right)\cdot\sin\left(\frac{\theta+2\alpha-\theta}{2}\right)} = \frac{m+n}{m-n}$$

$$\left[\begin{array}{l}\therefore \ \sin C + \sin D = 2\sin\frac{C+D}{2}\cos\frac{C-D}{2} \ and \\ \sin C - \sin D = 2\cos\frac{C+D}{2}\sin\frac{C-D}{2}\end{array}\right]$$

$$\Rightarrow \frac{\sin(\theta+\alpha)\cdot\cos\alpha}{\cos(\theta+\alpha)\cdot\sin\alpha} = \frac{m+n}{m-n}$$

$$\Rightarrow \tan(\theta+\alpha)\cdot\cot\alpha = \frac{m+n}{m-n}$$

Hence, proved.

20. Prove that $\frac{\tan A + \sec A - 1}{\tan A - \sec A + 1} = \frac{1+\sin A}{\cos A}$.

[NCERT Exemplar]

Ans. L.H.S. $= \frac{\tan A + \sec A - 1}{\tan A - \sec A + 1}$

$$= \frac{\tan A + \sec A - (\sec^2 A - \tan^2 A)}{(\tan A - \sec A + 1)}$$

$[\therefore \quad \sec^2 A - \tan^2 A = 1]$

$$= \frac{\tan A + \sec A - \{(\sec A - \tan A)(\sec A + \tan A)\}}{(\tan A - \sec A + 1)}$$

$[\therefore \quad a^2 - b^2 = (a-b)(a+b)]$

$$= \frac{(\sec A + \tan A)(1 - \sec A + \tan A)}{1 - \sec A + \tan A}$$

$= \sec A + \tan A$

$$= \frac{1}{\cos A} + \frac{\sin A}{\cos A} = \frac{1+\sin A}{\cos A} = \text{R.H.S.}$$

Hence, proved.

SHORT ANSWER Type-II Questions (SA-II)

[3 marks]

21. If $\tan x = \frac{b}{a}$, then find the value of $\sqrt{\frac{a+b}{a-b}} + \sqrt{\frac{a-b}{a+b}}$. [NCERT Exemplar]

Ans. Given, $\tan x = \frac{b}{a}$

$$\sqrt{\frac{a+b}{a-b}} + \sqrt{\frac{a-b}{a+b}} = \frac{\sqrt{(a+b)^2} + \sqrt{(a-b)^2}}{\sqrt{(a-b)(a+b)}}$$

$$= \frac{(a+b)+(a-b)}{\sqrt{a^2-b^2}}$$

$$= \frac{2a}{\sqrt{a^2-b^2}}$$

$$= \frac{2a}{a\sqrt{1-\left(\frac{b}{a}\right)^2}}$$

$$= \frac{2}{\sqrt{1-\tan^2 x}} \qquad \left[\because \ \frac{b}{a} = \tan x\right]$$

$$= \frac{2\cos x}{\sqrt{\cos^2 x - \sin^2 x}}$$

$$= \frac{2\cos x}{\sqrt{\cos 2x}} \qquad [\therefore \quad \cos 2x = \cos^2 x - \sin^2 x]$$

22. Find the value of $m \sin x + n \cos x$, if $\tan \frac{x}{2} = \frac{m}{n}$.

Ans. We have, $\tan\frac{x}{2} = \frac{m}{n}$

and, $$\sin x = \frac{2\tan\frac{x}{2}}{1+\tan^2\frac{x}{2}} = \frac{2\frac{m}{n}}{1+\frac{m^2}{n^2}} = \frac{2mn}{m^2+n^2}$$

$$\cos x=\sqrt{1-\left(\frac{2mn}{m^2+n^2}\right)^2}=\sqrt{\frac{(m^2+n^2)^2-4m^2n^2}{(m^2+n^2)^2}}$$

$$=\frac{m^2-n^2}{m^2+n^2}$$

$$\therefore\ m\sin x+n\cos x=m\left(\frac{2mn}{m^2+n^2}\right)+n\left(\frac{m^2-n^2}{m^2+n^2}\right)$$

$$=\frac{2m^2n}{m^2+n^2}+\frac{nm^2}{m^2+n^2}-\frac{n^3}{m^2+n^2}=\frac{3m^2n-n^3}{m^2+n^2}$$

23. Find the value of $\tan\left(\frac{41\pi}{4}\right)$ and $\sin\left(-\frac{17\pi}{43}\right)$.

Ans. $\tan\left(\frac{41\pi}{4}\right)=\tan\left(10\pi+\frac{\pi}{4}\right)$

$$=\tan\left(\frac{\pi}{4}\right)=1.$$

And $\sin\left(-\frac{17\pi}{43}\right)=-\sin\left(\frac{17\pi}{43}\right)$

$$=-\sin\left(4\pi+\frac{\pi}{4}\right)=-\sin\frac{\pi}{4}=-\frac{1}{\sqrt{2}}.$$

24. If $\frac{2\sin a}{1+\cos a+\sin a}=y$, then prove that $\frac{1-\cos a+\sin a}{1+\sin a}$ is also equal to y. **[NCERT Exemplar]**

Ans. Given, $\frac{2\sin a}{1+\cos a+\sin a}=y$

Now, $\frac{1-\cos a+\sin a}{1+\sin a}$

$$=\frac{(1-\cos a+\sin a)}{1+\sin a}\cdot\frac{(1+\cos a+\sin a)}{(1+\cos a+\sin a)}$$

$$=\frac{\{(1+\sin a)-\cos a\}}{1+\sin a}\cdot\frac{\{(1+\sin a)+\cos a\}}{1+\cos a+\sin a}$$

$$=\frac{(1+\sin a)^2-\cos^2 a}{(1+\sin a)(1+\cos a+\sin a)}$$

$$=\frac{(1+\sin^2 a+2\sin a)-\cos^2 a}{(1+\sin a)(1+\cos a+\sin a)}$$

$$=\frac{(1+\sin^2 a+2\sin a)-(1-\sin^2 a)}{(1+\sin a)(1+\cos a+\sin a)}$$

$$=\frac{2\sin^2 a+2\sin a}{(1+\sin a)(1+\cos a+\sin a)}$$

$$=\frac{2\sin a(\sin a+1)}{(1+\sin a)(1+\cos a+\sin a)}$$

$$=\frac{2\sin a}{1+\cos a+\sin a}=y$$

Hence, proved.

25. cos 46° cos 14° – sin 46° sin 14° + sin 75°.

Ans. We know, cos (*A* + *B*) = cos *A* cos *B* – sin *A* sin *B*

So using this formula,

cos 46° cos 14° – sin 46° sin 14°

= cos (46° + 14°)

= cos 60°

And $\cos 60°=\frac{1}{2}$ ...(i)

Now, sin 75° = sin (45° + 30°)

= sin 45° cos 30° + cos 45° sin 30°

[∴ sin (*A* + *B*) = sin *A* cos *B* + cos *A* sin *B*]

$$=\frac{1}{\sqrt{2}}\cdot\frac{\sqrt{3}}{2}+\frac{1}{\sqrt{2}}\cdot\frac{1}{2}$$

$$\left[\because\ \sin 30°=\frac{1}{2},\ \cos 30°=\frac{\sqrt{3}}{2}\text{ and } \sin 45°=\cos 45°=\frac{1}{\sqrt{2}}\right]$$

$$=\frac{\sqrt{3}}{2\sqrt{2}}+\frac{1}{2\sqrt{2}}=\frac{\sqrt{3}+1}{2\sqrt{2}}$$ ...(ii)

On adding eq.(i) and eq.(ii), we get

cos 47° cos 13° – sin 47° sin 13° + sin 75°

$$=\frac{1}{2}+\frac{\sqrt{3}+1}{2\sqrt{2}}$$

$$=\frac{1}{2}+\frac{(\sqrt{3}+1)\times\sqrt{2}}{2\sqrt{2}\times\sqrt{2}}$$

$$=\frac{1}{2}+\frac{\sqrt{2}(\sqrt{3}+1)}{4}$$

26. If $a\cos\theta+b\sin\theta=m$ and $a\sin\theta-b\cos\theta=n$, then show that $a^2+b^2=m^2+n^2$. **[NCERT Exemplar]**

Ans. Given, $a\cos\theta+b\sin\theta=m$ ...(i)

And $a\sin\theta-b\cos\theta=n$ ...(ii)

Squaring and adding of eqs (i) and (ii), we get

$m^2+n^2=(a\cos\theta+b\sin\theta)^2+(a\sin\theta-b\cos\theta)^2$

$\Rightarrow m^2+n^2=a^2\cos^2\theta+b^2\sin^2\theta+2ab\cos\theta\sin\theta+a^2\sin^2\theta+b^2\cos^2\theta-2ab\sin\theta\cos\theta$

$\Rightarrow m^2+n^2=a^2(\cos^2\theta+\sin^2\theta)+b^2(\sin^2\theta+\cos^2\theta)$

$\Rightarrow m^2+n^2=a^2+b^2$

Hence, proved.

27. Prove that: sin a + sin b + sin c – sin ($a + b + c$) $= 4 \sin\frac{a+b}{2} \sin\frac{b+c}{2} \sin\frac{a+c}{2}$

Ans. L.H.S = (sin a + sin b) + (sin c – sin ($a + b + c$))

$$= \left(2\sin\frac{(a+b)}{2}\cos\frac{(a-b)}{2}\right) + \left(2\cos\frac{(c+a+b+c)}{2}\sin\frac{(c-a-b-c)}{2}\right)$$

$$= 2\sin\frac{(a+b)}{2}\cos\frac{(a-b)}{2} - 2\cos\frac{(a+b+2c)}{2}\sin\frac{(a+b)}{2}$$

$$= 2\sin\frac{(a+b)}{2}\left[\cos\frac{(a-b)}{2} - \cos\frac{(a+b+2c)}{2}\right]$$

$$= 2\sin\frac{(a+b)}{2}\left[\left(-2\sin\frac{(a-b+a+b+2c)}{2}\right)\sin\frac{(a-b-a-b-2c)}{4}\right]$$

$$= 2\sin\left(\frac{a+b}{2}\right)\left[2\sin\frac{(a+c)}{2}\sin\frac{(b+c)}{2}\right]$$

$$= 4\sin\left(\frac{a+b}{2}\right)\sin\left(\frac{a+b}{2}\right)\sin\left(\frac{b+c}{2}\right) = \text{R.H.S.}$$

LONG ANSWER Type Questions (LA)

[4 & 5 marks]

28. Prove that $\cos\theta\cos\frac{\theta}{2} - \cos 3\theta\cos\frac{9\theta}{2} = \sin 7\theta \sin 8\theta$. **[NCERT Exemplar]**

Ans. L.H.S. $= \cos\theta\cos\frac{\theta}{2} - \cos 3\theta\cos\frac{9\theta}{2}$

$$= \frac{1}{2}\left[2\cos\theta\cos\frac{\theta}{2} - 2\cos 3\theta\cos\frac{9\theta}{2}\right]$$

$$= \frac{1}{2}\left[\cos\left(\theta+\frac{\theta}{2}\right) + \cos\left(\theta-\frac{\theta}{2}\right) - \left\{\cos\left(3\theta+\frac{9\theta}{2}\right) + \cos\left(3\theta-\frac{9\theta}{2}\right)\right\}\right]$$

[∵ 2 cos A cos B = cos ($A + B$) + cos ($A – B$)]

$$= \frac{1}{2}\left(\cos\frac{3\theta}{2} + \cos\frac{\theta}{2} - \cos\frac{15\theta}{2} - \cos\frac{3\theta}{2}\right)$$

$$= \frac{1}{2}\left(\cos\frac{\theta}{2} - \cos\frac{15\theta}{2}\right)$$

$$= -\frac{1}{2}\left[2\sin\left(\frac{\theta+15\theta}{2}\right)\sin\left(\frac{\theta-15\theta}{2}\right)\right]$$

$\left[\because \cos C - \cos D = -2\sin\frac{C+D}{2}\sin\frac{C-D}{2}\right]$

$= -\{\sin 8\theta \sin(-7\theta)\}$

$= \sin 8\theta \sin 7\theta$ [∵ $\sin(-\theta) = -\sin\theta$]

= R.H.S.

Hence, proved.

29. If $\cos(\alpha+\beta) = \frac{4}{5}$ and $\sin(\alpha-\beta) = \frac{5}{13}$, where α, β lie between 0 and $\frac{\pi}{4}$, then find that value of tan 2α. **[NCERT Exemplar]**

Ans. Given, $\cos(\alpha+\beta) = \frac{4}{5}$ and $\sin(\alpha-\beta) = \frac{5}{13}$

$$\Rightarrow \sin(\alpha+\beta) = \sqrt{1-\frac{16}{25}} = \sqrt{\frac{9}{25}} = \pm\frac{3}{5}$$

$$\therefore \sin(\alpha+\beta) = \frac{3}{5}$$

And $\cos(\alpha-\beta) = \sqrt{1-\frac{25}{169}} = \sqrt{\frac{144}{169}} = \pm\frac{12}{13}$

$$\therefore \cos(\alpha-\beta) = \frac{12}{13}$$

Now, $\tan(\alpha+\beta) = \frac{\sin(\alpha+\beta)}{\cos(\alpha+\beta)}$ $\left[\because 0 < \alpha < \frac{\pi}{4}\right]$

$$= \frac{\frac{3}{5}}{\frac{4}{5}} = \frac{3}{4}$$

And $\tan(\alpha-\beta) = \frac{\sin(\alpha-\beta)}{\cos(\alpha-\beta)} = \frac{\frac{5}{13}}{\frac{12}{13}} = \frac{5}{12}$

$\therefore$ tan 2α = tan ($\alpha + \beta + \alpha - \beta$)

$$= \frac{\tan(\alpha+\beta) + \tan(\alpha-\beta)}{1-\tan(\alpha+\beta)\tan(\alpha-\beta)}$$

$$= \frac{\frac{3}{4}+\frac{5}{12}}{1-\frac{3}{4}\cdot\frac{5}{12}} = \frac{\frac{(36+20)}{48}}{\frac{(48-15)}{48}}$$

$$= \frac{56}{33}$$

30. Find the value of cot 105° and cot 15°.

Ans. $\therefore$ cot (105)° = cot (60° + 45°)

We know $\cot(A+B)=\dfrac{\cot A\cot B-1}{\cot B+\cot A}$

So Applying the formula in cot (60° + 45°)

We get, $\cot(60°+45°)=\dfrac{\cot 60°\cot 45°-1}{\cot 60°+\cot 45°}$

$$=\frac{\frac{1}{\sqrt{3}}\times 1-1}{\frac{1}{\sqrt{3}}+1}\quad\left\{\cot 60°=\frac{1}{\sqrt{3}},\cot 45°=1\right\}$$

$$=\frac{\frac{1}{\sqrt{3}}-1}{\frac{1+\sqrt{3}}{\sqrt{3}}}=\frac{\frac{1-\sqrt{3}}{\sqrt{3}}}{\frac{1+\sqrt{3}}{\sqrt{3}}}$$

$$=\frac{1-\sqrt{3}}{1+\sqrt{3}}$$

$$=\frac{(1-\sqrt{3})^2}{1-3}\qquad\text{[On Rationalisation]}$$

$$=\frac{1+3-2\sqrt{3}}{-2}=\frac{4-2\sqrt{3}}{-2}$$

$$=-2+\sqrt{3}=\sqrt{3}-2$$

Now, cot 15°

We have, $\cot(A-B)=\dfrac{\cot A\cdot\cot B+1}{\cot B-\cot A}$

$$\Rightarrow (\cot 60°-45°)=\frac{\cot 60°\cdot\cot 45°+1}{\cot 45°-\cot 60°}$$

$$\Rightarrow \cot(15°)=\frac{\frac{1}{\sqrt{3}}\times 1+1}{1-\frac{1}{\sqrt{3}}}$$

$$\Rightarrow \cot(15°)=\frac{\frac{1}{\sqrt{3}}+1}{1-\frac{1}{\sqrt{3}}}$$

$$\Rightarrow \cot(15°)=\frac{\frac{1+\sqrt{3}}{\sqrt{3}}}{\frac{\sqrt{3}-1}{\sqrt{3}}}$$

$$\Rightarrow \cot(15°)=\frac{\sqrt{3}+1}{\sqrt{3}-1}$$

$$\Rightarrow \cot(15°)=\frac{(\sqrt{3}+1)^2}{(\sqrt{3})^2-1^2}\qquad\text{[On Rationalisation]}$$

$$\Rightarrow \cot(15°)=\frac{3+1+2\sqrt{3}}{3-1}$$

$$\Rightarrow \cot(15°)=\frac{4+2\sqrt{3}}{2}=\frac{2(2+\sqrt{3})}{2}$$

$$\therefore\ \cot 15°=2+\sqrt{3}$$

4 Complex Numbers and Quadratic Equations

The voltage produced by a battery is characterized by one real number (called potential), such as +12 volts or –12 volts. But the "AC" voltage in a home requires two parameters. One is a potential, such as 120 volts, and the other is an angle (called phase). The voltage is said to have two dimensions. A 2-dimensional quantity can be represented mathematically as either a vector or as a complex number (known in the engineering context as phasor)

Topic Notes

- *Complex numbers and its Planar Representation*
- *Quadratic Equations of Complex Number*

COMPLEX NUMBERS AND ITS PLANAR REPRESENTATION 1

TOPIC 1

COMPLEX NUMBER

Imaginary Numbers

"An imaginary number is a number whose square is less than or equal to zero".

e.g. $\sqrt{-1}, \sqrt{-2}$ ..... etc.

Here, $\sqrt{-1}$ can be defined as *i* (*iota*).

Integral power *i*(*iota*)

$i^\circ = 1$

$i^1 = i$

$i^2 = -1$

$i^3 = -i$

$i^4 = 1$

$i^5 = i^4 \times i = i$

$i^6 = i^4 . i^2 = -1$

$i^7 = i^4 . i^3 = -i$

$i^8 = i^4 . i^4 = 1$

and so on.

Power of *i*: $i^1\ i^2\ i^3\ i^4\ i^5\ i^6\ i^7$ ....

Simplified form: $i, -1, -i, 1, i, -1, -i,$

To simplify, i^{-n} we can write $i^{-n} = \frac{1}{i^n}$ which can be simplified as above.

Complex Number

"A complex number is a combination of real and imaginary numbers which can be represented as *x* + *iy* where *a* and *b* real numbers". Such expressions are known as a Cartesian form of the complex number.

Here, *a* is the real part and *b* is the imaginary part.

So, $z = a + ib$ is a complex number.

Purely Real and Purely Imaginary Complex Numbers

A complex number $z = x + iy$ is a purely real if its imaginary part is 0, *i.e.* $Im(z) = 0$ and purely imaginary if its real part is 0 *i.e.* $Re(z) = 0$.

Equality of Complex Number

Two complex number $z_1 = x_1 + iy_1$ and $z_2 = x_2 + iy_2$ are said to be equal, if $x_1 = x_2$ and $y_1 = y_2$.

i.e. $Re(z_1) = Re(z_2)$ and $Im(z_1) = Im(z_2)$.

Thus, two complex numbers are equal if and only if, their real parts are equal and their imaginary parts are also equal.

Caution

➥ *Other relation 'greater than' and 'less than' are not defined for complex number.*

Algebra of Complex Number

Let $z_1 = x_1 + iy_1$ and $z_2 = x_2 + iy_2$ be any two complex numbers.

Addition of Complex Numbers

$$z_1 + z_2 = (x_1 + iy_1) + (x_2 + iy_2)$$
$$= (x_1 + x_2) + i(y_1 + y_2)$$

Real parts are added together and the imaginary parts together

Properties of Addition

Closure $z_1 + z_2$ is also a complex number.

(i) Commutative $z_1 + z_2 = z_2 + z_1$

(ii) Associative $z_1(z_2 + z_3) = (z_1 + z_2) + z_3$

(iii) Existence of additive identity $z + 0 = z = 0 + z$

Here, 0 is an additive identity.

(iv) Existence of Additive inverse $z + (-z) = 0 = (-z) + z$

Here, $-z$ is additive inverse.

Subtraction of Complex Numbers

$$z_1 - z_2 = (x_1 + iy_1) - (x_2 + iy_2) = (x_1 - x_2) + i(y_1 - y_2)$$

Multiplication of Complex Numbers

$$z_1z_2 = (x_1 + iy_1)(x_2 + iy_2)$$
$$= (x_1x_2 - y_1y_2) + i(x_1y_2 + x_2y_1)$$

Properties of Multiplication

(i) Closure: z_1z_2 is also a complex number.

(ii) Commutative : $z_1z_2 = z_2z_1$

(iii) Associative: $z_1(z_2z_3) = (z_1z_2)z_3$

(iv) Existence of multiplicative identity

$z . 1 = z = 1 . z$

Here, 1 is multiplicative identity.

(v) Existence of Multiplicative inverse For every non-zero complex number *z*, there exists a complex z_1 such that $z . z_1 = 1 = z_1 . z$

(vi) Distributive $z_1(z_2 + z_3) = z_1z_2 + z_1z_3$

Division of Complex Numbers

$$\frac{z_1}{z_2}=\frac{x_1+iy_1}{x_2+iy_2}=\frac{(x_1x_2+y_1y_2)+i(x_2y_1-x_1y_2)}{x_2^2+y_2^2}$$

Where, $z_2 \neq 0$

Conjugate and Modulus

Let $z = a + ib$ be a complex number, then the conjugate of z, denoted by $\bar{z}$ is defined as the complex number

$a - ib$ _

So, $\bar{z} = a - ib$

In other words, the conjugate of a complex number can be obtained by changing the sign of.

Properties of Conjugate

(i) $(\bar{z}) = z$

(ii) $z + \bar{z} = 2Re(z), z - \bar{z} = 2i\, Im(z)$

(iii) $z = \bar{z}$, if z is purely real

(iv) $z + \bar{z} = 0 \Leftrightarrow z$ is purely imaginary

(v) $\overline{z_1 + z_2} = \bar{z}_1 + \bar{z}_2$

(vi) $\overline{z_1 - z_2} = \bar{z}_1 - \bar{z}_2$

(vii) $\overline{z_1 z_2} = \bar{z}_1 \cdot \bar{z}_2$

(viii) $1\left(\frac{z_1}{z_2}\right) = \frac{z_1}{\bar{z}_1}, z_2 \neq 0$

(ix) $z.\bar{z} = \{Re(z)\}^2 + Im(z)\}^2$

(x) $z_1\bar{z}_2 + \bar{z}_1 z_2 = 2Re(\bar{z}_1 z_2) = 2Re(z_1\bar{z}_2)$

(xi) If $z = f(z_1)$, then $\bar{z} = f(z_1)\ f(\bar{z}_1)$

(xii) $(\bar{z})^n = (\overline{z^n})$

Modulus

Let $z = a + ib$ be a complex number. Then the modulus of z is defined as the non-negative real number $\sqrt{a^2+b^2}$. It is denoted by $|z|$.

So, $|z| = \sqrt{a^2+b^2}$

Properties of Modulus

(i) $|z| \geq 0$

(ii) If $|z| \geq 0$, then $z = 0$ *i.e.* $Re(z) = 0 = Im(z)$

(iii) $-|z| \leq Re(z) \leq |z|$ and $-|z| \leq |Im(z)| \leq |z|$

(iv) $|z| = |\bar{z}| = |-z| = |-\bar{z}|$

(v) $z.\bar{z} = |z|^2$

(vi) $|z_1 z_2| = |z_1||z_2|^2$

(vii) $\left|\frac{z_1}{z_2}\right| = \frac{|z_1|}{|z_2|},\ z_2 \neq 0$

(viii) $|z_1 + z_2|^2 = |z_1|^2 + |z_2|^2 + 2Re\ (z_1\bar{z}_2)$

(ix) $|z_1 - z_2|^2 = |z_1|^2 + |z_2|^2 - 2Re\ (z_1\bar{z}_2)$

(x) $|z_1 + z_2| \leq |z_1| + |z_2|$

(xi) $|z_1 - z_2| \geq |z_1| - |z_2|$

Example 1.1: Express the the given complex number in the form $a + ib$:

(A) $a + ib : i^{-39}$ (B) $(1 - i)^4$ [NCERT]

Ans. (A) $i^{-39} = \frac{1}{i^{39}}$

$= \frac{1}{(i^{38}) \times i}$

$= \frac{1}{(i^2)^{19} \times i}$

Putting $i^2 = -1$

$= \frac{1}{(-1)^{19} \times i}$

$= \frac{1}{-1 \times i}$

$= \frac{1}{-i}$ Multiplying and dividing by $-i$

$= \frac{1}{-i} \times \frac{-i}{-i}$

$= \frac{-i}{i^2}$ Putting $i^2 = -1$

$= \frac{-i}{(-1)} = i$

$= 0 + i$

(B) $(1 - i)^4$

$= ((1 - i)^2)^2$

$= (1 - i)^2(1 - i)^2$

Using $(a - b)^2 = a^2 + b^2 - 2ab$

$= (1^2 + i^2 - 2 \times 1 \times i)\ (1^2 + i^2 - 2 \times 1 \times i)$

$= (1 + i^2 - 2i)\ (1 + i^2 - 2i)$

$= (1 - 1 - 2i)\ (1 - 1 - 2i)$ (putting $i^2 = -1$)

$= (0 - 2i)\ (0 - 2i)$

$= (-2i)\ (-2i)$

$= 4i^2$

Putting $i^2 = -1$

$= 4 \times -1$

$= -4$

$= -4 + 0$

$= -4 + 0i$

Example 1.2: **(A) Find the multiplicative inverse of the complex number $\sqrt{5}+3i$.**

(B) Express the following expression in the form of *a* + *ib*.

$$\frac{(3+i\sqrt{5})(3-i\sqrt{5})}{(\sqrt{3}+\sqrt{2}i)-(\sqrt{3}-i\sqrt{2})}.$$ **[NCERT]**

Ans. (A) Multiplicative inverse of $z = z^{-1}$

Multiplicative inverse of $z = \frac{1}{z}$

Putting $z = \sqrt{5}+3i$

Multiplicative inverse of $\sqrt{5}+3i = \frac{1}{\sqrt{5}+3i}$

Rationalizing

$$= \frac{1}{\sqrt{5}+3i} \times \frac{\sqrt{5}-3i}{\sqrt{5}-3i}$$

$$= \frac{\sqrt{5}-3i}{(\sqrt{5}+3i)(\sqrt{5}-3i)}$$

[∵ Using $(a-b)(a+b) = a^2 - b^2$]

$$= \frac{\sqrt{5}-3i}{(\sqrt{5}+3i)(\sqrt{5}-3i)}$$

$$= \frac{\sqrt{5}-3i}{(\sqrt{5})^2-(3i)^2}$$ Putting $i^2 = -1$

$$= \frac{\sqrt{5}-3i}{5-9(-1)}$$

$$= \frac{\sqrt{5}-3i}{5+9}$$

$$= \frac{\sqrt{5}-3i}{14}$$

$$= \frac{\sqrt{5}}{14} - \frac{3}{14}i$$

(B) $$\frac{(3+i\sqrt{5})(3-i\sqrt{5})}{(\sqrt{3}+\sqrt{2}i)-(\sqrt{3}-i\sqrt{2})}$$

[∵ Using $(a+b)(a-b) = a^2 - b^2$]

$$= \frac{(3)^2-(i\sqrt{5})^2}{\sqrt{3}+\sqrt{2}i-\sqrt{3}+i\sqrt{2}}$$

$$= \frac{9^2-i^2\times 5}{\sqrt{3}-\sqrt{3}+\sqrt{2}i+i\sqrt{2}}$$

Putting $i^2 = -1$

$$= \frac{9-(-1)\times 5}{0+\sqrt{2}i+i\sqrt{2}}$$

$$= \frac{9+5}{\sqrt{2}i+\sqrt{2}i}$$

$$= \frac{14}{2\sqrt{2}i}$$

$$= \frac{14}{2\sqrt{2}i} \times \frac{2\sqrt{2}i}{2\sqrt{2}i}$$

$$= \frac{28\sqrt{2}i}{4\times 2\times i^2}$$

$$= \frac{28\sqrt{2}i}{8\times i^2}$$

$$= \frac{28\sqrt{2}i}{-8}$$ (putting $i^2 = -1$)

$$= \frac{28\sqrt{2}i}{-8}$$

$$= \frac{-7\sqrt{2}i}{2}$$

$$= \frac{-7\sqrt{2}}{2}i$$

$$= 0+\left(\frac{-7\sqrt{2}}{2}\right)i$$

TOPIC 2

ARGAND PLANE

A complex number $z = x + iy$ can be represented by a unique point $P(x, y)$ in the Cartesian plane, referred to a pair of rectangular axes. The representation of complex numbers as points in the plane is known as argand diagram. The plane, representing complex numbers as points, is called complex plane or argand plane or Gaussian plane.

A purely real number *x*, *i.e.* $(x + 0i)$ is represented by the point $(x, 0)$ on *x-axis*. Therefore, *x-axis* is called the real axis, while a is the intersection (common) of two axes called zero complex number *i.e.* $z = 0 + 0i$.

If two complex numbers Z_1 and Z_2 are represented by the points *P* and *Q* in the complex plane, then $|Z_1 - Z_2|$ = *PQ* = distance between *P* and *Q*.

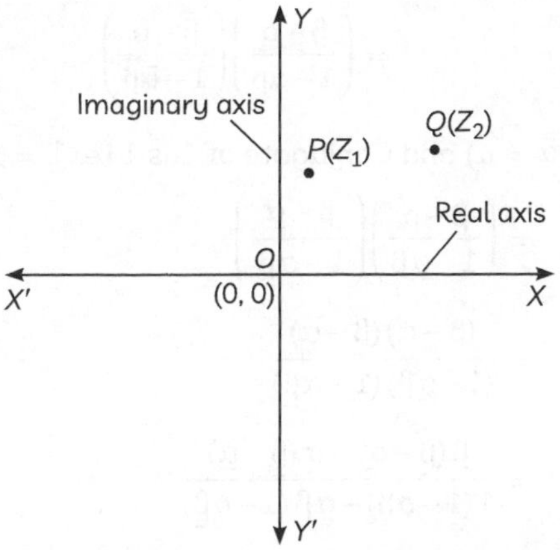

Representation of Complex Number on Argand Plane

The complex number $z = x + iy$ and its conjugate $\bar{z} = x - iy$ *can be represented* in the Argand plane. The complex number and conjugate are the points $P(x, y)$ and $Q(x, -y)$ respectively.

Geometrically, the point $(x, -y)$ is the mirror image of the point (x, y) on the real axis.

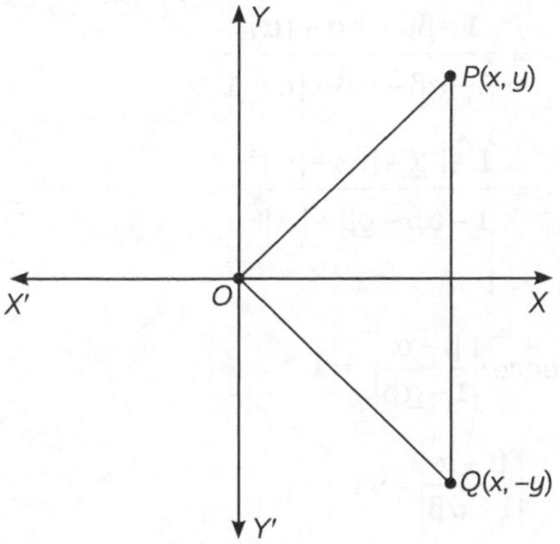

A complex number satisfying $-\pi < \theta \leq \pi$ is called Principal argument denoted by α.

Properties of Argand Plane

The qualities of the argand plane listed below can help you better comprehend the argand plane.

1. The axes of the argand plane are comparable to the axes of ordinary coordinates.
2. The origin is the place where the real and imaginary axes of the argand plane intersect.
3. The argand plane's real and imaginary axes are perpendicular to one other.
4. The real and imaginary axes of the argand plane split it into four quadrants in the same way as the coordinate axis does.
5. The distance and midpoint formulas are the same in the argand plane as they are in the coordinate axes.
6. Cartesian coordinates or polar coordinates are used to represent the points in the argand plane.

Example 1.3: Find the modulus and the argument of the complex number $z = -\sqrt{3} + i$. [NCERT]

Ans. $z = x + iy$

Modulus of $z = |z| = \sqrt{x^2 + y^2}$

Method (1) to calculating modulus of z

$$z = -\sqrt{3} + i$$

Complex number z is of the form $x + iy$

Where $x = -\sqrt{3}$ *and* $y = 1$

Modulus of $z = |z|$

$$= \sqrt{x^2 + y^2}$$

$$= \sqrt{(-\sqrt{3})^2 + (1)^2}$$

$$= \sqrt{3+1}$$

$$= \sqrt{4}$$

Or, $|z| = 2$

Hence, Modulus of $z = 2$

Method (2)

Given $z = -\sqrt{3} + i$ ...(1)

Let $z = r(\cos\theta + i\sin\theta)$ ...(2)

Here, r is modulus, and θ is argument

From (1) and (2)

$$-\sqrt{3} + i = r(\cos\theta + i\sin\theta)$$

$$-\sqrt{3} + i = r\cos\theta + ir\sin\theta$$

$-\sqrt{3}$	i	$r\cos\theta$	$ir\sin\theta$
↓	↓	↓	↓
Real part	Imaginary part	Real Part	Imaginary part

Comparing Real parts

$$-\sqrt{3} = r\cos\theta$$

Squaring both sides

$$(\sqrt{3})^2 = (r\cos\theta)^2$$

$$3 = r^2\cos^2\theta \quad ...(3)$$

Similarly, comparing imaginary parts

$$1 = r\sin\theta$$

Squaring both sides

$$(1)^2 = (r\sin\theta)^2$$

$$1 = r^2\sin^2\theta \quad ...(4)$$

Adding (3) and (4)

$$3 + 1 = r^2\cos^2\theta + r^2\sin^2\theta$$

$$4 = r^2\cos^2\theta + r^2\sin^2\theta$$

$$4 = r^2(\cos^2\theta + \sin^2\theta)$$

$$4 = r^2 \times 1 \ (\cos^2\theta + \sin^2\theta = 1)$$

$$4 = r^2$$
$$r = 2$$
Hence, modulus = 2

Finding argument

$$-\sqrt{3} + i = r\cos\theta + i\,r\sin\theta$$

$$\underbrace{-\sqrt{3}}_{\text{Real part}} \quad \underbrace{i}_{\text{Imaginary part}} \quad \underbrace{r\cos\theta}_{\text{Real Part}} \quad \underbrace{ir\sin\theta}_{\text{Imaginary part}}$$

Comparing real part

$$-\sqrt{3} = r\cos\theta$$

Putting $r = 2$

$$-\sqrt{3} = 2\cos\theta$$
$$-\sqrt{3} = 2\cos\theta$$
$$\cos\theta = -\frac{\sqrt{3}}{2}$$

Comparing imaginary parts

$$1 = r\sin\theta$$

Putting $r = 2$

$$1 = 2 \times \sin\theta$$
$$\frac{1}{2} = \sin\theta$$
$$\sin\theta = \frac{1}{2}$$

Hence, $\sin\theta = \frac{1}{2}$ and $\cos\theta = -\frac{\sqrt{3}}{2}$

Since $\sin\theta$ is positive and $\cos\theta$ is negative,
Argument will be in IInd quadrant

Argument = 180° – 30°

= 150°

$$= 150 = 150 \times \frac{\pi}{180}$$
$$= \frac{5\pi}{6}$$

Example1. 4: If α and β are different complex numbers with $|\beta| = 1$, then find $\left|\frac{\beta-\alpha}{1-\bar{\alpha}\beta}\right|$.

Ans. We know that $|z|^2 = (z)(\bar{z})$

$z = x + iy$, $\bar{z}$ = conjugate

$\bar{z} = x - iy$, $|z|$ = modulus, $|z| = \sqrt{x^2+y^2}$

$$\left|\frac{\beta-\alpha}{1-\bar{\alpha}\beta}\right|^2 = \left(\frac{\beta-\alpha}{1-\bar{\alpha}\beta}\right)\overline{\left(\frac{\beta-\alpha}{1-\bar{\alpha}\beta}\right)}$$
$$= \left(\frac{\beta-\alpha}{1-\bar{\alpha}\beta}\right)\left(\frac{\overline{\beta-\alpha}}{\overline{1-\bar{\alpha}\beta}}\right)$$
$$= \left(\frac{\beta-\alpha}{1-\bar{\alpha}\beta}\right)\left(\frac{\bar{\beta}-\bar{\alpha}}{1-\bar{\bar{\alpha}}\bar{\beta}}\right)$$

($(\bar{\bar{\alpha}} = \alpha)$ and Conjugate of 1 is 1 i.e. $\bar{1} = 1$

$$= \left(\frac{\beta-\alpha}{1-\bar{\alpha}\beta}\right)\left(\frac{\bar{\beta}-\bar{\alpha}}{1-\alpha\bar{\beta}}\right)$$
$$= \frac{(\beta-\alpha)(\bar{\beta}-\bar{\alpha})}{(1-\bar{\alpha}\beta)(1-\alpha\bar{\beta})}$$
$$= \frac{\beta(\bar{\beta}-\bar{\alpha})-\alpha(\bar{\beta}-\bar{\alpha})}{1(1-\alpha\bar{\beta})-\bar{\alpha}\beta(1-\alpha\bar{\beta})}$$
$$= \frac{\beta\bar{\beta}-\beta\bar{\alpha}-\alpha\bar{\beta}+\alpha\bar{\alpha}}{1-\alpha\bar{\beta}-\bar{\alpha}\beta+\alpha\bar{\alpha}\beta\bar{\beta}}$$

(As $|z| = (z)(\bar{z})$)

$$= \frac{|\beta|^2-\beta\bar{\alpha}-\bar{\beta}\alpha+|\alpha|^2}{1-\alpha\bar{\beta}-\bar{\alpha}\beta+|\alpha|^2|\beta|^2}$$

Given that $|\beta| = 1$

So, $|\beta|^2 = 1$

$$= \frac{1-\beta\bar{\alpha}-\bar{\beta}\alpha+|\alpha|^2}{1-\alpha\bar{\beta}-\bar{\alpha}\beta+|\alpha|^2 1}$$
$$= \frac{1-\beta\bar{\alpha}-\bar{\beta}\alpha+|\alpha|^2}{1-\alpha\bar{\beta}-\bar{\alpha}\beta+|\alpha|^2}$$
$$= 1$$

Hence $\left|\frac{\beta-\alpha}{1-\bar{\alpha}\beta}\right|^2 = 1$

$$\left|\frac{\beta-\alpha}{1-\bar{\alpha}\beta}\right| = \sqrt{1}$$
$$\left|\frac{\beta-\alpha}{1-\bar{\alpha}\beta}\right| = 1$$

Example 1.5: Express the given complex number in the form *a + ib*.

$$\left(\frac{1}{5}+i\frac{2}{5}\right)-\left(4+i\frac{5}{2}\right)$$ **[NCERT]**

Ans. Let $z = \left(\frac{1}{5}+i\frac{2}{5}\right)-\left(4+i\frac{5}{2}\right)$

$$= \frac{1}{5}+i\frac{2}{5}-4-i\frac{5}{2}$$
$$= \frac{1}{5}-4+i\frac{2}{5}-i\frac{5}{2}$$
$$= \left(\frac{1}{5}-4\right)+\left(i\frac{2}{5}-i\frac{5}{2}\right)$$
$$= \left(\frac{1-4\times5}{5}\right)+i\left(\frac{2\times2-5\times5}{10}\right)$$

$$= \left(\frac{1-20}{5}\right)+i\left(\frac{4-25}{10}\right)$$

$$= \left(\frac{-19}{5}\right)+\left(\frac{-21}{10}i\right)$$

Example 1.6: Express the complex number given form $a + i\,b$.

$$\left(-2-\frac{1}{3}i\right)^3$$ **[NCERT]**

Ans. Let $z = \left(-2-\frac{1}{3}i\right)^3$

$$= -1\left(2+\frac{1}{3}i\right)^3$$

It is of the form $(a + b)^3$

[$\because$ Using $(a + b)^3 = a^3 + b^3 + 3ab(a + b)$]

Here, $a = 2$ and $b = \frac{1}{3}i$

$$z = -1\left((2)^3+\left(\frac{1}{3}i\right)^3+3\times2\times\frac{1}{3}i\left(2+\frac{1}{3}i\right)\right)$$

$$= -1\left(8+\left(\frac{1}{3}\right)^3\times(i)^3+2i\left(2+\frac{1}{3}i\right)\right)$$

$$= -1\left(8+\frac{1}{27}i^3+4i+\frac{2}{3}i^2\right)$$

$$= -1\left(8+\frac{1}{27}i\times i^2+4i+\frac{2}{3}i^2\right)$$

Putting $i^2 = -1$

$$= -1\left(8+\frac{1}{27}i(-1)+4i+\frac{2}{3}(-1)\right)$$

$$= -1\left(8-\frac{1}{27}i+4i-\frac{2}{3}\right)$$

$$= -8+\frac{1}{27}i-4i+\frac{2}{3}$$

$$= -8+\frac{2}{3}+\frac{1}{27}i-4i$$

$$= \left(-8+\frac{2}{3}\right)+\left(\frac{1}{27}-4\right)i$$

$$= \left(\frac{-24+2}{3}\right)+\left(\frac{1-4\times27}{27}\right)i$$

$$= \frac{-22}{3}+\left(\frac{1-108}{27}\right)i$$

$$= \frac{-22}{3}+\left(\frac{-107}{27}\right)i$$

$$= \frac{-22}{3}-\frac{107}{27}i$$

Example 1.7: Solve the equations: $x^2 - x + 2 = 0$.

Ans. The given equation is $x^2 - x + 2 = 0$

which is of the form

$ax^2 + bx + c = 0$

Comparing $a = 1, b = -1, c = 2$

$$x = \frac{-b\pm\sqrt{b^2-4ac}}{2a}$$

$$x = \frac{-(-1)\pm\sqrt{(-1)^2-4\times1\times2}}{2\times1}$$

$$= \frac{1\pm\sqrt{1-8}}{2}$$

$$= \frac{1\pm\sqrt{-7}}{2}$$

$$= \frac{1\pm\sqrt{-1\times7}}{2}$$

$$= \frac{1\pm\sqrt{-1}\times\sqrt{7}}{2}$$

$$= \frac{1\pm\sqrt{7}\,i}{2}$$

Thus, $x = \frac{1\pm\sqrt{7}\,i}{2}$

Example 1.11: If $a + ib = \frac{(x-i)^2}{2x^2+1}$ prove that $a^2 + b^2 = \frac{(x^2+1)^2}{(2x^2+1)^2}$. **[NCERT]**

Ans. Given that

$$a + ib = \frac{(x-i)^2}{2x^2+1}$$

$$\Rightarrow |a + ib| = \left|\frac{(x-i)^2}{2x^2+1}\right|$$

[On taking modulus on both sides]

$$\Rightarrow |a + ib| = \left|\frac{(x-i)\ \ (x-i)}{2x^2+1}\right|$$

$$\Rightarrow |a + ib| = \frac{|(x-i)(x-i)|}{|2x^2+1|}$$

$$\Rightarrow |a + ib| = \frac{|x-i||x-i|}{2x^2+1}$$

$\Rightarrow \sqrt{a^2+b^2} = \frac{\sqrt{x^2+1}\sqrt{x^2+1}}{2x^2+1}$

$\Rightarrow \sqrt{a^2+b^2} = \frac{x^2+1}{2x^2+1}$

$= a^2+b^2 = a^2+b^2 = \frac{(x^2+1)^2}{(2x^2+1)^2}$

[on squaring both sides]

Hence, proved.

OBJECTIVE Type Questions

[1 mark]

Multiple Choice Questions

1. $\sqrt{p+iq} = a+ib$ **then** $\sqrt{p-iq}$ **is:**

(a) a^2+b^2 **(b)** $\sqrt{a^2+b^2}$

(c) $a+ib$ **(d)** $a-ib$

Ans. *(d)* $a-ib$

Explanation: If $\sqrt{p+iq} = a+ib$

Then, $\sqrt{p-iq} = a-ib$

So, option *(d)* is correct.

2. **If** $a+ib = \frac{(p^2+1)^2}{2p-i}$ **then** a^2+b^2 **is equal to:**

(a) $\frac{(p^2+1)^4}{4p^2+1}$ **(b)** $\frac{(p+1)^2}{4p+1}$

(c) $\frac{(p-1)^2}{(4p-1)^2}$ **(d) None of these**

Ans. *(a)* $\frac{(p^2+1)^4}{4p^2+1}$

Explanation: $a+ib = \frac{(p^2+1)^2}{2p-i}$

Then

$a-ib = \frac{(p^2+1)^2}{2p+i}$ Multiplying we get,

$$a^2+b^2 = \frac{(p^2+1)^2}{2p-i} \times \frac{(p^2+1)^2}{2p+i}$$

$$= \frac{(p^2+1)^4}{4p^2+1}$$

Hence, option *(a)* is correct.

3. **If** $(a+ib)^{1/3} = p+iq$ **then** $\frac{a}{p}+\frac{b}{q}$ **is:**

(a) 0 **(b) 1**

(c) –1 **(d) None of these**

Ans. *(d) None of these*

Explanation: If then $a+ib = (p+iq)^3$

$$a+ib = p^3 + (iq)^3 + 3p^2iq + 3p(iq)^2$$

$$= p^3 - iq^3 + 3p^2qi - 3pq^2$$

$$a+ib = (p^3 - 3pq^2) + i(3p^2q - q^3)$$

Thus, $a = p^3 - 3pq^2, b = 3p^2q - q^3$

So,

$$\frac{a}{p}+\frac{b}{q} = \frac{p(p^2-3q^2)}{p} + \frac{q(3p^2-q^2)}{q}$$

$$= p^2 - 3q^2 + 3p^2 - q^2$$

$$= 4(p^2 - q^2)$$

Hence, option *(d)* is correct.

4. $(\sqrt{-4})(\sqrt{-2})$ **is equal to:**

(a) $\sqrt{8}$ **(b)** $-\sqrt{8}$

(c) $i\sqrt{8}$ **(d) None of these**

Ans. *(b)* $-\sqrt{8}$

Explanation: $(\sqrt{-4})(-\sqrt{2}) = i\sqrt{4}.i\sqrt{2}$

$$= i^2\sqrt{8} = -\sqrt{8}$$

Hence, option *(b)* is correct.

5. **If** $a+ib = 3-4i$ **then Re and *Im* part of the complex number is:**

(a) 3, 4 **(b) 3, –4**

(c) 4, 3 **(d) 4, –3**

Ans. *(b)* 3, –4

Explanation: Here complex number

$a + ib = 3 - 4i$

So, a general complex number can be written as Re + *i*(*Im*).

So Re = 3

And Im = –4

Hence, option (b) is correct

6. **The value of** i^9 **is:**

(a) 1 **(b)** i

(c) –1 **(d) none**

Ans. *(b) i*

Explanation: Here, i^9 can be written as

$i^4 . i^4 . i$

We know that $i^4 = 1$

So $i^9 = i$

Hence, option (b) is correct

7. **If $\frac{1-in}{1+in} = a + ib$ then $a^2 + b^2 =$**

(a) 1 (b) –1

(c) 0 (d) None of these

Ans. *(a) 1*

Explanation: If $\frac{1-in}{1+in} = a+ib$ then

$$\frac{1+in}{1-in} = a - ib$$

$$a^2 + b^2 = \left(\frac{1-in}{1+in}\right)\left(\frac{1+in}{1-in}\right) = 1$$

Hence, $a^2 + b^2 = 1$, so option (a) is correct.

8. **The value of $(2 + i)^4 - (2 - i)^4$ is:**

(a) 8 (b) 4

(c) –8 (d) –4

Ans. *(c) –8*

Explanation: $(2 + i)^4 - (2 - i)^4$

$= ((2 + i)^2)^2 - ((2 - i)^2)^2$

$= (i^2 + 4 + 4i)^2 - (4 + i^2 - 4i)^2$

$= (2i)^2 - (-2i)^2$

$= 4i^2 + 4i^2$

$= 8i^2 = -8$

So, option (c) is correct.

9. **The real value of θ for which the expression $\frac{1+i\cos\theta}{1-2i\cos\theta}$ is a real number is:**

(a) $n\pi \pm \frac{\pi}{4}$ (b) $n\pi \pm \frac{\pi}{2}$

(c) $n\pi \pm \frac{\pi}{2}$ (d) $2n\pi \pm \frac{\pi}{4}$

[DIKSHA]

Ans. (c) $n\pi \pm \frac{\pi}{2}$

Explanation: Let $z = \frac{1+i\cos\theta}{1-2i\cos\theta}$

$$= \frac{(1+i\cos\theta)(1+2i\cos\theta)}{(1-2i\cos\theta)(1+2i\cos\theta)}$$

$$= \frac{1-2\cos^2\theta + i3\cos\theta}{1+4\cos^2\theta}$$

$$= \frac{1-2\cos^2\theta}{1+4\cos^2\theta} + i\left(\frac{3\cos\theta}{1+4\cos^2\theta}\right)$$

purely real, then

$Im(z) = 0$

$3\cos\theta = 0$

$\theta = \frac{(2n\pm1)\pi}{2}$ where $n \in N$

10. **If $\left(\frac{1+i}{1-i}\right)^x = 1$, then:**

(a) $x = 2n$ (b) $x = 2n + 1$

(c) $x = 4n$ (d) $x = 4n + 1$

[DIKSHA]

Ans. (c) $x = 4n$

Explanation: If $\left(\frac{1+i}{1-i}\right)^x = 1$

Multiplying and dividing with $(1 + i)^x$

$$= \left[\frac{(1+i)(1+i)}{(1-i)(1+i)}\right]^x$$

$$= \left(\frac{1-1+2i}{2}\right)^x$$

$$= i^x$$

But $i^x = 1 = i^4$,

or $i^x = 1^{4n}$ $(n \in z)$

Therefore $x = 4n$, $n \in z$

Hence, option (c) is correct.

11. **The real value of α for which the expression $\frac{1-i\sin\alpha}{1+2i\sin\alpha}$ is purely real is:**

(a) $(n+1)\frac{\pi}{2}$ (b) $(2n+1)\frac{\pi}{2}$

(c) $n\pi$ (d) None of these

[NCERT Exemplar]

Ans. (c) $n\pi$

Explanation: Rationalizing the denominator

$$\Rightarrow \frac{(1-i\sin\alpha)(1-2i\sin\alpha)}{(1+2i\sin\alpha)(1-2i\sin\alpha)}$$

$$= \frac{1-i\sin\alpha - 2i\sin\alpha + 2i^2\sin^2\alpha}{1-4i^2\sin^2\alpha}$$

$$= \frac{1-3i\sin\alpha - 2\sin^2\alpha}{1+4\sin^2\alpha}$$

$$= \frac{1-2\sin^2\alpha}{1+4\sin^2\alpha} - \frac{3i\sin\alpha}{1+4\sin^2\alpha}$$

It is given that z is purely real.

$$\Rightarrow \quad \frac{-3i \sin\alpha}{1+4\sin^2\alpha} = 0$$

$$\Rightarrow \quad -3\sin\alpha = 0$$

$$\Rightarrow \quad \sin\alpha = 0$$

$$\alpha = n\pi, n \in 1$$

Assertion-Reason (A-R)

DIRECTION: In the following questions, a statement of assertion (A) is followed by a statement of the reason (R). Mark the correct choice as:

(a) Both assertion (A) and reason (R) are true and reason (R) is the correct explanation of assertion (A).

(b) Both assertion (A) and reason (R) are true but reason (R) is not the correct explanation of assertion (A).

(c) Assertion (A) is true but reason (R) is false.

(d) Assertion (A) is false but reason (R) is true.

12. Assertion (A): Simplest form of i^{35} is $-i$.

Reason (R): Additive inverse of $(1 - i)$ is equal to $-1 + i$.

Ans. *(d) Assertion (A) is false but reason (R) is true.*

Explanation: $i^{35} = \frac{1}{i^{-35}} = \frac{1}{(i^2)^{17} i} = \frac{1}{-i} \times \frac{i}{i} = \frac{i}{-i^2} = i$

Additive inverse of z is $-z$.

So addictive inverse of $(1 - i)$ is $-1 + i$.

Hence, assertion is false and reason is true.

13. Assertion (A): If $z_1 = 2 + 3i$ and $z_2 = 3 - 2i$ then $z_1 - z_2 = -1 + 5i$.

Reason(R): If $z_1 = (a + ib)$ and $z_2(c + id)$ then $z_1 - z_2 = (a - c) + i(b - a)$.

Ans. *(a) Both assertion (A) and reason (R) are true and reason (R) is the correct explanation of assertion (A).*

Explanation: Given $z_1 = 2 + 3i$, $z_2 = 3 - 2i$ then $z_1 - z_2 = -1 + 5i$

Hence, assertion and reason both are true and reason is the correct explanation of assertion.

14. Assertion (A): If $(1 + i)^6 = a + ib$ then $b = -8$.

Reason (R): If $(1 - i)^3 = a + ib$ then $\frac{a}{b} = 1$.

Ans. *(b) Both assertion (A) and reason (R) are true but reason (R) is not the correct explanation of assertion (A).*

Explanation: $(1 + i)^6 = ((1 + i)^2)^3 = (2i)^3 = 8i^3$

$= -8i = a + ib, b = -8$

$(1 - i)^3 = 1^3 - i^3 - 3(1)^2 i + 3(1)i^2$

$= -2 - 2i$

$= a + ib, a = -2$ and $b = -2$

Hence, assertion and reason both are true but reason is not the correct explanation of assertion.

15. Assertion (A): Multiplicative inverse of $2 - 3i$ is $2 + 3i$.

Reason (R): If $z = 3 + 4i$ then $\underline{z} = 3 - 4i$.

Ans. *(d) Assertion (A) is false but reason (R) is true.*

Explanation: $z^{-1} = \frac{z}{|z|^2} = \frac{2+3i}{13} = \frac{2}{13} + \frac{3}{13}i$

$z = a + ib$

then $\underline{z} = a - ib$

$z = 3 + 4i$

then $z = 3 - 4i$

Hence, assertion is false and reason is true.

CASE BASED Questions (CBQs)

[4 & 5 marks]

Read the following passages and answer the questions that follow:

16. *Two complex numbers $Z_1 = a + ib$ and $Z_2 = c + id$ are said to be equal if $a = c$ and $b = d$.*

(A) If $(2a + 2b) + i(b - a) = -4i$, then find the real values of a and b.

(B) If $(x + y) + i(x - y) = 4 + 6i$, then find xy.

Ans. (A) We have $(2a + 2b) + i(b - a) = -4i$

Here

$2a + 2b = 0$

$\Rightarrow \quad a + b = 0$

and $\quad b - a = -4$

So,

$a = 2$ and $b = -2$

(B) Given that $(x + y) + i(x - y) = 4 + 6i$

Hence,

$x + y = 4$

$x - y = 6$

by solving equations

$x = 5, y = -1$

then $xy = -5$

17. *A complex number z is pure real if and only if $\underline{z} = z$ and is pure imaginary if and only if $\underline{z} = -z$.*

(A) If $(1 + i)z = (1 - i)\bar{z}$, then $-i\bar{z}$ is:

(a) $-\bar{z}$ (b) z

(c) $\bar{z}$ (d) z^{-1}

(B) $\overline{z_1 z_2}$ is:

(a) $\overline{z_1}\,\overline{z_2}$ (b) $\overline{z_1} + \overline{z_1}$

(c) $\dfrac{\overline{z_1}}{\overline{z_2}}$ (d) $\dfrac{1}{\overline{z_1 z_2}}$

(C) If x and y are real numbers and the complex number

$$\frac{(2+i)x-i}{4+i}+\frac{(1-i)y+2i}{4i}$$

is pure real, the relation between x and y is:

(a) $8x - 17y = 16$

(b) $8x + 17y = 16$

(c) $17x - 8y = 16$

(d) $17x - 8y = -16$

(D) If $z = \dfrac{3+2i\sin\theta}{1-2i\sin\theta}\left(0<\theta\le\dfrac{\pi}{2}\right)$ is pure imaginary, then θ is equal to:

(a) $\dfrac{\pi}{4}$ (b) $\dfrac{\pi}{6}$

(c) $\dfrac{\pi}{3}$ (d) $\dfrac{\pi}{12}$

Ans. (A) *(b)* z

Explanation: Since, $(1 + i)z = (1 - i)\bar{z}$

$$\Rightarrow \frac{z}{\bar{z}}=\frac{1-i}{1+i}\times\frac{1-i}{1-i}=\frac{(1-i)^2}{1-i^2}$$

$$=\frac{1+i^2-2i}{1+1}=-i$$

$$\Rightarrow z=-i\bar{z}$$

(B) *(a)* $\overline{z_1}\,\overline{z_2}$

Explanation: $\because \overline{z_1 z_2}=\overline{z_1}\,\overline{z_2}$

(C) *(a)* $8x - 17y = 16$

Explanation: Let

$$z=\frac{(2+i)x-i}{4+i}+\frac{(1-i)y+2i}{4i}$$

$$=\frac{2x+(x-1)i}{4+i}+\frac{y+(2-y)i}{4i}\times\frac{i}{i}$$

$$=\frac{(2x+(x-1)i)(4-i)}{(4+i)(4-i)}+\frac{-iy+(2-y)}{4}$$

$$=\frac{8x+x-1+i(4x-4-2x)}{16+1}+\frac{(2-y)-iy}{4}$$

$$=\frac{9x-1+i(2x-4)}{17}+\frac{2-y-iy}{4}$$

Since, z is real $\Rightarrow \bar{z}=z$

$\Rightarrow$ $Im z = 0$

$$\Rightarrow \frac{2x-4}{17}-\frac{y}{4}=0$$

$\Rightarrow$ $8x - 16 = 17y$

$\Rightarrow$ $8x - 17y = 16$

(D) *(c)* $\dfrac{\pi}{3}$

Explanation: $z=\dfrac{3+2i\sin\theta}{1-2i\sin\theta}\times\dfrac{(1+2i\sin\theta)}{(1+2i\sin\theta)}$

$$=\frac{(3+2i\sin\theta)(1+2i\sin\theta)}{1+4\sin^2\theta}$$

$$=\frac{(3-4\sin^2\theta)+i(8\sin\theta)}{1+4\sin^2\theta}$$

Since, z is pure imaginary.

$\Rightarrow$ $Re(z) = 0$

$$\Rightarrow \frac{3-4\sin^2\theta}{1+4\sin^2\theta}=0$$

$$\Rightarrow \sin^2\theta=\frac{3}{4}$$

$$\Rightarrow \sin\theta=\pm\frac{\sqrt{3}}{2}$$

$$\Rightarrow \theta=\frac{\pi}{3}\left(since, 0<\theta\le\frac{\pi}{2}\right)$$

VERY SHORT ANSWER Type Questions (VSA)

[**1** mark]

18. Reduce $\dfrac{(4+i\sqrt{3})(4-i\sqrt{3})}{(\sqrt{3}+\sqrt{2}i)-(\sqrt{3}-\sqrt{2}i)}$ to the standard form.

Ans. $=\dfrac{(4+i\sqrt{3})(4-i\sqrt{3})}{(\sqrt{3}+\sqrt{2}i)-(\sqrt{3}-\sqrt{2}i)}=\dfrac{16-3i^2}{\sqrt{3}+\sqrt{2}i-\sqrt{3}+\sqrt{2}i}$

$$=\frac{16+3}{2\sqrt{2}i}=\frac{19}{2\sqrt{2}i}=\frac{19}{2\sqrt{2}i}\times\frac{2\sqrt{2}i}{2\sqrt{2}i}=\frac{38\sqrt{2}i}{8i^2}=\frac{-19\sqrt{2}i}{4}.$$

19. **Write the additive inverse of $6i - i\sqrt{-49}$.**

Ans. Given, $6i-i\sqrt{-49}$

$= 6i - i(7i)$
$= 6i - 7i^2$
$= 6i + 7$

Additive inverse $= -6i - 7$

20. Write the value of $i + i^{10} + i^{20} + i^{30}$.

Ans. $i + i^{10} + i^{20} + i^{30} = i + (i^2)^5 + (i^2)^{10} + (i^2)^{15}$
$= -i + (-1)^5 + (-1)^{10} + (-1)^{15}$
$= i - 1 + 1 - 1 \quad [\because i^2 = -1]$
$= i - 1$

21. Using conjugate and modulus of a complex number $z = 4 - 3i$, find the multiplicative inverse of $4 - 3i$.

Ans. Let $z = 4 - 3i$

Then, $\underline{z} = 4 + 3i$ and $|z| = \sqrt{(4)^3 + (-3)^3} = 5$

Now, $z\underline{z} = |z|^2$

$$\Rightarrow \frac{1}{z} = \frac{\underline{z}}{|z|^2} = \frac{4+3i}{(5)^2} = \frac{4}{25} + \frac{3}{25}i.$$

Hence, the multiplicative inverse of $4 - 3i$ is $\frac{4}{25} + \frac{3}{25}i$.

22. If $(1 + i)z = (1 - i)\underline{z}$, then show that $z = -i\underline{z}$. [NCERT Exemplar]

Ans. We have, $(1 + i)z = (1 - i)\underline{z}$

$$\Rightarrow z = \frac{1-i}{1+i}\underline{z} = \frac{(1-i)(1-i)}{(1+i)(1-i)}\underline{z} = \frac{(1-i)^2}{(1-i^2)}\underline{z}$$

$$= \frac{1-2i+i^2}{1+1}\underline{z} = \frac{1-2i-1}{2}\underline{z} = -i\underline{z}$$

$z = i\underline{z}$

SHORT ANSWER Type-I Questions (SA-I)

[2 marks]

23. Find the conjugate of the following:

(A) $p + iq$ (B) $3 - 7i$

Ans. (A) Let $z = p + iq$

Then, the conjugate of z is $\underline{z} = p - iq$.

(B) Let $z = 3 - 7i$

Then, the conjugate of z is $\underline{z} = 3 + 7i$.

24. For what values a and b are $(1 - i)a + (1 + i)b$ and $1 - 3i$ equal?

Ans. Let $(1 - i)a + (1 + i)b = 1 - 3i$

$\Rightarrow \quad a - ia + b + ib = 1 - 3i$

$\Rightarrow (a + b) + i(-a + b) = 1 - 3i$

So, the real and imaginary parts of the above complex numbers must be equal.

$\therefore$ We have,

$$\left.\begin{matrix} a+b=1 \\ -a+b=-3 \end{matrix}\right\} \Rightarrow a = 2, b = -1$$

Hence, $a = 2, b = -1$.

25. Find the conjugate of the following:

(A) $\frac{1}{2+4i}$ (A) $(2 + 5i)^2$

Ans. (A)

$$\text{Let } z = \frac{1}{2+4i} = \frac{(2-4i)}{(2+4i)(2-4i)} = \frac{2-4i}{4-16i^2}$$

$$= \frac{2-4i}{20} = \frac{2}{20} - \frac{4}{20}i.$$

Then, the conjugate of z is $\underline{z} = \frac{2}{20} + \frac{4}{20}i$.

(B) We have $(2 + 5i)^2$

$= (2)^2 + 2.2.5i + (5i)^2 = 4 + 20i - 25$
$= -21 + 20i$

$\therefore$ Complex conjugate of

$(2 + 5i)^2 = \underline{(-21+20i)}$
$= -21 - 20i$

26. If $z_1 = \sqrt{2}(\cos 30° + i \sin 60°)$

$z_2 = \sqrt{3}(\cos 60° + i \sin 30°)$

Ans. Given,

$z_1 = \sqrt{2}(\cos 30° + i \sin 60°)$ and

$z_2 = \sqrt{3}(\cos 60° + i \sin 30°)$

$$\therefore z_1 z_2 = \left[\sqrt{2}(\cos 30° + i \sin 60°)\right]\left[\sqrt{3}(\cos 60° + i \sin 30°)\right]$$

$= \sqrt{6}$ [(cos 30° cos 60° – sin 30° sin 60°) + i (cos 30° sin 30°) + (sin 60° cos° 60°)]

$$= \sqrt{6}\left[\cos(60° + 30°) + i\left(\frac{\sqrt{3}}{2}\cdot\frac{1}{2} + \frac{\sqrt{3}}{2}\cdot\frac{1}{2}\right)\right]$$

$[\because \cos(A + B) = \cos A \cos B - \sin A \sin B]$

$$= \sqrt{6}\left[\cos 90^\circ + i\left(\frac{\sqrt{3}}{2}\right)\right]$$

$$= \sqrt{6}\left[0 + i\left(\frac{\sqrt{3}}{2}\right)\right]$$

$$= 0 + i\left(\frac{\sqrt{6}(\sqrt{3})}{2}\right) = \frac{0 + 3\sqrt{2i}}{2}$$

$\therefore$ $Re(z_1 z_2) = 0$

27. Solve the equation $|z| = z + 1 + 2i$ **[NCERT Exemplar]**

Ans. We have, $|z| = z + 1 + 2i$

Putting $z = x + iy$, we get

$$|x + iy| = x + iy + 1 + 2i$$

$$\Rightarrow \sqrt{x^2 + y^2} = (x + 1) + i(y + 2)$$

$$[\because |z| = \sqrt{x^2 + y^2}]$$

Comparing real and imaginary parts, we get

$$\sqrt{x^2 + y^2} = x + 1;$$

And $0 = y + 2 \Rightarrow y = -2$

Putting this value of y in $\sqrt{x^2 + y^2} = x + 1$ we get

$$x^2 + (-2)^2 = (x + 1)^2$$

$$\Rightarrow \quad x^2 + 4 = x^2 + 2x + 1$$

$$\Rightarrow \quad x = 3/2$$

$$z = x + iy = 3/2 - 2i$$

28. Find the modulus of $\frac{1+i}{1-i} - \frac{1-i}{1+i}$.

Ans. $\frac{1+i}{1-i} - \frac{1-i}{1+i} = \frac{(1+i)^2 - (1-i)^2}{(1-i)(1+i)}$

$$= \frac{(1 + i^2 + 2i) - (1 + i^2 - 2i)}{1 - i^2} = \frac{4i}{2} = 0 + 2i.$$

Hence, $\left|\frac{1+i}{1-i} - \frac{1-i}{1+i}\right| = \sqrt{(0)^2 + (2)^2} = 2$

SHORT ANSWER Type-II Questions (SA-II)

[**3** marks]

29. Find the real numbers x and y such that $(x - iy)(3 + 5i)$ is the conjugate of $-6 + 24i$.

Ans. Given that $(x - iy)(3 + 5i)$ is the conjugate of $-6 + 24i$.

$\therefore$ $(x - iy)(3 + 5i) = -6 + 24i$

$\Rightarrow$ $3x + 5ix - 3iy - 5i^2 y = -6 + 24i$

$\Rightarrow$ $(3x + 5y) + i(5x - 3y) = -6 + 24i$

So, the real and imaginary parts of the above complex numbers must be equal.

$$\left.\begin{aligned} 3x + 5y &= -6 \\ 5x - 3y &= 24 \end{aligned}\right\} \Rightarrow x = 3,\ y = -3$$

$\therefore$ We have,

Hence, $x = 3$, $y = -3$

30. Find real value of x and y,

If $\frac{(1+i)x - 2i}{3+i} + \frac{(2-3i)y + i}{3-i} = i$

Ans. We have,

$$\frac{(1+i)x - 2i}{3+i} + \frac{(2-3i)y + i}{3-i} = i$$

$$\frac{\{(1+i)x - 2i\}(3-i) + \{(2-3i)y + i\}(3+i)}{(3+i)(3-i)} = i$$

$$\frac{\{x + i(x-2)\}(3-i) + \{2y + i(1-3y)(3+i)\}}{(3+i)(3-i)} = i$$

$$\frac{(3 + 3i - i - i^2)x - (6i - 2i^2) + (6 - 9i + 2i - 3i^2)y + (3i + i^2)\}}{3^2 - i^2} = i$$

$(4 + 2i)x - (6i + 2) + (9 - 7i)y + (3i - i) = i(9 + 1)$

$4x + 2xi - 6i - 2 + 9y - 7yi + 3i - 1 = 10i$

$$\frac{(4x + 9y - 3) + i(2x - 7y - 3)}{10} = 0 + i$$

$$\frac{4x + 9y - 3}{10} = 0 \text{ and } \frac{2x - 7y - 3}{10} = 1$$

$4x + 9y - 3 = 0$ and $2x - 7y - 13 = 0$

$x = 3$ and $y = -1$

31. Find the modulus of each of the following:

(A) $12i - 5$ **(B) $(2 - i)^2$**

Ans. (A) Let $z = 12i - 5 = -5 + 12i$

Then, the modulus of

z is $|z| = \sqrt{(-5)^2 + (12)^2} = \sqrt{169} = 13$

(B) Let $z = (2 - i)^2 = 4 + i^2 - 4i = 3 - 4i$

Then, the modulus of

z is $|z| = \sqrt{(3) + (-4)^2} = \sqrt{25} = 5$

32. **If the real part of $\frac{z+2}{z-1}$ is 4, then show that the locus of the point representing z in the complex plane is a circle.**

[NCERT Exemplar]

Ans. Let $z = x + iy$

Now,

$$\frac{z+2}{z-1} = \frac{x-iy+2}{x-iy-1} = \frac{[(x+2)-iy][(x-1)+iy]}{[(x-1)-iy][(x-1)+iy]}$$

$$= \frac{(x-1)(x+2)+y^2+i[(x+2)y-(x-1)y]}{(x-1)^2+y^2}$$

Given that the real part is 4.

$$\Rightarrow \frac{(x-1)(x+2)+y^2}{(x-1)^2+y^2} = 4$$

$$\Rightarrow x^2+x-2+y^2 = 4(x^2-2x+1+y^2)$$

$$\Rightarrow 3x^2+3y^2-9x+6=0,$$

which represents a circle

Hence, locus of z is a circle.

33. **Find the number of non-zero integral solutions of the equation $|3^{1/2}-i|^x = 4^x$.**

Ans. $|3^{1/2}-i|^x = 4^x$

$$\Rightarrow [(\sqrt{(3^{1/2})^2+(-1)^2})]^x = 4^x$$

$$\Rightarrow (\sqrt{4})^x = 4^x$$

$$\Rightarrow 4^{x/2} = 4^x$$

$$\Rightarrow \frac{x}{2} = x$$

$$\Rightarrow x - \frac{x}{2} = 0$$

$$\Rightarrow x = 0$$

Hence, the given equation does not have a non-zero integral solution.

LONG ANSWER Type Questions (LA)

[**4** & **5** marks]

34. **If $x+iy = \sqrt{\frac{p+iq}{a+ib}}$, prove that $(x^2+y^2)^2 = \frac{p^2+q^2}{a^2+b^2}$.**

Ans. Given, $x + iy = \sqrt{\frac{p+iq}{a+ib}}$

$$\Rightarrow (x+iy)^2 = \left(\frac{p+iq}{a+ib}\right)^2 \quad \text{[on squaring both sides]}$$

$$\Rightarrow |(x+iy)^2| = \left|\frac{p+iq}{a+ib}\right|^2$$

[on taking modulus on both sides]

$$\Rightarrow |(x+iy)(x+iy)| = \left|\frac{p+iq}{a+ib}\right|^2$$

$$\Rightarrow |x+iy||x+iy| = \left|\frac{p+iq}{a+ib}\right|^2$$

$$\Rightarrow \sqrt{x^2+(y)^2}\sqrt{x^2+(y)^2} = \frac{\sqrt{p^2+(q)^2}}{\sqrt{a^2+(b)^2}}$$

$$\Rightarrow \sqrt{x^2+y^2}\sqrt{x^2+y^2} = \frac{\sqrt{p^2+q^2}}{\sqrt{a^2+b^2}}$$

$$\Rightarrow x^2+y^2 = \frac{\sqrt{p^2+q^2}}{\sqrt{a^2+b^2}}$$

$$\Rightarrow (x^2+y^2)^2 = \frac{p^2+q^2}{a^2+b^2} \quad \text{[on squaring both sides]}$$

Hence, proved.

35. **If $x - iy = \frac{(a+7)^2}{2a+i}$ find the value of $x^2 + y^2$.**

Ans. Given, $x - iy = \frac{(a+7)^2}{2a+i}$

We know that if two complex numbers are equal, then their conjugates are also.

Taking conjugate of both sides, we get

$$x + iy = \frac{(a+7)^2}{2a-i}$$

Multiplying corresponding sides of both equations (1) and (2), we get

$$(x-iy)(x+iy)$$

$$= \frac{(a+7)^2}{2a+i} \times \frac{(a+7)^2}{2a-i}$$

$$\Rightarrow x^2 - i^2y^2 = \frac{(a+7)^4}{(2a)^2-i^2}$$

$$\Rightarrow \quad x^2 + y^2 = \frac{(a+7)^4}{4a^2+1}$$

36. Show that | z – 2/z – 3| = 2 represents a circle. Find its center and radius.

[NCERT Exemplar]

Ans. We have $|z - 2/z - 3| = 2$

Putting $= x + iy$, we get

$$\left|\frac{x+iy-2}{x+iy-3}\right| = 2$$

$$\Rightarrow |x - 2 + iy| = 2\,|x - 3 + iy|$$

$$\Rightarrow \sqrt{(x-2)^2 + y^2} = 2\sqrt{(x-3)^2 + y^2}$$

$$\Rightarrow x^2 - 4x + 4 + y^2 = 4(x^2 - 6x + 9 + y^2)$$

$$\Rightarrow 3x^2 + 3y^2 - 20x + 32 = 0$$

$$\Rightarrow x^2 + y^2 - \frac{20}{3}x + \frac{32}{3} = 0$$

$$\Rightarrow \left(x - \frac{10}{3}\right)^2 + y^2 + \frac{32}{3} - \frac{100}{9} = 0$$

$$\Rightarrow \left(x - \frac{10}{3}\right)^2 + (y-0)^2 = \frac{4}{9}$$

Hence, center of the circle is $\left(\frac{10}{3}, 0\right)$ and radius is $\frac{2}{3}$.

QUADRATIC EQUATIONS OF COMPLEX NUMBER 2

TOPIC 1

SOLUTION OF QUADRATIC EQUATION

Quadratic means "involving the second power and no higher power of an unknown quantity or a variable".

An Equation of the Form

$ax^2 + bx + c = 0$ where $a \neq 0$ is called quadratic equation and a, b, c are called coefficients.

The values of x which satisfy the given quadratic equation are called the roots of that quadratic equation.

$= \dfrac{-b \pm \sqrt{D}}{2a}$ here, D is called Discriminant and

$D = b^2 - 4ac$

If $D > 0$ then the roots are real.

$D = 0$ then the roots are equal.

$D < 0$ then the roots are imaginary.

Important

➥ *A polynomial equation has at least one root.*

Caution

➥ *A Polynomial equation of degree n has n roots.*

Example 2.1: Solve the equation $2x^2 + x + 1 = 0$

Ans. Given equation is $2x^2 + x + 1 = 0$

The above equation is of the form

$ax^2 + bx + c = 0$

where $a = 2, b = 1, c = 1$

Using, $x = \dfrac{-b \pm \sqrt{b^2 - 4ac}}{2a}$

$$x = \frac{-1 \pm \sqrt{(1)^2 - 4 \times 2 \times 1}}{2 \times 2}$$

$$= \frac{-1 \pm \sqrt{1-8}}{4}$$

$$= \frac{-1 \pm \sqrt{-7}}{4}$$

$$= \frac{-1 \pm \sqrt{-1 \times 7}}{4}$$

$$= \frac{-1 \pm \sqrt{-1} \times \sqrt{7}}{4} = \frac{-1 \pm \sqrt{7}i}{4}$$

Thus, $x = \dfrac{-1 \pm \sqrt{7}i}{4}$

Example 2.2: Solve the following quadratic equations:

(A) $x^2 - x - 6 = 0$ **(B)** $25x^2 + 30x + 7 = 0$

(B) $9x^2 - 12x + 4 = 0$

Ans. (A) The given equation is $x^2 - x - 6 = 0$

Which is of the form $ax^2 + bx + c = 0$ where $a = 1, b = -1, c = -6$

Then, the roots of the given equation are

$$x = \frac{-b \pm \sqrt{b^2 - 4ac}}{2a}$$

$$= \frac{-(-1) \pm \sqrt{(-1)^2 - 4(1)(-6)}}{2(1)}$$

$$= \frac{1 \pm \sqrt{25}}{2} = 3, -2$$

(B) The given equation is $25x^2 + 30x + 7 = 0$

Which is of the form $ax^2 + bx + c = 0$ where $a = 25, b = 30, c = 7$.

Then, the roots of the given equation are

$$x = \frac{-b \pm \sqrt{b^2 - 4ac}}{2a}$$

$$= \frac{-30 \pm \sqrt{(30)^2 - 4(25)(7)}}{2(25)}$$

$$= \frac{-30 \pm \sqrt{200}}{50}$$

$$= \frac{-30 \pm 10\sqrt{2}}{50} = \frac{-3+\sqrt{2}}{5}, \frac{-3-\sqrt{2}}{5}$$

(C) Given equation is

$$9x^2 - 12x + 4 = 0$$

Which is of the form $ax^2 + bx + c = 0$ where $a = 9, b = -12, c = 4$

Then, the roots of the given equation are

$$x = \frac{-b \pm \sqrt{b^2 - 4ac}}{2a}$$

$$= \frac{12 \pm \sqrt{(-12)^2 - 4(9)(4)}}{2(9)}$$

$$= \frac{12 \pm 0}{18} = \frac{2}{3}, \frac{2}{3}.$$

Example 2.3: Solve the equation $x^2 - x + 2 = 0$

Ans. Given equation is $x^2 - x + 2 = 0$

The above equation is of the form

$ax^2 + bx + c = 0$

Where $a = 1, b = -1, c = 2$

$$= \frac{-b \pm \sqrt{b^2 - 4ac}}{2a}$$

$$x = \frac{-(-1) \pm \sqrt{(-1)^2 - 4 \times 1 \times 2}}{2 \times 1}$$

$$= \frac{1 \pm \sqrt{1-8}}{2}$$

$$= \frac{1 \pm \sqrt{-7}}{2}$$

$$= \frac{1 \pm \sqrt{-1 \times 7}}{2}$$

$$= \frac{1 \pm \sqrt{-1} \times \sqrt{7}}{2}$$

$$= \frac{1 \pm i\sqrt{7}}{2}$$

Thus, $x = \frac{1 \pm i\sqrt{7}}{2}$

Example 2.4: Solve the equation $x^2 + x + \frac{1}{\sqrt{2}} = 0$

Ans. Given equation is $x^2 + x + \frac{1}{\sqrt{2}} = 0$

Multiplying both sides by $\sqrt{2}$

$$\sqrt{2}x^2 + \sqrt{2}x + \sqrt{2} \times \frac{1}{\sqrt{2}} = 0 \times \sqrt{2}$$

$$\sqrt{2}x^2 + \sqrt{2}x + 1 = 0$$

The above equation is of the form

$ax^2 + bx + c = 0$

Where $a = \sqrt{2}, b = \sqrt{2}, and\ c = 1$

$$x = \frac{-b \pm \sqrt{b^2 - 4ac}}{2a}$$

$$x = \frac{-\sqrt{2} \pm \sqrt{(\sqrt{2})^2 - 4 \times \sqrt{2} \times 1}}{2 \times \sqrt{2}}$$

$$x = \frac{-\sqrt{2} \pm \sqrt{(\sqrt{2})^2 - 4 \times \sqrt{2} \times 1}}{2 \times \sqrt{2}}$$

$$x = \frac{-\sqrt{2} \pm (\sqrt{(2 - 4\sqrt{2})}}{2\sqrt{2}}$$

$$x = \frac{-\sqrt{2} \pm \sqrt{2}\left(\sqrt{1 - 2\sqrt{2}}\right)}{2\sqrt{2}}$$

Thus $x = \frac{-1 \pm ix\sqrt{(2\sqrt{2}) - 1}}{2}$

$$x = \frac{-\sqrt{2}(-1 \pm (\sqrt{1 - 2\sqrt{2}})}{2\sqrt{2}}$$

$$x = \frac{-1 \pm \sqrt{1 - 2\sqrt{2}}}{2}$$

$$x = \frac{-1 \pm \sqrt{-(2\sqrt{2} - 1)}}{2}$$

(since $2\sqrt{2} = 2 \times 1.14 > 1$)

$$x = \frac{-1 \pm \sqrt{-1 \times (2\sqrt{2} - 1)}}{2}$$

$$x = \frac{-1 \pm \sqrt{-1} \times \sqrt{(2\sqrt{2} - 1)}}{2}$$

Example 2.6: Solve the equation $27x^2 - 10x + 1 = 0$.

Ans. Given equation is $27x^2 - 10x + 1 = 0$

The above equation is of the form

$ax^2 + bx + c = 0$

Where $a = 27$, $b = -10$ and $c = 1$

$$x = \frac{-b \pm \sqrt{b^2 - 4ac}}{2a}$$

$$x = \frac{-(-10) \pm \sqrt{(-10)^2 - 4 \times (27) \times (1)}}{2 \times 27}$$

$$x = \frac{10 \pm \sqrt{100 - 108}}{2 \times 27}$$

$$x = \frac{10 \pm \sqrt{-8}}{2 \times 27}$$

$$x = \frac{10 \pm \sqrt{-2 \times 4}}{2 \times 27}$$

$$x = \frac{10 \pm 2\sqrt{-2}}{2 \times 27}$$

$$x = \frac{2(5 \pm \sqrt{-2})}{2 \times 27}$$

$$x = \frac{5 \pm \sqrt{-2}}{27}$$

$$x = \frac{5 \pm \sqrt{2x - 1}}{27}$$

$$x = \frac{5 \pm \sqrt{2} \times \sqrt{-1}}{27}$$

$$x = \frac{5 \pm i\sqrt{2}}{27}$$

Thus, $x = \frac{5 \pm i\sqrt{2}}{27}$

Example 2.7 **Solve the equation $x^2 - 2x + \frac{3}{2} = 0$.**

Ans. Given equation is $x^2 - 2x + \frac{3}{2} = 0$

Multiplying whole equation by 2

$$2 \times x^2 - 2 \times 2x + 2 \times \frac{3}{2} = 0 \times 2$$

$$2x^2 - 4x + 3 = 0$$

The above equation is of the form

$$ax^2 + bx + c = 0$$

Where $a = 2$, $b = -4$ and $c = 3$

$$x = \frac{-b \pm \sqrt{b^2 - 4ac}}{2a}$$

$$x = \frac{-(-4) \pm \sqrt{(-4)^2 - 4 \times 2 \times 3}}{2 \times 2}$$

$$x = \frac{4 \pm \sqrt{16 - 24}}{4}$$

$$x = \frac{4 \pm \sqrt{-8}}{4}$$

$$x = \frac{4 \pm \sqrt{-4 \times 2}}{4}$$

$$x = \frac{4 \pm \sqrt{-1 \times 4 \times 2}}{4}$$

$$x = \frac{4 \pm \sqrt{-1} \times \sqrt{4} \times \sqrt{2}}{4}$$

$$x = \frac{4 \pm i \times 2 \times \sqrt{2}}{4}$$

$$x = \frac{4 \pm i2\sqrt{2}}{4}$$

$$x = \frac{2(2 \pm i\sqrt{2})}{4}$$

$$x = \frac{2 \pm i\sqrt{2}}{2}$$

Thus, $x = \frac{2 \pm i\sqrt{2}}{2}$

OBJECTIVE Type Questions

[**1** mark]

Multiple Choice Questions

1. **If a, b are roots of quadratic equation $x^2 + x + 1 = 0$ then $\frac{(a^2 + b^2)}{2} = ?$**

(a) 1 (b) 2

(c) –1 (d) 3

Ans. *(a)* 1

Explanation: $D = b^2 - 4ac = 1^2 - 4 \times 1 \times 1$

$= 1 - 4 = -3$

$$x = \frac{-b \pm \sqrt{D}}{2a} = \frac{-1 \pm \sqrt{-3}}{2}$$

$$a = \frac{-1 + \sqrt{-3}}{2} \quad b = \frac{-1 - \sqrt{-3}}{2}$$

Hence, $\frac{(a^2 + b^2)}{2} = \frac{2}{2} = 1$

So, option *(a)* is correct.

2. **If α, β are roots of $4x^2 + 3x + 7 = 0$ then $\frac{1}{\alpha} + \frac{1}{\beta} = ?$**

(a) $\frac{7}{3}$ (b) $\frac{-7}{3}$

(c) $\frac{3}{7}$ (d) $\frac{-3}{7}$

Ans. *(d)* $\frac{-3}{7}$

Explanation: $4x^2 + 3x + 7 = 0$ then

$D = 3^2 - 4 \times 4 \times 7$

$= 9 - 112$

$= -103$

$$x = \frac{-3 \pm \sqrt{-103}}{8}$$

$$\alpha = \frac{-3 + \sqrt{-103}}{8}, \beta = \frac{-3 - \sqrt{-103}}{8}$$

$$\alpha + \beta = \frac{-3 + \sqrt{-103}}{8} + \frac{-3 - \sqrt{-103}}{8}$$

$$= \frac{-3 + \sqrt{-103} - 3 - \sqrt{103}}{8} = \frac{-6}{8}$$

$= \frac{-3}{4}$

$\alpha\beta = \frac{7}{4}$

Then $\frac{1}{\alpha} + \frac{1}{\beta} = \frac{-3}{7}$

So option (d) is correct.

3. The least value of k which makes the roots of the equation $2x^2 + 10x + 2k = 0$ imaginary is:

(a) 4 **(b)** 5

(c) 6 **(d)** 7

Ans. *(d) 7*

Explanation: $2x^2 + 10x + 2k = 0$

$x^2 + 5x + k = 0$

$D = 25 - 4 \times 1 \times k$

$D = 25 - 4k$

For imaginary roots

$D < 0$

$25 - 4k < 0$

$25 < 4k$

$\frac{25}{4} < k$

$6.5 < k$

Hence, option *(d)* is correct.

4. Roots of $8x^2 + 16 = 0$ are:

(a) $\pm\sqrt{2}i$ **(b)** 2

(c) 2i **(d)** None

Ans. *(a)* $\pm\sqrt{2}i$

Explanation: $8x^2 + 16 = 0$

$x^2 + 2 = 0$

$D = 0^2 - 4 \times 1 \times 2$

$D = -8$

$x = \frac{-b \pm \sqrt{D}}{2a}$

$= \frac{\pm\sqrt{-8}}{2}$

$= \frac{\pm 2\sqrt{2}i}{2}$

$= \pm\sqrt{2}i$

Option *(a)* is correct.

5. Roots of $x^2 + 3x + 9 = 0$ are:

(a) $\frac{-3 \pm 3\sqrt{3}i}{2}$ **(b)** $\frac{3 \pm 3\sqrt{3}i}{2}$

(c) $\frac{3 \pm \sqrt{3}i}{2}$ **(d)** $\frac{-3 \pm \sqrt{3}i}{2}$

Ans. *(a)* $\frac{-3 \pm 3\sqrt{3}i}{2}$

Explanation: $x^2 + 3x + 9 = 0$

$D = 3^2 - 4 \times 1 \times 9$

$= 9 - 36$

$= -27$

$x = \frac{-b \pm \sqrt{D}}{2a}$

$= \frac{-3 \pm \sqrt{-27}}{2}$

$= \frac{-3 \pm 3\sqrt{3}i}{2}$

$= \frac{3(-1 \pm \sqrt{3}i)}{2}$

Hence, option *(a)* is correct.

6. Roots of $x^2 + x + 1 = 0$ are:

(a) $\frac{-1 \pm \sqrt{3}i}{2}$ **(b)** $\frac{1 \pm \sqrt{3}i}{2}$

(c) $\frac{2 \pm \sqrt{3}i}{2}$ **(d)** $\frac{-2 \pm \sqrt{3}i}{2}$

Ans. *(a)* $\frac{-1 \pm \sqrt{3}i}{2}$

Explanation: $x^2 + x + 1 = 0$

$D = 1^2 - 4 \times 1 \times 1$

$= 1 - 4$

$D = -3$

$x = \frac{-b \pm \sqrt{D}}{2a}$

$= \frac{-1 \pm \sqrt{-3}}{2}$

$= \frac{-1 \pm \sqrt{3}i}{2}$

Hence, option *(a)* is correct.

7. Roots of $\sqrt{2}x^2 + x + \sqrt{2} = 0$ are given by:

(a) $\frac{-1 \pm i\sqrt{7}}{2\sqrt{2}}$ **(b)** $\frac{-1 \pm i\sqrt{7}}{\sqrt{2}}$

(c) $\frac{1 \pm \sqrt{7}i}{2}$ **(d)** None

Ans. *(a)* $\frac{-1 \pm i\sqrt{7}}{2\sqrt{2}}$

Explanation: $\sqrt{2}x^2 + x + \sqrt{2} = 0$

$D = 1^2 - 4 \times \sqrt{2} \times \sqrt{2}$

$= 1 - 8$
$= -7$

$$x = \frac{-b \pm \sqrt{D}}{2a}$$

$$= \frac{-1 \pm \sqrt{-7}}{2\sqrt{2}}$$

$$= \frac{-1 \pm i\sqrt{7}}{2\sqrt{2}}$$

Hence, option (*a*) is correct.

8. Roots of $(y + 1)(y - 3) + 7 = 0$ are given by:

(a) $-1 \pm \sqrt{3}i$ **(b)** $1 \pm \sqrt{3}i$

(c) $1 \pm \sqrt{2}i$ **(d)** $-1 \pm \sqrt{2}i$

Ans. (*b*) $1 \pm \sqrt{3}i$

Explanation: $(y + 1)(y - 3) + 7 = 0$

$y^2 - 2y - 3 + 7 = 0$

$y^2 - 2y + 4 = 0$

$D = 4 - 4 \times 1 \times 4$

$= 4 - 16$

$= -12$

$$x = \frac{-b \pm \sqrt{D}}{2a}$$

$$= \frac{+2 \pm \sqrt{-12}}{2}$$

$$= \frac{2 \pm 2\sqrt{3}i}{2}$$

$$= 1 \pm \sqrt{3}i$$

Hence, option (*b*)is correct.

9. Question 9. Solution of the equation $x^2 + 3x + 5 = 0$ is given by.

(a) $(-3 \pm \sqrt{13i})/2$ **(b)** $(-2 \pm \sqrt{13i})/2$

(c) $\frac{-3 \pm \sqrt{-11i}}{2}$ **(d)** $\frac{-2 \pm 11i}{2}$ **[DIKSHA]**

Ans. (*c*) $\frac{-3 \pm \sqrt{-11i}}{2}$

Explanation: The given quadratic equation is

$x^2 + 3x + 5 = 0$

Hence, comparing the equation with

$ax^2 + bx + c = 0$

$a = 1, b = 3, c = 5$

$D = b^2 - 4ac$

$D = 3^2 - 4 \times 1 \times 5$

$D = 9 - 20$

$D = -11$

$$\text{Roots} = \frac{-b \pm \sqrt{b^2 - 4ac}}{-2a}$$

$$\text{Roots} = \frac{-3 \pm \sqrt{11i^2}}{2 \times 1}$$

$$= \frac{-3 \pm \sqrt{-11i}}{2}$$

$$= \frac{-3 \pm i\sqrt{11}}{2}$$

$$\text{Roots are } \frac{-3 + \sqrt{11i}}{2}, \frac{-3 - \sqrt{11i}}{2}$$

Hence option (*c*) is correct.

Assertion-Reason (A-R)

DIRECTION: In the following questions, a statement of assertion (A) is followed by a statement of the reason (R). Mark the correct choice as:

(a) Both assertion (A) and reason (R) are true and reason (R) is the correct explanation of assertion (A).

(b) Both assertion (A) and reason (R) are true but reason (R) is not the correct explanation of assertion (A).

(c) Assertion (A) is true but reason (R) is false.

(d) Assertion (A) is false but reason (R) is true.

10. Assertion (A): If $3x^2 + 4x + 2 = 0$ then the equation has imaginary roots.

Reason (R): If $ax^2 + bx + c = 0$, $D = b^2 - 4ac$ is less than zero then the equation will have imaginary roots.

Ans. (*a*) *Both assertion (A) and reason (R) are true and reason (R) is the correct explanation of assertion (A).*

Explanation: $3x^2 + 4x + 2 = 0$

$a = 3, b = 4, c = -2$

$D = b^2 - 4ac$

$= 16 - 24$

$= -8$

$D < 0$ *i.e.* roots are imaginary.

Thus, assertion and reason both are true and reason is the correct explanation of assertion. Hence, the correct option is (*a*).

11. Assertion (A): Roots of the quadratic equation $x^2 + 3x + 5 = 0$ is $x = \frac{-3 \pm i\sqrt{11}}{2}$.

Reason (R): If $x^2 - x + 2 = 0$ is a quadratic equation, its roots are $\frac{1 \pm i\sqrt{7}}{2}$.

Ans. *(b) Both assertion (A) and reason (R) are true but reason (R) is not the correct explanation of assertion (A).*

Explanation: $x^2 + 3x + 5 = 0$

$$a = 1, b = 3, c = 5$$
$$D = b^2 - 4ac$$
$$= 9 - 20$$
$$= -11$$
$$D < 0$$
$$x = \frac{-3 \pm i\sqrt{11}}{2}$$

On comparing given equation

$$a = 1, b = -1, c = 2$$
$$D = b^2 - 4ac$$
$$= 1 - 8 = -7 < 0$$
$$x = \frac{-(-1) \pm \sqrt{-7}}{2}$$
$$= \frac{1 \pm \sqrt{7}i}{2}$$

12. Assertion (A): If $x^2 - x + 2 = 0$ has $\frac{1 \pm i\sqrt{7}}{2}$ roots.

Reason (R): If $D < 0$ then the equation has imaginary roots.

Ans. *(a) Both assertion (A) and reason (R) are true and reason (R) is the correct explanation of assertion (A).*

Explanation: $x^2 - x + 2 = 0$

$$D = 1 - 4 \times 1 \times 2$$
$$= 1 - 8$$
$$= -7$$
$$x = \frac{+1 \pm \sqrt{-7}}{2} = \frac{+1 \pm \sqrt{7}i}{2}$$

(R) If $D < 0$ then roots are imaginary.

Thus, assertion and reason both are true and the reason is the correct explanation of assertion. Hence, the correct option is (a).

13. Assertion (A): If $x^2 - x - 6 = 0$ has 3, –2 roots.

Reason (R): If $D > 0$ the equation has real and distinct roots.

Ans. *(a) Both assertion (A) and reason (R) are true and reason (R) is the correct explanation of assertion (A).*

Explanation: $x^2 - x - 6 = 0$

$$D = 1 - 4 \times 1 \times -6$$
$$= 1 + 24$$
$$= 25$$
$$x = \frac{-b \pm \sqrt{D}}{2a}$$
$$= \frac{1 \pm \sqrt{25}}{2}$$
$$= \frac{6}{2} = 3$$
$$= \frac{-4}{2} = -2$$

(R) If $D > 0$ roots are real and distinct.

CASE BASED Questions (CBQs)

[**4** & **5** marks]

Read the following passages and answer the questions that follow:

14. *An equation of the form $ax^2 + bx + c$, $a \neq 0$ is called a quadratic equation in variable, x where a, b and c are numbers (real and complex).*

The roots of the quadratic equation $ax^2 + bx + c = 0$, $a \neq 0$ are

$$\alpha = \frac{-b + \sqrt{b^2 - 4ac}}{2a}$$

and

$$\beta = \frac{-b - \sqrt{b^2 - 4ac}}{2a}$$

Now, if we look at these roots of the quadratic equation $ax^2 + bx + c = 0$; $a \neq 0$, we observe that the roots depend upon the value of the quantity $b^2 - 4ac$. This quantity is known as the discriminant of the quadratic equation and denoted by D.

There are the following cases:

Case I: If $b^2 - 4ac = 0$ i.e. $D = 0$, then $a = b = -\frac{b}{2a}$.

Thus, if $b^2 - 4ac = 0$, then the quadratic equation has real and equal roots, and each equal to $-b/2a$.

Case II: If a, b and c are rational numbers and $b^2 - 4ac > 0$ and it is a perfect square, then $D = \sqrt{b^2 - 4ac}$ is a rational number, and hence α and β are rational and unequal.

Case III: If $b^2 - 4ac > 0$, and it is not a perfect square, then roots are irrational and unequal.

Case IV: If $b^2 - 4ac < 0$, then the roots are complex conjugate of each other.

(A) Find the roots of a quadratic equation $2x^2 - 2\sqrt{3}x + \frac{21}{8} = 0$.

(B) Find the roots of a quadratic equation $25x^2 - 30x + 11 = 0$.

Ans. (A) We have, $2x^2 - 2\sqrt{3}x + \frac{21}{8} = 0$ ...(1)

On comparing equation (1) with

$ax^2 + bx + c = 0$

We get

$a = 2, b = -2\sqrt{3}$ and $c = \frac{21}{8}$

$\because \quad x = \frac{-b \pm \sqrt{b^2 - 4ac}}{2a}$

$\therefore \quad x = \frac{-(-2\sqrt{3}) \pm \sqrt{(-2\sqrt{3})^2 - 4 \times 2 \times \frac{21}{8}}}{2 \times 2}$

$= \frac{2\sqrt{3} \pm \sqrt{12-21}}{4} = \frac{2\sqrt{3} \pm \sqrt{-9}}{4}$

$= \frac{2\sqrt{3} \pm 3i}{4} = \frac{\sqrt{3}}{2} \pm \frac{3}{4}i \qquad [\because \sqrt{-1} = i]$

Hence, the roots are $\frac{\sqrt{3}}{2} + \frac{3}{4}i$ and $\frac{\sqrt{3}}{2} - \frac{3}{4}i$.

(B) Given, $25x^2 - 30x + 11 = 0$ ...(i)

On comparing equation (i) with

$ax^2 + bx + c = 0$

We get

$a = 25, b = -30$ and $c = 11$

$\because \quad x = \frac{-b \pm \sqrt{b^2 - 4ac}}{2a}$

$\therefore \quad x = \frac{30 \pm \sqrt{(-30)^2 - 4 \times 25 \times 11}}{2 \times 25}$

$\Rightarrow \quad x = \frac{30 \pm \sqrt{900 - 1100}}{50}$

$\Rightarrow \quad x = \frac{30 \pm \sqrt{-200}}{50}$

$\Rightarrow \quad x = \frac{30 \pm 10i\sqrt{2}}{50} \qquad [\because \sqrt{-1} = i]$

$\Rightarrow \quad x = \frac{3}{5} \pm \frac{\sqrt{2}}{5}i$

Hence, the roots are $\frac{3}{5} + \frac{\sqrt{2}}{5}i$ and $\frac{3}{5} - \frac{\sqrt{2}}{5}i$.

15. *A quadratic equation can be defined as an equation of degree 2. This means that the highest exponent of the polynomial in it is 2. The standard form of a quadratic equation is $ax^2 + bx + c = 0$, where a ,b and c are real numbers and $a \neq 0$. Every quadratic equation has two roots depending on the nature of its discriminant, $D = b^2 - 4ac$.*

(A) Which of the following quadratic equation have no real roots?

(a) $-4x^2 + 7x - 4 = 0$

(b) $-4x^2 + 7x - 2 = 0$

(c) $-2x^2 + 5x - 2 = 0$

(d) $3x^2 + 6x + 2 = 0$

(B) Which of the following quadratic equation have rational roots?

(a) $x^2 + x - 1 = 0$

(b) $x^2 - 5x + 6 = 0$

(c) $4x^2 - 3x - 2 = 0$

(d) $6x^2 - x + 11 = 0$

(C) Which of the following quadratic equation have irrational roots?

(a) $3x^2 + 2x + 2 = 0$

(b) $4x^2 - 7x + 3 = 0$

(c) $6x^2 - 3x - 5 = 0$

(d) $2x^2 + 3x - 2 = 0$

(D) Which of the following quadratic equations have equal roots?

(a) $x^2 - 3x + 4 = 0$

(b) $2x^2 - 2x + 1 = 0$

(c) $5x^2 - 10x + 1 = 0$

(d) $9x^2 + 6x + 1 = 0$

(E) Which of the following quadratic equations has two distinct real roots?

(a) $x^2 + 3x + 1 = 0$

(b) $-x^2 + 3x - 3 = 0$

(c) $4x^2 + 8x + 4 = 0$

(d) $3x^2 + 6x + 4 = 0$

Ans. (A) *(a) $-4x^2 + 7x - 4 = 0$*

Explanation: To have no real roots, discriminant ($D = b^2 - 4ac$) should be <0.

(a) $D = 7^2 - 4(-4)(-4) = 49 - 64 = -15 < 0$

(b) $D = 7^2 - 4(-4)(-2) = 49 - 32 = 17 > 0$

(c) $D = 5^2 - 4(-2)(-2) = 25 - 16 = 9 > 0$

(d) $D = 6^2 - 4(3)(2) = 36 - 24 = 12 > 0$

(B) *(b) $x^2 - 5x + 6 = 0$*

Explanation: To have rational roots, discriminant ($D = b^2 - 4ac$) should be > 0 and also a perfect square.

(a) $D = 1^2 - 4(1)(-1) = 1 + 4 = 5$, which is not a perfect square.

(b) $D = (-5)^2 - 4(1)(6) = 25 - 24 = 1$, which is a perfect square.

(c) $D = (-3)^2 - 4(4)(-2) = 9 + 32 = 41$, which is not a perfect square.

(d) $D = (-1)^2 - 4(6)(11) = 1 - 264 = -263$, which is not a perfect square.

(C) (c) $6x^2 - 3x - 5 = 0$

Explanation: To have irrational roots, discriminant ($D = b^2 - 4ac$) should be > 0 but not a perfect square.

(a) $D = 2^2 - 4(3)(2) = 4 - 24 = -20 < 0$,

(b) $D = (-7)^2 - 4(4)(3) = 49 - 48 = 1 > 0$, and also a perfect square.

(c) $D = (-3)^2 - 4(6)(-5) = 9 + 120 = 12 > 0$, and also not a perfect square.

(d) $D = 3^2 - 4(2)(-2) = 9 + 16 = 25 > 0$, and also a perfect square.

(D) (d) $9x^2 + 6x + 1 = 0$

Explanation: To have equal roots, discriminant ($D = b^2 - 4ac$) should be = 0.

(a) $D = (-3)^2 - 4(1)(4) = 9 + 16 = -7 < 0$

(b) $D = (-2)^2 - 4(2)(1) = 4 - 8 = -4 < 0$

(c) $D = (-10)^2 - 4(5)(1) = 100 - 20 = 80 > 0$

(d) $D = 6^2 - 4(9)(1) = 36 - 36 = 0$

(E) (a) $x^2 + 3x + 1 = 0$

Explanation: To have two distinct real roots, discriminant ($D = b^2 - 4ac$) should be > 0.

(a) $D = 3^2 - 4(1)(1) = 9 - 4 = 5 > 0$

(b) $D = 3^2 - 4(-1)(-3) = 9 - 12 = -3 < 0$

(c) $D = 8^2 - 4(4)(4) = 64 - 64 = 0$

(d) $D = 6^2 - 4(3)(4) = 36 - 48 = -12 < 0$

VERY SHORT ANSWER Type Questions (VSA)

[1 mark]

16. Solve the quadratic equation $3x^2 + x + 2 = 0$.

Ans. Here $a = 3, b = 1, c = 2$

So,
$$D = 1^2 - 4 \times 3 \times 2 = 1 - 24 = -23$$

So,
$$x = \frac{-b \pm \sqrt{D}}{2a} = \frac{-1 \pm \sqrt{-23}}{2 \times 3}$$

$$x = \frac{-1 \pm \sqrt{23}i}{6}$$

17. Find the value of P such that the difference of the roots of the equation $x^2 - Px + 8 = 0$ is 2. [NCERT Exemplar]

Ans. If $ax^2 + bx + c = 0$ is a quadratic equation then the sum of roots = $-b/a$ and the product of roots = c/a.

Let α, β be the roots of the equation

$x^2 - Px + 8 = 0$

Therefore $\alpha + \beta = P$ and $\alpha.\beta = 8$

Now $\alpha - \beta = \pm\sqrt{(\alpha+\beta)^2 - 4\alpha\beta}$

Or, $2 = \pm\sqrt{P^2 - 32}$

Squaring both sides, we have

$\Rightarrow$ $P^2 - 32 = 4$, i.e., $P = \pm 6$.

18. Solve the following quadratic equation $\sqrt{3}x^2 + 2x + \sqrt{3} = 0$.

Ans. Here $a = \sqrt{3}, b = 2, c = \sqrt{3}$

So,
$$D = 2^2 - 4 \times \sqrt{3} \times \sqrt{3} = 4 - 12 = -8$$

$$x = \frac{-b \pm \sqrt{D}}{2a} = \frac{-2 \pm \sqrt{-8}}{2\sqrt{3}} = \frac{-1 \pm \sqrt{2}i}{\sqrt{3}}$$

19. Solve $2x^2 + 4x + 5 = 0$.

Ans. Here $a = 2, b = 4, c = 5$

So,
$$D = 4^2 - 4 \times 2 \times 5 = 16 - 40 = -24$$

So,
$$x = \frac{-b \pm \sqrt{D}}{2a} = \frac{-4 \pm \sqrt{-24}}{4} = \frac{-2 \pm \sqrt{6}i}{2}$$

20. Find the value of a such that the sum of the squares of the roots of the equation $x^2 - (a - 2)x - (a + 1) = 0$ is least. [NCERT Exemplar]

Ans. Let α, β be the roots of the equation

Therefore, $\alpha + \beta = a - 2$ and $\alpha\beta = -(a + 1)$

Now $\alpha^2 + \beta^2 = (\alpha + \beta)^2 - 2\alpha\beta$

$= (a - 2)^2 + 2(a + 1)$

$= (a - 1)^2 + 5$

Therefore, $\alpha^2 + \beta^2$ will be minimum if $(a - 1)^2 = 0$, i.e. when $a = 1$.

21. Solve $3x^2 - 5x + \frac{10}{3} = 0$.

Ans. Here $a = 3, b = -5, c = \frac{10}{3}$

So, $D = b^2 - 4ac = 25 - 4 \times 3 \times \frac{10}{3}$

$x = 25 - 0$

$= -15$

So, $x = \frac{3 \pm \sqrt{-15}}{6} = \frac{3 \pm i\sqrt{15}}{6}$

SHORT ANSWER Type-I Questions (SA-I)

[**2** marks]

22. Solve the following quadratic equations by factorization method:

$2x^2 - 7ix - 6 = 0$

Ans. The given equation is

$2x^2 - 7ix - 6 = 0$

$\Rightarrow 2x^2 - 7ix - 6 = 0$

Splitting the middle term we have,

$\Rightarrow 2x^2 - 3ix - 4ix + 6i^2 = 0$

$\Rightarrow x(2x - 3i) - 2i(2x - 3i) = 0$

$\Rightarrow (2x - 3i)(x - 2i) = 0$

$\Rightarrow 2x - 3i = 0, x - 2i = 0$

$\Rightarrow x = 3i/2, x = 2i$

Hence, the roots of the equation are $3i/2$ and $2i$.

23. Solve the quadratic equation: $4x^2 + 3\underline{ix} - 3 = 0$.

Ans. Given equation $4x^2 + 3\underline{ix} - 3$,

Which is of the form $ax^2 + bx + c = 0$ where

$a = 4, b = 3i, c = -3$

Then, the roots of the given equation are

$$x = \frac{-b \pm \sqrt{b^2 - 4ac}}{2a} = \frac{-3i \pm \sqrt{(3i)^2 - 4.4.(-3)}}{2(4)}$$

$$= \frac{-3i \pm \sqrt{39}}{8}$$

Hence, $\frac{-3i + \sqrt{39}}{8}$ and $\frac{-3i - \sqrt{39}}{8}$ are the roots of the given equation.

24. Solve the equation $4x^2 - 4x + 2 = 0$ by using the general expressions for the roots of a quadratic equation.

Ans. Given equation is $4x^2 - 4x + 2 = 0$

Comparing the given equation with the general form $ax^2 + bx + c = 0$, we get

$a = 4, b = -4, c = 2$

Substituting the values of a, b, c in

$$\alpha = \frac{-b + \sqrt{b^2 - 4ac}}{2a} \text{ and } \beta = \frac{-b - \sqrt{b^2 - 4ac}}{2a}$$

we get

$$\alpha = \frac{4 + \sqrt{16 - 32}}{8} \text{ and } \beta = \frac{4 - \sqrt{16 - 32}}{8}$$

$$\Rightarrow \alpha = \frac{4 + \sqrt{-16}}{4} \text{ and } \beta = \frac{4 - \sqrt{-16}}{4}$$

$$\Rightarrow \alpha = \frac{4 + 4i}{4} \text{ and } \beta = \frac{4 - 4i}{4}$$

$\Rightarrow \alpha = 1 + i$ and $\beta = 1 - i$

Hence, the roots of the given equation are $1 + i$ and $1 - i$.

25. Solve the equation $3x^2 - 4x + 20/3$. **[DIKSHA]**

Ans. The given quadratic equation is

$3x^2 - 4x + 20/3 = 0$

The given equation can also be written as

$9x^2 - 12x + 20 = 0$

Comparing with $ax^2 + bx + c = 0$, we get

$a = 9, b = -12, c = 20$

$D = b^2 - 4ac = (-12)^2 - 4(9)(20)$

$= 144 - 720$

$= -576$

Therefore, the required solution is

$$x = \frac{-b \pm \sqrt{b^2 - 4ac}}{2a}$$

$$x = \frac{[-(-12) \pm \sqrt{-576}]}{(2 \times 9)}$$

$x = \frac{[12 \pm \sqrt{576 i}]}{2 \times 9}$

$x = \frac{[12 \pm 24i]}{2 \times 9}$

$x = \frac{6[2 \pm 4i]}{2 \times 9}$

$x = \frac{[2 \pm 4i]}{3}$

SHORT ANSWER Type-II Questions (SA-II)

[3 marks]

26. Solve the equation $9x^2 + 25 = 0$ by factorization method.

Ans. We have,

$9x^2 + 25 = 0$

$\Rightarrow 9x^2 - 25i^2 = 0$

$\Rightarrow (3x)^2 - (5i)^2 = 0$

$\Rightarrow (3x + 5i)(3x - 5i) = 0$

$\Rightarrow 3x + 5i = 0$ or $3x - 5i = 0$

$\Rightarrow x = -\frac{5}{3}i$, or $x = \frac{5}{3}i$

Hence, the roots of the given equation are $-\frac{5}{3}i$ and $\frac{5}{3}$.

27. Solve the equation $2x^2 - 10x + 8 = 0$ by factorization method.

Ans. We have, $2x^2 - 10x + 8 = 0$

$\Rightarrow 2x^2 - 8x - 2x + 8 = 0$

$\Rightarrow 2x(x - 4) - 2(x - 4) = 0$

$\Rightarrow (2x - 2)(x - 4) = 0$

$\Rightarrow 2x - 2 = 0$ or $x - 4 = 0$

Thus, $x = 1$ or $x = 4$

28. Solve the equation $9x^2 - 12x + 13 = 0$ by the factorization method only.

Ans. $9x^2 - 12x + 13 = 0$

$\Rightarrow 9x^2 - 12x + 4 + 9 = 0$

$\Rightarrow (3x - 2)^2 + 9 = 0$

$\Rightarrow (3x - 2)^2 - 9i^2 = 0$

$\Rightarrow \{(3x - 2) + 3i\}\{(3x - 2) - 3i\} = 0$

$\Rightarrow (3x - 2 + 3i)(3x - 2 - 3i) = 0$

$\Rightarrow 3x - 2 + 3i = 0$, or $3x - 2 - 3i = 0$

$\Rightarrow 3x = 2 - 3i$, or $3x = 2 + 3i$

$\Rightarrow x = 2 - \frac{3i}{3}$ and $x = 2 + \frac{3i}{3}$

LONG ANSWER Type Questions (LA)

[4 & 5 marks]

29. Find the square roots of the following complex number

$$x^2 + \frac{1}{x^2} - \frac{4}{i}\left(x - \frac{1}{x}\right).$$

Ans. Here, $x^2 + \frac{1}{x^2} - \frac{4}{i}\left(x - \frac{1}{x}\right)$

The above expression can be written in the form of

$a^2 + 2ab + b^2$

So, we get

$$= \left(x - \frac{1}{x}\right)^2 + (2i)^2 + 2.\left(\frac{-2}{i}\right).\left(x - \frac{1}{x}\right)$$

$$= \left(x - \frac{1}{x}\right)^2 + 2.\left(\frac{-2}{i}\right)\left(x - \frac{1}{x}\right) + \left(\frac{-2}{i}\right)^2$$

Here $a = \left(x - \frac{1}{x}\right)$ and $b = \left(\frac{-2}{i}\right)$

Now, applying formula

$a^2 + 2ab + b^2 = (a^2 + b^2)$

We get

$$\left(x - \frac{1}{x} - \frac{2}{i}\right)^2$$

Hence roots are

$$\left(x - \frac{1}{x} - \frac{2}{i}\right) \text{and} \left(x - \frac{1}{x} - \frac{2}{i}\right)$$

30. $z = p + iq$ and $z^2 = x + iy$ where p, q, x, y are real number show that

$$2p^2 = x + \sqrt{x^2 + y^2}.$$

Ans. Here,

$z = p + iq$

Squaring both sides, we get

$$z^2 = (p + iq)^2$$

$$\Rightarrow \quad z^2 = p^2 + (iq)^2 + 2pqi \quad ...(1)$$

As per the question $z^2 = x + iy$ ...(2)

Comparing (1) and (2) we get,

$\Rightarrow \; p^2 - q^2 + 2pqi = x + iy$

Comparing the real and imaginary part of both sides we get

$$p^2 - q^2 = x \quad ...(3)$$

$$2pq = y$$

Also,

$$p^2 + q^2 = \sqrt{x^2 + y^2} \quad ...(4)$$

Adding (3) and (4) we get, $2p^2 = x + \sqrt{x^2 + y^2}$.

Hence Proved.

31. Solve the following quadratic equation

$(2 + i)x^2 + (i - 5)x + (1 - i) = 0$

Ans. Comparing the given equation with the standard form of quadratic equation, we get

$$a = 2 + i$$

$$b = i - 5$$

$$c = (1 - i)$$

Now, $D = b^2 - 4ac$

$$\Rightarrow \quad D = (i - 5)^2 - 4(2 + i)(1 - i)$$

$$D = (-1 + 25 - 10i) - 4(2 + i)(1 - i)$$

$$= (24 - 10i) - 4(2 - i - 2i + 1)$$

$$= (24 - 10i) - 4(3 - 3i)$$

$$= 24 - 10i - 12 + 12i$$

$$= 12 + 2i$$

Or, $\sqrt{D} = \sqrt{12 + 2i}$

Therefore, the required solution is

$$x = \frac{-b \pm \sqrt{D}}{2a}$$

$$x = \frac{-(i-5) \pm (\sqrt{12+2i})}{2(2+i)}$$

5 Linear Inequalities

Linear inequations can be found all around us—we just need to know where to look. Consider the following scenario: On the highway, there are speed limits. When discussing these situations, we frequently use limits, such as "the speed limit is 55 miles per hour." However, we are not required to travel at 55 miles per hour on the highway.

Topic Notes

- *Linear Inequalities and their Algebraic Solutions*

LINEAR INEQUALITIES AND THEIR ALGEBRAIC SOLUTIONS

TOPIC 1

INTRODUCTION TO LINEAR INEQUALITY

An inequality is said to be linear, if the variable (s) occurs in first degree only and there is no term involving the product of the variables. e.g. $ax + b \leq 0$, $ax + by + c > 0$, $ax \leq 6$.

Two real numbers or two algebraic expression connected by the symbol '<' (less than), '>' (greater than), '≤' (less than or equal) or '≥' (greater than or equal) form a_n in equality or inequality.

An inequality can be of the following forms:

$a < b$ (read as 'a is less than b')

$a > b$ (read as 'a is greater than b')

$a \leq b$ (read as 'a is less than or equal to b')

$a \geq b$ (read as 'a is greater than or equal to b')

Inequality

Two real numbers or two algebraic expression related by the symbols

'<', '>', '≤' or '≥' from an inequality.

Linear Inequality

An inequality is said to be linear, if each variable occurs in first degree only and there is no term involving the product of the variables.

e.g., $ax + b \leq 0$, $ax + by + c > 0$, $ax \leq 4$.

Example 1: $\dfrac{3(x-2)}{5} \leq \dfrac{5(2-x)}{3}$ **[NCERT]**

Ans. We have, $\dfrac{3(x-2)}{5} \leq \dfrac{5(2-x)}{3} \Rightarrow \dfrac{3x-6}{5} \leq \dfrac{10-5x}{3}$

$\Rightarrow 9x - 18 \leq 50 - 25x$

Transposing the terms $(-25x)$ to LHS and the term (-18) to RHS,

$\Rightarrow 9x + 25x \leq 50 + 18$

$\Rightarrow 34x \leq 68$

$\Rightarrow x \leq \dfrac{68}{34}$

$\Rightarrow x \leq 2$

$\therefore$ Solution set = $(-\infty, 2)$

Example 2: $\dfrac{1}{2}\left(\dfrac{3x}{5}+4\right) \geq \dfrac{1}{3}(x-6)$. **[NCERT]**

Ans. We have,

$$\frac{1}{2}\left(\frac{3x}{5}+4\right) \geq \frac{1}{3}(x-6)$$

$$\Rightarrow \frac{1}{2}\left(\frac{3x}{5}+\frac{4}{1}\right) \geq \frac{1}{3}(x-6)$$

Taking LCM in LHS,

$$\frac{1}{2}\left(\frac{3x+20}{5}\right) \geq \frac{1}{3}(x-6)$$

$$\Rightarrow \frac{3x+20}{10} \geq \frac{x-6}{3}$$

$\Rightarrow 3(3x + 20) \geq 10(x - 6)$

$\Rightarrow 9x + 60 \geq 10x - 60$

Transposing the term $10x$ to LHS and the term 60 to RHS,

$9x - 10x \geq -60 - 60 \Rightarrow -x \geq -120$

Multiplying both sides by -1, we get

$x \leq 120$

$\therefore$ Solution set = $(-\infty, 120]$.

Example 3: $2(2x + 3) - 10 < 6(x - 2)$. **[NCERT]**

Ans. We have,

$2(2x + 3) - 10 < 6(x - 2)$

$\Rightarrow 4x + 6 - 10 < 6x - 12$

$\Rightarrow 4x - 4 < 6x - 12$

Transposing the term $6x$ to LHS and (-4) to RHS,

$\Rightarrow 4x - 6x < -12 + 4$

$\Rightarrow -2x < -8$

Dividing both sides by -2,

$$\Rightarrow \frac{-2x}{-2} > \frac{-8}{-2}$$

$\Rightarrow x > 4$

$\therefore$ Solution set = $(4, \infty)$.

TOPIC 2

ALGEBRAIC SOLUTION OF LINEAR INEQUALITIES IN ONE VARIABLE AND THEIR GRAPHICAL REPRESENTATION

Let us consider the inequality $15x < 200$

Obviously, x cannot be a negative integer or a fraction. Left-hand side (L.H.S) of this inequality is $15x$ and right-hand side (RHS) is 200. Therefore, we have

For $x = 0$, L.H.S. $= 15(0) = 0 < 200$ (R.H.S), which is true.

For $x = 1$, L.H.S. $= 15(1) = 15 < 200$ (R.H.S), which is true.

For $x = 2$, L.H.S. $= 15(2) = 30 < 200$, which is true.

For $x = 3$, L.H.S. $= 15(3) = 45 < 200$, which is true.

For $x = 4$, L.H.S. $= 15(4) = 60 < 200$, which is true.

For $x = 5$, L.H.S. $= 15(5) = 75 < 200$, which is true.

For $x = 6$, L.H.S. $= 15(6) = 90 < 200$, which is true.

In the above situation, we find that the values of x, which makes the above inequality a true statement, are 0, 1, 2, 3, 4, 5, 6. These values of x, which make above inequality a true statement, are called solutions of inequality and the set {0, 1, 2, 3, 4, 5, 6} is called its solution set.

As a result, any solution of an inequality in one variable is a variable value, making the proposition true.

We discovered the answer to the aforementioned inequality using a time-consuming trial and error process.

Important

- *Equal numbers can be added (or subtracted) to (from) both sides of an inequality.*
- *A non-zero number can be multiplied (or divided) on both sides of an inequality.*
- *Equal numbers can be added to (or withdrawn from) both sides of an inequality without changing its sign.*
- *An inequality can be multiplied (or divided) by the same positive value on both sides. The sign of inequality is reversed when both sides are multiplied or divided by a negative value.*
- *Any solution of an inequality in one variable is a value of the variable which makes it a true statement.*

Example 4: **$5x - 3 \geq 3x - 5$.** **[NCERT]**

Ans. We have, $5x - 3 \geq 3x - 5$

Transposing the term $3x$ to LHS and the term (-3) to RHS,

$$5x - 3x \geq -5 + 3$$

$$\Rightarrow \quad 2x \geq -2$$

$$\Rightarrow \quad \frac{2x}{2} \geq -\frac{2}{2}$$

$$\Rightarrow \quad x \geq \frac{-2}{2}$$

$$x \geq -1$$

$x \geq -1$

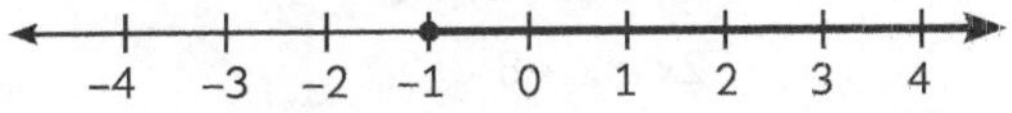

All the numbers on the right side of -1 will be greater than it.

$\therefore$ Solution set $= [-1, \infty)$.

Example 5: **$3(1 - x) < 2(x + 4)$.** **[NCERT]**

Ans. We have, $3(1 - x) < 2(x + 4) \Rightarrow 3 - 3x < 2x + 8$

Transposing the term $2x$ to the LHS and the term 3 to RHS,

$$-3x - 2x < 8 - 3$$

$$\Rightarrow \quad -5x < 5$$

$$\Rightarrow \quad \frac{-5x}{-5} > \frac{5}{-5}$$

$$\Rightarrow \quad x > \frac{-5}{5}$$

$$\Rightarrow \quad x > -1$$

$x > -1$ or $-1 < x$

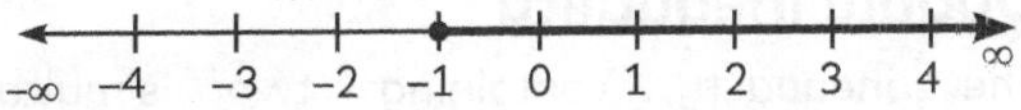

$\therefore$ Solution set $= (-1, \infty)$.

Example 6: **A man wants to cut three lengths from a single piece of board of length 91 cm. The second length is to be 3 cm longer than the shortest and the third length is to be twice as long as the shortest. What are the possible lengths of the shortest board if the third piece is to be at least 5cm longer than the second?**

[Hint: If x is the length of the shortest board, then x, (x + 3) and 2x are the lengths of the second and third piece, respectively. Thus, $x + (x + 3) + 2x \geq 91$ and $2x \geq (x + 3) + 5$]

Ans. Let the length of the shortest board be x cm.

Length of second board 3 cm longer than the shortest side $= x + 3$ cm

and length of the third board = Twice the shortest board

$= 2x$ cm

Given that maximum sum of length of the boards can be 91 cm.

i.e., sum of length of boards ≤ 91

$$x + (x + 3) + 2x \leq 91$$

$$4x + 3 \leq 91$$

$$4x \leq 91 - 3$$

$$4x \leq 88$$

$$x \le \frac{88}{4}$$

$$x \le 22$$

Also, the third piece is at least 5cm longer than the second piece.

$$2x \ge (x + 3) + 5$$

$$2x \ge x + 8$$

$$2x - x \ge 8$$

$$x \ge 8$$

Hence, $x \le 22$ and $x \ge 8$

i.e., $8 \le x \le 22$

Thus, the possible length of the shortest board is greater than or equal to 8cm but less than or equal to 22 cm.

TOPIC 3
TYPES OF INEQUALITIES

Strict Inequality

The inequality containing < or > is called strict inequality. A strict inequality can be of the following forms:

$a < b$ or $a > b$

Slack Inequality

The inequality containing ≤ or ≥ is called slack inequality. A slack inequality can be of the following forms:

$a \le b$ or $a \ge b$

Double Inequality

The inequality containing two simultaneous inequalities is called double inequality. A double inequality can be of the following forms:

$a < b < c$ or $a \le b < c$ or $a < b \le c$ or $a \le b \le c$

or $a > b > c$ or $a \ge b > c$ or $a > b \ge c$ or $a \ge b \ge c$

Linear Inequality in one Variable

An inequality of the form

$ax + b < 0$ or $ax + b \le 0$ or $ax + b > 0$ or $ax + b \ge 0$

Where $a, b \in R$ $(a \ne 0)$ and x is a real variable, is called linear inequality in one variable x.

Linear Inequality in two Variables

An inequality of the form

$ax + by + c < 0$ or $ax + by + c \le 0$

or $ax + by + c > 0$ or $ax + by + c \ge 0$

Where $a, b, c \in R$ $(a \ne 0, b \ne 0)$ and x, y are real variables, is called linear inequality in two variables x and y.

Quadratic Inequality in one Variable

An inequality of the form

$ax^2 + bx + c < 0$ or $ax^2 + bx + c \le 0$

or $ax^2 + bx + c > 0$ or $ax^2 + bx + c \ge 0$

Where $a, b, c \in R$ $(a \ne 0)$ and x is a real variable, is called quadratic inequality in one variable x.

Important

- ***Solution of an inequality:*** *The value(s) of the variable(s) that make the inequality a true statement is called the solution of the given inequality.*
- ***Solution set of an inequality:*** *The set of all possible solutions of an inequality is called the solution set of the given inequality.*

Concept of Intervals

Let's start with the most basic definition: In mathematics, an interval is a set of real numbers between two given numbers, called the endpoints of the interval. It is formed by all the numbers lying between the two endpoints of the set.

In mathematics, a (real) interval is a set of real numbers that contains all real numbers lying between any two numbers of the set. For example, the set of numbers x satisfying $0 \le x \le 1$ is an interval which contains 0, 1, and all numbers in between.

Interval notation is used to express the set of inequalities. There are 3 types of interval notation: open interval closed interval, and half-open interval. The interval with no infinity symbol is called a bounded interval. The interval containing the infinity symbol is called an unbounded interval.

Compound Inequality

An inequality that contains at least two inequalities separated by either 'and' or 'or' is called compound inequalities.

The solution set of a compound inequality with an 'and' represents the intersection of the solution sets of the individual linear inequalities. The compound inequality of the form '$x > a$ and $x < b$' can be expressed as '$x > a, x < b$' or '$a < x < b$'.

The solution set of a compound inequality with an 'or' represents the union of the solution sets of the individual linear inequalities. For instance, the compound inequality of the form '$x > 2$ or $x > 3$' can be expressed as '$x > 2$'.

Absolute Value Inequality

Absolute value of a Real number: Let x be any real number. Then, the absolute value of x is given by

$$|x| = \begin{cases} x & \text{if } \geq 0 \\ -x & \text{if } x < 0 \end{cases}$$

Clearly, $|x| \geq 0$. Also, $|x|$ represents the distance of x from 0.

For instance, $|-2| = |2| = 2$. Also, both -2 and 2 are two units from zero.

We have the following four types of absolute-value inequalities:

1. $|x| < a$, where a is any positive real number.

   This inequality represents that the distance of x from 0 is less than a.

   Hence, the solution set of given inequality $= \{x \in R: -a < x < a\} = (-a, a)$.

   On the number line $(-a, a)$ may be represented as shown below:

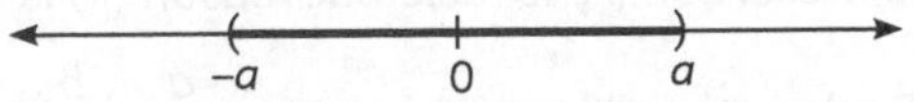

2. $|x| \leq a$, where a is any positive real number.

   This inequality represents that the distance of x from 0 is less than or equal to a.

   Hence, the solution set of given inequality $= \{x \in R: -a \leq x \leq a\} = [-a, a]$.

   On the number line $[-a, a]$ may be represented as shown below:

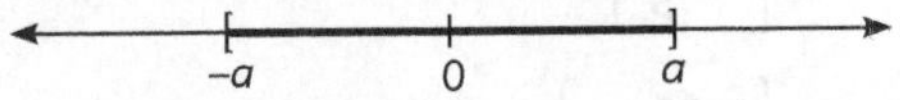

3. $|x| > a$, where a is any positive real number.

   This inequality represents that the distance of x from 0 is greater than a.

   Hence, the solution set of given inequality $= \{x \in R: x < -a \text{ or } x > a\} = (-\infty, -a) \cup (a, \infty)$.

   The representation on the number line of the solution is as shown below:

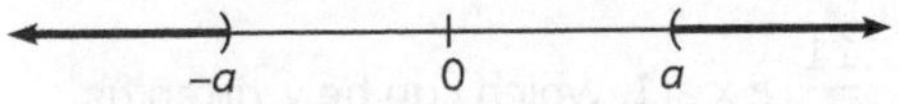

4. $|x| \geq a$, where a is any positive real number.

   This inequality represents that the distance of x from 0 is greater than or equal to a.

   Hence, the solution set of given inequality $= \{x \in R: x \leq -a \text{ or } x \geq a\} = (-\infty, -a] \cup [a, \infty)$.

   The representation on the number line of the solution is as shown below:

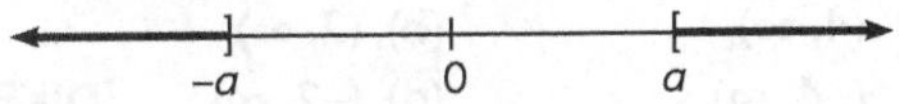

OBJECTIVE Type Questions

[1 mark]

Multiple Choice Questions

1. If $|3 - 6x| \geq 9$, then $x \in$:

(a) $(-\infty, -1) \cup (3, \infty)$ (b) $(-\infty, 1] \cup (2, \infty)$

(c) $(-\infty, -1) \cup (0, \infty)$ (d) $(-\infty, -1) \cup (2, \infty)$

Ans. *(d) $(-\infty, -1) \cup (2, \infty)$*

Explanation: We have, $|3 - 6x| \geq 9$

$\Rightarrow 3 - 6x \leq -9$ or $3 - 6x \geq 9$

$\Rightarrow -6x \leq -12$ or $-6x \geq 6$

$\Rightarrow x \geq 2$ or $x \leq -1$

$\Rightarrow (-\infty, -1) \cup (2, \infty)$

2. If x is a real number and $|x| < 3$, then x lies between:

(a) $x \geq 3$ (b) $x \leq -3$

(c) $-3 \leq x \leq 3$ (d) $-3 < x < 3$ [DIKSHA]

Ans. *(d) $-3 < x < 3$*

Explanation: $|x| < 3$

Here, x is a real number

So,

$x < 3$

$-x < 3 \Rightarrow x > -3$

$x \in (-3, 3)$

Hence, option (d) is correct.

3. If $2x - 1 < 6 + x$, $4 - 3x \leq 1$, then $x \in$

(a) $[1, 7]$ (b) $[-1, 7]$

(c) $[1, 7)$ (d) $(1, 7)$

Ans. *(c) $[1, 7)$*

Explanation: We have, $2x - 1 < 6 + x$

$\Rightarrow x < 7$

Also, we have $4 - 3x \leq 1$

$\Rightarrow -3x \leq -3$

$\Rightarrow x \geq 1$

Thus, solution of the given system are all real number lying between 1 and 7 including 1, i.e., $1 \leq x < 7$.

$\therefore x \in [1, 7)$

4. If $-8 \leq 5x - 3 < 7$, then $x \in$:

(a) $(-1, 2)$ (b) $[-1, 2)$

(c) $[-2, \infty)$ (c) $[-2, 0)$

Ans. *(b) $[-1, 2)$*

Explanation: We have, $-8 \leq 5x - 3 < 7$

$\Rightarrow -5 \leq 5x < 10$

$\Rightarrow -1 \leq x < 2 \therefore x \in [-1, 2)$

5. If $-3 \leq \frac{5-3x}{2} \leq 4$, then x:

(a) $\left[1, \frac{11}{3}\right]$ (b) $[-5, 5]$

(c) $\left[-\frac{11}{3}, \infty\right]$ (d) $[-\infty, \infty]$

Ans. (a) $\left[1, \frac{11}{3}\right]$

Explanation: We have, $-3 \leq \frac{5-3x}{2} \leq 4$

$\Rightarrow -6 \leq 5 - 3x \leq 8$ or $-11 \leq -3x \leq 3$

$\Rightarrow \frac{11}{3} \geq x \geq 1$, which can be written as

$\frac{11}{3} \geq x \geq 1.$

$\therefore\ x \in 1, \frac{11}{3}$

6. The given inequality for the real x : $4x + 3 < 5x + 7$. The solution set is:

(a) $(4, \infty)$ (b) $(2, \infty)$

(c) $(-4, \infty)$ (d) $(-2, \infty)$ [DIKSHA]

Ans. *(c) $(-4, \infty)$*

Explanation: $4x + 3 < 5x + 7$

$\Rightarrow \quad 3 - 7 < 5x - 4x$

$-4 < x$ or, $x > -4$

$x \in (-4, \infty)$

Hence, option (c) is correct.

7. If $3x - 1 < 5 + x$, $6 - 5x \leq 1$, then $x \in$:

(a) $[1, 3]$ (b) $[-1, 3]$

(c) $[1, 3)$ (d) $(1, 3)$

Ans. *(c) $[1, 3)$*

Explanation: We have, $3x - 1 < 5 + x \Rightarrow x < 3$

Also, we have $6 - 5x \leq 1 \Rightarrow -5x \leq -5 \Rightarrow x \geq 1$

Thus, solution of the given system are all real number lying between 1 and 3 including 1, i.e., $1 \leq x < 3$.

$\therefore\ x \in [1, 3)$

Hence, option (c) is correct.

8. If $\frac{x+3}{x+5} > 3$, then $x \in$:

(a) $(-6, 5)$ (b) $(-6, -\infty)$

(c) $(-6, \infty)$ (d) $(6, 12)$

Ans. *(b) $(-6, -\infty)$*

Explanation: We have, $x + 3 > 3x + 15$

$\Rightarrow -12 > 2x \Rightarrow -6 > x$

$\Rightarrow x < -6$

Hence, option (b) is correct.

Assertion-Reason (A-R)

DIRECTION: In the following questions, a statement of assertion (A) is followed by a statement of the reason (R). Mark the correct choice as:

(a) Both assertion (A) and reason (R) are true and reason (R) is the correct explanation of assertion (A).

(b) Both assertion (A) and reason (R) are true but reason (R) is not the correct explanation of assertion (A).

(c) Assertion (A) is true but reason (R) is false.

(d) Assertion (A) is false but reason (R) is true.

9. Assertion: If $a < b$, $c < 0$ then $\frac{a}{c} < \frac{b}{c}$.

Reason: If both sides are divided by the same negative quantity, then the inequality is reversed.

Ans. *(d) Assertion (A) is false but reason (R) is true.*

Explanation: If $a < b$, $c < 0$ then $\frac{a}{c} > \frac{b}{c}$.

10. Assertion: If $-5 \leq 2x + 9 \leq 2$, then $x \in [-7, -3.5]$.

Reason: The representation on the number line of $-5 \leq 2x + 9 \leq 2$ is

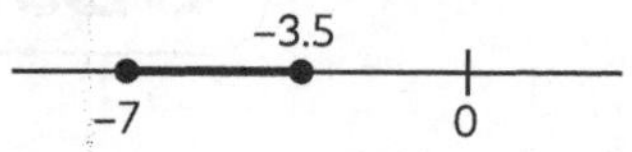

Ans. *(a) Both assertion (A) and reason (R) are true and reason (R) is the correct explanation of assertion (A).*

Explanation: We have $-5 \leq 2x + 9 \leq 2$

$\Rightarrow -14 \leq 2x \leq -7$

$\Rightarrow -7 \leq x \leq \frac{-7}{2}$

$\therefore\ x \in \left[-7, \frac{-7}{2}\right]$

11. Assertion: If $11x - 9 \leq 68$, then $x \in (-\infty, 7)$.

Reason: If an inequality consists of sign $\leq$ or $\geq$, then the point on the line are also included in the solution region.

Ans. *(d) Assertion (A) is false but reason (R) is true.*

Explanation: We have $11x - 9 \leq 68$,

$\Rightarrow 11x \leq 77$

$\Rightarrow x \leq 7$

$\therefore\ x \in (-\infty, 7]$

So, assertion is false but the reason is true.

12. **Assertion:** $|3x - 5| > 9$

$$\Rightarrow x \in \left(-\infty, \frac{-4}{3}\right) \cup \left(\frac{14}{3}, \infty\right).$$

Reason: The reason containing all the solutions of an inequality is called the solution region.

Ans. (b) *Both assertion (A) and reason (R) are true but reason (R) is not the correct explanation of assertion (A).*

Explanation: We have $|3x - 5| > 9$

$\Rightarrow 3x - 5 < -9$ or $3x - 5 > 9$

$\Rightarrow 3x < -4$ or $3x > 14$

$\Rightarrow x < \frac{-4}{3}$ or $x > \frac{14}{3}$

$\therefore\ x \in \left(-\infty, \frac{-4}{3}\right) \cup \left(\frac{14}{3}, \infty\right)$

CASE BASED Questions (CBQs)

[**4** & **5** marks]

Read the following passages and answer the questions that follow:

13. *Reema went to a stationery shop with Rs 100 to buy notebooks. The price of each notebook is Rs 25. Let x denotes the number of notebooks.*

(A) The inequality which represents the above situation is:

(a) $25x > 100$ (b) $25x \geq 100$

(c) $25x < 100$ (d) $25x \leq 100$

(B) The maximum number of notebooks that Reema can buy is:

(a) 2 (b) 3

(c) 4 (d) 5

(C) The graph representing the above situation is:

(a) 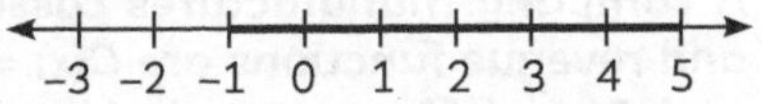

(b) 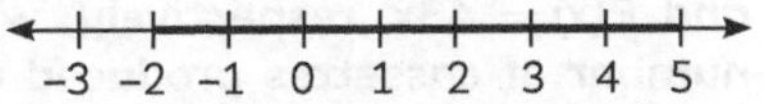

(c) 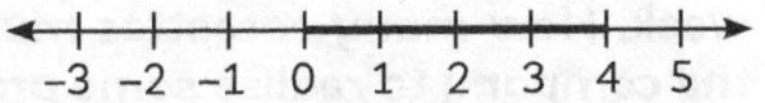

(d) 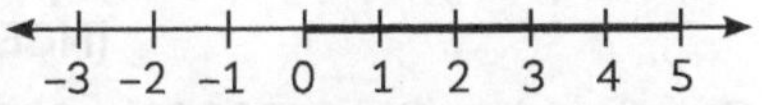

(D) If Reema gets discount of ₹ 5 on each notebook, then the maximum number of notebooks that she can buy is:

(a) 2 (b) 3

(c) 4 (d) 5

(E) If Reema gets ₹ 25 extra from her mother, then the inequality representing the given situation is:

(a) $25x \geq 125$ (b) $25x \leq 125$

(c) $25x \geq 100$ (d) $25x \leq 100$

Ans. (A) *(d) $25x \leq 100$*

Explanation: Here, x denotes the number of notebooks.

Cost of one notebook = ₹ 25

Total amount spent by her = ₹ $25x$

As she has the total amount of ₹ 100

$\therefore$ Required inequality is $25x \leq 100$

(B) *(c) 4*

Explanation: We have, $25x \leq 100$

$\Rightarrow x \leq 4$, where x is the number of notebooks

$\therefore$ The maximum number of notebooks that Reema can buy is 4.

(C) *(c)* 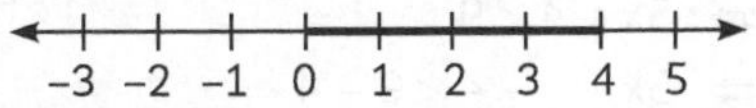

Explanation: As, x represent the number of notebooks

$\therefore\quad x \geq 0$ ...(1)

Also, $x \leq 4$ ...(2)

Combining (1) and (2), we get

$0 \leq x \leq 4$

(D) *(d) 5*

Explanation: If Reema gets discount of ₹ 5 on each notebook, then the cost of one notebook = ₹ 20

Also, $20x \leq 100$

$\Rightarrow x \leq 5$

$\therefore$ The maximum number of notebooks that

Reema can buy is 5.

(E) *(b) $25x \leq 125$*

Explanation: If Reema gets ₹ 25 extra from her mother, then she has the total amount of ₹ 125.

Required inequality is $25x \leq 125$.

14. *Amit's mother gave him ₹ 200 to buy some packets of rice and maggie from the market. The cost of one packet of rice is ₹ 30 and that of one packet of maggie is ₹ 20. Let x denotes the number of packet of rice and y denotes the number of packets of maggie.*

(A) Find the inequality that represents the given situation.

(B) If he buys 4 packets of rice and spends entire amount of Rs 200, then find the maximum number of packets of maggie that he can buy.

Ans. (A) Total amount = ₹ 200

Cost of one packet of rice = ₹ 30

And cost of one packet of maggie = ₹ 20

Here, x and y denote the number of packets of rice and maggie respectively,

Total amount spent by Amit is $30x + 20y$.

$\therefore$ Required inequality is $30x + 20y \leq 200$

(B) If he spends his entire amount, then

We have, $30x + 20y = 200$

Since, number of packet of rice = 4

$\therefore$ At $x = 4$, equation (1) becomes

$30 \times 4 + 20y = 200$

$\Rightarrow \quad 120 + 20y = 200$

$\Rightarrow \quad 20y = 200 - 120$

$\Rightarrow \quad 20y = 80$

$\therefore$ Maximum number of packets of maggie that he can buy is 4.

VERY SHORT ANSWER Type Questions (VSA)

[1 mark]

15. Solve the following inequality:

$10x + 4 < 5x + 9$.

Ans. We have, $10x + 4 < 5x + 9$

$\Rightarrow 10x + 4 - 5x < 5x + 9 - 5x$

[On subtracting 5x from both sides]

$\Rightarrow 5x + 4 < 9$

$\Rightarrow 5x + 4 - 4 < 9 - 4$

[On subtracting 4 from both sides]

$\Rightarrow 5x < 5$

$\Rightarrow \frac{5x}{5} < \frac{5}{5}$ [On dividing both sides by 5]

$\Rightarrow x < 1$

Hence, the solution set of given inequality $= \{x \in R : x < 1\} = (-\infty, 1)$.

16. Solve the following equation:

$3x + 17 \leq 2\,(1 - x)$.

Ans. We have

$3x + 17 \leq 2\,(1 - x)$

$\Rightarrow \quad 3x + 17 \leq 2 - 2x$

$\Rightarrow \quad 3x + 2x \leq 2 - 17$

[$\because$ Transposing $-2x$ to LHS and 17 to RHS]

$\Rightarrow \quad 5x \leq -15$

$\Rightarrow \quad \frac{5x}{5} \leq \frac{-15}{5}$

$\Rightarrow \quad x \leq -3$

$\Rightarrow x \in (-\infty, -3]$

Hence, the solution set of the given in equation is $(-\infty, -3]$, which can be represent on real line as shown in figure.

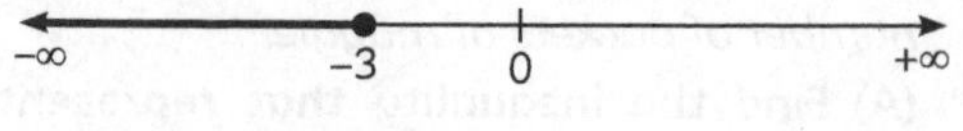

17. $4x + 3 \geq 2x + 17$, $3x - 5 < -2$.

[NCERT Exemplar]

Ans. We have, $4x + 3 \geq 2x + 17$

$\Rightarrow 4x - 2x \geq 17 - 3 \Rightarrow 2x \geq 14$

$\Rightarrow x \geq \frac{14}{2}$

$\Rightarrow x \geq 7$ ...(i)

Also, we have $3x - 5 < -2$

$\Rightarrow 3x < -2 + 5 \Rightarrow 3x < 3$

$\Rightarrow x < 1$ ...(ii)

On combining eq. (i) and (ii) we see that solution is not possible because nothing is common between these two solutions, (i.e., $x < 1, x \geq 7$).

18. A company manufactures cassettes. Its cost and revenue functions are $C(x) = 26000 + 30x$ and $R(x) = 43x$, respectively, where x is the number of cassettes produced and sold in a week. How many cassettes must be sold by the company to realise some profit?

[NCERT Exemplar]

Ans. Cost function, $C(x) = 26000 + 30x$ and Revenue function, $R(x) = 43x$

For profit, $R(x) >$

or, $C(x) < R(x)$

$\Rightarrow 26000 + 30x < 43x$

$\Rightarrow 30x - 43x < -26000$

$\Rightarrow -13x < -26000$

$\Rightarrow 13x > 26000$

$\Rightarrow x > \frac{26000}{13}$

$\therefore \quad x > 2000$

Hence, more than 2000 cassettes must be produced to get profit.

SHORT ANSWER Type-I Questions (SA-I)

[2 marks]

19. Solve $-15x > 45$, when

(A) x is a natural number.

(B) x is an integer.

Ans. We have, $-15x > 45$

$$\Rightarrow \frac{-15x}{-15} < \frac{45}{-15}$$

[On dividing both sides by -15]

$\Rightarrow x < -3$

(A) Given that x is a natural number, i.e., $x \in N$.

Hence, the solution set of given inequality $= \{x \in N : x < -3\}$ = No Solution.

(B) Given that x is an integer, i.e., $x \in Z$.

Hence, the solution set of given inequality $= \{x \in Z : x < -3\} = \{......, -5, -4\}$.

20. Solve $40x < 100$. when

(A) x is a natural number.

(B) x is an integer.

Ans. We have, $40x < 100$

$$\Rightarrow \frac{40x}{40} < \frac{100}{40}$$ [On dividing both sides by 24]

$$\Rightarrow x < \frac{5}{2}$$

(A) Given that x is a natural number, i.e., $x \in N$.

Hence, the solution set of given inequality

$$= \left\{x \in N : x < \frac{5}{2}\right\} = \{1, 2\}$$

(B) Given that x is an integer, i.e., $x \in Z$.

Hence, the solution set of given inequality

$$= \left\{x \in Z : x < \frac{5}{2}\right\} = \{......, -2, -1, 0, 1, 2\}.$$

21. The water acidity in a pool is considered normal when the average pH reading of three daily measurements is between 8.2 and 8.5. If the first two pH readings are 8.48 and 8.35, then find the range of pH value for the third reading that will result in the acidity level being normal. [NCERT Exemplar]

Ans. Given, first pH value = 8.48 and second pH value = 8.35

Let third pH value be x.

Since, it is given that average pH value lies between 8.2 and 8.5.

$$\therefore \ 8.2 < \frac{8.48 + 8.35 + x}{3} < 8.5$$

$$\Rightarrow 8.2 < \frac{16.83 + x}{3} < 8.5$$

$\Rightarrow 3 \times 8.2 < 16.83 + x < 8.5 \times 3$

$\Rightarrow 24.6 < 16.83 + x < 25.5$

$\Rightarrow 24.6 - 16.83 < x < 25.5 - 16.83$

$\Rightarrow 7.77 < x < 8.67$

Thus, third pH value lies between 7.77 and 8.67.

22. Find $x^2 + 4ax + 4 > 0$ for all x. [DIKSHA]

Ans. Given, $x^2 + 4ax + 4 > 0$

$\Rightarrow x^2 + 4ax + 4a^2 + 4 - 4a^2 > 0$

$\Rightarrow (x + 2a)^2 + (4 - 4a^2)^2 > 0$

$\Rightarrow 4 - 4a^2 > 0$

$\Rightarrow 4 > 4a^2$

$\Rightarrow 1 > a^2$

$\Rightarrow |a| < 1 - 1 < a < 1$

SHORT ANSWER Type-II Questions (SA-II)

[3 marks]

23. Solve: $-5 \le \frac{2-3x}{4} \le 9$. [NCERT Exemplar]

Ans. We have, $-5 \le \frac{2-3x}{4} \le 9$

$$\Rightarrow -5 \times 4 \le \frac{2-3x}{4} \times 4 \le 9 \times 4$$

[Multiplying throughout by 4]

$\Rightarrow -20 \le 2 - 3x \le 36$

$\Rightarrow -20 - 2 \le 2 - 3x - 2 \le 36 - 2$

[Subtracting 2 throughout]

$\Rightarrow -22 \le -3x \le 34$

$$\Rightarrow \frac{-22}{-3} \ge \frac{-3x}{-3} \ge \frac{34}{-3}$$

[Dividing throughout by – 3]

$$\Rightarrow \frac{22}{3} \ge x \ge \frac{-34}{3}$$

$$\Rightarrow \frac{-34}{3} \le x \le \frac{22}{3}$$

$\Rightarrow x \in \left[\frac{-34}{3}, \frac{22}{3}\right]$

Hence, the interval $\left[\frac{-34}{3}, \frac{22}{3}\right]$ is the solution set of the given system of in equations.

24. Solve $-11 \le 4x - 3 \le 13$.

Ans. We have,

$- 11 \le 4x - 3 \le 13 \Leftrightarrow -11 \le 4x - 3$ and $4x - 3 \le 13$

Thus, we have two inequalities and we wish to solve them simultaneously. Instead of solving these inequalities by using the method discussed in the first three examples, let us solve them directly in a different way as given below.

We have,

$- 11 \le 4x - 3 \le 13$

$\Rightarrow -11 + 3 \le 4x - 3 + 3 \le 13 + 3$ [Adding 3 throughout]

$\Rightarrow -8 \le 4x \le 16$

$\Rightarrow \frac{-8}{4} \le x \le \frac{16}{4}$ [Dividing by 4 throughout]

$\Rightarrow -2 \le x \le 4$

$\Rightarrow x \in [-2, 4]$

Hence, the interval [–2, 4] is the solution set of the given system of in equations.

25. Solve the following system of inequalities $\frac{2x+1}{7x-1} > 5$, $\frac{x+7}{x-8} > 2$. [NCERT Exemplar]

Ans. The given system of inequalities is

$$\frac{2x+1}{7x-1} > 5 \quad ...(i)$$

and

$$\frac{x+7}{x-8} > 2 \quad ...(ii)$$

Now, $\frac{(2x+1) - 5(7x-1)}{7x-1} > 0$

$\Rightarrow \frac{2x+1-35x+5}{7x-1} > 0$

$\Rightarrow \frac{-33x+6}{7x-1} > 0$

$\Rightarrow \frac{33x-6}{7x-1} < 0$

$\Rightarrow x \in \left(\frac{1}{7}, \frac{6}{33}\right)$ ...(iii)

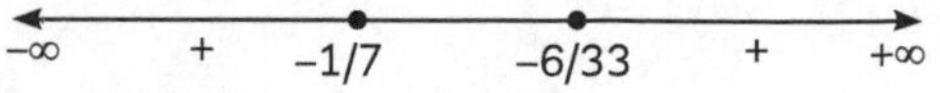

and $\frac{x+7}{x-8} > 2$

$\Rightarrow \frac{x+7}{x-8} - 2 > 0$

$\Rightarrow \frac{x+7-2(x-8)}{x-8} > 0$

$\Rightarrow \frac{x+7-2x+16}{x-8} > 0$

$\Rightarrow \frac{-x+23}{x-8} > 0$

$\Rightarrow \frac{x-23}{x-8} < 0$

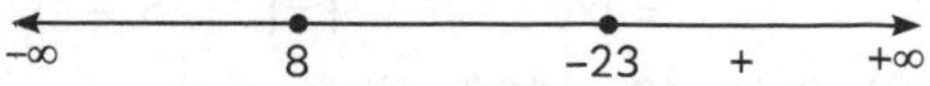

In the figure (–23 should be 23)

$\Rightarrow x \in (8, 23)$ ...(iv)

Since, the intersection of eq. (iii) and (iv) is the null set. Hence, the given system of equation has no solution.

26. Solve the following system of in equations: $|x - 1| \le 5$, $|x| \ge 2$ [NCERT Exemplar]

Ans. The given system of inequalities is

$|x - 1| \le 5$ ...(i)

$|x - 1| \ge 2$ ...(ii)

Now, $|x - 1| \le 5$ $[|x - 1| \le r \Leftrightarrow a - r \le a + r]$

Thus, the solution set of (i) is the interval

$x \in [-4, 6]$

And, $|x| \ge 2 \Leftrightarrow x \le -2$, or $x \ge 2$

$[|x| \ge a \Rightarrow x \le -a$ or $x \le a]$

$\Leftrightarrow x \in (-\infty, -2] \cup [2, \infty)$.

Thus, the solution set of (ii) is $(-\infty, -2] \cup [2, \infty)$.

The solution sets of inequalities (i) and (ii) are represented graphically in figure (i) and (ii) respectively. The interaction of these two is

$[-4, -2] \cup [2, 6]$

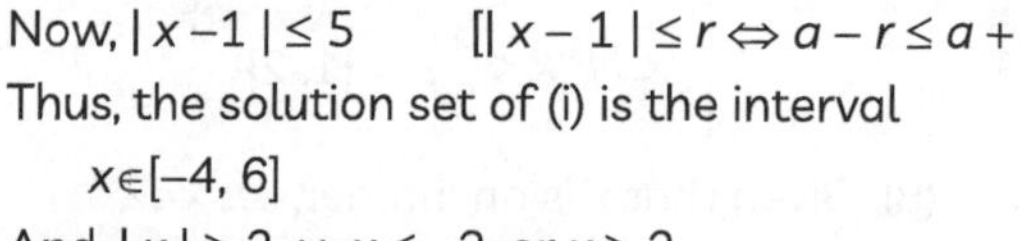

Hence, the solution set of the given system of in equations is $[-4, -2] \cup [2, 6]$.

LONG ANSWER Type Questions (LA)

[4 & 5 marks]

27. A solution of 9% acid is to be diluted by adding 3% acid solution to it. The resulting mixture is to be more than 5% but less than 7% acid. If there is 460L of the 9% solution, how many litres of 3% solution will have to be added? [NCERT Exemplar]

Ans. Let x L of 3% solution be added to 460 L of 9% solution of acid.

Then, the total quantity of mixture = $(460 + x)$ L

Total acid content in the $(460 + x)$ L of mixture

$$= \left(460 \times \frac{9}{100} + x \times \frac{3}{100}\right)$$

It is given that acid content in the resulting mixture must be more than 5% but less than 7% acid.

Therefore,

$$5\% \text{ of } (460 + x) < 460 \times \frac{9}{100} + \frac{3x}{100} < 7\% \text{ of } (460 + x)$$

$$\Rightarrow \frac{5}{100} \times (460 + x) < 460 \times \frac{9}{100} + \frac{3}{100}x < \frac{7}{100} \times (460 + x)$$

$$\Rightarrow 5 \times (460 + x) < 460 \times 9 + 3x < 7 \times (460 + x)$$ (multiplying by 100)

$$\Rightarrow 2300 + 5x < 4140 + 3x < 3220 + 7x$$

Taking first two inequalities,

$$2300 + 5x < 4140 + 3x$$

$$\Rightarrow 5x - 3x < 4140 - 2300$$

$$\Rightarrow 2x < 1840$$

$$\Rightarrow x < \frac{1840}{2}$$

$$\Rightarrow x < 920$$

Taking last two inequalities,

$$4140 + 3x < 3220 + 7x$$

$$\Rightarrow 3x - 7x < 3220 - 4140$$

$$\Rightarrow -4x < -920$$

$$\Rightarrow 4x > 920$$

$$\Rightarrow x > \frac{920}{4}$$

$$\Rightarrow x > 230 \quad ...(ii)$$

Hence, the number of litres of the 3% solution of acid must be more than 230 L and less than 920 L.

28. During preparation, a solution of 6% alcohol is to be diluted by adding 2% concentrated solution to it. The resulting mixture is to be more than 4% but less than 6% acid. If there is 660L of the 7% solution, how many litres of 2% solution will have to be added?

Ans. Let xL of 2% solution be added to $660L$ of 6% solution of acid.

Then, the total quantity of mixture = $(660 + x)L$

Total acid content in the $(660 + x)L$ of mixture

$$= (660 \times \frac{6}{100} + x \times \frac{2}{100})$$

It is given that acid content in the resulting mixture must be more than 4% but less than 7% acid.

Therefore,

$$4\% \text{ of } (660 + x) < 660 \times \frac{6}{100} + \frac{2x}{100} < 7\% \text{ of } (660 + x)$$

$$\Rightarrow \frac{4}{100} \times (660 + x) < 660 \times \frac{6}{100} + \frac{2}{100}x < \frac{7}{100} \times (660 + x)$$

$$\Rightarrow 4 \times (660 + x) < 660 \times 6 + 2x < 7 \times (660 + x)$$ (multiplying by 100)

$$\Rightarrow 2540 + 4x < 3960 + 2x < 4620 + 7x$$

Taking first two inequalities,

$$2540 + 4x < 3960 + 2x$$

$$\Rightarrow 4x - 2x < 3960 - 2540$$

$$\Rightarrow 2x < 1420$$

$$\Rightarrow x < \frac{1420}{2}$$

$$\Rightarrow x < 710$$

Taking last two inequalities,

$$3960 + 2x < 4620 + 7x$$

$$\Rightarrow -7x + 2x < 4620 - 3960$$

$$\Rightarrow -5x < 660$$

$$\Rightarrow x > \frac{660}{5}$$

$$\Rightarrow x > 132 \quad ...(ii)$$

Hence, the number of litres of the 2% solution of acid must be more than 132 L and less than 710 L.

6 Permutations & Combinations

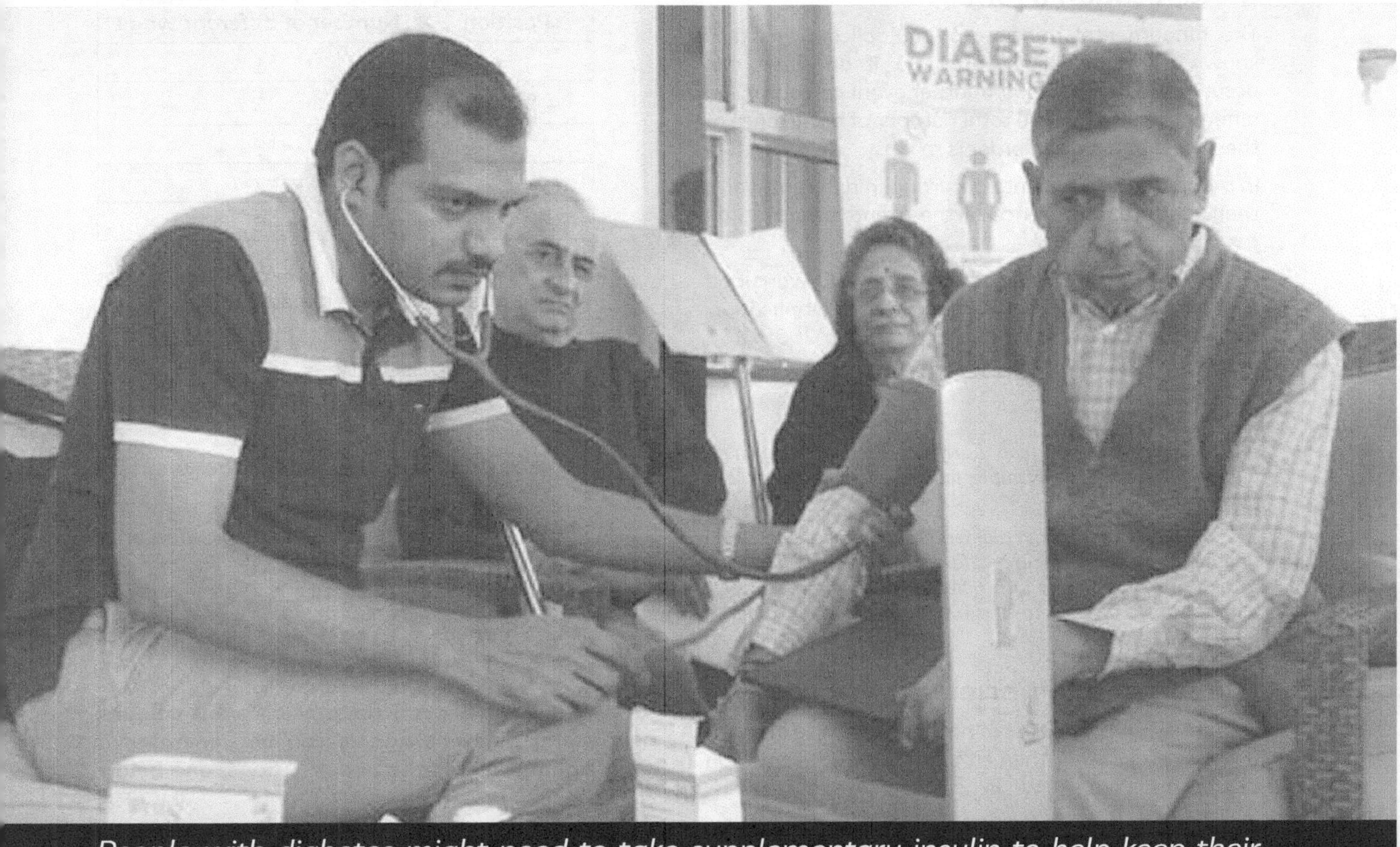

People with diabetes might need to take supplementary insulin to help keep their blood sugar levels within a normal range. Insulin is a kind of protein that is present in humans. Its job is to keep the quantity of sugar in the body in check so that it doesn't become too high or too low. Insulin is made up of 51 amino acids that are organized in a certain order or permutation. Any rearrangement that differs from this usual sequence renders the protein defective, resulting in illnesses like diabetes. The body has a system in place to guarantee that this sequence is followed and that the proper protein is produced.

Topic Notes

- *Fundamental of Counting and Permutation*
- *Combination and its Applications*

FUNDAMENTALS OF COUNTING AND PERMUTATION 1

TOPIC 1

FUNDAMENTAL PRINCIPLE OF COUNTING

The foundation of permutations and combinations are two essential ideas of counting.

Fundamental Principle of Multiplication (FPM)

The fundamental principle of multiplication is also known as multiplication principle. If an event can occur in m different ways, another event can occur in n different ways, then the total number of occurrence of the events in the given order is $m \times n$.

In a and b are two events occurring in different ways, then the total occurrence of the events are given by $a \times b$.

Here, the teacher can select a boy in 200 ways and a girl in 150 ways. So, by principle of multiplication, the teacher can select a boy and a girl in $200 \times 150 = 30000$ ways.

Important

- *The above principle can be generalized for any finite number of events. For example, for 3 events, the principle is as follows:*
- *'If an event can occur in a different ways, following which another event can occur in b different ways, following which a third event can occur in p different ways, then the total number of occurrence to 'the events in the given order is $a \times b \times p$'.*

Fundamental Principle of Addition

Let two events are performing independently in a and b ways respectively, then either of the two events can be occurred in $(a + b)$ ways.

Example 1.1: How many 5-digit telephone numbers can be constructed using the digits 0 to 9 if each number starts with 67 and no digit appears more than once? [NCERT]

Ans. The telephone number is of 5 digits and first 2 numbers are 6 and 7

Hence, number is of the form

6	7	___	___	___
↓	↓	↓	↓	↓
1st digit	2nd digit	3rd digit	4th digit	5th digit

Position	Number of different ways
1st fix	1
2nd fix	1
3rd	8
4th	7
5th	6

Digits between 0 to 9 = 0, 1, 2, 3, 4, 5, 6, 7, 8, 9

Total number of digits between 0 to 9 = 10

Now,

1st and 2nd place is fix.

3rd place: After fixing 67, only 8 ways to (10 – 2) fill 3rd place.

4th place: After fixing 6, 7 and 3rd place only 7 ways (10 – 3) to fill 4th place.

5th place: After fixing 6, 7, 3rd and 4th place, only 6 ways (10 – 4) to fill 5th place.

Thus, the Number of telephone number that can be formed

$= 1 \times 1 \times 8 \times 7 \times 6 = 336$

Example 1.2: Given 5 flags of different colours, how many different signals can be generated if each signal requires the use of 2 flags, one below the other? [NCERT]

Ans. A signal can have only 2 flags

→ First flag

→ Second Flag

Flag Position	Number of different ways
First	5
Second	4

The required number of signals

$= 5 \times 4 = 20$

TOPIC 2

PERMUTATION

A permutation is an arrangement of a number of objects in a definite order, taken some or all at a time.

The number of permutation of n different objects, taken r at a time when, $0 < r \leq n$ is given by

$${}^nP_r = \frac{n!}{(n-r)!}$$

Here ! is termed as factorial i.e.,

$$5! = 5 \times 4 \times 3 \times 2 \times 1 = 5 \times 4! = 5 \times 4 \times 3!$$

$$4! = 4 \times 3 \times 2 \times 1 = 4 \times 3! = 4 \times 3 \times 2!$$

$$1! = 1$$

$$0! = 1$$

Factorial Notations

In earlier classes, we came across the products of number in the form 1×2, 2×1 etc. So to make this more convenient, we use a special notation, i.e.,

$$1! = 1$$

$$2! = 1 \times 2$$

$$3! = 3 \times 2 \times 1$$

and so on.

Important

The notation n! represent the product of first n natural numbers.

Zero Factorial

It does not make any sense to define 0! as product of the integers from 1 to 0. So, we define $0! = 1$.

Caution

Students should know that factorial of fractions or negative integers are not defined. n! is defined only for whole, i.e., for non-negative integers.

Example 1.3: Evaluate:

(A) $8!$ (B) $4! + 3!$

(C) $\frac{8!}{610!23!}$

Ans. (A) $8! = 8 \times 7 \times 6 \times 5 \times 4 \times 3 \times 2 \times 1 = 720$

(B) $4! - 3! = (4 \times 3 \times 2 \times 1) - (3 \times 2 \times 1)$

$= 24 - 6$

$= 18$

(C) $\frac{8!}{6!2!} = \frac{8 \times 7 \times 6!}{6! \times 2 \times 1} = 28.$

Example 1.4: If $\frac{1}{6!} + \frac{1}{7!} = \frac{x}{8!}$, **find x,**

Ans. We have,

$$\frac{1}{6!} + \frac{1}{7!} = \frac{x}{8!}$$

$$\Rightarrow \frac{8!}{6!} + \frac{8!}{7!} = x$$

$$\Rightarrow \frac{8 \times 7 \times 6!}{6!} + \frac{8 \times 7!}{7!} = x$$

$$\Rightarrow 6 + 8 = x$$

$$\Rightarrow x = 64.$$

Permutations when all the Objects are Distinct

Theorem 1

The number of permutations of n different objects taken r at a time, where $0 < r \leq n$ and the objects do not repeat, is $n(n-1)(n-2) \ldots (n-r+1)$, which is denoted by ${}^nP_r$ or $P(n, r)$.

i.e., $P(n, r) = {}^nP_r = \frac{n!}{(n-r)!}, 0 \leq r \leq n$

Proof: We know that

$$P(n, r) = {}^nP_r = n(n-1)(n-2)(n-3) \ldots [n-(r-1)]$$

On multiplying numerator and denominator by

$(n-r)(n-r-1) \ldots 3 \times 2 \times 1$, we get

$${}^nP_r = \left[\frac{n(n-1)(n-2)\ldots(n-(r-1)) \times (n-r)(n-(r+1))\ldots3.2.1}{(n-r)(n-(r+1))\ldots3.2.1}\right]$$

$$= \frac{n(n-1)(n-2)\ldots3.2.1}{(n-r)(n-r-1)\ldots3.2.1}$$

$$= \frac{n!}{(n-r)!}$$

Where, $0 \leq r \leq n$

In Particular,

(i) When $r = 0$, then ${}^nP_0 = \frac{n!}{(n-0)!} = \frac{n!}{n!} = 1$

(ii) When $r = n$, then ${}^nP_n = \frac{n!}{(n-n)!} = \frac{n!}{0!} = n!$

$[\because 0! = 1]$

Important

Number of permutations of n different things, taken all at a time = n!

Permutations with Repetitions

When repetition of objects is allowed, then the number of permutations can be obtained with the help of the following theorem.

Theorem 2

The number of permutation of n different objects taken r at a time, when each may be repeated any number of times in each arrangement, is n^r (permutation with repetitions).

Important

The number of permutations of n different objects, all at a time, when each may be repeated any number of times in each arrangement, is n^r.

When all the Values are not Distinct

When all the items are not distinct, i.e. some of them are of the same kind, we can use the following theorems to calculate the number of permutations.

Theorem 3

The number of permutations of n objects, where p objects are of the same kind and rest are all different $= \frac{n!}{p!}$.

In fact, we have a more general theorem.

Theorem 4

The number of permutations of n objects, where P_1 objects are of one kind, P_2 are of second kind, ..., P_k are of kth kind and the rest, if any, are of different kind is

$$\frac{n!}{p_1!p_2!....p_k!}$$

Example 1.6: Find the number of 4-digit numbers that can be formed using the digits 1, 2, 3, 4,5 if no digit is repeated. How many of these will be even? [NCERT]

Ans. Let the 4 digit number be

__ __ __ __

Total number of digits (1, 2, 3, 4, 5) = 5

So, $n = 5$

We need to make 4-digit number, so we take 4 digits at a time,

So, $r = 4$

Number of 4-digit numbers $= {}^nP_r$

$$= {}^5P_4$$

$$= \frac{5!}{(5-4)!}$$

$$= \frac{5!}{1!}$$

$$= 5!$$

$$= 5 \times 4 \times 3 \times 2 \times 1$$

$$= 120$$

Thus, number of 4-digit numbers = 120

Now, we have to find even 4-digit numbers

__ __ __ __

In an even number, last digit should be even

So, here units place should be even.

In our digits (1, 2, 3, 4, 5), only 2, 4 are even.

Hence, either 2 or 4 can be at the unit place

So, we fix 2 at unit place and then find the total ways.

Numbers where Digit at unit place = 2

__ __ __ 2

Remaining 3 places are to be filled with digits (1, 3, 4, 5)

Hence,

n = number of digits left = 4

and r = number of digits to be taken = 3

Number of ways remaining 3 places are filled

$$= {}^4P_3$$

$$= \frac{4!}{(4-3)!}$$

$$= \frac{4!}{1!}$$

$$= 4 \times 3 \times 2$$

$$= 24$$

Similarly, if we fix digit at unit place as 4,

Number of ways = 24

Total number to 4 digit even number

= 24 + 24 = 48

Example 1.7: In how many ways can the letters of the word PERMUTATIONS be arranged if the

(A) words start with P and end with S,

(B) vowels are all together,

(C) there are always 4 letters between P and S? [NCERT]

Ans. (A) Let first position be P and last position be S (both are fixed)

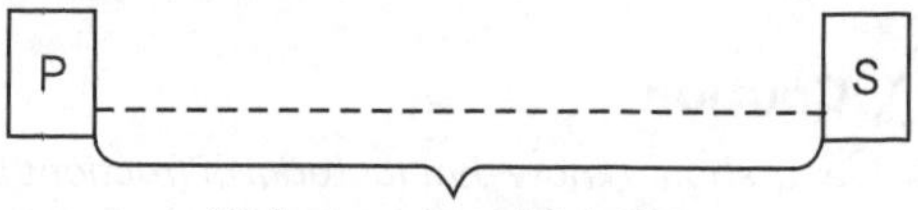

10 letters in which 2T

Since letters are repeating

Hence, we use this formula $\frac{n!}{p_1!p_2!p_3!}$

Total number of letters = n = 10

and since, 2T

Therefore, $p_1 = 2$

Now,

Total arrangements $= \frac{10!}{2!}$

= 1814400

(B) Vowels are a, e, i, o, u.

Vowels in word PERMUTATION = ($EUAIO$)

We write EUAIO as a single object

So, our letters become EAUIOPRMTTNC

Let's arrange them now

Arranging 5 vowels	Arranging remaining letters
Since, vowels are coming together, they can be EAUIO, OAEUI, AEIOU and so on.	Number we need to arrange = 7 + 1 = 8 Here are 2T,

Total letter in AEIOU = 5 Total permutations of 5 letters $= {}^5P_5$ $= \frac{5!}{(5-5)!}$ $= \frac{5!}{0!} = \frac{5!}{1}$ = 120	since letter are repeating, We use this formula $= \frac{n!}{p_1!p_2!p_3!}$ Total letters = n = 8 As, 2T $\therefore p_1 = 2$ Total arrangements $= \frac{8!}{2!}$

Hence,

Total number of arrangements

$$= \frac{8!}{2!} \times 120 = 2419200$$

(C)

Position of *p*	Position of *S*
1st	6th
2nd	7th
3rd	8th
4th	9th
5th	10th
6th	11th
7th	12th
8th	13th (Not possible as there are only 12 digits)

So, there are total 7 cases where there are 4 digits between *P* and *S* but that is when *P* is before *S*.

There can be a case where S is before *P*.

Thus, total cases = 7 × 2 = 14 *cases*

Now, lets find Permutation of letters in 1 case

Since Position of *P* and *S* are fixed we need to arrange remaining letters *i.e.*, (*E, R, M, U, T, A, T, I, O, N*).

Since, T is repeating, we use this formula

$$= \frac{n!}{p_1!p_2!p_3!}$$

Number of letters = 10

$n = 10$

Here 2*T*'s

$p_1 = 2$

Number of arrangements $= \frac{10!}{2!}$

Thus, Total number of arrangements

$$= 14 \times \frac{10!}{2!}$$

$$= 14 \times \frac{10!}{(2 \times 1)}$$

$$= 7 \times 10!$$

$$= 25401600$$

Important

- *If r particular things out of n different things are to be together, then we count these r particular things as one things and remaining (n – r) things as separate things.*

Then, total number of things = (n – r) + 1

= n – r + 1.

But, r particular things can also be arranged among themselves in r! ways.

∴ *Required number of permutations = (n – r + 1)! r!*

If r particular things are identical, then the required number of permutations = (n – r + 1)!

- *The number of permutations of n objects taken r at a time, when a particular object is taken in each arrangement, is r.* ${}^{n-1}P_{r-1}$.
- *The number of permutations of n objects taken r at a time, when a particular object is never taken in each arrangement, is* ${}^{n-1}P_r$
- *The number of permutations of n different objects taken r at a time in which two specific objects always occur together, is 2!(r – 1).* ${}^{n-2}P_{r-2}$.

Example 1.8: In the different permutations of all the letters of the word EXAMINATION are listed as in a dictionary, how many words are there in this list before the first word starting with E? [NCERT]

Ans. In dictionary, words are given alphabetically, we need to find words starting before E i.e., starting with *A, B, C* or *D*.

In EXAMINATION, there is no *B, C* or *D*, hence words should start with *A*.

Words in the list before the word starting with *E*

= words starting with letter *A*

Words starting with letter *A*

A _ _ _ _ _ _ _ _ _ _ (10 letters in which E, X)

Since, letters are repeating,

Hence, we use this formula $= \frac{n!}{p_1!p_2!p_3!}$

Remaining letters = n = 10

Since, 2*I*, 2*N*

Therefore, $p_1 = 2, p_2 = 2$

Number of words formed by these letters

$$= \frac{n!}{p_1!p_2!}$$

$= \frac{10!}{2!2!}$

$= 907200$

Thus,

Words in the list before the word starting with E

= words starting with letter A

$= 907200$

OBJECTIVE Type Questions

[1 mark]

Multiple Choice Questions

1. The number of six digit numbers whose all digits are odd is:

(a) 6^5 **(b) 5^6**

(c) $\frac{6!}{2!}$ **(d) None**

Ans. *(b) 5^6*

Explanation: Since, six-digit numbers whose all digits are odd are to be formed, suggests that repetition of digits is a must as available digit are 1, 3, 5, 7 and 9.

Hence, the required number is 5^6.

Option (b) is correct.

2. The sum of the digits in unit place of all the numbers formed with the help of 3, 4, 5 and 6 taken all at a time is:

(a) 432 **(b) 108**

(c) 36 **(d) 18**

[NCERT Exemplar]

Ans. *(b) 108*

Explanation: The sum of the digits in unit place of all the numbers formed with the help of 3, 4, 5 and 6 taken all at a time

$= (3 + 4 + 5 + 6)3!$

$= 108$

Hence, option (b) is the correct answer.

3. Evaluate (i) 5! (ii) 7!

	(i)	(ii)
(a)	**120**	**5040**
(b)	**720**	**40320**
(c)	**115**	**5020**
(d)	**121**	**5000**

Ans. *(a) 120, 5040*

Explanation:

(i) $5! = 5 \times 4 \times 3 \times 2 \times 1 = 120$

(ii) $7! = 7 \times 6 \times 5 \times 4 \times 3 \times 2 \times 1 = 5040$

So option (a) is correct.

4. Compute $\frac{9!}{6!}$.

(a) 420 **(b) 400**

(c) 504 **(d) 440**

Ans. *(c) 504*

Explanation: We have $\frac{9!}{6!} = \frac{9 \times 8 \times 7 \times 6!}{6!} = 504$

Hence, option (c) is correct.

5. A boy has 9 trousers and 12 shirts. In how many different ways can he select a trouser and a shirt?

(a) 101 **(b) 108**

(c) 105 **(d) 106** **[DIKSHA]**

Ans. *(b) 108*

Explanation: The boy can select one trouser in 9 ways.

The boy can select one shirt in 12 ways.

The number of ways in which he can select one trouser and one shirt is

$= 9 \times 12$ ways

$= 108$ ways

6. A five digit number divisible by 3 is to be formed using the numbers 0, 1, 2, 3, 4 and 5 without repetitions. The total number of ways this can be done is:

(a) 216 **(b) 600**

(c) 240 **(d) 3125**

[NCERT Exemplar]

[Hint: 5 digit numbers can be formed using digits 0, 1, 2, 3, 4, 5 or by using digits 1, 2, 3, 4, 5 since the sum of digits in these cases is divisible by 3].

Ans. *(a) 216*

Explanation: 5-digit numbers that can be formed using digits 0, 1, 2, 3, 4

4	4	3	2	1

$4 \times 4 \times 3 \times 2 \times 1 = 96$

5-digit numbers can be formed using digits 1, 2, 3, 4, 5 = 5!

Total number of ways = 5! + 96

$= 120 + 96$

$= 216$

Hence, option (a) is correct.

7. **Find value of x such that $\frac{{}^{x}P_4}{{}^{x-1}P_4} = \frac{5}{3}$, x > 4.**

(a) 11 (b) 15

(c) 12 (d) 10

Ans. *(d) 10*

Explanation: Given that $\frac{{}^{x}P_4}{{}^{x-1}P_4} = \frac{5}{3}$

$3x(x-1)(x-2)(x-3) = 5(x-1)(x-2)(x-3)(x-4)$

$3x = 5(x-4)$ as $((x-1)(x-2)(x-3) \neq 0, x > 4)$

$x = 10$

Hence, option (d) is correct.

8. **How many three letter words are formed using the letters of the word "TIME"?**

(a) 20 (b) 24

(c) 26 (d) 12 [DIKSHA]

Ans. *(b) 24*

Explanation: The number of letters in the given word is 4.

The number of 3 letter words that can be formed using these four letters is ${}^4P_3$

$= 4 \times 3 \times 2$

$= 24$

9. **Find r if $5\ {}^4P_{r+1} = {}^5P_{r-1}$.**

(a) 2 (b) 4

(c) 3 (d) None of the above

Ans. *(d) None of the above*

Explanation: We have $5\ {}^4P_{r+1} = {}^5P_{r-1}$

$$5 \times \frac{4!}{(4-r)!} = \frac{5!}{(5-r+1)!}$$

$(6-r)(5-r) = 0$

$r = 6$ or 5

Hence, option (*d*) is correct.

Assertion-Reason (A-R)

DIRECTION: In the following questions, a statement of assertion (A) is followed by a statement of the reason (R). Mark the correct choice as:

(a) Both assertion (A) and reason (R) are true and reason (R) is the correct explanation of assertion (A).

(b) Both assertion (A) and reason (R) are true but reason (R) is not the correct explanation of assertion (A).

(c) Assertion (A) is true but reason (R) is false.

(d) Assertion (A) is false but reason (R) is true.

10. **Assertion: Number of lines formed by joining *n* points on a circle ($n \geq 2$) is $\frac{n(n-1)}{2}$.**

Reason: $C(n, 3) = \frac{n(n-1)}{2}$.

Ans. *(c) Assertion (A) is true but reason (R) is false.*

Explanation: Number of lines is ${}^nC_2 = \frac{n(n-1)}{2}$

$$C(n, 3) = \frac{n!}{3!(n-3)!} = \frac{n(n-1)(n-2)}{6}$$

11. **Assertion: The product of five consecutive natural numbers is divisible by 4!**

Reason: Product of *n* consecutive natural numbers is divisible by (*n* + 1)!.

Ans. *(c) Assertion (A) is true but reason (R) is false.*

Explanation: Product of *n* consecutive natural numbers

$= (m+1)(m+2)(m+3) \dots (m+n), m \in W$

$$= \frac{(m+n)!}{m!} = n! \times \frac{(m+n)!}{m!n!} = n! \times {}^{m+n}C_m$$

⇒ Product is divisible by *n*! and so it is always divisible by (*n* – 1)! but not by (*n* + 1)!

12. **Assertion: Number of rectangles on a chess board is ${}^8C_2 \times {}^8C_2$.**

Reason: To form a rectangle, we have to select any two of the horizontal line and any two of the vertical line.

Ans. *(d) Assertion (A) is false but reason (R) is true.*

Explanation: In a chess board, there are 9 horizontal and 9 vertical lines. Number of rectangles of any size are ${}^9C_2 \times {}^9C_2$.

13. **Assertion: If *n* is a positive integer, then $n(n^2 - 1)(n + 2)$ is divisible by 24.**

Reason: Product of *r* consecutive whole numbers is divisible by *r*.

Ans. *(a) Both assertion (A) and reason (R) are true and reason (R) is the correct explanation of assertion (A).*

Explanation: $n(n^2 - 1)(n + 2) = (n - 1)n(n + 1)(n + 2)$ is the product of four consecutive whole numbers and hence it is divisible by 24.

14. **Assertion: The number of ways of distributing 10 identical balls is 4 distinct boxes such that no box is empty is ${}^9C_3$.**

Reason: The number of ways of choosing any 3 places, from 9 different places is ${}^9C_3$.

Ans. (a) *Both assertion (A) and reason (R) are true and reason (R) is the correct explanation of assertion (A).*

Explanation: Let the number of ways of distributing n identical objects among r persons such that each person gets at least one object is same as the number of ways of selecting $(r-1)$ places out of $(n-1)$ different places, i.e., ${}^{n-1}C_{r-1}$.

CASE BASED Questions (CBQs)

[**4** & **5** marks]

Read the following passages and answer the questions that follow:

15. *A dentist conducts a team to take surveys of people in his locality about using toothpaste. A survey team has some persons and the survey team owner makes a team out of total persons available at that time. If he has a group of 5 persons available at that time out of which 2 are men and 3 are women.*

(A) If a committee of 3 persons is to be constituted from the available group. In how many ways can this be done? How many of these committees would consist of 1 man and 2 women?

(B) If $P(2n-1, n) : P(2n+1, n-1) = 22:7$. find n.

Ans (A) Here order does not matter, so we can use combinations to count.

$\therefore$ Required number of ways $= {}^5C_3 = \dfrac{5!}{3!2!}$

$$= \frac{5\times4}{2\times1} = 10$$

We have,

1 man can be selected from 2 men by ${}^2C_1 = 2$ ways

And 2 women can be selected from 3 women by ${}^3C_2 = \dfrac{3!}{2!1!} = 3$ *ways*

$\therefore$ Required number of committee
$2 \times 3 = 6$ *ways*

(B) We have.

$${}^{2n-1}P_n : {}^{2n+1}P_{n-1} = 22:7$$

$$\frac{\dfrac{(2n-1)!}{(2n-1-n)!}}{\dfrac{(2n+1)}{(2n+1-n+1)!}} = \frac{27}{7}$$

$$\frac{(2n-1)!}{(n-1)!} \times \frac{(n+2)!}{(2n+1)!} = \frac{22}{7}$$

$$\Rightarrow \quad \frac{(2n-1)!}{(n-1)!} \times \frac{(n+2)(n+1)n(n-1)!}{(2n+1)(2n)(2n-1)!} = \frac{22}{7}$$

$$\Rightarrow \quad \frac{(n+2)(n+1)n}{(2n+1)(2n)} = \frac{22}{7}$$

$$\Rightarrow \quad \frac{(n+1)(n+2)}{2(2n+1)} = \frac{22}{7}$$

$$7(n^2 + 3n + 2) = 44(2n+1)$$

$$7n^2 + 21n + 14 = 88n + 44$$

$$7n^2 - 67n - 30 = 0$$

$$7n^2 - 70n + 3n - 30 = 0$$

$$7n(n-10) + 3(n-10) = 0$$

$$\Rightarrow \quad (n-10)(7n+3) = 0$$

$$\Rightarrow \quad n = 10, \text{ or } n = \frac{-3}{7}$$

$\therefore \quad n = 10 \qquad [\because n \text{ can't be negative}]$

16. *Sumit works at a book shop. While arranging some books on the book shelf, he observed that there are 5 History books, 3 Mathematics books and 4 Science books which are to be arranged on the shelf.*

(A) In how many ways can he select either a History or a maths book?

(a) 10 **(b) 8**
(c) 20 **(d) 60**

(B) If he selects 2 History books, 1 Math book and 1 Science book to arrange them, then find the number of ways in which selection can be made.

(a) 200 **(b) 220**
(c) 240 **(d) 260**

(C) Find the number of ways, if the books of the same subject are put together.

(a) 4! .2! .3! **(b) 2! .3! .2! .5!**
(c) 5! .2! .4! **(d) 3! .5! .4!**

(D) If we are given the number of arrangement of books are ${}^5P_2 \times {}^3P_1 \times {}^4P_1$, then the arrangement is in the manner:

(a) 2 History books, 2 Maths books, 3 Science books respectively.

(b) 2 History books, 3 Maths books, 2 Science books respectively.

(c) 3 History books, 2 Maths books, 2 Science books respectively.

(d) None of these

Ans. (A) *(b) 8*

Explanation: A History book can be selected in 5 ways and a Math book can be selected in 3 ways.

Required number of ways = 5 + 3 = 8

[Using addition Principle]

(B) *(c) 240*

Explanation: Now, 2 History books can be chosen in $^5P_2$ ways, 1 Maths book can be chosen in $^3P_1$ ways and 1 Science book can be chosen in $^4P_1$ ways.

∴ Required number of ways = $^5P_2 \times {}^3P_1 \times {}^4P_1$

= 240

(C) *(d) 3! .5! .4!*

Explanation: Number of ways of arranging History books = 5!

Number of ways of arranging Maths books = 3!

Number of ways of arranging Science books = 4!

∴ Required number of ways if the books of same subject are put together = 3! .5! .4!

(D) *(d) None of these*

Explanation: The number of arrangements of books $^5P_2 \times {}^3P_1 \times {}^4P_1$ represents the arrangement of 2 History books, 1 Maths book and 1 Science book respectively.

VERY SHORT ANSWER Type Questions (VSA)

[**1** mark]

17. How many rectangles can be formed from the chess board of any size?

Ans. In a chess board, there are 9 horizontal and 9 vertical lines. Number of rectangles of any size are $^9C_2 \times {}^9C_2$.

= 36 × 36 = 1296

18. If $^{16}P_{r-1}\,P : {}^{15}P_{r-1} = 16 : 7$ then find *r*.

Ans. We know that $^nP_r = \dfrac{n!}{(n-r)!}$

Hence

$$^{16}P_{r-1} : {}^{15}P_{r-1} = 16 : 7$$

$$\frac{16!}{(16-r+1)} \times \frac{(15-r+1)!}{15!} = \frac{16}{7}$$

$$\frac{16}{(17-r)!} \times (16-r)! = \frac{16}{7}$$

$$\frac{16}{17-r} = \frac{16}{7}$$

$$17 - r = 7$$

$$10 = r$$

Hence, $r = 10$

19. Evaluate 2.5! – 3.4!

Ans. 2.5! – 3.4! = 2 × 5 × 4 × 3 × 2 × 1 – 3 × 4 × 3 × 2 × 1

= 240 – 72

= 168

20. Find the number of integers greater than 7000 that can be formed with the digits 3, 5, 7, 8 and 9 where no digits are repeated.

[**Hint:** Besides 4-digit integers greater than 7000, five digit integers are always greater than 7000]. **[NCERT Exemplar]**

Ans. According to the question,

digits that can be used = 3, 5, 7, 8, 9

Since, no digits can be repeated.

The number of integers is $^5P_5$ = 5!

= 120

For a four-digit integer to be greater than 7000, the four-digit integer should begin with 7, 8 or 9.

The number of such integer

= 3 × $^4P_3$

= 3(24)

= 72

Therefore, the total no. of ways

= 120 + 72

= 192

21. How many numbers can be made which lie between 500 and 1000, without repetition, using digits 2, 3, 4, 5, 6, 8 and 0. [DIKSHA]

Ans. There are total 7 digits given: 2, 3, 4, 5, 6, 8 and 0

Between 500 and 1000 means from 501 to 999.

All of them are 3 digit numbers.

First digit	Second digit	Third digit
5, 6 or 8 i.e., 3 possibilities (1 digit gets used here)	Anyone from 7 – 1 = 6 remaining digits i.e., 6 possibilities	Anyone from 6 – 1 = 5 remaining digits i.e., 5 possibilities.

Therefore, the total possible numbers

$= 3 \times 6 \times 5 = 90$

22. **Evaluate $\frac{6}{5}.5! - \frac{5}{4}.4!$**

Ans. $\frac{6}{5}.5! - \frac{5}{4}.4!$

$= \frac{6}{5} \times 5 \times 4 \times 3 \times 2 \times 1 - \frac{5}{4} \times 4 \times 3 \times 2 \times 1$

$= 144 - 30$

$= 114$

23. **Find the number of different four digit numbers that can be formed with digits 2, 3, 4, 7 and using each digit only once.** **[NCERT Exemplar]**

Ans. We know that,

$${}^nP_r = \frac{n!}{(n-r)!}$$

Four digit numbers that can be formed with digits 2, 3, 4, 7 and using each digit only once

$= {}^4P_4$

$= 4!$

$= 24$

SHORT ANSWER Type-I Questions (SA-I)

[2 marks]

24. **If ${}^{12}P_{x+1} > 2\ {}^{12}P_x$ then find the set of values of x.**

Ans. We have ${}^{12}P_{x+1} > 2\ {}^{12}P_x$

$$\frac{12!}{(11-x)!} > 2\frac{12!}{(12-x)(11-x)!}$$

$$1 > 2\frac{1}{(12-x)}$$

$(12 - x) > 2$

$x < 10$

$x = 10, 9, 8, 7, 6, 5$

25. **Find r, if ${}^nP_r = 600$ and ${}^nC_r = 100$.**

Ans We know that ${}^nP_r = {}^nC_r\ r!$.

Given that ${}^nP_r = 600$ and ${}^nC_r = 100$

$\therefore\ 600 = 100 \times r!$

$\Rightarrow r! = 6$

$\Rightarrow r! = 3!$

$\Rightarrow r = 3$

26. **Find the number of different words that can be formed from the letters of the word 'TRIANGLE' so that no vowels are together.** **[NCERT Exemplar]**

Ans. know that,

$${}^nP_r = \frac{n!}{(n-r)!}$$

According to the question,

Total number of vowels letter = 3(A, E, I)

Total number of consonants letter = 5

T	*R*	*I*	*A*	*N*	*G*	*L*	*E*

The vowels can be placed in

$${}^6P_3 = \frac{6!}{3!}$$

$= 120$

The number of ways, consonants can be arranged placed = 5! = 120

Therefore, total number of ways it can be arranged $= 5! \times {}^6P_3$

$= 120 \times 120$

$= 14400$

27. **Find r, if $7\,{}^6P_r = \frac{1}{3}\,{}^7P_{r+2}$.**

Ans. We have,

$$7\,{}^6P_r = \frac{1}{3}\,{}^7P_{r+2}.$$

$$\Rightarrow\ 7\frac{6!}{(6-r)!} = \frac{1}{3} \times \frac{7!}{[7-(r+2)]!}$$

$$\Rightarrow\ 7\frac{6!}{(6-r)!} = \frac{1}{3} \times \frac{7!}{(5-r)!}$$

$$\Rightarrow\ \frac{1}{(6-r)} = \frac{1}{3}$$

$\Rightarrow\ (6 - r) = 3$

$\Rightarrow\ r = 3$

28. **Find the number of positive integers greater than 6000 and less than 7000 which are divisible by 5, provided that no digit is to be repeated.** **[NCERT Exemplar]**

Ans. (i) Thousand's Place can be filled with 6 alone.

Hence, the number of ways = 1

6			

Unit place can be filled with either 0 or 5.

Hence, number of way = 2

6			0 or 5

Hundred's place can be filled with the remaining 8 digits.

Hence, number of way = 8

6	9, 8, 7, 4, 3, 2, 1		(0 or 5)

Ten's place can be filled with 7 digits.

Number of ways = 7

6	9, 8, 7, 4, 3, 2, 1	Remaining 7	0 or 5

Thus, required number will be

$= 1 \times 8 \times 7 \times 2$

$= 112$

29. Find the sum of all four digit numbers that can be formed by the digits 1, 3, 5, 7, 9 without repetition. **[DIKSHA]**

Ans. The given digits are 1, 3, 5, 7, 9

Sum of r digit number = ${}^{n-1}P_{r-1}$

(sum of all n digits) × (1111 ... r times)

N is the number of non zero digits.

Here $n = 5, r = 4$

The sum of 4 digit numbers

$= {}^4P_3\,(1 + 3 + 5 + 7 + 9)(1111) = 666600.$

30. There are 10 persons named P_1, P_2, P_3, ... P_{10}. Out of 10 persons, 5 persons are to be arranged in a line such that in each arrangement P_1 must occur whereas P_4 and P_5 do not occur. Find the number of such possible arrangements. [Hint: Required number of arrangement = ${}^7C_4 \times 5!$]. **[NCERT Exemplar]**

Ans. We know that,

$${}^nC_r = \frac{n!}{r!(n-r)!}$$

According to the question,

There are 10 person named $P_1, P_2, P_3, \ldots, P_{10}$

Number of ways in which P_1 can be arranged

$= 5! = 120$

Number of ways in which others can be arranged, ${}^7C_4 = \frac{7!}{(4!3!)} = 35$

Therefore, the required number of arrangement

$= {}^7C_4 \times 5!$

$= 35 \times 120$

$= 4200$

31. How many words, with or without meaning, can be formed using all the letters of the word EQUATION, using each letter exactly once? **[DIKSHA]**

Ans. Number of letters in word EQUATION'= 8

$n = 8$

If all letters of the word used at a time

$r = 8$

Different numbers formed = ${}^nP_r$

$= {}^8P_8$

$= \frac{8!}{(8-8)!}$

$= \frac{8!}{0!}$

$= \frac{8!}{1}$

$= 8!$

$= 8 \times 7 \times 6 \times 5 \times 4 \times 3 \times 2 \times 1$

$= 40320$

SHORT ANSWER Type-II Questions (SA-II)

[3 marks]

32. Evaluate

(A) ${}^5P_2$ (B) ${}^{40}P_{40}$ (C) P(7, 3)

Ans. (A) ${}^5P_2 = \frac{5!}{(5-2)!} = \frac{5!}{3!} = \frac{5 \times 4 \times 3!}{3!} = 20$

(B) ${}^{40}P_{40} = \frac{40!}{(40-40)!} = \frac{40!}{0!} = 40!$

(C) $P(7, 3) = \frac{7!}{(7-3)!} = \frac{7!}{4!} = \frac{7 \times 6 \times 5 \times 4!}{4!} = 210$

33. How many automobile licence plates can be made if each plate contains two different letters followed by three different digits? **[NCERT Exemplar]**

Ans. According to the question,

number of letters in automobile licence plates $= 2$

We know that,

There are 26 alphabets.

so, letters can be arranged without repetition in the following number of ways,

$= 26 \times 25$

$= 650$

Number of digits in automobile licence plates $= 3$

We know that, there are 10 digits

0	1	2	3	4	5	6	7	8	9

Hence the number of digits without repetitions

$= 10 \times 9 \times 8$

$= 720$

Therefore, the total number of way automobile licence plates

$= 720 \times 650$

$= 468000$

34. Find the value of n such that $\frac{^nP_5}{^{n-1}P_5} = \frac{4}{3}, n > 4$.

Ans. We have,

$$\frac{^nP_5}{^{n-1}P_5} = \frac{4}{3}$$

$$\Rightarrow \quad 3\,{}^nP_5 = 4\,{}^{n-1}P_5$$

$$\Rightarrow \quad 3 \times \frac{n!}{(n-5)!} = 4 \times \frac{(n-1)!}{[(n-1)-5]!}$$

$$\Rightarrow \quad 3 \times \frac{n!}{(n-5)!} = 4 \times \frac{(n-1)!}{(n-6)!}$$

$$\Rightarrow \quad 3 \times \frac{n(n-1)!}{(n-5)(n-6)!} = 4 \times \frac{(n-1)!}{(n-6)!}$$

$$\Rightarrow \quad \frac{3n}{n-5} = 4$$

$$\Rightarrow \quad 3n = 4n - 20$$

$$\Rightarrow \quad n = 20$$

35. If the letters of the word RACHIT are arranged in all possible ways as listed in dictionary. Then what is the rank of the word RACHIT?

[Hint: In each case number of words beginning with A, C, H, I is 5!]

[NCERT Exemplar]

Ans. According to the question,

R	*A*	*C*	*H*	*I*	*T*

Arranging in alphabetical order, we get

ACHIRT

Number of words that can start with $A = 5!$

Number of words that can start with $C = 5!$

Number of words that can start with $H = 5!$

Number of words that can start with $I = 5!$

Total $= 5! + 5! + 5! + 5!$

$= 120 + 120 + 120 + 120$

$= 480$

Since, the word that can start with *R* is *RACHIT*

Number of words that can start with $R = 1$

Hence, we obtain that,

The rank of the word *RACHIT* $= 480 + 1 = 481$

LONG ANSWER Type Questions (LA)

[**4** & **5** marks]

36. Eight chairs are numbered 1 to 8. Two women and 3 men wish to occupy one chair each. First the women choose the chairs from amongst the chairs 1 to 4 and then men select from the remaining chairs. Find the total number of possible arrangements. [NCERT Exemplar]

Ans. We know that,

$$^nP_r = \frac{n!}{(n-r)!}$$

According to the question,

W_1 can occupy chairs marked 1 to 4 in 4 different ways.

Chair	1	2	3	4	5	6	7	8
People	W_1, W_2	W_1, W_2	W_1, W_2	W_1, W_2				

W_2 can occupy 3 chairs marked 1 to 4 in 3 different ways.

So, total no. of ways in which women can occupy the chairs,

$$^4P_2 = \frac{4!}{(4-2)!}$$

$$= \frac{(4 \times 3 \times 2 \times 1)}{(2 \times 1)}$$

$$^4P_2 = 12$$

Now, 6 chairs will be remaining.

Chair	1	2	3	4	5	6	7	8
People	W_1	W_2						

M_1 can occupy any of the 6 chairs in 6 different ways,

M_2 can occupy any of the remaining 5 chairs in 5 different ways.

M_3 can occupy any of the remaining 4 chairs in 4 different ways.

So, total no. of ways in which men can occupy the chairs.

$$^6P_3 = \frac{6!}{(6-3)!}$$

$$= 120$$

Hence, total number of ways in which men and women can be seated

$$^4P_2 \times {}^6P_3 = 120 \times 12$$
$$= 1440$$

37. How many 5-letter words, with or without meaning, containing 3 vowels and 2 consonants can be formed using the letters of the word EQUATION so that the vowels and consonants occur together?

Ans. The word EQUATION consists of 5 vowels (*E, U, A, I, O*)and 3 consonants (*Q, T, N*).

We choose 3 vowels and 2 consonants from 5 vowels and 3 consonants.

Here, the order is not important. So, each selection is a combination.

Number of ways of selecting 3 vowels from 5 vowels $= {}^5C_3 = \frac{5!}{3!2!} = 10.$

Number of ways of selecting 2 consonants from 3 consonants $= {}^3C_2 = \frac{3!}{2!1!} = 3$

So, number of such combinations = 10 × 3 = 30.

We count words formed in which all the vowels and consonants occur together.

We consider the 3 vowels as a single object *X* and the 2 consonants as a single object *Y*, and count the arrangements possible with *X* and *Y* taken all at a time.

Here, The order is important and the repetition of letters is not allowed.

So, each arrangement is a permutation.

So, number of arrangements with these 2 objects $= {}^2P_2 = \frac{2!}{0!} = 2$

We count the number of arrangements possible in the object *X*.

We arrange 3 vowels taken all at a time.

Here, the order is important. So, each arrangement is a permutation.

So, number of arrangements in object

$$X = {}^3P_3 = \frac{3!}{0!} = 6$$

We count the number of arrangements possible in the object *Y*.

We arrange 2 consonants taken all at a time.

Here, the order is important and the repetition of letters is not allowed.

So, each arrangement is a permutation.

So, number of arrangements in object

$$Y = {}^2P_2 = \frac{2!}{0!} = 2$$

Thus, number of arrangements possible with each combination = 2 × 6 × 2 = 24

Hence, required number of words

= 30 × 24 = 720

38. In how many ways can 8 men and 7 women be seated along a round table if no two women sit together?

Ans. To arrange 8 men and 7 women, taken all at a time, along a round table such that no two women sit together.

Here, each arrangement is a stationary circular permutation.

We arrange 8 men along a circle. So, we arrange 8 men, taken all at a time.

So, number of ways in which men are arranged

$$= \frac{^8P_8}{8}$$
$$= \frac{8!}{8 \times 0!}$$
$$= 5040$$

We arrange 7 women so that the women occupy the empty places.

We first choose 7 places and then arrange 7 women in them.

(i) we choose 7 places from 8 places, for the women to sit.

Here, the order is not important.

So, each selection is a combination.

Number of ways of selecting 7 places from 8 places $= {}^8C_7 = \frac{8!}{7!1!} = 8$

So, number of such combinations = 8

(ii) We arrange women on the places in each of the above combinations.

Here, the order is important and the repetition of women cannot be done.

So, each arrangement is a permutation.

We arrange 7 women, taken all at a time.

Number of arrangements for each combination $= {}^7P_7 = \frac{7!}{0!} = 5040$

So, number of ways in which women are arranged = 8 × 5040 = 40320.

COMBINATION AND ITS APPLICATIONS 2

TOPIC 1

COMBINATION

A combination is an unordered collection of some or all of the objects in a set.

The number of combination of r objects that can be selected from n different objects where $(0 < r \leq n)$ is given by

$$^nC_r = \frac{n!}{r!(n-r)!}$$

and

$$^nC_a = {^nC_b}$$

Here, $n = a + b$

Difference between Combination and Permutation

This will help you to understand clearly the difference between permutations and combinations.

Selection Combination	Arrangement Permutation
ABC	ABC, ACB, BAC, BCA, CAB, CBA
ABD	ABD, ADB, BAD, BDA, DAB, DBA
ACD	ACD, ADC, CAD, CDA, DAC, DCA
BCD	BCD, BDC, CBD, CDB, DBC, DCB
Total 4 combinations	24 permutations

Theorem 1

$$^nP_r = {^nC_r}.\, r!, 0 < r \leq n$$

Proof: The number of combinations of n distinct objects taken r at a time is, ^nC_r. In these combinations, r things can be arranged among themselves in $r!$ ways. So, we have $r!$ permutations.

Therefore, the total number of permutations of n different things taken r at a time is $^nC_r \times r!$, which is equal to ^nP_r.

$\therefore \quad {^nP_r} = r! \times {^nC_r}, 0 < r \leq n$

Hence, proved.

Theorem 2

$$^nC_r = {^nC_{n-r}}, 0 \leq r \leq n$$

Important

➥ *This theorem is used to simplify the calculation when r is large.*

Theorem 3

$$^nC_r + {^nC_{r-1}} = {^{n+1}C_r}$$

Proof

$$\text{L.H.S.} = {^nC_r} + {^nC_{r-1}}$$

$$= \frac{n!}{r!(n-r)!} + \frac{n!}{(r-1)!(n-r+1)!}$$

$$= \frac{n!(n-r+1)}{r!(n-r+1)(n-r)!} + \frac{n!r}{r(r-1)!(n-r+1)!}$$

$$= \frac{n!(n-r+1)}{r!(n-r+1)!} + \frac{n!r}{r!(n-r+1)!}$$

$$= n!\left[\frac{n-r+1+r}{r!(n-r+1)!}\right]$$

$$= \frac{(n+1)n!}{r!(n+1-r)!}$$

$$= \frac{(n+1)!}{r!(n+1-r)!}$$

$$= {^{n+1}C_r} = \text{R.H.S}$$

Hence, proved.

Theorem 4

If $^nC_x = {^nC_y}$, then either $x = y$ or $x + y = n$.

Example 1: If $^nC_8 = {^nC_6}$, find $^nC_2$.

Ans. If $^nC_x = {^nC_y}$ and $x + y = n$.

$\therefore \quad {^nC_8} = {^nC_6}$

$\Rightarrow \quad n = (8 + 6) = 14$

Now, $\quad {^nC_2} = {^{14}C_2}$

$$= \frac{14}{2} \times \frac{13}{1} \times {^{12}C_0}$$

$$\left[\because \ {^nC_r} = \frac{n}{r} \cdot {^{n-1}C_{r-1}}\right]$$

$$= \frac{14}{2} \times \frac{13}{1} \times 1 = 91.$$

Example 2: How many words with or without meaning, each 2 of vowels and 3 consonants, can be formed from the letters of the word DAUGHTER? [NCERT]

Ans. There are 3 vowels and 5 consonants in the word DAUGHTER out of which 2 vowels and 3 consonants can be chosen in $^3C_2 \times {^5C_3}$ ways. These selected five letters can now be arranged in 5! Ways.

Hence, the required number of words

$$= {^3C_2} \times {^5C_3} \times 5! = 3 \times 10 \times 120 = 3600$$

Example 3: **The English alphabet has 5 vowels and 21 consonants. How many words with two different vowels and 2 different consonants can be formed from the alphabets?** **[NCERT]**

Ans. Out of 5 vowels and 21 consonants, 2 vowels and 2 consonants can be chosen in ${}^5C_2 \times {}^{21}C_2 \times 4! = 10 \times 210 \times 24 = 50400$.

Example 4: **In how many ways can 5 girls and 3 boys be seated in a row so that no two boys are together?** **[NCERT]**

Ans. Since, boys are to be separated. Therefore, let us first seat 5 girls. This can be done in 5! ways. For each such arrangement, three boys can be seated only at the cross-marked places.

× G × G × G × G × G ×

There are 6 crossed marked places and three boys can be seated in ${}^6C_3 \times 3!$ ways. Hence, by the fundamental principles of counting, the total number of ways is $5! \times {}^6C_3 \times 3!$

$= 14400.$

Example 5: **If the ratio ${}^{2n}C_3 : {}^nC_3$ is equal to 11 : 1, find *n*.** **[NCERT]**

Ans. We have,

$${}^{2n}C_3 : {}^nC_3 = 11 : 1$$

$$\Rightarrow \frac{{}^{2n}C_3}{{}^nC_3} = \frac{11}{1}$$

$$\Rightarrow \frac{\dfrac{(2n)!}{(2n-3)!3!}}{\dfrac{n!}{(n-3)!(3!)}} = \frac{11}{1}$$

$$\Rightarrow \frac{(2n)!}{(2n-3)!} \times \frac{(n-3)!}{n!} = \frac{11}{1}$$

$$\Rightarrow \frac{(2n)(2n-1)(2n-2)(2n-3)!}{(2n-3)!} \times \frac{(n-3)!}{n(n-1)(n-2)(n-3)!} = \frac{11}{1}$$

$$\Rightarrow \frac{(2n)(2n-1)(2n-2)}{n(n-1)(n-2)} = \frac{11}{1}$$

$$\frac{4(2n-1)}{n-2} = \frac{11}{1}$$

$$\Rightarrow 8n - 4 = 11n - 22$$

$$\Rightarrow 3n = 18$$

$$\Rightarrow n = 6$$

OBJECTIVE Type Questions

[**1** mark]

Multiple Choice Questions

1. **Evaluate ${}^{22}C_2$.**

(a) 231 **(b) 232**

(c) 233 **(d) 234**

Ans. *(a) 231*

Explanation: $${}^{22}C_2 = \frac{22!}{20!2!} = \frac{22 \times 21 \times 20!}{20! \times 2 \times 1}$$

$$= \frac{22 \times 21}{2} = 21 \times 11$$

$$= 231$$

2. **If ${}^{12}C_x < 2\ {}^{12}C_{x+1}$ then set of values of *x* is:**

(a) [1, 10] **(b) (7, ∞)**

(c) {1, 2, 3} **(d) [1, 8]**

Ans. *(d) [1, 8]*

Explanation: We have ${}^{12}C_x < 2\ {}^{12}C_{x+1}$

$$\frac{12!}{x!(12-x)!} < 2\frac{12!}{(11-x)!(x+1)!}$$

$$\frac{1}{12-x} < 2\frac{1}{x+1}$$

$$x + 1 < 24 - 2x$$

$$x < \frac{23}{3}$$

$x = 7.65$ ... ...

Hence option (d) is correct.

3. **A committee has 5 men and 6 women. What are the number of ways of selecting 2 men and 3 women from the given committee?**

(a) 100 **(b) 204**

(c) 200 **(d) 300** **[DIKSHA]**

Ans. *(c) 200*

Solution: The number of ways to select two men and three women = ${}^5C_2 \times {}^6C_3$

$$= \frac{(5 \times 4)}{(2 \times 1)} \times \frac{(6 \times 5 \times 4)}{(3 \times 2)}$$

$$= 200$$

4. **If ${}^{2x+3}C_{2x} - {}^{2x+2}C_{2x-1} = 15(2x + 1)$, then *x* =**

(a) 13 **(b) 14**

(c) 27 **(d) 15**

Ans. *(b) 14*

Explanation: We have

$$^{2x+3}C_{2x} - {}^{2x+2}C_{2x-1} = 15\ (2x + 1)$$

$$\frac{(2x+3)!}{2x!3!} - \frac{(2x+2)!}{(2x-1)!3!} = 15(2x+1)$$

$$\frac{(2x+2)(2x+1)}{2} = 15(2x+1)$$

$$\Rightarrow \quad x + 1 = 15$$

$$x = 14$$

Hence, option (b) is correct.

5. If $^nC_{12} = {}^nC_8$, then n is equal to:

(a) 20 **(b) 12**

(c) 6 **(d) 30**

[NCERT Exemplar]

Ans. *(a) 20*

Explanation: According to the question,

$$^nC_{12} = {}^nC_8$$

We know that,

$$^nC_r = \frac{n!}{r!(n-r)!}$$

$$n - 8 = 12$$

$$n = 20$$

Hence, option (a) is the correct answer.

6. If $^nC_{10} = {}^nC_9$ then find $^nC_{19}$.

(a) 1 **(b) 2**

(c) 0 **(d) 3**

Ans. *(a) 1*

Explanation: Here, $^nC_P = {}^nC_k$

$$n = P + k \text{ or } P = k$$

$$^nC_{10} = {}^nC_9$$

$$\Rightarrow \quad n = 10 + 9 = 19$$

Then $^{19}C_{19} = 1$

Hence option (a) is correct.

7. The number of diagonals of a polygon of 17 sides is:

(a) 225 **(b) 350**

(c) 119 **(d) 210**

Ans. *(c) 119*

Explanation: Here required number is

$^{17}C_2 - 17 = 119$

Hence option (c) is correct.

8. $^nP_r = 840$, $^nC_r = 35$, then $r = ?$

(a) 2 **(b) 4**

(c) 3 **(d) 5** **[DIKSHA]**

Ans. *(b) 4*

Explanation:

$$P_r^n = r!C_r^n$$

$$r! = \frac{840}{35} = 24$$

$$r! = 4!$$

$$r = 4$$

9. Total number of words formed by 2 vowels and 3 consonants taken from 4 vowels and 5 consonants is equal to:

(a) 60 **(b) 120**

(c) 7200 **(d) 720**

[NCERT Exemplar]

Ans. *(c) 7200*

Explanation: We know that,

$$^nC_r = \frac{n!}{r!(n-r)!}$$

Total number of given vowels = 4

Total number of given consonant = 5

Total number of words that can be formed by 2 vowels and 3 consonants $= {}^4C_2 . {}^5C_3$

$$= \frac{4!}{2!2!} \times \frac{5!}{3!2!}$$

Total number of words $= 5! \times \frac{4!}{2!2!} \times \frac{5!}{3!2!}$

$$= 7200$$

Hence, option (c) is the correct answer.

10. If $^{x-1}C_3 + {}^{x-1}C_4 > {}^xC_3$ then x is:

(a) $x > 5$ **(b) $x > 6$**

(c) $x > 7$ **(d) None**

Ans. *(c) $x > 7$*

Explanation: We have,

$$^{x-1}C_3 + {}^{x-1}C_4 > {}^xC_3$$

$$^xC_4 > {}^xC_3$$

$$\Rightarrow \quad \frac{x!}{(x-4)!4!} > \frac{x!}{(x-3)!3!}$$

$$\frac{1}{4} > \frac{1}{x-3}$$

$$x - 3 > 4$$

$$x > 7$$

Hence option (c) is correct.

11. Everybody in a room shakes hands with everybody else. The total number of handshakes is 66. The total number of persons in the room is:

(a) 11 **(b) 12**

(c) 13 **(d) 14**

[NCERT Exemplar]

Ans. *(b) 12*

Explanation: We know that,

$$^nC_r = \frac{n!}{r!(n-r)!}$$

Let the total time of handshakes $= {}^nC_2 = 66$

$$\frac{n!}{2!(n-2)!} = 66$$

$$\Rightarrow \quad \frac{n(n-1)}{2} = 66$$

$\Rightarrow$ $n^2 - n = 132$

$\Rightarrow$ $(n-12)(n+11) = 0$

$n = 12$ or $n = -11$

Therefore, $n = 12$

Hence, option (b) is the correct answer.

CASE BASED Questions (CBQs)

[4 & 5 marks]

Read the following passages and answer the questions that follow:

12. *Riya and her 5 friends went for a trip to Shimla. They stayed in a hotel. There were 4 vacant rooms A, B, C and D. Out of these 4 vacant rooms, two rooms A and B were double share rooms and two rooms C and D can contain one person each.*

(A) The number of ways in which in which room A can be filled is:

(a) 10 (b) 15

(c) 20 (d) 25

(B) If room A and B are already filled each, then find the number of ways in which room C and be filled.

(a) 2 (b) 4

(c) 6 (d) 8

(C) The total number of ways of accommodating Riya and her friends in these 4 vacant rooms is:

(a) 150 (b) 160

(c) 170 (d) 180

(D) If room A is filled with 2 persons, then find the number in which rooms C and D can be filled.

(a) 4 (b) 12

(c) 8 (d) 10

Ans. (A) *(b) 15*

Explanation: Total members = 6

$\because$ Room *A* is a double shared room.

$\therefore$ The number of ways in which room *A* can be filled = ${}^6C_2 = 15$

(B) *(a) 2*

Explanation: Now, rooms *A* and *B* can be filled with 2 members each and room *C* can be filled with 1 person.

$\therefore$ Required number of ways = ${}^2C_1 = 2$

(C) *(d) 180*

Explanation: Required number of ways

$= 15 \times 6 \times 2 \times 1 = 180$

(D) *(b) 12*

Explanation: As, room A is filled with 2 persons

Now, the remaining persons = 4

Given that room C and D can occupy 1 person each.

$\therefore$ The number of ways in which rooms C and D can be filled = ${}^4C_1 \times {}^3C_1 = 12$

13. *Two friends Swati and Komal are playing cards. Swati asks Komal to choose any four cards from a pack of 52 cards. Now, based on this answer the following:*

(A) In how many ways can Komal select 4 cards from same suite and she select all 4 cards from different suites?

(B) In how many ways can she select all face cards?

Ans. (A) Komal can select 4 cards from same suite either 4 hearts or 4 diamonds or 4 spades or 4 clubs.

i.e., ${}^{13}C_4 + {}^{13}C_4 + {}^{13}C_4 + {}^{13}C_4 = 4 \times {}^{13}C_4$

She can select 4 cards from different suites as 1 heart, 1 diamond, 1 spade and 1 club

i.e., ${}^{13}C_1 \times {}^{13}C_1 \times {}^{13}C_1 \times {}^{13}C_1$

$= 13 \times 13 \times 13 \times 13 = (13)^4$

(B) In a pack of 52 cards 12 are face cards and 40 are non-face cards.

$\therefore$ Number of ways of selecting 4 face cards from 12 face cards

$${}^{12}C_4 = \frac{12!}{4!8!} = \frac{12\times11\times10\times9\times8!}{4\times3\times2\times1\times8!} = 495$$

VERY SHORT ANSWER Type Questions (VSA)

[1 mark]

14. Find r, if ${}^nP_r = 2880$ and ${}^nC_r = 120$.

Ans. We know that ${}^nP_r = {}^nC_r\, r!$.

Given that ${}^nP_r = 2880$ and ${}^nC_r = 120$

$\therefore$ $2880 = 120 \times r!$

$\Rightarrow$ $r! = 24$

$\Rightarrow$ $r! = 4!$

$\Rightarrow$ $r = 4$

15. How many committees of five persons with a chairperson can be selected from 12 persons? [Hint: Chairman can be selected in 12 ways and remaining in $^{11}C_4$].

[NCERT Exemplar]

Ans. We know that,

$$^nC_r = \frac{n!}{r!(n-r)!}$$

Number of ways a chairperson can be selected $= 12$

Selection of 4 other people

$$= {}^{11}C_4 = \frac{11!}{4!7!} = 330$$

Selection of 5 people

$$= 330 \times 12 = 3960$$

16. Find r, if $^{10}C_{2r} = {}^{10}C_{r+2}$.

Ans. We know that if $^nC_a = {}^nC_b$, then either

$a = b$ or $n = a + b$

Given that, $^{10}C_{2r} = {}^{10}C_{r+2}$

Then, either $2r = r + 2$ or $10 = 2r + (r + 2)$.

i.e., either $r = 2$ or $r = \frac{8}{3}$.

But, $r = \frac{8}{3}$ is not possible, as r is always an integer.

Hence, $r = 2$.

17. If there are 30 students in a group. If all shake hands with one another, how many handshakes are possible? [DIKSHA]

Ans. There are 30 people. A handshake needs 2 people.

This simply means in how many ways 2 people can be selected out of 30.

So, the answer is $^{30}C_2$

$$^nC_r = \frac{n!}{r!(n-r)!}$$

$$\therefore \quad ^{30}C_2 = \frac{30!}{2!(30-2)!}$$

$$= \frac{30 \times 29}{2}$$

$= 435$

$=$ Number of handshakes

⚠ Caution

➥ *Students should know if there are n people and they shake hands only once with each other, then*

Number of handshakes $= {}^nC_2 = \frac{n(n-1)}{2}$

SHORT ANSWER Type-I Questions (SA-I)

[**2** marks]

18. In how many ways can a student choose a programme of 7 courses if 9 course 5 optional and 4 compulsory) are available and 4 specific courses are compulsory for every student?

Ans. To choose a programme of 7 courses (3 optional and 4 compulsory) from 9 courses (including 5 optional and 4 compulsory).

Here, the order is not important.

So, each selection is a combination.

Number of ways of selecting 3 optional from 5

optional $= {}^5C_3 = \frac{5!}{3!2!}$

$= 10$

Number of ways of selecting 4 compulsory from 4 compulsory $= {}^4C_4$

$= 1$

Hence, required number of ways $= 10 \times 1$

$= 10$

19. A candidate is required to answer 7 questions out of 12 questions, which are divided into two groups, each containing 6 questions. He is not permitted to attempt more than 5 questions from either group. Find the number of different ways of doing questions.

[NCERT Exemplar]

Ans. We know that

$$^nC_r = \frac{n!}{r!(n-r)!}$$

No of questions in group $A = 6$

No of questions in group $B = 6$

According to the question,

The different ways in which the question can be attempted are,

Group A	2	3	4	5
Group B	5	4	3	1

Hence, the number of different ways of doing questions,

$= ({}^6C_2 \times {}^6C_5) + ({}^6C_3 \times {}^6C_4) + ({}^6C_4 \times {}^6C_3) + ({}^6C_5 \times {}^6C_2)$

$= (15 \times 6) + (20 \times 15) + (15 \times 20) + (6 \times 15)$

$= 780$

20. Out of 18 points in a plane, no three points are in the same line except five points which are collinear. Find the number of lines that can be formed joining the point.

Ans. We know that,

$${}^nC_r = \frac{n!}{r!(n-r)!}$$

According to the question,

Number of points = 18

Number of collinear points = 5

Number of lines formed by 18 points = ${}^{18}C_2$

For 5 points to be collinear = ${}^5C_2$

The number of lines that can be formed joining the point, = ${}^{18}C_2 - {}^5C_2 + 1$

$$= \frac{18!}{2!16!} - \frac{5!}{2!3!} + 1$$

$= 153 - 10 + 1$

$= 144$

21. There are two identical red, two identical black, and two identical white balls. In how many different ways can the balls be placed in the cells (Each cell to contain one ball) shown above such that balls of the same color do not occupy any two consecutive cells? [DIKSHA]

Ans. Case I: 2 balls of the same colour and two balls of a different colour are arranged.

Two balls of the same colour and two balls of different colours can be arranged together in which two balls of the same colour are adjacent

$= 4! / (2! \times 2!) = 6$ ways

Therefore, total number of arrangements

$= 6 \times 3 = 18$ ways

Case II: Two colors out of 3 can be selected in

$= {}^3C_1 = 3$ ways

Now 2 balls of each colour can be arranged alternatively in 2 ways

Thus 4 balls can be arranged (two of each colours) $= 3 \times 2 = 6$ ways

Hence total number of arrangements

$= 18 + 6 = 24$ ways

22. Determine n, if ${}^{2n}C_4 : {}^nC_3 = 12 : 1$.

Ans. We have, ${}^{2n}C_4 : {}^nC_3 = 12 : 1$

$$\Rightarrow \frac{{}^{2n}C_4}{{}^nC_3} = \frac{12}{1}$$

$$\Rightarrow {}^{2n}C_4 = 12\,{}^nC_3$$

$$\Rightarrow \frac{(2n)!}{4!(2n-4)!} = 12 \times \frac{n!}{3!(n-3)!}$$

$$\Rightarrow \frac{(2n)(2n-1)(2n-2)(2n-3)(2n-4)!}{4 \times 3 \times 2!(2n-4)!} = 12 \times \frac{n(n-1)(n-2)(n-3)!}{2!(n-3)!}$$

$\Rightarrow 4(2n-1)(2n-3) = 6(n-1)(n-2)$ $[\because n \neq 0]$

$\Rightarrow 2n(5n-7) = 0$ $[\because n \neq 1, \text{ as } 3 \leq 2n]$

$\Rightarrow n = 7/5$ or 0

SHORT ANSWER Type-II Questions (SA-II)

[**3** marks]

23. A boy has 4 movie tickets and 9 movie of his interest in the theater. Of these 9, he does not want to see Marvels Part II, unless Marvels Part I is also seen. In how many ways can he choose the 3 movies to be seen?

Ans. To choose 4 movies from 9 movies. Marvel's Part II is not to be seen, unless Marvels Part I is also seen.

Here, the order is not important.

So, each selection is a combination.

Case I: Marvels Part II is seen.

In this case, Marvels Part I is also seen.

Number of ways of selecting 2 movies from 7 movie = ${}^7C_2$

$$= \frac{7!}{2!5!}$$

$= 21$

Case II: Marvels Part II is not seen.

In this case, Marvels Part I may or may not be seen.

Number of ways of selecting 4 movies from 8 movies = ${}^8C_4$

$$= \frac{8!}{4!4!}$$

$= 70$

Hence, the required number of ways

$= 21 + 70$

$= 91.$

24. We wish to select 6 persons from 8, but if the person A is chosen, then B must be chosen. In how many ways can selections be made? [NCERT Exemplar]

Ans. We know that,

$$^nC_r = \frac{n!}{r!(n-r)!}$$

According to the question,

Case I: If both A and B are selected

$$= 1 \times 1 \times {^6C_4}$$

$$= \frac{6!}{4!(6-4)!}$$

$$= \frac{6!}{4!2!}$$

$$= 1$$

Case II: If neither A nor B are selected $= {^6C_6} = 1$

If B is selected, but A is not selected $= 1 \times {^6C_5}$

$$= \frac{6!}{5!(6-5)!}$$

$$= 6$$

Adding the result of both A and B being selected, neither A nor B being selected and B being selected but A not being selected.

We get,

$15 + 1 + 6 = 22$

25. Prove that: $\frac{^nC_r}{^{n-1}C_{r-1}} = \frac{n}{r}$.

Ans. L.H.S. $= \frac{^nC_r}{^{n-1}C_{r-1}} = \frac{\left[\frac{n!}{r!(n-r)!}\right]}{\left[\frac{(n-1)!}{(r-1)![(n-1)-(r-1)]!}\right]}$

$$= \frac{\left[\frac{n!}{r!(n-r)!}\right]}{\left[\frac{(n-1)!}{(r-1)!(n-r)!}\right]}$$

$$= \frac{n!}{r!(n-r)!} \times \frac{(r-1)!(n-r)!}{(n-1)!}$$

$$= \frac{n(n-1)!}{r(r-1)!(n-r)!} \times \frac{(r-1)!(n-r)!}{(n-1)!}$$

$$= \frac{n}{r}$$

$= \text{R.H.S.}$

26. A convex polygon has 44 diagonals. Find the number of its sides. [Hint: Polygon of *n* sides has ($^nC_2 - n$) number of diagonals]. [NCERT Exemplar]

Ans. We know that,

$$^nC_r = \frac{n!}{r!(n-r)!}$$

Let the number of sides the given polygon have $= n$

Now,

The number of line segments obtained by joining n vertices $= {^nC_2}$

So, number of diagonals of the polygon

$$= {^nC_2} - n$$

$$= 44$$

$$\frac{n!}{2!(n-2)!} - n = 44$$

$$\frac{n(n-1)(n-2)!}{2(n-2)!} - n = 44$$

$$\frac{n(n-1)}{2} - n = 44$$

$$n^2 - 3n - 88 = 0$$

$$(n-11)(n+8) = 0$$

$$n = 11 \text{ or } n = -8$$

The polygon has 11 sides.

27. Evaluate:

(A) $^6C_2$ **(B)** $^{40}C_{40}$

(C) $^{13}C_3$

Ans. (A) $^6C_2 = \frac{6!}{2!(6-2)!}$

$$= \frac{6!}{2!4!}$$

$$= \frac{6 \times 5 \times 4!}{2 \times 1 \times 4!}$$

$$= 15$$

(B) $^{40}C_{40} = \frac{40!}{40!(40-40)!}$

$$= \frac{40!}{40!0!}$$

$$= 1$$

(C) $^{13}C_3 = \frac{13!}{3!(13-3)!}$

$$= \frac{13!}{3!10!}$$

$$= \frac{13 \times 12 \times 11 \times 10!}{3 \times 2 \times 1 \times 10!}$$

$$= 286.$$

28. A bag contains six white marbles and five red marbles. Find the number of ways in which four marbles can be drawn from the bag if:

(A) **They can be of any color**

(B) **Two must be white and two red and**

(C) **They must all be of the same color.**

[NCERT Exemplar]

Ans. We know that:

$$^nC_r = \frac{n!}{r!(n-r)!}$$

According to the question,

Number of white marbles = 6

Number of red marbles = 5

Total number of marbles = 6 white + 5 red = 11 marbles

(A) If they can be of any color

Then, any 4 marbles out of 11 can be selected,

Therefore, the required number of ways $= {}^{11}C_4$

(B) Two must be white and two red

Number of ways of choosing two white and two red $= {}^6C_2 \times {}^5C_2$

(C) They must all be of the same color

Then, four white marbles out of 6 can be selected $= {}^6C_4$

Or, 4 red marbles out of 5 can be selected $= {}^5C_4$

Therefore, the required number of ways $= {}^6C_4 + {}^5C_4$

LONG ANSWER Type Questions (LA)

[**4** & **5** marks]

29. What is the number of ways of choosing 4 cards from a pack of 52 playing cards? In how many of these

(A) four cards are of different color?

(B) four cards belong to four different suits?

(C) four cards are face cards?

(D) two are red cards and two are black cards?

(E) cards are of the same colour?

Ans. Four cards can be chosen from 52 playing cards in ${}^{52}C_4$ ways.

Now, $${}^{52}C_4 = \frac{52!}{48!4!} = \frac{49 \times 50 \times 51 \times 52}{2 \times 3 \times 4} = 270725$$

Hence, required number of ways = 270725

(A) There are four suits (diamond, spade, club and heart) of 13 cards each. Therefore, there are ${}^{13}C_4$ ways of choosing 4 diamond cards, ${}^{13}C_4$ ways of choosing 4 club cards, ${}^{13}C_4$ ways of choosing 4 spade cards and ${}^{13}C_4$ ways of choosing heart cards.

∴ Required number of ways

$$= {}^{13}C_4 + {}^{13}C_4 + {}^{13}C_4 + {}^{13}C_4$$

$$= 4 \times \frac{13!}{9!4!}$$

$$= 2860$$

(B) There are 13 cards in each suit. Four cards drawn belong to four different units means one card is drawn from each suit. Out of 13 diamond cards one card can be drawn in ${}^{13}C_1$ ways.

Similarly, there are ${}^{13}C_1$ ways of choosing one club card, ${}^{13}C_1$ ways of choosing one spade card and ${}^{13}C_1$ ways of choosing one heart card.

∴ Number of ways of selecting one card from each suit $= {}^{13}C_1 \times {}^{13}C_1 \times {}^{13}C_1 \times {}^{13}C_1$

$$= 4 \times {}^{13}C_1$$

$$= 4 \times \frac{13!}{1!12!}$$

$$= 4 \times 13$$

$$= 52$$

(C) There are 12 face cards out of which 4 cards can be chosen in ${}^{12}C_4$ ways.

∴ Required number of ways

$$= {}^{12}C_4$$

$$= \frac{12!}{4!8!}$$

$$= 495$$

(D) There are 26 red cards and 26 black cards. Therefore, 2 red cards can be chosen in ${}^{26}C_2$ ways and 2 black cards can be chosen in ${}^{26}C_2$ ways. Hence, 2 red and 2 black cards can be chosen in ${}^{26}C_2 \times {}^{26}C_2$

$$= \left(\frac{26!}{24!2!}\right)^2$$

$$= (325)^2$$

= 105625 ways.

(E) Out of 26 red cards, 4 red cards can be chosen in ${}^{26}C_4$ ways. Similarly, 4 black cards can be chosen in ${}^{26}C_4$ ways.

Hence, 4 red or 4 black cards can be chosen in ${}^{26}C_4 + {}^{26}C_4$

$$= 2 \times \frac{26!}{4!22!} = 29900 \text{ ways.}$$

30. If ${}^nC_{r-1} = 36$, ${}^nC_r = 84$ and ${}^nC_{r+1} = 126$, then find ${}^rC_2$.

[Hint: From equation using ${}^nC_r / {}^nC_{r+1}$ and ${}^nC_r / {}^nC_{r-1}$ to find the value of r].

[NCERT Exemplar]

Ans. We know that,

$$ {}^nC_r = \frac{n!}{r!(n-r)!} $$

According to the question,

$$ {}^nC_{r-1} = 36, $$

$$ {}^nC_r = 84, $$

$$ {}^nC_{r+1} = 126 $$

$$ \frac{{}^nC_r}{{}^nC_{r+1}} = \frac{84}{126} $$

$$ \Rightarrow \frac{\frac{n!}{r!(n-r)!}}{\frac{n!}{(r+1)!(n-r-1)!}} = \frac{84}{126} = \frac{2}{3} $$

$$ 2n - 2r = 3r + 3 $$

$$ \Rightarrow 2n - 3 = 5r \quad \text{...(i)} $$

$$ \frac{{}^nC_r}{{}^nC_{r-1}} = \frac{84}{36} $$

$$ \Rightarrow \frac{\frac{n!}{r!(n-r)!}}{\frac{n!}{(r-1)!(n-r+1)!}} = \frac{7}{3} $$

$$ = 3n - 3r + 3 = 7r $$

$$ 3n + 3 = 10r \quad \text{...(ii)} $$

From (i) and (ii),

We get

$$ 2(2n - 3) = 3n + 3 $$

$$ 4n - 3n - 6 - 3 = 0 $$

$$ n = 9 $$

And $r = 3$

Now ${}^rC_2 = {}^3C_2 = 3! / 2!$

$= 3$

7 Binomial Theorem

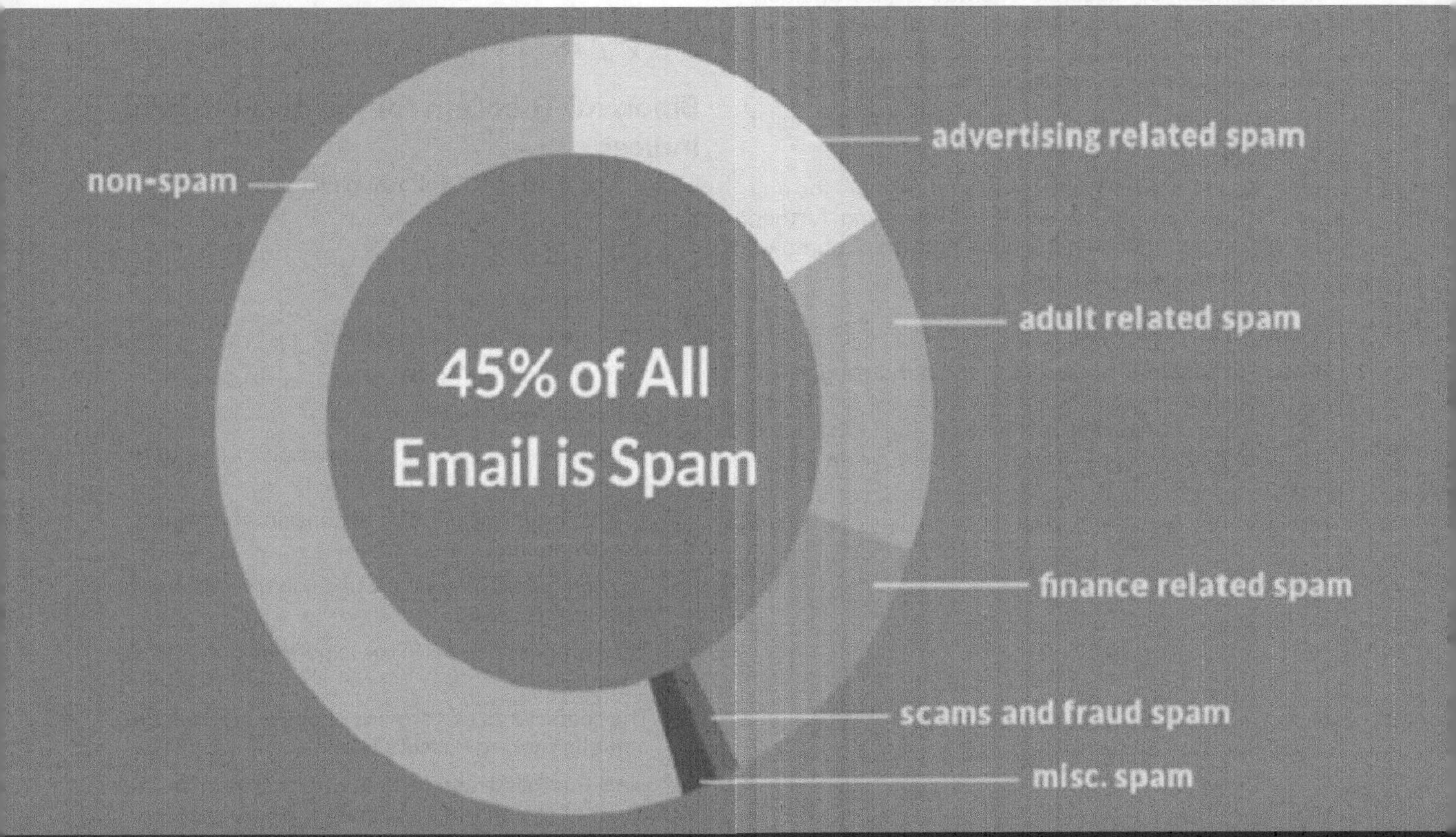

The prediction of the wide variety of spam emails obtained via way of means of someone is one of the prominent examples of a binomial distribution. This is due to the fact an electronic mail has possibilities, i.e., either it could be a spam email or not.

Topic Notes

- *Basics of Binomial Theorem*

BASICS OF BINOMIAL THEOREM

TOPIC 1

BINOMIAL THEOREM FOR POSITIVE INTEGER

Introduction

In mathematics, an algebraic expression is an expression built up from constants, variables, and a finite number of algebraic operations (like addition, subtraction, etc). An algebraic expression that contains only two terms is called a binomial. In this chapter, we shall discover the answer to the following question:

"What happens when you multiply a binomial by itself (as many times as you want)?"

In other words, we want to expand $(x + y)^n$ for any positive integral index n. Before proceeding further, let us first understand a beautiful pattern of numbers known as 'Pascal's Triangle'.

Pascal's Triangle

Pascal's triangle, in algebra, a triangular arrangement of numbers that gives the coefficients in the expansion of any binomial expression, such as $(x + y)^n$. It is named for the 17th-century French mathematician Blaise Pascal

1
1 1
1 2 1
1 3 3 1
1 4 6 4 1
1 5 10 10 5 1
1 6 15 20 15 6 1
1 7 21 35 35 21 7 1

Binomial Theorem for Positive Integral Index

The Binomial Theorem helps us to expand any positive integral power of the binomial expression. It was first given by English mathematician Issac Newton. The Binomial Theorem for positive integral index can be states as follows:

For every positive integer n, we have

$$(x+y)^n = \sum_{r=0}^{n} {}^nC_r x^{n-r} y^r$$

$$= {}^nC_0 x^n y^0 + {}^nC_1 x^{n-1} y^1 + \ldots + {}^nC_{n-1} x^1 y^{n-1} + {}^nC_n x^0 y^n.$$

Binomial Theorem for any Positive Integer *n*

Binomial theorem states that for any given positive integer n, the expression of the nth power of the sum of any two numbers a and b may take place as the sum of $n + 1$ terms of the particular form

$$(x+y)^n = \sum_{r=0}^{n} {}^nC_r x^{n-r} y^r$$

$$= {}^nC_0 x^n y^0 + {}^nC_1 x^{n-1} y^1 + \ldots + {}^nC_{n-1} x^1 y^{n-1} + {}^nC_n x^0 y^n.$$

Binomial Theorem for Positive Integral Indices

Let us now observe the following identities:

$$(x + y)^0 = 1$$
$$(x + y)^1 = x + y$$
$$(x + y)^2 = x^2 + 2xy + y^2$$
$$(x + y)^3 = x^3 + 3x^2y + 3xy^2 + y^3$$
$$(x + y)^4 = x^4 + 4x^3y + 6x^2y^2 + 4xy^3 + y^4$$

One can easily observe that

(i) The exponent of x in the expansion of $(x + y)^n$ is decreasing by 1 from n to 0.

(ii) The exponent of y in the expansion of $(x + y)^n$ is increasing by 1 from 0 to n.

(iii) The sum of exponents of x and y in the expansion of $(x + y)^n$ is always n.

(iv) The number of terms in the expansion of $(x + y)^n$ is always $n + 1$.

(v) The coefficients of terms in above expression are actually making Pascal's Triangle.

So, using Pascal's triangle one can easily write the expansion of $(x + y)^5$, $(x + y)^6$ and other exponents as follows:

$$(x + y)^5 = x^5 + 5x^4 y + 10x^3y^2 + 10x^2y^3 + 5xy^4 + y^5$$
$$(x + y)^6 = x^6 + 6x^5y + 15x^4y^2 + 20x^3y^3 + 15x^2y^4 + 6xy^5 + y^6$$

But, working with Pascal's Triangle can be very time-consuming if the exponent is a very large number (say, 100). So, we require a formula to find the value at any place in Pascal's Triangle. In fact, there is such a formula available.

The value at $(n + 1)^{th}$ row and $(r + 1)^{th}$ place of Pascal's Triangle is

$${}^nC_r = \frac{n!}{r!(n-r)!}$$

For example, the value at the 5th row and 3rd place is ${}^4C_2 = \frac{4!}{2!(4-2)!} = 6$, which can be verified to be correct from the above triangle.

This formula is very useful, as one can now work out any value in Pascal's Triangle directly (without calculating the whole triangle above it).

With this understanding, we are now in a position to write the expansion of $(x + y)^n$ for any positive integral index n.

Example 1: Expand the expression $(1 - 2x)^5$. [NCERT]

Ans. By using Binomial Theorem, the expression $(1 - 2x)^5$ can be expanded as

$$(1 - 2x)^5$$

$$= {}^5C_0(1)^5 - {}^5C_1(1)^4(2x) + {}^5C_2(1)^3(2x)^2 - {}^5C_3(1)^2(2x)^3 + {}^5C_4(1)^1(2x)^4 - {}^5C_5(2x)^5$$

$$= 1 - 5(2x) + 10(4x^2) - 10(8x^3) + 5(16x^4) - (32x^5)$$

$$= 1 - 10x + 40x^2 - 80x^3 + 80x^4 - 32x^5$$

Which is the required expansion.

Example 2: Expand the expression $\left(\frac{2}{x} - \frac{x}{2}\right)^5$. [NCERT]

Ans. By using Binomial Theorem, the expression $\left(\frac{2}{x} - \frac{x}{2}\right)^5$ can be expanded as

$$\left(\frac{2}{x} - \frac{x}{2}\right)^5 = {}^5C_0\left(\frac{2}{x}\right)^5 - {}^5C_1\left(\frac{2}{x}\right)^4\left(\frac{x}{2}\right) + {}^5C_2\left(\frac{2}{x}\right)^3\left(\frac{x}{2}\right)^2 - {}^5C_3\left(\frac{2}{x}\right)^2\left(\frac{x}{2}\right)^3 + {}^5C_4\left(\frac{2}{x}\right)\left(\frac{x}{2}\right)^4 - {}^5C_5\left(\frac{x}{2}\right)^5$$

$$= \frac{32}{x^5} - 5\left(\frac{16}{x^4}\right)\left(\frac{x}{2}\right) + 10\left(\frac{8}{x^3}\right)\left(\frac{x^2}{4}\right) - 10\left(\frac{4}{x^2}\right)\left(\frac{x^3}{8}\right) + 5\left(\frac{2}{x}\right)\left(\frac{x^4}{16}\right) - \frac{x^5}{32}$$

$$= \frac{32}{x^5} - \frac{40}{x^3} + \frac{20}{x} - 5x + \frac{5}{8}x^3 - \frac{x^5}{32}$$

Example 3: Evaluate $\left(\sqrt{3} + \sqrt{2}\right)^6 - \left(\sqrt{3} - \sqrt{2}\right)^6$. [NCERT]

Ans. Firstly, the expression $(a + b)^6 - (a - b)^6$ is simplified by using Binomial Theorem. This can be done as

$$(a + b)^6 = {}^6C_0a^6 + {}^6C_1a^5b + {}^6C_2a^4b^2 + {}^6C_3a^3b^3 + {}^6C_4a^2b^4 + {}^6C_5a^1b^5 + {}^6C_6b^6$$

$$= a^6 + 6a^5b + 15a^4b^2 + 20a^3b^3 + 15a^2b^4 + 6ab^5 + b^6$$

$$(a - b)^6 = {}^6C_0a^6 - {}^6C_1a^5b + {}^6C_2a^4b^2 - {}^6C_3a^3b^3 + {}^6C_4a^2b^4 - {}^6C_5a^1b^5 + {}^6C_6b^6$$

$$= a^6 - 6a^5b + 15a^4b^2 - 20a^3b^3 + 15a^2b^4 - 6ab^5 + b^6$$

$$\therefore\ [(a + b)^6 - (a - b)^6 = 2[6a^5b + 20a^3b^3 + 6ab^5]$$

Putting $a = \sqrt{3}$ and $b = \sqrt{2}$, we obtain

$$\left(\sqrt{3} + \sqrt{2}\right)^6 - \left(\sqrt{3} - \sqrt{2}\right)^6$$

$$= 2\left[6\left(\sqrt{3}\right)^5\left(\sqrt{2}\right) + 20\left(\sqrt{3}\right)^3\left(\sqrt{2}\right)^3 + 6\left(\sqrt{3}\right)\left(\sqrt{2}\right)^5\right]$$

$$= 2[54\sqrt{6} + 120\sqrt{6} + 24\sqrt{6}]$$

$$= 2 \times 198\sqrt{6}$$

$$= 396\sqrt{6}$$

Example 4: Prove that. $\sum_{r=0}^{n} 3^r\ {}^nC_r = 4^n$. [NCERT]

Ans. By Binomial Theorem,

$$\sum_{r=0}^{n} {}^nC_r\, a^{n-r}b^r = (a + b)^n$$

By putting $b = 3$ and $a = 1$ in the above equation, we obtain

$$\sum_{r=0}^{n} {}^nC_r(1)^{n-r}(3)^r = (1 + 3)^n$$

$$\Rightarrow \sum_{r=0}^{n} 3^r\ {}^nC_r = 4^n$$

Hence, proved.

Example 5: Show that $9^{n+1} - 8n - 9$ is divisible by 64, whenever n is a positive integer. [NCERT]

Ans. In order to show that $9^{n+1} - 8n - 9$ is divisible by 64, it has to be proved that,

$9^{n+1} - 8n - 9 = 64k$, where k is some natural number

By Binomial Theorem,

$$(1 + 8)^{n+1} = {}^{n+1}C_0 + {}^{n+1}C_1(8) + {}^{n+1}C_2(8)^2 + \ldots + {}^{n+1}C_{n+1}(8)^{n+1}$$

$$\Rightarrow 9^{n+1} = 1 + (n + 1)(8) + 8^2\,[{}^{n+1}C_2 + {}^{n+1}C_3 \times 8 + \ldots + {}^{n+1}C_{n+1}(8)^{n-1}]$$

$$\Rightarrow 9^{n+1} = 9 + 8n + 64[{}^{n+1}C_2 + {}^{n+1}C_3 \times 8 + \ldots + {}^{n+1}C_{n+1}(8)^{n-1}]$$

$$\Rightarrow 9^{n+1} - 8n - 9 = 64k, \text{ where } k = {}^{n+1}C_2 + {}^{n+1}C_3 \times 8 + \ldots + {}^{n+1}C_{n+1}(8)^{n-1}$$

is a natural number.

Thus, $9^{n+1} - 8n - 9$ is divisible by 64, whenever n is a positive integer.

OBJECTIVE Type Questions

[1 mark]

Multiple Choice Questions

1. If P and Q are the coefficient of a^r and a^{n-r} respectively in the expansion of $(1 + a)^n$, then:

(a) $P = Q$ (b) $P \neq Q$

(c) $P = \lambda Q$ for some λ (d) None of these

Ans. *(a) $P = Q$*

Explanation: We have,

P = coeffcient of a^r in the expansion of

$(1 + a)^n = {}^nC_r$

Q = coeffcient of a^{n-r} in the expansion of

$(1 + a)^n = {}^nC_{n-r}$

Now, ${}^nC_r = {}^nC_{n-r} \Rightarrow P = Q.$

Hence, option (a) is the correct answer.

2. The number of terms in the expansion of $(4 + 4x + x^2)^{20}$, when expanded in descending powers of x, is:

(a) 20 (b) 21

(c) 40 (d) 41

Ans. *(d) 41*

Explanation: We have

$$(4 + 4x + x^2)^{20} = [(2 + x)^2]^{20} = (2 + x)^{40}.$$

Therefore, there are 41 terms in the expansion of $(4 + 4x + x^2)^{20}$.

Hence, option (d) is the correct answer.

3. The largest coefficient in the expansion of $(a + b)^{18}$ is:

(a) ${}^{18}C_{18}$ (b) ${}^{18}C_{12}$

(c) ${}^{18}C_9$ (d) ${}^{18}C_6$

Ans. *(c) ${}^{18}C_9$*

Explanation: We know that if n is even then ${}^nC_r$ is greatest for $r = \frac{n}{2}$. Therefore ${}^{18}C_r$ is greatest for $r = 9$. Hence, the greatest coefficient is ${}^{18}C_9$.

Hence, option (c) is the correct answer.

4. The number of terms in the expansion of $(1 + q)^9 + (1 - q)^9$ is:

(a) 5 (b) 7

(c) 9 (d) 10

Ans. *(a) 5*

Explanation: We have,

$(p + q)^9 + (p - q)^9$

$= 2({}^9C_0 + {}^9C_2\,(q)^2 + \ldots + {}^9C_8\,(q)^8)$

Thus, it has 5 terms.

Hence, option (a) is the correct answer.

5. The total number of terms in the expansion of $(x + a)^{100} + (x - a)^{100}$ after simplification is:

(a) 50 (b) 202

(c) 51 (d) None of these

[NCERT Exemplar]

Ans. *(c) 51*

Explanation: Given,

$(x + a)^{100} + (x - a)^{100}$

$= ({}^{100}C_0x^{100} + {}^{100}C_1x^{99}a + {}^{100}C_2\,x^{98}\,a^2 + \ldots) + ({}^{100}C_0\,x^{100} - {}^{100}C_1\,x^{99}\,a + {}^{100}C_2\,x^{98}\,a^2 + \ldots)$

$= 2({}^{100}C_0\,x^{100} + {}^{100}C_2\,x^{98}\,a^2 + \ldots + {}^{100}C_{100}\,a^{100})$

So, there are 51 terms.

Hence, option (c) is the correct answer.

6. Given the integers $r > 1$, $n > 2$, and coefficient of $(3r)^{th}$ and $(r + 2)^{nd}$ terms in the binomial expansion of $(1 + x)^{2n}$ are equal, then:

(a) $n = 2r$ (b) $n = 3r$

(c) $n = 2r + 1$ (d) None of these

[NCERT Exemplar]

Ans. *(a) $n = 2r$*

Explanation: Given $(1 + x)^{2n}$

$T_{3r} = T_{(3r-1)+1} = {}^{2n}C_{3r-1}\,x^{3r-1}$

and $T_{r+2} = T_{(r+1)+1} = {}^{2n}C_{r+1}\,x^{r+1}$

Given, ${}^{2n}C_{3r-1} = {}^{2n}C_{r+1}$

$3r - 1 + r + 1 = 2n$

$[\because\ {}^nC_x = {}^nC_y \Rightarrow x + y = n]$

Or, $n = 2r$

Hence, option (a) is the correct answer.

Assertion-Reason (A-R)

DIRECTION: In the following questions, a statement of assertion (A) is followed by a statement of the reason (R). Mark the correct choice as:

(a) Both assertion (A) and reason (R) are true and reason (R) is the correct explanation of assertion (A).

(b) Both assertion (A) and reason (R) are true but reason (R) is not the correct explanation of assertion (A).

(c) Assertion (A) is true but reason (R) is false.

(d) Assertion (A) is false but reason (R) is true.

7. Assertion: The coefficient of a^4b^5 in the expansion of $(a + b)^9$ is ${}^9C_4$.

Reason: The formula of $(a + b)^n$ is ${}^nC_0a^nb^0 + {}^nC_1a^{n-1}b^1 + \ldots\ldots\ {}^nC_n\,a^n$.

Ans. *(a) Both assertion (A) and reason (R) are true and reason (R) is the correct explanation of assertion (A).*

Explanation: Since a^4b^5 occurs in 5th term of $(a + b)^9$, therefore coefficient of a^4b^5 is ${}^9C_4$.

Formula for $(a + b)^n$ is correct.

8. Assertion: Let x be a true integer. If the coefficient of 2nd, 3rd and 4th term of expansion $(1 + x)^3$ are in A.P then the value of x is 7.

Reason: The common difference of A.P. are different.

Ans. *(c) Assertion (A) is true but reason (R) is false.*

Explanation: As ${}^xC_1, {}^xC_2$ and ${}^xC_3$ are in A.P

$\Rightarrow \quad 2{}^xC_2 = {}^nC_1 + {}^nC_3$

$$x(x-1) = x + \frac{(x)(x-1)(x-2)}{6}$$

$$x - 1 = \frac{1+(x-1)(x-2)}{6}$$

$$6x - 6 = 6 + x^2 - 3x + 2$$

$$x^2 - 9x + 14 = 0$$

$$(n-2)(n-7) = 0$$

$$n = 2 \text{ or } 7$$

The common difference of an A.P is always same.

Hence, assertion is true but reason is false.

9. Assertion: The sum of the last eight coefficients in the expansion of $a(1 + x)^{16}$ is 2^{15}.

Reason: If x is an odd integer, then $({}^2C_0 - {}^2C_1 - 1{}^2C_2 - {}^2C_3 + \ldots + (-1))^x \cdot {}^2C_x \neq 0$.

Ans. *(c) Assertion (A) is true but reason (R) is false.*

Explanation: We have,

${}^{16}C_0 + {}^{16}C_1 + \ldots + {}^{16}C_{16} = 2^{16}$ (putting $x = 1$)

$\Rightarrow 2({}^{16}C_8 + {}^{16}C_9 + \ldots + {}^{16}C_{16}) = 2^{16}$

$\Rightarrow {}^{16}C_8 + {}^{16}C_9 + \ldots + {}^{16}C_{16} = 2^{15}$

Reason is false as

$${}^2C_0 - {}^2C_1 + {}^2C_2 - {}^2C_3 + \ldots (-1)^x\, {}^2C_x = 0$$

Hence, assertion is true but reason is false.

CASE BASED Questions (CBQs)

[4 & 5 marks]

Read the following passages and answer the questions that follow:

10. *Ms. Khushi and Mr. Daksh decide to construct a Pascal triangle with the help of binomial theorem. They use the formula for the expansion is* $(x + y)^n = \sum_{r=0}^{n} {}^nC_r x^{n-r} y^r$

$$= {}^nC_0 x^n y^0 + {}^nC_1 x^{n-1} y^1 + \ldots + {}^nC_{n-1} x^1 y^{n-1} + {}^nC_n x^0 y^n.$$

(A) The coefficient of x^k $(0 \le k \le n)$ in the expansion of $E = 1 + (1 + x) + (1 + x)^2 + \ldots (1 + x)^n$ is:

(a) ${}^{n+1}C_{k+1}$ (b) ${}^nC_k$

(c) ${}^{n+1}C_{n-k-1}$ (d) None of these

(B) The coefficient of y is the expansion of $\left(y^2 + \frac{c}{y}\right)^5$ is:

(a) $10\ c^3$ (b) $20\ c^2$

(c) $10\ c$ (d) $20\ c$

(C) The number of terms in the expansion of $(1+\sqrt{5}x)^7 + (1-\sqrt{5}x)^7$ are:

(a) 4 (b) 8

(c) 5 (d) 9

(D) The sum of coefficient of even powers x in the expansion of $\left(x - \frac{1}{x}\right)^{2n}$ is:

(a) $11 \times {}^{11}C_5$ (b) $\frac{11}{2} \times {}^{11}C_6$

(c) $11({}^{11}C_5 + {}^{11}C_6)$ (d) 0

Ans. (A) *(a)* ${}^{n+1}C_{k+1}$

Explanation:

$$E = \frac{(1+x)^{n+1} - 1}{(1+x) - 1}$$

$$= \frac{{}^{n+1}C_0 + {}^{n+1}C_1 x + {}^{n+1}C_2 x^2 + \ldots - 1}{x}$$

$$= {}^{n+1}C_1 + {}^{n+1}C_2 x + {}^{n+1}C_3 x^2 + \ldots$$

Coeffcient of $x^4 = {}^{n+1}C_{k+1}$

Hence, option (a) is the correct answer.

(B) *(a)* $10\ c^3$

Explanation:

$$(y^2 + c/y)^5 = {}^5C_0\left(\frac{c}{y}\right)^0 (y^2)^{5-0} + {}^5C_1\left(\frac{c}{y}\right)^1 (y^2)^{5-1} + \ldots + {}^5C_5\left(\frac{c}{y}\right)^5 (y^2)^{5-5}$$

$$= \sum_{r=0}^{5} {}^5C_r \left(\frac{c}{y}\right)^r (y^2)^{5-r}$$

We need coeffcient of $y \Rightarrow 2(5 - r) - r = 1$

$\Rightarrow 10 - 3r = 1$

$\Rightarrow r = 3$

So, coeffcient of $y = {}^5C_3 . c^3$

$= 10c^3$

Hence, option (a) is the correct answer.

(C) *(a) 4*

Explanation: Given expansion is

$$\left(1+\sqrt{5}x\right)^7 + \left(1-\sqrt{5}x\right)^7.$$

Here, $n = 7$, which is odd.

$$\text{Total number of terms} = \frac{n+1}{2} = \frac{7+1}{2} = \frac{8}{2} = 4$$

Hence, option (a) is the correct answer.

(D) *(d) 0*

Explanation: $(r + 1)^{th}$ term $= {}^{11}C_r (x)^{11-r}.x^{-r}$

$= {}^{11}C_r . x^{11-2r}$

Even power of x exists only if $11 - 2r =$ an even number which is not possible

Thus, Sum of coefficient = 0

Hence, option (*d*) is the correct answer.

11. *Ms. Tanvi and Mr. Dhruv play a game to make the equations by observing some condition they make some equations. From the above information solve the following questions:*

(A) Expand, $(1 - x + x^2)^4$.

(B) Expand the expression, $(1 - 3x)^7$.

Ans. (A) We have,

$(1 - x + x^2)^4 = [(1 - x) + x^2]^4$

$= {}^4C_0(1 - x)^4 + {}^4C_1(1 - x)^3 (x^2) + {}^4C_2(1 - x)^2 (x^2)^2 + {}^4C_3(1 - x) (x^2)^3 + {}^4C_4(x^2)^4$

$= (1 - x)^4 + 4x^2 (1 - x)^3 + 6x^4(1 - x)^2 + 4x^6 (1 - x) + 1x^8$

$= (1 - 4x + 6x^2 - 4x^3 + x^4) + 4x^2 (1 - 3x + 3x^2 - x^3) + 6x^4 (1 - 2x + x^2) + 4 (1 - x)x^6 + x^8$

$= 1 - 4x + 6x^2 - 4x^3 + x^4 + 4x^2 - 12x^3 + 12x^4 - 4x^5 + 6x^4 - 12x^5 + 6x^6 + 4x^6 - 4x^7 + x^8$

$= 1 - 4x + 10x^2 - 16x^3 + 19x^4 - 16x^5 + 10x^6 - 4x^7 + x^8$

(B) Here, $a = 1, b = 3x$, and $n = 7$

Given, $(1 - 3x)^7 = {}^7C_0(1)^7 - {}^7C_1(1)^6 (3x)^1 + {}^7C_2(1)^5 (3x)^2 - {}^7C_3(1)^1 (3x)^3 + {}^7C_4(1)^3 (3x)^4 - {}^7C_5(1)^2 (3x)^5 + {}^7C_6(1)^1 (3x)^6 - {}^7C_7(1)^0 (3x)^7$

$= 1 - 21x + 189x^2 - 945x^3 + 2835x^4 - 5103x^5 + 5103x^6 - 2187x^7.$

VERY SHORT ANSWER Type Questions (VSA)

[1 mark]

12. Find the coefficient of x in the expansion of $(1 - 3x + 7x^2)(1 - x)^{16}$. [NCERT Exemplar]

Ans. Given $(1 - 3x + 7x^2)(1 - x)^{16}$

$= (1 - 3x + 7x^2)({}^{16}C_0 - {}^{16}C_1 x^1 + {}^{16}C_2 x^2 + ... + {}^{16}C_{16} x^{16})$

$= (1 - 3x + 7x^2)(1 - 16x + 120x^2 + ...)$

Coefficient of $x = - 19$

13. Find the coefficient of x^{15} in the expansion of $(x - x^2)^{10}$. [NCERT Exemplar]

Ans. Given $(x - x^2)^{10}$

$T_{r+1} = {}^{10}Cr\, x^{10-r} (-x^2)^r = (-1)^r\, {}^{10}C_r x^{10-r} x^{2r}$

$= (-1)^r\, {}^{10}C_r x^{10+r}$

For the coefficient of x^{15}, we have

$10 + r = 15 \Rightarrow r = 5$

$T_{5+1} = (-1)^5\, {}^{10}C_5\, x^{15}$

Coefficient of

$$x^{15} = -\frac{10\times9\times8\times7\times6\times5!}{5\times4\times3\times2\times1\times5!} = -252$$

14. Find the 3rd term from beginning in the expansion of $(x^3 + 3a)^5$.

Ans. The 3rd term is

$= {}^5C_2 (x^3)^3 (3a)^2$

$= 10(x^9)\, 9(a)^2$

15. Find the number of terms in the expansion $(1 - 3x + 3x^2 - x^3)^9$.

Ans. We have, $(1 - 3x + 3x^2 - x^3)^9$

$= ((1 - x)^3)^9 = (1 - x)^{27}$

$\therefore$ Total number of terms $= \dfrac{51+1}{2} = 26$

SHORT ANSWER Type-I Questions (SA-I)

[2 marks]

16. Using Binomial theorem, find the value of $(0.98)^{14}$ upto 4 places of decimal.

Ans. $(0.98)^{14} = (1 - 0.02)^{14}$

$= 1 + {}^{14}C_1(-0.02)^1 + {}^{14}C_2(-0.02)^2 + {}^{14}C_3(-0.02)^3$

[Neglecting higher powers of (0. 01)]

$= 1 - 14(0.02) + 91(0.0004) - 364(0.000008)$

$= 1 - 0.28 + 0.0364 - 0.002912 = 0.753488.$

17. For what value of 'p', the coefficients of $(2p + 1)^{th}$ and $(4p + 5)^{th}$ terms in the expansion of $(1 + a)^{10}$ are equal?

Ans. Coeff. of $(2p + 1)^{th}$ term in $(1 + a)^{10} = {}^{10}C_{2p}$

And coeff. of $(4p + 5)^{th}$ term in $(1 + a)^{10}$

$= {}^{10}C_{4p+4}.$

By the question, ${}^{10}C_{2p} = {}^{10}C_{4p+4}$

thus, either $10 = 2p + (4p + 4)$ or $2p = 4p + 4$

$\Rightarrow 6p = 6$ or $2p = -4$

$\Rightarrow p = 1$ or $p = -2.$

But p can't be – ve.

Hence, $p = 1$.

18. Expand $\left(y^2 + \frac{2}{y}\right)^5, y \neq 0.$

Ans. By using binomial theorem, we have

$\left(y^2 + \frac{2}{y}\right)^5$

$= {}^5C_0(y^2)^5 + {}^5C_1(y^2)^4\left(\frac{2}{y}\right)^1 + {}^5C_2(y^2)^3\left(\frac{2}{y}\right)^2 + {}^5C_3(y^2)^2\left(\frac{2}{y}\right)^3 + {}^5C_4(y^2)^1\left(\frac{2}{y}\right)^4 + {}^5C_5(y^2)^0\left(\frac{2}{y}\right)^5$

$\Rightarrow y^7 + 5y^8\left(\frac{2}{y}\right) + 10y^6\left(\frac{2}{y}\right)^2 + 10y^4\left(\frac{2}{y}\right)^3 + 5y^2\left(\frac{2}{y}\right)^4 + \left(\frac{2}{y}\right)^5$

$\Rightarrow y^7 + 10y^7 + 40y^4 + 80y + \frac{80}{y^2} + \frac{32}{y^5}$

19. Which is larger $(1.01)^{10,000,00}$ or 20,000.

Ans. $(1.01)^{10,00000} = (1 + 0.01)^{10,00000}$

$= {}^{10,0000}C_0 + {}^{10,00000}C_1(0.01)$

+ other positive term

$= 1 + 10,00000 \times 0.01$

$= 10,001$

Hence, $(1.01)^{10,00000} < 20,000$.

SHORT ANSWER Type-II Questions (SA-II)

[3 marks]

20. Find out which one is larger $99^{50} + 100^{50}$ or 101^{50}. (DIKSHA)

Ans. Let's try to find out $101^{50} - 99^{50}$ in terms of remaining term *i.e.*

$101^{50} - 99^{50} = (100 + 1)^{50} - (100 - 1)^{50}$

$= (C_0.\,100^{50} + C_1.\,100^{49} + C_2.\,100^{48} + ...)$

$= (C_0.\,100^{50} - C_1.\,100^{49} + C_2.\,100^{48} ...)$

$= 2(C_1.\,100^{49} + C_3.\,100^{47} + ...)$

$= 2(50.\,100^{49} + C_3.\,100^{47} + ...)$

$= 100^{50} + 2(C_3.\,100^{47} + ...)$

$= 100^{50}$

$\Rightarrow 101^{50} > 99^{50} + 100^{50}$

21. Evaluate $(102)^4$.

Ans. Given: $(102)^4$.

Here, 102 can be written as the sum or the difference of two number, such that the binomial theorem can be applied.

Therefore $102 = 100 + 2$

Hence, $(102)^4 = (100 + 2)^4$

Now, by applying binomial theorem, we get:

$(102)^4 = (100 + 2)^4 = {}^4C_0(100)^4 + {}^4C_1(100)^3(2) + {}^4C_2(100)^2(2)^2 + {}^4C_3(100)^1(2)^3 + {}^4C_4(2)^4$

$= (100)^4 + 8(100)^3 + 24(100)^2 + 32(100) + 16$

$= 100000000 + 8000000 + 240000 + 3200 + 16$

$= 108243216$

22. Using binomial theorem, expand $(x + y)^6 - (x - y)^6$. Hence, find the value of $\left(\sqrt{3} + 1\right)^6 - \left(\sqrt{3} - 1\right)^6$.

Ans. $(x+y)^6 - (x-y)^6 = {}^6C_0x^6 + {}^6C_1x^5y + {}^6C_2x^4y^2 + {}^6C_3x^3y^3 + {}^6C_4x^2y^4 + {}^6C_5xy^5 + {}^6C_6x^0y^6 - [{}^6C_0x^6 + {}^6C_1x^5(-y)^1 + {}^6C_2x^4(-y)^2 + {}^6C_3x^3(-y)^3 + {}^6C_4x^2(-y)^4 + {}^6C_5x(-y)^5 + {}^6C_6x^0(-y)^6]$

$= 2(6x^5y + 20x^3y^3 + 6xy^5)$

$= 4xy(3x^4 + 10x^2y^2 + 3y^4)$

On substituting $x = \sqrt{3}$ and $y = 1$, we get

$= 4\times\sqrt{3}\times 1\left(3(\sqrt{3})^4 + 10(\sqrt{3})^2(1)^2 + 3(1)^4\right)$

$= 4\sqrt{3}(3\times 9 + 10\times 3 + 3)$

$= 4\sqrt{3}(27+30+3)$

$= 4\sqrt{3}(60)$

$= 240\sqrt{3}$

LONG ANSWER Type Questions (LA)

[**4** & **5** marks]

23. Using the binomial theorem, show that $6^n - 5n$ always leaves remainder 1 when divided by 25.

Ans. For any two numbers, say a and b, we can find numbers x and y such that $a = bx + y$, then we say that c divides a with x as quotient and y as remainder. Thus, in over to show that $6^n - 5n$ leaves remainder 1 when divided by 25, we should prove that $6^n - 50 = 25k + 1$, where K is some natural number.

We know that,

$(1+a)^n = {}^nC_0 + {}^nC_1 a + {}^nC_2 a^2 + ... + {}^nC_n a^n$

Now, for $a = 5$, we get:

$(1+5)^n = {}^nC_0 + {}^nC_1 5 + {}^nC_2 (5)^2 + ... + {}^nC_n (5)^n$

Now the above from can be written as :

$6^n = 1 + 5n + 5^2\,{}^nC_2 + 5^3\,{}^nC_3 + ... + 5^n$

Now, bring $5n$ to the L.H.S., we get

$6^n - 5n = 1 + 5^2\,{}^nC_2 + 5^3\,{}^nC_3 + ... + 5^n$

$6^n - 5n = 1 + 5^2({}^nC_2 + 5\,{}^nC_3 + ... + 5^{n-2})$

$6^n - 5n = 1 + 25({}^nC_2 + 5\,{}^nC_3 + ... + 5^{n-2})$

$6^n - 5n = 1 + 25K$

(Where $k = {}^nC_2 + 5\,{}^nC_3 + ... + 5^{n-2}$)

Hence, proved.

24. Using binomial theorem, expand the following expansion.

(A) $(x^2 + 2a)^4$

(B) $\left(2+\sqrt{3}\right)^7 + \left(2-\sqrt{3}\right)^7$

(C) $\left(x^2 + 3 + 2\sqrt{3}x\right)^3$

(D) $(x^2 - 2x + 1)^3$

Ans. (A) Here, $a = x^2$, $b = 2a$ and $n = 4$

Given, $(x^2+2a)^4 = {}^4C_0(x^2)^4 + {}^4C_1(x^2)^3(2a)^1 + {}^4C_2(x^2)^2(2a)^2 + {}^4C_3(x^2)^1(2a)^3 + {}^4C_4(x^2)^0(2a)^4$

$= 1(x^8) + 4(x^6)(2a) + 6x^4\,4a^2 + 4x^2\,8a^3 + 16a^4$

$= x^8 + 8x^6a + 24x^4a^2 + 32x^2a^3 + 16a^4$

(B) $\left(2+\sqrt{3}\right)^7$

$= {}^7C_0(2)^7\times(\sqrt{3})^0 + {}^7C_1(2)^6\times(\sqrt{3})^1 + {}^7C_2(2)^5(\sqrt{3})^2 + {}^7C_3(2)^4(\sqrt{3})^3 + {}^7C_4(2)^3(\sqrt{3})^4 + {}^7C_5(2)^2(\sqrt{3})^5 + {}^7C_6(2)^1(\sqrt{3})^6 + {}^7C_7(2)^0(\sqrt{3})^7$

and $\left(2-\sqrt{3}\right)^7$

$= {}^7C_0(2)^7(\sqrt{3})^0 + {}^7C_1(2)^6(\sqrt{3})^1 - {}^7C_2(2)^5(\sqrt{3})^2 - {}^7C_3(2)^4(\sqrt{3})^3 + {}^7C_4(2)^3(\sqrt{3})^4 - {}^7C_5(2)^2(\sqrt{3})^5 + {}^7C_6(2)^1(\sqrt{3})^6 - {}^7C_7(2)^0(\sqrt{3})^7.$

Now, $(2+\sqrt{3})^7 + (2-\sqrt{3})^7$ we get,

$= 2[{}^7C_0(2)^7(\sqrt{3})^0 + {}^7C_2(2)^5(\sqrt{3})^2 + {}^7C_4(2)^3(\sqrt{3})^4 + {}^7C_6(2)^1(\sqrt{3})^6]$

$= 10084$

(C) $\left(x^2 + 3 + 2\sqrt{3}x\right)^3 = \left(x+\sqrt{3}\right)^6$

$= {}^6C_0(x)^6\times(\sqrt{3})^0 + {}^6C_1x^5(\sqrt{3})^1 + {}^6C_2x^4(\sqrt{3})^2 + {}^6C_3x^3(\sqrt{3})^3 + {}^6C_4x^2(\sqrt{3})^4 + {}^6C_5x^1(\sqrt{3})^5 + {}^6C_6(\sqrt{3})^6$

$= x^6 + 6\sqrt{3}x^5 + 45x^4 + 60\sqrt{3}x^3 + 135x^2 + 54\sqrt{3}x + 27.$

(D) We have, $(x^2 - 2x + 1)^3 = [(x-1)^2]^3 = (x-1)^6$

$= {}^6C_0(x)^6 - {}^6C_1(x^5)(1) + {}^6C_2(x)^4 - {}^6C_3(x)^3 + {}^6C_4(x)^2 - {}^6C_5(x)^1 + {}^6C_6(1)^6$

$= x^6 - 6x^5 + 15x^4 - 20x^3 + 15x^2 - 6x + 1.$

8 Sequence and Series

Sequence and series are useful because they can be used to model real-world situations. Geometric series occur in real life when each actor in a system behaves independently and is fixed. If each person decides not to have another child based on the current population, the annual population increase is geometric.

Topic Notes

- *Arithmetic Mean and Geometric Progression*
- *Relation Between A.M. and G.M.*

ARITHMETIC MEAN AND GEOMETRIC PROGRESSION 1

TOPIC 1

SEQUENCE AND MEAN

Sequence and Series are two mathematical words that are generally considered implying the same thing, a set of numbers arranged in some definite order.

(1) *A sequence is a function whose domain is as the subset of the set of natural numbers N and range is as the subset of real number R.*

(2) *A sequence is an ordered list of numbers.*

Important

➥ *The numbers in the list are called terms*

➥ *a_n is called nth term of sequence a_1, a_2, a_3......*

➥ *The nth term is also called the general term of the sequence*

(3) *A sequence is said to be a progression if the term of the sequence can be expressed by some explicit formula.*

Series

If a_1, a_2, a_3.....be a sequence, then the expression $a_1 + a_2 + a_3 + ...$ is called the series associated with the sequence.

TOPIC 2

ARITHMETIC MEAN

(1) If a, A and b are in AP, then $A = (a + b)/2$ is called the arithmetic mean of a and b.

(2) If a_1, a_2, a_3, a_n are n numbers, then their AM is given by,

$$d = \frac{b-a}{n+1}$$

$$A_1 = a + d = \frac{na+b}{n+1}$$

$$A_2 = a + 2d = \frac{(n-1)a+2b}{n+1}$$

$$\ldots A_n = a + nd = \frac{a+nd}{n+1}$$

(3) If $a, A_1, A_2, A_3, \ldots, A_n, b$ are in AP, then $A_1, A_2, A_3, \ldots, A_n$ are n arithmetic mean between a and b, where

$$d = \frac{a+nd}{n+1}$$

$$A_1 = a + d = \frac{na+b}{n+1}$$

$$A_2 = a + 2d = \frac{(n-1)a+2b}{n+1}$$

$$\ldots A_n = a + nd = \frac{a+nb}{n+1}$$

(4) Sum of n AM's between a and b is nA

i.e., $A_1 + A_2 + A_3 + \ldots + = nA$

Important Results on AP

(i) If $a_p = q$ and $a_q = p$, then $a_{p+q} = 0$, $T_r = p + q - r$

(ii) If $pT_p = qT_q$, then $a_{p+q} = 0$

(iii) If $a_p = \frac{1}{p}$ and $a_q = \frac{1}{p}$, then $a_{pq} = 1$

(iv) If $S_p = q$ and $S_q = p$, then $S_{p+q} = -p + q$

(v) If $S_p = s_q$, then $S_{p+q} = 0$

Example 1.1: Show that the sequence whose nth term is $a_n = n_{n+2}$ is not an *A.P.* **[NCERT]**

Ans. Given $a_n = n (n + 2) = n^2 + 2n$.

Then, $a_{n+1} = (n + 1)^2 + 2 (n + 1) = (n^2 + 2n + 1) + (2n + 2)$

$= n^2 + 4n + 3.$

Now, $a_{n+1} - a_n = (n^2 + 4n + 3) - (n^2 + 2n)$

$= 2n + 3$

which is dependent on n.

Hence, the given sequence is not an A.P.

Example 1.2: If $\frac{a^n + b^n}{a^{n-1} + b^{n-1}}$ is A.M. of a and b. Then find the value of n. **[NCERT]**

Ans. Given that $\frac{a^n + b^n}{a^{n-1} + b^{n-1}}$ is the A.M. of a and b.

$$\therefore \quad \frac{a^n + b^n}{a^{n-1} + b^{n-1}} = \frac{a+b}{2}$$

$\Rightarrow \quad 2a^n + 2b^n = (a + b)(a^{n-1} + b^{n-1})$

$\Rightarrow \quad 2a^n + 2b^n = a^n + ab^{n-1} + ba^{n-1} + b^n$

$\Rightarrow \quad a^n + b^n = ab^{n-1} + ba^{n-1}$

$\Rightarrow \quad a^n - ba^{n-1} = ab^{n-1} - b^n$

$\Rightarrow \quad a^{n-1}(a - b) = b^{n-1}(a - b)$

$\Rightarrow \quad a^{n-1} = b^{n-1}$

$\Rightarrow \quad \frac{a^{n-1}}{b^{n-1}} = 1$

$\Rightarrow \quad \left(\frac{a}{b}\right)^{n-1} = \left(\frac{a}{b}\right)^0$

$\Rightarrow \quad n - 1 = 0$

$\Rightarrow \quad n = 1$

Example 1.3: Between 1 and 31 are inserted *m* arithmetic means so that the ratio of the 7th and (*m* - 1)th means is 5: 9. Find the value of *m*. **[NCERT]**

Ans. Let $A_1, A_2, \ldots A_m$ be *m* arithmetic means between 1 and 31. Then $1, A_1, A_2 \ldots A_m, 31$ is an *A.P.* with common difference *d* given by

$$d = \frac{31-1}{m+1} = \frac{30}{m+1}$$

Now, $A_7 = 1 + 7d = 1 + \frac{7\times 30}{m+1} = \frac{m+211}{m+1}$

And, $A_{m-1} = 1 + (m - 1)d$

$$= 1 + \frac{30(m-1)}{m+1} = \frac{31m-29}{m+1}$$

It is given that

$$\frac{A_7}{A_{m-1}} = \frac{5}{9}$$

$$\frac{m+211}{31m-29} = \frac{5}{9}$$

$\Rightarrow \quad 9m + 1899 = 155m - 145$

$\Rightarrow \quad 146m = 2044$

$\Rightarrow \quad m = 14$

Example 1.4: In an *A.P* if m^{th} the term is *n* and the nth term is *m*, where $m \neq n$, find the pth term. **[NCERT]**

Ans. Let *a* be the first term and *d* be the common difference of the given *A.P.*

Given that the mth term is *n* and the nth term is *m*, where $m \neq n$,

$\therefore \quad a_m = n$

$\Rightarrow \quad a + (m - 1)d = n$ ...(1)

$\therefore \quad a_n = m$

$\Rightarrow \quad a + (n - 1)d = m$ ...(2)

On subtracting (2) from (1), we get

$(m - 1)d - (n - 1)d = n - m$

$\Rightarrow \quad (m - 1 - n + 1)d = n - m$

$\Rightarrow \quad d = -1$ ...(3)

Putting value of *d* in (1), we get

$a - (m - 1) = n$

$\Rightarrow \quad a = n + m - 1$ ....(4)

So, the pth term of the *A.P*, is given by

$a_p = a + (p - 1)d$

$= (n + m - 1 + (p - 1)(-1)$

$= n + m - 1 - p + 1 = n + m - p$

[using (3) and (4)]

TOPIC 3

GEOMETRIC PROGRESSION

A sequence $a_1, a_2, a_3, \ldots, a_n$ is called a geometric progression. If each term is non-zero and follows a relation $\frac{a_{k+1}}{a_k} = r$ where *r* is a constant for all $k \in N$

$\Rightarrow$ "*r*" is called the common ratio.

Geometric progressions happen whenever each agent of a system acts independently.

Here are some examples:

(i) The amount on your savings account ;

(ii) The amount of money in your piggy bank if you deposit the same amount each week (a bank account with regular deposits leads you to arithmetic-geometric sequences)

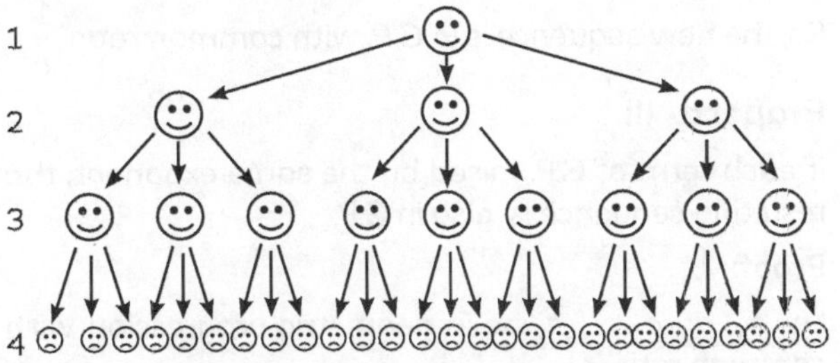

Properties of G.P

In this section, we will discuss important properties of geometric progressions and geometric series.

Property I

If all the terms of G.P. be multiplied or divided by the same non-zero constant, then the resulting sequence remains in G.P. with the same common ratio.

Proof:

Let $a_1, a_2, a_3, \ldots, a_n$ be in geometric progression with common ratio 'r'.

$$\frac{a_{n+1}}{a_n}, \text{ for all } n \in N \quad \text{...(i)}$$

Let 'k' be any non-zero constant by which we are multiplying each term of G.P. So we get,

$$ka_1, ka_2, ka_3, \ldots, ka_n$$

So equation (i) $\Rightarrow \dfrac{ka_{n+1}}{ka_n}$, for all $n \in N$

which is same as $\dfrac{a_{n+1}}{a_n} = r.$

new sequence formed is also in G.P. with common ratio 'r'.

Property II

The reciprocal of the terms of a given G.P. from a G.P.

Proof:

Let $a_1, a_2, a_3, \ldots, a_n$ be in geometric progression with common ratio 'r'.

$$\frac{a_{n+1}}{a_n}, \text{ for all } n \in N \quad \text{...(i)}$$

Now the sequence formed by reciprocal will be

$$\frac{1}{a_1}, \frac{1}{a_2}, \frac{1}{a_3}, \ldots, \frac{1}{a_n}.$$

The common ratio

$$= \frac{\frac{1}{a_{n+1}}}{\frac{1}{a_n}} = \frac{a_n}{a_{n+1}} = \frac{1}{r}$$

So, the new sequence is in G.P. with common ratio $\dfrac{1}{r}$.

Property III

If each term of G.P. raised by the same exponent, the resulting sequence is also in G.P.

Proof:

Let $a_1, a_2, a_3, \ldots, a_n$ be in geometric progression with common ratio 'r'.

$$\frac{a_{n+1}}{a_n}, \text{ for all } n \in N \quad \text{...(i)}$$

Let each term of G.P. is raised by exponent, 'k' then the sequence becomes $a_1^k, a_2^k, a_3^k, \ldots, a_n^k$

$$\frac{a^k_{n+1}}{a_n^k} = \left(\frac{a_{n+1}}{a_n}\right)^k = r^k \text{ for all } n \in N$$

$\therefore$ $a_1^k, a_2^k, a_3^k, \ldots, a_n^k$ is in G.P. with common ratio r^k.

Property IV

In a finite G.P., the product of the terms equidistant from the beginning and the end is always the same and equal to the product of the first and the last term.

Proof:

Let $a_1, a_2, a_3, \ldots, a_n$ be in geometric progression with common ratio 'r'.

Kth term from the beginning $= a_k = a_1 r^{k-1}$

Kth term from the end $= a_{n-k+1} = a_1 r^{n-k}$

$\therefore$ Product of kth term from the beginning and kth term from the end

$$= a_1 r^{k-1} \times a_1 r^{n-k}$$

$$= a_1^2 r^{k-1+n-k}$$

$$= a_1^2 r^{n-1} \text{ for } K = 2, 3, 4, \ldots (n-1)$$

Hence, the product of the terms equidistant from the beginning and the end is always the same and is equal to the product of first and the last term.

Property V

Three non-zero numbers a, b, c are in G.P. if and only if $b^2 = ac$.

Proof: a, b, c are in G.P.

$\therefore$ Common ration $= \dfrac{b}{a} = \dfrac{c}{b}$

$\therefore$ $b^2 = ac$

Property VI

If the terms of a given G.P. are chosen at regular intervals, then the new sequence so formed also forms G.P.

Property VII

If $a_1, a_2, a_3, \ldots, a_n$ be in geometric progression, then $\log a_1, \log a_2, \log a_3, \ldots, \log a_n$ is an arithmetic progression and vice-versa.

Sum of *n* terms of a G.P.

If,

a = the first term.

r = Common ratio.

Then, sum of n terms of a G.P.

$$a_n = ar^{n-1}$$

$$S_n = a\left(\frac{r^n - 1}{r - 1}\right) \text{ if } r > 1$$

$$S_n = a\left(\frac{1 - r^n}{1 - r}\right) \text{ if } r < 1$$

Sum of infinite terms

$S_n = a_n$ if $r = 1$

Geometric Mean

(1) If a, b and c are in G.P, then, b is called the geometric mean and it is given by

$$b = \sqrt{ab}$$

(2) If $G_1, G_2, G_3, \ldots, G_n$ are n numbers between positive numbers a and b then

$$\text{Common ratio, } r = \left(\frac{b}{a}\right)^{\frac{1}{n+1}}$$

$$\text{and } G_n = a\left(\frac{b}{a}\right)^{\frac{n}{n+1}}$$

Example 1.5: Show that the sequence 5, 10, 20, 40, ..., is a G.P. Write its general term. [NCERT]

Ans. Given sequence is 5, 10, 20, 40, . . .

Since, $\frac{10}{5} = 2, \frac{20}{10} = 2, \frac{40}{20} = 2, \ldots.$

So, the given sequence is a G.P. with a common ratio, $r = 2$.

Also, the first term of G.P. is $a = 5$.

Hence, the general term of the G.P. is given by

$$a_n = ar^{n-1} = 5\,(2^{n-1}).$$

Example 1.6: If $-\frac{2}{7}, x, -\frac{7}{2}$ are in G.P. find x? [NCERT]

Ans. Given that $-\frac{2}{7}, x, -\frac{7}{2}$ are in G.P.

$$\therefore \quad \frac{x}{\left(-\frac{2}{7}\right)} = \frac{\left(-\frac{7}{2}\right)}{x}$$

$$\Rightarrow x^2 = 1$$

$$\Rightarrow x = \pm 1$$

Example 1.7: Show that the sequence whose n^{th} term is $a_n = 3^n$ is a G.P. Find its common ratio. [NCERT]

Ans. Given, $a_n = 3^n$

Then, $a^{n+1} = 3^{n+1}$

Now, $\frac{a_{n+1}}{a_n} = \frac{3^{n+1}}{3^n} = 3$, which is an independent of n.

Hence, the given sequence is a G.P. with a common ratio of 3.

Example 1.8: Find the number of terms in the G.P. 2, 6, 18, ...,13122. [NCERT]

Ans. Given G.P. is 2, 6, 18, ..., 13122

Since, $\frac{6}{2} = 3, \frac{18}{6} = 3, \ldots$

So, the common ratio of the given G.P. is $r = 3$.

Also, the first term of the G.P. is $a = 2$.

Let the number of terms in the given G.P. be n.

Then,

$$a_n = 13122$$

$$\Rightarrow ar^{n-1} = 13122$$

$$\Rightarrow 2\,(3^{n-1}) = 13122 \qquad [\because a = 2, r = 3]$$

$$\Rightarrow 3^{n-1} = 6561$$

$$\Rightarrow 3^{n-1} = 3^8$$

$$\Rightarrow n - 1 = 8$$

$$\Rightarrow n = 9$$

Hence, the number of terms in the given G.P. is 9.

Example 1.9: If the 4th, 10th and 16th terms of a G.P. are x, y and z, respectively. Prove that x, y, z are in G.P. [NCERT]

Ans. Let a be the first term and r be the common ratio of the given G.P.

Given that 4th, 10th and 16th terms of the G.P. are x, y and z respectively.

$$\therefore \quad a_4 = x$$

$$\Rightarrow \quad ar^3 = x$$

$$\therefore \quad a_{10} = y$$

$$\Rightarrow \quad ar^9 = y$$

$$\therefore \quad a_{16} = z$$

$$\Rightarrow \quad ar^{15} = z$$

Since, $\frac{y}{x} = \frac{ar^9}{ar^3} = r^6$ and $\frac{z}{y} = \frac{ar^{15}}{ar^9} = r^6$

$$\therefore \quad \frac{y}{x} = \frac{z}{y}$$

Hence, x, y, z are in G.P.

Example 1.10: If, $\frac{a+bx}{a-bx} = \frac{b+cx}{b-cx} = \frac{c+dx}{c-dx}$ $(x \neq 0)$ then show that a, b, c and d are in G.P. [NCERT]

Ans. We have,

$$\frac{a+bx}{a-bx} = \frac{b+cx}{b-cx} = \frac{c+dx}{c-dx}$$

Applying componendo- dividendo

$$\frac{a+bx+a-bx}{(a+bx)-(a-bx)} = \frac{b+cx+(b-cx)}{b+cx-(b-cx)} = \frac{c+dx+(c-dx)}{c+dx-(c-dx)}$$

$$\frac{a+a+bx-bx}{bx+bx-a+a} = \frac{b+b+cx-cx}{cx+cx-b+b} = \frac{c+dx+c-dx}{dx+dx-c+c}$$

$$\frac{2a+0}{2bx+0}=\frac{2b+0}{2cx+0}=\frac{2c+0}{2dx+0}$$

$$\frac{2a}{2bx}=\frac{2b}{2cx}=\frac{2c}{2dx}$$

$$\frac{a}{bx}=\frac{b}{cx}=\frac{c}{dx}$$

$$\frac{a}{b}=\frac{b}{c}=\frac{c}{d}$$

$$\frac{b}{a}=\frac{c}{b}=\frac{d}{c}$$

As the common ratio is same, thus *a, b, c* and *d* are in *G.P.*

OBJECTIVE Type Questions

[**1** mark]

Multiple Choice Questions

1. **The nth term of a G.P 5, 25, 125, ...is:**

(a) 5^n **(b)** 5^{n-1}

(c) 5^{n+1} **(d)** 5^{n-2}

Ans. *(a)* 5^n

Explanation: Here

$a = 5$

$r = 5$

So, $a_n = ar^{n-1}$

$= 5(5^{n-1})$

$= 5^n$

Hence, option (a) is correct.

2. **If the third term of G.P. is 4,Then the product of its first 5 terms is:**

(a) 4^3 **(b)** 4^4

(c) 4^5 **(d)** None of these

[DIKSHA]

Ans. *(c)* 4^5

Explanation: Here

$a_3 = 4$

$ar^2 = 4$

Product of first 5 terms

$= a.\ ar.\ ar^2.\ ar^3.\ ar^4$

$= a^5 . r^{10}$

$= (ar^2)^5$

$= (4)^5$

Hence, option (c) is correct.

3. **In a G.P, the 3rd is 24 and the 6th term is 192. Then the 10th term is:**

(a) 1084 **(b)** 3290

(c) 3072 **(d)** 2340

Ans. *(c) 3072*

Explanation: Here,

$a_3 = 24$ and $a_6 = 192$

So, $ar^2 = 24$ and $ar^5 = 192$

So, dividing we get,

$r^3 = 8$

$r = 2, a = 6$

$a_{10} = ar^9$

$= (6.\ 2^9)$

$= 3072$

Hence, option (c) is correct.

4. **If the 8th term of G.P is 192 with a common ratio of 2, then the 12th term is:**

(a) 1640 **(b)** 2084

(c) 3072 **(d)** 3126

Ans. *(c) 3072*

Explanation: Here,

$a_8 = 192$

and $r = 2$

So,

$ar^7 = 192$

$a2^7 = 192$

$a = \frac{192}{128}$

$a = \frac{3}{2}$

$a_{12} = ar^{11}$

$= \frac{3}{2} \times 2^{11}$

$= 3 \times 2^{10}$

$= 3 \times 1024 = 3072$

Hence, option (c) is correct.

5. **5120 is which term of the G.P 5, 10, 20, 40, ...**

(a) 11th **(b)** 10th

(c) 6th **(d)** 5th

Ans. *(a)* 11th

Explanation: Here $a = 5$, $r = 2$ and $a_n = 5120$

$a_n = ar^{n-1}$

$5120 = 5.\ 2^{n-1}$

$2^{n-1} = \frac{5120}{5}$

$2^{n-1} = 1024$

$2^{n-1} = 2^{10}$

$n = 11$

Hence, 11th term is 5120.

So, option (a) is correct.

6. **The 5th term from the end of the sequence 16, 8, 4, 2 ... $\frac{1}{16}$ is:**

(a) 1 (b) 2

(c) 3 (d) 4

Ans. *(a) 1*

Explanation: Here,

$$a = 16$$

$$r = \frac{1}{2}$$

So, 5th term

$$a_5 = ar^4$$

$$= 16 \times \left(\frac{1}{2}\right)^4$$

$$= 1$$

Hence, option (a) is correct.

7. **18th term from the end of the sequence 3, 6, 12,...25th term is:**

(a) 393216 (b) 393206

(c) 313216 (d) 303216

Ans. *(a) 393216*

Explanation: Here $a = 3, r = 2$

$m = 18$ and $n = 25$

We know that if a sequence has n term then m^{th} term from end is equal to $(n - m + 1)$.

$$a_{18} = ar^{18-1} = 3(2)^{18-1}$$

$$= 3\,(2)^{17}$$

$$= 3 \times 131072$$

$$= 393216$$

Hence, option (a) is correct.

8. **If *n* terms of a *G.P.* 3, 3^2, 3^3... are needed to give the sum 120, then the value of n is:**

(a) 2 (b) 3

(c) 4 (d) 5

Ans. *(c) 4*

Explanation: Here $S_n = 120, a = 3, r = 3$

So,

$$S_n = a\left(\frac{r^n - 1}{r - 1}\right)$$

$$120 = 3\left(\frac{3^n - 1}{3 - 1}\right)$$

$$240 = 3(3^n - 1)$$

$$80 = 3^n - 1$$

$$81 = 3^n$$

$$n = 4$$

Hence, option (c) is correct.

9. **If x, 2y, 3z are in *A.P.*, where the distinct numbers x, y, z are in *G.P.*, then the common ratio of the *G.P.* is:**

(a) 3 : 1 (b) 1 : 3

(c) 2 : 1 (d) 1 : 2

[NCERT Exemplar]

Ans. *(b) 1 : 3*

Since x, 2y, 3z are in A.P.

$\therefore \quad 2y - x = 3z - 2y$

$\Rightarrow \quad 4y = x + 3z$ ...(i)

Now, x, y, z are in G.P.

$\therefore \quad$ common ratio $r = \frac{y}{x} = \frac{z}{y}$ ...(ii)

$\therefore \quad y^2 = xz$

Putting the value of x from eq. (i), we get

$$y^2 = (4y - 3z)z$$

$\Rightarrow \quad y^2 = 4yz - 3z^2$

$\Rightarrow \quad 3z^2 - 4yz + y^2 = 0$

$\Rightarrow \quad 3z^2 - 3yz - yz + y^2 = 0$

$\Rightarrow \quad 3z\,(z - y) - y(z - y) = 0$

$\Rightarrow \quad (3z - y)\,(z - y) = 0$

$\Rightarrow \quad 3z - y = 0$ and $z - y = 0$

$\Rightarrow \quad 3z = y$ and $z \neq y$

[$\because$ z and y are distinct numbers]

$\Rightarrow \quad \frac{z}{y} = \frac{1}{3}$ (from eq. (ii))

$\Rightarrow \quad r = \frac{1}{3}$

Hence, the correct option is (b).

10. **The lengths of three unequal edges of a rectangular solid block are in *G.P.* If the volume of the block is 512 cm^3 and the total surface area is 232 cm^2, then the length of the longest edge is:**

(a) 8 cm (b) 12 cm

(c) 9 cm (d) 15 cm

Ans. *(a) 8 cm*

Explanation: Let the three unequal length of the block be A/r,A and Ar.

The volume A^3 equals to 512.

$\Rightarrow \quad A^3 = 512$

$\Rightarrow \quad A = 8$

Also, the total surface area = $2\left(\frac{A^2}{r} + A^2 + A^2r\right)$

Hence, $2\left(\frac{A^2}{r} + A^2 + A^2r\right) = 232$

$\Rightarrow \quad \frac{1}{r} + 1 + r = \frac{232}{2A^2}$

$$= \frac{232}{2 \times 64} = \frac{29}{16}$$

$\Rightarrow \quad \frac{1}{r}+1+r=\frac{29}{16}$

$\Rightarrow \quad \frac{1}{r}+r=\frac{29}{16}-1$

$\Rightarrow \quad \frac{1}{r}+r=\frac{13}{16}$

Hence, $r = 1$ or $\frac{13}{16}$

So, the longest side = 8 × 1 = 8 *cm*

11. The sum or difference of two *G.P.* s, is again a *G.P.*

(a) False **(b) True**

(c) May be **(d) None of the above**

Ans. *(a) False*

Explanation: Let two G.P.s are

$a, ar_1, ar_1^2, ar_1^3, \ldots$ and $b, br_2, br_2^2, br_2^3, \ldots$

Now sum of two G.P.s is

$a+b, (ar_1+br_2), (ar_1^2+br_2^2), \ldots$

Clearly, $\frac{ar_1+br_2}{a+b} \neq \frac{ar_1^2+br_2^2}{ar_1+br_2}$

Similarly, for difference of two *G.P.s*,

We get $\frac{ar_1-br_2}{a-b} \neq \frac{ar_1^2-br_2^2}{ar_1-br_2}$ So, the sum or difference of two *G.P.s* is not a *G.P.*

Assertion-Reason (A-R)

DIRECTION: In the following questions, a statement of assertion (A) is followed by a statement of the reason (R). Mark the correct choice as:

(a) Both assertion (A) and reason (R) are true and reason (R) is the correct explanation of assertion (A).

(b) Both assertion (A) and reason (R) are true but reason (R) is not the correct explanation of assertion (A).

(c) Assertion (A) is true but reason (R) is false.

(d) Assertion (A) is false but reason (R) is true.

12. Assertion (A): If 5th and 8th term of a *G.P* be 48 and 384 respectively, then the common ratio of *G.P* is 2.

Reason (R): If 18, *x*, 14 are in A.P, then *x* = 16.

Ans. *(b) Both assertion (A) and reason (R) are true but reason (R) is not the correct explanation of assertion (A).*

Explanation: $T_5 = 48$

$ar^4 = 48$

$T_8 = 384$

$ar^7 = 384$

So, $r^3 = 8$

$r = 2$

18, *n*, 14 are in *A.P*

So, $n - 18 = 14 - n$

$2n = 32$

$n = 16$

13. Assertion (A): The sum of the first 20 terms of an *A.P*, 4, 8, 12 is equal to 840.

Reason (R): Sum of *n* terms of an *A.P* is $\left[S_n=\frac{n}{2}(2a+(n-1)d\right]$.

Ans. *(a) Both assertion (A) and reason (R) are true and reason (R) is the correct explanation of assertion (A).*

Explanation: Given *A.P.* is 4, 8, 12

$a = 4, d = 4$

Now, $S_{20}=\frac{20}{2}(2\times4+(20-1)\times4) = 840$

14. Assertion (A): The sum of the series $\frac{3}{\sqrt{5}}+\frac{4}{\sqrt{5}}+\sqrt{5}+\ldots$ 25 term is $75\sqrt{5}$.

Reason (R): If 27, *n*, 3 are in G.P then *x* = ± 4.

Ans. *(c) Assertion (A) is true but reason (R) is false.*

Explanation:

$$S_n = \frac{3}{\sqrt{5}}+\frac{4}{\sqrt{5}}+\sqrt{5}+\ldots 25^{th} \text{ term}$$

$$a = \frac{3}{\sqrt{5}}$$

$$d = \frac{1}{\sqrt{5}}$$

So, $$S_n = \frac{25}{2}\left[2\times\frac{3}{\sqrt{5}}+(25-1)\frac{1}{\sqrt{5}}\right]$$

$$= 25\times\frac{15}{5}\times\sqrt{5}=75\sqrt{5}$$

Given, 27, *n*, 3 are in *G.P.*

$$\frac{n}{27}=\frac{3}{n}$$

So, $n^2 = 81 \Rightarrow n = \pm 9$

Hence, assertion is true but reason is false.

15. Assertion (A): If the number $\frac{-2}{7}, k, \frac{-7}{2}$ is in G.P then $k = \pm 1$.

Reason (R): If a_1, a_2, a_3 are in G.P then $\frac{a_2}{a_1} = \frac{a_3}{a_2}$.

Ans. (a) *Both assertion (A) and reason (R) are true, and reason (R) is the correct explanation of assertion (A).*

Explanation: If $\frac{-2}{7}, k, \frac{-7}{2}$ are in G.P.

$$\frac{a_2}{a_1} = \frac{a_3}{a_2}$$

$$\frac{k}{-2/7} = \frac{-7/2}{k}$$

$$14k^2 = 14$$

$$k^2 = 1$$

$$k = \pm 1$$

CASE BASED Questions (CBQs)

[**4** & **5** marks]

Read the following passages and answer the questions that follow:

16. *A.M. and G.M. Inequality*

Let a, b be two positive real numbers, then

$$(\sqrt{a} - \sqrt{b})^2 \geq 0$$

$$\Rightarrow a + b - 2\sqrt{ab} \geq 0$$

$$\Rightarrow \frac{a+b}{2} \geq \sqrt{ab}$$

$\Rightarrow$ A.M $\geq$ G.M.

Equality holds iff a = b

i.e., A.M. = G.M. iff a = b

The A.M. and G.M. inequality for two variables can be generalised to n variables.

If $a_1, a_2, a_3,...,a_n$ are n positive real numbers, then

$$\frac{a_1 + a_2 + a_3 + ... + a_n}{n} \geq (a_1 . a_2 . a_3 .... a_n)^{\frac{1}{n}}.$$

(A) If x, y, z are positive integers, then find value of the expression (x + y) (y + z) (z + x).

(B) Find the minimum value of the expression $3^x + 3^{1-x}$, $x \in R$ and if three positive real numbers a, b, c are in A.P. and abc = 4, then find the minimum possible value of b.

Ans. (A) $\because$ A.M. > G.M.

$$\therefore \quad \frac{x+y}{2} > \sqrt{xy}$$

$$\frac{y+z}{2} > \sqrt{yz}$$

And $\frac{z+x}{2} > \sqrt{zx}$ Multiplying three inequalities, we get,

$$\frac{x+y}{2}, \frac{y+z}{2}, \frac{z+x}{2} > \sqrt{(xy)(yz)(xz)}$$

$$\Rightarrow (x + y)(y + z)(z + x) > 8xyz$$

(B) $\because$ A.M. $\geq$ G.M.

$$\therefore \quad \frac{a_1 + a_2 + a_3 + ... + 2a_n}{n} \geq (a_1, a_2, a_3, .. 2a_n)^{1/n}$$

$$\Rightarrow \frac{3^x + 3^{1-x}}{2} \geq \sqrt{3^x . 3^{1-x}}$$

$$\Rightarrow 3^x + 3^{1-x} \geq 2\sqrt{3}$$

So, the minimum value of $3^x + 3^{1-x}$ is $2\sqrt{3}$.

Given a, b, c are in A.P.

So, $\quad 2b = a + c$

And abc = 4

We know that A.M. $\geq$ G.M.

So, $\frac{a+b+c}{3} \geq (abc)^{1/3}$

$$\Rightarrow \frac{2b+b}{3} \geq (4)^{1/3} \quad \text{[using (i) and (ii)]}$$

$$\Rightarrow \frac{3b}{3} \geq (2^2)^{1/3}$$

$$\Rightarrow b \geq 2^{\frac{2}{3}}$$

So, the minimum possible value of b is $2^{\frac{2}{3}}$.

17. *A sequence of non-zero numbers is said to be a geometric progression, if the ratio of each term, except the first one, by its preceding term is always constant. Rahul, being a plant lover, decides to open a nursery and he bought few plants and pots. He wants to place pots in such a way that the number of pots in the first row is 2, in second row is 4 and in the third row is 8 and so on.....*

(A) The constant multiple by which the number of pots is increasing in every row is:

(a) 2 (b) 4

(c) 8 (d) 1

(B) The number of pots in 8th row is:

(a) 156 (b) 256

(c) 300 (d) 456

(C) The difference in number of pots placed in 7th row and 5th row is:

(a) 86 (b) 50

(c) 90 (d) 96

(D) Total number of pots upto 10th row is:

(a) 1046 (b) 2046

(c) 1023 (d) 1024

(E) If Rahul wants to place 510 pots in total , then the total number of rows formed in this arrangement is:

(a) 7 (b) 8

(c) 9 (d) 5

Ans. (A) *(a) 2*

Explanation: The number of pots in each row is 2, 4, 8.... .

$\therefore$ This forms a geometric progression,

Where $a = 2, r = \frac{4}{2} = 2$

Hence, the constant multiple by which the number of pots is increasing in every row is 2.

(B) *(b) 256*

Explanation: Number of pots in 8th row $= a_8$

$$a_8 = ar^{8-1} = 2(2)^7 = 2^8 = 256$$

(C) *(d) 96*

Explanation: Number of pots in 7th row,

$$a_7 = 2(2)^{7-1} = 2.2^6 = 2^7 = 128$$

Number of pots in 5th row,

$$a_5 = 2(2)^{5-1} = 2.2^4 = 2^5 = 32$$

Required answer = 128 – 32 = 96

(D) *(b) 2046*

Explanation: Total number of pots upto 10th row

$$\therefore \quad S_{10} = \frac{a(r^{10}-1)}{r-1} = \frac{2(2^{10}-1)}{2-1}$$

$$= \frac{2(1024-1)}{1} = 2046$$

(E) *(b) 8*

Explanation: Let there be n number of rows.

$$\therefore \quad S_n = 510 = \frac{2(2^n-1)}{2-1}$$

$$\Rightarrow \quad \frac{510}{2} = 2^n - 1$$

$$\Rightarrow \quad 255 = 2^n - 1$$

$$\Rightarrow \quad 256 = 2^n$$

$$\Rightarrow \quad 2^8 = 2^n$$

$$\Rightarrow \quad n = 8$$

VERY SHORT ANSWER Type Questions (VSA)

[**1** mark]

18. Find the sum of the G.P. 0.15, 0.015, 0.0015, ... to 20 terms. **[NCERT Exemplar]**

Ans. Given *G.P.* is 0.15, 0.015, 0.0015, . . .

Since, $\frac{0.015}{0.15} = 0.1, \frac{0.0015}{0.015} = 0.1, \ldots$

So, the common ratio of the given *G. P* is $r = 0.1$.

Also, the first term of the *G.P.* is $a = 0.15$.

Hence, the sum of 20 terms of the *G.P.* is given by

$$S_{20} = \frac{a(1-r^{20})}{1-r} = \frac{(0.15)[1-(0.1)^{20}]}{1-0.1}$$

$$= \frac{1}{6}[1-(0.1)^{20}]$$

19. If a, b and c are in G.P. then find the value of $\frac{a-b}{b-c}$.

Ans. Since a, b and c are in G.P.

$$\therefore \quad \frac{b}{a} = \frac{c}{b} = r \quad \text{(constant)}$$

$\Rightarrow b = ar$ *and* $c = br$

$\Rightarrow c = ar.r = ar^2$

So, $$\frac{a-b}{b-c} = \frac{a-ar}{ar-ar^2} = \frac{a(1-r)}{ar(1-r)}$$

$$= \frac{1}{r} = \frac{a}{b} = \frac{b}{c}$$

Hence, the correct value of $\frac{a-b}{b-c}$ is $\frac{a}{b}$ or $\frac{b}{c}$.

20. Find the sum of the G.P. 1, $-a$, a^2, $-a^3$, ... to n terms.

Ans. Given *G.P.* is $1, -a, a^2, -a^3, \ldots$

Since, $\frac{-a}{1}=-a, \frac{a^2}{-a}=-a, \ldots$

So, the common ratio of the given G.P. is $r = -a$.

Also, the first term of the G.P. is $A = 1$.

Hence, the sum of n terms of the G.P. is given by

$$S_n = \frac{A(1-r^n)}{1-r} = \frac{(1)[1-(-a)^n]}{1-(-a)} = \frac{1-(-a)^n}{1+a}..$$

21. Find the sum to n terms of the G.P., whose k^{th} term is 5^k.

Ans. Given that k^{th} term of a G.P. is 5^k.

$\therefore \quad a_k = 5^k$

Putting $k = 1$ in (1) we get

$a_1 = 5$ ...(2)

Putting $k = 2$ in (1), we get

$a_2 = 25$

Then, the first term is $a = a_1 = 5$ and the common ratio is $r = \frac{a_2}{a_1} = \frac{25}{5} = 5$

Hence, the sum of n terms of the G.P. is given by

$$S_n = \frac{a(r^n-1)}{r-1} = \frac{(5)(5^n-1)}{5-1} = \frac{5}{4}(5^n-1)$$

22. Find the 9th term and the general term of the progression: $\frac{1}{4}, -\frac{1}{2}, 1, -2, \ldots$

Ans. The given progression is clearly a G.P. with the first term $a = \frac{1}{4}$ and common ratio $r = -2$.

$\therefore$ 9th term $= a_9 = ar^{9-1} = ar^8 = \frac{1}{4}(-2)^8 = 64$

And,

General term $= a_n = ar^{n-1}$

$= \frac{1}{4}(-2)^{n-1} = (-1)^{n-1}2^{n-3}$

SHORT ANSWER Type-I Questions (SA-I)

[2 marks]

23. If the pth, q^{th} and r^{th} terms of a G.P. are a, b and c respectively. Prove that $a^{q-r}\, b^{r-p}\, c^{p-q} = 1$.

Ans. Let A be the first term and R be the common ratio of the given G.P.

Given that p^{th}, q^{th} and r^{th} terms of the G.P are a, b and c respectively.

$\therefore \quad A_p = a$

$\Rightarrow \quad AR^{p-1} = a$ ...(i)

$\therefore \quad A_q = b$

$\Rightarrow \quad AR^{q-1} = b$ ...(ii)

$\therefore \quad A_r = c$

$\Rightarrow \quad AR^{r-1} = c$ ...(iii)

Hence, $a^{q-r}\, b^{r-p}\, c^{p-q} = (AR^{p-1})^{q-r}\,(AR^{q-1})^{r-p}\,(AR^{r-1})^{p-q}$

{Using (i), (ii) and (iii)}

$= A^{q-r+r-p+p-q}\, R^{(p-1)(q-r)+(q-1)(r-p)+(r-1)(p-q)}$

$= A^0\, R^{(pq-q-pr+r+qr-r-pq+p+pr-p-qr+q)}$

$= A^0\, R^0$

$= 1.$

24. The fourth, seventh, and the last term of a G.P. are 10, 80 and 2560 respectively. Find the first term and the number of terms in the G.P.

Ans. Let a be the first term and r be the common ratio of the given G.P. Then,

$a_4 = 10, a_7 = 80$

$\Rightarrow \quad ar^3 = 10$ and $ar^6 = 80$

$\Rightarrow \quad \frac{ar^6}{ar^3} = \frac{80}{10}$

$\Rightarrow \quad r^3 = 8$

$\Rightarrow \quad r = 2.$

Putting $r = 2$ in $ar^3 = 10$, we get:

$a(2)^3 = 10$

$\Rightarrow \quad a = \frac{10}{8} = \frac{5}{4}$

Let there be n terms in the given G.P. Then,

$a_n = 2560$

$\Rightarrow \quad ar^{n-1} = 2560$

$\Rightarrow \quad \frac{5}{4}(2^{n-1}) = 2560$

$\Rightarrow \quad 2^{n-4} = 256$

$\Rightarrow \quad 2^{n-4} = 2^8$

$\Rightarrow \quad n-4 = 8$

$\Rightarrow \quad n = 12$

25. If the 4th and 9th term of a G.P. be 54 and 13122 respectively, find the G.P.

Ans. Let a be the first term and r the common ratio of the given G.P. Then,

$a_4 = 54$ and $a_9 = 13122$

$\Rightarrow$ $ar^3 = 54$ and $ar^8 = 13122$

$\Rightarrow \quad \dfrac{ar^8}{ar^3} = \dfrac{13122}{54}$

$\Rightarrow \quad r^5 = 243$

$\Rightarrow \quad r^5 = 3^5$

$\Rightarrow \quad r = 3$

Putting $r = 3$ in $ar^3 = 54$, we get:

$a(3)^3 = 54$

$\Rightarrow a = 2$

Thus, the given G.P. is $a, ar, ar^2, ar^3, ...$ i.e. 2, 6, 18, 54.

26. The 5th, 8th and 11th terms of a G.P. are p, q and s respectively. Show that $q^2 = ps$.

Ans. Let a be the first term and r be the common ratio of the given G.P.

Given that 5th, 8th and 11th terms of the G.P. are p, q, and s respectively.

$\therefore \quad a_5 = p$

$\Rightarrow \quad ar^4 = p \quad$ ...(1)

$\therefore \quad a_8 = q$

$\Rightarrow \quad ar^7 = q \quad$ ...(2)

$\therefore \quad a_{11} = s$

$\Rightarrow \quad ar^{10} = s \quad$ ....(3)

Hence, $ps = (ar^4)(ar^{10})$ [Using (1) and (3)]

$= a^2 r^{14}$

$= (ar^7)^2$

$= q^2$ [Using (2)]

SHORT ANSWER Type-II Questions (SA-II)

[3 marks]

27. Show the products of the corresponding terms of the sequence $a, ar, ar^2, ..., ar^{n-1}$ and $A, AR, AR^2, ..., AR^{n-1}$ form a G.P. and find the common ratio.

Ans. The sequence formed by the products of the corresponding terms of the given sequence is

$aA, aArR, aAr^2R^2, ..., aAr^{n-1}R^{n-1})$

Or

$aA, aA(rR), aA(rR)^2, aA(rR)^3, ..., aA(rR)^{n-1}$

Clearly, the ratio of any term and preceding term in the above sequence is the same,

Common ration = rR.

So, it is a G.P. with a common ratio rR.

28. A side of an equilateral triangle is 20 cm long. A second equilateral triangle is inscribed in it by joining the mid-points of the sides of the first triangle. The process is continued as shown in the accompanying diagram. Find the perimeter of the sixth inscribed equilateral triangle. [NCERT Exemplar]

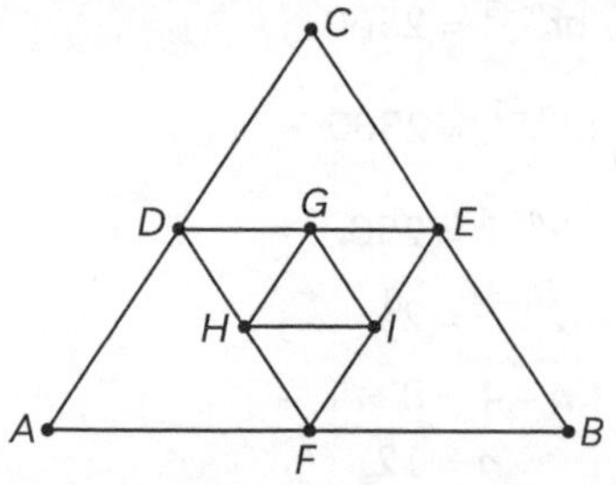

Ans. The side of the first equilateral ΔABC = 20 cm

By joining the mid-points of the sides of this triangle, we get the second equilateral triangle which each side $= \dfrac{20}{2} = 10$ cm.

[$\because$ The line joining the mid-points of two sides of a triangle is 1/2 and parallel to the third side of the triangle].

Similarly, each side of the third equilateral triangle $= \dfrac{10}{2} = 5$ cm

$\therefore$ Perimeter of first triangle = 20 × 3 = 60 cm

Perimeter of the second triangle

= 10 ×3 = 30 cm

And the perimeter of the third triangle

= 5 × 3 = 15 cm

Therefore, the series will be 60, 30, 15, . . .

Which is G.P. in which $a = 60$, and $r = \dfrac{30}{60} = \dfrac{1}{2}$

Now, we have to find the perimeter of the sixth inscribed equilateral triangle

$\therefore \quad a_6 = ar^{6-1}$

$= 60 \times \left(\dfrac{1}{2}\right)^5$

$= 60 \times \dfrac{1}{32}$

$= \dfrac{15}{8}$ cm.

Hence, the required perimeter $= \dfrac{15}{8}$ cm

29. If p^{th}, q^{th}, r^{th} and s^{th} terms of an A.P. are in G.P., then show that $(p - q)$, $(q - r)$, $(r - s)$ are also in G.P.

Ans. Let a be the first term and d be the common difference of the given A.P. Further, let a_p, a_q, a_r and a_s be its pth, q^{th}, r^{th} and s^{th} terms respectively.

Then,

$a_p = a + (p-1)d$, $a_q = a + (q-1)d$,

$a_r = a + (r-1)d$ and $a_s = a + (s-1)d$.

$\Rightarrow$ $a_p - a_q = (p-q)d$, $a_q - a_r = (q-r)d$

and $a_r - a_s = (r-s)d$

It is given that a_p, a_q, a_r and a_s are in G.P. Let A be the first term and R be the common ratio of the G.P. Then,

$A = a_p$, $AR = a_q$, $AR^2 = a_r$ and $AR^3 = a_s$.

$\therefore$ $A - AR = a_p - a_q$, $AR - AR^2 = a_q - a_r$

and $AR^2 - AR^3 = a_r - a_s$

$\Rightarrow$ $A(1-R) = a_p - a_q$, $AR(1-R) = a_q - a_r$

and $AR^2(1-R) = a_r - a_s$

$\Rightarrow$ $(a_q - a_r)^2 = \{AR(1-R)\}^2$

$= \{A(1-R)\}\{AR^2(1-R)\} = (a_p - a_q)(a_r - a_s)$

$\Rightarrow$ $(q-r)^2 d^2 = \{(p-q)d\}\{(r-s)d\}$

$\Rightarrow$ $(q-r)^2 = (p-q)(r-s)$

$\Rightarrow$ $p-q$, $q-r$, $r-s$ are in G.P.

30. Which term of the G.P. $\sqrt{3}, 3, 3\sqrt{3}, \ldots$ is 729?

Ans. Given G.P. is $\sqrt{3}, 3, 3\sqrt{3}, \ldots$

Since, $\frac{3}{\sqrt{3}} = \sqrt{3}, \frac{3\sqrt{3}}{3} = \sqrt{3}, \ldots$

So, the common ratio of the given G.P. is $r = \sqrt{3}$.

Also, the first term of the G.P. is $a = \sqrt{3}$

Let 729 be the nth term of the G.P.

Then, $a_n = 729$

$\Rightarrow$ $ar^{n-1} = 729$

$\Rightarrow$ $\sqrt{3}(\sqrt{3})^{n-1} = 729$ $[\because a = \sqrt{3}, r = \sqrt{3}]$

$\Rightarrow$ $(\sqrt{3})^n = 729$

$\Rightarrow$ $3^{n/2} = 3^6$

$\Rightarrow$ $\frac{n}{2} = 6$

$\Rightarrow$ $n = 12$

Hence, 729 is the 12th term of the given G.P.

31. If the continued product of three numbers in G.P. is 216 and the sum of their products in pairs is 156. Find the numbers.

Ans. Let the three numbers be $\frac{a}{r}$, a, ar. Then,

Product = 216

$\Rightarrow$ $\frac{a}{r}.(a).(ar) = 216$

$\Rightarrow$ $a^3 = 6^3$

$\Rightarrow$ $a = 6$

Sum of the products in pairs = 156

$\Rightarrow$ $\frac{a}{r}.a + a.ar + \frac{a}{r}.ar = 156$

$\Rightarrow$ $a^2\left(\frac{1}{r}+r+1\right) = 156$

$\Rightarrow$ $36\left(\frac{1+r^2+r}{r}\right) = 156$

$\Rightarrow$ $3(r^2+r+1) = 13r$

$\Rightarrow$ $3r^2 - 10r + 3 = 0$

$\Rightarrow$ $(3r-1)(r-3) = 0$

$\Rightarrow$ $r = \frac{1}{3}$ or, $r = 3$

Putting the values of a and r, the required numbers are 18,6,2 or 2,6,18.

LONG ANSWER Type Questions (LA)

[4 & 5 marks]

32. The length of three unequal edges of a rectangular solid block are in G.P. The volume of the block is 216 cm^3 and the total surface area is 252cm^2. Find the length of the largest edge. [NCERT Exemplar]

Ans. Let the length, breadth and height of a rectangular block be

$\frac{a}{r}$, a and ar. [Since they are in G.P.]

$\therefore$ Volume $= l \times b \times h$

$216 = \frac{a}{r} \times a \times ar$

$\Rightarrow$ $a^3 = 216$

$\Rightarrow$ $a = 6$

Now total surface area = $2[lb + bh + lh]$

$252 = 2\left[\frac{a}{r}\cdot a + a.ar + \frac{a}{r}\cdot ar\right]$

$\Rightarrow$ $252 = 2\left[\frac{a^2}{r} + a^2r + a^2\right]$

$\Rightarrow$ $252 = 2a^2\left[\frac{1}{r} + r + 1\right]$

$$\Rightarrow\ 252 = 2\times(6)^2\left[\frac{1+r^2+r}{r}\right]$$

$$\Rightarrow\ 252 = 72\left[\frac{1+r^2+r}{r}\right]$$

$$\Rightarrow\ \frac{252}{72} = \frac{1+r+r^2}{r}$$

$$\Rightarrow\ \frac{7}{2} = \frac{1+r+r^2}{r}$$

$$2 + 2r + 2r^2 = 7r$$

$$\Rightarrow\ 2r^2 - 5r + 2 = 0$$

$$\Rightarrow\ 2r^2 - 4r - r + 2 = 0$$

$$\Rightarrow\ 2r(r-2) - 1(r-2) = 0$$

$$\Rightarrow\ (r-2)(2r-1) = 0$$

$$\Rightarrow\ r - 2 = 0 \text{ and } 2r - 1 = 0$$

$$\therefore\ r = 2, \frac{1}{2}$$

Therefore, the three edges are:

If $r = 2$ then edges are 3, 6, 12.

If $r = \frac{1}{2}$ then edges are 12, 6, 3.

So, the length of the longest edge = 12

33. If the pth and q^{th} terms of a G.P. are q and p respectively, then show that its $(p + q)^{th}$ term is $\left(\frac{q^p}{p^q}\right)^{\frac{1}{p-q}}$. [NCERT Exemplar]

Ans. Let a be the first term and r be the common ratio of a G.P.

Given that $a_p = q$

$$\Rightarrow\ ar^{p-1} = q \quad \text{...(i)}$$

and $a_q = p$

$$\Rightarrow\ ar^{q-1} = p \quad \text{...(ii)}$$

Dividing eq.(i) by eq. (ii) we get,

$$\frac{ar^{p-1}}{ar^{q-1}} = \frac{q}{p}$$

$$\Rightarrow\ \frac{r^{p-1}}{r^{q-1}} = \frac{q}{p}$$

$$\Rightarrow\ r^{p-q} = \frac{q}{p}$$

$$\Rightarrow\ r = \left(\frac{q}{p}\right)^{\frac{1}{p-q}}$$

Putting the value of r in eq.(i), we get

$$a\left[\frac{q}{p}\right]^{\frac{1}{p-q}\times p-1} = q$$

$$a\left[\frac{q}{p}\right]^{\frac{p-1}{p-q}} = q$$

$$\therefore\ a = q.\left[\frac{p}{q}\right]^{\frac{p-1}{p-q}}$$

Now $T_{p+q} = ar^{p+q-1}$

$$= q\left[\frac{p}{q}\right]^{\frac{p-1}{p-q}}\left[\frac{q}{p}\right]^{\frac{1}{p-q}(p+q-1)}$$

$$= \left(\frac{p}{q}\right)^{\frac{p-1}{p-q}}.\left(\frac{q}{p}\right)^{\frac{p+q-1}{p-q}}$$

$$= q\left(\frac{p}{q}\right)^{\frac{p-1}{p-q}}.\left(\frac{p}{q}\right)^{\frac{-(p+q-1)}{p-q}}$$

$$= q\left(\frac{p}{q}\right)^{\frac{p-1}{p-q}-\frac{p+q-1}{p-q}}$$

$$= q\left(\frac{p}{q}\right)^{\frac{p-1-p-q+1}{p-q}}$$

$$= q\left(\frac{p}{q}\right)^{\frac{-q}{p-q}} = q\left(\frac{q}{p}\right)^{\frac{q}{p-q}}$$

$$= \frac{q^{\frac{q}{p-q}+1}}{p^{\frac{q}{p-q}}}$$

$$= \frac{q^{\frac{p}{p-q}}}{p^{\frac{q}{p-q}}} = \left[\frac{q^p}{p^q}\right]^{\frac{1}{p-q}}$$

Hence, the required term = $\left[\frac{q^p}{p^q}\right]^{\frac{1}{p-q}}$.

34. Find the sum of 5 + 5.5 + 5.5.5 . . . to n terms

Ans. Let S be the sum of the series 5 +5.5 + 5.55 + 5.555 + . . . to n terms.

S = 5 + 5.5 + 5.55 + 5.555 + . . . to n terms.

$\Rightarrow$ S = 5+(5 + 0.5) + (5 + 0.55) + (5 + 0.555) + ... to n terms

$\Rightarrow$ S = (5 + 5 + 5 + . . . to n terms) + {0.5 + 0.55 + 0.555 + ... to $(n - 1)$terms}

$\Rightarrow$ $S = 5n$ + 5{0.1 + 0 .11 + 0.111 + ... to $(n - 1)$ terms}

$$\Rightarrow\ S = 5n + \frac{5}{9}$$

{0.9 + 0.99 + 0.999 + to $(n - 1)$terms}

$$\Rightarrow S = 5n + \frac{5}{9}\left[\left(1-\frac{1}{10}\right)+\left(1-\frac{1}{100}\right)+\left(1-\frac{1}{1000}\right) + \ldots + \left(1-\frac{1}{10^{n-1}}\right)\right]$$

$$\Rightarrow \ S = 5n + \frac{5}{9}\left[(n-1) - \left(\frac{1}{10}+\frac{1}{10^2}+\frac{1}{10^3} + \ldots + \frac{1}{10^{n-1}}\right)\right]$$

$$\Rightarrow \ S = 5n + \frac{5}{9}\left[(n-1) - \frac{1}{10}\left\{\frac{1-\left(\frac{1}{10}\right)^{n-1}}{\left(1-\frac{1}{10}\right)}\right\}\right]$$

$$\Rightarrow \ S = 5n + \frac{5}{9}\left\{(n-1) - \frac{1}{9}\left(1-\frac{1}{10^{n-1}}\right)\right\}$$

35. If S be the sum, P the product, and R the sum of the reciprocals of *n* terms of a G.P., prove that $\left(\frac{S}{R}\right)^n = P^2$.

Ans. Let a be the first term and r be the common ratio of the G.P. Then,

$$S = a + ar + ar^2 + \ldots + ar^{n-1} = a\left(\frac{r^n-1}{r-1}\right)$$

$$P = a.\ ar\ ar^2 \ldots ar^{n-1}$$

$$= a^n r^{1+2+3+\ldots+(n-1)} = a^n r^{\frac{n(n-1)}{2}} \text{ and,}$$

$$R = \frac{1}{a} + \frac{1}{ar} + \frac{1}{ar^2} + \ldots + \frac{1}{ar^{n-1}}$$

$$\Rightarrow \ R = \frac{1}{a}\frac{\left\{\left(\frac{1}{r}\right)^n - 1\right\}}{\left\{\left(\frac{1}{r}\right) - 1\right\}} = \frac{1}{a}\left(\frac{1-r^n}{1-r}\right)\frac{1}{r^{n-1}}$$

$$\Rightarrow \ R = \frac{1}{a}\left(\frac{r^n-1}{r-1}\right)\frac{1}{r^{n-1}}$$

$$\therefore \quad \frac{S}{R} = a\left(\frac{r^n-1}{r-1}\right).a\left(\frac{r-1}{r^n-1}\right)r^{n-1} = a^2 r^{n-1}$$

$$\Rightarrow \quad \left(\frac{S}{R}\right)^n = a^{2n} r^{n(n-1)} = \left\{a^n r^{\frac{n(n-1)}{2}}\right\}^{-2} = P^2$$

Hence, $\left(\frac{S}{R}\right)^n = P^2$

RELATION BETWEEN A.M. AND G.M. 2

TOPIC 1

A.M. AND G.M.

Relation between Arithmetic Mean and Geometric Mean

The following results give the relation between arithmetic mean and geometric mean of two positive real numbers.

Result 1: The arithmetic mean of two positive real numbers is always greater than or equal to their geometric mean.

Proof: Let A and G denote the arithmetic mean and geometric mean of positive real numbers a and b.

Then, $A = \frac{a+b}{2}$ and $G = \sqrt{ab}$

Now, $A - G = \frac{a+b}{2} - \sqrt{ab} = \frac{a+b-2\sqrt{ab}}{2}$

$= \frac{(\sqrt{a})^2 + (\sqrt{b})^2 - 2\sqrt{a}\sqrt{b}}{2}$

$= \frac{(\sqrt{a}-\sqrt{b})^2}{2} \geq 0$

Hence, $A \geq G$.

Result 2: The arithmetic mean of two positive real number is equal to their geometric mean if and only if they are equal.

Proof: Let A and G denote the arithmetic mean and geometric mean of positive real numbers a and b.

Then, by previous result, we have

$A = G$

$\Leftrightarrow \quad A - G = 0$

$\Leftrightarrow \quad \frac{(\sqrt{a}-\sqrt{b})^2}{2} = 0$

$\Leftrightarrow \quad a = b$

Example 2.1: If A.M. and G.M. of roots of a quadratic equation are 8 and 5 respectively, then obtain the quadratic equation. (NCERT)

Ans. Let a and b be the roots of a quadratic equation.

Given that A.M. and G.M. of roots of quadratic equation are A=8 and G=5 respectively.

$A = 8$

$\Rightarrow \quad \frac{a+b}{2} = 8$

$\Rightarrow \quad a + b = 16$ ...(1)

$G = 5$

$\Rightarrow \quad \sqrt{ab} = 5$

$\Rightarrow \quad ab = 25$ ...(2)

Hence, the required quadratic equation is given by

$x^2 -$ (sum of roots) $x +$ (product of roots) $= 0$

$\Rightarrow x^2 - (a + b)x + ab = 0$

$\Rightarrow x^2 - 16x + 25 = 0$ (Using (1) and (2))

Example 2.2: Show that the products of the corresponding terms of the sequences $a, ar, ar^2, ar^3 ... ar^{n-1}$ and $A, AR, AR^2, AR^3 ... AR^{n-1}$ from a G.P, and find the common ratio. [NCERT]

Ans. 1st sequence is $a, ar, ar^2, ar^3 ... ar^{n-1}$

2nd sequence is $A, AR, AR^2, AR^3 ... AR^{n-1}$

	1st sequence	2nd sequence	Product of corresponding terms
1st term	a	A	$a \times A$
2nd term	ar	AR	$ar \times AR$
3rd term	ar^2	AR^2	$ar^2 \times AR^2$
n^{th} term	ar^{n-1}	AR^{n-1}	$ar^{n-1} \times AR^{n-1}$

Let P = Product of corresponding terms of 1st and 2nd sequence

$= a \times A, ar \times AR, ar^2 \times AR^2, ..., ar^{n-1} \times AR^{n-1}$

$= aA, arAR, ar^2 AR^2, ..., aA(r^{n-1} R^{n-1})$

$P = aA, arAR, ar^2 AR^2, ..., aA(r^{n-1} R^{n-1})$

Now, in $aA, arAR, ar^2 AR^2, ..., aA(r^{n-1} R^{n-1})$

$\frac{arAR}{aA} = rR$

and $\frac{ar^2AR^2}{arAR} = Rr$

Thus, $\frac{\text{Second term}}{\text{First term}} = \frac{\text{Third term}}{\text{Second term}}$,

i.e., common ratio is same

Thus, it is a G.P

Common ratio $= r = \frac{\text{second term}}{\text{first term}}$

$= \frac{arAR}{aA}$

$= rR$

Example 2.3: If S_1, S_2, S_3 are the sum of the first n natural numbers, their squared and their cubes respectively, show that $9S_2^2 = S_3(1 + 8S_1)$. [NCERT]

Ans. Given that S_1, S_2, S_3 are the sum of first n natural numbers, their squares and their cubes respectively.

$$S_1 = \frac{n(n+1)}{2}$$

$$S_2 = \frac{n(n+1)(2n+1)}{6}$$

$$S_3 = \left[\frac{n(n+1)}{2}\right]^2$$

Now, LHS = $9S_2^2 = 9\left[\frac{n(n+1)(2n+1)}{6}\right]^2$

Or, $9S_2^2 = \frac{n^2(n+1)^2(2n+1)^2}{4}$ ...(1)

Also, RHS= $S_3(1 + 8S_1)$

$$= \left[\frac{n(n+1)}{2}\right]^2 [1+4n(n+1)]$$

$$= \frac{n^2(n+1)^2}{4}[1+4n^2+4n]$$

Or, $S_3(1 + 8S_1) = \frac{n^2(n+1)^2(2n+1)^2}{4}$ ...(2)

From (1) and (2), we get

$$9S_2^2 = S_3(1+8S_1)$$

Hence, proved.

Example 2.4: If A and G be A.M and G.M., respectively between two positive numbers, prove that the numbers are $A \pm \sqrt{(A+G)(A-G)}$. [NCERT]

Ans. If a & b be two numbers

We need to show that the numbers are

$$A \pm \sqrt{(A+G)(A-G)}$$

i.e., a = $A+\sqrt{(A+G)(A-G)}$

$b = A-\sqrt{(A+G)(A-G)}$

Now we know that

Arithmetic mean = $A = \frac{a+b}{2}$

Geometric mean = $G = \sqrt{ab}$

Putting value of A and G in RHS we can prove that it is equal to a and b.

Solving

$$= A \pm \sqrt{(A+G)(A-G)}$$

$$= A \pm \sqrt{A^2 - G^2}$$

Putting $A = \frac{a+b}{2}$ and $G = \sqrt{ab}$

$$= \left(\frac{a+b}{2}\right) \pm \sqrt{\left(\frac{a+b}{2}\right)^2 - (\sqrt{ab})^2}$$

$$= \left(\frac{a+b}{2}\right) \pm \sqrt{\frac{(a+b)^2}{4} - ab}$$

$$= \left(\frac{a+b}{2}\right) \pm \sqrt{\frac{a^2+b^2+2ab-4ab}{4}}$$

$$= \left(\frac{a+b}{2}\right) \pm \sqrt{\frac{a^2+b^2-2ab}{4}}$$

[∵ Using $(x-y)^2 = x^2 + y^2 - 2xy$]

$$= \frac{a+b}{2} \pm \sqrt{\frac{(a-b)^2}{4}}$$

$$= \frac{a+b}{2} \pm \sqrt{\left(\frac{a-b}{2}\right)^2}$$

$$= \frac{a+b}{2} \pm \frac{a-b}{2}$$

Taking Positive Value	Taking Negative Value
$= \frac{a+b}{2} + \frac{a-b}{2}$	$= \frac{a+b}{2} - \left(\frac{a-b}{2}\right)$
$= \frac{a}{2} + \frac{b}{2} + \frac{a}{2} - \frac{b}{2}$	$= \frac{a}{2} + \frac{b}{2} - \frac{a}{2} + \frac{b}{2}$
$= \frac{a}{2} + \frac{a}{2} + \frac{b}{2} - \frac{b}{2}$	$= \frac{a}{2} - \frac{a}{2} + \frac{b}{2} + \frac{b}{2}$
$= \frac{a}{2} + \frac{a}{2} + 0$	$= 0 + \frac{b}{2} + \frac{b}{2}$
$= a$	$= b$

Thus, $A+\sqrt{(A+G)(A-G)} = a$

and $A-\sqrt{(A+G)(A-G)} = b$ Hence proved.

Example 2.5: The ratio of the A.M. and G.M. of two positive numbers a and b, is $m : n$. Show that $a : b = (m+\sqrt{m^2-n^2}) : (m-\sqrt{m^2-n^2})$ [NCERT]

Ans. Here, the two numbers be a and b

Arithmetic Mean = A.M. = $\frac{a+b}{2}$ and Geometric Mean = G.M. = $\sqrt{ab}$

According to the question,

$$\frac{A.M.}{G.M.} = \frac{m}{n}$$

$$\frac{a+b}{2\sqrt{ab}} = \frac{m}{n}$$

Applying componendo and dividendo, we get

$$\frac{a+b+2\sqrt{ab}}{a+b-2\sqrt{ab}}=\frac{m+n}{m-n}$$

$$\frac{(\sqrt{a})^2+(\sqrt{b})^2+2(\sqrt{a}\times\sqrt{b})}{(\sqrt{a})^2+(\sqrt{b})^2-2(\sqrt{a}\times\sqrt{b})}=\frac{m+n}{m-n}$$

[$\because$ $(x+y)^2=x^2+y^2+2xy$]

$(x-y)^2=x^2+y^2-2xy$

$$\frac{(\sqrt{a}+\sqrt{b})^2}{(\sqrt{a}-\sqrt{b})^2}=\frac{m+n}{m-n}$$

$$\left(\frac{\sqrt{a}+\sqrt{b}}{\sqrt{a}-\sqrt{b}}\right)^2=\frac{m+n}{m-n}$$

$$\frac{\sqrt{a}+\sqrt{b}}{\sqrt{a}-\sqrt{b}}=\sqrt{\frac{m+n}{m-n}}$$

$$\frac{\sqrt{a}+\sqrt{b}}{\sqrt{a}-\sqrt{b}}=\frac{\sqrt{m+n}}{\sqrt{m-n}}$$

Applying componendo and dividendo

$$\frac{(\sqrt{a}+\sqrt{b})+(\sqrt{a}-\sqrt{b})}{(\sqrt{a}+\sqrt{b})-(\sqrt{a}-\sqrt{b})}=\frac{\sqrt{m+n}+\sqrt{m-n}}{\sqrt{m+n}-\sqrt{m-n}}$$

$$\frac{2\sqrt{a}}{2\sqrt{b}}=\frac{\sqrt{m+n}+\sqrt{m-n}}{\sqrt{m+n}-\sqrt{m-n}}$$

$$\frac{\sqrt{a}}{\sqrt{b}}=\frac{\sqrt{m+n}+\sqrt{m-n}}{\sqrt{m+n}-\sqrt{m-n}}$$

Squaring both sides

$$\left(\frac{\sqrt{a}}{\sqrt{b}}\right)^2=\left(\frac{\sqrt{m+n}+\sqrt{m-n}}{\sqrt{m+n}-\sqrt{m-n}}\right)^2$$

$$\frac{(\sqrt{a})^2}{(\sqrt{b})^2}=\frac{(\sqrt{m+n}+\sqrt{m-n})^2}{(\sqrt{m+n}-\sqrt{m-n})^2}$$

[$\because$ $(x+y)^2=x^2+y^2+2xy$ $(x-y)^2$
$=x^2+y^2-2xy$]

$$\frac{a}{b}=\frac{(\sqrt{m+n})^2+(\sqrt{m-n})^2+2(\sqrt{m+n})(\sqrt{m-n})}{(\sqrt{m+n})^2+(\sqrt{m-n})^2-2(\sqrt{m+n})(\sqrt{m-n})}$$

$$\frac{a}{b}=\frac{m+n+m-n+2\sqrt{(m+n)(m-n)}}{m+n+m-n-2\sqrt{(m+n)(m-n)}}$$

$$\frac{a}{b}=\frac{m+m+n-n+2\sqrt{(m^2-n^2)}}{m+m+n-n-2\sqrt{(m^2-n^2)}}$$

$$\frac{a}{b}=\frac{2m+2\sqrt{(m^2-n^2)}}{2m-2\sqrt{(m^2-n^2)}}$$

$$\frac{a}{b}=\frac{2\left(m+\sqrt{(m^2-n^2)}\right)}{2\left(m-\sqrt{(m^2-n^2)}\right)}$$

$$\frac{a}{b}=\frac{m+\sqrt{(m^2-n^2)}}{m-\sqrt{(m^2-n^2)}}$$

Thus, $a:b=(m+\sqrt{m^2-n^2}):(m-\sqrt{m^2-n^2})$

Hence, proved.

Example 2.6: If a, b, c are in A.P., b, c, d are in G.P. and $\frac{1}{c},\frac{1}{d},\frac{1}{e}$ are in A.P. prove that a, c, e are in G.P.

[NCERT]

Ans. It is given that a, b, c are in A.P.

So, their common difference is same

$b-a=c-b$

$b+b=c+a$

$2b=c+a$

$$b=\frac{c+a}{2} \quad ...(1)$$

Also, given that b,c,d are in G.P.

So, their common ratio is same

$$\frac{c}{b}=\frac{d}{c}$$

$$c^2=bd \quad ...(2)$$

Also,

$\frac{1}{c},\frac{1}{d},\frac{1}{e}$ are in A.P.

So, their common difference is same

$$\frac{1}{d}-\frac{1}{c}=\frac{1}{e}-\frac{1}{d}$$

$$\frac{1}{d}+\frac{1}{d}=\frac{1}{e}+\frac{1}{c}$$

$$2\left(\frac{1}{d}\right)=\frac{c+e}{ec}$$

$$\frac{2}{d}=\frac{c+e}{ec}$$

$$\frac{d}{2}=\frac{ec}{c+e}$$

$$d=2\left(\frac{ec}{c+e}\right) \quad ...(3)$$

We need to show that a, c, e are in G.P. i.e., we need to show their common ratio is same

$$\frac{c}{a}=\frac{e}{c}$$

$$c^2=ae$$

So, we need to show $c^2=ae$.

From (2), we have

$$c^2 = bd$$

Putting value of $b = \dfrac{a+c}{2}$ and $d = \dfrac{2ce}{c+e}$

$$c^2 = \left(\frac{a+c}{2}\right)\left(\frac{2ce}{c+e}\right)$$

$$c^2 = \frac{(a+c)(2ce)}{2(c+e)}$$

$$c^2 = \frac{(a+c)(ce)}{(c+e)}$$

$$\frac{c^2}{c} = \frac{e(a+c)}{c+e}$$

$$c = \frac{e(a+c)}{c+e}$$

$$c(c+e) = e(a+c)$$

$$c^2 + ec = ea + ec$$

$$c^2 = ea + ec - ec$$

$$c^2 = ea + 0$$

$$c^2 = ea$$

Hence, proved

Thus, *a*, *c* and *e* are in *G.P.*

OBJECTIVE Type Questions

[1 mark]

Multiple Choice Questions

1. The nth term of an *A.P.* with first term *a* and common difference *d* is:

(a) $2a + (n-1)d$ **(b)** $a + (n-1)d$

(c) $\frac{n}{2}(2a+(n-1)d)$ **(d)** $n(2a + (n-1)d)$

Ans. (b) $a + (n-1)d$

Explanation: The nth term of an *A.P.* whose first term is *a* and common difference *d* is

$$a_n = a + (n-1)d$$

Hence, option (b) is correct.

2. The sum of *n* terms of a *G.P.* with first term *a* and common ratio *r* where *r* >1, is:

(a) $a\left(\frac{1-r^n}{1-r}\right)$ **(b)** $a\left(\frac{1-r}{1-r^n}\right)$

(c) $a\left(\frac{r^n-1}{r-1}\right)$ **(d)** None

Ans. (c) $a\left(\frac{r^n-1}{r-1}\right)$

Explanation: The formula of sum of *G.P.* of *n* term is

$$S_n = a\left(\frac{r^n-1}{r-1}\right) \text{ if } r>1$$

$$= a\left(\frac{1-r^n}{1-r}\right) \text{ if } r<1$$

Hence option (c) is correct.

3. $3^{\frac{1}{2}} \times 3^{\frac{1}{4}} \times 3^{\frac{1}{8}} \times \ldots$ upto infinite terms is equal to:

(a) 3^2 **(b)** 3

(c) 3^3 **(d)** 3^4

Ans. (b) 3

Explanation: Given

$$3^{\frac{1}{2}} \times 3^{\frac{1}{4}} \times 3^{\frac{1}{8}} \times \ldots$$

$$= 3^{\frac{1}{2}+\frac{1}{4}+\frac{1}{8}+\ldots}$$

$$= 3^{\frac{1}{2}\left(1+\frac{1}{2}+\left(\frac{1}{2}\right)^2+\left(\frac{1}{2}\right)^3+\ldots\right)}$$

$$= 3^{\frac{1}{2}\times\left(\frac{1}{1-\frac{1}{2}}\right)} \quad [\because a = 1 \text{ and } r = \frac{1}{2}]$$

$$= 3^{\frac{1}{2}\times\frac{2}{1}} = 3$$

Hence option (b) is correct.

4. The geometric mean of 2 and 8 is:

(a) 4 **(b)** 6

(c) 7 **(d)** 5

Ans. (a) 4

Explanation: The geometric mean of 2 and 8 is $\sqrt{16}$ *i.e.*, 4.

Hence option (a) is correct.

5. Four geometric means between 3 and 96 are:

(a) 6, 12, 24, 48 **(b)** 6, 10, 24, 48

(c) 6, 10, 40, 48 **(d)** 48, 24, 10, 5

Ans. *(a) 6, 12, 24, 48*

Explanation: Let G_1, G_2, G_3 and G_4 be the required GM's.

Then, 3 , G_1, G_2, G_3, G_4, 96 are in G.P.

Let r be the common ratio. Here, 96 is the 6th term.

$\therefore\ 96 = ar^{6-1} = 3r^5$

$\Rightarrow\ 32 = r^5 \Rightarrow (2)^5 = r^5 \Rightarrow r = 2$

$\therefore\ G_1 = ar = 3.2 = 6$

$G_2 = ar^2 = 3.2^2 = 12$

$G_3 = ar^3 = 3.2^3 = 24$

And $G_4 = ar^4 = 3.2^4 = 48$

Hence option (a) is correct.

6. The minimum value of $4^x + 4^{1-x}$, $x \in R$ is:

(a) 2 **(b) 4**

(c) 1 **(d) 0 [NCERT Exemplar]**

Ans. *(b) 4*

Explanation: We know that, $AM \geq GM$

$$\Rightarrow \frac{4^x + 4^{1-x}}{2} \geq \sqrt{4^x . 4^{1-x}}$$

$$\Rightarrow 4^x + 4^{1-x} \geq 2.2$$

$$\Rightarrow 4^x + 4^{1-x} \geq 4$$

Hence, option (b) is correct.

Assertion-Reason (A-R)

DIRECTION: In the following questions, a statement of assertion (A) is followed by a statement of the reason (R). Mark the correct choice as:

(a) Both assertion (A) and reason (R) are true and reason (R) is the correct explanation of assertion (A).

(b) Both assertion (A) and reason (R) are true but reason (R) is not the correct explanation of assertion (A).

(c) Assertion (A) is true but reason (R) is false.

(d) Assertion (A) is false but reason (R) is true.

7. Assertion (A): The sum of first n terms of the series 0.6 + 0.66 + 0.666 + ... is

$$\frac{2}{3}\left[n - \frac{1}{9}\left\{1 - \left(\frac{1}{10}\right)^n\right\}\right].$$

Reason (R): General term of a GP is $T_n = ar^{n-1}$, where a = first term and r = common ratio.

Ans. *(b) Both assertion (A) and reason (R) are true but reason (R) is not the correct explanation of assertion (A).*

Explanation: Let

$S = 0.6 + 0.66 + 0.666 + \ldots$ upto n terms

$S = 6(0.1 + 0.11 + 0.111 + \ldots$ upto n terms)

$$= \frac{6}{9}(0.9 + 0.99 + 0.999 + \ldots \text{ upto } n \text{ terms})$$

$$= \frac{2}{3}\left[\frac{9}{10} + \frac{99}{100} + \frac{999}{1000} + \ldots \text{upto } n \text{ terms}\right]$$

$$= \frac{2}{3}\left[\left(1 - \frac{1}{10}\right) + \left(1 - \frac{1}{100}\right) + \left(1 - \frac{1}{1000}\right) + \ldots \text{ upto } n \text{ terms}\right]$$

$$= \frac{2}{3}\Big[(1 + 1 + 1 + \ldots \text{ upto } n \text{ terms}) - \left(\frac{1}{10} + \frac{1}{100} + \frac{1}{1000} + \ldots \text{upto } n \text{ terms}\right)\Big]$$

$$= \frac{2}{3}\left[n - \frac{\frac{1}{10}\left\{1 - \left(\frac{1}{10}\right)^n\right\}}{1 - \frac{1}{10}}\right]$$

$$\left[\because \text{ sum of } GP = \frac{a(1 - r^n)}{1 - r}, r < 1\right]$$

$$= \frac{2}{3}\left[n - \frac{\frac{1}{10}\left\{1 - \left(\frac{1}{10}\right)^n\right\}}{\frac{9}{10}}\right]$$

$$= \frac{2}{3}\left[n - \frac{1}{9}\left\{1 - \left(\frac{1}{10}\right)^n\right\}\right]$$

8. Assertion (A): The sum of first n natural number is $1 + 2 + 3 + \ldots + n = n\left(\frac{n+1}{2}\right)$.

Reason (R): For n number of A.P. the sum $S_n = \frac{n}{2}\left[2a + (n-1)d\right]$.

Ans. *(a) Both assertion (A) and reason (R) are true and reason (R) is the correct explanation of assertion (A).*

Explanation: We know that the sum of first n natural number is $n\left(\frac{n+1}{2}\right)$

For A.P.

$1 + 2 + \ldots n$

$a = 1, d = 1$

$$S_n = \frac{n}{2}\left[2 \times 1 + (n-1)1\right]$$

$$= \frac{n}{2}[2+n-1]$$

$$= \frac{n}{2}[n+1]$$

Hence, both assertion and reason are true and reason is the correct explanation of assertion.

9. Assertion: Two sequence can be in both *A.P.* and *G.P.*

Reason: If the sum of n terms of a sequence is a quadratic expression, then it always represents an *A.P.*

Ans. *(c) Assertion (A) is true but reason (R) is false.*

Explanation: Two sequence can be in both *A.P.* and *G.P.* in some special cases.

If the sum of *n* term of a sequence is quadratic then it may or may not be represent an *A.P.*

CASE BASED Questions (CBQs)

[4 & 5 marks]

Read the following passages and answer the questions that follow:

10. *A person was employed in a company on the condition that he will be paid rupees 2, 4, 6, 8, 10, ... for the work done in the company on 1st, 2nd, 3rd, ... day.*

(A) Name the progression of amount received by the person.

(a) A.P. **(b) G.P.**
(c) A.P. and G.P. **(d) None**

(B) The common difference of the sequence is:

(a) 1 **(b) 2**
(c) 3 **(d) 4**

(C) The first term of the sequence is:

(a) 2 **(b) 4**
(c) 6 **(d) 8**

(D) The total amount received in 10 days in rupees is:

(a) 115 **(b) 105**
(c) 120 **(d) 110**

Ans. (A) *(a) A.P.*

Explanation: The given series 2, 4, 6, 8, ... is A.P. because the common difference is same as

$$a_2 - a_1 = 2$$
$$a_3 - a_2 = 2$$

Hence, option (a) is correct.

(B) *(b) 2*

Explanation: The common difference as the A.P. 2, 4, 6, 8,...

$$a_2 - a_1 = 4 - 2 = 2$$
$$a_3 - a_2 = 6 - 4 = 2$$
$$a_4 - a_3 = 8 - 6 = 2$$

Hence option (b) is correct.

(C) *(a) 2*

Explanation: The first term of A.P 2, 4, 6, 8 ,... is 2.

Hence, option (a) is correct.

(D) *(d) 110*

Explanation: Here $a = 2$, $d = 2$ and $n = 10$

So,

$$S_{10} = \frac{10}{2}\left[2\times2+(10-1)2\right]$$

$$= \frac{10}{2}[4+18]$$

$$= \frac{10}{2}[22]$$

$$= 10 \times 11 = ₹\,110$$

Hence, option (d) is correct.

11. *A group of students obtain the sum of first n natural number is $\frac{n(n+1)}{2}$ named as A_n, sum of square of n natural number is $\frac{n(n+1)(2n+1)}{6}$ named as B_n and sum of cubes of n natural number is $\left(\frac{n(n+1)}{2}\right)^3$ named as C_n.*

(A) Find the value of A_5 and B_3.

(B) Find the value of C_2 and the sum of first *n* natural number is also the sum of *n* numbers of *A.P* whose first term is 1 and common difference is also 1.

Ans. (A) $$A_n = \frac{n(n+1)}{2}$$

So, Put $n = 5$

We get

$$A_5 = \frac{5(5+1)}{2}$$

$$= \frac{5\times6}{2}$$
$$= 3 \times 5$$
$$= 15$$
$$B_n = \frac{n(n+1)(2n+1)}{6}$$

So put $n = 3$

$$B_3 = \frac{3(3+1)(6+1)}{6}$$
$$= \frac{3\times4\times7}{6}$$
$$= \frac{28}{2}$$
$$= 14$$

(B) $C_n = \left(\frac{n(n+1)}{2}\right)^3$

Put $n = 2$

$$C_2 = \left(\frac{2(2+1)}{2}\right)^3$$
$$= (3)^3$$
$$= 27$$
$$A_n = \frac{n(n+1)}{2}$$

and $S_n = 1 + 2 + 3 + ... n$

$$= \frac{n}{2}[2a+(n-1)d]$$
$$= \frac{n}{2}[2+(n-1)1]$$
$$= \frac{n}{2}[2+n-1]$$
$$= \frac{n(n+1)}{2}$$

Hence option (a) is correct.

VERY SHORT ANSWER Type Questions (VSA)

[1 mark]

12. The first term of a G.P. is 0.3 and the common ratio is 0.5. Find the sum to infinity of G.P.

Ans. Given that the first term of a G.P is $a = 0.3$ and the common ratio is $r = 0.5$ clearly, $|r| < 1$.

Hence, the sum to infinity of G.P. is $S_\infty = \frac{a}{1-r} = \frac{0.3}{1-0.5} = 0.6$

13. Find the sum of infinity of the G.P 5, $\frac{20}{7}, \frac{80}{49}$ ….

Ans. Given G.P. is 5, $\frac{20}{7}, \frac{80}{49}$ ....

Since, $\frac{\left(\frac{20}{7}\right)}{5} = \frac{4}{7} \cdot \frac{\left(\frac{80}{49}\right)}{\left(\frac{20}{7}\right)} = \frac{4}{7}$ Clearly, $|r| < 1$.

Also, the first term of G.P. is $a = 5$.

Hence, the sum of infinity of G.P. is $S_\infty = \frac{a}{1-r} = \frac{5}{1-\frac{4}{7}} = \frac{35}{3}$

14. Prove that $9^{1/2} \times 9^{1/4} \times 9^{1/8}$ ... ∞ = 9

Ans. Here

$$= 9^{1/2} \times 9^{1/4} \times 9^{1/8} ... \infty$$
$$= 9^{\left[\frac{1}{2}+\frac{1}{4}+\frac{1}{8}...\infty\right]}$$
$$= 9^{\left[\frac{1/2}{1-1/2}\right]} \qquad \because \frac{1}{2}+\frac{1}{4}+\frac{1}{8}...\infty = \frac{\frac{1}{2}}{1-\frac{1}{2}} = 1$$
$$= 9^1$$
$$= 9$$

15. The first term of a G.P is 4 and the sum of infinity is 8 find common ratio.

Ans. Given, $S_\infty = 8$

$$\Rightarrow \frac{a}{1-r} = 8$$
$$\Rightarrow \frac{4}{1-r} = 8$$
$$\Rightarrow 4 = 8 - 8r$$
$$-4 = -8r$$

Or, $\frac{1}{2} = r$

SHORT ANSWER Type-I Questions (SA-I)

[2 marks]

16. If x, y, z are distinct positive number, then prove that (x + y) (y + z) (z + x) > 8xyz. **[NCERT Exemplar]**

Ans. Using A.M > G.M., we obtain

$\frac{x+y}{2} > \sqrt{xy}, \frac{y+z}{2} > \sqrt{yz}$ *and* $\frac{z+x}{2} > \sqrt{zx}$ for the three pairs

$\Rightarrow$ $x+y > 2\sqrt{xy}, y+z > 2\sqrt{yz}$ *and* $z+x > 2\sqrt{zx}$

$\Rightarrow$ $(x+y)(y+z)(z+x) > 2\sqrt{xy} \times 2\sqrt{xy} \times, 2\sqrt{zx}$

$\Rightarrow$ $(x + y)(y + z)(z + x) > 8xyz$.

17. If $x \in R$, find the minimum value of the expression $3^x + 3^{1-x}$. **[NCERT Exemplar]**

Ans. We know that A.M. > G.M.

$\therefore \quad \frac{3^x+3^{1-x}}{2} \geq \sqrt{3^x \times 3^{1-x}}$ for all $x \in R$

$\Rightarrow \quad \frac{3^x+3^{1-x}}{2} \geq \sqrt{3}$ for all $x \in R$

$\Rightarrow \quad 3^x+3^{1-x} \geq 2\sqrt{3}$ for all $x \in R$

Hence, the minimum value of $3^x + 3^{1-x}$ for any $x \in R$ is $2\sqrt{3}$

18. Write the sum of 2 + 4 + 6 + 8 + ... + 2n.

Ans. Here, n^{th} term is $2n$

So, $\quad S_n = \sum 2n$

$= 2\sum n$

$= \frac{2n(n+1)}{2}$

$= n(n + 1)$

$= n^2 + n$

SHORT ANSWER Type-II Questions (SA-II)

[3 marks]

19. Find the sum of the sequence 2, 22, 222, 2222, ...

Ans. Let $S_n = 2 + 22 + 222 + 2222 + ...$

$= 2(1 + 11 + 111 + ...)$

$= \frac{2}{9}(9+99+999+...)$

$= \frac{2}{9}((10-1)+(10^2-1)+(10^3-1)+...)$

$= \frac{2}{9}(10+10^2+10^3+...-n)$

$= \frac{2}{9}\left[\frac{10}{9}(10^n-1)-n\right]$

20. Find the positive numbers whose difference is 32 and whose A.M exceeds the G.M. by 8.

Ans. Let the two numbers be a and b

Then, as per the question, $a - b = 32$

It is also given that

A.M. – G.M = 8

$\frac{a+b}{2} - \sqrt{ab} = 8$

Or, $\quad a+b-2\sqrt{ab} = 16$

Or, $\quad (\sqrt{a}-\sqrt{b})^2 = 16$

Or, $\quad \sqrt{a}-\sqrt{b} = \pm 4 \quad$ ...(1)

Now, $\quad a - b = 32$

$(\sqrt{a}+\sqrt{b})(\sqrt{a}-\sqrt{b}) = 32$

$(\sqrt{a}+\sqrt{b}) \times \pm 4 = 32$

$\sqrt{a}+\sqrt{b} = \pm 8 \quad$ ...(2)

So, solving (1) and (2) we get,

$a = 36$

$b = 4$

21. Find the sum of first n terms of the series $\frac{1}{2}+\frac{3}{4}+\frac{7}{8}+\frac{15}{16}+ ... + n$ terms

Ans. The given sequence is

$\frac{1}{2}+\frac{3}{4}+\frac{7}{8}+\frac{15}{16}+...+n$ terms

We can write each individuals as,

$\frac{1}{2} = 1-\frac{1}{2}$

$\frac{3}{4}=1-\frac{1}{4}$

$\frac{7}{8}=1-\frac{1}{8}$ and ... till n terms

Now writing each term in its new form, we get,

$$\left(1-\frac{1}{2}\right)+\left(1-\frac{1}{4}\right)+\left(1-\frac{1}{8}\right)+...+\left(1-\frac{1}{2^n}\right)$$

$$= (1+1+1 x... \ n \text{ terms})-\left(\frac{1}{2}+\frac{1}{4}+\frac{1}{8}+...+\frac{1}{2^n}\right)$$

$$= n-\left(\frac{1}{2}+\frac{1}{4}+\frac{1}{8}+...+\frac{1}{2^n}\right) \quad ...(i)$$

Now, $\left(\frac{1}{2}+\frac{1}{4}+\frac{1}{8}+...+\frac{1}{2^n}\right)$ in a G.P with common ratio = $\frac{1}{2}$ so,

$$\frac{1}{2}+\frac{1}{4}+\frac{1}{8}+...+\frac{1}{2^n}=\frac{\frac{1}{2}\left(1-\left(\frac{1}{2}\right)^n\right)}{1-\frac{1}{2}}$$

$$=\left[1-\left(\frac{1}{2}\right)^n\right]$$

Putting this value in eq. (i), we get

$$n-\left(\frac{1}{2}+\frac{1}{4}+\frac{1}{8}+...+\frac{1}{2^n}\right)$$

$$= n-\left[1-\left(\frac{1}{2}\right)^n\right]=n-1+\left(\frac{1}{2}\right)^n$$

22. Write first five terms of sequence of whose n^{th} term is = $\frac{1}{2}|2n-1|$.

Ans. Put $n = 1$

$$a_1 = \frac{1}{2}|2\times1-1|$$

$$= \frac{1}{2}$$

$$a_2 = \frac{1}{2}|2\times2-1|$$

$$= \frac{3}{2}$$

$$a_3 = \frac{1}{2}|2\times3-1|$$

$$= \frac{5}{2}$$

$$a_4 = \frac{1}{2}|2\times4-1|$$

$$= \frac{7}{2}$$

$$a_5 = \frac{1}{2}|2\times5-1|$$

$$= \frac{9}{2}$$

LONG ANSWER Type Questions (LA)

[**4** & **5** marks]

23. If A is the arithmetic mean and G_1, G_2 be two geometric means between any two numbers, then prove that [DIKSHA]

$$2A = \frac{G_1^2}{G_2}+\frac{G_2^2}{G_1}$$

Ans. Given A is the arithmetic mean and G_1, G_2 be two geometric means between any two numbers.

Let the two numbers be 'a' and 'b'.

The arithmetic mean is given by $A = \frac{a+b}{2}$ and the geometric mean is given by $G = \sqrt{ab}$.

We have to insert two geometric means between a and b.

Now, that we have the terms a, G_1, G_2, b

G_1 will be the geometric mean of a and G_2 and G_2 will be the geometric mean of G_1 and b.

Hence $G_1 = \sqrt{aG_2}$ amd $G_2 = \sqrt{G_1 b}$

Squaring both sides, $G_1 = \sqrt{aG_2}$

$$\Rightarrow \quad G_1^2 = aG_2 \quad ...(1)$$

Put $G_2 = \sqrt{G_1 b}$ in (1)

$$\Rightarrow \quad G_1^2 = a\sqrt{G_1 b}$$

Squaring on both sides we get

$$\Rightarrow \quad G_1^4 = a^2 (G_1 b)$$

$$\Rightarrow \quad G_1^3 = a^2 b$$

$$\Rightarrow \quad G_1 = a^{\frac{2}{3}} b^{\frac{1}{3}} \quad ...(2)$$

Put value of G_1 in $G_2 = \sqrt{G_1 b}$

$\Rightarrow \quad G_2 = \sqrt{a^{\frac{2}{3}} b^{\frac{1}{3}} b}$

$= \left(a^{\frac{2}{3}} b^{\frac{4}{3}}\right)^{\frac{1}{2}}$

$= a^{\frac{1}{3}} b^{\frac{2}{3}}$ ..(3)

Now, we have to prove that $2A = \frac{G_1^2}{G_2} + \frac{G_2^2}{G_1}$.

Consider RHS

$\Rightarrow \quad \text{RHS} = \frac{G_1^2}{G_2} + \frac{G_2^2}{G_1}$

Substitute values of G_1 and G_2 from (2) and (3)

$\Rightarrow \quad \text{RHS} = \frac{\left(a^{\frac{2}{3}} b^{\frac{1}{3}}\right)^2}{a^{\frac{1}{3}} b^{\frac{2}{3}}} + \frac{\left(a^{\frac{1}{3}} b^{\frac{2}{3}}\right)^2}{a^{\frac{2}{3}} b^{\frac{1}{3}}}$

$= \frac{a^{\frac{4}{3}} b^{\frac{2}{3}}}{a^{\frac{1}{3}} b^{\frac{2}{3}}} + \frac{a^{\frac{2}{3}} b^{\frac{4}{3}}}{a^{\frac{2}{3}} b^{\frac{1}{3}}}$

Taking LCM and simplify we get,

$= a^{\frac{4}{3}-\frac{1}{3}} b^{\frac{2}{3}-\frac{2}{3}} + a^{\frac{2}{3}-\frac{2}{3}} b^{\frac{4}{3}-\frac{1}{3}}$

$\Rightarrow \quad \text{RHS} = 2\frac{a+b}{2}$

But $\quad A = \frac{a+b}{2}$

Therefore

$\Rightarrow \quad \text{RHS} = 2A$

Hence, RHS = LHS

Hence proved.

24. (A) If *a, b, c, d* are four distinct positive quantities in *A.P.*, then show that *bc > ad*.

(B) If *a, b, c, d* are four distinct positive quantities in *G.P.*, then show that *a + b > b + c*.

Ans. (A) Given that *a, b, c, d* are four distinct positive quantities in *A.P.*

Since, *a, b, c* are in *A.P.*

So, $\frac{a+c}{2} = b]$

Now, A.M. > G.M. [$\because$ *a, c* are distinct]

$\Rightarrow \quad \frac{a+c}{2} > \sqrt{ac}$

$\Rightarrow \quad b > \sqrt{ac}$

$\Rightarrow \quad b^2 > ac$ ...(1)

Since, *b, c, d* are in *A.P.*

So, $\frac{b+d}{2} = c$

Now, *A.M.* > *G.M.* [$\because$ *b, d* are distinct]

$\Rightarrow \quad \frac{b+d}{2} > \sqrt{bd}$

$\Rightarrow \quad c > \sqrt{bd}$

$\Rightarrow \quad c_2 > bd$ ...(2)

Multiplying (1) and (2), we get

$b^2 c^2 > (ac)(bd)$

$\Rightarrow \quad bc > ad$

(B) Given *a, b, c, d* are four distinct positive quantities in *G.P.*

Since *a, b, c* are in *G.P.*

So, $\sqrt{ac} = b$

Now, *A.M.* > *G.M.* [$\because$ *a, c* are distinct]

$\Rightarrow \quad \frac{a+b}{2} > \sqrt{ac}$

$\Rightarrow \quad \frac{a+b}{2} > b$

$\Rightarrow \quad a + c > 2b$ ...(3)

Since *b, c, d* are in *G.P.*

So, $\sqrt{bd} = c$

Now, *A.M.* > *G.M.* [$\because$ *a, c* are distinct]

$\Rightarrow \quad \frac{b+d}{2} > \sqrt{bd}$

$\Rightarrow \quad \frac{b+d}{2} > c$

$\Rightarrow \quad b + d > 2c$ ...(4)

Adding (3) and (4), we get

$(a + c) + (b + d) > 2b + 2c$

$\Rightarrow \quad a + d > b + c.$

25. If p^{th}, q^{th} and r^{th} terms of an A.P. and G.P. are both a,b and c respectively, show that $a^{b-c} \cdot b^{c-a} \cdot c^{a-b} = 1$ [DIKSHA]

Ans. Let the first term of *A.P.* be *m* and common difference as *d*.

Let the *G.P.* first term *a* and common ratio *r*.

The nth term of an *A.P.* is given as $t_n = a + (n - 1)d$ where a is the first term and d is the common difference.

The nth term of a *G.P* is given by $t_n = ar^{n-1}$ where a is the first term and *r* is the common ratio.

The pth term (t^p) of both $A.P$ and $G.P$.

For $A.P.$

$\Rightarrow \quad t_p = m + (p - 1)d$

$\Rightarrow \quad a = m + (p - 1)d \quad ...1$

For $G.P.$

$\Rightarrow \quad t_p = ls^{p-1}$

$\Rightarrow \quad a = ld^{p-1} \quad ...2$

The qth term (t_q) of both $A.P.$ and $G.P.$ is b

For $A.P.$

$\Rightarrow \quad t_q = m + (q - 1)d$

$\Rightarrow \quad b = m + (q - 1)d \quad ...3$

For $G.P.$

$\Rightarrow \quad t_q = ls^{q-1}$

$\Rightarrow \quad b = ls^{q-1} \quad ...4$

The rth term (t_r) of both $A.P.$ and $G.P.$ is c

For $A.P.$

$\Rightarrow \quad t_r = m + (r - 1)d$

$\Rightarrow \quad c = m + (r - 1)d \quad ...5$

For GP

$\Rightarrow \quad t_r = ls^{r-1}$

$\Rightarrow \quad c = ls^{r-1} \quad ...6$

Let us find $b - c$, $c - a$ and $a - b$

Using 3 and 5

$\Rightarrow \quad b - c = (q - r)d \quad ...(i)$

Using 5 and 1

$\Rightarrow \quad c - a = (r - p)d \quad ...(ii)$

Using 1 and 3

$\Rightarrow \quad a - b = (p - q)d \quad ...(iii)$

We have to prove that $a^{b-c}. b^{c-a}. c^{a-b} = 1$

LHS $= a^{b-c}. b^{c-a}. c^{a-b}$

Using 2, 4 and 6

$\Rightarrow$ LHS$= (ls^{p-1})^{b-c}. (ls^{q-1})^{c-a}. (ls^{r-1})^{a-b}$

$$= \left(\frac{ls^p}{s}\right)^{b-c} . \left(\frac{ls^q}{s}\right)^{c-a} . \left(\frac{ls^r}{s}\right)^{a-b}$$

$$= \frac{l^{b-c}\, s^{p(b-c)}}{s^{b-c}} . \frac{l^{c-a}\, s^{q(c-a)}}{s^{c-a}} . \frac{l^{a-b}\, s^{r(a-b)}}{s^{a-b}}$$

$$= \frac{l^{b-c+c-a+a-b}}{s^{b-c+c-a+a-b}} . s^{p(b-c)} . s^{q(c-a)} . s^{r(a-b)}$$

$$= s^{p(b-c)} . s^{q(c-a)} . s^{r(a-b)}$$

Substituting values of $a - b$, $c - a$ and $b - c$ from (iii), (ii) and (i)

$= s^{p(q-r)d)} . s^{q(r-p)d)} . sr^{(p-q)d)}$

$= s^{pqd - prd} . s^{qrd - pqd} . s^{prd - qrd}$

$= s^{pqd - prd + qrd - pqd + prd - qrd}$

$= s^0 = 1$

$\Rightarrow$ LHS = RHS Hence proved.

9 Straight Lines

We observe the concept of lines every day in our daily life. When you go to a railway station you can observe the railway tracks. Railway tracks are usually constructed with horizontal supports. Their function is to secure the rail so that they won't shift under the heavy force of the moving trains

Topic Notes

- *Basics of a Straight Line*
- *Forms of Line*

BASICS OF A STRAIGHT LINE 1

TOPIC 1

SLOPE AND ANGLE OF A LINE

A straight line is a curve such that every point on the line segment joining any two points on it lies on it.

Slope of a Line

Slope of a line in terms of coordinates of any two points on it.

Let $P(x_1\ y_1)$ and $Q(x_2\ y_2)$ be two points on a line making an angle θ with the positive direction of x-axis

Then its slope is

$$m = \frac{y_2 - y_1}{x_2 - x_1}$$

The slope of a line passing through points $P(x_1, y_1)$ and $Q(x_2, y_2)$ is given by $m = \tan\theta = \left|\frac{y_2 - y_1}{x_2 - x_1}\right|$.

Example 1.1: Find the slope of a line, which passes through the origin, and the mid-point of the line segment joining the points P(0, –4) and B(8, 0). [NCERT]

Ans. Let M be the mid-point of P(0, –4) and B(8, 0).

We know that

Mid-point of (x_1, y_1) and (x_2, y_2)

$$= \left(\frac{x_1 + x_2}{2}, \frac{y_1 + y_2}{2}\right)$$

Mid-point M of (0, –4) and (8, 0) $= \left(\frac{0+8}{2}, \frac{-4+0}{2}\right)$

$$= \left(\frac{8}{2}, \frac{-4}{2}\right)$$

$$= (4, -2)$$

We know that slope of the line passing through

(x_1, y_1) and (x_2, y_2) is $m = \frac{y_2 - y_1}{x_2 - x_1}$

Slope of line between points O(0, 0) and M(4, -2).

Here,

$$x_1 = 0, y_1 = 0$$

$$x_2 = 4, y_2 = -2$$

Putting values

$$m = \frac{-2-0}{4-0}$$

$$= \frac{-2}{4}$$

$$= \frac{-1}{2}$$

Hence, slope of line is $\frac{-1}{2}$.

Example 1.2: Find the slope of the line, making an inclination of 60°with the positive direction of x-axis. [NCERT]

Ans. Given that inclination of a line with the positive direction of x-axis is 60°.

∴ θ = 60°

Hence, the slope of the line,

$$m = \tan\theta = \tan 60° = \sqrt{3}$$

Example 1.3: Find the angle between the x-axis and the line joining the points (3, –1) and (4, –2).

Ans. First we find slope of line joining the point (3, –1) and (4, –2).

We know that slope of line passing through (x_1, y_1) and (x_2, y_2) is

$$m = \frac{y_2 - y_1}{x_2 - x_1}$$

Here, $x_1 = 3, y_1 = -1$ and $x_2 = 4, y_2 = -2$

Slope of the joining (3, –1) and (4, –2) is

$$m = \frac{-2-(-1)}{4-3}$$

$$= \frac{-2+1}{4-3}$$

$$= \frac{-1}{1}$$

$$= -1$$

Now,

Slope = m = tan θ

Where θ is the angle between line and positive x-axis.

So,

$$m = \tan\theta$$

$$-1 = \tan\theta$$

$$\tan\theta = -1$$

$$\tan\theta = \tan(135)°$$

$$\theta = 135°$$

So, required angle = θ = 135°

Angle Between Two Lines

The angle θ between the lines having slope m_1 and m_2 is given by

$$\tan\theta = \left|\frac{m_2 - m_1}{1 + m_1 m_2}\right|$$

Case I: when angle θ is acute:

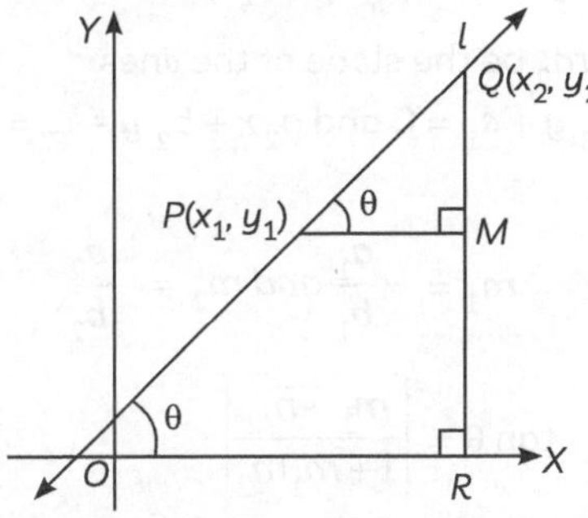

In the given figure $\angle MPQ = \theta$ ...(1)

Therefore, slope of line $l = m = \tan\theta$

But in ΔMPQ, we have $\tan\theta = \frac{MQ}{MP} = \frac{y_2 - y_1}{x_2 - x_1}$ ...(2)

From equations (1) and (2), we have

$$m = \frac{y_2 - y_1}{x_2 - x_1}.$$

Case II: When angle θ is obtuse:

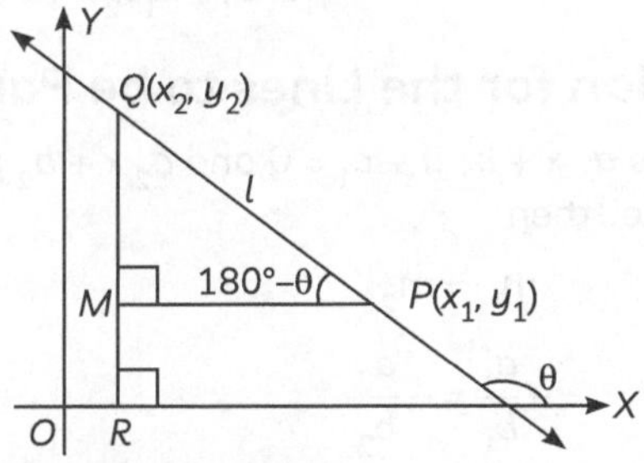

In the given figure, we have

$$\angle MPQ = 180° - \theta$$

Therefore, $\theta = 180° - \angle MPQ$

Now, slope of the line l

$$m = \tan\theta$$

$$= \tan(180° - \angle MPQ) = -\tan\angle MPQ$$

$$= -\frac{MQ}{MP} = -\frac{y_2 - y_1}{x_1 - x_2} = \frac{y_2 - y_1}{x_2 - x_1}$$

Consequently, we see that in both the cases the slope *m* of the line through the points

(x_1, y_1) and (x_2, y_2) is given by $m = \frac{y_2 - y_1}{x_2 - x_1}$

Condition of Parallelism of Lines

If two lines of slope m_1 and m_2 are parallel, then the angle θ between them is 0°.

$$\tan\theta = \tan 0° = 0$$

$$\frac{m_2 - m_1}{1 + m_1 m_2} = 0$$

$$m_2 = m_1$$

Thus, when two lines are parallel, their slopes are equal.

Condition of Perpendicularity of two Lines

If two lines of slopes m_1 and m_2 are perpendicular, then the angle θ between them is 90°.

Hence,

$$m_1 \times m_2 = -1$$

Example 1.4: The slope of a line is double of the slope of another line. If tangent of the angle between them is $\frac{1}{3}$, find the slopes of the lines.

[NCERT]

Ans. Let m_1 and m_2 be the slope of two lines.

We know that angles between two lines are

$$\tan\theta = \left|\frac{m_2 - m_1}{1 + m_1 m_2}\right|$$

Here, $\tan\theta = \frac{1}{3}$

and $m_2 = 2m_1$

Putting values

$$\tan\theta = \left|\frac{m_2 - m_1}{1 + m_1 m_2}\right|$$

$$\frac{1}{3} = \left|\frac{2m_1 - m_1}{1 + m_1(2m_1)}\right|$$

$$\frac{1}{3} = \left|\frac{m_1}{1 + 2m_1^2}\right|$$

$$\left|\frac{m_1}{1 + 2m_1^2}\right| = \frac{1}{3}$$

So, $\frac{m_1}{1 + 2m_1^2} = \frac{1}{3}$ or $\frac{m_1}{1 + 2m_1^2} = \frac{-1}{3}$

Solving $\frac{m_1}{1 + 2m_1^2} = \frac{1}{3}$	Solving $\frac{m_1}{1 + 2m_1^2} = \frac{-1}{3}$
$3m_1 = 1 + 2m_1^2$	$3m_1 = -1 - 2m_1^2$
$2m_1^2 + 1 - 3m_1 = 0$	$2m_1^2 + 1 + 3m_1 = 0$
$2m_1^2 - 3m_1 + 1 = 0$	$2m_1^2 + 3m_1 + 1 = 0$
$2m_1^2 - 2m_1 - m_1 + 1 = 0$	$2m_1^2 + 2m_1 + m_1 + 1 = 0$

$2m_1(m_1 - 1) - 1(m_1 - 1) = 0$

$(2m_1 - 1)(m_1 - 1) = 0$

So, $m_1 = \frac{1}{2}, m_1 = 1$

When, $m_1 = \frac{1}{2}$

$m_2 = 2m_1$

$m_2 = 2\left(\frac{1}{2}\right) = 1$

When, $m_1 = 1$

$m_2 = 2m_1$

$m_2 = 2(1) = 2$

$2m_1(m_1 + 1) + 1(m_1 + 1) = 0$

$(2m_1 + 1)(m_1 + 1) = 0$

So, $m_1 = \frac{-1}{2}, m_1 = -1$

When, $m_1 = \frac{-1}{2}$

$m_2 = 2m_1$

$m_2 = 2\left(\frac{-1}{2}\right) = -1$

When, $m_1 = -1$

$m_2 = 2m_1$

$m_2 = 2(-1) = -2$

Hence slope of lines are $\frac{1}{2}$ and 1 or 1 and 2 or $\frac{-1}{2}$ and -1 or -1 and -2.

Intersects of a Line on the Axes

If a straight line cuts x-axis at A and y-axis at B, then OA and OB are known as intersects of the line on x-axis and y-axis respectively.

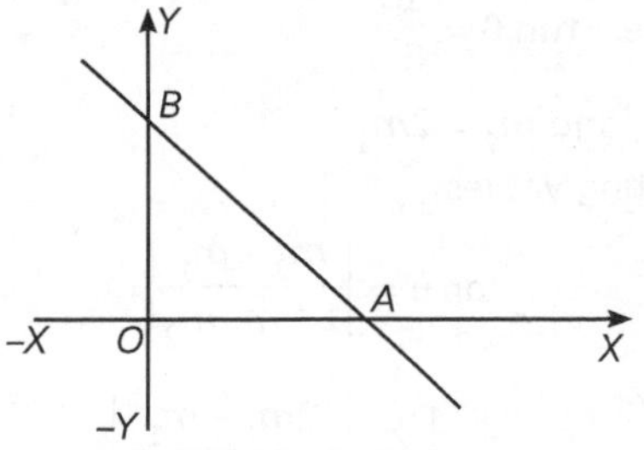

Point of Intersection of Two Lines

Let the equations of two lines be

$$a_1 x + b_1 y + c_1 = 0$$

and, $$a_2 x + b_2 y + c_2 = 0$$

Suppose these two lines intersect at a point, $P(x_1, y_1)$. Then, (x_1, y_1) satisfies each of the given equations.

$\therefore \quad a_1 x_1 + b_1 y_1 + c_1 = 0$ and $a_2 x_1 + b_2 y_1 + c_2 = 0$

Solving these two equations by cross-multiplication, we get

$$\frac{x_1}{b_1c_2 - b_2c_1} = \frac{y_1}{c_1a_2 - c_2a_1}$$

$$\Rightarrow \quad x_1 = \frac{b_1c_2 - b_2c_1}{a_1b_2 - a_2b_1}, y_1 = \frac{c_1a_2 - c_2a_1}{a_1b_2 - a_2b_1}$$

Hence, the coordinates of the point of intersection of the line (i) and (ii) are:

$$\left(\frac{b_1c_2 - b_2c_1}{a_1b_2 - a_2b_1}, \frac{c_1a_2 - c_2a_1}{a_1b_2 - a_2b_1}\right)$$

Angle between two Straight Lines When their Equations are given

The acute angle θ between the lines $a_1 x + b_1 y + c_1 = 0$ and $a_2 x + b_2 y + c_2 = 0$ is given by

$$\tan\theta = \left|\frac{a_2b_1 - a_1b_2}{a_1a_2 + b_1b_2}\right|$$

Let m_1 and m_2 be the slope of the lines

$$a_1 x + b_1 y + c_1 = 0 \text{ and } a_2 x + b_2 y + c_2 = 0$$

Then,

$$m_1 = -\frac{a_1}{b_1} \text{ and } m_2 = -\frac{a_2}{b_2}$$

Now, $$\tan\theta = \left|\frac{m_1 - m_2}{1 + m_1m_2}\right|$$

$$\Rightarrow \quad \tan\theta = \left|\frac{-\frac{a_1}{b_1} + \frac{a_2}{b_2}}{1 + \left(-\frac{a_1}{b_1}\right)\left(-\frac{a_2}{b_2}\right)}\right|$$

$$\Rightarrow \quad \tan\theta = \left|\frac{a_2b_1 - a_1b_2}{a_1a_2 + b_1b_2}\right|$$

$$\Rightarrow \quad \theta = \tan^{-1}\left|\frac{a_2b_1 - a_1b_2}{a_1a_2 + b_1b_2}\right|$$

Condition for the Lines to be Parallel

If the lines $a_1 x + b_1 y + c_1 = 0$ and $a_2 x + b_2 y + c_2 = 0$ are parallel, then

$$m_1 = m_2$$

$$\Rightarrow \quad -\frac{a_1}{b_1} = -\frac{a_2}{b_2}$$

$$\Rightarrow \quad \frac{a_1}{a_2} = \frac{b_1}{b_2}$$

Condition for the Lines to be Perpendicular

If the lines $a_1 x + b_1 y + c_1 = 0$ and $a_2 x + b_2 y + c_2 = 0$ are perpendiculars, then

$$m_1 m_2 = -1$$

$$\Rightarrow \quad -\frac{a_1}{b_1} \times -\frac{a_2}{b_2} = -1$$

$$a_1a_2 + b_1b_2 = 0$$

If follows from the above discussion that the lines $a_1 x + b_1 y + c_1 = 0$ and $a_2 x + b_2 y + c_2 = 0$ are:

(i) Coincident, if $\frac{a_1}{a_2} = \frac{b_1}{b_2} = \frac{c_1}{c_2}$

(ii) Parallel, if $\frac{a_1}{a_2} = \frac{b_1}{b_2} \neq \frac{c_1}{c_2}$

(iii) Intersecting, if $\frac{a_1}{a_2} \neq \frac{b_1}{b_2}$

(iv) Perpendicular, if $a_1 a_2 + b_1 b_2 = 0$

TOPIC 2

DISTANCE OF A POINT FROM A LINE

The length of the perpendicular from a point (x_1, y_1) to a line $ax + by + c = 0$ is $\left|\frac{ax_1 + by_1 + c}{\sqrt{a^2 + b^2}}\right|$.

Distance between Parallel Lines

If two lines are parallel, then the distance between them is the same throughout. Therefore, to find the distance between two parallel lines, choose an arbitrary point on one of them and find the length of the perpendicular on the other. In order to choose a point on a line, we give an arbitrary value to x or y and find the value of the other variable.

We may use the following algorithm to find the distance between two parallel lines.

Let the two parallel lines be, $ax + by + c_1 = 0$ and $ax + by + c_2 = 0$. To find the distance between these two lines, we use following working steps.

Step I: Choose a point on any one of the two lines by giving a particular value to x or y of your choice.

Step II: Find the length of the perpendicular from the chosen point in Step I to the other line.

Step III: The length obtained in Step II is the required distance between the parallel lines.

The distance between two parallel lines $ax + by + c_1 = 0$ and $ax + by + c_2 = 0$ is given by $\frac{|c_1 - c_2|}{\sqrt{a^2 + b^2}}$.

Example 1.5: The base of an equilateral triangle with side 2*a* lies along with the *y*-axis such that the mid-point of the base is at the origin. Find the vertices of the triangle. [NCERT]

Ans. Let ΔABC be the equilateral triangle with side $2a$ such that its base BC is along the y-axis and the mid-point of the base is at the origin O.

Then, point A lies on the x-axis and $OB = OC = a$.

The coordinates of points B and C are $(0, a)$ and $(0, -a)$ respectively.

Let $(x, 0)$be the coordinates of point A.

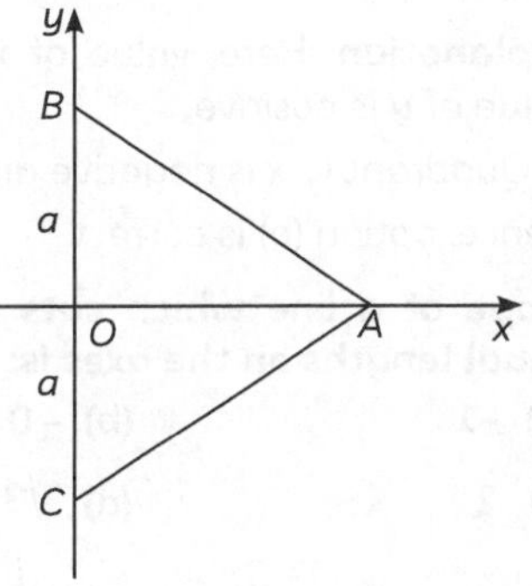

Since, $AB = 2a$

$\Rightarrow \sqrt{(0-x)^2 + (a-0)^2} = 2a$

$\Rightarrow \sqrt{x^2 + a^2} = 2a$

$\Rightarrow x^2 + a^2 = 4a^2$

$\Rightarrow x^2 = 3a^2$

$\Rightarrow x = \pm\sqrt{3}a$

So, the coordinates of point A are $(\sqrt{3}a, 0)$ or $(-\sqrt{3}a, 0)$.

Hence, vertices of the triangle are $(\sqrt{3}a, 0)$, $(0, a)$, $(0, -a)$ or $(-\sqrt{3}a, 0)$ $(0, a)$, $(0, -a)$.

Example 1.6: Find a point on the x-axis, which is equidistant from the point (7, 6) and (3, 4). [NCERT]

Ans. Point on x-axis $(a, 0)$.

Let $P(a, 0)$, $A(7, 6)$ and $B(3, 4)$

Here, $PA = PB$

$\sqrt{(7-a)^2 + (6-0)^2} = \sqrt{(3-a)^2 + (4-0)^2}$

$(7 - a)^2 + 36 = (3 - a)^2 + 16$

$49 + a^2 - 14a + 36 = 9 + a^2 - 6a + 16$

$49 - 16 + 36 - 9 = 14a - 6a$

$60 = 8a$

$\frac{60}{8} = a$

So point is $\left(\frac{15}{2}, 0\right)$

OBJECTIVE Type Questions

[1 mark]

Multiple Choice Questions

1. The point (–1. 5, 2. 56) lies in which quadrant?

(a) I (b) II

(c) III (d) IV

Ans. *(b) II*

Explanation: Here, value of x is negative and value of y is positive.

In Quadrant II, x is negative and y is positive.

Hence, option (b) is correct.

2. Slope of a line which cuts off intercepts of equal lengths on the axes is:

(a) –1 (b) – 0

(c) 2 (d) $\sqrt{3}$

[NCERT Exemplar]

Ans. *(a) –1*

Explanation: We know that the equation of line in intercept form is

$$\frac{x}{a}+\frac{y}{b}=1$$

Where a and b are the intercepts on the axis.

Given that $a = b$

$$\Rightarrow \quad \frac{x}{a}+\frac{y}{b}=1$$

$$\Rightarrow \quad \frac{x+y}{a}=1$$

$$\Rightarrow \quad x+y=a$$

$$\Rightarrow \quad y=-x+a$$

$$\Rightarrow \quad y=(-1)x+a$$

Comparing, with the standard form $y = mx + b$

So, the slope of the line $m = -1$.

3. The value of y, if the distance between points $P(0, 0)$ and $Q(6, y)$ is 10 units is:

(a) 3, –3 (b) 8, –8

(c) 0 (d) None

Ans. *(b) 8, –8*

Explanation: $P(0, 0)$ and $Q(6, y)$

$$PQ = 10$$

$$\sqrt{(6-0)^2+(y-0)^2}=10$$

$$36+y^2=100$$

$$y^2=64$$

$$y=8,-8$$

Hence option (b) is correct.

4. The point on x-axis which is equidistant from the point (3, 2) and (–5, –2) is:

(a) (1, 0) (b) (2, 0)

(c) (–1, 0) (d) (–2, 0)

Ans. *(c) (–1, 0)*

Explanation: $PA = PB$

$$\Rightarrow \quad PA^2 = PB^2$$

$$(3-x)^2+(2-0)^2=(-5-x)^2+(-2-0)^2$$

$$9+x^2-6x+4=25+x^2+10x+4$$

$$16x+16=0$$

$$x=-1$$

Since the point is on x – axis, so $y = 0$

Thus, the Point is (–1, 0)

Hence option (c) is correct.

5. The tangent of angle between the lines whose intercepts on the axes are a, $-b$ and b, $-a$, respectively, is:

(a) $\frac{a^2-b^2}{ab}$ (b) $\frac{b^2-a^2}{2}$

(c) $\frac{b^2-a^2}{2ab}$ (d) None of these

[NCERT Exemplar]

Ans. (c) $\frac{b^2-a^2}{2ab}$

Explanation: Let the first equation of line having intercepts on the axes a, $-b$ is

$$\frac{x}{a}+\frac{y}{-b}=1$$

$$\Rightarrow \quad \frac{x}{a}-\frac{y}{b}=1$$

$$\Rightarrow \quad bx-ay=ab \quad \text{...(i)}$$

Let the second equation of line having intercepts on the axes b, $-a$ is

$$\frac{x}{b}+\frac{y}{-a}=1$$

$$\Rightarrow \quad \frac{x}{b}-\frac{y}{a}=1$$

$$\Rightarrow \quad ax-by=ab \quad \text{...(ii)}$$

Now, we find the slope of equation (i)

$$bx-ay=ab$$

$$\Rightarrow \quad ay=bx-ab$$

$$\Rightarrow \quad y=\frac{b}{a}x-b$$

Since, the above equation is in $y = mx + b$ form.

So, the slope of equation (i) is

$$m_1 = \frac{b}{a}$$

Now, we find the slope of equation (ii),

$$ax - by = ab$$

$$\Rightarrow \quad by = ax - ab$$

$$\Rightarrow \quad y = \frac{a}{b}x - a$$

Since the above equation is in $y = mx + b$ form. So, the slope of eq. (i) is

$$m_2 = \frac{a}{b}$$

Let θ be the angle between the given two lines.

$$\tan\theta = \left|\frac{m_1 - m_1}{1 + m_1 m_2}\right|$$

Putting the values of m_1 and m_2 in the above equation, we get

$$\Rightarrow \quad \tan\theta = \left|\frac{\frac{b}{a} - \frac{a}{b}}{1 + \left(\frac{b}{a}\right)\left(\frac{a}{b}\right)}\right|$$

$$\Rightarrow \quad \tan\theta = \left|\frac{\frac{b^2 - a^2}{ab}}{1+1}\right|$$

$$\Rightarrow \quad \tan\theta = \left|\frac{b^2 - a^2}{2ab}\right|$$

$$\Rightarrow \quad \tan\theta = \frac{b^2 - a^2}{2ab}$$

Hence, the correct option is (c).

6. If the vertices (1, 3), (2, 5)and (3, –5) of a triangle, the centroid is:

(a) (1, 2) **(b) (1, 3)**

(c) (3, 1) **(d) (2, 1)**

Ans. *(d) (2, 1)*

Explanation: Centroid

$$= \left(\frac{x_1 + x_2 + x_3}{3}, \frac{y_1 + y_2 + y_3}{3}\right)$$

$$= \left(\frac{1+2+3}{3}, \frac{3+5-5}{3}\right)$$

$$= \left(\frac{6}{3}, \frac{3}{3}\right)$$

$$= (2, 1)$$

Hence, option (d) is correct.

7. The slope whose angle is 90° is:

(a) 1 **(b) 0**

(c) -1 **(d) Not defined**

Ans. *(d) Not defined*

Explanation: Here, it is given that θ = 90°, therefore, the slope of the line is:

$$m = \tan\theta$$

$$m = \tan 90°$$

$$= \text{Not defined}$$

Hence, option (d) is correct.

8. The slope of the lines which make an angle 45° with the line 3x – y + 5 = 0 is:

(a) $-2, \frac{1}{2}$ **(b)** $\frac{1}{2}, -3$

(c) $2, \frac{-1}{2}$ **(d)** $-3, \frac{1}{2}$ **[DIKSHA]**

Ans. *(a)* $-2, \frac{1}{2}$

Explanation: Slope of the line $3x - y + 5 = 0$ is 3.

$$\tan 45° = \left|\frac{m-3}{1+3m}\right|$$

$$1 = \left|\frac{m-3}{1+3m}\right|$$

$$|1 + 3m| = |(m - 3)|$$

$$1 + 3m = \pm (m - 3)$$

$$m = -2 \text{ or, } m = \frac{1}{2}$$

9. The area of a triangle whose vertices are (2, 4), (4, –2), and (–3, 10) is:

(a) 4 **(b) 9**

(c) 3 **(d) 10**

Ans. *(b) 9*

Explanation: Area of Triangle (2, 4), (4, –2), and (–3, 10)

$$= \frac{1}{2}\{x_1(y_2 - y_3) + x_2(y_3 - y_1) + x_3(y_1 - y_2)\}$$

$$= \frac{1}{2}|2(-2-10) + 4(10-4) + (-3)(4+2)|$$

$$= \left|\frac{-24+24-18}{2}\right|$$

$$= \left|\frac{-18}{2}\right| = 9$$

Hence option (b) is correct.

10. The slope of a line whose inclination is 30° is:

(a) $\frac{1}{\sqrt{3}}$ **(b) 1**

(c) $\sqrt{3}$ **(d) None**

Ans. *(a)* $\frac{1}{\sqrt{3}}$

Explanation: Let θ be the inclination of a line, then its slope = tan θ

at $\theta = 30°$

So, $m = \tan 30°$

$= \frac{1}{\sqrt{3}}$

Hence, option (a) is correct.

11. The distance between the parallel lines $3x - 4y + 7 = 0$ and $3x - 4y + 5 = 0$ is:

(a) $\frac{3}{4}$ **(b)** $\frac{7}{5}$

(c) $\frac{2}{5}$ **(d)** $\frac{3}{5}$ **[DIKSHA]**

Ans. (c) $\frac{2}{5}$

Explanation: Given that,

$a = 3, b = -4, c_1 = 7, c_2 = 5$

$$d = \frac{|c_1 - c_2|}{\sqrt{a^2 + b^2}}$$

$$d = \frac{|7-5|}{\sqrt{(3)^2 + (-4)^2}}$$

$$= \frac{2}{\sqrt{9+16}}$$

$$= \frac{2}{\sqrt{25}}$$

$$= \frac{2}{5}.$$

Hence, option (c) is correct.

12. The angle between x-axis and the line joining the points (3, –1) and (4, –2) is:

(a) 135° **(b) 145°**

(c) 270° **(d) None of these**

[DIKSHA]

Ans. *(a) 135°*

Explanation: The slope of the line joining the points

(3, –1) and (4, –2) is $m = \frac{-2-(-1)}{4-3}$

$= -2 + 1 = -1$

Now, the inclination (θ) of the line joining the points (3, –1) and (4, –2) is given by $\tan\theta = -1$

$\Rightarrow \theta = (90° + 45°) = 135°.$

A slope of the line is an inclination with the x-axis.

Thus, the angle between x – axis and the line joining the points (3,1) and (4,2) is 135°.

Assertion-Reason (A-R)

DIRECTION: In the following questions, a statement of assertion (A) is followed by a statement of the reason (R). Mark the correct choice as:

(a) Both assertion (A) and reason (R) are true and reason (R) is the correct explanation of assertion (A).

(b) Both assertion (A) and reason (R) are true but reason (R) is not the correct explanation of assertion (A).

(c) Assertion (A) is true but reason (R) is false.

(d) Assertion (A) is false but reason (R) is true.

13. Assertion (A): The angle between the line $x + 2y - 3 = 0$ and $3x + y + 1 = 0$ is $\tan^{-1}(1)$.

Reason (R): Angle between two lines is given by $\tan\theta = \pm\left(\frac{m_2 - m_1}{1 + m_1 m_2}\right)$

Ans. *(a) Both assertion (A) and reason (R) are true and reason (R) is the correct explanation of assertion (A).*

Explanation: Let m_1 and m_2 be the slopes of the straight lines $x + 2y - 3 = 0$ and $3x + y + 1 = 0$.

Then, $m_1 = -\frac{1}{2}$ and $m_2 = -3$

Let θ be the angle between the given lines.

Then, $\tan\theta = \pm\left(\frac{m_2 - m_1}{1 + m_1 m_2}\right)$

$$= \pm\left(\frac{-3+\frac{1}{2}}{1+\frac{3}{2}}\right) = \pm 1$$

$\Rightarrow \theta = \tan^{-1}(1)$

14. Assertion (A): A slope of line $3x - 4y + 10 = 0$ is $\frac{3}{4}$.

Reason (R): x-intercepts and y-intercepts of $3x - 4y + 10 = 0$ respectively are $\frac{-10}{3}$ and $\frac{5}{2}$.

Ans. *(b) Both assertion (A) and reason (R) are true but reason (R) is not the correct explanation of assertion (A).*

Explanation: Given equation $3x - 4y + 10 = 0$ can be written as

$$y = \frac{3}{4}x + \frac{5}{2} \quad ...(i)$$

Comparing Equation. (i) with $y = mx + c$, we have slope of the given line as $m = \frac{3}{4}$.

Equation $3x - 4y + 10 = 0$ can be written as

$$3x - 4y = -10 \text{ or } \frac{x}{-\frac{10}{3}} + \frac{y}{\frac{5}{2}} = 1 \quad ...(ii)$$

Comparing EQ. (ii) with $\frac{x}{a} + \frac{y}{b} = 1$, we have x-intercept as $a = -\frac{10}{3}$ and y-intersect as $b = \frac{5}{2}$.

15. Assertion (A): If $x \cos\theta + y \sin\theta = 2$ is perpendicular to the line $x - y = 3$ then one of the values of θ is $\frac{\pi}{4}$.

Reason (R): If two lines $y = m_1 x + c_1$ and $y = m_2 x + c_2$ are perpendicular then $m_1 = m_2$.

Ans. *(c) Assertion (A) is true but reason (R) is false.*

Explanation: Since, slope of line $x \cos\theta + y \sin\theta = 2$ is $-\cot\theta$ and slope of line $x - y = 3$ is 1. Also, these lines are perpendicular to each other.

$\therefore \quad (-\cot\theta)(1) = -1$

$\Rightarrow \cot\theta = 1 = \theta = \cot^{-1}\left(\cot\frac{\pi}{4}\right)$

$\Rightarrow \theta = \frac{\pi}{4}$

Condition of perpendicularity of two lines is $m_1 . m_2 = -1$ and not $m_1 = m_2$.

16. Assertion (A): The slope of the line $x + 7y = 0$ is $\frac{1}{5}$ and y-intercept is 0.

Reason (R): The slope of the line $6x + 3y - 5 = 0$ is -2 and y – intercept is $\frac{5}{2}$.

Ans. *(d) Assertion (A) is false but reason (R) is true.*

Explanation: Given equation is $x + 7y = 0$

$\Rightarrow y = \frac{-x}{7} + 0$

On comparing with $y = mx + c$, we get

Slope $(m) = \frac{-1}{7}$, y – intercept = 0

Given equation is $6x + 3y - 5 = 0$

$\Rightarrow y = -2x + \frac{5}{3}$

On comparing with $y = mx + c$, we get

Slope $(m) = -2$, y – intercept = $\frac{5}{3}$

Hence, assertion is false but reason is true.

CASE BASED Questions (CBQs)

[**4** & **5** marks]

Read the following passages and answer the questions that follow:

17. *Tross bridges are formed with a structure of connected elements that form triangular structure to make up the bridge. Trusses are the triangles that connect to the top and bottom cord and two endposts. Consider the ΔABC with vertices $A(1, 4)$, $B(2, -3)$ and $C(-1, -2)$.*

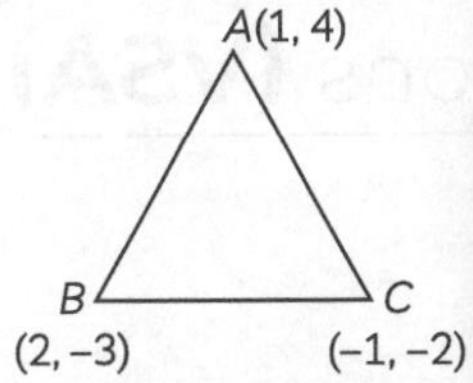

(A) Slope of BC is:

(a) $\frac{-1}{2}$ **(b)** $\frac{1}{3}$

(c) $\frac{-1}{3}$ **(d)** None

(B) Slope of AC is:

(a) 3 **(b)** 4

(c) 5 **(d)** 6

(C) Distance between A and C is:

(a) $\sqrt{10}$ **(b)** $2\sqrt{10}$

(c) $3\sqrt{10}$ **(d)** $4\sqrt{10}$

(D) Distance between B and C is:

(a) $\sqrt{5}$ **(b)** $\sqrt{7}$

(c) $\sqrt{9}$ **(d)** $\sqrt{10}$

Ans. (A) *(b)* $\frac{-1}{3}$

Explanation: Here $B(2, -3)$ and $C(-1, -2)$

So,

Slope of BC is $\frac{y_2 - y_1}{x_2 - x_1}$

$$= \frac{-2+3}{-1-2} = \frac{1}{-3} = \frac{-1}{3}$$

Hence, option (b) is correct.

(B) *(a)* 3

Explanation: Here, $A(1, 4)$ and $C(-1, -2)$.

So

Slope of AC is $\frac{y_2 - y_1}{x_2 - x_1}$

$$= \frac{-2-4}{-1-1} = \frac{-6}{-2} = 3$$

Hence, option (a) is correct.

(C) *(b)* $2\sqrt{10}$

Explanation: Here, $A(1, 4)$ and $C(-1, -2)$.

So

$$AC = \sqrt{(-1-1)^2 + (-2-4)^2}$$

$$= \sqrt{4+36}$$

$$= \sqrt{40}$$

$$= 2\sqrt{10}$$

Hence, option (b) is correct.

(D) *(d)* $\sqrt{10}$

Explanation: Here $B(2, -3)$ and $C(-1, -2)$

So

$$BC = \sqrt{(-1-2)^2 + (-2+3)^2}$$

$$= \sqrt{9+1}$$

$$= \sqrt{10}$$

Hence, option (d) is correct.

18. *The corner points of a square plot are (1, 2), (2, 3), (3, 1) (0, –4). Plot are in an industrial area to build a well known company showroom.*

Based on the above information, answer the following questions:

(A) Find the distance between (1, 2) and (3, 1) and also find the slope of (1, 2) and (3, 1).

(B) Find the distance between (2, 3) and (0, –4) and also find the slope of (2, 3) and (0, –4).

Ans. (A) $A = (1, 2)$

$B = (3, 1)$

$$AB = \sqrt{(3-1)^2 + (1-2)^2}$$

$$= \sqrt{4+1}$$

$$= \sqrt{5}$$

Here, $x_1 = 2, x_2 = 0$

$y_1 = 3, y_2 = -4$

$$m = \frac{y_2 - y_1}{x_2 - x_1}$$

$$= \frac{-4-3}{0-2}$$

$$= \frac{-7}{-2}$$

$$= \frac{7}{2}$$

(B) Here $A = (2, 3)$

$B = (0, -4)$

So,

$$AB = \sqrt{(0-2)^2 + (-4-3)^2}$$

$$= \sqrt{4+49}$$

$$= \sqrt{53}$$

Here $x_1 = 1, x_2 = 3$

$y_1 = 2, y_2 = 1$

$$m = \frac{y_2 - y_1}{x_2 - x_1}$$

$$= \frac{1-2}{3-1}$$

$$= \frac{-1}{2}$$

VERY SHORT ANSWER Type Questions (VSA)

[1 mark]

19. Determine x so that 4 is the slope of the line through (0, 2) and (x, 3).

Ans. The slope of the line through (0, 2) and (x, 3) is

$$\frac{3-2}{x-0} = 4$$

$$1 = 4x$$

$$x = \frac{1}{4}$$

20. Find the point on y-axis whose perpendicular distance from the line $4x - 3y - 12 = 0$ is 3. **[DIKSHA]**

Ans. Let the required point $P(0, \alpha)$. It is given that the length of the perpendicular from $P(0, \alpha)$ on $4x - 3y - 12 = 0$ is 3.

Now, perpendicular distance of a line $4x - 3y - 12 = 0$ from a point $(0, \alpha)$ is

$$D = \left|\frac{Ax_1 + By_1 + C}{\sqrt{A^2 + B^2}}\right|$$

$$\left|\frac{4 \times 0 - 3\alpha - 12}{\sqrt{4^2 + (-3)^2}}\right| = 3$$

$$|3\alpha + 12| = 15$$

$$|\alpha + 4| = 5$$

$$\alpha + 4 = \pm 5$$

$$\alpha = 1, -9$$

Hence, the points are (0, 1) and (0, -9).

21. If the sum of the distance of a moving point in a plane from the axes is 1, then find the locus of the point. [NCERT Exemplar]

Ans. Let the coordinates of a moving point P be (a, b).

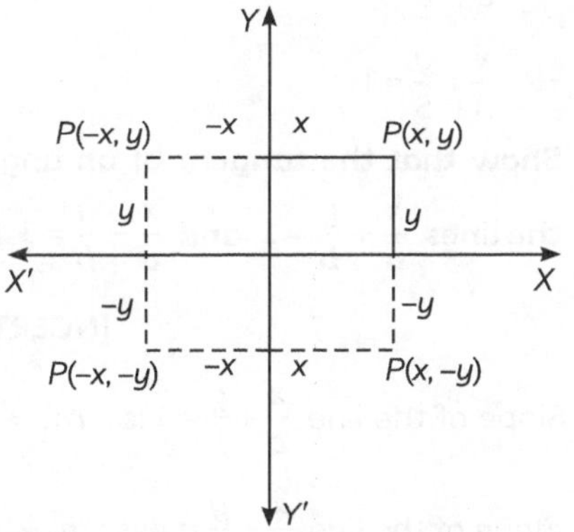

Given that the sum of the distance from the axes to the point is always 1.

$\therefore \quad |x| + |y| = 1$

$\Rightarrow \quad \pm x \pm y = 1$

$\Rightarrow -x - y = 1, x + y = 1, -x + y = 1$ and $x - y = 1$

Hence, these equations gives us the locus of the point P which is a square.

22. If $A(1, -1)$, $B(2, 3)$ and $C(-4, -2)$ are three points, find the angle between BA and BC.

Ans. Let m_1 and m_2 be the slopes of BA and BC respectively. Then,

$$m_1 = \frac{3+1}{2-(1)} = \frac{4}{1} = 4, \text{ and } m_2 = \frac{-2-3}{-4-2} = \frac{5}{6}$$

Let θ be the acute angle between BA and BC.

Then,

$$\tan\theta = \left|\frac{m_2 - m_1}{1 + m_1 m_2}\right|$$

$$= \left|\frac{\frac{5}{6} - 4}{1 + \frac{5}{6} \times 4}\right|$$

$$= \left|\frac{\frac{-19}{6}}{\frac{26}{6}}\right| = \left|\frac{-19}{26}\right|$$

$$\tan\theta = \frac{19}{26}$$

$$\Rightarrow \quad \theta = \tan^{-1}\left(\frac{19}{26}\right)$$

23. If a, b, c are in A.P., then find the points where the straight line $ax + by + c = 0$ will always pass. [NCERT Exemplar]

Ans. Given line is $ax + by + c = 0$ ...(i)

Since, a, b are c are in A.P., we get

$$b = \frac{a+c}{2}$$

Or, $\quad a - 2b + c = 0$ ...(ii)

On comparing Equation. (i) and (ii), we get

$$x = 1, y = -2$$

So, (1, –2) lies on the line.

24. Find the coordinates of a point on $x + y + 3 = 0$ whose distance from $x + 2y + 2 = 0$ is $\sqrt{5}$. [DIKSHA]

Ans. Let the required point be (x_1, y_1).

Since, it lies on $x + y + 3 = 0$

$x_1 + y_1 + 3 = 0$ ...(i)

Length of the perpendicular from (x_1, y_1) to $x + 2y + 2 = 0$ is $\sqrt{5}$.

$$\left|\frac{x_1 + 2y_1 + 2}{\sqrt{1^2 + 2^2}}\right| = \sqrt{5}$$

$x_1 + 2y_1 + 2 = \pm 5$ ...(ii)

or, $x_1 + 2y_1 - 3 = 0$ and $x_1 + 2y_1 + 7 = 0$

Solving eq. (i) and (ii), we get $x_1 = -9$, $y_1 = 6$ and $x_1 = 1$, $y_1 = -4$

Hence, the points are (–9, 6) and (1, –4)

SHORT ANSWER Type-I Questions (SA-I)

[**2** marks]

25. Find the obtuse angle between the lines $x - 2y + 3 = 0$ and $3x + y - 1 = 0$. [DIKSHA]

Ans. Let m_1 and m_2 be the slope of the straight lines $x - 2y + 3 = 0$ and $3x + y - 1 = 0$

$$m_1 = \frac{1}{2} \text{ and } m_2 = -3$$

Let θ be the angle between the given lines. Then

$$\tan\theta = \left|\frac{m_1 - m_2}{1+m_1m_2}\right| = \left|\frac{\frac{1}{2}+3}{1-\frac{3}{2}}\right|$$

$$\tan\theta = 7$$

$$\theta = \tan^{-1}(7)$$

The acute angle between the lines is $\tan^{-1}(7)$ and the obtuse angle is $\pi - \tan^{-1}(7)$.

26. If the angle between two lines is $\frac{\pi}{4}$ and the slope of the line is $\frac{1}{2}$, find the slope of other line. [DIKSHA]

Ans. We know that acute angle θ between two lines with slope m_1 and m_2 is given by

$$\tan\theta = \left|\frac{m_2 - m_1}{1+m_1m_2}\right|$$

Let, $m_1 = \frac{1}{2}$ and $m_2 = m$ slope of the other line.

It is given that $\theta = \frac{\pi}{4}$

Substituting $m_1 = \frac{1}{2}$, $m_2 = m$ and $\theta = \frac{\pi}{4}$, we obtain,

$$\tan\frac{\pi}{4} = \left|\frac{m-\frac{1}{2}}{1+m.\frac{1}{2}}\right|$$

$$1 = \left|\frac{2m-1}{2+m}\right|$$

$$\left|\frac{2m-1}{2+m}\right| = \pm 1$$

solving further, we obtain

$$m = 3 \text{ or } m = -\frac{1}{3}$$

Hence, slope of the line is 3 or $-\frac{1}{3}$.

27. A line passes through $P(1.5, 2.5)$such that its intercepts between the axes is bisected at P. Find the equation of the line.

Ans. Let the line make intercepts a and b with x and y-axis respectively.

Then, the line passes through the points $(a, 0)$ and $(0, b)$.

Given that the intercepts between the axes is bisected at $P(1.5, 2.5)$.

$$\therefore \frac{a+0}{2} = 1.5 \quad \text{and} \quad \frac{b+0}{2} = 2.5$$

$$\Rightarrow a = 3 \quad \text{and} \quad b = 5$$

Hence, the equation of the line in intercepts form is

$$\frac{x}{a}+\frac{y}{b}=1$$

$$\Rightarrow \frac{x}{3}+\frac{y}{5}=1$$

28. Show that the tangent of an angle between the lines $\frac{x}{a}+\frac{y}{b}=1$ and $\frac{x}{a}-\frac{y}{b}=1$ is $\frac{2ab}{a^2-b^2}$.

[NCERT Exemplar]

Ans. Slope of the line $\frac{x}{a}+\frac{y}{b}=1$ is : $m_1 = -\frac{b}{a}$

Slope of the line $\frac{x}{a}-\frac{y}{b}=1$ is : $m_2 = \frac{b}{a}$

Let θ be angle between the given lines. Then

$$\tan\theta = \left|\frac{m_1 - m_2}{1+m_1m_2}\right| = \left|\frac{-\frac{b}{a}-\frac{b}{a}}{1+\left(\frac{-b}{a}\right)\left(\frac{b}{a}\right)}\right| = \left|\frac{\frac{-2b}{a}}{\frac{a^2-b^2}{a^2}}\right|$$

Thus, , $\tan\theta = \frac{2ab}{a^2-b^2}$

29. Find the angle between the negative x-axis and the line joining the points (4, –2)and (5, –3).

Ans. Let m_1 be the slope of x-axis.

Then, $m_1 = 0$

Let m_2 be the slope of the line passing through the points (4, – 2)and (5, – 3).

Then, $m_2 = \frac{-3-(-2)}{5-4} = -1$

Let θ be the angle between the two lines.

Then, $\tan\theta = \left|\frac{m_1 - m_2}{1+m_1 m_2}\right| = \left|\frac{0-(-1)}{1+(0)(-1)}\right| = 1$

∴ $\theta = 45°$

Hence, the required angle is 45°.

30. In what direction should a line be drawn through the point (1, 2) so that its point of intersection with the line $x + y = 4$ is at a distance $\frac{\sqrt{6}}{3}$ from the given point.

[NCERT Exemplar]

Ans. Let the slope of the line be m. Also, the line passes through the point $A(1, 2)$.

∴ Equation of line is $y - 2 = m(x - 1)$

or $mx - y + 2 - m = 0$ ...(i)

Also the equation of the given line is

$x + y - 4 = 0$ (ii)

Let these lines meet at point B.

Solving (i) and (ii), we get $B = \left(\frac{m+2}{m+1}, \frac{3m+2}{m+1}\right)$

Now, given that $AB = \frac{\sqrt{6}}{3}$

⇒ $AB^2 = \frac{6}{9}$

⇒ $\left(\frac{m+2}{m+1} - 1\right)^2 + \left(\frac{3m+2}{m+1} - 2\right)^2 = \frac{6}{9}$

⇒ $\left(\frac{1}{m+1}\right)^2 + \left(\frac{m}{m+1}\right)^2 = \frac{2}{3}$

⇒ $\frac{1+m^2}{(1+m)^2} = \frac{2}{3}$

⇒ $3 + 3m^2 = 2 + 2m^2 + 4m$

⇒ $m^2 - 4m + 1 = 0$

∴ $m = \frac{4 \pm \sqrt{16-4}}{2} = 2 \pm \sqrt{3}$

$= 2+\sqrt{3}$ or $2-\sqrt{3}$

∴ $\tan\theta = 2+\sqrt{3}$ or $2-\sqrt{3}$

∴ $\theta = 75°$ or $\theta = 15°$.

SHORT ANSWER Type-II Questions (SA-II)

[**3** marks]

31. Find the angle between the lines $y = (2-\sqrt{3})(x+5)$ and $y = (2+\sqrt{3})(x-7)$

[NCERT Exemplar]

Ans. Given equations are $y = (2-\sqrt{3})(x+5)$ and $(2+\sqrt{3})(x-7)$.

The given equation can be written as

⇒ $y = (2-\sqrt{3})x + (2-\sqrt{3})5$ ...(1)

⇒ $y = (2+\sqrt{3})x - 7(2+\sqrt{3})$ ...(2)

Now, we have to find the slope of equation (1). Since, the quation 1 is in $y = mx + b$ form, we can easily see that the slope (m_1) is $(2-\sqrt{3})$.

Now, the slope (m_2) of equation (2) is $(2+\sqrt{3})$.

Let θ be the angle between the given two lines.

$\tan\theta = \left|\frac{m_1 - m_1}{1+m_1 m_2}\right|$

Putting the values of m_1 and m_2 in above equation, we get

⇒ $\tan\theta = \left|\frac{2-\sqrt{3}-(2+\sqrt{3})}{1+(2-\sqrt{3})(2+\sqrt{3})}\right|$

⇒ $\tan\theta = \left|\frac{2-\sqrt{3}-2-\sqrt{3}}{1+[(2)^2-(\sqrt{3})^2]}\right|$

[∵ $(a-b)(a+b) = (a^2-b^2)$]

⇒ $\tan\theta = \left|\frac{-2\sqrt{3}}{1+[4-3]}\right|$

On simplifying we get,

⇒ $\tan\theta = \left|\frac{-2\sqrt{3}}{1+1}\right|$

⇒ $\tan\theta = \left|\frac{-2\sqrt{3}}{2}\right|$

⇒ $\tan\theta = \sqrt{3}$ or $-\sqrt{3}$

⇒ $\theta = \tan^{-1}(\sqrt{3})$ or $(-\sqrt{3})$

⇒ $\theta = 60°$ or $120°$

Hence, the required angle are 60° or 120°.

32. If the angle between two lines is $\frac{5\pi}{4}$ and the slope of one of the lines is $\frac{1}{2}$, find the slope of the other line.

Ans. Given that slope of one line is $m_1 = \frac{1}{2}$.

Let, m_2 be the slope of the other line.

Also, given that the angle between the two lines is $\theta = \frac{\pi}{4}$

Now, $$\tan\theta = \left|\frac{m_1 - m_2}{1 + m_1 m_2}\right|$$

$$\Rightarrow \quad \tan\frac{\pi}{4} = \left|\frac{\frac{1}{2} - m_2}{1 + \left(\frac{1}{2}\right) m_2}\right|$$

$$\Rightarrow \quad 1 = \left|\frac{1 - 2m_2}{2 + m_2}\right|$$

$$\Rightarrow \quad \pm 1 = \frac{1 - 2m_2}{2 + m_2}$$

$$\therefore \quad \frac{1 - 2m_2}{2 + m_2} = 1$$

$$\Rightarrow \quad 1 - 2m_2 = 2 + m_2$$

$$\Rightarrow \quad m_2 = -\frac{1}{3}$$

$$\therefore \quad \frac{1 - 2m_2}{2 + m_2} = -1$$

$$\Rightarrow \quad 1 - 2m_2 = -2 - m_2$$

$$\Rightarrow \quad m_2 = 3$$

Hence, the slope of the other line is $-\frac{1}{3}$ or 3.

33. Find the points on the line $x + y = 4$ which lie at a unit distance from the line $4x + 3y = 10$ [NCERT Exemplar]

Ans. Let (x_1, y_1) be any point lying in the equation $x + y = 4$.

$$\therefore \quad x_1 + y_1 = 4 \qquad ...(1)$$

Distance of the point (x_1, y_1) from the equation $4x + 3y = 10$ is

$$d = \frac{|Ax_1 + By_1 + C|}{\sqrt{A^2 + B^2}}$$

$$\Rightarrow \quad 1 = \left|\frac{4x_1 + 3y_1 - 10}{\sqrt{(4)^2 + (3)^2}}\right|$$

On simplification we get

$$\Rightarrow \quad 1 = \left|\frac{4x_1 + 3y_1 - 10}{\sqrt{16 + 9}}\right|$$

$$\Rightarrow \quad 1 = \left|\frac{4x_1 + 3y_1 - 10}{5}\right|$$

$\Rightarrow$ $4x_1 + 3y_1 - 10 = \pm 5$

$4x_1 + 3y_1 - 10 = 5$ or $4x_1 + 3y_1 - 10 = -5$

$4x_1 + 3y_1 = 5 + 10$ or $4x_1 + 3y_1 = -5 + 10$

$4x_1 + 3y_1 = 15$ ...(2)

Or $4x_1 + 3y_1 = 5$ ...(3)

From equation (1), we have $y_1 = 4 - x_1$ ...(4)

Putting the value of y_1 in equation (2), we get

$$4x_1 + 3(4 - x_1) = 15$$

$$\Rightarrow \quad 4x_1 + 12 - 3x_1 = 15$$

$$\Rightarrow \quad x_1 = 15 - 12$$

$$\Rightarrow \quad x_1 = 3$$

Putting the value of x_1 in equation (4), we get

$$y_1 = 4 - 3$$

$$\Rightarrow \quad y_1 = 1$$

Putting the value of $y_1 = 4 - x_1$ in equation (3), we get

$$4x_1 + 3(4 - x_1) = 5$$

$$\Rightarrow \quad 4x_1 + 12 - 3x_1 = 5$$

$$\Rightarrow \quad x_1 = 5 - 12$$

$$\Rightarrow \quad x_1 = -7$$

Putting the value of x_1 in equation (4), we get

$$y_1 = 4 - (-7)$$

$$\Rightarrow \quad y_1 = 4 + 7$$

$$\Rightarrow \quad y_1 = 11$$

Hence, the required points on the given line are (3, 1) and (-7, 11).

34. Find the slope of the line, which makes an angle of 45° with the positive direction of y-axis measured anticlockwise.

Ans. Given that a line makes an angle of 45° with the positive direction of y - axis measured anticlockwise.

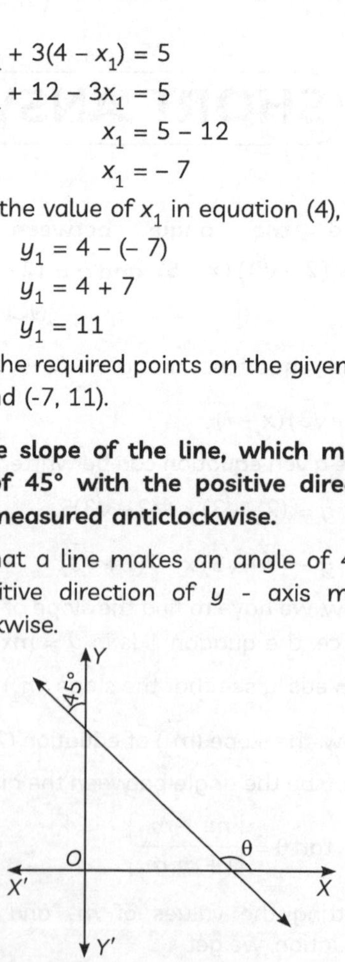

So, the line makes an angle of 135°with the positive direction of x-axis measured anticlockwise.

$\therefore \quad \theta = 135°$

Hence, slope of line, $m = \tan\theta$

$= \tan 135°$

$= \tan(90° + 45°)$

$= -\cot 45°$

$= -1$

LONG ANSWER Type Questions (LA)

[**4** & **5** marks]

35. Find the points on the x-axis, whose distance from the line $\frac{x}{3}+\frac{y}{4}=1$ are 4 units.

Ans. Given the equation of the line is

$$\frac{x}{3}+\frac{y}{4}=1$$

$\Rightarrow 4x + 3y - 12 = 0$

which is of the form $Ax + By + C = 0$ with

$A = 4, B = 3, C = -12.$

Let $(a, 0)$be the required point on x-axis.

Let, $x_1 = a$, $y_1 = 0$

Now, the distance of a point $(x_1, y_1)$from the given line is

$$d = \frac{|Ax_1+By_1+C|}{\sqrt{A^2+B^2}} = \frac{|(4)(a)+(3)(0)-12|}{\sqrt{(4)^2+(3)^2}}$$

$$= \frac{|4a-12|}{5}$$

Since the point $(a, 0)$ is at a distance of 4 units from the given line.

$\therefore \quad d = 4$

$\Rightarrow \quad \frac{|4a-12|}{5} = 4$

$\Rightarrow \quad |4a - 12| = 20$

$\Rightarrow \quad 4a - 12 = \pm 20$

$\Rightarrow \quad a = 8, -2$

Hence, the required points are $(8, 0)$and $(-2, 0)$.

36. A variable line passes through a fixed point P. The algebraic sum of the perpendiculars drawn from the points (2, 0),(0, 2) and (1, 1) on the line is zero. Find the coordinates of the point P. [NCERT Exemplar]

Ans. Let the variable line be $ax + by = 1$

We know that, length of the perpendicular from (p, q) to the line $ax + by + c = 0$ is

$$d = \left|\frac{ap+bq+c}{\sqrt{a^2+b^2}}\right|$$

Now, perpendicular distance from $A(2,0)$ is

$$d_1 = \left|\frac{2\times a+0\times b-1}{\sqrt{a^2+b^2}}\right|$$

$$= \frac{2a-1}{\sqrt{a^2+b^2}}$$

Now, perpendicular distance from $B(0,2)$ is

$$d_2 = \left|\frac{0\times a+2\times b-1}{\sqrt{a^2+b^2}}\right|$$

$$= \frac{2b-1}{\sqrt{a^2+b^2}}$$

Now, perpendicular distance from $C(1, 1)$ is

$$d_3 = \left|\frac{1\times a+1\times b-1}{\sqrt{a^2+b^2}}\right|$$

$$= \frac{a+b-1}{\sqrt{a^2+b^2}}$$

It is given that the algebraic sum of the perpendicular from the given points (2, 0), (0, 2) and (1, 1) to this line is zero.

$d_1 + d_2 + d_3 = 0$

Substituting the values we get

$$\therefore \quad \frac{2a-1}{\sqrt{a^2+b^2}}+\frac{2b-1}{\sqrt{a^2+b^2}}+\frac{a+b-1}{\sqrt{a^2+b^2}}=0$$

$\Rightarrow \quad 2a - 1 + 2b - 1 + a + b - 1 = 0$

$\Rightarrow \quad 3a + 3b - 3 = 0$

$\Rightarrow \quad a + b - 1 = 0$

$\Rightarrow \quad a + b = 1$

So, the equation $ax + by = 1$ represents a family of straight lines passing through a fixed point.

Comparing the equation $ax + by = 1$ and

$a + b = 1$, we get

$x = 1$ and $y = 1$

So, the coordinates of fixed points is (1, 1).

37. P_1, P_2 are points on either of the two lines $y-\sqrt{3}\,|x|=2$ at a distance of 5 units from their point of intersection. Find the coordinates of the foot of perpendiculars drawn from P_1, P_2 on the bisector of the angle between the given lines. [NCERT Exemplar]

Ans. Given lines are $y-\sqrt{3}|x|=2$. If $x \geq 0$, then

$$y-\sqrt{3}x=2 \quad ...(i)$$

If $x < 0$, then

$$y+\sqrt{3}x=2 \quad ...(ii)$$

On adding equation (i) and (ii), we get

$$y-\sqrt{3}x+y+\sqrt{3}x = 2+2$$

$\Rightarrow$ $2y = 4$

$\Rightarrow$ $y = 2$

Substituting the value of $y = 2$ in equation ...(ii), we get

$$2+\sqrt{3}x = 2$$

$\Rightarrow$ $\sqrt{3}x = 2-2$

$\Rightarrow$ $x = 0$

$\therefore$ Point of intersection of given lines is (0, 2).

Now, we find the slopes of given lines.

Slope of equation (i) is

$$y = \sqrt{3}x+2$$

Comparing the above equation with $y = mx + b$, we get

$$m = \sqrt{3}$$

And we know that, $m = \tan\theta$

$\therefore$ $\tan\theta = \sqrt{3}$

$\Rightarrow$ $\theta = 60°$ $[\because \tan 60° = \sqrt{3}]$

Slope of equation (ii) is

$$y = -\sqrt{3}x+2$$

Comparing the above equation with

$y = mx + b$, we get

$$m = -\sqrt{3}$$

And we know that, $m = \tan\theta$

$\therefore$ $\tan\theta = -\sqrt{3}$

$\Rightarrow$ $\theta = (180° - 60°)$

$\Rightarrow$ $\theta = 120°$

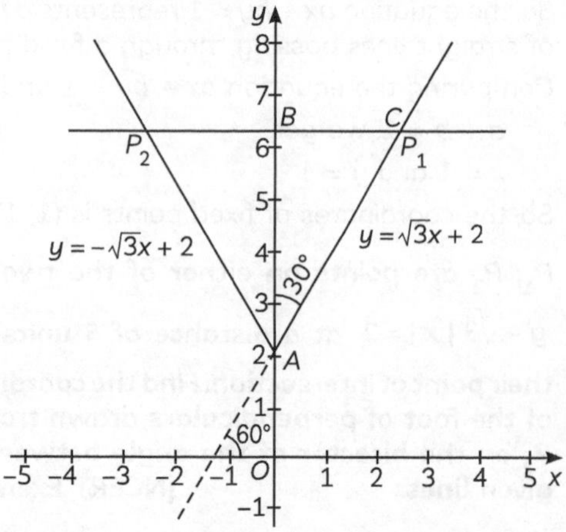

In ΔACB,

$$\cos 30° = \frac{BA}{AC}$$

Given $AC = 5$ units

$\Rightarrow$ $\frac{\sqrt{3}}{2} = \frac{BA}{5}$

$\Rightarrow$ $BA = \frac{5\sqrt{3}}{2}$

$\therefore$ $OB = OA + AB$

$$= 2+\frac{5\sqrt{3}}{2}$$

Hence, the coordinates of the foot of perpendicular $= \left(0, 2+\frac{5\sqrt{3}}{2}\right)$.

38. In the triangle ABC with vertices A(2, 3), B(4, –1), and C(1, 2), find the equation and length of altitude from vertex A.

Ans. Given a triangle ABC with vertices $A(2, 3)$, $B(4, -1)$, and $C(1, 2)$.

Lat AD be the perpendicular form the vertex A.

Now, slope of BC i.e.

$$m_1 = \frac{y_2-y_1}{x_2-x_1} = \frac{2-(-1)}{1-4} = \frac{3}{-3} = -1$$

Let m_2 be the slope of AD.

Since, AD is perpendicular to BC.

$$m_1m_2 = -1$$

$$-1m_2 = -1$$

$\Rightarrow$ $m_2 = 1$

So, slope of AD is 1.

Equation of line having one coordinate and slope is given by

$$y - y_1 = m(x - x_1)$$

So, equation of AD is

$$y - 3 = 1(x - 2)$$

$= \quad y = x + 1$

$= \quad -x + y - 1 = 0$

We know that the perpendicular distance of line $Ax + By + C = 0$ from point (x_1, y_1) is given by

$$d = \frac{|Ax_1+By_1+C|}{\sqrt{A^2+B^2}}$$

Now, length of AD from vertex $A(2, 3)$ is

$$\left|\frac{-3+2-1}{\sqrt{(-1)^2+1^2}}\right|$$

$$= \left|\frac{-2}{\sqrt{2}}\right|$$

$$= \sqrt{2}$$

Hence, length altitude AD is $\sqrt{2}$.

FORMS OF LINE 2

TOPIC 1

DIFFERENT FORMS OF EQUATIONS OF STRAIGHT LINE

Slope Intercept Form of a Line

The equation of a line with slope m and making an intercept c on y-axis is given by $y = mx + c$.

Let the given line intersects y-axis at Q and makes an angle θ with x-axis. Then $m = \tan\theta$. Let $P(x, y)$ be any point on the line. Draw PL perpendicular to x-axis and $QM \perp PM$.

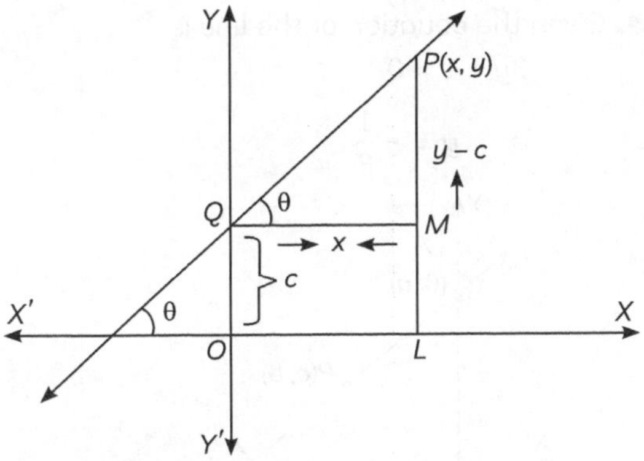

Clearly, $\angle MQP = \theta$, $QM = OL = x$

And, $PM = PL - ML = PL - OQ = y - c$

From triangle, PMQ, we have

$$\tan\theta = \frac{PM}{QM} = \frac{y-c}{x}$$

$$\Rightarrow \quad m = \frac{y-c}{x}$$

$\Rightarrow$ $y = mx + c$, which is the required equation of the line.

Two-Point form of a Line

The equation of a line passing through two points (x_1, y_1) and (x_2, y_2) is

$$y - y_1 = \left(\frac{y_2 - y_1}{x_2 - x_1}\right)(x - x_1)$$

Let m be the slope of the line passing through (x_1, y_1) and (x_2, y_2). Then,

$$m = \frac{y_2 - y_1}{x_2 - x_1}$$

So, the equation of the line is

$$y - y_1 = m(x - x_1)$$

Substituting the value of m, we obtain

$$y - y_1 = \frac{y_2 - y_1}{x_2 - x_1}(x - x_1)$$

This is the required equation of the line in two-point form.

Point-Slope Form of a Line

The equation of a line which passes through the point (x_1, y_1) and has the slope 'm' is $y - y_1 = m(x - x_1)$.

Let the line pass through the point $Q(x_1, y_1)$ and let $P(x, y)$ be any point on the line.

Then,

$$\text{Slope of the line is} = \frac{y - y_1}{x - x_1}$$

But, the slope of the line is m.

$$\therefore \quad m = \frac{y - y_1}{x - x_1} \Rightarrow y - y_1 = m(x - x_1)$$

Hence, $y - y_1 = m(x - x_1)$ is the required equation of the line.

Example 2.1: Find the equation of the line which passes through $(2, 2\sqrt{3})$ and inclined with the x-axis at an angle of 75°. [NCERT]

Ans. We know that

Equation of line passing through point (x_0, y_0) with slope m is

$$y - y_0 = m(x - x_0)$$

Here point $(x_0, y_0) = (2, 2\sqrt{3})$

Hence $x_0 = 2, y_0 = 2\sqrt{3}$

And slope $= m = \tan\theta$

Given $\theta = 75°$

$$\therefore \quad m = \tan(75°)$$

$$= \tan(45 + 30)°$$

$$= \frac{\tan 45° + \tan 30°}{1 - \tan 45° \tan 30°}$$

$$\left[\because \tan(A + B) = \frac{\tan A + \tan B}{1 - \tan A \tan B}\right]$$

$$= \frac{1 + \frac{1}{\sqrt{3}}}{1 - \frac{1}{\sqrt{3}}}$$

$$= \frac{\frac{\sqrt{3}+1}{\sqrt{3}}}{\frac{\sqrt{3}-1}{\sqrt{3}}}$$

$$= \frac{\sqrt{3}+1}{\sqrt{3}-1}$$

$$\therefore \quad m = \frac{\sqrt{3}+1}{\sqrt{3}-1}$$

Putting value of m in $(y - y_0) = m(x - x_0)$

$$(y - 2\sqrt{3}) = \frac{\sqrt{3}+1}{\sqrt{3}-1}(x-2)$$

$$(y - 2\sqrt{3})(\sqrt{3}-1) = (\sqrt{3}+1)(x-2)$$

$$y(\sqrt{3}-1) - 2\sqrt{3}(\sqrt{3}-1)$$

$$= x(\sqrt{3}+1) - 2(\sqrt{3}+1)$$

$$y(\sqrt{3}-1) - 2\sqrt{3}\times\sqrt{3} + 2\sqrt{3}$$

$$= x(\sqrt{3}+1) - 2\sqrt{3} - 2$$

$$y(\sqrt{3}-1) - 6 + 2\sqrt{3} = x(\sqrt{3}+1) - 2\sqrt{3} - 2$$

$$y(\sqrt{3}-1) = x(\sqrt{3}+1) - 2\sqrt{3} - 2 + 6 - 2\sqrt{3}$$

$$y(\sqrt{3}-1) = x(\sqrt{3}+1) - 4\sqrt{3} + 4$$

$$y(\sqrt{3}-1) - x(\sqrt{3}+1) = -4\sqrt{3} + 4$$

$$x(\sqrt{3}+1) - y(\sqrt{3}+1) = 4\sqrt{3} - 4$$

$$x(\sqrt{3}+1) - y(\sqrt{3}-1) = 4(\sqrt{3}-1)$$

The Intercept form of a Line

The equation of a line which cuts off intercepts a and b respectively from the x and y-axis is

$$\frac{x}{a} + \frac{y}{b} = 1..$$

Let AB be the line which cuts off intercepts $OA = a$ and $OB = b$ on the x and y-axes respectively. Let $P(x, y)$ be any point on the line. Draw $PL \perp OX$. Then, $OL = x$ and $PL = y$

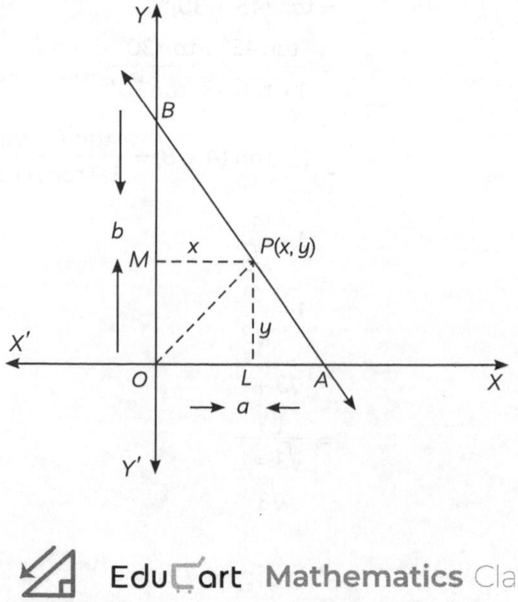

Clearly,

Area of ΔOAB = Area of ΔOPB

$$\Rightarrow \quad \frac{1}{2}OA.OB = \frac{1}{2}OA.PL + \frac{1}{2}OB.PM$$

$$\Rightarrow \quad \frac{1}{2}ab = \frac{1}{2}ay + \frac{1}{2}bx$$

$$\Rightarrow \quad ab = ay + bx$$

$$\Rightarrow \quad \frac{x}{a} + \frac{y}{b} = 1$$

This is the equation of the line in the intercept form.

Example 2.2: Reduce the equation 3y + 1 = 0 into intercepts form and find its intercepts on the axes. [NCERT]

Ans. Given the equation of the line is

$$3y + 1 = 0$$

$$y = -\frac{1}{3}$$

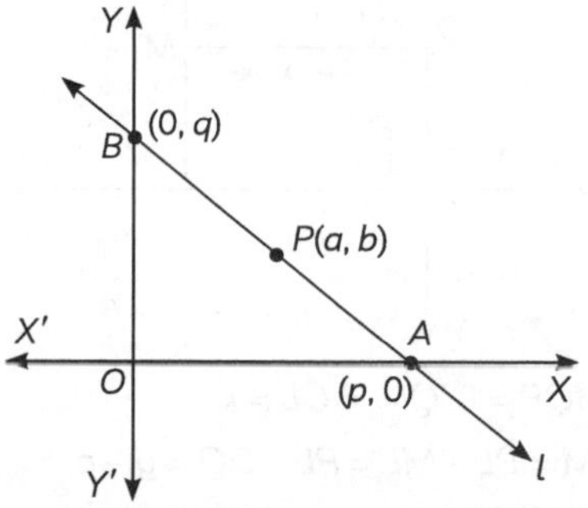

Which is the required intercept form. The given line has y-intercept as $-\frac{1}{3}$ but it has no x-intercept.

Example 2.3: P (a, b) is the midpoint of a line segment between axes. Show that equation of the line is $\frac{x}{a} + \frac{y}{b} = 2$ [NCERT]

Ans. Plotting x-axis and y-axis

Let l be a line intersecting x-axis at A and y-axis at 0.

Let, $P(a, b)$ be midpoint of AB.

Let, co-ordinates of A be $(p, 0)$.

Let, co-ordinates of B be $(0, q)$.

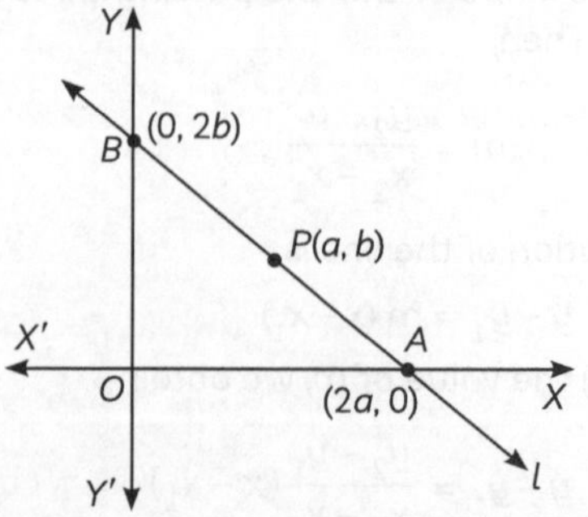

We know that mid-point of a line joining points (x_1, y_1) and (x_2, y_2) is $\left(\frac{x_1+x_2}{2}, \frac{y_1+y_2}{2}\right)$.

Mid-point of a line joining points $A(p, 0)$ and $B(0, q)$ is $P(a, b)$.

Putting values

$$(a, b) = \left(\frac{p+0}{2}, \frac{0+q}{2}\right)$$

$$(a, b) = \left(\frac{p}{2}, \frac{q}{2}\right)$$

$$a = \frac{P}{2}$$

$$2a = p$$

$$p = 2a$$

$$b = \frac{q}{2}$$

$$2b = q$$

$$q = 2b$$

Or,, $p = 2a, q = 2b$

So, points are

$$A = (p, 0) = (2a, 0)$$

$$B = (0, q) = (0, 2b)$$

Finding equation of line by two point equation of line

$$(y - y_1) = \frac{y_2 - y_1}{x_2 - x_1}(x - x_1)$$

For equation of line l passing through $(2a, 0)$ and $(0, 2b)$.

Here $x_1 = 2a, y_1 = 0$

$x_2 = 0, y_2 = 2b$

Putting values

$$(y - y_1) = \frac{y_2 - y_1}{x_2 - x_1}(x - x_1)$$

$$(y - 0) = \frac{2b - 0}{0 - 2a}(x - 2a)$$

$$(y - 0) = \frac{2b}{-2a}(x - 2a)$$

$$(y - 0) = \frac{-b}{a}(x - 2a)$$

$$ay = -bx + 2ab$$

$$ay + bx = 2ab$$

Dividing by ab

$$\frac{ay}{ab} + \frac{bx}{ab} = \frac{2ab}{ab}$$

$$\frac{y}{b} + \frac{x}{a} = 2$$

$$\frac{x}{a} + \frac{y}{b} = 2$$

So, the equation of line is $\frac{x}{a} + \frac{y}{b} = 2$

Hence, proved

Example 2.4: Find the distance of the line $4x + 7y + 5 = 0$ from the point (1, 2) along the line $2x - y = 0$.

Ans. There are two lines

Line CD: $2x - y = 0$ ...(i)

Line AB: $4x + 7y + 5 = 0$ ...(ii)

Both lines meet at Q.

Point $P(1, 2)$ is on line CD.

We need to find distance PQ, in PQ, P is (1, 2)

We need to find point Q.

To find PQ, we must find coordinates of point Q

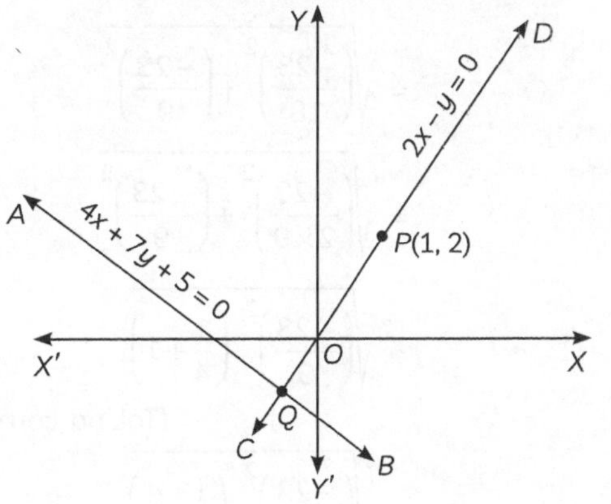

Point Q is the intersection of lines AB and CD.

From (i)

$$2x - y = 0$$

$$2x = y$$

$$y = 2x$$

Putting value of y in (ii)

$$4x + 7(2x) + 5 = 0$$

$$4x + 14x + 5 = 0$$

$$18x = -5$$

$$x = \frac{-5}{18}$$

Putting, $x = \frac{-5}{18}$ in (i)

$$2x - y = 0$$

$$2\left(\frac{-5}{18}\right) - y = 0$$

$$\frac{-5}{9} - y = 0$$

$$\frac{-5}{9} = y$$

$$y = \frac{-5}{9}$$

Hence, coordinates of point Q is $\left(\frac{-5}{18}, \frac{-5}{9}\right)$

Now, we have to find distance PQ.

We know that distance of points (x_1, y_1) and (x_2, y_2) is

$$d = \sqrt{(x_2 - x_1)^2 + (y_2 - y_1)^2}$$

Distance PQ where (1, 2) and $Q\left(\frac{-5}{18}, \frac{-5}{9}\right)$ is

$$PQ = \sqrt{\left(\frac{-5}{18} - 1\right)^2 + \left(\frac{-5}{9} - 2\right)^2}$$

$$= \sqrt{\left(\frac{-5-18}{18}\right)^2 + \left(\frac{-5-18}{9}\right)^2}$$

$$= \sqrt{\left(\frac{-23}{18}\right)^2 + \left(\frac{-23}{9}\right)^2}$$

$$= \sqrt{\left(\frac{-23}{2\times 9}\right)^2 + \left(\frac{-23}{9}\right)^2}$$

$$= \sqrt{\left(\frac{-23}{9}\right)^2 \cdot \left(\frac{1}{4} + 1\right)}$$

(Taking common)

$$= \sqrt{\left(\frac{-23}{9}\right)^2 \cdot \left(\frac{1+4}{4}\right)}$$

$$= \sqrt{\left(\frac{-23}{9}\right)^2 \cdot \left(\frac{5}{4}\right)}$$

$$= \frac{-23}{9}\sqrt{\frac{5}{4}}$$

$$= \frac{-23}{9}\sqrt{\frac{5}{2^2}}$$

$$= \frac{-23}{9}\frac{\sqrt{5}}{2}$$

$$= \frac{-23\sqrt{5}}{18}$$

But distance is always positive

Hence, distance of $PQ = \frac{23\sqrt{5}}{18}$.

Example 2.5: Find the distance between parallel lines $15x + 8y - 34 = 0$ and $15x + 8y + 31 = 0$. [NCERT]

Ans. The equation of the first line is

$$15x + 8y - 34 = 0,$$

which is of the form $Ax + By + C_1 = 0$

with $A = 15$, $B = 8$, $C_1 = -34$.

The equation of the second line is

$$15x + 8y + 31 = 0$$

Which is of the form $Ax + By + C_2 = 0$

with $A = 15$, $B = 8$, $C_2 = 31$.

Now, the distance between the given parallel lines is

$$d = \frac{|C_1 - C_2|}{\sqrt{A^2 + B^2}} = \frac{|-34 - 31|}{\sqrt{(15)^2 + (8)^2}} = \frac{65}{17}$$

Hence, the required distance $= \frac{65}{17}$ units.

Example 2.6: Find the equation of a line parallel to y-axis and passing through (–2, 5). [NCERT]

Ans. The equation of a line parallel to y-axis is of the form $x = a$. ...(1)

Given that the line passes through the point (–2, 5).

Putting $x = -2$ and $y = 5$ in (1), we get

$$-2 = a$$

Putting the value of a in (1), we get

$$x = -2.$$

Which is the required equation.

Example 2.7: Find the equation of the line which intersects the y-axis at a distance of 2 units above the origin and makes an angle of 30° with the positive direction of the x-axis. [NCERT]

Ans. Line AB intersects the y-axis 2 units above origin.

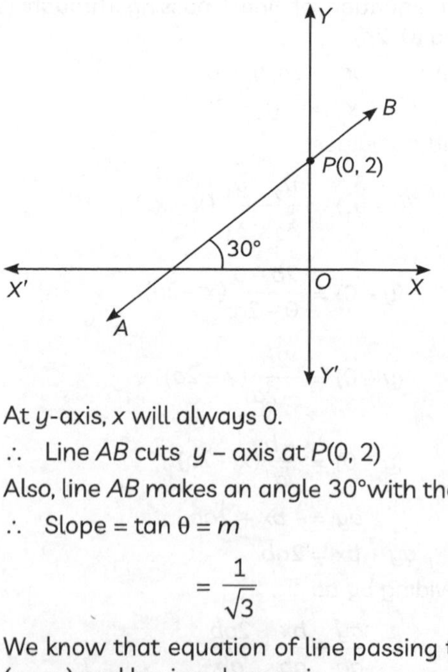

At y-axis, x will always 0.

∴ Line AB cuts y – axis at $P(0, 2)$

Also, line AB makes an angle 30°with the x-axis.

∴ Slope = tan θ = m

$$= \frac{1}{\sqrt{3}}$$

We know that equation of line passing through (x_0, y_0) and having slope m is

$$(y - y_0) = m(x - x_0)$$

Putting, $x_0 = 0, y_0 = 2$ and $m = \frac{1}{\sqrt{3}}$

We have

$$(y-2) = \frac{1}{\sqrt{3}}(x-0)$$

$$(y-2) = \frac{1}{\sqrt{3}}x$$

$$\sqrt{3}(y-2) = x$$

$$\sqrt{3}y - 2\sqrt{3} = x$$

$$\sqrt{3}y - x - 2\sqrt{3} = 0$$

Hence, the required equation is

$$\sqrt{3}y - x - 2\sqrt{3} = 0$$

Example 2.7: Find equation of the line through the point(0, 2) making an angle $\frac{2\pi}{3}$ with the positive x-axis. Also, find the equation of line parallel to it and crossing the y-axis at a distance of 2 units below the origin. [NCERT]

Ans. Let AB be the line passing through $P(0, 2)$ and making an angle $\frac{2\pi}{3}$ with positive x-axis.

Slope of line $AB = \tan\theta = m$

$$= \tan\left(\frac{2\pi}{3}\right)$$

$$= \tan(120°)$$

$$= \tan(180° - 60°)$$

$$= -\tan(60°)$$

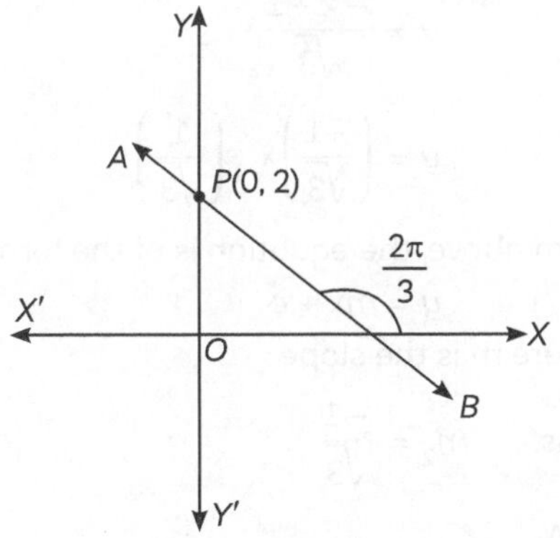

$$= -\sqrt{3} \quad (\tan 60° = \sqrt{3})$$

We know that

Equation of line passing through (x_0, y_0) and having slope m

$$(y - y_0) = m(x - x_0)$$

Equation of line AB passing through (0, 2) and having slope $m = -\sqrt{3}$.

$$(y-2) = -\sqrt{3}(x-0)$$

$$(y-2) = -\sqrt{3}x$$

$$y + \sqrt{3}x = 0 + 2$$

$$\sqrt{3}x + y = 2$$

$$\sqrt{3}x + y - 2 = 0$$

Hence, equation of line AB is $\sqrt{3}x + y - 2 = 0$.

Also,

We have to find equation of line which is parallel to line AB and crossing at a distance of 2 unit below the origin.

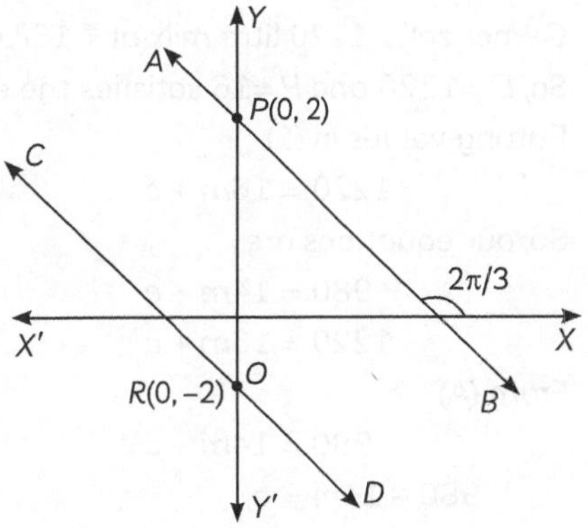

Let CD be the line parallel to AB and passing through point $R(0, -2)$.

We know that if two lines are parallel, thentheir slopes are equal

Therefore,

Slope of CD = Slope of AB

Slope of $CD = -\sqrt{3}$

Now,

Equation of line passing through point (x_0, y_0) and having slope m

$$(y - y_0) = m(x - x_0)$$

Equation of line CD passing through (0, –2) and slope $m = -\sqrt{3}$.

$$(y-(-2)) = -\sqrt{3}(x-0)$$

$$(y+2) = -\sqrt{3}(x)$$

$$y + \sqrt{3}x + 2 = 0$$

$$\sqrt{3}x + y + 2 = 0$$

Hence, equation of line $CD = \sqrt{3}x + y + 2 = 0$

Example 2.8: The owner of a milk store finds that he can sell 980 litres of milk each week at Rs 14/litre and 1220 litres of milk each week at Rs 16/Litre. Assuming a linear relationship between selling price and demand, how many litres could he sell weekly at 17/litre? [NCERT]

Ans. Let selling price be P along x-axis and demand of milk be D along y-axis.

We know that the equation of line is

$$y = mx + c$$

Here, P is along x-axis and D is along y-axis.

So, our equation becomes

$$D = mP + c \quad ...(1)$$

Now,

Owner sells 980 litre milk at ₹ 14/litre.

So, $D = 980$ and $P = 14$ satisfies the equation.

Putting values in (1)

$$980 = 14m + c \quad ...(A)$$

Owner sells, 1220 litre milk at ₹ 16/Litre.

So, $D = 1220$ and $P = 16$ satisfies the equation.

Putting values in (1)

$$1220 = 16m + c \quad ...(B)$$

So, our equations are

$$980 = 14m + c \quad ...(A)$$

$$1220 = 16m + c \quad ...(B)$$

From (A)

$$980 = 14m + c$$

$$980 - 14m = c$$

Putting value of c in (B)

$$1220 = 16m + 980 - 14m$$

$$1220 - 980 = 16m - 14m$$

$$240 = 2m$$

$$\frac{240}{2} = m$$

$$120 = m$$

$$m = 120$$

Putting, $m = 120$ in (A)

$$980 = 14m + c$$

$$980 - 14m = c$$

$$980 - 14(120) = c$$

$$980 - 1680 = c$$

$$-700 = c$$

$$c = -700$$

Putting value of m and c in (1)

$$D = mP + c$$

$$D = 120P - 700$$

Hence, the required is $D = 120P - 700$

We need to find how many litres could he sell weekly at Rs 17/litres.

I.e. we need to find D when $P = 17$

Putting $P = 17$ in the equation

$$D = 120P - 700$$

$$D = 120(17) - 700$$

$$D = 2040 - 700$$

$$D = 1340$$

Hence, when price is ₹ 17/litre, 1340 litres of milk could be sold.

Example 2.9: Find angles between the lines $\sqrt{3}x + y = 1$ and $x + \sqrt{3}y = 1$. **[NCERT]**

Ans. Given equation of lines,

$$\sqrt{3}x + y = 1 \quad ...(1)$$

$$x + \sqrt{3}y = 1 \quad ...(2)$$

We know that

Angle θ between two lines can be found by using formula

$$\tan\theta = \left|\frac{m_2 - m_1}{1 + m_2 m_1}\right|$$

Let slope of line (1) be m_1 and slope of line (2) be m_2

Calculating m_1

From (1), $\sqrt{3}x + y = 1$

$$y = -\sqrt{3}x + 1$$

From above, the equation is of the form

$$y = mx + c$$

Where m is the slope

Thus, $m_1 = -\sqrt{3}$

Calculating m_2

From (1)

$$x + \sqrt{3}y = 1$$

$$\sqrt{3}y = -x + 1$$

$$y = \frac{-x + 1}{\sqrt{3}}$$

$$y = \left(\frac{-1}{\sqrt{3}}\right)x + \left(\frac{1}{\sqrt{3}}\right)$$

From above, the equation is of the form

$$y = mx + c$$

Where m is the slope

Thus, $m_2 = \frac{-1}{\sqrt{3}}$

Now,

Angle between lines $\sqrt{3}x + y = 1$ *and* $x + \sqrt{3}y = 1$ is

$$\tan\theta = \left|\frac{m_2 - m_1}{1 + m_2 m_1}\right|$$

Putting values

$$\tan\theta = \left|\frac{-\sqrt{3} - \left(\frac{-1}{\sqrt{3}}\right)}{1 + (-\sqrt{3})\left(\frac{-1}{\sqrt{3}}\right)}\right|$$

$$\tan\theta = \left|\frac{-\sqrt{3}+\frac{1}{\sqrt{3}}}{1+1}\right|$$

$$\tan\theta = \left|\frac{\frac{(-\sqrt{3})(\sqrt{3})+1}{\sqrt{3}}}{2}\right|$$

$$\tan\theta = \left|\frac{-3+1}{2\sqrt{3}}\right|$$

$$\tan\theta = \left|\frac{-1}{\sqrt{3}}\right|$$

$$\tan\theta = \frac{1}{\sqrt{3}}$$

We know that $\tan 30° = \frac{1}{\sqrt{3}}$

$\tan\theta° = \tan 30°$

Hence $\theta = 30°$

Thus, the acute angle between the lines (1) and (2) is $\theta = 30°$

And obtuse angle (ϕ) between these two lines is

$\phi = 180° - \theta$

$\phi = 180° - 30°$

$\phi = 150°$

Thus, the required angle between the line is 30°or 150°.

Example 2.10 **Find the values of k for which the line $(k - 3)x - (4 - k^2)y + k^2 - 7k + 6 = 0$ is [NCERT]**

(A) Parallel to the x-axis

(B) Parallel to the y-axis

(C) Passing through origin

Ans. (A) Any line parallel to x-axis is of the form

$y = p$

Where p is constant

So, there is no term of x.

Since line

$(k - 3)x - (4 - k^2)y + k^2 - 7k + 6 = 0$ is

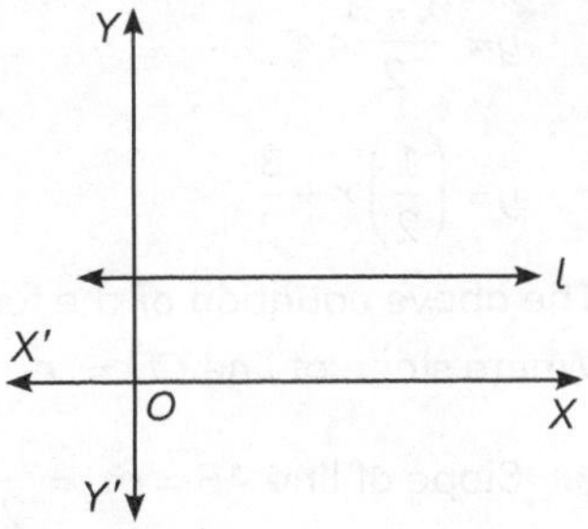

Parallel to x-axis

Hence,

$(k - 3)x = 0$

$k - 3 = \frac{0}{x} = k - 3 = 0$

$k = 3$

(B) Any line parallel to y-axis is of the form

$x = q$

Where q is constant

So, there is no term of y.

Since, line $(k - 3)x - (4 - k^2)y + k^2 - 7k + 6 = 0$ is

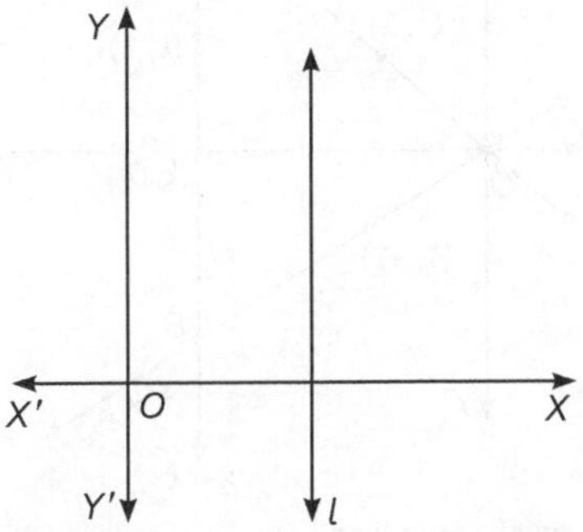

Parallel to y-axis

Hence,

$-(4 - k^2)y = 0$

$-(4 - k^2) = \frac{0}{y}$

$-4 + k^2 = 0$

$k^2 = 4$

$k = \sqrt{4}$

$k = \pm 2$

Hence $k = 2$ or -2

(C) If the line passing through the origin i.e. (0, 0) will satisfy the equation of line

Putting $x = 0$ and $y = 0$ in equation

$(k - 3)x - (4 - k^2)y + k^2 - 7k + 6 = 0$

$(k - 3)0 - (4 - k^2)0 + k^2 - 7k + 6 = 0$

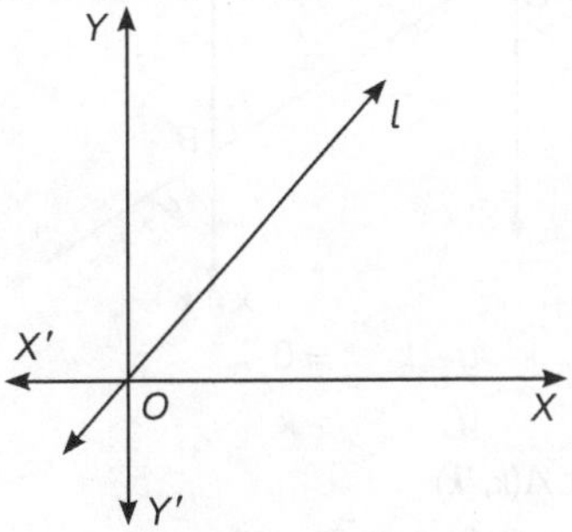

$k^2 - 7k + 6 = 0$

$k^2 - 6k - k + 6 = 0$

$k(k - 6) - 1(k - 6) = 0$

$(k - 1)(k - 6) = 0$

So, $k = 1$ or $k = 6$

Example 2.11 **Find the area of the triangle formed by the lines $y - x = 0$, $x + y = 0$ and $x - k = 0$. [NCERT]**

Ans. There are three lines given in the graph

$y - x = 0$ ..(1)

(0, 0) and (1, 1) satisfy this line

$x + y = 0$ ...(2)

(0, 0) and (1, – 1) satisfy this line

$x - k \quad = 0$ ...(3)

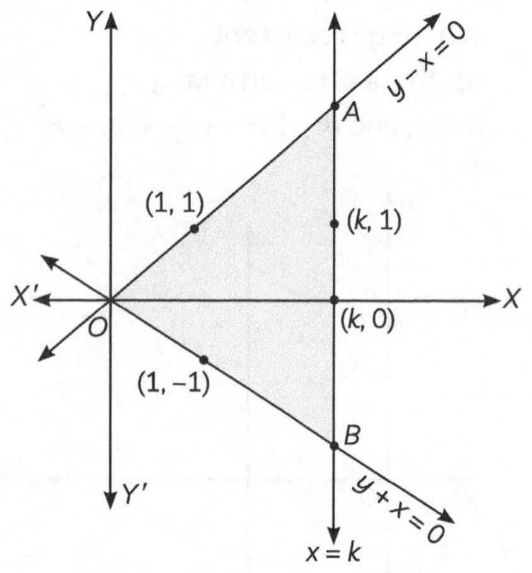

(k, 0) satisfy this line.

Let, line (1) and (3) intersect be point A and whereas line (2) and (3) intersect be point B

We need to find area triangle ΔOAB

We know O(0, 0)

We need to find coordinates of A and B

Coordinate of point A

Point A is the intersection of x = k and y – x = 0

Putting x = k in equation (1)

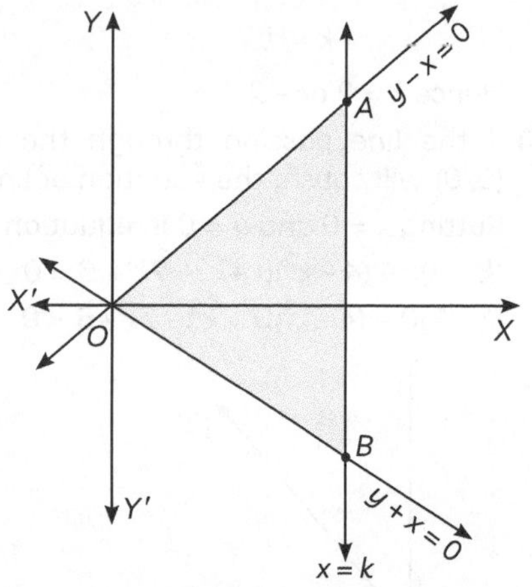

$y - k \quad = 0$

$y \quad = k$

So, point A(k, k)

Coordinate of point B

Point B is the intersection of x = k and y + x = 0

Putting x = k in equation (2)

$y + k \quad = 0$

$y \quad = -k$

So, point B(k, – k).

We know that

Area of triangle whose vertices are

(x_1, y_1), (x_2, y_2), and (x_3, y_3) is

$$= \frac{1}{2}|x_1(y_2 - y_3) + x_2(y_3 - y_1) + x_3(y_1 - y_2)|$$

For ΔAOB,

$(x_1, y_1) = O(0, 0)$

$(x_2, y_2) = A(k, k)$

$(x_3, y_3) = B(k, -k)$

Area of triangle ΔAOB whose vertices are (0, 0) (k, k) & (k,– k)

$$= \frac{1}{2}|0(k-(-k)+k(-k-0)+k(0-k)|$$

$$= \frac{1}{2}|0+k(-k)+k(-k)|$$

$$= \frac{1}{2}|-k^2-k^2|$$

$$= \frac{1}{2}|-2k^2|$$

$$= \frac{2k^2}{2}$$

$= k^2$ square units

Hence, required area of triangle is k^2 square units.

Example 2.12: If the lines $y = 3x + 1$ and $2y = x + 3$ are equally inclined to the line $y = mx + 4$, find the value of m. [NCERT]

Ans. Let line AB be $y = 3x + 1$

Line CD be $2y = x + 3$

and line PQ be $y = mx + 4$

Lines AB and CD area equally inclined to the line PQ

First we find slopes of lines

Slope of line AB

$y = 3x + 1$

The above equation is of the form $y = m_1 x + c_1$

Where slope of line AB = m_1

∴ Slope of line AB = $m_1 = 3$ ...(1)

Slope of line CD

$2y = x + 3$

$$y = \frac{x+3}{2}$$

$$y = \left(\frac{1}{2}\right)x + \frac{3}{2}$$

The above equation of the form $y = m_2x + c_2$

Where slope of line CD = m_2

∴ Slope of line AB = $m_2 = \frac{1}{23}$ ...(2)

Slope of line PQ

$y = mx + 4$

The above equation of the form $y = mx + c$

Where m is slope

Thus, slope of line PQ = m ...(3)

Now, given that lines

AB and CD are equally inclined to the line PQ

I.e. line AB and line CD make equal angle with line PQ

Angle between AB and PQ = angle between CD and PQ

We know that angle between two lines whose slope are m_1 and m_2 is

$$\tan\theta = \left|\frac{m_2 - m_1}{1 + m_2 m_1}\right|$$

Find angle between AB and PQ

Slope of $AB = m_1 = 3$

and slope of $PQ = m$

$$\tan\theta = \left|\frac{m-3}{1+3m}\right|$$

$$\left|\frac{m-3}{1+3m}\right| = \tan\theta \quad \text{...(A)}$$

Finding angle between CD and PQ

Slope of $PR = \frac{1}{2}$ and slope of $PQ = m$

$$\tan\theta = \left|\frac{m - \frac{1}{2}}{1 + \frac{1}{2}m}\right|$$

$$\tan\theta = \left|\frac{\frac{2m-1}{2}}{\frac{2+m}{2}}\right| = \left|\frac{2m-1}{2+m}\right| \quad \text{...(B)}$$

Since, angle (θ) are equal, so, $\tan\theta$ must be equal.

i.e. eq. A = eq. B

From (A) and (B)

$$\left|\frac{m-3}{1+3m}\right| = \left|\frac{2m-1}{2+m}\right|$$

So, $$\left(\frac{m-3}{1+3m}\right) = \left(\frac{2m-1}{2+m}\right)$$

or $$\left(\frac{m-3}{1+3m}\right) = -\left(\frac{2m-1}{2+m}\right)$$

Solving, $$\left(\frac{m-3}{1+3m}\right) = \left(\frac{2m-1}{2+m}\right)$$

$$\frac{m-3}{1+3m} = \frac{2m-1}{2+m}$$

$$(m-3)(2+m) = (2m-1)(1+3m)$$

$$m(2+m) - 3(2+m) = 2m + 6m^2 - 3m)$$

$$2m + m^2 - 6 - 3m = 2m + 6m^2 - 1 - 3m$$

$$-m + m^2 - 6 = -m + 6m^2 - 1$$

$$5m - 5m + m^2 - 6m^2 - 6 + 1 = 0$$

$$0 - 5m^2 - 5 = 0$$

$$-5m^2 = 5$$

$$m^2 = \frac{5}{-5}$$

$$m^2 = -1$$

This is not possible as the square of a number cannot be negative

Solving $$\left(\frac{m-3}{1+3m}\right) = -\left(\frac{2m-1}{2+m}\right)$$

$$\frac{m-3}{1+3m} = \frac{1-2m}{2+m}$$

$$(m-3)(2+m) = (1-2m)(1+3m)$$

$$m(2+m) - 3(2+m) = 1(1+3m) - 2m(1+3m)$$

$$2m + m^2 - 6 - 3m = 1 + 3m - 2m - 6m^2$$

$$m^2 - 6 - m = -6m^2 + m + 1$$

$$m^2 + 6m^2 - m - m - 6 - 1 = 0$$

$$7m^2 - 2m - 7 = 0$$

The above equation is of the form

$$ax^2 + bx + c = 0$$

Where solution is $x = \frac{-b \pm \sqrt{b^2 - 4ac}}{2a}$

Here $a = 7$, $b = -2$, $c = -7$ & $x = m$

So,

$$m = \frac{-(-2) \pm \sqrt{(-2)^2 - 4(7)(-7)}}{2(7)}$$

$$m = \frac{2 \pm \sqrt{4 - (7)\times(-7)}}{14}$$

$$m = \frac{2 \pm \sqrt{4(1+49)}}{14}$$

$$m = \frac{2(1 \pm \cdot\sqrt{50})}{14}$$

$$m = \frac{2(1 \pm \cdot\sqrt{5\times5\times2})}{14}$$

$$m = \frac{2(1 \pm \cdot\sqrt{5\times5\times2})}{14}$$

$$m = \frac{1}{7}(1 \pm 5\sqrt{2})$$

$$m = \frac{1 \pm 5\sqrt{2}}{7}$$

Thus, the required value of m is $\frac{1+5\sqrt{2}}{7}$ and $\frac{1-5\sqrt{2}}{7}$.

Example 2.13 **A person standing at the junction (crossing) of two straight paths represented by the equations $2x - 3 + 4 = 0$ and $3x + 4y - 5 = 0$ wants to reach the path whose equation is $6x - 7y + 8 = 0$ in the least time. Find the equation of the path that he should follow.** **[NCERT]**

Ans. Let equation of lines

$OA : 2x - 3y + 4 = 0$ ...(1)

$OB : 3x + 4y - 5 = 0$ ...(2)

$AB : 6x - 7y + 8 = 0$ ...(3)

The two paths cross at point O

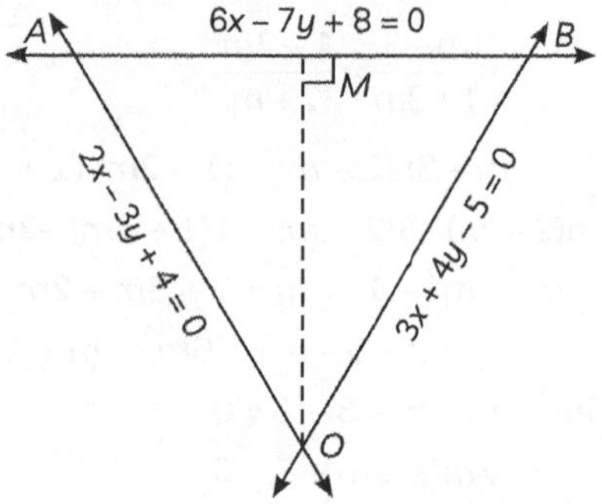

$\therefore$ The person in standing at point O

From point O, if he has to reach line AB in the least time, least distance from point O to line AB will be perpendicular distance.

Let $OM \perp AB$

We need to find equation of line OM.

First we find coordinates of point O.

Point O is the intersection of OA and OB.

From (1)

$$2x - 3y + 4 = 0$$
$$2x = 3y - 4$$
$$x = \frac{3y-4}{2}$$
$$x = \frac{3}{2}y - \frac{4}{2}$$
$$x = \frac{3}{2}y - 2$$

Putting value of x in (2)

$$3x + 4y - 5 = 0$$
$$3\left(\frac{3}{2}y - 2\right) + 4y - 5 = 0$$
$$\frac{9}{2}y - 6 + 4y - 5 = 0$$
$$\frac{9}{2}y + 4y - 11 = 0$$
$$\frac{9y+8y}{2} = 11$$
$$9y + 8y = 22$$
$$17y = 22$$
$$y = \frac{22}{17}$$

Putting value of y in (1)

$$2x - 3y + 4 = 0$$
$$2x - 3\left(\frac{22}{17}\right) + 4 = 0$$
$$2x - \frac{66}{17} + 4 = 0$$
$$2x = \frac{66}{17} - 4$$
$$2x = \frac{66 - 4(17)}{17}$$
$$2x = \frac{66-68}{17}$$
$$2x = \frac{-2}{17}$$
$$x = \frac{-2}{17\times 2}$$
$$x = \frac{-1}{17}$$

Thus, the coordinate of point O is $O\left(\frac{-1}{17}, \frac{22}{17}\right)$.

Now, line OM is perpendicular to line AB.

When two lines are perpendicular, then the product of their slopes are equal to –1.

Slope of OM × slope of $AB = -1$

$$\text{Slope of } OM = \frac{-1}{\text{slope of } AB}$$

Equation of AB is $6x - 7y + 8 = 0$

$$6x + 8 = 7y$$
$$7y = 6x + 8$$
$$y = \frac{6x+8}{7}$$
$$y = \left(\frac{6}{7}\right)x + \frac{8}{7}$$

The above equation is of the form

$$y = mx + c$$

Where m is slope of line

$$\text{Slope of } \quad AB = \frac{6}{7}$$

$$\text{Slope of } \quad OM = \frac{-1}{\text{slope of } AB}$$
$$= \frac{-1}{\frac{6}{7}}$$
$$= \frac{-7}{6}$$

Finding equation of OM.

We know that equation of line passing through (x_1, y_1) having slope m is equation of line OM passing through $O\left(\frac{-1}{17}, \frac{22}{17}\right)$ having slope $\frac{-7}{6}$ is

Equation of path OM is

$$y-\frac{22}{17}=\frac{-7}{6}\left(x-\left(\frac{-1}{17}\right)\right)$$

$$y-\frac{22}{17}=\frac{-7}{6}\left(x+\frac{1}{17}\right)$$

$$y-\frac{22}{17}=\frac{-7}{6}x-\frac{7}{6}\times\frac{1}{17}$$

$$y-\frac{22}{17}=\frac{-7}{6}x-\frac{7}{6\times17}$$

$$y+\frac{7}{6}x=\frac{22}{17}-\frac{7}{6\times17}$$

$$\frac{6y+7x}{6}=\frac{22(6)-7}{6\times17}$$

$$\frac{6y+7x}{6}=\frac{132-7}{6\times17}$$

$$\frac{6y+7x}{6}=\frac{125}{6\times17}$$

$$17(6y + 7x) = 125$$

$$17(6y) + 17(7x) = 125$$

$$102y + 119x = 125$$

Hence, the required equation is

$$119x + 102y = 125$$

OBJECTIVE Type Questions

[**1** mark]

Multiple Choice Questions

1. A line passes through (2,2) and is perpendicular to the line $3x + y = 3$. Its y-intercept is:

(a) $\frac{1}{3}$ (b) $\frac{2}{3}$

(c) 1 (d) $\frac{4}{3}$

[NCERT Exemplar]

Ans. (d) $\frac{4}{3}$

Explanation: Slope of given line $3x + y = 3$ is -3.

$\therefore$ Slope of perpendicular line $= \frac{1}{3}$

Thus, the equation of the required line is:

$$y-2=\frac{1}{3}(x-2)$$

$$\Rightarrow \quad x-3y+4=0$$

For y – intercept, put $x = 0$.

$$0-3y+4=0$$

$$\Rightarrow \quad y=\frac{4}{3},$$

which is y-intercept.

Hence, the option(d) is the correct answer.

2. Equation of the line passing through (1, 2) and parallel to the line $y = 3x - 1$ is:

(a) $y + 2 = x + 1$ (b) $y + 2 = 3(x + 1)$

(c) $y - 2 = 3(x - 1)$ (d) $y - 2 = x - 1$

[NCERT Exemplar]

Ans. (c) $y - 2 = 3(x - 1)$

Explanation: Line is parallel to $y = 3x - 1$ and passes through the point (1, 2). Hence, its slope is same as the given line i.e. $m = 3$

So, the equation of the line is: $y - 2 = 3(x - 1)$

Hence, the option(c) is the correct answer.

3. The equation line through point (0, 2) with slope −2 is:

(a) $y + 2x = 2$ (b) $y - 2x = 2$

(c) $2x - y = 2$ (d) $d = 0$

Ans. (a) $y + 2x = 2$

Explanation: Here $x_1 = 0, y_1 = 2$ and $m = -2$, the equation will be

$$y - y_1 = m(x - m)$$

$$y - 2 = -2(x - 0)$$

$$y - 2 = -2x$$

$$y + 2x = 2$$

Hence, the option(a) is the correct answer.

4. The equation of the straight line passing through the point (3, 2) and perpendicular to the line $y = x$ is:

(a) $x - y = 5$ (b) $x + y = 5$

(c) $x + y = 1$ (d) $x - y = 1$

[NCERT Exemplar]

Ans. *(b)* $x + y = 5$

Explanation: Given that straight line passing through the point (3, 2) and perpendicular to the line $y = x$.

Let the equation of line 'L' is

$$y - y_1 = m(x - x_1)$$

Since L is passing through the point (3, 2).

$$\therefore \quad y - 2 = m(x - 3) \qquad ...(i)$$

Now, given eq. is $y = x$

Since, the above equation is in $y = mx + b$ form.

So, the slope of this equation = 1

It is also given that line L and $y = x$ are perpendicular to each other.

We know that, when two lines are perpendicular, then

$$m_1 \times m_2 = -1$$

$$\therefore \quad m \times 1 = -1$$

$$\Rightarrow \quad m = -1$$

Putting the value of m in equation (i), we get

$$y - 2 = (-1)(x - 3)$$

$$\Rightarrow \quad y - 2 = -x + 3$$

$$\Rightarrow \quad x + y = 3 + 2$$

$$\Rightarrow \quad x + y = 5$$

Hence, the option(b) is the correct answer.

5. The equation of the line which has slope of 2 and cuts-off intercept of 6 on x-axis, is:

(a) $2x - y + 12 = 0$ (b) $2x + y + 12 = 0$

(c) $-2x + y + 12 = 0$ (d) $2x + y - 12 = 0$

[DIKSHA]

Ans. *(c)* $-2x + y + 12 = 0$

Explanation: Let a and b be the intercepts of the line on X and Y-axes, respectively.

Equation of the line will be $\frac{x}{a} + \frac{y}{b} = 1$

$$\frac{x}{a} + \frac{y}{b} = 1$$

$$\frac{x}{6} + \frac{y}{b} = 1$$

$$bx + 6y = 6b$$

$$y = \frac{6b - bx}{6}$$

$$= \frac{-bx + 6b}{6}$$

$$y = \frac{-b}{6}x + b$$

[Comparing it with $y = mx + c$]

$$\text{slope,} \quad m = \frac{-b}{6}$$

But, by the question $\frac{-b}{6} = 2$

$$\text{Or,} \quad -b = 12$$

$$b = -12$$

So,

$$\frac{x}{6} + \frac{y}{-12} = 1 \Rightarrow \frac{x}{6} - \frac{y}{12} = 1$$

$$\frac{2x - y}{12} = 1$$

$$2x - y = 12$$

$$\Rightarrow \quad -2x + y + 12 = 0$$

Hence, the option(c) is the correct answer

6. The equation of the line through (–2, 3) with slope –4 is:

(a) $x + 4y - 10 = 0$ (b) $y + 4x + 5 = 0$

(c) $x + y - 1 = 0$ (d) $3x + 4y - 6 = 0$

[DIKSHA]

Ans. *(b)* $y + 4x + 5 = 0$

Explanation: We know that

Equation of line passing through point (x_0, y_0) with slope m is

$$y - y_0 = m(x - x_0)$$

Here, slope $= m = -4$

Point $(x_0, y_0) = (-2, 3)$

Hence, $x_0 = -2, y_0 = 3$

Putting the values

$$(y - 3) = -4(x - (-2))$$

$$(y - 3) = -4(x + 2)$$

$$y - 3 = -4x - 8$$

$$y + 4x - 3 + 8 = 0$$

$$y + 4x + 5 = 0$$

Thuse, the required equation is $y + 4x + 5 = 0$.

Hence, the option(b) is the correct answer.

7. The equation of line passing through the points (1, 2) and (1, 3) is:

(a) 0 (b) Not defined

(c) $x - y = 2$ (d) $x + y = 2$

Ans. *(b)* Not defined

Explanation: Here $x_1 = 1, x_2 = 1$ and $y_1 = 2, y_2 = 3$.

So equation of line will be

$$y - y_1 = \frac{y_2 - y_1}{x_2 - x_1}(x - x_1)$$

$$y - 2 = \frac{3 - 2}{1 - 1}(x - 1)$$

$$y - 2 = \frac{1}{0}(x - 1)$$

Slope = 1/0 which is not defined.

Hence, the option(b) is the correct answer.

8. A line cutting of intercept –3 onthe y-axis and the tangent at angle to the x-axis is $\frac{3}{5}$ its equation is:

(a) $5y - 3x + 15 = 0$ (b) $3y - 5x + 15 = 0$
(c) $5y - 3x - 15 = 0$ (d) None of these

[NCERT Exemplar]

Ans. *(a) $5y - 3x + 15 = 0$*

Explanation: We know that,

Slope of a line, $m = \tan \theta$.

Given that $\tan \theta = \frac{3}{5}$

$\Rightarrow$ Slope of line, $m = \frac{3}{5}$

Since, the lines cut off intercepts = –3 on y-axis then the line is passing through the point (0, –3).

So, the equation of line is

$$y - y_1 = m(x - x_1)$$

$$\Rightarrow \quad y - (-3) = \frac{3}{5}(x - 0)$$

$$\Rightarrow \quad y + 3 = \frac{3}{5}x$$

$$\Rightarrow \quad 5y + 15 = 3x$$

$$\Rightarrow \quad 5y - 3x + 15 = 0$$

Hence, the option(a) is the correct answer

9. The distance of the point (4, –6) from the line $4x - 5y - 32 = 0$ is:

(a) $\frac{3}{7}$ (b) $\frac{14}{41}$

(c) $\frac{7}{5}$ (d) $\frac{14}{\sqrt{41}}$

Ans. *(d) $\frac{14}{\sqrt{41}}$*

Explanation: Given line is

$$4x - 5y - 32 = 0$$

Here $A = 4$, $B = -5$ and $C = -32$

Given point is (4, –6).

So

$$d = \left|\frac{Ax_1 + By_1 + C}{\sqrt{A^2 + B^2}}\right|$$

$$= \left|\frac{4 \times 4 + (-5)(-6) - 32}{\sqrt{16 + 25}}\right|$$

$$= \left|\frac{16 + 30 - 32}{\sqrt{41}}\right|$$

$$= \frac{14}{\sqrt{41}}$$

Hence, the option(d) is the correct answer

Assertion-Reason (A-R)

DIRECTION: In the following questions, a statement of assertion (A) is followed by a statement of the reason (R). Mark the correct choice as:

(a) Both assertion (A) and reason (R) are true and reason (R) is the correct explanation of assertion (A).

(b) Both assertion (A) and reason (R) are true but reason (R) is not the correct explanation of assertion (A).

(c) Assertion (A) is true but reason (R) is false.

(d) Assertion (A) is false but reason (R) is true.

10. Assertion (A): Slope of x-axis is zero and slope of y-axis is not defined.

Reason (R): Slope of x-axis is defined and slope of y-axis is zero.

Ans. *(c) Assertion (A) is true but reason (R) is false.*

Explanation: slope of x-axis is zero and hence defined but slope of y-axis not defined is correct.

So assertion is true but reason is false.

Hence, the option(c) is the correct answer.

11. Assertion (A): The distance between the line $4x + 3y = 11$ and $8x + 6y = 15$ is 7/10.

Reason (R): The distance between the line $ax + by = c_1$ and $ax + by = c_2$ is given by $\left|\frac{c_1 - c_2}{\sqrt{a^2 + b^2}}\right|$.

Ans. *(a) Both assertion (A) and reason (R) are true and reason (R) is the correct explanation of assertion (A).*

Explanation: Given lines are

$$4x + 3y = \frac{15}{2} \text{ then}$$

Distance between them is

$$= \left|\frac{11 - 15/2}{\sqrt{16 + 9}}\right|$$

$$= \left|\frac{7}{10}\right| = \frac{7}{10}$$

Hence, the option (a) is the correct answer.

CASE BASED Questions (CBQs)

[4 & 5 marks]

Read the following passages and answer the questions that follow:

12. *A triangular park has two of its vertices as B(–4, 1)and C(2, 11).The third vertex A is a point dividing the line joining the points (3, 1)and (6, 4)in the ratio 2 : 1.*

(A) Find the coordinates of third vertex *A*.

(B) Find the equation of passing through *B* and *C*.

Ans. (A)

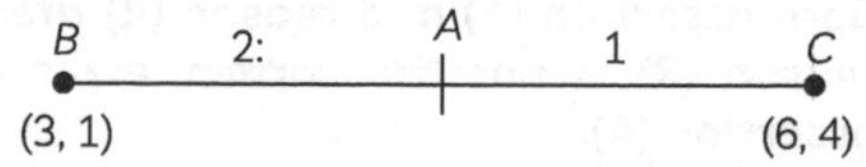

Coordinates of

$$A = \left(\frac{2\times6+1\times3}{2+1}, \frac{2\times4+1\times1}{2+1}\right)$$

i. e., (5, 3)

(B) Equation of line through $B(-4, 1)$and $C(2, 11)$ is

$$y-1=\frac{11-1}{2+4}(x+4)$$

$$\Rightarrow \quad y-1=\frac{5}{3}(x+4)$$

$$\Rightarrow \quad 3y - 3 = 5x + 20$$

$$\Rightarrow \quad 5x - 3y + 23 = 0$$

13. *India faces a major population crisis due to the growing population. If we ware to estimate, we can say that almost 17% of the population of the world lives in India alone. India ranks second in the list of most populated countries. Population vs year graph given below:*

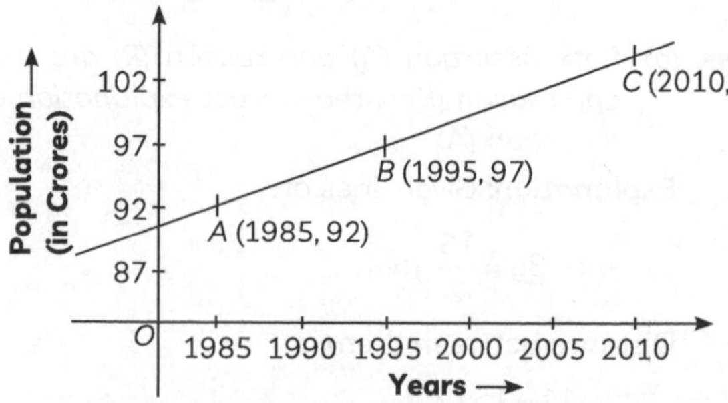

Based on the above information, answer the following questions.

(A) The slope of line *AB* is:

(a) 2 (b) 1

(c) 1/2 (d) 1/3

(B) The equation of line *AB* is:

(a) $x + 2y = 1791$ (b) $x - 2y = 1801$

(c) $x - 2y = 1791$ (d) $x - 2y + 1801 = 0$

(C) The population in the year 2010 is (in crores):

(a) 104.5 (b) 119.5

(c) 109.5 (d) None of these

(D) The equation of line perpendicular to line *AB* and passing through (1995, 97) is:

(a) $2x - y = 4087$ (b) $2x + y = 4087$

(c) $2x + y = 1801$ (d) None of the above

Ans. (A) *(c) 1/2*

Explanation: Slope of line

$$AB = \frac{y_2-y_1}{x_2-x_1} = \frac{97-92}{1995-1985}$$

$$= \frac{5}{10} = \frac{1}{2}$$

(B) *(b) $x - 2y = 1801$*

Explanation: Equation of line *AB* is

$$y - y_1 = m(x - x_1)$$

$$\therefore \quad y - 92 = \frac{1}{2}(x-1985)$$

$$2y - 184 = x - 1985$$

$$x - 2y = 1801$$

(C) *(a) 104.5*

Explanation: Let the population in year 2010 is *P*.

Since, *A, B, C* are collinear

$\therefore$ Slope of *AB* = Slope of *BC*

$$\frac{97-92}{1995-1985} = \frac{P-97}{2010-1995}$$

$$\Rightarrow \frac{1}{2} = \frac{P-97}{15}$$

$$\Rightarrow 7.5 = P - 97$$

$$\Rightarrow P = 97 + 7.5 = 104.5 \text{ crores}$$

(D) *(b) $2x + y = 4087$*

Explanation: $\because$ Slope of $AB = \frac{1}{2}$

Slope of line perpendicular to *AB* passing through (1995, 97) is

$$y - 97 = -2(x - 1995)$$

$$\Rightarrow \quad y - 97 = -2x + 3990$$

$$\Rightarrow \quad 2x + y = 4087$$

VERY SHORT ANSWER Type Questions (VSA)

[1 mark]

14. Find the equation of a line with slope (–3) and cutting off an intercept of 3 units on the negative y-axis.

Ans. Here $m = -3$, $c = -3$

So equation of line is

$$y = -3x - 3$$

Or $3x + y + 3 = 0$

15. Determine the equation line through the point (–2, –1) and parallel to x-axis.

Ans. Here, m=0

$$x_1 = -2, y_1 = -1$$

So the equation of line is

$$y - y_1 = m(x - x_1)$$

$$y + 1 = 0(x + 2)$$

$$y + 1 = 0$$

16. Find the equation of the line, which makes intercepts of 2 and –3 on the x and y-axis respectively.

Ans. Given that a line makes intercepts 2 and –3 on the x and, y-axis respectively.

Then, $a = 2$ and $b = -3$

Hence, the equation of line intercepts form is

$$\frac{x}{a} + \frac{y}{b} = 1$$

$$\frac{x}{2} - \frac{y}{3} = 1$$

17. Write the equation of the line for which $\tan\theta = \frac{1}{2}$, where θ is the inclination of the line and x-intercept is 4.

Ans. Given that $\tan\theta = \frac{1}{2}$, where θ is the inclination of the line.

Then, the slope of a line, $m = \tan\theta = \frac{1}{2}$

Also, given that x-intercept is $d = 4$.

Hence, the equation of the line in slope-intercept form is

$$y = m(x - d)$$

$$\Rightarrow \quad y = \frac{1}{2}(x - 4)$$

18. Find the equation of the line passing through the point (1, 2) and perpendicular to the line $x + y + 1 = 0$. [NCERT Exemplar]

Ans. Given that line passing through the point (1, 2) And perpendicular to the line $x + y + 1 = 0$.

Let the equation of line 'L' is

$$x - y + k = 0 \quad ...(i)$$

Since, L is passing through the point (1, 2)

$$\therefore \quad 1 - 2 + k = 0$$

$$\Rightarrow \quad k = 1$$

Putting the value of k in equation (i), we get

$$x - y + 1 = 0$$

Or $y - x - 1 = 0$.

19. Find the equation of the line through (2, 3) so that the segment of the line intercepted between the axes is bisected at this point. [DIKSHA]

Ans. Let the equation of the line be $\frac{x}{a} + \frac{y}{b} = 1$.

Which meets the x and y axes at $A(a, 0)$ and $B(0, b)$ respectively. The coordinate of the mid-point of AB are $\left(\frac{a}{2}, \frac{b}{2}\right)$. It is given that the point (2, 3) bisects AB

$$\frac{a}{2} = 2 \quad \text{and} \quad \frac{b}{2} = 3$$

$a = 4$ and $b = 6$ putting, $a = 4$ and $b = 6$ in $\frac{x}{a} + \frac{y}{b} = 1$, we get

$$\frac{x}{4} + \frac{y}{6} = 1 \quad \text{or} \quad 3x + 2y = 12$$

Hence the equation is $3x + 2y = 12$.

20. Find the equation of the line intersecting the y-axis at a distance of 4 units above the origin and making an angle of 30° with the positive direction of the x-axis.

Ans. Then, the slope of the line is $m = \tan 30° = \frac{1}{\sqrt{3}}$.

Also, given that the line intersects the y-axis at a distance of 4 units above the origin.

So, the y–intercept is $c = 4$.

Hence, the equation of the line in slope-intercept form is

$$y = mx + c$$

$$\Rightarrow \quad y = \frac{x}{\sqrt{3}} + 4.$$

21. **Find the equation of lines passing through (1, 2) and making angle 30° with y-axis** **[NCERT Exemplar]**

Ans. Given that line passing through (1, 2) making an angle 30° with y-axis.

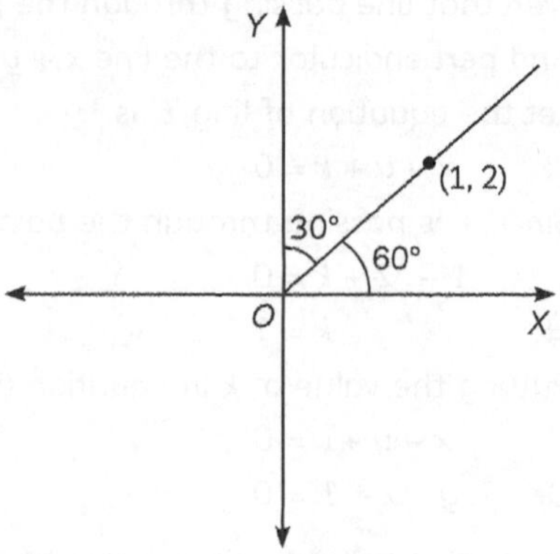

Angle made by the line with x-axis is (90° – 30°) = 60°

∴ Slope of the line, $m = \tan 60° = \sqrt{3}$

So, the equation of the line passing through the point (x_1, y_1) and having slope 'm' is

$$y - y_1 = m(x - x_1)$$

Here, $(x_1, y_1) = (1, 2)$

and $m = \sqrt{3}$

$\Rightarrow \quad y - 2 = \sqrt{3}(x - 1)$

$\Rightarrow \quad y - 2 = \sqrt{3}x - \sqrt{3}$

$\Rightarrow \quad y - \sqrt{3}x + \sqrt{3} - 2 = 0$

22. **A straight line moves so that the sum of the reciprocals of its intercepts made on axes is constant. Show that the line passes through a fixed point.** **[NCERT Exemplar]**

Ans. We know that intercepts form of a straight line is

$$\frac{x}{a} + \frac{y}{b} = 1$$

Where a and b are the intercepts on the axes.

Given that $\frac{1}{a} + \frac{1}{b} = \frac{1}{k}$ (let)

On cross multiplication we get

$\Rightarrow \quad \frac{k}{a} + \frac{k}{b} = 1$

This shows that the line is passing through the fixed point (k, k).

SHORT ANSWER Type-I Questions (SA-I)

[**2** marks]

23. **Find the equation of the straight line which passes through the point (1, –2) and cuts off equal intercepts from axes.** **[NCERT Exemplar]**

Ans. The equation of line in intercept form is

$$\frac{x}{a} + \frac{y}{b} = 1$$

Where a and b are the intercepts on the axis

Given that $a = b$

$\Rightarrow \quad \frac{x}{a} + \frac{y}{a} = 1$

The above equation can be written as

$\Rightarrow \quad \frac{x+y}{a} = 1$

On cross multiplication we get

$\Rightarrow \quad x + y = a \quad$ ...(1)

If equation (1) passes through the point (1, –2), we get

$x = 1$ and $y = -2$

$1 + (-2) = a$

$\Rightarrow \quad 1 - 2 = a$

$\Rightarrow \quad a = -1$

Putting the value of a in equation 1, we get

$$x + y = -1$$

$\Rightarrow \quad x + y + 1 = 0$

Hence, the equation of straight line is $x + y + 1 = 0$ which passes through the point (1, –2).

24. **A straight line cuts intercepts from the axes of the coordinate, the sum of whose reciprocals is a constant. Show that it always passes through a fixed point.**

Ans. Let the equation of the line be $\frac{x}{a} + \frac{y}{b} = 1$

Its intercepts on x and y axes are a and b respectively. It is given that

$$\frac{1}{a} + \frac{1}{b} = \text{constant} = p \text{ (say)}$$

$\therefore \quad \frac{1}{pa} + \frac{1}{pb} = 1$

$\Rightarrow \quad \frac{\frac{1}{p}}{a} + \frac{\frac{1}{p}}{b} = 1$

$\Rightarrow \left(\frac{1}{p}, \frac{1}{p}\right)$ satisfies the equation $\frac{x}{a}+\frac{y}{b}=1$

Hence, the line (i) passes through the fixed point $\left(\frac{1}{p}, \frac{1}{p}\right)$.

25. Find the equation of the line for which tan $\theta = \frac{1}{2}$, where θ is the inclination of the line and

(A) x-intercept equal to 4.

(B) y-intercept is $-\frac{3}{2}$ **[NCERT Exemplar]**

Ans. (A) Clearly, the line passes through (4, 0) and has slope = $\frac{1}{2}$.

So, the equation of the line is

$$y - 0 = \frac{1}{2}(x-4)$$

[putting $x_1 = 4$, $y_1 = 0$ and $m = \frac{1}{2}$ in $y - y_1 = m\,(x - x_1)$]

$$\Rightarrow \quad x - 2y - 4 = 0$$

(B) The line passes through $\left(0, -\frac{3}{2}\right)$ and has slope $= \frac{1}{2}$.

So, it equation is

$$y - \frac{3}{2} = \frac{1}{2}(x - 0)$$

[putting $x_1 = 0$, $y_1 = -\frac{3}{2}$ and $m = \frac{1}{2}$ in $y - y_1 = m(x - x_1)$]

$$\Rightarrow \quad 2y + 3 = x \text{ or, } x - 2y + 3 = 0$$

26. Find the equations of the straight lines which pass through the origin and trisect the intercept of the line $9x + 12y = 36$ between the axes.

Ans. The equation of the given line is

$$9x + 12y = 36 \text{ or, } \frac{x}{4}+\frac{y}{3}=1$$

It cuts the coordinate axes at $A(4, 0)$ and $B(0, 3)$.

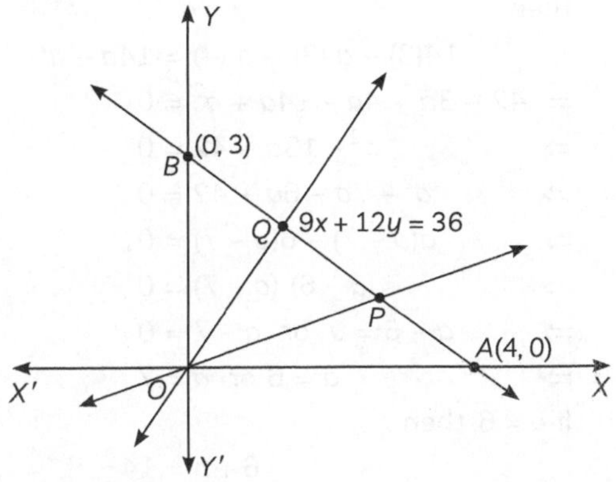

The portion AB of the given line intercepted between the axes is trisected by points P and Q.

$$\therefore \quad \frac{AP}{AB}=\frac{1}{2} \text{ and } \frac{AQ}{QB}=\frac{2}{1}$$

$\Rightarrow$ P and Q divide AB internally in the ratio 1 : 2 and 2 : 1 respectively.

So, coordinates P and Q are

$$P\left(\frac{1\times0+2\times4}{1+2}, \frac{1\times3+2\times0}{1+2}\right)$$

$$=\left(P\frac{8}{3},1\right), Q\left(\frac{2\times0+1\times4}{2+1}, \frac{2\times3+1\times0}{2+1}\right)=Q\left(\frac{4}{3},2\right)$$

Hence, the equation of OQ is

$$y-0=\frac{2-0}{\frac{4}{3}-0}(x-0) \text{ or, } 3x-2y=0$$

SHORT ANSWER Type-II Questions (SA-II)

[**3** marks]

27. Find the equation of the lines which passes through the point (3, 4) and cuts off intercepts from the coordinates axes such that their sum is 14. **[NCERT Exemplar]**

Ans. The equation of line in intercept form is

$$\frac{x}{a}+\frac{y}{b}=1$$

Where a and b are the intercepts on the axis.

Given that $a + b = 14$

The above equation can be written as

$\Rightarrow b = 14 - a$

Substituting the value of a and b in equation 1 we get

So, equation of line is

$$\frac{x}{a}+\frac{y}{14-a}=1$$

Taking LCM

$$\Rightarrow \frac{x(14-a)+ay}{(a)(14-a)}=1$$

$\Rightarrow 14x - ax + ay = 14a - a^2$ ...(2)

If equation 2 passes through the point (3, 4) then

$$14(3) - a(3) + a(4) = 14a - a^2$$

$\Rightarrow 42 - 3a + 4a - 14a + a^2 = 0$

$\Rightarrow a^2 - 13a + 42 = 0$

$\Rightarrow a^2 - 7a - 6a + 42 = 0$

$\Rightarrow a(a - 7) - 6(a - 7) = 0$

$\Rightarrow (a - 6)(a - 7) = 0$

$\Rightarrow a - 6 = 0$ or $a - 7 = 0$

$\Rightarrow a = 6$ or $a = 7$

If $a = 6$, then

$$6 + b = 14$$

$\Rightarrow b = 14 - 6 = 8$

If $a = 7$, then

$$7 + b = 14$$

$\Rightarrow b = 14 - 7$

$\Rightarrow 7$

If $a = 6$ and $b = 8$, then equation of line is

$$\frac{x}{6}+\frac{y}{8}=1$$

$$\Rightarrow \frac{4x+3y}{24}=1$$

$\Rightarrow 4x + 3y = 24$

If $a = 7$ and $b = 7$, then equation of line is

$$\frac{x}{7}+\frac{y}{7}=1$$

$\Rightarrow x + y = 7$

28. Find the equation of the line passing through the point (5, 2) and perpendicular to the line joining the points (2, 3) and (3, –1). **[NCERT Exemplar]**

Ans. Given points are $A(5, 2)$, $B(2, 3)$ and $C(3, -1)$.

Firstly, we find the slope of the line joining the points (2, 3) and (3, –1).

Slope of the line joining two points $= \frac{y_2 - y_1}{x_2 - x_1}$

$$\therefore m_{BC} = \frac{-1-3}{3-2} = -\frac{4}{1} = -4$$

It is given that line passing through the point (5, 2) is perpendicular to BC

$$m_1 m_2 = -1$$

$\Rightarrow -4 \times m_2 = -1$

$\Rightarrow m_2 = \frac{1}{4}$

Therefore slope of the required line $= \frac{1}{4}$

Now, we have to find the equation of line passing though point (5, 2)

Equation of line : $y - y_1 = m(x - x_1)$

$\Rightarrow y - 2 = \frac{1}{4}(x-5)$

$\Rightarrow 4y - 8 = x - 5$

$\Rightarrow x - 5 - 4y + 8 = 0$

$\Rightarrow x - 4y + 3 = 0$

Hence, the equation of line passing through the point (5, 2) is $x - 4y + 3 = 0$.

29. Find the equations of the altitudes of the triangle whose vertices are $A(7, -1)$, $B(-2, 8)$ and $C(1,2)$.

Ans. Let AD, BE and CF be three altitude of triangle ABC. Let m_1, m_2 and m_3 be the Slopes of AD, BE and CF, respectively. Then,

$AD \perp BC \Rightarrow$ Slope of $AD \times$ Slope of $BC = -1$

$$\Rightarrow m_1 \times \left(\frac{2-8}{1+2}\right) = -1$$

$$\Rightarrow m_1 = \frac{1}{2}$$

$BE \perp AC \Rightarrow$ Slope of $BE \times$ Slope of $AC = -1$

$$\Rightarrow m_2 \times \left(\frac{-1-2}{7-1}\right) = -1$$

$\Rightarrow m_2 = 2$

and $CF \perp AB \Rightarrow$ Slope of CF slope of $AB = -1$

$$\Rightarrow m_3 \times \left(\frac{-1-8}{7+2}\right) = -1$$

$\Rightarrow m_3 = 1$

Since AD passes through $A(7, -1)$ and has slope

$$m_1 = \frac{1}{2}$$

So, its equation is

$$y + 1 = \frac{1}{2}(x-7)$$

$\Rightarrow x - 2y - 9 = 0$

Similarly, equation of BE is

$y - 8 = 2(x + 2)$

$\Rightarrow 2x - y + 12 = 0$

equation of CF is $(x - 1)$

$\Rightarrow x + y + 1 = 0$

30. A line passing through the point A(3, 0) makes 30° angle with the positive direction of x-axis. If this line is rotated through an angle 15° in a clockwise direction. Find its equation in new position.

Ans. Let AB be in the given line and AC be its new position. Clearly, AC makes an angle of 15° with the positive direction of X-axis.

$\therefore \quad m = \text{Slope of } AC = \tan 15°$

$\Rightarrow \quad m = \tan(45° - 30°)$

$$\Rightarrow \quad m = \frac{\tan 45° - \tan 30°}{1 + \tan 45° \tan 30°}$$

$$\Rightarrow \quad m = \frac{1 - \frac{1}{\sqrt{3}}}{1 + \frac{1}{\sqrt{3}}} = \frac{\sqrt{3}-1}{\sqrt{3}+1}$$

$$\Rightarrow \quad m = \frac{(\sqrt{3}-1)^2}{(\sqrt{3}+1)(\sqrt{3}-1)}$$

$$= \frac{4-2\sqrt{3}}{2} = 2-\sqrt{3}$$

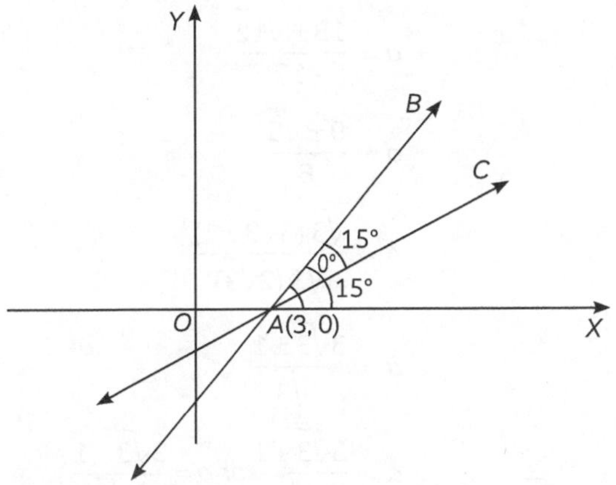

Clearly, AC passes through $A(3, 0)$ and has slope $m = 2-\sqrt{3}$. So, its equation is

$$y - 0 = (2-\sqrt{3})(x-3)$$

or, $\quad (2-\sqrt{3})x - y - 3(2-\sqrt{3}) = 0$

LONG ANSWER Type Questions (LA)

[**4** & **5** marks]

31. In what direction should a line be drawn through the point (1, 2) so that its point of intersection with the line x + y = 4 is at a distance $\frac{\sqrt{6}}{3}$ from the given point.

[NCERT Exemplar]

Ans. Let the given line $x + y = 4$ and the required line 'l' intersect at $B(a, b)$

Slope of line 'l' is

$$m = \frac{y_2 - y_1}{x_2 - x_1} = \frac{b-2}{a-1}$$

And we also know that, $m = \tan\theta$

$$\therefore \quad \tan\theta = \frac{b-2}{a-1} \quad \text{...(i)}$$

Given that $AB = \frac{\sqrt{6}}{3}$

So, by distance formula for point $A(1, 2)$ and $B(a, b)$, we get

$$d = \sqrt{(x_2-x_1)^2 + (y_2-y_1)^2}$$

$$\Rightarrow \quad \frac{\sqrt{6}}{3} = \sqrt{(a-1)^2 + (b-2)^2}$$

On squaring both the sides, we get

$$\Rightarrow \quad \frac{6}{9} = (a-1)^2 + (b-2)^2$$

Using $(a - b)^2$ formula we get

$$\Rightarrow \quad \frac{2}{3} = a^2 + 1 - 2a + b^2 + 4 - 4b$$

On cross multiplication, we get

$\Rightarrow \quad 2 = 3a^2 + 3 - 6a + 3b^2 + 12 - 12b$

$\Rightarrow \quad 2 = 3a^2 + 3b^2 - 6a - 12b + 15$

$\Rightarrow \quad 3a^2 + 3b^2 - 6a - 12b + 13 = 0 \quad$ ...(ii)

Point $B(a, b)$ also satisfies the equation $x + y = 4$.

$\therefore \quad a + b = 4$

$\Rightarrow \quad b = 4 - a \quad$ ...(iii)

Putting the value of b in equation (ii), we get

$3a^2 + 3(4 - a)^2 - 6a - 12(4 - a) + 13 = 0$

Computing and simplifying we get

$\Rightarrow \quad 3a^2 + 3(16 + a^2 - 8a) - 6a - 48 + 12a + 13 = 0$

$\Rightarrow \quad 3a^2 + 48 + 3a^2 - 24a - 6a - 48 + 12a + 13 = 0$

$\Rightarrow \quad 6a^2 - 18a + 13 = 0$

Now, we solve the above equation by using this formula

$$x = \frac{-b \pm \sqrt{b^2 - 4ac}}{2a}$$

$$a = \frac{-(-18) \pm \sqrt{(-18)^2 - 4 \times 6 \times 13}}{2 \times 6}$$

$$a = \frac{18 \pm \sqrt{324-312}}{12}$$

$$a = \frac{18 \pm \sqrt{12}}{12}$$

$$a = \frac{9 \pm \sqrt{3}}{6}$$

$$a = \frac{\sqrt{3}\,(3\sqrt{3} \pm 1)}{\sqrt{3}\,(2\sqrt{3})}$$

$$a = \frac{3\sqrt{3} \pm 1}{2\sqrt{3}}$$

$$\Rightarrow \quad a = \frac{3\sqrt{3}+1}{2\sqrt{3}} \text{ or } a = \frac{3\sqrt{3}-1}{2\sqrt{3}})$$

Putting the value of a in equation (iii), we get

$$b = 4 - \frac{3\sqrt{3}+1}{2\sqrt{3}}$$

Taking *LCM* and simplifying we get

$$\Rightarrow \quad b = \frac{8\sqrt{3} - 3\sqrt{3} \pm 1}{2\sqrt{3}}$$

$$\Rightarrow \quad b = \frac{5\sqrt{3} \pm 1}{2\sqrt{3}}$$

$$\Rightarrow \quad b = \frac{5\sqrt{3}+1}{2\sqrt{3}} \text{ or } b = \frac{5\sqrt{3}-1}{2\sqrt{3}}$$

Now, putting the value of a and b in equation (i), we get

$$\tan\theta = \frac{b-2}{a-1}$$

$$\Rightarrow \quad \tan\theta = \frac{\frac{5\sqrt{3} \pm 1}{2\sqrt{3}} - 2}{\frac{3\sqrt{3} \pm 1}{2\sqrt{3}} - 1}$$

Taking *LCM* and simplifying we get

$$\Rightarrow \quad \tan\theta = \frac{\frac{5\sqrt{3} \pm 1 - 4\sqrt{3}}{2\sqrt{3}}}{\frac{3\sqrt{3} \pm 1 - 2\sqrt{3}}{2\sqrt{3}}}$$

$$\Rightarrow \quad \tan\theta = \frac{\sqrt{3} \pm 1}{\sqrt{3} \pm 1}$$

$$\Rightarrow \quad \tan\theta = \frac{\sqrt{3}+1}{\sqrt{3}-1} \qquad ...(1)$$

$$\tan\theta = \frac{\sqrt{3}-1}{\sqrt{3}+1} \qquad ...(2)$$

We solve the equation (1) to get the value of θ, we get

We know that,

$$\tan^{-1}x - \tan^{-1}y = \tan^{-1}\left(\frac{x-y}{1+xy}\right)$$

$$\tan^{-1}\left(\frac{x-y}{1+xy}\right)$$

If $x = \sqrt{3}$ and $y = 1$

$$= \tan^{-1}\left(\frac{\sqrt{3}-1}{1+(\sqrt{3})1}\right)$$

$$= \tan^{-1}\left(\frac{\sqrt{3}-1}{1+\sqrt{3}}\right)$$

We have,

$$\theta = \tan^{-1}\left(\frac{\sqrt{3}-1}{\sqrt{3}+1}\right)$$

$$\theta = \tan^{-1}(\sqrt{3}) - \tan^{-1}(1)$$

$$\theta = \tan^{-1}\tan 60° - \tan^{-1}\tan 45°$$

$$\theta = 60° - 45°$$

$$\theta = 15°$$

Now, we solve the equation(2)

We know that,

$$\tan^{-1}x + \tan^{-1}y = \tan^{-1}\left(\frac{x+y}{1-xy}\right)$$

$$\tan^{-1}\left(\frac{x+y}{1-xy}\right)$$

If $\quad x = \sqrt{3}$ and $y = 1$

$$= \tan^{-1}\left(\frac{\sqrt{3}+1}{1-(\sqrt{3})(1)}\right)$$

$$= \tan^{-1}\left(\frac{\sqrt{3}+1}{1-\sqrt{3}}\right)$$

We have,

$$\theta = \tan^{-1}\left(\frac{\sqrt{3}+1}{\sqrt{3}-1}\right)$$

$$\theta = \tan^{-1}(\sqrt{3}) + \tan^{-1}(1)$$

$$\theta = \tan^{-1}\tan 60° + \tan^{-1}\tan 45°$$

$$\theta = 60° + 45°$$

$$\theta = 105°$$

32. Find the equation of the line which passes through the point (-5, 4) and the portion of the line intercepted between the axes is divided internally in the ratio 5 : 4 by this point.

Ans. Let AB be a line passing through a point $(-5, 4)$ and meets x-axis at $A(a, 0)$ and y-axis at $B(0, b)$.

Using the section formula for internal division, we have

$$(x, y) = \left(\frac{m_1 x_2 + m_2 x_1}{m_1 + m_2}, \frac{m_1 y_2 + m_2 y_1}{m_1 + m_2}\right) \quad ...(i)$$

Here, $m_1 = 5, m_2 = 4$

$(x_1, y_1) = (a, 0)$ and $(x_2, y_2) = (0, b)$

Substituting the above values in the above formula, we get

$$\Rightarrow \quad x = \frac{5(0)+4(a)}{5+4}, y = \frac{5(b)+4(0)}{5+4}$$

$$\Rightarrow \quad -5 = \frac{4a}{9}, 4 = \frac{5b}{9}$$

$$\Rightarrow \quad -45 = 4a \text{ or } 36 = 5b$$

$$\Rightarrow \quad -a = -\frac{45}{4} \text{ or } b = \frac{36}{5}$$

We know that intercept of the line is

$$\frac{x}{a} + \frac{y}{b} = 1$$

Substituting the value of a and b in above equation, we get

$$\frac{x}{-\frac{45}{4}} + \frac{y}{\frac{36}{5}} = 1$$

On simplification, we get

$$\Rightarrow \quad \frac{-4x}{45} + \frac{5y}{36} = 1$$

Taking LCM

$$\Rightarrow \quad \frac{-4x \times 4 + 5 \times 5y}{9 \times 5 \times 4} = 1$$

On cross multiplication we get

$$\Rightarrow \quad -16x + 25y = 180$$

Which is the required equation of the line.

10 Conic Sections

Because they curve in just one direction, roller coasters are wonderful examples of parabolas. This conic form is excellent for roller coasters because it provides riders the feeling of climbing a hill, reaching the peak, then coasting down at high speeds

Topic Notes

- *Circle and Parabola*
- *Ellipse and Hyperbola*

CIRCLE AND PARABOLA 1

TOPIC 1

SECTIONS OF A CONE

Circle , Ellipse, Parabola: When the plane cuts the nappe (other than the vertex) of the cone, we have the following situations:

(a) When $\beta = 90°$, the section is a circle (As shown in figure)

(b) When $\alpha < \beta < 90°$, the section is an ellipse (As shown in figure)

(c) When $\beta = \alpha$; the section is a parabola (As shown in figure)

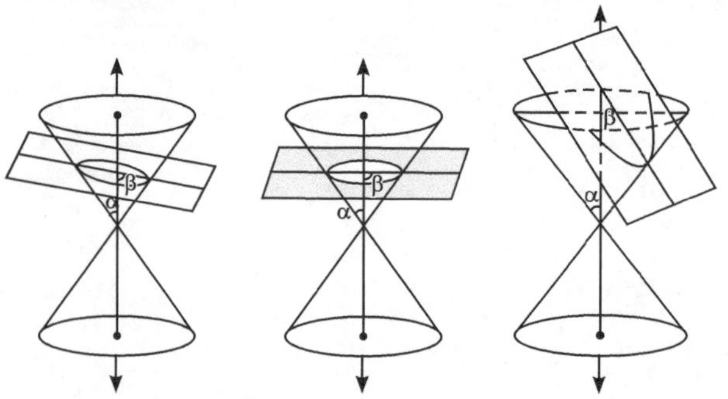

Important

➥ *Degenerated conic sections:*

(1) *When $\alpha < \beta \leq 90°$, then the section is a point (As shown in figure____)*

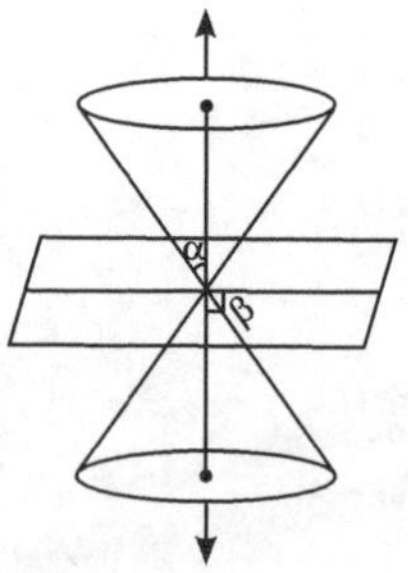

(2) *When $\beta = \alpha$, the plane contains a generator of the cone and the section is a straight line*

It is the degenerated case of a parabola. (As shown in figure____)

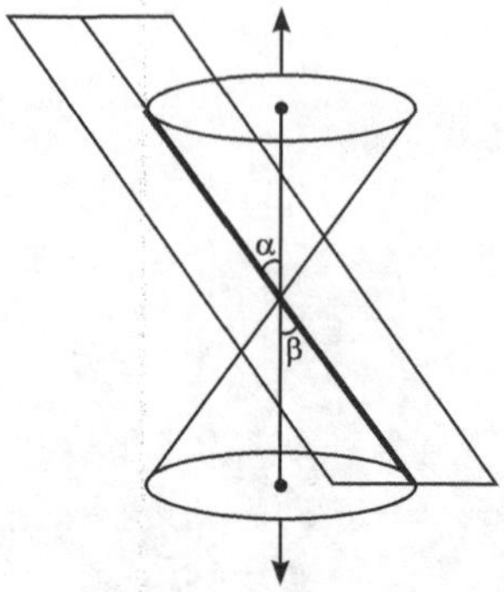

Conic

(1) The locus of a point which moves in a plane such that the ratio of its distance from a fixed point to its perpendicular distance from a fixed straight line is always constant, is known as a conic section or a conic.

(2) The fixed point (S) is called focus of the conic, the fixed line (l) is called directrix of the conic and the constant ratio is called eccentricity of the conic.

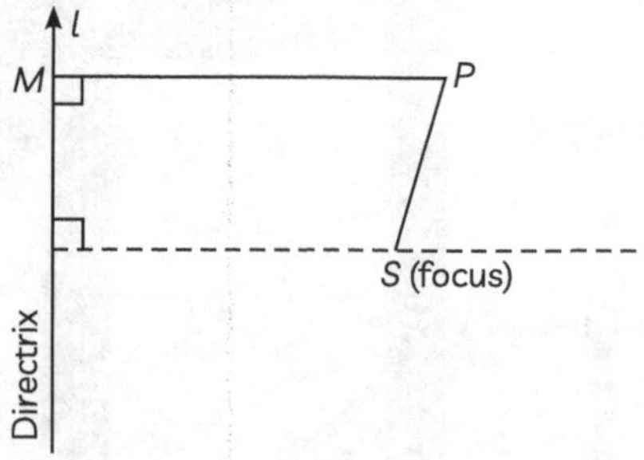

TOPIC 2

CIRCLE

A circle is the locus of a point which moves in a plane so that its distance from a fixed point remains constant. The fixed point and the constant distance are called center and radius of the circle, respectively.

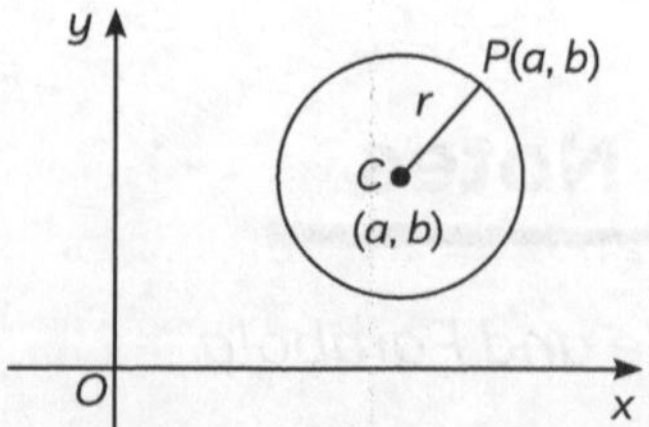

Equation of Circle

(1) Equation of circle if coordinates of the end points of the diameter are $(x_1, y_1),(x_2, y_2)$ is given by $(x - x_1)(x - x_2) + (y - y_1)(y - y_2) = 0$ whose center is $\left(\dfrac{x_1 + x_2}{2}, \dfrac{y_1 + y_2}{2}\right)$ and radius is $\dfrac{\left(\sqrt{(x_1 - x_2)^2 + (y_1 - y_2)^2}\right)}{2}$.

(2) The equation of circle with center (h, k) and radius a is

$$(x - h)^2 + (y - k)^2 = a^2 \quad ...(i)$$

If Center Coincide with Origin

As $h = k = 0$, then equation of circle be $x^2 + y^2 = a^2$

When Circle Touches x-axis

As $C(h, k)$ be the center of the circle and touches x-axis.

$\therefore \quad a = k$, then $(x - h)^2 + (y - k)^2 = a^2$ reduces to

$$(x - h)^2 + (y - a)^2 = a^2$$

Or, $\quad x^2 + y^2 - 2xh - 2ay + h^2 = 0$

When Circle Passes Through (0, 0)

Then the equation of circle (i) reduces to

$$(x - h)^2 + (y - k)^2 = h^2 + k^2$$

Or, $\quad x^2 + y^2 - 2hx - 2ky = 0$

When Circle Touches y-axis

As circle touches y-axis

$\therefore \quad h = a$ and equation of circle is

$(x - h)^2 + (y - k)^2 = a^2$ reduces to

$$x^2 + y^2 - 2ax - 2ky + k^2 = 0$$

Equation of Circle Touches Both Axis

In this case $h = k = a$ and equation of circle

$(x - h)^2 + (y - k)^2 = a^2$ reduces to

$$(x - a)^2 + (y - a)^2 = a^2$$

Or $\quad x^2 + y^2 - 2a(x + y) = -a^2$

Equation of Circle Passing Through (0, 0) and Centered at x-axis

Then $k = 0$, $h = a$ and equation $(x - h)^2 + (y - k)^2 = a^2$ reduces to $x^2 + y^2 - 2ax = 0$

Equation of Circle Passes Through (0, 0) and Centered at y-axis

In this case $h = 0$, $k = a$ then the equation $(x - h)^2 + (y - k)^2 = a^2$ reduces to $x^2 + y^2 - 2ay = 0$

Parametric form of Equation of Circle Centered at Origin:

$x = a \cos \theta$, $y = a \sin \theta$

Example 1.1: Finds the equation of the circle with radius 5 whose center lies on x-axis and passes through the point (2, 3). **[NCERT]**

Ans. Let the equation of the required circle be

$$(x - h)^2 + (y - k)^2 = r^2.$$

Since the radius of the circle is 5 and its center lies on the x-axis, $k = 0$ and $r = 5$.

Now, the equation of the circle becomes

$$(x - h)^2 + y^2 = 25. \quad ...(i)$$

It is given that the circle passes through point (2, 3).

$\therefore \quad (2 - h)^2 + 3^2 = 25$

$\Rightarrow \quad (2 - h)^2 = 25 - 9$

$\Rightarrow \quad (2 - h)^2 = 16$

$\Rightarrow \quad 2 - h = \pm\sqrt{16} = \pm 4$

If $2 - h = 4$, then $h = -2$.

If $2 - h = -4$, then $h = 6$.

When $h = -2$, the equation of the circle given by equation (i) becomes

$$(x + 2)^2 + y^2 = 25$$
$$x^2 + 4x + 4 + y^2 = 25$$
$$x^2 + y^2 + 4x - 21 = 0$$

When $h = 6$, the equation of the circle becomes

$$(x - 6)^2 + y^2 = 25$$
$$x^2 - 12x + 36 + y^2 = 25$$
$$x^2 + y^2 - 12x + 11 = 0$$

Example 1.2: Finds the equation of the circle with center $\left(\frac{1}{2}, \frac{1}{4}\right)$ and radius $\frac{1}{12}$. **[NCERT]**

Ans. The equation of a circle with center (h, k) and radius r is given as $(x - h)^2 + (y - k)^2 = r^2$

It is given that centre $(h, k) = \left(\dfrac{1}{2}, \dfrac{1}{4}\right)$ and radius

$(r) = \dfrac{1}{12}$

Therefore, the equation of the circle is

$$\left(x - \frac{1}{2}\right)^2 + \left(y - \frac{1}{4}\right)^2 = \left(\frac{1}{12}\right)^2$$

$$x^2 - x + \frac{1}{4} + y^2 - \frac{y}{2} + \frac{1}{16} = \frac{1}{144}$$

$$x^2 - x + \frac{1}{4} + y^2 - \frac{y}{2} + \frac{1}{16} - \frac{1}{144} = 0$$

$$144x^2 - 144x + 36 + 144y^2 - 72y + 9 - 1 = 0$$

$$144x^2 - 144x + 144y^2 - 72y + 44 = 0$$

$$36x^2 - 36x + 36y^2 - 18y + 11 = 0$$

$$36x^2 + 36y^2 - 36x - 18y + 11 = 0$$

Example 1.3: Finds the equation of the circle with centre (1, 1) and radius $\sqrt{2}$. **[NCERT]**

Ans. The equation of a circle with centre (h, k) and radius r is given as $(x - h)^2 + (y - k)^2 = r^2$

It is given that centre $(h, k) = (1, 1)$ and radius $\sqrt{2}$.

Therefore, the equation of the circle is

$$(x-1)^2+(y-1)^2=(\sqrt{2})^2$$

$$x^2-2x+1+y^2-2y+1=2$$

$$x^2+y^2-2x-2y=0$$

Example 1.4: Finds the centre and radius of the circle $x^2 + y^2 - 8x + 10y - 12 = 0$. **[NCERT]**

Ans. The equation of the given circle is

$$x^2+y^2-8x+10y-12=0$$

$$\Rightarrow \quad (x^2-8x)+(y^2+10y)=12$$

$$\Rightarrow \quad \{x^2-2(x)(4)+4^2\}+\{y^2+2(y)(5)+5^2\}-16-25=12$$

$$\Rightarrow \quad (x-4)^2+(y+5)^2=53$$

$$\Rightarrow \quad (x-4)^2+\{y-(-5)\}^2=(\sqrt{53})^2$$

Which is of the form $(x-h)^2+(y-k)^2=r^2$,

where $h = 4$, $k = -5$ and $r = \sqrt{53}$

Thus, the center of the given circle is (4, – 5), while its radius is $\sqrt{53}$.

Example 1.5: Find the center and radius of the circle $2x^2 + 2y^2 - x = 0$. **[NCERT]**

Ans. The equation of the given circle is

$$2x^2+2y^2-x=0$$

$$\Rightarrow \quad (2x^2-x)+2y^2=0$$

$$\Rightarrow \quad 2\left[\left(x^2-\frac{x}{2}\right)+y^2\right]=0$$

$$\Rightarrow \quad \left\{x^2-2.x\left(\frac{1}{4}\right)+\left(\frac{1}{4}\right)^2\right\}+y^2-\left(\frac{1}{4}\right)^2=0$$

$$\Rightarrow \quad \left(x-\frac{1}{4}\right)^2+(y-0)^2=\left(\frac{1}{4}\right)^2$$

Which is of the form $(x-h)^2+(y-k)^2=r^2$, where $h = 1/4$, $k = 0$ and $r = 1/4$.

Thus, the center of the given circle is (1/4, 0), while its radius is 1/4.

Parabola

A parabola is the set of all points in a plane that are equidistant from a fixed line and a fixed point. The fixed line is called the directrix and the fixed point is called the focus of the parabola.

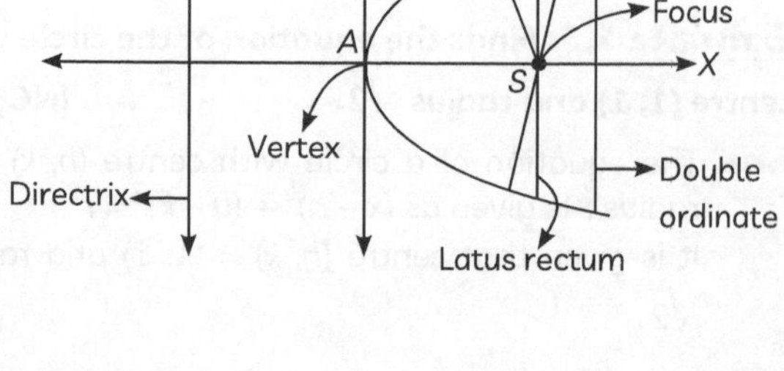

In conic section, a parabola is the set of all points in a plane that are equidistant from a fixed line and a fixed point (not on the line) in the plane. The fixed line is called the directrix, and the fixed point (F) is called the parabola's focus. A line through the focus and perpendicular to the directrix is called the axis of the parabola. Also, the vertex is the point of intersection of a parabola with the axis. As we know, the standard equation of the parabola is used in solving a variety of problems in maths. In this article, you will learn how to write the standard equations for parabola in different cases and how to solve questions based on these equations.

$y^2 = 4ax$, $y^2 = -4ax$, $x^2 = 4ay$, $x^2 = -4ay$ as the standard equation of parabola.

Latus Rectum

In the conic section, the latus rectum is the chord through the focus, and parallel to the directrix. The word latus rectum is derived from the Latin word "latus" which means "side", and the "rectum" which means "straight". Half the latus rectum is called the semi latus rectum. The diagram above shows the latus rectum of a parabola.

Length of Latus Rectum of Parabola

Let the ends of the latus rectum of the parabola, $y^2 = 4ax$ be L and L'. The x-coordinates of L and L' are equal to 'a' as $S = (a, 0)$

Assume that $L = (a, b)$.

We know that L is a point of the parabola, we have

$$b^2 = 4a(a) = 4a^2$$

Take square root on both sides, we get $b = \pm 2a$

Therefore, the ends of the latus rectum of a parabola are $L = (a, 2a)$ and $L' = (a, -2a)$

Hence, the length of the latus rectum of a parabola, 'LL'' is $4a$.

Caution

➥ *The standard equations of parabolas have focus on one of the coordinate axes; the vertex at the origin and thereby the directrix is parallel to the other coordinate axis.*

Standard Equation of Parabola

If a parabola has a horizontal axis, the standard form of the equation of the parabola is this:

$$(y-k)^2 = 4p(x-h), \text{ where } p \neq 0.$$

The vertex of this parabola is at (h, k). The focus is at $(h + p, k)$.

Standard equation	$y^2 = 4ax$	$y^2 = -4ax$	$x^2 = 4ay$	$x^2 = -4ay$
Graph	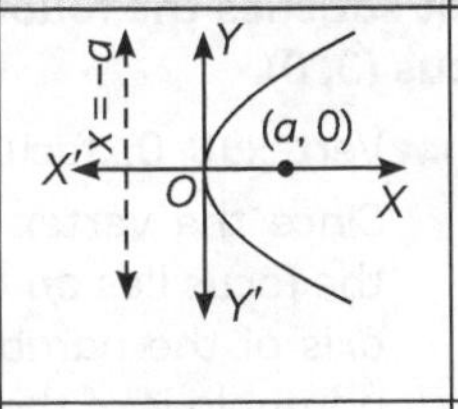	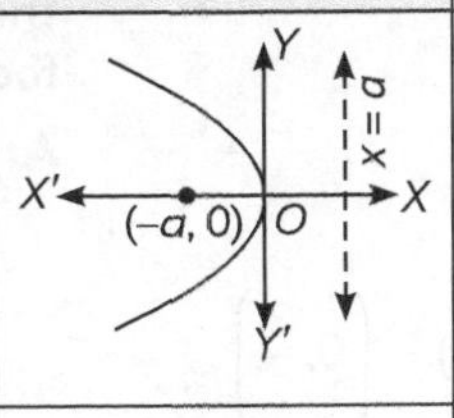	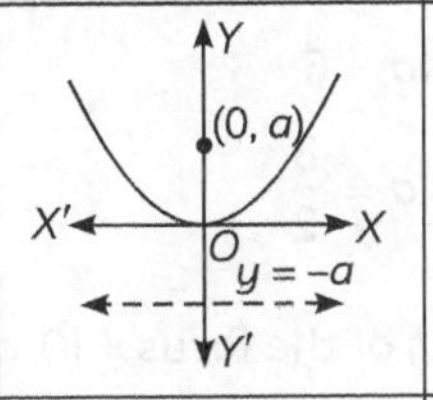	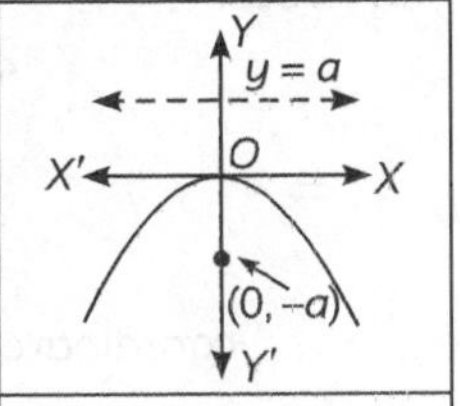
Eccentricity	$e = 1$	$e = 1$	$e = 1$	$e = 1$
Coordination of focus	$(a, 0)$	$(-a, 0)$	$(0, a)$	$(0, -a)$
Equation of directrix	$x + a = 0$	$x - a = 0$	$y + a = 0$	$y - a = 0$
Equation of axis	$y = 0$	$y = 0$	$x = 0$	$x = 0$
Coordination of vertex	$(0, 0)$	$(0, 0)$	$(0, 0)$	$(0, 0)$
Extremities of latus rectum	$(a, \pm 2a)$	$(-a, \pm 2a)$	$(\pm 2a, a)$	$(\pm 2a, -a)$
Length of latus rectum	$4a$	$4a$	$4a$	$4a$
Equation of latus rectum	$x - a = 0$	$x + a = 0$	$y - a = 0$	$y + a = 0$

Example 1.6: Find the equation of the parabola that satisfies the following conditions: Vertex (0, 0) passing through (2, 3) and axis is along x-axis. [NCERT]

Ans. Since the vertex is (0, 0) and the axis of the parabola is the x-axis, the equation of the parabola is either of the form

$$y^2 = 4ax \text{ or } y^2 = -4ax.$$

The parabola passes through point (2, 3), which lies in the first quadrant.

Therefore, the equation of the parabola is of the form $y^2 = 4ax$, while point (2, 3) must satisfy the equation $y^2 = 4ax$.

$$\therefore \quad 3^2 = 4a(2)$$

$$\Rightarrow \quad a = \frac{9}{8}$$

Thus, the equation of the parabola is

$$y^2 = 4\left(\frac{9}{8}\right)x$$

$$y^2 = \frac{9}{2}x$$

$$2y^2 = 9x$$

Example 1.7: Find the equation of the parabola that satisfies the following condition: Vertex (0, 0), passing through (5, 2) and symmetric with respect to y-axis. [NCERT]

Ans. Since the vertex is (0, 0) and the parabola is symmetric about the y-axis, the equation of the parabola is either of the form

$$x^2 = 4ay \text{ or } x^2 = -4ay.$$

The parabola passes through point (5, 2), which lies in the first quadrant.

Therefore, the equation of the parabola is of the form $x^2 = 4ay$, while point (5, 2) must satisfy the equation $x^2 = 4ay$.

$$\therefore \quad (5)^2 = 4 \times a \times 2$$

$$\Rightarrow \quad 25 = 8a$$

$$\Rightarrow \quad a = \frac{25}{8}$$

Thus, the equation of the parabola is

$$x^2 = 4\left(\frac{25}{8}\right)y$$

$$2x^2 = 25y$$

Example 1.8: Find the coordinates of the focus, axis of the parabola, the equation of directrix and the length of the latus return for $y^2 = 12x$. [NCERT]

Ans. The given equation is $y^2 = 12x$.

Here, the coefficient of x is positive. Hence, the parabola opens towards the right.

On comparing this equation with, $y^2 = 4ax$, we obtain

$$4a = 12$$

$$\Rightarrow \quad a = 3$$

$\therefore$ Coordinates of the focus = (a, 0) = (3, 0)

Since the given equation involves, y^2, the axis of the parabola is the x-axis.

Equation of directrix,

$$x = -a \text{ i.e., } x = -3 \text{ i.e., } x + 3 = 0$$

Length of latus rectum = $4a = 4 \times 3 = 12$

Example 1.9: Find the coordinates of the focus, axis of the parabola, the equation of directrix and the length of the latus rectum for $x^2 = 6y$. [NCERT]

Ans. The given equation is $x^2 = 6y$.

Here, the coefficient of y is positive. Hence, the parabola opens upwards.

On comparing this equation with, $x^2 = 4ay$, we obtain

$$4a = 6$$

$$\Rightarrow \quad a = \frac{3}{2}$$

$\therefore$ coordinates of the focus = $(0, a) = \left(0, \frac{3}{2}\right)$

Since the given equation involves x^2, the axis of the parabola is the y-axis.

Equation of directrix, $y = -a$ i.e., $y = -\frac{3}{2}$

Length of latus rectum = $4a = 6$

Example 1.10: Find the equation of the parabola that satisfies the following conditions: Vertex (0, 0) focus (–2, 0). **[NCERT]**

Ans. Vertex (0, 0); focus (–2, 0)

Since the vertex of the parabola is (0, 0) and the focus lies on the negative x-axis, x-axis is the axis of the parabola, while the equation of the parabola is of the form $y^2 = -4ax$. Since the focus is (–2, 0), $a = 2$.

Thus, the equation of the parabola is

$y^2 = -4(2)x$, i.e.,

$y^2 = -8x$

Example 1.11: Find the equation of the parabola that satisfies the following conditions: Vertex (0, 0); focus (3, 0). **[NCERT]**

Ans. Vertex (0, 0); focus (3, 0)

Since the vertex of the parabola is (0, 0) and the focus lies on the positive x-axis, x-axis is the axis of the parabola while the equation of the parabola is of the form $y^2 = 4ax$. Since the focus is (3, 0), $a = 3$.

Thus, the equation of the parabola is

$y^2 = 4 \times 3 \times x$, i.e., $y^2 = 12x$

Example 1.12: Find the equation of the parabola that satisfies the following conditions: Focus (0, – 3); directrix $y = 3$. **[NCERT]**

Ans. Focus = (0, –3); directrix $y = 3$

Since the focus lies on the y-axis, the y-axis is the axis of the parabola.

Therefore, the equation of the parabola is either of the form $x^2 = 4ay$ or $x^2 = -4ay$. It is also seen that the directrix, $y = 3$ is above the x-axis, while the focus (0, – 3) is below the x-axis. Hence, the parabola is of the form $x^2 = -4ay$.

Here, $a = 3$

Thus, the equation of the parabola is of the form $x^2 = -4ay$.

Here, $a = 3$

Thus, the equation of the parabola is $x^2 = -12y$.

OBJECTIVE Type Questions

[1 mark]

Multiple Choice Questions

1. Equation of a circle whose center is (–1.5, –2.6) and radius is 5 is:

(a) $(x - 1.5)^2 + (y + 2.6)^2 = 5$

(b) $(x + 1.5)^2 + (y - 2.6)^2 = 25$

(c) $(x + 1.5)^2 + (y + 2.6)^2 = 25$

(d) None

Ans. *(c)* $(x + 1.5)^2 + (y + 2.6)^2 = 25$

Explanation: Equation of a circle is

$(x - h)^2 + (y - k)^2 = r^2$

Here, $h = -1.5$, $k = -2.6$ and $r = 5$

So,

equation will be

$(x + 1.5)^2 + (y + 2.6)^2 = 25$

Hence, option(c) is the correct answer.

2. If the focus of a parabola is (0, –2a) and its directrix is $y = 2a$ then its equation is:

(a) $x^2 = -8a^2 y$ **(b) $x^2 = 8a^2 y$**

(c) $y^2 = -8a^2 x$ **(d) $y^2 = 8a^2 x$**

Ans. *(a)* $x^2 = -8a^2 y$

Explanation: Focus (0, –2a) then equation of parabola = $x^2 = -4ay$

Now the equation will be $x^2 = -8a^2 y$

Hence, option (a) is the correct answer.

3. If the parabola passes through the point (–3, –2) then the length of its latus rectum is, if equation is $y^2 = 4ax$:

(a) $-\frac{2}{3}$ **(b) $-\frac{4}{3}$**

(c) $-\frac{1}{3}$ **(d) – 4**

Ans. *(b)* $-\frac{4}{3}$

Explanation: Here equation of parabola

$y^2 = 4ax$

It passes through (–3, –2), so, putting

$x = -3, y = -2$

$4 = -12a$

$$-\frac{1}{3} = a$$

Then Length of latus rectum = $4a$

$$= 4 \times -\frac{1}{3} = -\frac{4}{3}$$

Hence, option (b) is the correct answer.

4. Equation of a circle whose center is (0, 0) and radius r is:

(a) $x^2 + y^2 = a^2$ **(b) $x^2 + y^2 = r^2$**

(c) $y^2 - x^2 = r^2$ **(d) None**

Ans. *(b)* $x^2 + y^2 = r^2$

Explanation: Equation of circle is

$(x - h)^2 + (y - k)^2 = r$

Here $h = 0, k = 0, r = r$

So equation will be $x^2 + y^2 = r^2$

Hence, option(b) is the correct answer.

5. Equation of a circle with center $(-a, -b)$ and radius = 100 is:

(a) $(x - a)^2 + (y - b)^2 = 100$

(b) $(x + a)^2 + (y + b)^2 = 10000$

(c) $x^2 + y^2 = 100$

(d) None

Ans. *(b)* $(x + a)^2 + (y + b)^2 = 10000$

Explanation: Here $h = -a, k = -b$ and $r = 100$

So equation will be $(x - h)^2 + (y - k)^2 = 100^2$

$(x + a)^2 + (y + b)^2 = 10000$

Hence, option(b) is the correct answer.

6. Latus rectum of the parabola $y^2 = 8x$ is:

(a) 2 **(b) 4**

(c) 6 **(d) 8** **[DIKSHA]**

Ans. *(d) 8*

Explanation: Equation of parabola is $y^2 = 8x$

Comparing with standard form

$y^2 = 4ax$ or, $4a = 8$

We know that length of latus rectum = $4a = 8$

Hence, option (d) is the correct answer.

7. Equation of circle with center (2, –3) and radius 8 is:

(a) $x^2 + y^2 - 4x + 6y - 51 = 0$

(b) $x^2 + y^2 - 4x - 6y + 51 = 0$

(c) $x^2 + y^2 + 4x - 6y - 51 = 0$

(d) $x^2 + y^2 - 4x + 6y + 51 = 0$ **[DIKSHA]**

Ans. *(a)* $x^2 + y^2 - 4x + 6y - 51 = 0$

Explanation: Equation of a circle is $(x - h)^2 + (y - k)^2 = r^2$

Here, $h = 2, k = -3$ and $r = 8$

So, equation will be

$$(x - 2)^2 + (y + 3)^2 = 64$$

$$x^2 + 4 - 4x + y^2 + 9 + 6y = 64$$

$$x^2 + y^2 - 4x + 6y - 51 = 0$$

Hence, option(a) is the correct answer.

8. The value of eccentricity for the parabola is:

(a) 1

(b) Less than 1

(c) More than 1

(d) Don't have eccentricity **[DIKSHA]**

Ans. *(a) 1*

Explanation: The eccentricity of parabola is 1.

Hence, option(a) is the correct answer.

Assertion-Reason (A-R)

DIRECTION: In the following questions, a statement of assertion (A) is followed by a statement of the reason (R). Mark the correct choice as:

(a) Both assertion (A) and reason (R) are true and reason (R) is the correct explanation of assertion (A).

(b) Both assertion (A) and reason (R) are true but reason (R) is not the correct explanation of assertion (A).

(c) Assertion (A) is true but reason (R) is false.

(d) Assertion (A) is false but reason (R) is true.

9. Assertion: A line through the focus and perpendicular to the directrix is called the x-axis of the parabola.

Reason: The point of intersection of parabola with axis is called the vertex of the parabola.

Ans. *(d) Assertion (A) is false but reason (R) is true.*

Explanation: A line through the focus and perpendicular to the directrix is called the axis of the parabola. The point of intersection of the parabola with the axis is called the vertex of the parabola.

Hence, option (d) is the correct answer.

10. Parabola is symmetric with respect to the axis of the parabola.

Assertion: If the equation of standard parabola has a term y^2, then the axis of symmetry is along the x-axis.

Reason: If the equation of standard parabola has a term x^2, then the axis of symmetry is along the x-axis.

Ans. *(c) Assertion (A) is true but reason (R) is false.*

Explanation: If the equation has a term y^2, then the axis of symmetry is along the x-axis and if the equation has a term x^2, then the axis of symmetry is along the y-axis.

Hence, option (c) is the correct answer.

11. Assertion: The eccentricity of a parabola is 1.

Reason: The eccentricity of a circle is greater than 1.

Ans. *(c) Assertion (A) is true but reason (R) is false.*

Explanation: The eccentricity of a parabola is exactly 1.

The eccentricity of a circle is 0.

Hence, assertion is true but reason is false.

Hence, option (c) is the correct answer.

12. Assertion: The parabola $y^2 = 8x$ where the value of a is 2.

Reason: The equation of a circle $x^2 + y^2 = 25$ having center on + ve x-axis and radius is 5.

Ans. *(c) Assertion (A) is true but reason (R) is false.*

Explanation: The parabola $y^2 = 8x$ here $4a = 8$ or, $a = 2$

The equation of circle $x^2 + y^2 = 25$ having centre center (0, 0) means at origin and radius is 5.

Hence, option (c) is the correct answer.

CASE BASED Questions (CBQs)

[4 & 5 marks]

13. *Neeraj Chopra an athlete won a gold medal in Javelin throw, He is the first athlete who won gold medal in Javelin throw from India at Olympics.*

(A) Name the shape of the path followed by a Javelin.

(a) Half ellipse **(b) Parabola**

(c) Circle **(d) None**

(B) If the equation of a curve is given by $y^2 = -24x$ the coordinate of the focii are:

(a) (6, 0) **(b) (0, 6)**

(c) (0, – 6) **(d) (–6, 0)**

(C) The equation of directrix is:

(a) $y - 6 = 0$ **(b) $y + 6 = 0$**

(c) $x + 6 = 0$ **(d) $x - 6 = 0$**

(D) The length of Latus Rectum is:

(a) –6 **(b) –24**

(c) 6 **(d) 24**

Ans. (A) *(b) Parabola*

Explanation: The path followed by Javelin is Parabolic.

Hence, option (b) is the correct answer.

(B) *(d) (–6, 0)*

Explanation: Here, $y^2 = -24x$

Equation of parabola is $y^2 = -4ax$

So, $4a = 24$ or, $a = 6$

Here, coordinate of focii = $(-a, 0) = (-6, 0)$

Hence, option (d) is the correct answer.

(C) *(d) $x - 6 = 0$*

Explanation: If $a = 6$ for $y^2 = -4ax$ then

Equation of directrix will $x - a = 0$

i.e., $x - 6 = 0$

Hence, option (d) is the correct answer.

(D) *(d) 24*

Explanation: Length of latus rectum for $y^2 = -4ax$

$4a$ i.e., = 24

Hence, option (d) is the correct answer.

VERY SHORT ANSWER Type Questions (VSA)

[1 mark]

14. Find the center and radius of the circle whose equation is $(x - \sqrt{7})^2 + (y - \sqrt{3})^2 = 48$.

Ans. General equation of circle is

$$(x - h)^2 + (y - k)^2 = r^2$$

Here, (h, k) is center and radius is r.

So, $(x - \sqrt{7})^2 + (y - \sqrt{3})^2 = (\sqrt{48})^2$

Center = $(\sqrt{7}, \sqrt{3})$ and radius = $\sqrt{48}$

15. Find the equation of parabola whose vertex is (0, 0) and focus is $(\sqrt{3}, 0)$.

Ans. Equation of parabola is $y^2 = 4ax$

Here, $a = \sqrt{3}$

so, equation will be

$$y^2 = 4\sqrt{3}x$$

16. Find the coordinates of a point on the parabola $y^2 = 8x$, whose focal distance is 4. [NCERT Exemplar]

Ans. Given parabola is $y^2 = 8x$ ...(i)

$$8x = 4ax$$

$\Rightarrow$ $a = 2$

$\therefore$ Focal distance = $|x + a| = 4$

$\Rightarrow$ $|x + 2| = 4$

$\Rightarrow$ $x + 2 = \pm 4$

$\Rightarrow$ $x = 2, -6$

But $x \neq -6$

For $x = 2, y^2 = 8 \times 2$

$\therefore$ $y^2 = 16$

$\Rightarrow$ $y = \pm 4$

So, the points are (2, 4) and (2, –4).

17. Find the equation of the circle having (1, –2) as its center and passing through 3x + y = 14, 2x + 5y = 18. [NCERT Exemplar]

Ans. Given that, center of the circle is (1, – 2) and the circle passing through the lines

$3x + y = 14$ ...(i)

And $2x + 5y = 18$ ...(ii)

Solving (i) and (ii), we get $x = 4$ and $y = 2$

$\therefore$ Radius of the circle $= \sqrt{(4-1)^2 + (2+2)^2}$

$= \sqrt{9+16} = 5$

Now, equation of the circle is $C(1, -2)$ and radius 5.

$(x - 1)^2 + (y + 2)^2 = 5^2$

$\Rightarrow$ $x^2 - 2x + 1 + y^2 + 4y + 4 = 25$

$\Rightarrow$ $x^2 + y^2 - 2x + 4y - 20 = 0$

18. Find the vertex of the parabola $4x^2 + y = 0$.

Ans. $4x^2 + y = 0$

$4x^2 = -y$

$x^2 = \frac{-1}{4}y$

Here, $4a = \frac{-1}{4}$

$a = \frac{-1}{16}$

So the vertex will be = (0, 0)

19. Find the equation of the parabola with vertex at (0, 0) and focus at (0, –2.5).

Ans. Equation of the parabola is

$x^2 = -4ay$

$\Rightarrow$ $x^2 = -4(2.5)y$ [$\because$ focus $(0, -a) = (0, -2.5)$]

$\Rightarrow$ $x^2 = -10y$

SHORT ANSWER Type-I Questions (SA-I)

[2 marks]

20. Find the co-ordinate of focus, and length of latus rectum of parabola $10y^2 = -60x$.

Ans. Given, equation of the parabola is $10y^2 = -60x$

$\Rightarrow$ $y^2 = -\frac{60}{10}x$

$\Rightarrow$ $y^2 = -4.\frac{3}{2}.x$

Comparing with $y^2 = -4ax$

Here, $a = \frac{3}{2}$

$\therefore$ focus $= (-a, 0) = \left(-\frac{3}{2}, 0\right)$

And length of latus rectum = $4a = -6$.

21. Find the equation of the circle which passes through the origin and cut off intercepts 3 and 4 on positive axes.

Ans. Here, passing points are (3, 0) and (0, 4) and center is at (0, 0)

So, the equation of circle is

$x^2 + y^2 + 2gx + 2fy + c = 0$

For (3, 0)

$9 + 6g = 0$

$\Rightarrow$ $g = \frac{-3}{2}$

For (0, 4)

$16 + 8f = 0$

$\Rightarrow$ $f = -2$

Hence, equation will be

$x^2 + y^2 - 3x - 4y = 0$

$\Rightarrow$ $\left(x - \frac{3}{2}\right)^2 + (y - 2)^2 = \left(\frac{5}{2}\right)^2$

22. If a circle passes through the points (0, 0), (*a*, 0) and (0, *b*), then find the co-ordinates of its centre. [NCERT Exemplar]

Ans. Let, the equation of circle is

$x^2 + y^2 + 2gx + 2fy + c = 0$ ...(i)

Since, this circle passes through the points $A(0, 0)$, $B(a, 0)$ and $C(0, b)$.

Putting (0, 0) we get $c = 0$

Putting $(a, 0)$ we get $a^2 + 2ag = 0$ ...(ii)

and putting $(0, b)$ we get $b^2 + 2bf = 0$ ...(iii)

From Eq.(ii), $a + 2g = 0$

$\Rightarrow$ $g = -a/2$

From Eq.(iii), $b + 2f = 0$

$\Rightarrow$ $f = -b/2$

$\left(\frac{a}{2}, \frac{b}{2}\right)$ is the centre of the circle.

23. Prove that the points (1, 2), (3, –4),(5, –6) and (11, – 8) are concyclic. [NCERT Exemplar]

Ans. Let, the equation of the required circle be

$$x^2 + y^2 + 2gx + 2fy + c = 0 \quad ...(1)$$

We get the equation of circle passing through (1, 2),(3, –4) and (5, –6) as

$$x^2 + y^2 - 22x - 4y + 25 = 0 \quad ...(2)$$

Also, point (11, – 8) lies on (2).

$$[\because x^2 + y^2 - 22x - 4y + 25 = 121 + 64 - 242 + 32 + 25 = 0]$$

Hence, the given points are concyclic.

24. Find the equation of the circle which passes through the points (1, –2) and (4, –3) has its centre on the line 3x + 4y = 7. [DIKSHA]

Ans. Let center is (h, k)

So,

$$(h-1)^2 + (k+2)^2 = (h-4)^2 + (k+3)^2$$

$$\Rightarrow \quad 6h - 2k = 20$$

$$\Rightarrow \quad 3h - k = 10 \quad ...(1)$$

The center is also lying on

$$3h + 4k = 7 \quad ...(2)$$

So, from equation (1) and (2)

$$h = \frac{47}{15}, k = \frac{-3}{5}$$

And, radius $= \sqrt{\frac{293}{45}}$

So equation will be

$$\left(x - \frac{47}{15}\right)^2 + \left(y + \frac{3}{5}\right)^2 = \frac{293}{45}$$

$$\Rightarrow \quad 15x^2 + 15y^2 - 94x + 18y + 33 = 0$$

SHORT ANSWER Type-II Questions (SA-II)

[3 marks]

25. Find the value of k such that the line x cos θ + y sin θ – k = 0 touches the circle $x^2 + y^2 - 2ax \cos\theta - 2ay \sin\theta = 0$.

Ans. Given equation of circle is

$$x^2 + y^2 - 2ax\cos\theta - 2ay\sin\theta = 0$$

Which represents a circle (in general form) with centre $(a\cos\theta, a\sin\theta)$

and radius $\sqrt{a^2cos^2\theta + a^2sin^2\theta - 0} = a$

Given that the line $x\cos\theta + y\sin\theta - k = 0$ touches the given circle.

So, the perpendicular distance of the line form $(a\cos\theta, a\sin\theta)$ is equal to the radius r of the circle.

$$\therefore \quad r = \left|\frac{(a\cos\theta)\cos\theta + (a\sin\theta)\sin\theta - k}{\sqrt{\cos^2\theta + \sin^2\theta}}\right|$$

$$\Rightarrow \quad a = |a - k|$$

$$\Rightarrow \quad \pm a = a - k$$

$$\Rightarrow \quad k = 0, 2a.$$

26. Find the equation of the circle which touches x-axis and whose center is (1, 2).

Ans. Given that, centre of the circle is (1, 2).

$$(x-h)^2 + (y-k)^2 = r^2$$

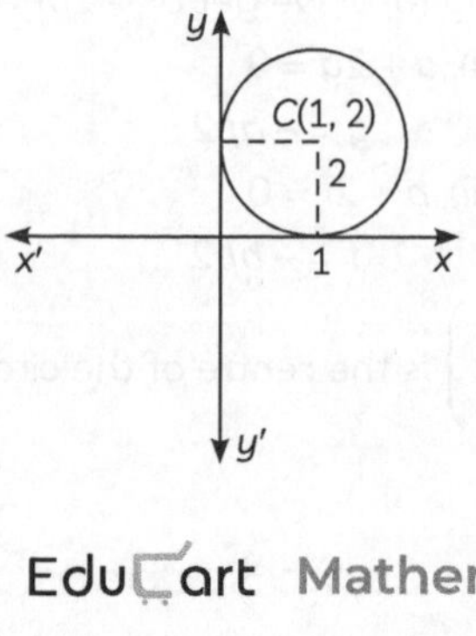

Put, $h = 1, k = 2$

$\because \quad r = 2$

So, the equation of circle is

$$(x-1)^2 + (y-2)^2 = 2^2$$

$$\Rightarrow \quad x^2 - 2x + 1 + y^2 - 4y + 4 = 4$$

$$\Rightarrow \quad x^2 - 2x + y^2 - 4y + 1 = 0$$

$$\Rightarrow \quad x^2 + y^2 - 2x - 4y + 1 = 0$$

27. Find the equation of the circle which touches the both axes in first quadrant and whose radius is a. [NCERT Exemplar]

Ans. Given that radius of the circle is a i.e., (h, k)

$$(x-h)^2 + (y-x)^2 = r^2$$

Put, $h = k = r = a$

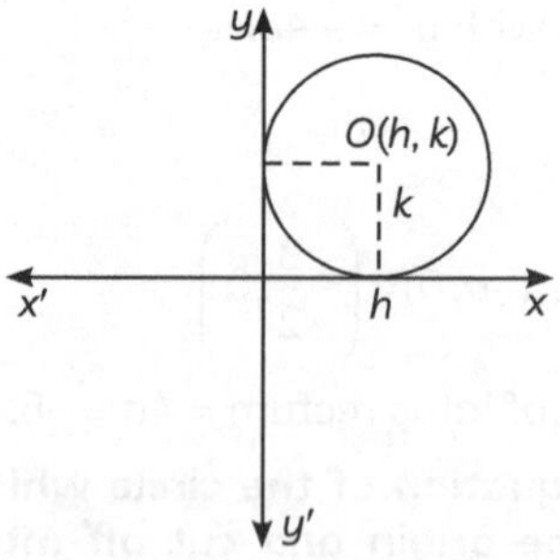

So, the equation of required circle is

$$(x-a)^2 + (y-a)^2 = a^2$$

$$\Rightarrow \quad x^2 - 2ax + a^2 + y^2 - 2ay + a^2 = a^2$$

$$\Rightarrow \quad x^2 + y^2 - 2ax - 2ay + a^2 = 0$$

28. If the points (0, 4) and (0, 2) are respectively the vertex and focus of a parabola, then find the equation of the parabola. [NCERT Exemplar]

Ans. Given that the coordinates, vertex of the parabola (0, 4) and focus of the parabola (0, 2).

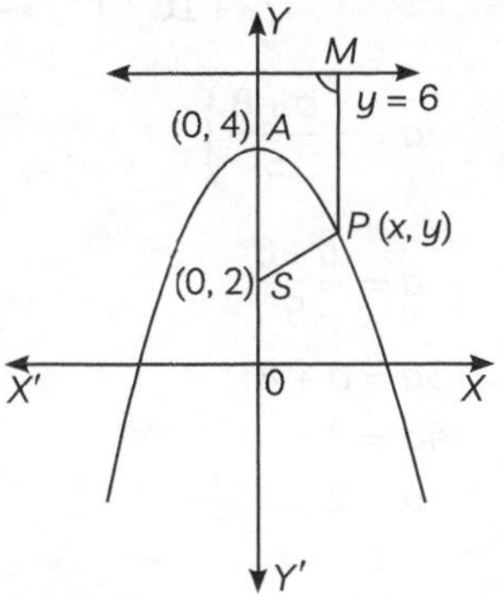

$PM = PS$.

$$\Rightarrow \quad \left|\frac{0+y-6}{\sqrt{0+1}}\right| = \sqrt{(x-0)^2+(y-2)^2}$$

$$\Rightarrow \quad |y-6| = \sqrt{x^2+y^2-4y+4}$$

$$\Rightarrow \quad x^2+y^2-4y+4 = y^2+36-12y$$

$$\Rightarrow \quad x^2+8y = 32$$

LONG ANSWER Type Questions (LA)

[**4** & **5** marks]

29. Find the equation of the parabola whose vertex is the point (0, 2) and the directrix is the line $x + y - 3 = 0$.

Ans. Given, vertex of parabola is (0, 2) and directrix of parabola is

$$x + y - 3 = 0 \quad ...(i)$$

Then, slope of directrix $= -1 = m_1$ (say)

Since, axis of parabola is perpendicular to the directrix.

So, slope of axis $= -\dfrac{1}{m_1} = 1 = m_2$ (say)

Then, the equation of axis is of the form

$y = m_2x + c$, i.e., $y = x + c$.

Since, axis passes through the vertex (0, 2).

$\therefore \quad 2 = 0 + c$

$\Rightarrow \quad c = 2$

So, the equation of axis of parabola is

$$y = x + 2. \quad ...(ii)$$

On solving (i) and (ii), we get $x = 1/2$, $y = 5/2$

The point of intersection of the directrix and axis is D(1/2, 5/2).

Let, F(α, β) be the coordinates of the focus.

The mid-point of FD is $\left(\dfrac{\alpha+1/2}{2}, \dfrac{\beta+5/2}{2}\right)$

We know that the vertex V is the mid-point of FD.

$\therefore \quad \dfrac{\alpha+1/2}{2} = 0$ and $\dfrac{\beta+5/2}{2} = 2$ i.e., $\alpha = -1/2$ and $\beta = 3/2$.

So, the coordinates of focus of parabola are (−1/2, 3/2).

Let, $P(x, y)$ be any point on the parabola.

Then, by definition of parabola, we have

Distance of $P(x, y)$ from (−1/2, 3/2) = Perpendicular distance of $P(x, y)$ from $x + y - 3 = 0$

$$\Rightarrow \quad \sqrt{(x+1/2)^2+(y-3/2)^2} = \left|\frac{x+y-3}{\sqrt{(1)^2+(1)^2}}\right|$$

$$\Rightarrow \quad \sqrt{(x+1/2)^2+(y-3/2)^2} = \left|\frac{x+y-3}{\sqrt{2}}\right|$$

$$\Rightarrow \quad (x+1/2)^2+(y-3/2)^2 = \frac{(x+y-3)^2}{2}$$

$$\Rightarrow \quad 2(x^2 + x + 1/4 + y^2 - 3y + 9/4) = x^2 + y^2 + 9 + 2xy - 6x - 6y$$

$$\Rightarrow \quad x^2 - 2xy + y^2 + 8x - 4 = 0$$

Which is the required equation of parabola.

30. Find the coordinates of focus, axis of parabola, the equation of directrix, coordinate of vertex of the parabola $x^2 - 2x - 4y - 11 = 0$.

Ans. Given, equation of the parabola is

$$x^2 - 2x - 4y - 11 = 0$$

$$\Rightarrow (x^2 - 6x + 4) - 4 - 4y - 11 = 0$$

$$\Rightarrow \quad (x-2)^2 = 4y + 20$$

$$\Rightarrow \quad (x-2)^2 = 4(y+5) = 4 \times 1 \times (y+5)$$

For vertex, $x - 2 = 0$

$\Rightarrow \quad x = 2$

$y + 5 = 0$

$\Rightarrow \quad y = -5$

Axis of parabola $x - 2 = 0$

$\Rightarrow \quad x = 2$

For directrix, $y + 5 = -1$

$\Rightarrow \quad y + 6 = 0$

And for focus, $y + 5 = 1$ and $x - 2 = 0$,

$\Rightarrow \quad y = -4$

$\Rightarrow \quad x = 2$

$\therefore$ focus = (2, – 4), axis of parabola is $x = 2$, equation of directrix is $y + 6 = 0$ and co-ordinates of vertex are (2, –5).

31. Find the equation of a circle which touches both the axes and the line $3x - 4y + 8 = 0$ and lies in the third quadrant. [NCERT Exemplar]

Ans. Let a be the radius of the circle. Then, the coordinates of the circle are $(-a, -a)$. Now, perpendicular distance from C to the line AB = Radius of the circle.

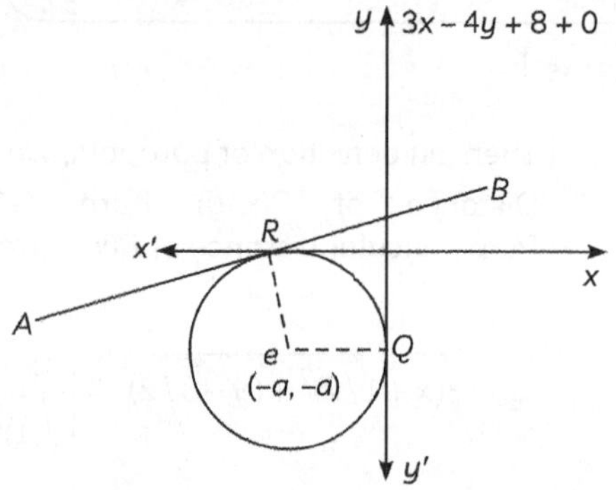

$$d = \left|\frac{-3a + 4a + 8}{\sqrt{9+16}}\right| = \left|\frac{a+8}{5}\right|$$

$$\because \quad a = \left(\frac{a+8}{5}\right)$$

$$a = \frac{a+8}{5}$$

$\Rightarrow \quad 5a = a + 8$

$\Rightarrow \quad 4a = 8$

$\Rightarrow \quad a = 2$

Or

$$a = \frac{-(a+8)}{5}$$

$5a = -a - 8$

$6a = -8$

$a = -8/6$

$a \neq -8/6$

So, the equation of circle is

$$(x + 2)^2 + (y + 2)^2 = 2^2$$

$\Rightarrow \quad x^2 + 4x + 4 + y^2 + 4y + 4 = 4$

$\Rightarrow \quad x^2 + y^2 + 4x + 4y + 4 = 0$

ELLIPSE AND HYPERBOLA 2

TOPIC 1

ELLIPSE

An ellipse is the set of all points in a plane, the sum of whose distances from two fixed points in the plane is a constant. The two fixed points are called the foci of the ellipse.

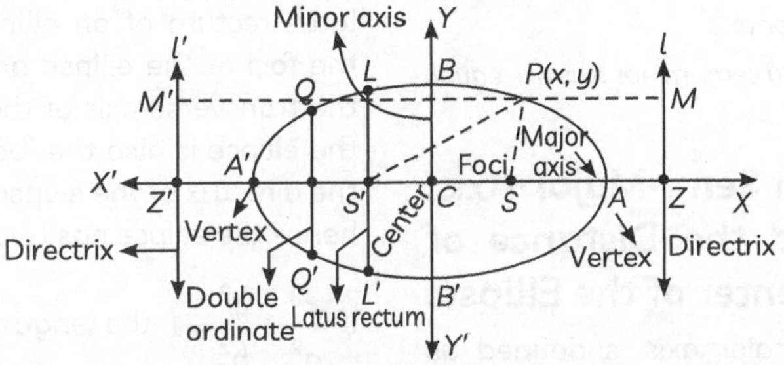

Standard equation	$\frac{x^2}{a^2}+\frac{y^2}{b^2}=1$, $a>b$	$\frac{x^2}{b^2}+\frac{y^2}{a^2}=1$, $a<b$
Graph	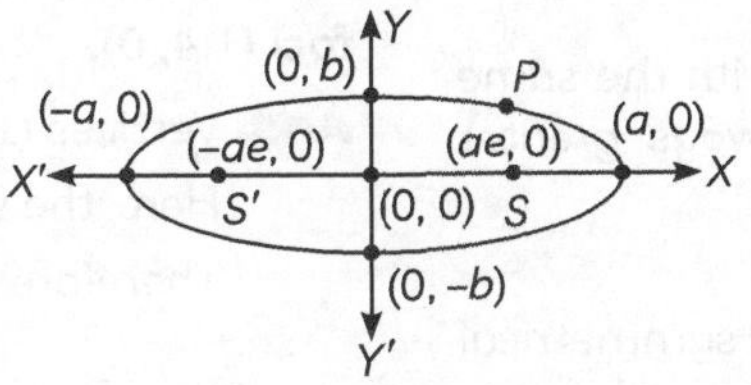	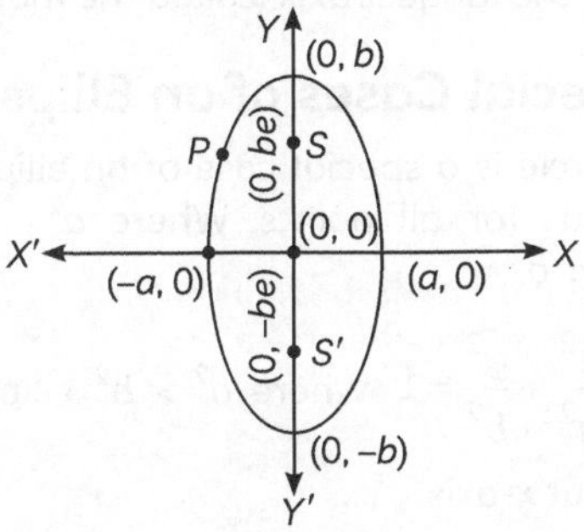
Coordinates of the centre	(0, 0)	(0, 0)
Coordinates of the vertices	$(\pm a, 0)$	$(0, \pm b)$
Length of major axis	$2a$	$2b$
Length of minor axis	$2b$	$2a$
Coordinates of foci	$(\pm ae, 0)$	$(0, \pm be)$
Equation of directrices	$x=\pm\left(\frac{a}{e}\right)$	$y=\pm\left(\frac{b}{e}\right)$
Eccentricity	$e=\sqrt{1-\frac{b^2}{a^2}}$	$e=\sqrt{1-\frac{a^2}{b^2}}$
Length of latus rectum	$\frac{2b^2}{a}$	$\frac{2a^2}{b}$
Ends of latus rectum	$\left(\pm ae, \pm\frac{b^2}{a}\right)$	$\left(\pm\frac{a^2}{b}, \pm be\right)$
Focal distance or radii	$\mid SP\mid=(a-ex_1)$ and $\mid S'P\mid=(a+ex_1)$	$\mid SP\mid=(b-ey_1)$ and $\mid S'P\mid=(b+ey_1)$
Sum of focal radii = | SP | + | SP |	$2a$	$2b$
Distance between foci	$2ae$	$2be$

Caution

➥ *The constant which is the sum of the distances of a point on the ellipse from the two fixed points is always greater than the distance between the two fixed points.*

Important

➥ *If length of major axis is 2a, length of minor axis is 2b and distance between the foci is 2c, then $a^2 = b^2 + c^2$.*

➥ *Ellipse is symmetric w.r.t. both the coordinate axes.*

➥ *The foci always lie on the major axis.*

➥ *If length of semi-major axis and semi-minor axis are equal, then the ellipse become circle.*

Relationship between Semi-Major Axis, Semi-minor Axis and the Distance of the Focus from the Center of the Ellipse.

For any ellipse, the semi-major axis is defined as one-half the sum of the perihelion and the aphelion, the semi-major axis is the distance from the origin to either side of the ellipse along the x-axis, or just one-half the longest axis (called the major axis).

Special Cases of an Ellipse

A circle is a special case of an ellipse, with the same radius for all points. Where a^2 is always greater than b^2.

If $\frac{x^2}{a^2}+\frac{y^2}{b^2}=1$ where $a^2 > b^2$ ellipse is symmetrical about x-axis.

$\frac{x^2}{b^2}+\frac{y^2}{a^2}=1$ where $a^2 > b^2$ ellipse is symmetrical about y-axis.

Eccentricity

The eccentricity of an ellipse is, most simply, the ratio of the distance c between the center of the ellipse and each focus to the length of the semi-major axis a.

If the distance of the focus from the center of the ellipse is 'c' and the distance of the end of the ellipse from the center is 'a', then eccentricity $e=\frac{c}{a}$.

Standard Equations of an Ellipse

When the centre of the ellipse is at the origin (0, 0) and the foci are on the x-axis and y-axis, then we can easily derive the ellipse equation. The equation of the ellipse is given by;

$$\frac{x^2}{a^2}+\frac{y^2}{b^2}=1.$$

Standard Forms of the Equation of an Ellipse with Center (h, k) The standard form of the equation of an ellipse with center (h, k) and major axis parallel to the x-axis is $\frac{(x-h)^2}{a^2}+\frac{(y-k)^2}{b^2}=1$.

Latus Rectum

The chord of the ellipse through its one focus and perpendicular to the major axis (or parallel to the directrix) is called the latus rectum of the ellipse. It is a double ordinate passing through the focus.The latus rectum of an ellipse is a line passing through the foci of the ellipse and is drawn perpendicular to the transverse axis of the ellipse. The latus rectum of the ellipse is also the focal chord, which is parallel to the directrix of the ellipse. The ellipse has two foci and hence the ellipse has two latus rectums.

If $\frac{x^2}{a^2}+\frac{y^2}{b^2}=1$ the length of latus ractum is $\frac{2b^2}{a}$

If $\frac{x^2}{b^2}+\frac{y^2}{a^2}=1$ the length of latus ractum is $\frac{2a^2}{b}$

Example 2.1: Finds the equation for the ellipse that satisfies the given conditions: Vertices (± 6, 0), foci (± 4, 0). [NCERT]

Ans. Vertices (±6, 0) and foci (±4, 0).

Here, the vertices are on the x-axis.

Therefore, the equation of the ellipse will be of the form $\frac{x^2}{a^2}+\frac{y^2}{b^2}=1$, where a is the semi-major axis.

Accordingly, $a = 6$, $c = 4$

It is known that $a^2 = b^2 + c^2$

$\therefore \quad 6^2 = b^2 + 4^2$

$\Rightarrow \quad 36 = b^2 + 16$

$\Rightarrow \quad b^2 = 36 - 16$

$\Rightarrow \quad b = \sqrt{20}$

Thus, the equation of the ellipse is

$$\frac{x^2}{6^2}+\frac{y^2}{(\sqrt{20})^2}=1 \text{ or } \frac{x^2}{36}+\frac{y^2}{20}=1$$

Example 2.2: Find the equation for the ellipse that satisfies the given conditions: Vertices (±5, 0), foci (±4, 0). [NCERT]

Ans. Vertices (± 5, 0), foci (± 4, 0)

Here, the vertices are on the x-axis.

Therefore, the equation of the ellipse will be of the form $\frac{x^2}{a^2}+\frac{y^2}{b^2}=1$ where a is the semi-major axis.

Accordingly, $a = 5$, $c = 4$

It is known that $a^2 = b^2 + c^2$

$\therefore \quad 5^2 = b^2 + 4^2$

$\Rightarrow \quad 25 = b^2 + 16$

$\Rightarrow \quad b^2 = 25 - 16$

$\Rightarrow \quad b = \sqrt{9} = 3$

Thus, the equation of the ellipse is $\frac{x^2}{5^2}+\frac{y^2}{3^2}=1$

or $\frac{x^2}{25}+\frac{y^2}{9}=1$

Example 2.3: Find the coordinates of the foci, the vertices, the length of major axis, the minor axis, the eccentricity and the length of the latus rectum of the ellipse $\frac{x^2}{16}+\frac{y^2}{9}=1$ **[NCERT]**

Ans. The given equation is $\frac{x^2}{16}+\frac{y^2}{9}=1$ or $\frac{x^2}{4^2}+\frac{y^2}{3^2}=1$

Here, the denominator of $\frac{x^2}{16}$ is greater than the denominator of $\frac{y^2}{9}$.

Therefore, the major axis is along the x-axis, while the minor axis is along the y-axis. On comparing the given equation with

$\frac{x^2}{a^2}+\frac{y^2}{b^2}=1$, we obtain $a = 4$ and $b = 3$.

$\therefore \quad c=\sqrt{a^2-b^2}=\sqrt{16-9}=\sqrt{7}$

Therefore,

The coordinates of the foci are $(\pm\sqrt{7},0)$

The coordinates of the vertices are $(\pm 4, 0)$

Length of major axis = $2a = 8$

Length of minor axis = $2b = 6$

Eccentricity, $e=\frac{c}{a}=\frac{\sqrt{7}}{4}$

Length of latus rectum = $\frac{2b^2}{a}=\frac{2\times 9}{4}=\frac{9}{2}$

Example 2.4: Find the coordinates of the focii, the vertices, the length of major axis, the minor axis, the eccentricity and the length of the latus rectum of the ellipse $\frac{x^2}{36}+\frac{y^2}{16}=1$ **[NCERT]**

Ans. The given equation is $\frac{x^2}{36}+\frac{y^2}{16}=1$

Here, the denominator of $\frac{x^2}{36}$ is greater than the denominator of $\frac{y^2}{16}$

Therefore, the major axis is along the x-axis, while the minor axis is along the y-axis. On comparing the given equation with

$\frac{x^2}{a^2}+\frac{y^2}{b^2}=1$,

$\therefore \quad c=\sqrt{a^2-b^2}=\sqrt{36-16}=\sqrt{20}=2\sqrt{5}$

we obtain $a = 6$ and $b = 4$.

Therefore,

The coordinates of the foci are $(2\sqrt{5},0)$ and $(-2\sqrt{5},0)$

The coordinates of the vertices are (6, 0) and (-6, 0)

Length of major axis = $2a = 12$

Length of minor axis = $2b = 8$

Eccentricity, $e=\frac{c}{a}=\frac{2\sqrt{5}}{6}=\frac{\sqrt{5}}{3}$

Length of latus rectum = $\frac{2b^2}{a}=\frac{2\times 16}{6}=\frac{16}{3}$

TOPIC 2

HYPERBOLA

A hyperbola is the set of all points in a plane, the difference of whose distance from two fixed points is constant.

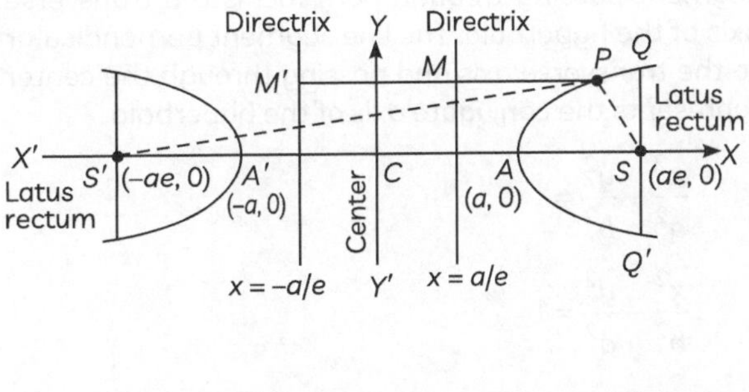

Fundamental terms	Hyperbola	Conjugate Hyperbola
Standard equation	$\frac{x^2}{a^2}-\frac{y^2}{b^2}=1$	$\frac{y^2}{b^2}-\frac{x^2}{a^2}=1$
Graph	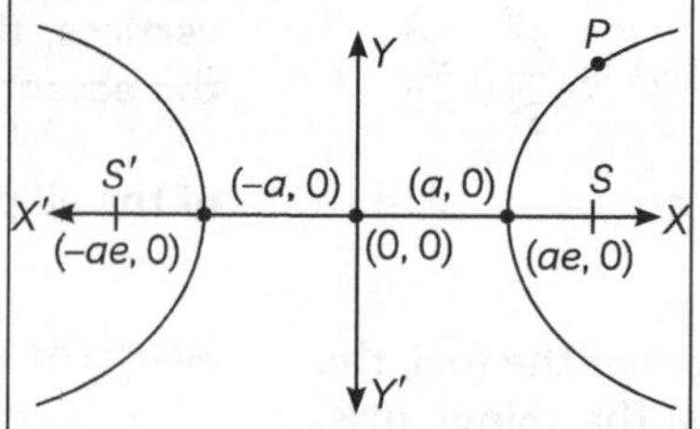	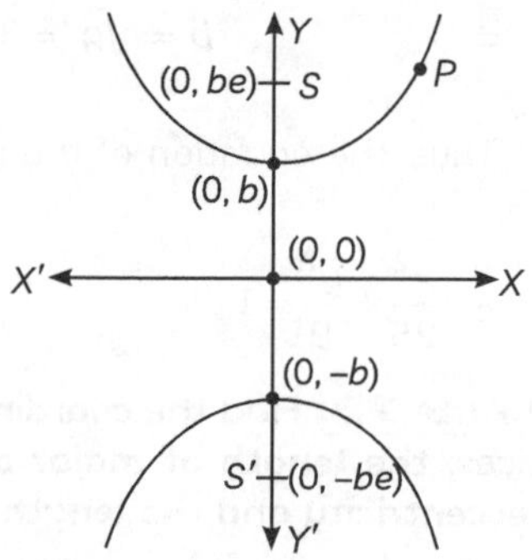
Coordinates of the centre	(0, 0)	(0, 0)
Coordinates of the vertices	$(\pm a, 0)$	$(0, \pm b)$
Length of transverse axis	$2a$	$2b$
Length of conjugate axis	$2b$	$2a$
Coordinates of foci	$(\pm ae, 0)$	$(0, \pm be)$
Equation of directrices	$x=\pm\left(\frac{a}{e}\right)$	$y=\pm\left(\frac{b}{e}\right)$
Eccentricity	$e=\sqrt{1+\frac{b^2}{a^2}}$	$e=\sqrt{1+\frac{a^2}{b^2}}$
Length of latus rectum	$\frac{2b^2}{a}$	$\frac{2a^2}{b}$
Ends of latus rectum	$\left(\pm ae, \pm\frac{b^2}{a}\right)$	$\left(\pm\frac{a^2}{b}, \pm be\right)$
Difference of focal radii = | SP | – | S'P |	$2a$	$2b$
Distance between foci	$2ae$	$2be$

Standard Equation of Hyperbola

A hyperbola is the locus of all those points in a plane such that the difference in their distances from two fixed points in the plane is a constant.

When both the foci are joined with the help of a line segment then the mid-point of this line segment joining the foci is known as the center, O represents the center of an ellipse in the figure given above. The line segment passing through both foci is the transverse axis of the hyperbola. The line segment perpendicular to the transverse axis and passing through the center represents the conjugate axis of the hyperbola.

$$\frac{x^2}{a^2}-\frac{y^2}{b^2}=1$$

$$\frac{x^2}{b^2}-\frac{y^2}{a^2}=1$$

These are the standard equations of hyperbola.

Latus Rectum

The line segments perpendicular to the transverse axis through any of the foci such that their endpoints lie on the hyperbola are defined as the latus rectum of a hyperbola.

Length of Latus Rectum of Hyperbola

Latus rectum of a hyperbola is defined analogously as in the case of parabola and ellipse.

The ends of the latus rectum of a hyperbola are $\left(\pm ae, \pm\frac{b^2}{a^2}\right)$, and the length of the latus rectum is $\frac{2b^2}{a}$.

Important

➥ *A hyperbola in which a = b is called a rectangular hyperbola.*

➥ *Hyperbola is symmetric w.r.t. both the axes.*

➥ *The foci are always on the transverse axis.*

Example 2.5: Find the equation of the hyperbola satisfy the given conditions: Vertices (± 2, 0), foci (± 3, 0). **[NCERT]**

Ans. Vertices (±2, 0), foci (±3, 0)

Here, the vertices are on the x-axis.

Therefore, the equation of the hyperbola is of the form $\frac{x^2}{a^2}-\frac{y^2}{b^2}=1$

Since the vertices are (±2, 0), $a = 2$

Since the foci are (±3, 0), $c = 3$.

We know that $a^2 + b^2 = c^2$

$\therefore \quad 2^2 + b^2 = 3^2$

$b^2 = 9 - 4 = 5$

Thus, the equation of the hyperbola is $\frac{x^2}{4}-\frac{y^2}{5}=1$

Example 2.6: Find the equation of the hyperbola satisfying the given conditions: Vertices (0, ±5), foci (0, ±8). **[NCERT]**

Ans. Vertices (0, ±5), foci (0, ±8)

Here, the vertices are on the y-axis.

Therefore, the equation of the hyperbola is of the form $\frac{y^2}{a^2}-\frac{x^2}{b^2}=1$

Since the vertices are (0, ±5), $a = 5$.

Since the foci are (0, ±8), $c = 8$.

We know that $a^2 + b^2 = c^2$.

$\therefore \quad 5^2 + b^2 = 8^2$

$b^2 = 64 - 25 = 39$

Thus, the equation of the hyperbola is

$$\frac{y^2}{25}-\frac{x^2}{39}=1.$$

Example 2.7: Find the coordinates of the foci and the vertices, the eccentricity, and the length of the latus rectum of the hyperbola $49y^2 - 16x^2 = 784$ **[NCERT]**

Ans. The given equation is $49y^2 - 16x^2 = 784$

It can be written as

$49y^2 - 16x^2 = 784$

Or, $\frac{y^2}{16}-\frac{x^2}{49}=1$

Or, $\frac{y^2}{4^2}-\frac{x^2}{7^2}=1$ ...(1)

On comparing equation (1) with the standard equation of hyperbola i.e., $\frac{y^2}{a^2}-\frac{x^2}{b^2}=1$, we obtain $a = 4$ and $b = 7$.

We know that $a^2 + b^2 = c^2$

$\therefore \quad c^2 = 16 + 49 = 65$

$\Rightarrow \quad c = \sqrt{65}$

Therefore,

The coordinates of the foci are $(0, \pm\sqrt{65})$.

The coordinates of the vertices are (0, ± 4).

Eccentricity, $e = \frac{c}{a} = \frac{\sqrt{65}}{4}$

Length of latus rectum $= \frac{2b^2}{a} = \frac{2\times 49}{4} = \frac{49}{2}$

OBJECTIVE Type Questions

[1 mark]

Multiple Choice Questions

1. If the ellipse $\frac{x^2}{4}+\frac{y^2}{1}=1$ meets the ellipse $\frac{x^2}{1}+\frac{y^2}{a^2}=1$ in four distinct points and $a = b^2 - 10b + 25$, then the value of b does not satisfy:

(a) $(-\infty, 4)$ **(b) [4, 6]**

(c) $(6, \infty)$ **(d) None of these**

Ans. *(b) [4, 6]*

Explanation: Now according to condition $a > 1$

$\Rightarrow b^2 - 10b + 25 = a > 1$

$\Rightarrow b^2 - 10b + 24 > 0$

$\Rightarrow (b - 4)(b - 6) > 0$

$\Rightarrow b < 4$ or $b > 6$

$\Rightarrow b \notin [4, 6]$

Hence, option (b) is the correct answer.

2. The sum of the distance of any point on the ellipse $3x^2 + 4y^2 = 24$ from its foci is:

(a) $4\sqrt{2}$ **(b) 8**

(c) $16\sqrt{2}$ **(d) $2\sqrt{2}$**

Ans. *(a)* $4\sqrt{2}$

Explanation: Given equation of ellipse is

$$\frac{x^2}{8}+\frac{y^2}{6}=1$$

$$\Rightarrow \quad a^2 = 8$$

$$\Rightarrow \quad a = 2\sqrt{2}$$

The sum of focal distances of a point of the ellipse = length of major axis = $2a = 4\sqrt{2}$

Hence, option(a) is the correct answer.

3. Find the coordinates of the focii and eccentricity of the ellipse $\frac{x^2}{25}+\frac{y^2}{9}=1$.

(a) $(0, \pm 4), \frac{4}{5}$ (b) $(\pm 4, 0), \frac{4}{5}$

(c) $(0, \pm 4), \frac{4}{3}$ (d) $(0, \pm 2), \frac{4}{5}$

Ans. *(b)* $(\pm 4, 0), \frac{4}{5}$

Explanation: From the given equation of ellipse, we have $a = 5$ and $b = 3$

$$\therefore \quad e=\sqrt{1-\frac{b^2}{a^2}}=\frac{4}{5}$$

Therefore, the coordinates of the foci are, $(\pm ae, 0)$ i.e., $(\pm 4, 0)$

Hence, option (b) is the correct answer.

4. If the length of the major axis of an ellipse is $\frac{17}{8}$ times the length of the minor axis, then the eccentricity of the ellipse is:

(a) $\frac{8}{17}$ (b) $\frac{15}{17}$

(c) $\frac{9}{17}$ (d) $\frac{2\sqrt{2}}{17}$

Ans. *(b)* $\frac{15}{17}$

Explanation: Length of major axis = $\frac{17}{8}$ × length of minor axis

$$\Rightarrow \quad 2a=\frac{17}{8}\times 2b$$

$$\Rightarrow \quad \frac{b}{a}=\frac{8}{17}$$

$$\Rightarrow \quad e=\sqrt{1-\frac{b^2}{a^2}}=\sqrt{1-\frac{64}{289}}=\sqrt{\frac{225}{289}}=\frac{15}{17}$$

Hence, option (b) is the correct answer.

5. Coordinates of focii of $9x^2 - 16y^2 = 144$ are:

(a) (3, 0); (–3, 0) (b) (4, 0); (–4, 0)

(c) (5, 0); (–5, 0) (d) (12, 0); (–12, 0)

[DIKSHA]

Ans. *(c) (5, 0); (–5, 0)*

Explanation: $9x^2 - 16y^2 = 144$

$$\frac{x^2}{16}-\frac{y^2}{9}=1$$

$$a^2 = 16$$

$$b^2 = 9$$

$$c = \pm 5$$

So coordinate of focii is $(\pm c, 0)$

i.e., $(\pm 5, 0)$

Hence, option (c) is the correct answer.

6. The equation $\frac{x^2}{1-r}-\frac{y^2}{1+r}=1$, $|r| < 1$ represents *a/an*:

(a) Ellipse (b) Hyperbola

(c) Circle (d) None of these

Ans. *(b) Hyperbola*

Explanation: Since $|r| < 1$, $1 - r$ and $1 + r$ are both positive.

So we put $1 - r = a^2$, $1 + r = b^2$.

Then the given equation becomes, $\frac{x^2}{a^2}-\frac{y^2}{b^2}=1$

which represents a hyperbola.

Hence, option (b) is the correct answer.

7. The eccentricity of the hyperbola $\frac{x^2}{a^2}-\frac{y^2}{b^2}=1$ which passes through the points (3, 0) and $(3\sqrt{2}, 2)$ is:

(a) $\frac{1}{\sqrt{13}}$ (b) $\sqrt{13}$

(c) $\frac{\sqrt{13}}{2}$ (d) $\frac{\sqrt{13}}{3}$

Ans. *(d)* $\frac{\sqrt{13}}{3}$

Explanation: Given that the hyperbola $\frac{x^2}{a^2}-\frac{y^2}{b^2}=1$ passes through the points (3, 0) and $(3\sqrt{2}, 2)$, so we get $a^2 = 9$ and $b^2 = 4$.

Again, we know that $b^2 = a^2 (e^2 - 1)$. This gives

$$4 = 9(e^2 - 1) \Rightarrow e^2 = \frac{13}{9} \Rightarrow e = \frac{\sqrt{13}}{3}$$

Hence, option (d) is the correct answer.

8. If e_1 is the eccentricity of the conic $9x^2 + 4y^2 = 36$ and e_2 is the eccentricity of the conic, $9x^2 - 4y^2 = 36$ then which is true?

(a) $e_1^2 + e_2^2 = 2$ **(b) $3 < e_1^2 + e_2^2 < 4$**

(c) $e_1^2 + e_2^2 > 4$ **(d) None of these**

Ans. *(b) $3 < e_1^2 + e_2^2 < 4$*

Explanation: We have, $\frac{x^2}{4} + \frac{y^2}{9} = 1$

$\therefore \quad e_1^2 = \frac{9-4}{9}$

$= \frac{5}{9}$

and

$\frac{x^2}{4} - \frac{y^2}{9} = 1$

$\therefore \quad e_2^2 = \frac{4+9}{4} = \frac{13}{4}$

Now $e_1^2 + e_2^2 = \left(\frac{5}{9}\right) + \left(\frac{13}{4}\right) = \frac{137}{36} > 3$ but < 4

$\therefore \quad 3 < e_1^2 + e_2^2 < 4$

Hence, option (b) is the correct answer.

9. The eccentricity of the hyperbola $x^2 - y^2 = 2004$ is:

(a) $\sqrt{3}$ **(b) 2**

(c) $2\sqrt{2}$ **(d) $\sqrt{2}$**

Ans. *(d) $\sqrt{2}$*

Explanation: Given equation of hyperbola is

$x^2 - y^2 = 2004$

Or $\frac{x^2}{(\sqrt{2004})^2} - \frac{y^2}{(\sqrt{2004})^2} = 1$

$\therefore \quad a = \sqrt{2004}$ and $b = \sqrt{2004}$

Using, $b^2 = a^2 (e^2 - 1)$

or, $e^2 - 1 = 1$

or, $e^2 = 2$ or, $e = \sqrt{2}$

Hence, option (d) is the correct answer.

10. Eccentricity of $9x^2 - 16y^2 = 144$ is:

(a) $\frac{2}{3}$ **(b) $\frac{3}{4}$**

(c) $\frac{4}{5}$ **(d) $\frac{5}{4}$** **[DIKSHA]**

Ans. *(d) $\frac{5}{4}$*

Explanation: $\frac{x^2}{16} - \frac{y^2}{9} = 1$

$a^2 = 16$

$b^2 = 9$

$c^2 = a^2 + b^2$

$c^2 = 25$

$e = \frac{c}{a}$

$e = \frac{5}{4}$

Hence, option (d) is the correct answer.

11. Find the equation of the ellipse with foci at $(\pm 5, 0)$ and $x = \frac{36}{5}$ as one of the directrices.

(a) $\frac{x^2}{36} + \frac{y^2}{11} = 4$ **(b) $\frac{x^2}{6} + \frac{y^2}{11} = 1$**

(c) $\frac{x^2}{36} + \frac{y^2}{11} = 1$ **(d) $\frac{x^2}{36} + \frac{y^2}{4} = 1$**

Ans. *(c) $\frac{x^2}{36} + \frac{y^2}{11} = 1$*

Explanation: We have $ae = 5$, $\frac{a}{e} = \frac{36}{5}$, which gives $a = 6$ and $e = \frac{5}{6}$.

Now, $b = a\sqrt{1-e^2} = 6\sqrt{1-\frac{25}{36}} = \sqrt{11}$

Thus, the equation of ellipse is $\frac{x^2}{36} + \frac{y^2}{11} = 1$.

Hence, option (c) is the correct answer.

Assertion-Reason (A-R)

DIRECTION: In the following questions, a statement of assertion (A) is followed by a statement of the reason (R). Mark the correct choice as:

(a) Both assertion (A) and reason (R) are true and reason (R) is the correct explanation of assertion (A).

(b) Both assertion (A) and reason (R) are true but reason (R) is not the correct explanation of assertion (A).

(c) Assertion (A) is true but reason (R) is false.

(d) Assertion (A) is false but reason (R) is true.

12. Assertion: The sum of focal distances of a point on the ellipse $9x^2 + 4y^2 - 18x - 24y + 9 = 0$ is 4.

Reason: The equation $9x^2 + 4y^2 - 18x - 24y + 9 = 0$ can be expressed as $9(x - 1)^2 + 4(y - 3)^2 = 36$.

Ans. *(d) Assertion (A) is false but reason (R) is true.*

Explanation: We have,

$$9x^2 + 4y^2 - 18x - 24y + 9 = 0$$

$$\Rightarrow \quad 9(x-1)^2 + 4(y-3)^2 = 36$$

$$\Rightarrow \quad \frac{(x-1)^2}{2^2} + \frac{(y-3)^2}{3^2} = 1$$

Here, $b > a$

$\therefore$ Sum of focal distance of a point is $2b = 6$.

Hence, option (d) is the correct answer.

13. Assertion: The length of major and minor axes of the ellipse $5x^2 + 9y^2 - 54y + 36 = 0$ are 6 and, 10, respectively.

Reason: The equation $5x^2 + 9y^2 - 54y + 36 = 0$ can be expressed as $5x^2 + 9(y - 3)^2 = 45$.

Ans. *(d) Assertion (A) is false but reason (R) is true.*

Explanation: We have,

$$5x^2 + 9y^2 - 54y + 36 = 0$$

$$\Rightarrow \quad 5x^2 + 9(y-3)^2 = 45$$

$$\Rightarrow \quad \frac{x^2}{3^2} + \frac{(y-3)^2}{(\sqrt{5})^2} = 1$$

$\therefore$ Length of major axis = $2 \times 3 = 6$

And length of minor axis = $2 \times \sqrt{5} = 2\sqrt{5}$

Hence, option(d) is the correct answer.

14. If the distance of foci and vertex of hyperbola from the centre are c and a respectively, then

Assertion: Eccentricity is always less than 1.

Reason: Foci are at a distance of ae from the center.

Ans. *(d) Assertion (A) is false but reason (R) is true.*

Explanation: Since, $c \geq a$, the eccentricity is near less than one. In terms of the eccentricity, the foci are at a distance of ae from the centre.

Hence, option (d) is the correct answer.

15. Assertion: The focii of the hyperbola $9x^2 - 16y^2 = 144$ is $(\pm 5, 0)$.

Reason: The formula to find the focii of a parabola is $c^2 = a^2 + b^2$.

Ans. *(a) Both assertion (A) and reason (R) are true and reason (R) is the correct explanation of assertion (A).*

Explanation: Here, $a^2 = 16, b^2 = 9$

So, $c^2 = 16 + 9 = 25$

$c = \pm 5,$

Hence, coordinate of focii is $(\pm 5, 0)$

To find the coordinate of focii we have to use $c^2 = a^2 + b^2$.

Hence, option(a) is the correct answer.

CASE BASED Questions (CBQs)

[**4** & **5** marks]

Read the following passages and answer the questions that follow:

16. *Arun was playing a football match. When he kicked the football, the path formed by the football from ground level is parabolic, which is shown in the following graph. Consider the coordinates of point A as (3, –2).*

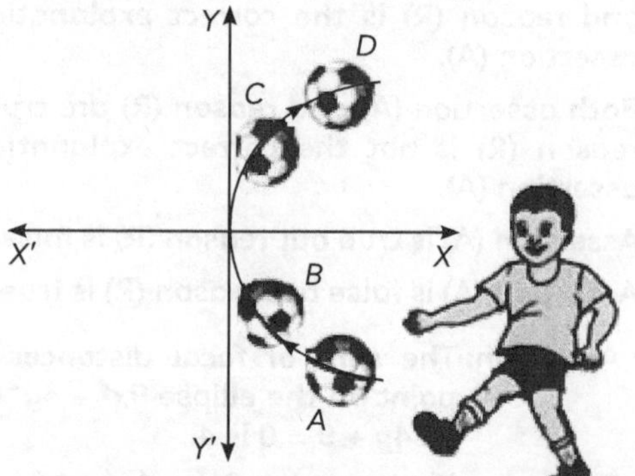

(A) The equation of path formed by the football is:

(a) $y^2 = x + 1$ (b) $3x^2 = 4y$

(c) $3y^2 = 4x$ (d) $x^2 = y - 1$

(B) The equation of directrix of path formed by football is:

(a) $x - \frac{4}{3} = 0$ (b) $x + \frac{2}{3} = 0$

(c) $x + 3 = 0$ (d) $x + \frac{1}{3} = 0$

(C) The extremities of latus rectum of given curve are:

(a) $\left(\frac{1}{3}, \pm\frac{2}{3}\right)$ (b) $\left(\frac{2}{3}, \pm\frac{1}{3}\right)$

(c) $\left(\pm\frac{1}{3}, 1\right)$ (d) $\left(\pm\frac{1}{3}, \frac{4}{3}\right)$

(D) The length of latus rectum of a given curve is:

(a) $\frac{2}{3}$ (b) $\frac{5}{3}$

(c) 3 (d) $\frac{4}{3}$

Ans. (A) (c) $3y^2 = 4x$

Explanation: The path formed by football is in the shape of parabola. We know that general equation of parabola is $y^2 = 4ax$.

Since, it passes through (3, –2)

$\therefore \quad (-2)^2 = 4 \times a \times 3$

$\Rightarrow \quad a = \frac{1}{3}$

$\Rightarrow$ Hence, required equation of path formed by football is $y^2 = \frac{4x}{3}$

$\Rightarrow \quad 3y^2 = 4x$

(B) (d) $x + \frac{1}{3} = 0$

Explanation: Since, $a = \frac{1}{3}$. Therefore, the equation of its directrix is $x + \frac{1}{3} = 0$.

(C) (a) $\left(\frac{1}{3}, \pm\frac{2}{3}\right)$

Explanation: The extremities of latus rectum are $(a, \pm 2a) \equiv \left(\frac{1}{3}, \pm\frac{2}{3}\right)$

(D) (d) $\frac{4}{3}$

Explanation: The length of latus rectum $= 4a = 4 \times \frac{1}{3} = \frac{4}{3}$

17. *Karan, the student of class XI was studying in his house. He felt hungry and found that his mother was not at home. So, he went to the nearby shop and purchased a packet of chips. While eating the chips, he observed that one piece of the chips is in the shape of hyperbola. Consider the vertices of the hyperbola at (± 5, 0) and focii at (± 7, 0).*

(A) Find the equation of hyperbolic curve and the length of conjugate axis formed by a given piece of chip.

(B) Find the eccentricity and length of latus rectum of the hyperbolic curve formed by a given piece of chips.

Ans. (A) We have, $a = 5$ and $ae = 7$

Now, $b^2 = a^2e^2 - a^2$

$= 49 - 25$

$= 24$

So, equation is $\frac{x^2}{25} - \frac{y^2}{24} = 1$

Length of conjugate axis $= 2b$

$= 2 \times 2\sqrt{6}$

$= 4\sqrt{6}$

(B) Eccentricity,

$$e = \sqrt{1 + \frac{b^2}{a^2}} = \sqrt{1 + \frac{24}{25}} = \sqrt{\frac{49}{25}} = \frac{7}{5}$$

Length of latus rectum $= \frac{2b^2}{a} = \frac{48}{5} = 9.6$

VERY SHORT ANSWER Type Questions (VSA)

[1 mark]

18. If the latus rectum of an ellipse is equal to half of the minor axis, then find its eccentricity. **[NCERT Exemplar]**

Ans. Consider the equation of the ellipse $\frac{x^2}{a^2} + \frac{y^2}{b^2} = 1$

It is given that, length of latus rectum = half of minor axis

$\Rightarrow \quad \frac{2b^2}{a} = b$

$\Rightarrow \quad a = 2b$

Now, $\quad b^2 = a^2(1 - e^2)$

$\Rightarrow \quad b^2 = 4b^2(1 - e^2)$

$\Rightarrow \quad 1 - e^2 = \frac{1}{4}$

$\Rightarrow \quad e^2 = \frac{3}{4}$

$\therefore \quad e = \frac{\sqrt{3}}{2}$

19. Find the equation of ellipse whose focus is (0, 17) and vertex is (0, 300).

Ans. Here $\quad c = 17$

$c^2 = a^2 - b^2$

$17^2 = a^2 - b^2$

$289 - 300 = -b^2$

$-11 = -b^2$

Hence, required ellipse is

$b^2 = 11$

$$\frac{x^2}{11} + \frac{y^2}{300} = 1$$

20. Given the ellipse with equation,

$9x^2 + 25y^2 = 225$,

find the eccentricity and focii.

[NCERT Exemplar]

Ans. Given equation of ellipse, $9x^2 + 25y^2 = 225$

Or $\frac{x^2}{25}+\frac{y^2}{9}=1$

So, $a = 5, b = 3$

Now, $b^2 = a^2(1-e^2)$

$\Rightarrow 9 = 25(1-e^2)$

$\Rightarrow \frac{9}{25} = 1-e^2$

$\Rightarrow e^2 = 1-\frac{9}{25} = \frac{16}{25}$

$\therefore e = \frac{4}{5}$

Foci $\equiv (\pm ae, 0) \equiv (\pm 5 \times (4/5), 0) \equiv (\pm 4, 0)$

21. Find the equation of hyperbola whose length of transverse axis 10 and conjugate axis is 16.

Ans. Length of transverse axis $= 2a$

$= 2a = 10$

$a = 5$

Length of conjugate axis $= 2b$

$= 2b = 16$

$b = 8$

Hence required equation of hyperbola is

$$\frac{x^2}{25}-\frac{y^2}{64}=1$$

SHORT ANSWER Type-I Questions (SA-I)

[**2** marks]

22. If the eccentricity of the hyperbola is $\sqrt{2}$. Then, find the general equation of hyperbola.

Ans. Given, eccentricity $e = \sqrt{2}$

$\Rightarrow \sqrt{1+\frac{b^2}{a^2}} = \sqrt{2}$

$\Rightarrow \sqrt{a^2+b^2} = \sqrt{2}a$

$\Rightarrow a^2+b^2 = 2a^2$

$\Rightarrow a^2 = b^2$

$\therefore$ Equation of the hyperbola is

$$\frac{x^2}{a^2}-\frac{y^2}{a^2}=1 \text{ or } \frac{y^2}{a^2}-\frac{x^2}{a^2}=1$$

$\Rightarrow x^2-y^2 = a^2$

$\Rightarrow y^2-x^2 = a^2$

23. If the distance between the foci of a hyperbola is 16 and its eccentricity is $\sqrt{2}$, then obtain the equation of the hyperbola. [NCERT Exemplar]

Ans. Let the equation of the hyperbola be $\frac{x^2}{a^2}-\frac{y^2}{b^2}=1$

Foci are $(\pm ae, 0)$

Distance between foci $= 2ae = 16$ (given)

$\Rightarrow ae = 8$

Also, $e = \sqrt{2}$ (Given)

$\Rightarrow a\times\sqrt{2} = 8$

$\Rightarrow a = \frac{8}{\sqrt{2}}$

$\therefore a = 4\sqrt{2}$

We know that, $b^2 = a^2(e^2-1)$

$\Rightarrow b^2 = (4\sqrt{2})^2\left[(\sqrt{2})^2-1\right]$

$= 16 \times 2(2-1) = 32$

So, the equation of hyperbola is: $\frac{x^2}{32}-\frac{y^2}{32}=1$ or

$x^2-y^2 = 32.$

24. Find the coordinate of foci, vertex, length of major axis of the ellipse

$$\frac{x^2}{90}+\frac{y^2}{9}=1.$$

Ans. From the equation $\frac{x^2}{90}+\frac{y^2}{9}=1$

$a^2 = 90$

$\Rightarrow a = \sqrt{90}$

$\Rightarrow a = 3\sqrt{10}$

$b^2 = 9$

$\Rightarrow b = 3$

Now $c = \sqrt{a^2-b^2}$

$= \sqrt{90-9} = \sqrt{81} = 9$

Coordinate of foci are $(\pm c, 0) = (\pm 9, 0)$

Vertex $(\pm a, 0) = (\pm\sqrt{90}, 0)$

Length of major axis $= 2a$

$= 2\times 3\sqrt{10}$

$= 6\sqrt{10}$

25. Find the equation of ellipse whose eccentricity is 2/3, latus rectum is 5 and the centre is (0, 0). **[NCERT Exemplar]**

Ans. Let equation of the ellipse be $\frac{x^2}{a^2}+\frac{y^2}{b^2} = 1$

$(a > b)$

Given that, $\Rightarrow e = \frac{2}{3}$ and latus rectum = 5

$$\therefore \quad \frac{2b^2}{a} = 5$$

$$b^2 = \frac{5a}{2}$$

We know that, $b^2 = a^2 (1 - e^2)$

$$\Rightarrow \quad \frac{5a}{2} = a^2\left(1-\frac{4}{9}\right)$$

$$\Rightarrow \quad \frac{5}{2} = \frac{5a}{9}$$

$$\Rightarrow \quad a = \frac{9}{2}$$

$$\therefore \quad b^2 = \frac{5\times 9}{2\times 2}=\frac{45}{4}$$

So, the required equation of the ellipse is

$$\frac{4x^2}{81}+\frac{4y^2}{45} = 1.$$

SHORT ANSWER Type-II Questions (SA-II)

[**3** marks]

26. Find the equation of hyperbola for which the length of the transverse axis along *x*-axis with centre at origin of a hyperbola is 7 and it passes through the point (5, –2).

Ans. Let $\frac{x^2}{a^2}-\frac{y^2}{b^2}=1$ represent the hyperbola.

According to the given condition, the length of transverse axis i.e., $2a = 7 \Rightarrow a = \frac{7}{2}$

Also, the point (5, –2) lies on the hyperbola, so, we have

$$\frac{4}{49}(25)-\frac{4}{b^2} = 1$$

which gives

$$\Rightarrow \quad \frac{100}{49}-\frac{4}{b^2} = 1$$

$$\frac{100}{49}-1 = \frac{4}{b^2}$$

$$\Rightarrow \quad \frac{4}{b^2} = \frac{51}{49}$$

$$b^2 = \frac{196}{51}$$

Hence equation of hyperbola is

$$\frac{4}{49}x^2-\frac{51}{196}y^2=1.$$

27. Write the equation of directrix of the ellipse $\frac{x^2}{a^2}+\frac{y^2}{b^2}=1$ such that $a > b$.

Ans. The given equation of the ellipse is

$$\frac{x^2}{a^2}+\frac{y^2}{b^2}=1, a>b$$

$\therefore$ Equation of the directrices $x=\pm\frac{a}{e}$.

The equation of directrices of the hyperbola

$\frac{x^2}{a^2}+\frac{y^2}{b^2}=1$ is also $x=\pm\frac{a}{e}$.

28. Check whether the line 2x + 3y = 12 touches the ellipse $\frac{x^2}{9}+\frac{y^2}{4}=2$ at the point (3, 2). **[NCERT Exemplar]**

Ans. Given line is $2x + 3y = 12$ and the ellipse is $4x^2 + 9y^2 = 72$

Solving line and ellipse, we get

$$(12 - 3y)^2 + 9y^2 = 72$$

$$\Rightarrow \quad (4 - y)^2 + y^2 = 8$$

$$\Rightarrow \quad 16 - 8y + y^2 + y^2 = 8$$

$$\Rightarrow \quad 2y^2 - 8y + 8 = 0$$

$$\Rightarrow \quad y^2 - 4y + 4 = 0$$

$$\Rightarrow \quad (y - 2)^2 = 0$$

$$\Rightarrow \quad y = 2$$

$$\Rightarrow \quad 2x = 12 - 3(2)$$

$$\Rightarrow \quad 2x = 6$$

(from the equation of line)

$$\Rightarrow \quad x = 3$$

So, point of contact is (3, 2)

Hence, verified.

29. If the line $y = mx + 1$ is tangent to the parabola $y^2 = 4x$ then find the value of *m*. **[NCERT Exemplar]**

Ans. Given that, line $y = mx + 1$ is tangent to the parabola $y^2 = 4x$.

Solving line with parabola, we have

$$(mx + 1)^2 = 4x$$

$\Rightarrow \quad m^2x^2 + 2mx + 1 = 4x$

$\Rightarrow \quad m^2x^2 + x(2m - 4) + 1 = 0$

Since the line touches the parabola, above equation must have equal roots.

$\therefore$ Discriminant, $D = 0$

$\Rightarrow \quad (2m - 4)^2 - 4m^2 = 0$

$\Rightarrow \quad 4m^2 - 16m + 16 - 4m^2 = 0$

$\Rightarrow \quad 16m = 16$

$\therefore \quad m = 1$

LONG ANSWER Type Questions (LA)

[**4** & **5** marks]

30. Find the equation for the ellipse that satisfies the given condition: major axis on the x-axis and passes through the points (2, 1) and (3, 2).

Ans. Let the equation of the ellipse with major axis on x-axis be

$$\frac{x^2}{a^2}+\frac{y^2}{b^2} = 1 \quad ...(i) \quad (a > b)$$

Since the ellipse passes through (2, 1) and (3, 2).

$$\therefore \quad \frac{4}{a^2}+\frac{1}{b^2} = 1 \quad ...(ii)$$

$$\text{And} \quad \frac{9}{a^2}+\frac{4}{b^2} = 1 \quad ...(iii)$$

On solving eq. (ii) and (iii), we obtain

$$\Rightarrow a^2 = \frac{5}{3} \text{ and } b^2 = \frac{5}{7}$$

$\therefore$ Thus, the equation of an ellipse is $\frac{3x^2}{5}+\frac{7y^2}{5}=1$, which is the required equation of the ellipse.

31. Find the equation of the ellipse centre is at origin and the major axis, which passes through the points (–3, 1) and (2, –2). [NCERT Exemplar]

Ans. As origin is the center of ellipse, so $\frac{x^2}{a^2}+\frac{y^2}{b^2}=1$ be the equation of ellipse.

Since this ellipse passes through (–3, 1) and (2, – 2) so,

$$\frac{9}{a^2}+\frac{1}{b^2}=1 \text{ and } \frac{4}{a^2}+\frac{4}{b^2}=1$$

$$\Rightarrow \frac{9}{a^2}+\frac{1}{b^2}=1 \text{ and } \frac{1}{a^2}+\frac{1}{b^2}=\frac{1}{4}$$

$$\text{Which gave } \frac{8}{a^2}=\frac{3}{4} \Rightarrow a^2=\frac{32}{3}$$

$$\text{And } \frac{1}{b^2}=1-\frac{9}{a^2}=1-\frac{9}{\frac{32}{3}}=1-\frac{27}{32}=\frac{5}{32}$$

$$\Rightarrow b^2=\frac{32}{5}$$

Hence, equation of ellipse is

$$\frac{x^2}{\frac{32}{3}}+\frac{y^2}{\frac{32}{5}}=1 \Rightarrow 3x^2+5y^2=32..$$

32. Find the equation of the hyperbola whose conjugate axis is 6 and distance between the focii is 12.

Ans. Let the equation of the ellipse be

$$\frac{x^2}{a^2}-\frac{y^2}{b^2}=1 \quad ...(i) \quad [a > b]$$

Length of conjugate axis = 6

$\Rightarrow 2b = 6 \quad \Rightarrow b = 3$

And distance between the focii = 12

$\Rightarrow \quad 2c = 12$

$\Rightarrow \quad c = 6$

Since, $\quad c^2 = a^2 + b^2$

$\Rightarrow \quad a^2 = c^2 - b^2 = 36 - 9 = 27$

$\Rightarrow \quad a^2 = 27$

$$\therefore \quad \frac{x^2}{27}-\frac{y^2}{9} = 1$$

$\frac{x^2}{27}-\frac{y^2}{9}=1$, is the required equation of the Hyperbola.

33. If the eccentricity of an ellipse is 5/8 and the distance between its foci is 10, then find latus rectum of the ellipse. [NCERT Exemplar]

Ans. Let equation of the ellipse be $\frac{x^2}{a^2}+\frac{y^2}{b^2}=1(a>b)$

Given that, eccentricity, $e=\frac{5}{8}$

Now, the foci of this ellipse are $(\pm ae, 0)$

Distance between foci = 10 (Given)

$\therefore \quad 2ae = 10 \Rightarrow ae = 5$

$$\Rightarrow \frac{5}{8}a = 5 \Rightarrow a = 8$$

We know that, $b^2 = a^2(1 - e^2)$

$$\Rightarrow b^2 = 64\left(1-\frac{25}{64}\right) = 64 - 25 = 39$$

$\therefore$ Length of latus rectum of ellipse

$$= \frac{2b^2}{a}=2\times\frac{39}{8}=\frac{39}{4}.$$

11 Introduction to Three Dimensional Geometry

If you're a tech enthusiast, you've probably heard of the term 'Virtual Reality' (VR). As the name suggests, it creates non-physical materiality that is very similar to reality. 3D VR is created or produced digitally. 3D environments are created by using computer software and artificial intelligence with the help of three dimensional geometry to replicate the real world or to create entirely new environments. These environments, like a game, can be thoroughly explored by the user. Users have the ability to interact with the environment, avatars, and items.

Topic Notes

- *Coordinate Planes in 3-D Space.*

COORDINATE PLANES IN 3-D SPACE

TOPIC 1

COORDINATE AXES

In a straight line chapter we have discussed that in order to locate the position of a point in a plane, we need to fix mutually perpendicular lines in the plane and two real numbers, which are the distances of the point from these lines.

These lines are called coordinate axes and the two numbers are called coordinates of the point with respect to the axes. Similarly or 3 axes we require three real numbers which are the distances of the points from the two adjacent walls. These three numbers are called coordinates of the point. So a point in space has three coordinates.

3-Dimensional geometry involves the mathematics of shapes in 3D space and involves 3 coordinates in the *XYZ* plane which are *x*-coordinate, *y*-coordinate, and *z*-coordinate. The shapes that occupy space are called 3D shapes. 3D shapes can also be defined as solid shapes having three dimensions length, width, and height.

Coordinate of a Point in Space

Thus, for each point in space there exists an ordered 3-tuple of real numbers for its representation.

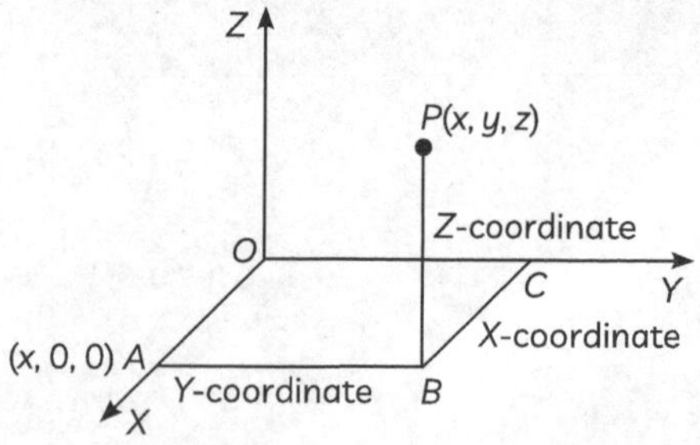

In the figure the co-ordinates of *P* are given by (*x*, *y*, *z*). The coordinates of the origin *O* is (0, 0, 0). Also the coordinates of the point *A* is given by (*x*, 0, 0) as *A* lies completely on the *x*-axis.

Coordinate Axis and Coordinate Plane in Space

The three coordinate axes determine the three coordinate planes illustrated in figure. The *xy*-plane is the plane that contains the *x*- and *y*-axes; the *yz*-plane contains the *y*- and *z*-axes; the *xz*-plane contains the *x* and *z*-axes. These three coordinate planes divide space into eight parts, called octants.

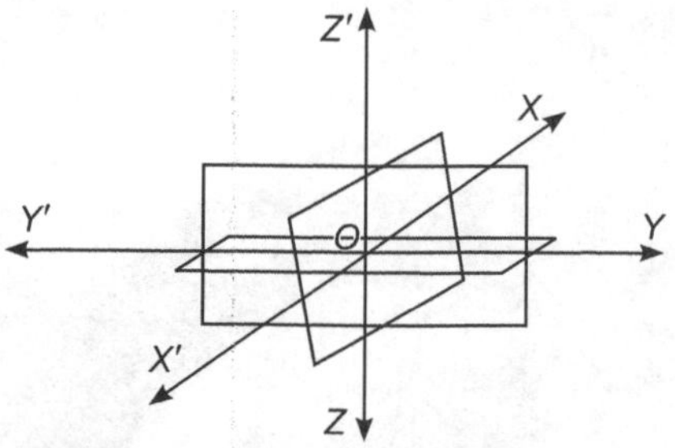

The following table shows the signs of coordinates of points in various octants:

Octants Coordinates	I	II	III	IV	V	VI	VII	VIII
x	+	–	–	+	[illegible]	–	–	+
y	+	+	–	–	[illegible]	+	–	–
z	+	+	+	+	[illegible]	–	–	–

TOPIC 2

DISTANCE FORMULA

If a point *P* lies in *xy*-plane, then by the definition of coordinates of a point, *z*-coordinate of *P* is zero. Therefore, the coordinates of a point on *xy*-plane are of the form (*x*, *y*, 0) and we may take the equation of *xy*-plane as $z = 0$. Similarly, the coordinates of any point in *yz* and *zx*-planes are of the forms (0, *y*, *z*) and (*x*, 0, *z*) respectively and their equations may be taken as $x = 0$ and $y = 0$ respectively.

If a point lies on the *x*-axis, then its *y* and *z*-coordinates are both zero. Therefore, the coordinates of a point on *x*-axis are of the form (*x*, 0, 0) and we may take the equation of *x*-axis as $y = 0$, $z = 0$. Similarly, the coordinates of a point on *y* and *z*-axes are of the form (0, *y*, 0) and (0, 0, *z*) respectively and their equations may be taken as $x = 0$, $z = 0$ and $x = 0$, $y = 0$ respectively.

We have the following working rule:

Step I: Using first two coordinates of the point, find quadrant number.

Step II: If third coordinates is positive, then octant number = quadrant number.

Step III: If third coordinate is negative, then octant number = quadrant number + 4.

Remarks:

1. The coordinates of a point lying on x-axis are of the form $(x, 0, 0)$.
2. The coordinates of a point lying on y-axis are of the form $(0, y, 0)$.
3. The coordinates of a point lying on z-axis are of the form $(0, 0, z)$
4. The coordinates of a point lying on yz-plane are of the form $(0, y, z)$.
5. The coordinates of a point lying on xz-plane are of the form $(x, 0, z)$.
6. The coordinates of a point lying on xy-plane are of the form $(x, y, 0)$.

The distance between the points $P(x_1, y_1, z_1)$ and $Q(x_2, y_2, z_2)$ is given by

$$PQ = \sqrt{(x_2 - x_1)^2 + (y_2 - y_1)^2 + (z_2 - z_1)^2}$$

Example 1: Name the octants in which the following points lie:

(A) (1, 2, 3) **(B) (–4, 2, 5)**
(C) (–3, –1, 6) **(D) (4, –2, 5)**
(E) (4, 2, –5) **(F) (–4, 2, –5)**
(G) (–2, –4, –7) **(H) (4, –2, –5)**

Ans. (A) I octant
(B) II octant
(C) III octant
(D) IV octant
(E) V octant
(F) VI octant
(G) VII octant
(H) VIII octant

Example 2. Find the coordinates of a point on Y-axis which is at a distance of $5\sqrt{2}$ from the point $P(3, -2, 5)$. **[NCERT]**

Ans. Let the point be $A(0, y, 0)$. Then,

$$AP = 5\sqrt{2}$$

$$\Rightarrow \sqrt{(0-3)^2 + (y+2)^2 + (0-5)^2} = 5\sqrt{2}$$

$$\Rightarrow 9 + (y + 2)^2 + 25 = 50$$

$$\Rightarrow (y + 2)^2 = 16$$

$$\Rightarrow y + 2 = \pm 4$$

$$\Rightarrow y = 2, -6$$

Hence, the coordinates of the required point are (0, 2, 0) and (0, – 6, 0).

Example 3. Find the distance between the points $P(2, 3, 5)$ and (4, 3, 1). **[NCERT]**

Ans. Given point are $P(2, 3, 5)$ and $Q(4, 3, 1)$.

Then, the distance between P and Q is given by

$$PQ = \sqrt{(4-2)^2 + (3-3)^2 + (1-5)^2}$$

$$= \sqrt{4+0+16}$$

$$= \sqrt{20} \text{ units.}$$

Example 4. Find the lengths of the medians of the triangle with vertices $A(0, 0, 6)$, $B(0, 4, 0)$ and $C(6, 0, 0)$. **[NCERT]**

Ans. Let D, E and F be the mid-points of sides, BC, CA and AB respectively.

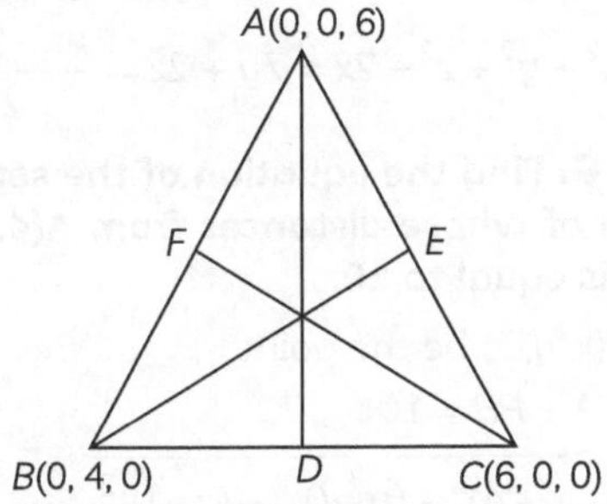

The coordinates of D, E and F are

$$D\left(\frac{0+6}{2}, \frac{4+0}{2}, \frac{0+0}{2}\right) = (3, 2, 0)$$

$$E\left(\frac{6+0}{2}, \frac{0+0}{2}, \frac{0+6}{2}\right) = (3, 0, 3)$$

And $$F\left(\frac{0+0}{2}, \frac{0+4}{2}, \frac{6+0}{2}\right) = (0, 2, 3)$$

$$\therefore \quad AD = \sqrt{(0-3)^2 + (0-2)^2 + (6-0)^2}$$

$$= \sqrt{9+4+36} = 7$$

$$BE = \sqrt{(0-3)^2 + (4-0)^2 + (0-3)^2}$$

$$= \sqrt{9+16+9} = \sqrt{34}$$

$$CF = \sqrt{(6-0)^2 + (0-2)^2 + (0-3)^2}$$

$$CF = \sqrt{36+4+9} = 7$$

Example 5: If A and B be the point (3, 4, 5) and (–1, 3, –7), respectively, find the equation of the set of points P such that $PA^2 + PB^2 = k^2$, where k is constant. **[NCERT]**

Ans. The coordinates of point A and B are given as (3, 4, 5) and (–1, 3, –7) respectively. Let the coordinates of point p be (x, y, z).

On using distance formula, we obtain

$$PA^2 = (x - 3)^2 + (y - 4)^2 + (z - 5)^2$$

$$= x^2 + 9 - 6x + y^2 + 16 - 8y + z^2 + 5^2 - 10z$$

$$= x^2 + y^2 + z^2 - 6x - 8y - 10z + 50$$

$$PB^2 = (x + 1)^2 + (y - 3)^2 + (z + 7)^2$$

$$= x^2 + 1 + 2x + y^2 + 9 - 6y + z^2 + 49 + 14z$$

$$= x^2 + y^2 + z^2 + 2x - 6y + 14z + 59$$

Now, if $PA^2 + PB^2 = K^2$, then

$$(x^2 + y^2 + z^2 - 6x - 8y - 10z + 50) + (x^2 + y^2 + z^2 + 2x - 6y + 14z + 59)$$

$$\Rightarrow\ 2x^2 + 2y^2 + 2z^2 - 4x - 14y + 4z + 109 = K^2$$

$$\Rightarrow\ 2(x^2 + y^2 + z^2 - 2x - 7y + 2z) + 109 = k^2$$

$$\Rightarrow\ 2(x^2 + y^2 + z^2 - 2x - 7y + 2z) = K^2 - 109$$

$$\Rightarrow\ x^2 + y^2 + z^2 - 2x - 7y + 2z = \frac{k^2 - 109}{2}$$

Thus, the required equation is

$$x^2 + y^2 + z^2 - 2x = 7y + 2z = \frac{k^2 - 109}{2}$$

Example 6: Find the equation of the set of points *P*, the sum of whose distances from *A*(4, 0, 0) and *B*(–4, 0, 0) is equal to 10. [NCERT]

Ans. Let $P(x, y, z)$ be the point

$$\therefore\ PA + PB = 10$$

$$\Rightarrow\ \sqrt{(x-4)^2 + (y-0)^2 + (z-0)^2} + \sqrt{(x+4)^2 + (y-0)^2 + (z-0)^2} = 10$$

$$\Rightarrow\ \sqrt{(x-4)^2 + y^2 + z^2} + \sqrt{(x+4)^2 + y^2 + z^2} = 10$$

$$\Rightarrow\ \sqrt{(x-4)^2 + y^2 + z^2} = 10 - \sqrt{(x+4)^2 + y^2 + z^2}$$

$$\Rightarrow\ (x-4)^2 + y^2 + z^2 = 100 - 20\sqrt{(x+4)^2 + y^2 + z^2} + (x+4)^2 + y^2 + z^2$$

$$\Rightarrow\ (x-4)^2 - (x+4)^2 - 100 = -20\sqrt{(x+4)^2 + y^2 + z^2}$$

$$\Rightarrow\ x^2 - 8x + 16 - x^2 - 8x - 16 - 100 = -20\sqrt{(x+4)^2 + y^2 + z^2}$$

$$\Rightarrow\ (4x + 25) = 5\sqrt{(x+4)^2 + y^2 + z^2}$$

$$\Rightarrow\ (4x + 25)^2 = 25(x + 4)^2 + 25y^2 + 25z^2$$

$$\Rightarrow\ 16x^2 + 200x + 625 = 25x^2 + 200x + 400 + 25y^2 + 25z^2$$

$$\Rightarrow\ 9x^2 + 25y^2 + 25z^2 = 225$$

Example 7: Verify the following

(A) (0, 7, –10), (1, 6, –6) and (4, 9, –6) are the vertices of an isosceles triangle.

(B) (0, 7, 10), (–1, 6, 6) and (–4, 9, 6) are the vertices of a right angled triangle. [NCERT]

Ans. (A) Let the given points be $A(0, 7, -10)$, $B(1, 6, -6)$ and $C(4, 9, -6)$.

$$AB = \sqrt{(0-1)^2 + (7-6)^2 + (-10+6)^2} = \sqrt{1+1+16} = \sqrt{18} = 3\sqrt{2}$$

$$BC = \sqrt{(1-4)^2 + (6-9)^2 + (-6+6)^2} = \sqrt{9+9+0} = \sqrt{18} = 3\sqrt{2}$$

$\therefore$ $AB = BC$, so ΔABC is isosceles.

(B) Let the given points be $A(0, 7, 10)$, $B(-1, 6, 6)$ and $C(-4, 9, 6)$.

$$AB = \sqrt{(0+1)^2 + (7-6)^2 + (10-6)^2} = \sqrt{1+1+16} = \sqrt{18}$$

$$BC = \sqrt{(-1+4)^2 + (6-9)^2 + (6-6)^2} = \sqrt{9+9+0} = \sqrt{18}$$

$$CA = \sqrt{(-4-0)^2 + (9-7)^2 + (6-10)^2} = \sqrt{16+4+16} = \sqrt{36}$$

Since $AB^2 + BC^2 = CA^2$ so, ΔABC is right-angled.

Example 8: If the vertices of a parallelogram *ABCD* are *A*(1, 2, 3), *B*(–1, –2, –1) and *C*(2, 3, 2), then find the fourth vertex *D*. [NCERT]

Ans. Let the fourth vertex of the parallelogram $ABCD$ is $D(x, y, z)$. Then, the mid-point of AC is P.

$$P\left(\frac{1+2}{2}, \frac{2+3}{2}, \frac{3+2}{2}\right) \text{ i.e., } P\left(\frac{3}{2}, \frac{5}{2}, \frac{5}{2}\right)$$

Mid-point of BD is also P (as diagonal bisect each other)

$$\frac{3}{2} = \frac{-1+x}{2} \Rightarrow x = 4$$

$$\frac{5}{2} = \frac{-2+y}{2} \Rightarrow y = 7$$

$$\frac{5}{2} = \frac{-1+z}{2} \Rightarrow z = 6$$

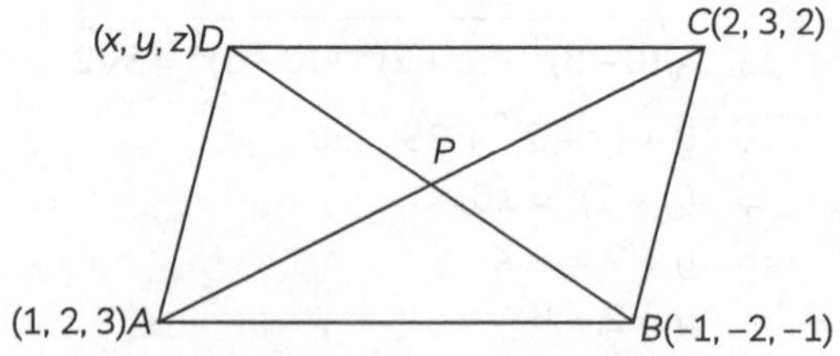

$\therefore$ The coordinates of fourth vertex is (4, 7, 6).

OBJECTIVE Type Questions

[1 mark]

Multiple Choice Questions

1. In the given figure, if P is (2, 4, 5), find the coordinates of F.

(a) (2, 4, 5) **(b) (4, 0, 5)**

(c) (2, 0, 5) **(d) (4, 2, 5)**

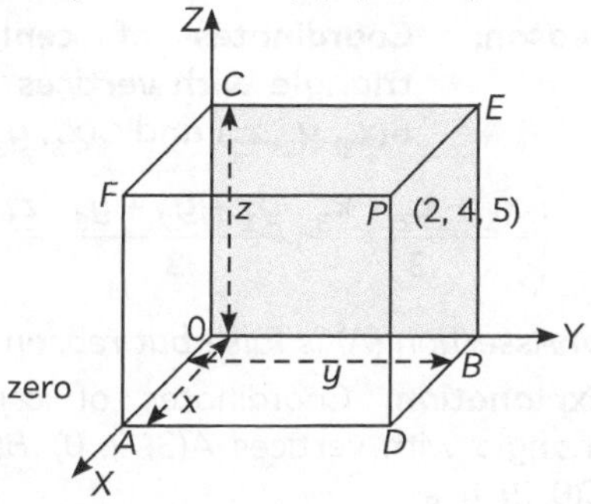

Ans. *(c) (2, 0, 5)*

Explanation: For the point F, the distance measured along OY is zero. Therefore, the coordinates of F are (2, 0, 5).

2. The octants in which the points (–3.5, 1.5, 2.5) and (–3.2, 1.2, –2.2) lie are respectively:

(a) Second, fourth **(b) Sixth, second**

(c) Fifth, sixth **(d) Second, sixth**

Ans. *(d) Second, sixth*

Explanation: The point (–3.5, 1.5, 2.5) lies in second octant $(-x, y, z)$ and the point (–3.2, 1.2, –2.2) lies in sixth octant $(-x, y, -z)$.

3. Let L, M, N be the feet of the perpendiculars drawn from a point P(7.2, 9.3, 3.4) on the x, y and z-axes respectively. Find the coordinates of L, M and N respectively.

(a) (7.2, 0, 0), (0, 9.3, 0), (0, 0, 3.4)

(b) (7, 0, 0), (0, 0, 9), (0, 4, 0)

(c) (0, 7, 0), (0, 0, 9), (4, 0, 0)

(d) (0, 0, 7), (0, 9, 0), (4, 0, 0)

Ans. *(a) (7.2, 0, 0), (0, 9.3, 0), (0, 0, 3.4)*

Explanation: Since L is the foot of perpendicular from P on the x-axis, so its y and z-coordinates are zero. So, the coordinates of L is (7.2, 0, 0). Similarly, the coordinates of M and N are (0, 9.3, 0) and (0, 0, 3.4), respectively.

4. The point A(–4, –3, –2) is present in:

(a) V-octant **(b) VI-octant**

(c) VII-octant **(d) VIII-octant**

[DIKSHA]

Ans. *(c) VII-octant*

Explanation: Octant of (–4, –3, –2)

1st oct $\rightarrow (+++)$

2nd oct $\rightarrow (-++)$

3rd oct $\rightarrow (--+)$

4th oct $\rightarrow (+-+)$

5th oct $\rightarrow (++-)$

6th oct $\rightarrow (-+-)$

7th oct $\rightarrow (---)$

8th oct $\rightarrow (+--)$

Therefore, (–4, –3, –2) lies in 7th octant.

5. What is the perpendicular distance of the point P(5, 6, 7) from xy-plane?

(a) 8 units **(b) 7 units**

(c) 6 units **(d) 5 units**

Ans. *(b) 7 units*

Explanation: Let L be the foot of perpendicular drawn from the point P(5, 6, 7) on the xy-plare, i.e. $z = o$

Then coordinates of $L \equiv (5, 6, 0)$

$\therefore$ Required distance PL

$$= \sqrt{(5-5)^2+(6-6)^2+(7-0)^2} = 7 \text{ units.}$$

6. Let A, B, C be the feet of the perpendicular segments drawn from a point P(1, 2, 5) on the xy, yz and zx-planes, respectively. The distance of the points A, B, C from the point P (in units) respectively are:

(a) 5, 2, 4 **(b) 3, 4, 5**

(c) 5, 1, 4 **(d) 3, 5, 4**

Ans. *(c) 5, 1, 4*

Explanation: We have, coordinates of A = (1, 2, 0), coordinates of B = (0, 2, 5), coordinates of C = (1, 0, 5)

Now, P = (1, 2, 5)

$$\therefore \quad PA = \sqrt{(1-1)^2+(2-2)^2+(5-0)^2} = 5 \text{ units}$$

$$PB = \sqrt{(1-0)^2+(2-2)^2+(5-5)^2} = 1 \text{ units}$$

$$PC = \sqrt{(1-1)^2+(2-0)^2+(5-5)^2} = 4 \text{ units}$$

7. The distance between (3, 2, –1) and (–1, –1, –1) is:

(a) 5 **(b) 6**

(c) 7 **(d) 8** **[DIKSHA]**

Ans. *(a) 5*

Explanation: The distance between the points $P(x_1, y_1, z_1)$ and $Q(x_2, y_2, z_2)$ is given by

$$PQ = \sqrt{(x_2-x_1)^2+(y_2-y_1)^2+(z_2-z_1)^2}$$

Two points are (3, 2, –1) and (–1, –1, –1), then

$$d = \sqrt{(3+1)^2 + (2+1)^2 + (-1+1)^2}$$

$$= \sqrt{16+9+0} = \sqrt{25}$$

$$= 5 \text{ units}$$

Hence, option (a) is the correct answer..

8. Find the distance between the points *P*(0, 3, 4) and *Q*(4, 1, 0).

(a) 5 units (b) 4 units

(c) 6 units (d) 2 units

Ans. *(c) 6 units*

Explanation: The distance between the points *P*(0, 3, 4) and *Q*(4, 1, 0) is

$$PQ = \sqrt{(4-0)^2 + (1-3)^2 + (0-4)^2}$$

$$= \sqrt{16+4+16} = \sqrt{36} = 6 \text{ units}$$

9. The space is divided into .... part by placing three axes perpendicular to each others.

(a) 3 (b) 4

(c) 6 (d) 8 [DIKSHA]

Ans. *(d) 8*

Assertion-Reason (A-R)

DIRECTION: In the following questions, a statement of assertion (A) is followed by a statement of the reason (R). Mark the correct choice as:

(a) Both assertion (A) and reason (R) are true and reason (R) is the correct explanation of assertion (A).

(b) Both assertion (A) and reason (R) are true but reason (R) is not the correct explanation of assertion (A).

(c) Assertion (A) is true but reason (R) is false.

(d) Assertion (A) is false but reason (R) is true.

10. Assertion: The points *A*(1, –1, 3), *B*(2, –4, 5) and *C*(5, –13, 11) are collinear.

Reason: If *AB* + *BC* = *AC*, then *A*, *B*, *C* are collinear.

Ans. *(a) Both assertion (A) and reason (R) are true and reason (R) is the correct explanation of assertion (A).*

Explanation: $|AB| = \sqrt{(1)^2 + (-3)^2 + (2)^2}$

$$= \sqrt{1+9+4} = \sqrt{14}$$

$$|BC| = \sqrt{(3)^2 + (-9)^2 + (6)^2}$$

$$= \sqrt{9+81+36} = 3\sqrt{14}$$

$$|AC| = \sqrt{(4)^2 + (-12)^2 + (8)^2}$$

$$\sqrt{16+144+64} = 4\sqrt{14}$$

$\because$ $AB + BC = 4\sqrt{14} = AC$

$\therefore$ Points *A*, *B* and *C* are collinear.

11. Assertion: Coordinates of centroid of a triangle formed by the vertices *A*(3, 2, 0), *B*(5, 3, 2) and *C*(0, 2, 4) is $\left(\frac{8}{3}, \frac{8}{3}, \frac{8}{3}\right)$.

Reason: Coordinates of centroid of a triangle with vertices $A(x_1, y_1, z_1)$, $B(x_2, y_2, z_2)$ and $C(x_3, y_3, z_3)$ is

$$\left(\frac{x_1+x_2+x_3}{3}, \frac{y_1+y_2+y_3}{3}, \frac{z_1+z_2+z_3}{3}\right)$$

Ans. *(d) Assertion (A) is false but reason (R) is true.*

Explanation: Coordinates of centroid of a triangle with vertices *A*(3, 2, 0), *B*(5, 3, 2) and *C*(0, 2, 4) is

$$\left(\frac{3+5+0}{3}, \frac{2+3+2}{3}, \frac{0+2+4}{3}\right) = \left(\frac{8}{3}, \frac{7}{3}, 2\right).$$

Hence, option(d) is the correct option.

12. Assertion: The foot of perpendicular drawn from the point *A*(1, 2, 8) on the *xy*-plane is (1, 2, 0).

Reason: Equation of *xy*-plane is *y* = 0.

Ans. *(c) Assertion (A) is true but reason (R) is false.*

Explanation: We know that in *xy*-plane, *z*-co-ordinte is 0. So, coordinate of foot of perpendicular drawn from point *A*(1, 2, 8) on *xy*-plane is (1, 2, 0).

Equation of *xy*-plane is *z* = 0

$\therefore$ Reason is wrong.

Hence, option(c) is the correct option.

13. Assertion: The distance between the points $(1+\sqrt{11}, 0, 0)$ and (1, –2, 3) is $2\sqrt{6}$ units.

Reason: Distance between any two points $A(x_1, y_1, z_1)$ and $B(x_2, y_2, z_2)$ is,

$$|AB| = \sqrt{(x_2+x_1)^2 + (y_2+y_1)^2 + (z_2+z_1)^2}$$

Ans. *(c) Assertion (A) is true but reason (R) is false.*

Explanation: Let $A \equiv (1+\sqrt{11}, 0, 0)$ and $B \equiv$ (1, –2, 3)

$$\therefore \ AB = \sqrt{(1-1-\sqrt{11})^2 + (-2-0)^2 + (3-0)^2}$$

$$= \sqrt{11+4+9} = \sqrt{24} = 2\sqrt{6} \text{ units}$$

Hence, option(c) is the correct option.

14. Assertion: The points $A(3, -1, 2)$, $B(1, 2, -4)$, $C(-1, 1, 2)$ and $D(1, -2, 8)$ are the vertices of a parallelogram.

Reason: Coordinates of mid-point of a line joining the points $A(x_1, y_1, z_1)$ and $B(x_2, y_2, z_2)$ is:

$$\left(\frac{x_1+x_2}{2}, \frac{y_1+y_2}{2}, \frac{z_1+z_2}{2}\right).$$

Ans. (a) *Both assertion (A) and reason (R) are true and reason (R) is the correct explanation of assertion (A).*

Explanation: Mid-point of

$$AC = \left(\frac{3-1}{2}, \frac{-1+1}{2}, \frac{2+2}{2}\right)$$

$$= (1, 0, 2)$$

$$\text{Mid-point of } BD = \left(\frac{1+1}{2}, \frac{2-2}{2}, \frac{-4+8}{2}\right) = (1, 0, 2)$$

$\because$ Mid-points of AC and BD coincides.

$\therefore$ $ABCD$ is a parallelogram.

CASE BASED Questions (CBQs)

[**4** & **5** marks]

Read the following passages and answer the questions that follow:

15. *Pankaj and his father were walking in a large park. They saw a kite flying in the sky. The position of Kite, Pankaj and Pankaj's father are at (20, 30, 10), (4, 3, 7) and (5, 3, 7) respectively.*

(A) The distance between Pankaj and Kite is:

(a) 41.32 units **(b) 31.52 units**

(c) 38.32 units **(d) 40.39 units**

(B) The distance between Pankaj's father and kite is:

(a) 31.30 units **(b) 38.43 units**

(c) 31.03 units **(d) 29.00 units**

(C) The co-ordinates of Pankaj lie in:

(a) IV quadrant **(b) III quadrant**

(c) II quadrant **(d) I quadrant**

(D) If co-ordinate of Kite, Pankaj and Pankaj's father form a triangle, then find the centroid of it.

(a) (9.67, 12, 8) **(b) (9.6, 8, 12)**

(c) (12, 8, 10) **(d) (7, 9, 7.2)**

(E) The co-ordinates of points in the *XY*-plane are of the form:

(a) $(0, 0, z)$ **(b) $(x, y, 0)$**

(c) $(x, 0, y)$ **(d) $(0, x, y)$**

Ans. (A) *(b) 31.52 units*

Explanation: Required distance

$$= \sqrt{(20-4)^2+(30-3)^2+(10-7)^2}$$

$$= \sqrt{16^2+27^2+3^2}$$

$$= \sqrt{256+729+9}$$

$$= \sqrt{994}$$

$$= 31.52 \text{ units}$$

(B) *(c) 31.03 units*

Explanation: Required distance

$$= \sqrt{(20-5)^2+(30-3)^2+(10-7)^2}$$

$$= \sqrt{15^2+27^2+3^2}$$

$$= \sqrt{255+729+9}$$

$$= \sqrt{963}$$

$$= 31.03 \text{ units}$$

(C) *(d) I quadrant*

Explanation: Because in (4, 3, 7); all are positive.

Thus, the coordinate lies in the I quadrant.

(D) *(a) (9.67, 12, 8)*

Explanation: Centroid

$$= \left(\frac{20+4+5}{3}, \frac{30+3+3}{3}, \frac{10+7+7}{3}\right)$$

$$= (9.67, 12, 8)$$

(E) *(b) (x, y, 0)*

Explanation: For *XY*-plane, $z = 0$

$\Rightarrow$ The co-ordinates are of the form $(x, y, 0)$.

16. *Vikas and his friends went for camping for 2 and 3 days. There they set up a tent which is triangular in shape. The vertices of the tent are A(4, 5, 9), B(3, 2, 5), C(5, 2, 5), D(–3, 2, –5) and E(–4, 5, –9) respectively.*

The vertex A is tied up by the rope at the ends F and G and the vertex E is tied up at the ends I and H.

(A) If *M* denotes the position of their bags inside the tent and it is just in middle of the vertices B and D, then find the coordinates of *M* and the length *AE*.

(B) If the length of the rope by which *E* is tied up with *H* is $5\sqrt{2}$ units, then find the equation denotes the set of point of *H* and the length *BC*.

Ans. (A) As, *M* is the middle point of *B*(3, 2, 5) and *D*(–3, 2, –5)

$\therefore$ The coordinates of *M* are

$$\left(\frac{3-3}{2}, \frac{2+2}{2}, \frac{5-5}{2}\right) = (0, 2, 0)$$

The length *AE* is

$$= \sqrt{(-4-4)^2 + (5-5)^2 + (-9-9)^2}$$

$$= \sqrt{64+0+324}$$

$$= \sqrt{388}$$

$$= 2\sqrt{97} \text{ units}$$

(B) As, the distance of *H*(*x*, *y*, *z*) from *E*(–4, 5, –9) is $5\sqrt{2}$ units.

$\therefore$ $EH = 5\sqrt{2}$

$\Rightarrow$ $\sqrt{(x+4)^2 + (y-5)^2 + (z+9)^2} = 5\sqrt{2}$

Squaring both sides, we get

$(x + 4)^2 + (y - 5)^2 + (z + 9)^2 = 25 \times 2$

$x^2 + y^2 + z^2 + 8x - 10y + 18z + 122 = 50$

$\Rightarrow$ $x^2 + y^2 + z^2 + 8x - 10y + 18z + 72 = 0$

The length

$$BC = \sqrt{(5-3)^2 + (2-2)^2 + (5-5)^2}$$

$$= \sqrt{4+0+0}$$

= 4 units

VERY SHORT ANSWER Type Questions (VSA)

[1 mark]

17. Find the length of the perpendicular drawn from the point *P*(2, 3, 4) on *y*-axis.

Ans. Given point is *P*(2, 3, 4).

Let *Q* be the foot of perpendicular drawn from the point *P*(2, 3, 4) on *y*-axis.

Then the coordinates of *Q* are (0, 3, 0)

Hence, the length of the perpendicular is given by

$$PQ = \sqrt{(0-2)^2 + (3-3)^2 + (0-4)^2}$$

$$= \sqrt{4+0+16} = \sqrt{20} \text{ units.}$$

18. Using distance formula, check wether the points *A*(0, 3, 5), *B*(1, 0, 3) and *C*(7, 0, 1) are collinear or not.

Ans. Given points are *A*(0, 3, 5), *B*(1, 0, 3) and *C*(7, 0, 1).

Then, $AB = \sqrt{(1-0)^2 + (0-3)^2 + (3-5)^2}$

$$= \sqrt{1+9+4} = \sqrt{14}$$

$$BC = \sqrt{(7-1)^2 + (0-0)^2 + (1-3)^2}$$

$$= \sqrt{36+0+4} = \sqrt{40} = 2\sqrt{10}$$

$$AC = \sqrt{(7-0)^2 + (0-3)^2 + (1-5)^2}$$

$$= \sqrt{49+9+16} = \sqrt{74}.$$

Since, *AB* + *BC* is not equal to *AC*.

Hence, the points *A*, *B* and *C* are not collinear.

19. If the origin is the centroid of a ΔABC having vertices *A*(*a*, 1, 3), *B*(–2, *b*, –5) and *C*(4, 7, *c*), then find values of *a*, *b*, *c*. [NCERT Exemplar]

Ans. Given that origin is the centroid of the ΔABC i.e., *G*(0, 0, 0).

$\because$ $0 = \dfrac{a-2+4}{3}$

$\Rightarrow$ $a = -2$

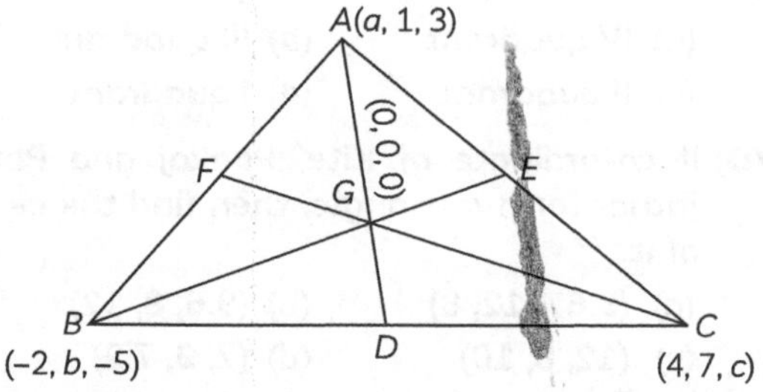

$0 = \dfrac{1+b+7}{3} \Rightarrow b = -8$

$0 = \dfrac{3-5+c}{3} \Rightarrow c = 2$

$\therefore$ $a = -2$, $b = -8$ and $c = 2$

20. Show that, if $x^2 + y^2 = 1$, then the point $(x, y, \sqrt{1-x^2-y^2})$ is at a distance of 1 unit from the origin. [NCERT Exemplar]

Ans. Given that, $x^2 + y^2 = 1$

The distance between the points $P(x_1, y_1, z_1)$ and $Q(x_2, y_2, z_2)$ is given by

$$PQ=\sqrt{(x_2-x_1)^2+(y_2-y_1)^2+(z_2-z_1)^2}$$

$\therefore$ Distance of the point $(x, y, \sqrt{1-x^2-y^2})$ from origin is given as

$$PQ=\sqrt{(x-0)^2+(y-0)^2+(\sqrt{1-x^2-y^2}-0)^2}$$

$$=\sqrt{x^2+y^2+1-x^2-y^2}$$

$$=1$$

Hence, proved.

SHORT ANSWER Type-I Questions (SA-I)

[2 marks]

21. Find the point on *x*-axis which is equidistant from the points *A*(0, 3, 2) and *B*(5, 0, 4).

Ans. Let *P*(*x*, 0, 0) be the point on *x*-axis which is equidistant from the point *A*(0, 3, 2) and *B*(5, 0, 4).

$\therefore$ $AP = BP$

$\Rightarrow$ $\sqrt{(x-0)^3+(0-3)^2+(0-2)^2}$

$= \sqrt{(x-5)^2+(0-0)^2+(0-4)^2}$

On squaring both sides, we get

$(x-0)^2+9+4=(x-5)^2+0+16$

$\Rightarrow$ $x^2+13=x^2+25-10x+16$

$\Rightarrow$ $10x=28$

$\Rightarrow$ $x=\frac{14}{5}$

Hence, the required point is $\left(\frac{14}{5}, 0, 0\right)$.

22. Find the equation of the set of the points *P* such that its distances from the points *A*(2, 0, –5) and *B*(0, 1, 4) are equal.

Ans. Given points are *A*(2, 0, –5) and *B*(0, 1, 4).

Let *P*(*x*, *y*, *z*) be any point such that its distance from the points *A* and *B* are equal.

$\therefore$ $AP = BP$

$\Rightarrow$ $\sqrt{(x-3)+(y-0)^2+(z+5)^2}$

$=\sqrt{(x+0)^2+(y-1)^2+(z-4)^2}$

On squaring both sides, we get

$(x-3)^2+(y)^2+(z+5)^2=(x)^2+(y-1)^2+(z-4)^2$

$\Rightarrow$ $-6x+2y+18z+17=0$

Which is the required equation.

23. Show that the point *A*(1, –1, 3), *B*(2, –4, 5) and *C*(5, –13, 11) are collinear. [NCERT Exemplar]

Ans. $AB=\sqrt{(1-2)^2+(-1+4)^2+(3-5)^2}$

$=\sqrt{1+9+4}=\sqrt{14}$

$BC=\sqrt{(2-5)^2+(-4+13)^2+(5-11)^2}$

$=\sqrt{9+18+36}=\sqrt{126}$

$AC=\sqrt{(1-5)^2+(-1+13)^2+(3-11)^2}$

$=\sqrt{16+144+64}=\sqrt{224}$

If *AB* + *BC* = *AC*, the *A*, *B*, *C* are collinear.

$\Rightarrow$ $\sqrt{14}+\sqrt{126}=\sqrt{224}$

$\Rightarrow$ $\sqrt{14}+3\sqrt{14}=4\sqrt{14}$

So, the points *A*, *B* and *C* are collinear.

24. If *A*, *B*, *C* be the feet of perpendicular from a point *P* on the *X*, *Y* and *Z*-axes respectively, then find the coordinates of *A*, *B* and *C* in each of the following where the point *P* is

(A) *A*(3, 4, 2) (B) B(–5, 3, 7)

(C) *C*(4, –3, –5) [NCERT Exemplar]

Ans. The coordinates of *A*, *B* and *C* are the following

(A) *A*(3, 0, 0), *B*(0, 4, 0), *C*(0, 0, 2)

(B) *A*(–5, 0, 0), *B*(0, 3, 0), *C*(0, 0, 7)

(C) *A*(4, 0, 0), *B*(0, –3, 0), *C*(0, 0, –5)

SHORT ANSWER Type-II Questions (SA-II)

[3 marks]

25. If the distance between the points (*a*, 0, 2) and (1, 1, 0) is $\sqrt{14}$, then find the value of *a*.

Ans. Let the given points be *A*(*a*, 0, 2) and *B*(1, 1, 0).

Given that the distance between *A* and *B* is 5.

$\therefore$ $AB = 5$

$\Rightarrow \quad \sqrt{(1-a)^2+(1-0)^2+(0-2)^2} = \sqrt{14}$

$\Rightarrow \quad (1-a)^2 + 1 + 4 = 14$

$\Rightarrow \quad 1 + a^2 - 2a + 5 = 14$

$\Rightarrow \quad a^2 - 2a - 8 = 0$

$\Rightarrow \quad (a+4)(a-2) = 0$

$\Rightarrow \quad a = -4, 2.$

26. If the origin is the centroid of ΔPQR with vertices $P(a, 0, 6)$, $Q(4, b, -1)$and $R(2, 4, c)$, then find the values of a, b and c.

Ans. Given vertices of ΔPQR are $P(a, 0, 6)$, $Q(4, b, -1)$ and $R(2, 4, c)$.

Then, the coordinates of the centroid of ΔPQR are given by

$$\left(\frac{a+4+2}{3}, \frac{0+b+4}{3}, \frac{6-1+c}{3}\right)$$

i.e., $\left(\frac{a+6}{3}, \frac{b+4}{3}, \frac{c+5}{3}\right)$

Given that the centroid of ΔPQR is the point (0, 0, 0).

$\therefore \quad \frac{a+6}{3} = 0$

$\Rightarrow \quad a = -6$

$\frac{b+4}{3} = 0$

$\Rightarrow \quad b = -4$

$\frac{c+5}{3} = 0$

$\Rightarrow \quad c = -5$

Hence, $a = -6$, $b = -4$ and $c = -5$.

27. If A, B and C be the feet of perpendicular from a point P on the XY, YZ and ZX-planes respectively, then find the coordinates of A, B and C in each of the following where the point P is

(A) (3, 4, 5) (B) (–5, 3, 7)

(C) (4, –3, –5) [NCERT Exemplar]

Ans. On XY-plane $Z = 0$, on YZ-plane, $x = 0$ and on ZX-plane, $y = 0$, coordinate of A, B and C are

(A) $A(3, 4, 0)$, $B(0, 4, 5)$, $C(3, 0, 5)$

(B) $A(-5, 3, 0)$, $B(0, 3, 7)$, $C(-5, 0, 7)$

(C) $A(4, -3, 0)$, $B(0, -3, -5)$, $C(4, 0, -5)$

28. Find the point P on z-axis such that $PA = PB$ where $A(1, 5, 7)$, $B(5, 1, -4)$. [DIKSHA]

Ans. Given that :-

$A = (1, 5, 7) \quad B = (5, 1, -4)$

To find:

A point at z-axis, equidistant from A and B.

Consider the point be P having co-ordinates , as it is on z-axis.

By the Question, $\underline{PA} = \underline{PB}$ on, $(PA)^2 = (PB)^2$

$\Rightarrow \quad (1-0)^2 + (5-0)^2 + (7-a)^2 = (5-0)^2 + (1-0)^2 + (-4-a)^2$

$\Rightarrow \quad 1 + 25 + 49 + a^2 - 14a = 25 + 1 + 16 + a^2 + 8a$

$\Rightarrow \quad 14a + 8a = 49 - 16$

$\Rightarrow \quad 22a = 33$

$\Rightarrow \quad a = 3/2$

Therefore, point 'p' is (0, 0, 3/2)

LONG ANSWER Type Questions (LA)

[**4** & **5** marks]

29. Find the centroid of a triangle, the mid-point of whose sides are $D(1, 2, -3)$, $E(3, 0, 1)$ and $F(-1, 1, -4)$.

Ans. Given that, mid-point of sides are $D(1, 2, -3)$ and $F(-1, 1, -4)$.

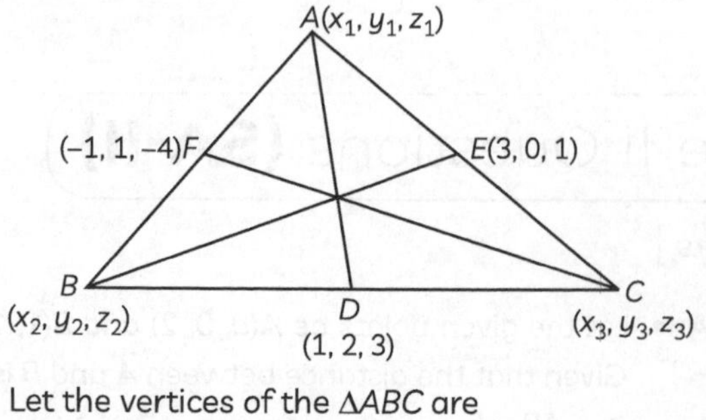

Let the vertices of the ΔABC are

$A(x_1, y_1, z_1)$, $B(x_2, y_2, z_2)$ and $C(x_3, y_3, z_3)$

Then, mid-point of BC are (1, 2, –3).

$\therefore \quad 1 = \frac{x_2+x_3}{2}$

$\Rightarrow \quad x_2 + x_3 = 2 \quad$ ...(i)

$2 = \frac{y_2+y_3}{2}$

$\Rightarrow \quad y_2 + y_3 = 4 \quad$ ...(ii)

$-3 = \frac{z_2+z_3}{2}$

$\Rightarrow \quad z_2 + z_3 = -6 \quad$ ...(iii)

Now the mid-points of AC & AB

$\Rightarrow \quad -1 = \dfrac{x_1 + x_2}{2}$

$\Rightarrow \quad x_1 + x_2 = -2$ ...(iv)

$\Rightarrow \quad 1 = \dfrac{y_1 + y_2}{2}$

$\Rightarrow \quad y_1 + y_2 = 2$ ...(v)

$\Rightarrow \quad -4 = \dfrac{z_1 + z_2}{2}$

$\Rightarrow \quad z_1 + z_2 = -8$ ...(vi)

$\Rightarrow \quad 3 = \dfrac{x_1 + x_3}{2}$

$\Rightarrow \quad x_1 + x_3 = 6$ ...(vii)

$\Rightarrow \quad 0 = \dfrac{y_1 + y_3}{2}$

$\Rightarrow \quad y_1 + y_3 = 0$ ...(viii)

$\Rightarrow \quad 1 = \dfrac{z_1 + z_3}{2}$

$\Rightarrow \quad z_1 + z_3 = 2$ ...(ix)

On adding eqn.(i) and (iv), we get

$x_1 + 2x_2 + x_3 = 0$ ...(x)

On adding Eqs. (ii) and (v), we get

$y_1 + 2y_2 + y_3 = 6$ ...(xi)

On adding eqn. (iii) and (vi), we get

$z_1 + 2z_2 + z_3 = -14$ ...(xii)

From eqn. (vii) and (x),

$2x_2 = -6 \Rightarrow x_2 = -3$

If $x_2 = -3$, then $x_3 = 5$

If $x_3 = 5$, then $x_1 = 1, x_2 = -3, x_3 = 5$

From eqn. (xi) and (viii)

$2y_2 = 6 \Rightarrow y_2 = 3$

If $y_2 = 3$, then $y_1 = -1$ if y_1

$= -1$, then $y_3 = 1, y_2 = 3, y_3 = 1$

From eqn. (xii) and (ix)

$2z_2 = -16 \Rightarrow z_2 = -8$

$z_2 = -8$, then $z_1 = 2$

$z_1 = 0$, then $z_3 = 0$

$z_1 = 0, z_2 = -8, z_3 = 2$

So, the points are $A(1, -1, 0)$, $B(-3, 3, -8)$ and $C(5, 1, 2)$.

$\therefore$ Centroid of the triangle

$$= G\left(\frac{1-3+5}{3}, \frac{-1+3+1}{3}, \frac{0-8+2}{3}\right)$$

i.e., $G(1, 1, -2)$.

30. If a parallelepiped is formed by planes drawn through the points (5, 8, 10) and (3, 6, 8) parallel to the coordinate planes, then find the length of edges and diagonal of the parallelepiped by using distance formula.

Ans. Let $P = (3, 6, 8)$ and $Q = (5, 8, 10)$

PE = Distance between parallel lines $ABCP$ and $FQDE$

= |10 – 8| [$\because$ These planes are perpendicular to Z-axis]

= 2 units.

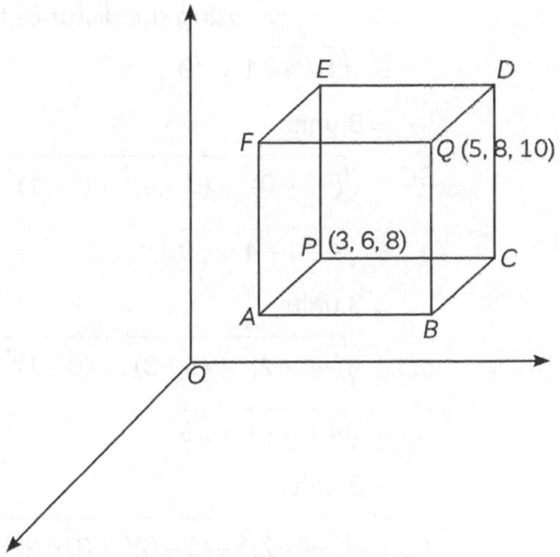

PE = Distance between parallel planes $ABQF$ and $PCDE$

= |5–3| [$\because$ these planes are perpendicular to X-axis]

= 2 units

PC Distance between parallel planes APEF and BCDQ

= |8 – 6| [$\because$ these planes are perpendicular to Y-Axis]

= 2 units

$\therefore$ Length of diagonal = Distance between P and Q.

$= \sqrt{(5-3)^2 + (8-6)^2 + (10\ 8)^2}$

[$\because$ using the distance formula]

$= \sqrt{2^2 + 2^2 + 2^2}$

$= \sqrt{4+4+4}$

$= \sqrt{12}$

$= 2\sqrt{3}$ units

Hence, the length of each edge of parallelepiped is 2 units and the length of its diagonal is $2\sqrt{3}$ units.

31. Show that the points (–2, 6, –2), (0, 4, –1), (–2, 3, 1) and (–4, 5, 0) are the vertices of a square.

Ans. Let $A(-2, 6, -2)$, $B(0, 4, -1)$, $C(-2, 3, 1)$ and $D(-4, 5, 0)$ be the given points.

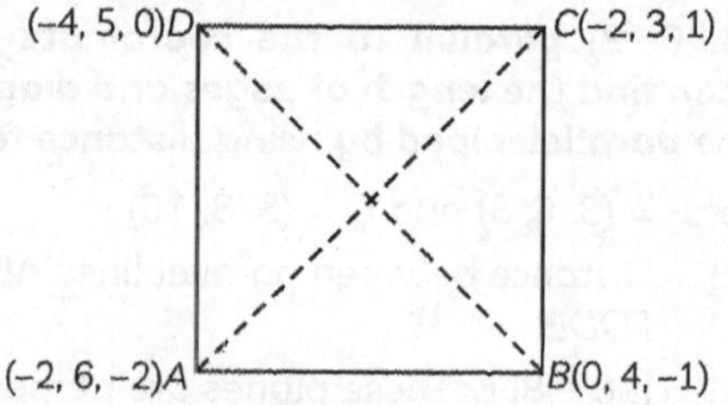

$\therefore \quad AB = \sqrt{(0+2)^2+(4-6)^2+(-1+2)^2}$

[∵ using the distance formulas]

$= \sqrt{4+4+1} = \sqrt{9}$

= 3 units

$BC = \sqrt{(-2-0)^2+(3-4)^2+(1+1)^2}$

$= \sqrt{4+1+4} = \sqrt{9}$

= 3 units

$CD = \sqrt{(-4+2)^2+(5-3)^2+(0-1)^2}$

$= \sqrt{4+4+1} = \sqrt{9}$

= 3 units

$AD = \sqrt{(-4+2)^2+(5-6)^2+(0+2)^2}$

$= \sqrt{4+1+4} = \sqrt{9}$

= 3 units.

Here, $AB = BC = CD = DA$.

So, $ABCD$ is a square or a rhombus.

Now, $AC = \sqrt{(-2+2)^2+(3-6)^2+(1+2)^2}$

$= \sqrt{0+9+9}$]

$= \sqrt{18}$ units

and $BD = \sqrt{(-4,-0)^2+(5-4)^2+(0+1)^2}$

$= \sqrt{16+1+1}$

$= \sqrt{18}$ units

Since, diagonal AC = diagonal BD

Hence, $ABCD$ is a square.

32. Show that the triangle ABC with vertices $A(0, 4, 1)$, $B(2, 3, -1)$ and $C(4, 5, 0)$ is right angled.

Ans. Points are $A(0, 4, 1)$, $B(2, 3, -1)$ and $C(4, 5, 0)$

$x_1 = 0 x_2 = 2 \qquad x_3 = 4$

$y_1 = 4 y_2 = 3 \qquad y_3 = 5$

$z_1 = 1 y_3 = -1 \qquad z_3 = 0$

If $P(x_1, y_1, z_1)$ and $Q(x_2, y_2, z_2)$ are the two points then the distance between these points can be given by the distance formula.

$PQ = \sqrt{(x_1-x_2)^2+(y_1-y_2)^2+(z_1-z_2)^2}$

$\Rightarrow \quad AB = \sqrt{(0-2)^2+(4-3)^2+(1-(-1))^2}$

$= \sqrt{(-2)^2+(1)^2+(2)^2}$

$= \sqrt{4+1+4}$

$= \sqrt{9}$

$\Rightarrow \quad BC = \sqrt{(2-4)^2+(3-5)^2+(-1-0)^2}$

$BC = \sqrt{(-2)^2+(-2)^2+(-1)^2}$

$BC = \sqrt{9}$

$BC = 3$

$\Rightarrow \quad AC = \sqrt{(0-4)^2+(4-5)^2+(1-0)^2}$

$= \sqrt{(-4)^2+(-1)^2+(1)^2}$

$= \sqrt{16+1+1}$

$= \sqrt{18}$

$= 3\sqrt{2}$

In a right angle triangle, sum of the square of two sides is equal to the square of the largest side.

$\Rightarrow \quad (AB)^2 + (BC)^2 = (AC)^2$

$\Rightarrow \quad (3)^2 + (3)^2 = (3\sqrt{2})^2$

$\Rightarrow \quad 9 + 9 = 18$

$\Rightarrow \quad 18 = 18$

Since, $(AB)^2 + (BC)^2 = (AC)^2$

Hence, ΔABC is right angled triangle.

12 Limits and Derivatives

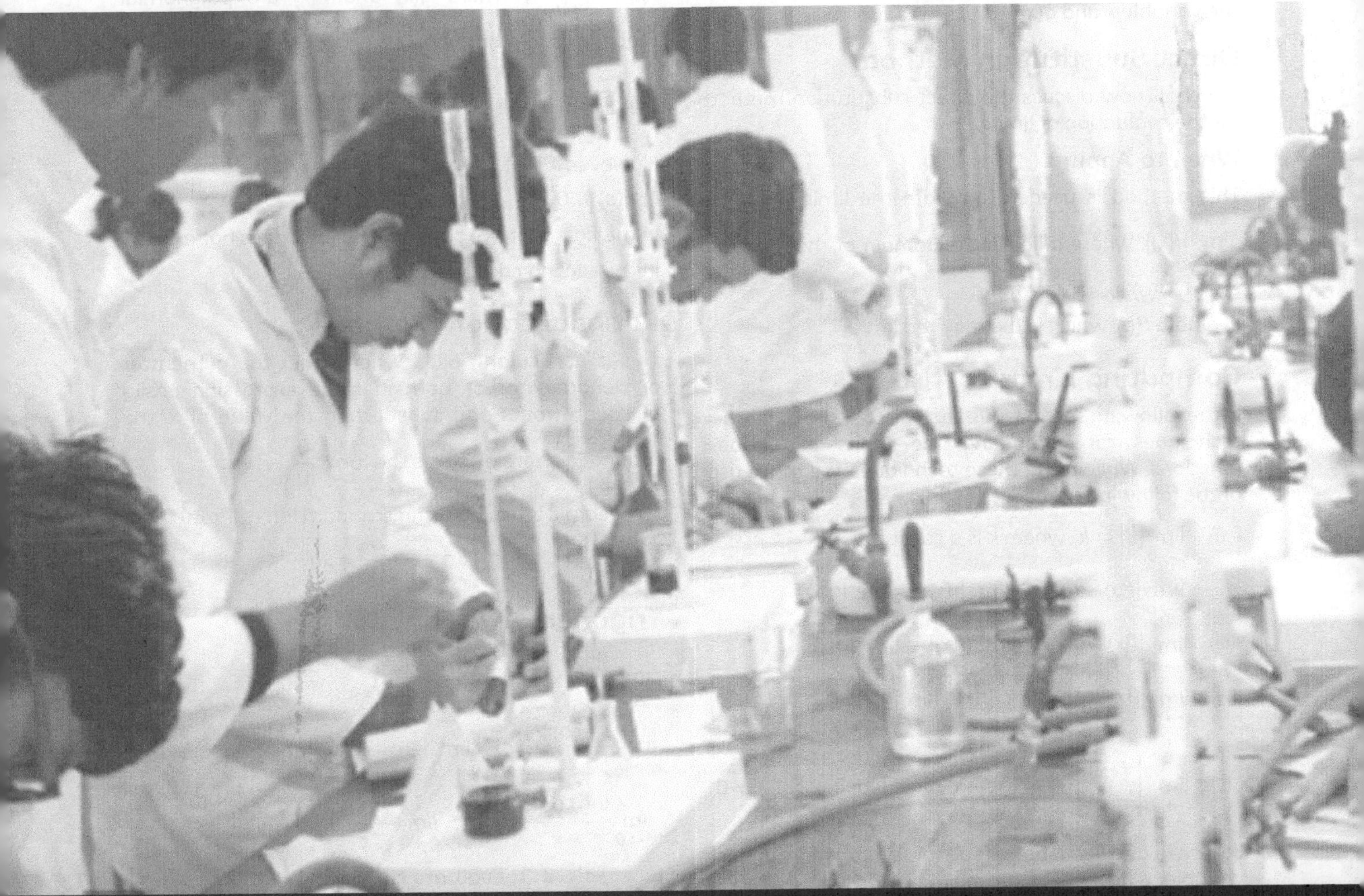

Every time a real-world application gets close to a stable solution, the real-life bounds are applied. A chemical reaction that starts in a beaker and involves two separate chemicals reacting to create a new compound is an example of a limit. The amount of the newly created compound has a limit now that time is getting closer to infinity.

Topic Notes

- *Fundamental of Limits*
- *Differentiation*

FUNDAMENTAL OF LIMITS 1

TOPIC 1

LIMITS OF ALGEBRAIC FUNCTIONS

In this section, we shall discuss various methods to evaluate the limits involving algebraic expressions of the form $\frac{p(x)}{q(x)}$, where $p(x)$ and $q(x)$ are expressions in the variable x and $g(x) \neq 0$.

Direct Substitution Method

We shall now discuss the direct substitution method for the evaluation of limits.

When to Apply

This method is used to evaluate the limits of form $\lim_{x \to a} [f(x)]$, where a lies in the domain of the function $f(x)$ (i.e., $f(a)$ exists).

Evaluate $f(a)$, which is the required limit.

Computing Limits

In the following sections, we shall discuss the algebraic techniques for computing the limits of various functions. While using these techniques, we make use of the following properties of limits:

(i) $\lim_{x \to a} [k] = k$, where k is a constant.

(ii) $\lim_{x \to a} [f(x) + g(x)] = \lim_{x \to a} [f(x)] + \lim_{x \to a} [g(x)]$.

(iii) $\lim_{x \to a} [f(x) - g(x)] = \lim_{x \to a} [f(x)] - \lim_{x \to a} [g(x)]$.

(iv) $\lim_{x \to a} [f(x)g(x)] = \lim_{x \to a} [f(x)] \lim_{x \to a} [g(x)]$.

(v) $\lim_{x \to a} \left[\frac{f(x)}{g(x)}\right] = \frac{\lim_{x \to a} [f(x)]}{\lim_{x \to a} [g(x)]}$ provided $\lim_{x \to a} [g(x)] \neq 0$.

Let $a \in R$ and let f be a real-valued function in real variable x defined at the points in an open interval containing a except possibly at a. Then, we say that the limit of the function $f(x)$ is a real number L, as x tends to a, if the value of $f(x)$ approaches L as x approaches a. It is denoted by $\lim_{x \to a} f(x)$ and is read as 'limit of $f(x)$ as x tends to a'.

Limits of a Polynomial Function

A function f is said to be a polynomial function if $f(x)$ is a zero function or if $f(x) = a_0 + a_1x + a_2x^2 + ... + a_nx^n$, where a_i, s are real number such that $a_n \neq 0$.

Then, limit of polynomial functions is

$$f(x) = \lim_{x \to a} f(x) = \lim_{x \to a} [a_0 + a_1x + a_2x^2 + ... + a_nx^n]$$

$$= a_0 + a_1a + a_2a^2 + ... + a_na^n = f(a)$$

Limits of Rational Functions

A function f is said to be a rational function, if $f(x) = \frac{g(x)}{h(x)}$, where $g(x)$ and $h(x)$ are polynomial functions such that $h(x) \neq 0$.

Then, $\lim_{x \to a} f(x) = \lim_{x \to a} \frac{g(x)}{h(x)} = \frac{\lim_{x \to a} g(x)}{\lim_{x \to a} h(x)} = \frac{g(a)}{h(a)}$

However, if $h(a) = 0$, then there are two cases arise,

(i) $g(a) \neq 0$ (ii) $g(a) = 0$

In the first case, we say that the limit does not exist.

In the second case, we can find a limit.

Rationalization Method

This is particularly used when either the numerator or denominator or both in value expression easily of square roots and substituting the value of x, the rational expression takes the form $\frac{0}{0}, \frac{\infty}{\infty}$, etc.

* Algebraic limits by using standard limits if $n \in \theta$ then

$$\lim_{x \to a} \frac{x^n - a^n}{x - a} = xa^{n-1}$$

Trigonometric Functions

$$\lim_{x \to 0} \frac{\sin x}{x} = 1, \quad \lim_{x \to 0} \frac{\tan x}{x} = 1$$

$$\lim_{x \to 0} \frac{1 - \cos x}{x} = 1, \quad \lim_{x \to 0} \frac{a^x - 1}{x} = \log_e a$$

$$\lim_{x \to 0} \frac{\log_e(1+n)}{x} = 1, \quad \lim_{x \to 0} \frac{e^x - 1}{x} = 1.$$

Example 1.1: Evaluate the given limit:

$$\lim_{x \to 0} \frac{\cos 2x - 1}{\cos x - 1}.$$ **[NCERT]**

Ans. $\lim_{x \to 0} \frac{\cos 2x - 1}{\cos x - 1}$

$$= \lim_{x \to 0} \frac{(1 - 2\sin^2 x) - 1}{\cos x - 1}$$

[$\because$ $\cos 2x = 1 - 2\sin^2 x$]

$$= \lim_{x \to 0} \frac{-2\sin^2 x}{\cos x - 1}$$

$$= \lim_{x \to 0} \frac{-2(1 - \cos^2 x)}{\cos x - 1}$$

[$\because$ $\sin^2 x = 1 - \cos^2 x$]

$$= \lim_{x\to 0} \frac{-2(1-\cos^2 x)}{-1(1-\cos x)}$$

$$= \lim_{x\to 0} \frac{2(1^2-\cos^2 x)}{1-\cos x}$$

$$= \lim_{x\to 0} 2(1+\cos x)$$

Putting $x = 0$

$$= 2(1 + \cos 0)$$
$$= 2(1 + 1)$$
$$= 2 \times 2$$
$$= 4$$

Example 1.2: Evaluate the given limit:

$$\lim_{x\to 3} \frac{x^4-81}{2x^2-5x-3}.$$ **[NCERT]**

Ans. $\lim_{x\to 3} \frac{x^4-81}{2x^2-5x-3}$

Putting $x = 3$

$$= \frac{(3)^4-81}{2(3)^2-5(3)-3}$$

$$= \frac{81-81}{18-15-3}$$

$$= \frac{0}{0}$$

Since, it is of the $\frac{0}{0}$ form.

We simplify as

$$\lim_{x\to 3} \frac{x^4-81}{2x^2-5x-3} = \lim_{x\to 3} \frac{(x^2)^2-(9)^2}{2x^2-6x+x-3}$$

$[\because\ a^2 - b^2 = (a - b)(a + b)]$

$$= \lim_{x\to 3} \frac{(x^2-9)(x^2+9)}{2x(x-3)+1(x-3)}$$

$$= \lim_{x\to 3} \frac{(x^2-9)(x^2+9)}{2x(x-3)+1(x-3)}$$

$$= \lim_{x\to 3} \frac{(x-3)(x+3)(x^2+9)}{(2x+1)(x-3)}$$

$$= \lim_{x\to 3} \frac{(x+3)(x^2+9)}{2x+1}$$

Putting $x = 3$

$$= \frac{(3+3)[(3)^2+9]}{2\times 3+1}$$

$$= \frac{6(9+9)}{6+1}$$

$$= \frac{6(18)}{7}$$

$$= \frac{(108)}{7}$$

Example 1.3: Evaluate the given limit $\lim_{z\to 1} \frac{z^{\frac{1}{3}}-1}{z^{\frac{1}{6}}-1}$. **[NCERT]**

Ans. $\lim_{z\to 1} \frac{z^{\frac{1}{3}}-1}{z^{\frac{1}{6}}-1}$

$$= \frac{(1)^{\frac{1}{3}}-1^1}{(1)^{\frac{1}{6}}-1}$$

$$= \frac{1-1}{1-1}$$

$$= \frac{0}{0}$$

Since, it is form $\frac{0}{0}$,

We can solve it by using

$$\lim_{x\to a} \frac{x^n-a^n}{x-a} = na^{n-1}$$

Hence,

$$\lim_{z\to 1} \frac{z^{\frac{1}{3}}-1}{z^{\frac{1}{6}}-1}$$

$$= \lim_{z\to 1} z^{\frac{1}{3}}-1 \div \lim_{z\to 1} z^{\frac{1}{6}}-1$$

$$= \lim_{z\to 1} [z^{\frac{1}{3}}-(1)^{\frac{1}{3}}] \div \lim_{z\to 1} [z^{\frac{1}{6}}-(1)^{\frac{1}{6}}]$$

Multiplying and dividing by $z - 1$

$$= \lim_{z\to 1} \frac{z^{\frac{1}{3}}-(1)^{\frac{1}{3}}}{z-1} \div \lim_{z\to 1} \frac{z^{\frac{1}{6}}-(1)^{\frac{1}{6}}}{z-1}$$

$[\because\ \lim_{z\to 1} \frac{x^n-a^n}{x-a} = na^{n-1}]$

$$\lim_{z\to 1} \frac{z^{\frac{1}{3}}-(1)^{\frac{1}{3}}}{z-1} \qquad \lim_{z\to 1} \frac{z^{\frac{1}{6}}-(1)^{\frac{1}{6}}}{z-1}$$

$$= \frac{1}{3}(1)^{\frac{1}{3}-1} \qquad = \frac{1}{6}(1)^{\frac{1}{6}-1}$$

$$= \frac{1}{3} \times 1 \qquad = \frac{1}{6} \times 1$$

$$= \frac{1}{3} \qquad = \frac{1}{6}$$

Hence, our equation becomes

$$= \lim_{z\to 1}\frac{z^{\frac{1}{3}}-(1)^{\frac{1}{3}}}{z-1} \div \lim_{z\to 1}\frac{z^{\frac{1}{6}}-(1)^{\frac{1}{6}}}{z-1}$$

$$= \frac{1}{3} \div \frac{1}{6}$$

$$= \frac{1}{3} \times \frac{6}{1}$$

$$= 2$$

Example 1.4: Evaluate the given limit: $\lim_{x\to 0}\frac{\sin ax}{\sin bx}$ $a, b \neq 0$. **[NCERT]**

Ans. $\lim_{x\to 0}\frac{\sin ax}{\sin bx}$

$$\lim_{x\to 0}\sin ax \lim_{x\to 0}\frac{1}{\sin bx}$$

Multiply and dividing by ax

$$\lim_{x\to 0}\frac{\sin ax}{ax}\times \lim_{x\to 0}\frac{1}{\sin bx}ax$$

$$= 1 \times \lim_{x\to 0}\frac{ax}{\sin bx} \qquad [\because \lim_{x\to 0}\frac{\sin x}{x} = 1]$$

$$= \lim_{x\to 0}\frac{ax}{\sin bx}$$

Replacing x by ax

$$\left[\lim_{x\to 0}\frac{\sin ax}{ax} = 1\right]$$

Multiplying and dividing by bx

$$= \lim_{x\to 0}\frac{ax}{\sin bx}\times\frac{bx}{bx}$$

$$= \lim_{x\to 0}\frac{bx}{\sin bx}\times\frac{a}{b}$$

$$= \frac{a}{b}\times \lim_{x\to 0}\frac{bx}{\sin bx}$$

$$= \frac{a}{b}\div \lim_{x\to 0}\frac{\sin bx}{bx}$$

[using $\lim_{x\to 0}\frac{\sin x}{x} = 1$ Replacing x by ax $\lim_{x\to 0}\frac{\sin ax}{bx} = 1$]

$$= \frac{a}{b}\div 1$$

$$= \frac{a}{b}$$

Example 1.5: Evaluate $\lim_{x\to 0} f(x)$, where

$$f(x) = \begin{cases}\frac{|x|}{x}, x \neq 0\\ 0, x = 0\end{cases}$$ **[NCERT]**

Ans. Finding limit at $x = 0$

LHL at x 0

$$\lim_{x\to 0} f(x) = \lim_{h\to 0} f(0-h)$$

$$= \lim_{h\to 0} f(-h)$$

$$= \lim_{h\to 0}\frac{|-h|}{-h}$$

$$= \lim_{h\to 0}\frac{h}{-h}$$

$$= \lim_{h\to 0} -1$$

$$= -1$$

RHL at $x \to 0$

$$\lim_{h\to 0} f(x) = \lim_{h\to 0} f(0+h)$$

$$= \lim_{h\to 0} f(h)$$

$$= \lim_{h\to 0}\frac{|h|}{h}$$

$$= \lim_{h\to 0}\frac{h}{h}$$

$$= \lim_{h\to 0} 1$$

$$= 1$$

Since Left Hand Limit (LHL) $\neq$ Right Hand Limit (RHL)

$\therefore \lim_{h\to 0} f(x)$ doesn't exist.

Example 1.6: Suppose $f(x) = \begin{cases} a+bx, x<1\\ 4, x=1\\ b-ax, x>1\end{cases}$ and if $\lim_{x\to 1} f(x) = f(1)$, what are possible values of a and b? **[NCERT]**

Ans. Here, limit exist at $x \to 1$

i.e., LHL = RHL = $f(1)$ = 4 ....(1)

LHL at $x \to 1$

$$\lim_{x\to 1} f(x) = \lim_{x\to 1} f(1-h)$$

$$= \lim_{h\to 0} a+b(1-h)$$

$$= a + b(1 - 0)$$

$$= a + b \quad ...(2)$$

From (1) and (2)

$$a + b = 4$$

RHL at $x \to 1$

$$\lim_{x\to 1} f(x) = \lim_{h\to 0} f(1+h)$$

$$= \lim_{h\to 0} b-a(1+h)$$

$$= b - a(1 + 0)$$

$$= b - a \quad ...(3)$$

From (1) and (3)

$$b - a = 4$$

Adding both

$$a + b + b - a = 4 + 4$$

$$2b = 8$$

$$b = 4$$

Also,

$$a + b = 4$$

$$a + 4 = 4$$

$$a = 0$$

Thus, $a = 0$ and $b = 4$.

Example 1.7: If $f(x) = \begin{cases} mx^2 + n, x < 0 \\ nx + m, 0 \le x \le 1 \\ nx^3 + m, x > 1 \end{cases}$, for what integers m and n does $\lim_{x \to 0} f(x)$ and $\lim_{x \to 1} f(x)$ exist? **[NCERT]**

Ans. Given limit exists at $x = 0$ and $x = 1$.

At, $x = 0$

Limit exists at $x = 0$ if

Left-hand limit = right-hand limit

$$f(x) = \begin{cases} mx^2 + n, x < 0 \\ nx + m\ \ 0 \le x \le 1 \\ nx^3 + m, x > 1 \end{cases}$$

LHL at $x \to 0$

$$\lim_{x \to 0} f(x) = \lim_{h \to 0} f(0 - h)$$

$$= \lim_{h \to 0} f(-h)$$

$$= \lim_{h \to 0} m(-h)^2 + n$$

$$= m(0)^2 + n$$

$$= n$$

RHL at $x \to 0$

$$\lim_{x \to 0} f(x) = \lim_{h \to 0} f(0 + h)$$

$$= \lim_{h \to 0} f(h)$$

$$= \lim_{h \to 0} nh + m$$

$$= n(0) + m$$

$$= m$$

Since for limit to exist, LHL = RHL

$\therefore\ m = n$

So, $\lim_{x \to 0} f(x)$ exists if $m = n$.

Now, a limit exists at $x = 1$.

Therefore,

Left-hand limit = Right-hand limit

$$f(x) = \begin{cases} mx^2 + n, x < 0 \\ nx + m\ \ 0 \le x \le 1 \\ nx^3 + m, x > 1 \end{cases}$$

LHL at $x \to 1$

$$\lim_{x \to 0} f(x) = \lim_{h \to 0} f(1 - h)$$

$$= \lim_{h \to 0} n(1 - h) + m$$

$$= n(1 - 0) + m$$

$$= n + m$$

RHL at $x \to 1$

$$\lim_{h \to 0} f(x) = \lim_{h \to 0} f(1 + h)$$

$$= \lim_{h \to 0} n(1 + h)^3 + m$$

$$= n(1 - 0)^3 + m$$

$$= n + m$$

Since, for limit to exist, LHL = RHL

$$m + n = m + n$$

Which is always true.

So, $\lim_{x \to 1} f(x)$ exists at all integral values of m and n.

Example 1.8: Evaluate the given limit: $\lim_{x \to 1}$ $(\text{cosec}\, x - \cot x)$. **[NCERT]**

Ans. $\lim_{x \to 0} (\text{cosec}\, x - \cot x)$

$$= \lim_{x \to 0} \left(\frac{1}{\sin x} - \frac{\cos x}{\sin x} \right)$$

$$\left[\because\ \text{cosec}\, \theta = \frac{1}{\sin \theta}, \cot \theta = \frac{\cos \theta}{\sin \theta} \right]$$

$$= \lim_{x \to 0} \frac{1 - \cos x}{\sin x}$$

Putting $x = 0$

$$= \frac{1 - \cos 0}{\sin 0}$$

$$= \frac{1 - 1}{0}$$

$$= \frac{0}{0}$$

Thus, we proceed as under

$\lim_{x \to 0} (\text{cosec}\, x - \cot x)$

$$= \lim_{x \to 0} \frac{1 - \cos x}{\sin x}$$

$$= \lim_{x \to 0} \frac{2 \sin^2 \frac{x}{2}}{\sin x}$$

$$= \lim_{x \to 0} \frac{2 \sin^2 \frac{x}{2}}{2 \sin \frac{x}{2} \cos \frac{x}{2}}$$

$$= \lim_{x \to 0} \frac{\sin \frac{x}{2}}{\cos \frac{x}{2}}$$

$$= \lim_{x \to 0} (\tan x/2)$$

$$= 0$$

Example 1.9: Evaluate the given limit: $\lim_{x \to 0} x \sec x$. **[NCERT]**

Ans. $\lim_{x \to 0} x \sec x$

$$= \lim_{x \to 0} x . \frac{1}{\cos x} \quad \left[\because \sec\theta = \frac{1}{\cos\theta}\right]$$

$$= \lim_{x \to 0} \frac{x}{\cos x}$$

Putting $x = 0$

$$= \frac{0}{\cos x}$$

$$= \frac{0}{1} \quad (\cos 0 = 1)$$

$$= 0$$

OBJECTIVE Type Questions

[**1** mark]

Multiple Choice Questions

1. The value of $\lim_{x \to 3} (4x^3 - 2x^2 - x + 1)$ is equal to:

(a) 40 **(b) 20**
(c) 38 **(d) 88**

Ans. *(d) 88*

Explanation:

We have $\lim_{x \to 3} (4x^3 - 2x^2 - x + 1)$

Putting, $x = 3$, then

$$= 4(3)^3 - 2(3)^2 - 3 + 1$$

$$= 4 \times 27 - 2 \times 9 - 3 + 1$$

$$= 108 - 18 - 2$$

$$= 90 - 2$$

$$= 88$$

So, option (d) is the correct answer.

2. If $f(x) = \frac{|x-9|}{x-9}$, then find $f(x)$ of $x = 3$ for left-hand limit.

(a) 1 **(b) –1**
(c) 2 **(d) 0**

Ans. *(b) –1*

Explanation:

We have $f(x) = \frac{|x-9|}{x-9}$

The LHL $= \frac{-(x-9)}{x-9}$

$$= -1$$

So, option (b) is the correct answer.

3. The value of $\lim_{x \to 2} \frac{x^3 - 8}{x - 2}$ is equal to:

(a) 10 **(b) 11**
(c) 12 **(d) 13**

Ans. *(c) 12*

Explanation:

We have, $\lim_{x \to 2} \frac{x^3 - 8}{x - 2}$

then $\frac{x^3 - 2^3}{x - 2} = \frac{(x-2)(x^2 + 2^2 + 2x)}{x-2}$

$$= x^2 + 4 + 2x$$

$$= 2^2 + 4 + 4$$

$$= 12$$

So, option (c) is the correct answer.

4. The value of x $\lim_{x \to \frac{1}{2}} \frac{4x^2 - 1}{2x - 1}$ is equal to:

(a) 1 **(b) 2**
(c) 3 **(d) 4**

Ans. *(b) 2*

Explanation:

We have,

$$\lim_{x \to \frac{1}{2}} \frac{4x^2 - 1}{2x - 1} = \frac{(2x)^2 - 1^2}{2x - 1}$$

$$= \frac{(2x-1)(2x+1)}{2x-1}$$

$$= 2x + 1$$

$$= 2 \times \frac{1}{2} + 1$$

$$= 2$$

So, option (b) is the correct answer.

5. **The value of $\lim_{x\to 5}\left(\frac{x^2-25}{x-5}\right)$ is:**

(a) 0 (b) ∞
(c) 10 (d) 5 **[DIKSHA]**

Ans. *(c) 10*

Explanation: $\lim_{x\to 5}\left(\frac{x^2-25}{x-5}\right)$

$\lim_{x\to 5}\frac{(x+5)(x-5)}{x-5}$

$\lim_{x\to 5} x+5 = 5+5 = 10$

So, option (c) is the correct answer.

6. **If $\lim_{x\to 2}\frac{x^n-2^n}{x-2} = 80$ then n is equal to:**

(a) 1 (b) 3
(c) 5 (d) 7

Ans. *(c) 5*

Explanation: We have $\lim_{x\to 2}\frac{x^n-2^n}{x-2} = 80$

So, $n \,.\, 2^{(n-1)} = 80$

$= n.2^{(n-1)} = 5 \times 16$

$n.2^{n-1} = 5 \times 2^{5-1}$

$n = 5$

So, option (c) is the correct answer.

7. **The value of $\lim_{x\to 0}\frac{(x+2)^{1/3}-2^{1/3}}{x}$ is equal to:**

(a) $\frac{1}{3(2)^{3/2}}$ (b) $\frac{1}{3(2)^{2/3}}$

(c) $\frac{1}{2(3)^{2/3}}$ (d) $\frac{1}{3\sqrt{3}}$

Ans. *(b)* $\frac{1}{3(2)^{2/3}}$

Explanation: We have $\lim_{x\to 0}\frac{(x+2)^{1/3}-2^{1/3}}{x}$

So we can write $\frac{(x+2)^{1/3}-2^{1/3}}{(x+2)-2}$

Now, using $\lim_{x\to a}\frac{x^n-a^n}{x-a} = na^{n-1}$

$= \frac{1}{3}(2)^{\frac{1}{3}-1}$

$= \frac{1}{3}2^{\frac{-2}{3}}$

$= \frac{1}{3.2^{2/3}}$

So, option (b) is the correct answer.

8. **The value of $\lim_{x\to 0}\left(\frac{\tan^2 3x}{x^2}\right)$ is:**

(a) 0 (b) 3
(c) ∞ (d) 9 **[DIKSHA]**

Ans. *(d) 9*

Explanation: Given, $\lim_{x\to 0}\left(\frac{\tan^2 3x}{x^2}\right)$

We know that $\lim_{x\to 0}\frac{\tan ax}{ax}$

$\lim_{x\to 0} 9\frac{\tan^2 3x}{9x^2}$

$\lim_{x\to 0} 9\left(\frac{\tan 3x}{3x}\right)^2$

$= 9 \times 1$

$= 9$

So, option (*d*) is the correct answer.

9. **The value of $\lim_{x\to 0}\left[\frac{\sqrt{3+x}-\sqrt{3}}{x}\right]$ is equal to**

(a) $\frac{1}{3(2)^{\frac{1}{2}}}$ (b) $\frac{1}{2(3)^{\frac{1}{2}}}$

(c) $\frac{1}{4}$ (d) $\frac{1}{5}$

Ans. *(b)* $\frac{1}{2(3)^{\frac{1}{2}}}$

Explanation: We have, $\lim_{x\to 0}\left[\frac{\sqrt{3+x}-\sqrt{3}}{x}\right]$

We can write as $\frac{(3+x)^{1/2}-(3)^{1/2}}{(x+3)-(3)}$

Now, using $\lim_{x\to a}\frac{x^n-a^n}{x-a} = na^{n-1}$

Given limit $= \frac{1}{2}(3)^{1/2-1}$

$= \frac{1}{2}(3)^{\frac{-1}{2}}$

$$= \frac{1}{2(3)^{\frac{1}{2}}}$$

So, option (b) is the correct answer.

10. $\lim\limits_{x \to 0} \frac{1 - \cos 4x}{x^2}$ **is equal to:**

(a) 8 (b) 1

(c) 2 (d) 3

Ans. *(a) 8*

Explanation: We have, $\frac{1-\cos 4x}{x^2} = \frac{2\sin^2 2x}{x^2}$

$$= 2\left(\frac{\sin 2x}{2x}\right)^2 \times 4$$

$$= 8(1)^2 = 8$$

So, option (a) is the correct answer.

11. The value of $\lim\limits_{x \to 1} \frac{(\sqrt{x}-1)(2x-3)}{2x^2+x-3}$ **is :**

(a) $\frac{1}{10}$ (b) $\frac{-1}{10}$

(c) 1 (d) None of these

[NCERT Exemplar]

Ans. *(b)* $\frac{-1}{10}$

Explanation: Given, $\lim\limits_{x \to 1} \frac{(\sqrt{x}-1)(2x-3)}{2x^2+x-3}$

$$= \lim_{x \to 1} \frac{(\sqrt{x}-1)(2x-3)}{x(2x+3)-1(2x+3)}$$

$$= \lim_{x \to 1} \frac{(\sqrt{x}-1)(2x-3)}{(x-1)(2x+3)}$$

$$= \lim_{x \to 1} \frac{(\sqrt{x}-1)(\sqrt{x}+1)(2x-3)}{(x-1)(\sqrt{x}+1)(2x+3)}$$

$$= \lim_{x \to 1} \frac{(x-1)(2x-3)}{(x-1)(\sqrt{x}+1)(2x+3)}$$

$$= \lim_{x \to 1} \frac{2x-3}{(\sqrt{x}+1)(2x+3)}$$

Taking limit we have

$$= \frac{2(1)-3}{(\sqrt{1}+1)(2\times1+3)} = \frac{-1}{2\times5} = \frac{-1}{10}$$

So, option (b) is the correct answer.

12. $\lim\limits_{x \to 0} \frac{|\sin x|}{x}$ **is equal to:**

(a) 1 (b) –1

(c) Does not exist (d) None of these

[NCERT Exemplar]

Ans. *(c) Does not exist*

Explanation: Given, $\lim\limits_{x \to 0} \frac{|\sin x|}{x}$

$$\text{LHL} = \lim_{x \to 0^-} \frac{-\sin x}{x} = -1 \quad [\because \lim_{x \to 0} \frac{\sin x}{x} = 1]$$

$$\text{RHL} = \lim_{x \to 0^+} \frac{\sin x}{x} = 1$$

LHL $\neq$ RHL so the limit does not exist.

So, option (c) is the correct answer.

13. If $f(x) = \begin{cases} x^2-1, & 0 < x < 2 \\ 2x+3, & 2 \le x \le 3' \end{cases}$ **then the quadratic equations whose roots are** $\lim\limits_{x \to 2^-} f(x)$ **and** $\lim\limits_{x \to 2^+} f(x)$ **is:**

(a) $x^2 - 6x + 9 = 0$ (b) $x^2 - 7x + 8 = 0$

(c) $x^2 - 14x + 49 = 0$ (d) $x^2 - 10x + 21 = 0$

[NCERT Exemplar]

Ans. *(d)* $x^2 - 10x + 21 = 0$

Explanation: Given, $\begin{cases} x^2-1, & 0 < x < 2 \\ 2x+3, & 2 \le x \le 3 \end{cases}$

$$\therefore \quad \lim_{x \to 2^-} f(x) = \lim_{x \to 2^-} (x^2-1)$$

$$\lim_{h \to 0} [(2-h)^2] = \lim_{h \to 0} (4+h^2-4h-1)$$

$$= \lim_{h \to 0} (h^2 - 4h + 3) = 3$$

and $\lim\limits_{x \to 2^+} f(x) = \lim\limits_{x \to 2^+} (2x+3) = \lim\limits_{h \to 0} [2(2+h)+3]$

$$= 7$$

Therefore, the quadratic equation whose roots are 3 and 7 is $x^2 - (3 + 7)x + 3 \times 7 = 0$ i.e., $x^2 - 10x + 21 = 0$.

So, option (d) is the correct answer.

14. $\lim\limits_{x \to 0} \frac{\tan 2x - x}{3x - \sin x}$ **is equal to:**

(a) 2 (b) $\frac{1}{2}$

(c) $-\frac{1}{2}$ (d) $\frac{1}{4}$

[NCERT Exemplar]

Ans. *(b)* $\frac{1}{2}$

Explanation: Given, $\lim_{x\to 0}\frac{\tan 2x - x}{3x-\sin x} = \left(\frac{0}{0}\right)$ form.

Now, applying *L* 'Hospital's rule we get,

$$= \lim_{x\to 0}\frac{2\sec^2 2x - 1}{3-\cos x}$$

$$= \frac{2-1}{2}$$

$$= \frac{1}{2}$$

So, option (b) is the correct answer.

Assertion-Reason (A-R)

DIRECTION: In the following questions, a statement of assertion (A) is followed by a statement of the reason (R). Mark the correct choice as:

(a) Both assertion (A) and reason (R) are true and reason (R) is the correct explanation of assertion (A).

(b) Both assertion (A) and reason (R) are true but reason (R) is not the correct explanation of assertion (A).

(c) Assertion (A) is true but reason (R) is false.

(d) Assertion (A) is false but reason (R) is true.

15. Assertion (A): $\lim_{x\to 1}\frac{ax^2+bx+c}{cx^2+bx+a}$ **is equal to 1, where** $a+b+c \neq 0$.

Reason (R): $\lim_{x\to -2}\frac{\frac{1}{x}+\frac{1}{2}}{x+2}$ **is equal to** $\frac{1}{4}$.

Ans. *(c) Assertion (A) is true but reason (R) is false.*

Explanation: Given, $\lim_{x\to 1}\frac{ax^2+bx+c}{cx^2+bx+a}$

$$= \frac{a\times(1)^2+b\times 1+c}{c\times(1)^2+b\times 1+a}$$

$$= \frac{a+b+c}{c+b+a} = 1$$

$$= \lim_{x\to -2}\frac{\frac{1}{x}+\frac{1}{2}}{x+2}$$

$$= \lim_{x\to -2}\frac{(2+x)}{2x(x+2)} = \lim_{x\to -2}\frac{1}{2x}$$

$$= \frac{1}{2(-2)} = -\frac{1}{4}$$

So, option (c) is the correct answer.

16. Assertion (A): $\lim_{x\to 0}\frac{\sin ax}{bx}$ **is equal to** $\frac{a}{b}$.

Reason (R): $\lim_{x\to 0}\frac{\sin x}{x} = 1$.

Ans. *(a) Both assertion (A) and reason (R) are true and reason (R) is the correct explanation of assertion (A).*

Explanation: Given, $\lim_{x\to 0}\frac{\sin ax}{bx} = \lim_{x\to 0}\frac{(a)\sin ax}{b(ax)}$

[dividing and multiplying by a]

$$= \frac{a}{b}\times 1 = \frac{a}{b}\left[\because \lim_{x\to 0}\frac{\sin ax}{ax} = 1\right]$$

Hence, option *(a)* is the correct answer.

17. Assertion (A): $\lim_{x\to 0}\frac{\sin ax + bx}{ax+\sin bx}$ **is equal to –2.**

Reason (R): $\lim_{x\to 1}(5x^3+5x+1)$ **is equal to 11.**

Ans. *(d) Assertion (A) is false but reason (R) is true.*

Explanation: $\lim_{x\to 0}\frac{\sin ax + bx}{ax+\sin bx}$

Dividing each term by x, we get

$$= \lim_{x\to 0}\frac{\frac{\sin ax}{x}+\frac{bx}{x}}{\frac{ax}{x}+\frac{\sin bx}{x}} = \lim_{x\to 0}\frac{\frac{a\sin ax}{ax}+b}{a+\frac{b\sin bx}{bx}}$$

$$= \frac{a\times 1+b}{a+b\times 1} = \frac{a+b}{a+b} = 1\left[\because \lim_{x\to 0}\frac{\sin x}{x} = 1\right]$$

$$\lim_{x\to 1}(5x^3+5x+1)$$

$$= 5(1)^3+5(1)+1 = 5+5+1 = 11$$

So, option (d) is the correct answer.

18. Assertion (A): $\lim_{x\to \pi}\frac{\sin(\pi - x)}{\pi(\pi - x)}$ **is equal to** π.

Reason (R): $\lim_{x\to 0}\frac{\cos x}{\pi - x}$ **is equal to** $\frac{1}{\pi}$.

Ans. *(d) Assertion (A) is false but reason (R) is true.*

Explanation: Given, $\lim_{x\to \pi}\frac{\sin(\pi - x)}{\pi(\pi - x)}$

Let, $\pi - x = h$, As $x \to \pi$, then $h \to 0$,

$$\therefore \quad \lim_{x\to \pi}\frac{\sin(\pi - x)}{\pi(\pi - x)} = \lim_{h\to 0}\frac{\sin h}{\pi h}$$

$$= \lim_{h\to 0}\frac{1}{\pi}\times\frac{\sin h}{h}$$

$$= \frac{1}{\pi}\times 1 = \frac{1}{\pi}\left[\because \lim_{h\to 0}\frac{\sin h}{h} = 1\right]$$

Given, $\lim_{x\to 0}\frac{\cos x}{\pi - x}$

Putting, the limit directly, we get

$$\frac{\cos 0}{\pi - 0} = \frac{1}{\pi}$$

So, option (d) is the correct answer.

CASE BASED Questions (CBQs)

[**4** & **5** marks]

Read the following passages and answer the questions that follow:

19. *A function f is said to be a rational function, if*

$f(x) = \frac{g(x)}{h(x)}$, where g(x) and h(x) are polynomial functions such that $h(x) \neq 0$.

Then, $\lim_{x\to a} f(x) = \lim_{x\to a}\frac{g(x)}{h(x)}$

$$= \frac{\lim_{x\to a} g(x)}{\lim_{x\to a} h(x)} = \frac{g(a)}{h(a)}$$

However, if h(a) = 0, then there are two cases arise,

(i) $g(a) \neq 0$ (ii) $g(a) = 0$

In the first case, we say that the limit does not exist.

In the second case, we can find limit.

(A) Find the value of $\lim_{x\to -2}\left[\frac{x^2-4}{x^3-4x^2+4x}\right]$.

(B) Find $\lim_{x\to -1}\frac{x^7-2x^5+1}{x^3-3x^2+2}$.

Ans. (A) Consider $f(x) = \frac{x^2-4}{x^3-4x^2+4x}$

On putting x = 2, we get

$f(2) = \frac{4-4}{8-16+8} = \frac{0}{0}$ i.e., it is the form $\frac{0}{0}$.

So, let us first factorise it.

Consider, $\lim_{x\to 2}\frac{x^2-4}{x^3-4x^2+4x}$

$$= \lim_{x\to 2}\frac{(x+2)(x-2)}{x(x-2)^2}$$

$$= \lim_{x\to 2}\frac{(x+2)}{x(x-2)}$$

$$= \frac{2+2}{2(2-2)} = \frac{4}{0}$$

which is not defined.

$\therefore \lim_{x\to 2}\left[\frac{x^2-4}{x^3-4x^2+4x}\right]$ does not exist.

(B) Given $\lim_{x\to 1}\frac{x^7-2x^5+1}{x^3-3x^2+2}$ $\left[\frac{0}{0}\text{form}\right]$

$$= \lim_{x\to 1}\frac{x^7-x^5-x^5+1}{x^3-x^2-2x^2+2}$$

$$= \lim_{x\to 1}\frac{x^5(x^2-1)-1(x^5-1)}{x^2(x-1)-2(x^2-1)}$$

On dividing numerator and denominator by (x – 1), then

$$= \lim_{x\to 1}\frac{\frac{x^5(x^2-1)}{(x-1)} - \frac{1(x^5-1)}{(x-1)}}{\frac{x^2(x-1)}{(x-1)} - \frac{2(x^2-1)}{(x-1)}}$$

$$= \frac{\lim_{x\to 1} x^5(x+1) - \lim_{x\to 1}\left(\frac{x^5-1}{x-1}\right)}{\lim_{x\to 1} x^2 - \lim_{x\to 1} 2(x+1)}$$

$$= \frac{1\times 2 - 5\times(1)^4}{1-2\times 2} = \frac{2-5}{1-4}$$

$$\left[\because \lim_{x\to a}\frac{x^n-a^n}{x-a} = na^{n-1}\right]$$

$$= \frac{-3}{-3} = 1$$

20. *A class teacher Shinu Sharma of Class XI writes Let $f : R \to [0, \infty)$ be a function defined as f(x) = |x| and g(x) = f(x + 1) + f(x – 1), ∀∈ R. and asked students to answer the following question based on the above information*

(A) The value of *g(x)* is:

(a) 1 **(b)** 1

(c) 1 **(d)** 1

(B) If $\lim_{x\to -1} g(x) = a$, then the value of *a* is:

(a) 0 **(b)** -2

(c) 2 **(d)** Does not exist

(C) The value of $\lim_{x\to 1^+} g(x)$ is:

(a) 0 (b) 2

(c) –2 (d) Does not exist

(D) The value of $\lim_{x\to 1^-} g(x)$ is:

(a) 0 (b) 2

(c) –2 (d) Does not exist

Ans. (A) *(a) 1*

Explanation: Given $f(x) = |x|$ and $g(x) = f(x+1) + f(x-1)$

So,

$$g(x) = |x + 1| + |x - 1|$$

$$g(x) = \begin{cases} -(x+1)-(x-1), & \text{if } x<-1 \\ (x+1)-(x-1), & \text{if } -1\le x<1 \\ (x+1)+(x-1), & \text{if } x\ge 1 \end{cases}$$

$$\Rightarrow g(x) = \begin{cases} -2x & \text{if } x<-1 \\ 2 & \text{if } -1\le x<1 \\ 2x & \text{if } x\ge 1 \end{cases}$$

$\therefore$ Option (*a*) is the correct answer.

(B) *(c) 2*

Explanation: For $\lim_{x\to -1} g(x)$ to exist

$$\lim_{x\to -1^-} g(x) = \lim_{x\to -1^+} g(x)$$

$$\Rightarrow \lim_{x\to -1^-} (-2x) = \lim_{x\to -1^+} 2$$

$$\Rightarrow 2 = 2$$

$\lim_{x\to -1} g(x)$ exists and equal to $2 \Rightarrow a = 2$

$\therefore$ Option (*c*) is the correct answer.

(C) *(b) 2*

Explanation: $\lim_{x\to 1^+} g(x) = \lim_{x\to 1^+} 2x = 2$

$\therefore$ Option (*b*) is correct answer.

(D) *(b) 2*

Explanation: $\lim_{x\to 1^-} g(x) = \lim_{x\to 1^-} 2 = 2$

$\therefore$ Option (*b*) is correct answer.

VERY SHORT ANSWER Type Questions (VSA)

[**1** mark]

21. **Evaluate:** $\lim_{x\to 0}\left[\frac{9x\cos x - 3\sin x}{4x^2 - \tan x}\right]$.

Ans. $\lim_{x\to 0}\left[\frac{9x\cos x-3\sin x}{4x^2-\tan x}\right] = \lim_{x\to 0}\left[\frac{9\cos x - 3\frac{\sin x}{x}}{4x-\frac{\tan x}{x}}\right]$

[on dividing the numerator and denominator by *x*]

$$= \frac{9\lim_{x\to 0}[\cos x] - 3\lim_{x\to 0}\left[\frac{\sin x}{x}\right]}{4\lim_{x\to 0}[x] - \lim_{x\to 0}\left[\frac{\tan x}{x}\right]} = \frac{9(1)-3(1)}{4(0)-(1)} = -6$$

22. **Evaluate:** $\lim_{x\to\pi/6}\left[\frac{\cos^2 x - 4}{\cos x - 2}\right]$.

Ans. $\lim_{x\to\pi/6}\left[\frac{\cos^2 x-4}{\cos x-2}\right] = \lim_{x\to\pi/6}\left[\frac{(\cos x+2)(\cos x-2)}{\cos x-2}\right]$

$$= \lim_{x\to\pi/6}(\cos x + 2)$$

$$= \lim_{x\to\pi/6}[\cos x+2] = \cos\frac{\pi}{6}+2$$

$$= \frac{\sqrt{3}}{2} + 2.$$

23. $\lim_{x\to 0}\left(\frac{\sqrt{2+x}-\sqrt{2}}{x}\right)$. **[DIKSHA]**

Ans. Given, $\lim_{x\to 0}\left(\frac{\sqrt{2+x}-\sqrt{2}}{x}\right)$

$$\lim_{x\to 0}\left(\frac{\sqrt{2+x}-\sqrt{2}}{x}\right)\times\left(\frac{\sqrt{2+x}+\sqrt{2}}{\sqrt{2+x}+\sqrt{2}}\right)$$

$$= \lim_{x\to 0}\left(\frac{(2+x)-2}{x(\sqrt{2+x}+\sqrt{2})}\right)$$

$$= \lim_{x\to 0}\left(\frac{1}{\sqrt{2+x}+\sqrt{2}}\right)$$

$$= \left(\frac{1}{2\sqrt{2}}\right)$$

24. **Evaluate:** $\lim_{x\to 8}\left[\frac{e^x - e^4}{x-4}\right]$.

Ans. Let $L = \lim_{x\to 8}\left[\frac{e^x-e^4}{x-4}\right]$

Putting, $x = 4 + y$

Then, $y = x - 4$ and $y \to 0$ and as $x \to 4$

$$\therefore \quad L = \lim_{y\to 0}\left[\frac{e^{4+y}-e^4}{y}\right] = \lim_{y\to 0}\left[\frac{e^4e^y-e^4}{y}\right]$$

$$= \lim_{y\to 0}\left[\frac{e^4(e^y-1)}{y}\right]$$

$$= e^4 \lim_{y\to 0}\left[\frac{e^y-1}{y}\right] = e^4(1) = e^4.$$

25. **Evaluate;** $\lim_{x\to 0}\left[\frac{\log(1+5x)}{3x}\right]$.

Ans. $\lim_{x\to 0}\left[\frac{\log(1+5x)}{3x}\right] = \lim_{x\to 0}\left[\frac{5}{3}\times\frac{\log(1+5x)}{5x}\right]$

{multiplying and dividing by 5}

$$= \frac{5}{3}\lim_{x\to 0}\left[\frac{\log(1+5x)}{5x}\right]$$

$$= \frac{5}{3}\lim_{5x\to 0}\left[\frac{\log(1+5x)}{5x}\right] \quad [\because \; 5x\to 0 \text{ as } x\to 0]$$

$$= \frac{5}{3}(1) = \frac{5}{3}$$

26. **Evaluate:** $\lim_{x\to a}\frac{(2+x)^{5/2}-(a+2)^{5/2}}{x-a}$.

[NCERT Exemplar]

Ans. $\lim_{x\to a}\frac{(2+x)^{5/2}-(a+2)^{5/2}}{(2+x)-(a+2)}$

$$= \lim_{2+x\to a+2}\frac{(2+x)^{5/2}-(a+2)^{5/2}}{(2+x)-(a+2)}$$

$$= \frac{5}{2}(a+2)^{5/2-1} = \frac{5}{2}(a+2)^{3/2}$$

$$\left[\because \lim_{x\to a}\frac{x^n-a^n}{x-a} = n\cdot a^{n-1}\right]$$

Hence, the required answer is $\frac{5}{2}(a+2)^{3/2}$.

27. $\lim_{x\to 0}\frac{(1+x)^6-1}{(1+x)^5-1}$. **[DIKSHA]**

Ans. Given, $\lim_{x\to 0}\frac{(1+x)^6-1}{(1+x)^5-1}$

$$= \lim_{x\to 0}\left(\frac{(1+x)^6-1}{(1+x)-1}\right)\left(\frac{(1+x)-1}{(1+x)^5-1}\right)$$

$$= \frac{6(1)^{6-1}}{5(1)^{5-1}}$$

$$= \frac{6}{5}$$

28. **Evaluate:** $\lim_{x\to\frac{\pi}{3}}\frac{\sqrt{1-\cos 6x}}{\sqrt{2}\left(\frac{\pi}{3}-x\right)}$. **[NCERT Exemplar]**

Ans. Given that $\lim_{x\to\frac{\pi}{3}}\frac{\sqrt{1-\cos 6x}}{\sqrt{2}\left(\frac{\pi}{3}-x\right)}$

$$= \lim_{x\to\frac{\pi}{3}}\frac{\sqrt{2\sin^2 3x}}{\sqrt{2}\left(\frac{\pi}{3}-x\right)} \quad [\because \; 1-\cos\theta = 2\sin^2\theta/2]$$

$$= \lim_{x\to\frac{\pi}{3}}\frac{\sqrt{2}\sin 3x}{\sqrt{2}\left(\frac{\pi-3x}{3}\right)} = \lim_{x\to\frac{\pi}{3}}\frac{3\cdot\sin(\pi-3x)}{\pi-3x}$$

$$\left[\because \lim_{x\to 0}\frac{\sin x}{x} = 1\right]$$

$= 3$

Hence, the required answer is 3.

SHORT ANSWER Type-I Questions (SA-I)

[**2** marks]

29. **If** $\lim_{x\to 1}\left[\frac{x^4-1}{x-1}\right] = \lim_{x\to k}\left[\frac{x^3-k^3}{x^2-k^2}\right]$**, then find the value of** k**.** **[NCERT Exemplar]**

Ans. Given that $\lim_{x\to 1}\left[\frac{x^4-1}{x-1}\right] = \lim_{x\to k}\left[\frac{x^3-k^3}{x^2-k^2}\right]$

$$\Rightarrow \quad 4(1)^{4-1} = \lim_{x\to k}\left[\frac{\left(\frac{x^3-k^3}{x-k}\right)}{\left(\frac{x^2-k^2}{x-k}\right)}\right]$$

$$\Rightarrow \quad 4 = \frac{\lim_{x \to k}\left[\frac{x^3 - k^3}{x - k}\right]}{\lim_{x \to k}\left[\frac{x^2 - k^2}{x - k}\right]}$$

$$\Rightarrow \quad 4 = \frac{3k^2}{2k}$$

$$\Rightarrow \quad 4 = \frac{3k}{2}$$

$$\Rightarrow \quad k = \frac{8}{3}.$$

30. Evaluate the given limits: $\lim_{x \to 3} \frac{x^2 - 9}{2x^2 - 5x - 3}$.

Ans. $\lim_{x \to 3} \frac{x^2 - 9}{2x^2 - 5x - 3}$

$$\lim_{x \to 3} \frac{x^2 - 9}{2x^2 - 5x - 3} = \lim_{x \to 3} \frac{(x)^2 - (3)^2}{2x^2 - 6x + x - 3}$$

$$= \lim_{x \to 3} \frac{(x-3)(x+3)}{2x(x-3) + 1(x-3)}$$

$$= \lim_{x \to 3} \frac{(x+3)}{(2x+1)}$$

Putting $x = 3$

$$= \frac{(3+3)}{2 \times 3 + 1}$$

$$= \frac{6}{6+1}$$

$$= \frac{6}{7}$$

31. Find $\lim_{x \to 0} [f(x)]$, where

$$f(x) = \begin{cases} 2x + 3 \text{ if } x \leq 0 \\ 3(x+1) \text{ if } x > 0 \end{cases}$$

Ans. Given

R.H.L. $= \lim_{x \to 0+} [f(x)]$

$= \lim_{x \to 0+} [3(x + 1)]$

$= \lim_{x \to 0} [3(0 + h + 1)]$

[By putting $x = 0 + h$]

L.H.L. $= \lim_{x \to 0-} [f(x)]$

$= \lim_{x \to 0-} [2x + 3]$

$= \lim_{h \to 0} [2(0 - h) + 3]$ [By putting $x = 0 - h$]

$= 3$

Since, $\lim_{x \to 0+} [f(x)] = \lim_{x \to 0-} [f(x)] = 3$

Hence, $\lim_{x \to 0} [f(x)] = 3$

32. Find $\lim_{x \to 5} [f(x)]$, where $f(x) = |x| - 5$.

Ans. Given $f(x) = |x| - 5 = \begin{cases} x - 5 \text{ if } x \geq 0 \\ -x - 5 \text{ if } x < 0 \end{cases}$

R.H.L. $= \lim_{x \to 5+} [f(x)]$

$= \lim_{x \to 5+} [x - 5]$

$= \lim_{x \to 0} [5 + h - 5]$ [But putting $x = 5 + h$]

L.H.L. $= \lim_{x \to 5-} [f(x)]$

$= \lim_{x \to 5-} [x - 5]$

$= \lim_{h \to 0} [5 - h - 5]$ [But putting $x = 5 - h$]

$= 0$

Since, $\lim_{x \to 5+} [f(x)] = \lim_{x \to 5-} [f(x)] = 0$

Hence, $\lim_{x \to 5} [f(x) = 0]$

33. Evaluate: $\lim_{x \to 0} \frac{\sin 2x + 3x}{2x + \tan 3x}$. **[NCERT Exemplar]**

Ans. Given that: $\lim_{x \to 0} \frac{\sin 2x + 3x}{2x + \tan 3x}$

$$= \lim_{x \to 0} \frac{\left(\frac{\sin 2x + 3x}{2x}\right) \times 2x}{\left(\frac{2x + \tan 3x}{3x}\right) \times 3x}$$

$$= \lim_{x \to 0} \frac{\left(\frac{\sin 2x}{2x} + \frac{3x}{2x}\right) \times 2x}{\left(\frac{2x}{3x} + \frac{\tan 3x}{3x}\right) \times 3x}$$

$$= \frac{\left(\lim_{x \to 0} \frac{\sin 2x}{2x} + \frac{3}{2}\right)}{\left[\frac{2}{3} + \lim_{x \to 0} \frac{\tan 3x}{3x}\right)} \times \frac{2}{3} \quad \left[\because \lim_{x \to 0} \frac{\sin x}{x} = 1\right]$$

$$= \frac{\left(1 + \frac{3}{2}\right)}{\left(\frac{2}{3} + 1\right)} \times \frac{2}{3} = \frac{5/2}{5/3} \times \frac{2}{3} = \frac{3}{2} \times \frac{2}{3} = 1$$

34. Evaluate: $\lim_{x \to \frac{1}{2}} \left(\frac{8x - 3}{2x - 1} - \frac{4x^2 + 1}{4x^2 - 1}\right)$.

[NCERT Exemplar]

Ans. Given that $\lim_{x \to \frac{1}{2}} \left(\frac{8x - 3}{2x - 1} - \frac{4x^2 + 1}{4x^2 - 1}\right)$

$$= \lim_{x\to\frac{1}{2}}\left[\frac{(8x-3)(2x+1)-(4x^2+1)}{(4x^2-1)}\right]$$

$$= \lim_{x\to\frac{1}{2}}\left[\frac{16x^2-6x+8x-3-4x^2-1}{4x^2-1}\right]$$

$$= \lim_{x\to\frac{1}{2}}\left[\frac{12x^2+2x-4}{4x^2-1}\right] = \lim_{x\to\frac{1}{2}}\frac{2(6x^2+x-2)}{4x^2-1}$$

$$= \lim_{x\to\frac{1}{2}}\frac{2\left[6x^2+4x-3x-2\right]}{(2x+1)(2x-1)}$$

$$= \lim_{x\to\frac{1}{2}}\frac{2\left[2x(3x+2)-1(3x+2)\right]}{(2x+1)(2x-1)}$$

$$= \lim_{x\to\frac{1}{2}}\frac{2(3x+2)(2x-1)}{(2x+1)(2x-1)} = \lim_{x\to\frac{1}{2}}\frac{2(3x+2)}{(2x+1)}$$

Taking limit, we have

$$= \frac{2\left(3\times\frac{1}{2}+2\right)}{2\times\frac{1}{2}+1} = \frac{2\left(\frac{7}{2}\right)}{2} = \frac{7}{2}$$

Hence, the required answer is $\frac{7}{2}$.

SHORT ANSWER Type-II Questions (SA-II)

[**3** marks]

35. Evaluate: $\lim\limits_{x\to 0}\left[\dfrac{\sin 5x-\sin 3x}{\tan 7x}\right]$.

Ans. $$\lim_{x\to0}\left[\frac{\sin 5x-\sin 3x}{\tan 7x}\right] = \lim_{x\to0}\left[\frac{\frac{\sin 5x}{x}-\frac{\sin 3x}{x}}{\frac{\tan 7x}{x}}\right]$$

[on dividing numerator and denominator by x]

$$\lim_{x\to0}\left[\frac{5\frac{\sin 5x}{5x}-3\frac{\sin 3x}{3x}}{7\frac{\tan 7x}{7x}}\right]$$

$$= \frac{5\lim\limits_{x\to0}\left[\frac{\sin 5x}{5x}\right]-3\lim\limits_{x\to0}\left[\frac{\sin 3x}{3x}\right]}{7\lim\limits_{x\to0}\left[\frac{\tan 7x}{7x}\right]}$$

$$= \frac{5\lim\limits_{5x\to0}\left[\frac{\sin 5x}{5x}\right]-3\lim\limits_{3x\to0}\left[\frac{\sin 3x}{3x}\right]}{7\lim\limits_{7x\to0}\left[\frac{\tan 7x}{7x}\right]}$$

[$\because$ $5x\to0, 3x\to0, 7x\to0$ as $x\to0$]

$$= \frac{5(1)-3(1)}{7(1)} = \frac{2}{7}$$

36. Find $\lim\limits_{x\to0}[f(x)]$**, where** $f(x) = \begin{cases}\frac{|x|}{x} \text{ if } x\neq0\\ 0 \text{ if } x=0\end{cases}$.

Ans. $$f(x) = \begin{cases}\frac{|x|}{x}\text{ if } x\neq0\\ 0\text{ if } x=0\end{cases} = \begin{cases}\frac{x}{x}\text{ if } x>0\\ -\frac{x}{x}\text{ if } x=0\\ 0\text{ if } x=0\end{cases} = \begin{cases}1\text{ if } x>0\\ -1\text{ if } x<0\\ 0\text{ if } x=0\end{cases}$$

Given R.H.L. = $\lim\limits_{x\to0}[f(x)]$

$= \lim\limits_{x\to0}[1] = 1$

L.H.L. = $\lim\limits_{x\to0}[f(x)]$

$= \lim\limits_{x\to0}[-1] = -1$

Since, $\lim\limits_{x\to0}[f(x)] \neq \lim\limits_{x\to0}[f(x)]$

Hence, $\lim\limits_{x\to0}[f(x)]$ does not exist.

37. Evaluate: $\lim\limits_{x\to0}\left[\dfrac{\tan x-2\tan 3x+\tan 5x}{x}\right]$.

Ans. $$\lim_{x\to0}\left[\frac{\tan x-2\tan 3x+\tan 5x}{x}\right]$$

$$= \lim_{x\to0}\left[\frac{\tan x}{x}-\frac{2\tan 3x}{x}+\frac{\tan 5x}{x}\right]$$

$$= \lim_{x\to0}\left[\frac{\tan x}{x}-6\frac{\tan 3x}{3x}+5\frac{\tan 5x}{5x}\right]$$

$$= \lim_{x\to0}\left[\frac{\tan x}{x}\right]-6\lim_{x\to0}\left[\frac{\tan 3x}{3x}\right]+5\lim_{x\to0}\left[\frac{\tan 5x}{5x}\right]$$

$$= \lim_{x\to 0}\left[\frac{\tan x}{x}\right] - 6\lim_{3x\to 0}\left[\frac{\tan 3x}{3x}\right] + 5\lim_{5x\to 0}\left[\frac{\tan 5x}{5x}\right]$$

$[\because \to 0.5x\ 0 \text{ as } x \to 0]$

$= 1 - 6(1) + 5(1) = 0$

38. Evaluate: $\lim_{x\to a}\frac{\sin x - \sin a}{\sqrt{x}-\sqrt{a}}$. **[NCERT Exemplar]**

Ans. $\lim_{x\to a}\frac{\sin x - \sin a}{\sqrt{x}-\sqrt{a}} \times \frac{\sqrt{x}+\sqrt{a}}{\sqrt{x}+\sqrt{a}}$

$$= \lim_{x\to a}\frac{(\sin x - \sin a)(\sqrt{x}+\sqrt{a})}{x-a}$$

$$= \lim_{x\to a}\frac{\left(2\cos\frac{x+a}{2}\cdot\sin\frac{x-a}{2}\right)(\sqrt{x}+\sqrt{a})}{x-a}$$

$$= \lim_{x\to a}\left(2\cos\frac{x+a}{2}\cdot\frac{\sin\frac{x-a}{2}}{2\times\frac{x-a}{2}}\right)(\sqrt{x}+\sqrt{a})$$

$$= \lim_{x\to a}\cos\left(\frac{x+a}{2}\right)(\sqrt{x}+\sqrt{a})$$

$$\left[\because \lim_{\frac{x-a}{2}\to 0}\frac{\sin\frac{x-a}{2}}{\frac{x-a}{2}} = 1\right]$$

Taking limit we have

$$= \cos\left(\frac{a+a}{2}\right)(\sqrt{a}+\sqrt{a}) = \cos a \times 2\sqrt{a} = 2\sqrt{a}\cdot\cos a$$

Hence, required answer is $2\sqrt{a}\cdot\cos a$.

39. Evaluate: $\lim_{x\to 0}\frac{\sqrt{2}-\sqrt{1+\cos x}}{\sin^2 x}$.

[NCERT Exemplar]

Ans. Given that $\lim_{x\to 0}\frac{\sqrt{2}-\sqrt{1+\cos x}}{\sin^2 x}$

$$= \lim_{x\to 0}\frac{\sqrt{2}-\sqrt{1+\cos x}}{\sin^2 x}\times\frac{\sqrt{2}+\sqrt{1+\cos x}}{\sqrt{2}+\sqrt{1+\cos x}}$$

$$= \lim_{x\to 0}\frac{2-(1+\cos x)}{\sin^2 x\left[\sqrt{2}+\sqrt{1+\cos x}\right]}$$

$$= \lim_{x\to 0}\frac{1-\cos x}{\sin^2 x\left[\sqrt{2}+\sqrt{1+\cos x}\right]}$$

$$= \lim_{x\to 0}\frac{2\sin^2 x/2}{(2\sin x/2\cos x/2)^2}\times\frac{1}{\left[\sqrt{2}+\sqrt{1+\cos x}\right]}$$

$$= \lim_{x\to 0}\frac{2\sin^2 x/2}{(4\sin^2 x/2\cos^2 x/2)^2}\times\frac{1}{\left[\sqrt{2}+\sqrt{1+\cos x}\right]}$$

$$= \lim_{x\to 0}\frac{2}{4\cos^2\frac{x}{2}}\times\frac{1}{\left[\sqrt{2}+\sqrt{1+\cos x}\right]}$$

Taking limit, we get

$$= \frac{2}{4\cos^2 0}\times\frac{1}{(\sqrt{2}+\sqrt{2})} = \frac{1}{2}\times\frac{1}{2\sqrt{2}} = \frac{1}{4\sqrt{2}}$$

Hence, the required answer is $\frac{1}{4\sqrt{2}}$.

LONG ANSWER Type Questions (LA)

[**4** & **5** marks]

40. Evaluate: $\lim_{x\to 3}\frac{x^3-7x^2+15x-9}{x^4-5x^3+27x-27}$.

Ans. When, $x=3$, the expression $\lim_{x\to 3}\frac{x^3-7x^2+15x-9}{x^4-5x^3+27x-27}$ assumes the form $\frac{0}{0}$.

So, (x − 3) is a factor of numerator and denominator. Factorising the numerator and denominator,

we get

$$\lim_{x\to 3}\frac{x^3-7x^2+15x-9}{x^4-5x^3+27x-27} \quad \left(\text{form}\frac{0}{0}\right)$$

$$= \lim_{x\to 3}\frac{(x-3)(x^2-4x+3)}{(x-3)(x^3-2x^2-6x+9)} \quad \left(\text{form}\frac{0}{0}\right)$$

$$= \lim_{x\to 3}\frac{x^2-4x+3}{x^3-2x^2-6x+9} \quad \left(\text{form}\frac{0}{0}\right)$$

$$= \lim_{x\to 3}\frac{(x-3)(x-1)}{(x-3)(x^2+x-3)} \quad \left(\text{form}\frac{0}{0}\right)$$

$$= \lim_{x\to 3}\frac{x-1}{x^2+x-3} = \frac{3-1}{9+3-3} = \frac{2}{9}$$

41. Evaluate: $\lim_{x\to a}\left[\frac{\log x - \log a}{x-a}\right]$.

Ans. We have, $\lim_{x\to a}\left[\frac{\log x-\log a}{x-a}\right]$

Put $x = a + y$

Then, $y = x - a$ and $y \to 0$ as $x \to a$

$$\lim_{x\to 0}\left[\frac{\log x-\log a}{x-a}\right]=\lim_{y\to 0}\left[\frac{\log(a+y)-\log a}{y}\right]$$

$$=\lim_{y\to 0}\left[\frac{\log\left(\frac{a+y}{a}\right)}{y}\right]$$

$$=\lim_{y\to 0}\left[\frac{\log\left(1+\frac{y}{a}\right)}{a\left(\frac{y}{a}\right)}\right]$$

$$=\frac{1}{a}\lim_{y\to 0}\left[\frac{\log\left(1+\frac{y}{a}\right)}{\left(\frac{y}{a}\right)}\right]$$

$$=\frac{1}{a}\lim_{(y/a)\to 0}\left[\frac{\log\left(1+\frac{y}{a}\right)}{\left(\frac{y}{a}\right)}\right]$$

$$=\left[\because \frac{y}{a}\to 0 \text{ as } y\to 0\right]$$

$$=\frac{1}{a}(1)=\frac{1}{a}$$

42. Evaluate: $\lim_{x\to\pi/3}\left[\frac{\sqrt{1-\cos 6x}}{\sqrt{2}\left(\frac{\pi}{3}-x\right)}\right]$.

Ans. Given:

Let $L = \lim_{x\to\pi/3}\left[\frac{\sqrt{1-\cos 6x}}{\sqrt{2}\left(\frac{\pi}{3}-x\right)}\right]$

Put $x = \frac{\pi}{3} - y$

Then, $y = \frac{\pi}{3} - x$ and $y \to 0$ as $x \to \frac{\pi}{3}$

$$\therefore \quad L=\lim_{y\to 0}\left[\frac{\sqrt{1-\cos(2\pi-6y)}}{\sqrt{2}y}\right]$$

$$=\lim_{y\to 0}\left[\frac{\sqrt{1-\cos 6y}}{\sqrt{2}y}\right]$$

$$=\lim_{y\to 0}\left[\frac{\sqrt{2\sin^2 3y}}{\sqrt{2}y}\right]$$

$$=\lim_{y\to 0}\left[\frac{\sin 3y}{y}\right]$$

$$=\lim_{y\to 0}\left[\frac{3\sin 3y}{3y}\right]$$

$$=\lim_{y\to 0}\left[\frac{\sin 3y}{3y}\right]$$

$$=3\lim_{3y\to 0}\left[\frac{\sin 3y}{3y}\right] \qquad [\because 3y\ 0 \text{ as } y\ 0]$$

$$=3(1)=3$$

43. Differentiate cos(x^2 + 1)s with respect to 'x' using first principal method.

[NCERT Exemplar]

Ans. Let $f(x) = \cos(x^2 + 1)$ ...(i)

$\Rightarrow \quad f(x + \Delta x) = \cos[(x + \Delta x)^2 + 1]$ ...(ii)

Subtracting equation (i) from equation (ii) we get

$f(x + \Delta x) - f(x) = \cos[(x + \Delta x)^2 + 1] - \cos(x^2 + 1)$

Dividing both sides by Δx we get

$$=\frac{f(x+\Delta x)-f(x)}{\Delta x}=\frac{[\cos[(x+\Delta x)^2+1]-\cos(x^2+1)]}{\Delta x}$$

$$=\lim_{\Delta x\to 0}\frac{f(x+\Delta x)-f(x)}{\Delta x}$$

$$=\lim_{\Delta x\to 0}\frac{\cos[(x+\Delta x)^2+1)]-\cos(x^2+1)}{\Delta x}$$

$$=f'(x)=\lim_{\Delta x\to 0}\frac{\cos[(x+\Delta x)^2+1]-\cos(x^2+1)}{\Delta x}$$

$$=\lim_{\Delta x\to 0}-2\sin\left[\frac{(x+\Delta x)^2+1+x^2+1}{2}\right]\times\frac{\sin\left[\frac{(x+\Delta x)^2+1-x^2-1}{2}\right]}{\Delta x}$$

$$\left[\because \cos C-\cos D=-2\sin\frac{C+D}{2}.\sin\frac{C-D}{2}\right]$$

$$=\lim_{\Delta x\to 0}-2\sin\left[\frac{x^2+\Delta x^2+2x.\Delta x+x^2+2}{2}\right]\times\frac{\sin[\frac{x^2+\Delta x^2+2x.\Delta x-x^2}{2}}{\Delta x}$$

$$=\lim_{\Delta x\to 0}\frac{-2\sin\frac{[x^2+\frac{\Delta x^2}{2}+x.\Delta x-1]}{2}\sin\left[\Delta x\frac{(\Delta x+2x)}{2}\right]}{\Delta x}$$

$$=-2\sin\left[x^2+\frac{\Delta x^2}{2}+x\Delta x+1\right]$$

$$= \lim_{\Delta x \to 0} \frac{\sin\left[\Delta x \frac{(\Delta x + 2x)}{2}\right]}{\Delta x\left[\frac{\Delta x + 2x}{2}\right]} \times \left(\frac{\Delta x + 2x}{2}\right)$$

$$= \lim_{\Delta x \to 0} -2\sin\left[x^2 + \frac{\Delta x^2}{2} + x\Delta x + 1\right]$$

$$.\sin\frac{\left[\Delta x \frac{(\Delta x + 2x)}{2}\right]}{\Delta x\left[\frac{\Delta x + 2x}{2}\right]} \times \left[\frac{\Delta x + 2x}{2}\right]$$

$$\therefore \; \Delta x\left[\frac{\Delta x + 2x}{2}\right] \to 0$$

Taking limit, we have

$= -2 \sin (x^2 + 1) \cdot 1 \cdot (x) = -2x \sin (x^2 + 1)$

$$\left[\because \lim_{x \to 0} \frac{\sin x}{x} = 1\right]$$

Hence, the required answer is $-2x \sin (x^2 + 1)$.

DIFFERENTIATION 2

TOPIC 1

DERIVATIVE AT A POINT

Let $f(x)$ be a real valued function defined on an open interval (a, b) and let $c \in (a, b)$. Then, $f(x)$ is said to be differentiable or derivable at $x = c$, if

$$\lim_{x \to c} \frac{f(x) - f(c)}{x - c} \text{ exists finitely.}$$

This limit is called the derivative or differentiation of $f(x)$ at $x = c$ and is denoted by $f'(c)$ or $Df(c)$ or $\left\{\frac{d}{dx} f(x)\right\} x = c$.

That is,

$$f'(c) = \lim_{x \to c} \frac{f(x) - f(c)}{x - c}, \text{ provided that the limit exists.}$$

Throughout this chapter it will be assumed that a given function $f(x)$ is differentiable at every point in its domain, i.e. $\lim_{x \to c} \frac{f(x) - f(c)}{x - c}$ exists for all c in its domain.

$$\therefore \quad f'(c) = \lim_{x \to c^+} \frac{f(x) - f(c)}{x - c} = \lim_{x \to c^-} \frac{f(x) - f(c)}{x - c}$$

$$\Rightarrow \quad f'(c) = \lim_{h \to 0} \frac{f(c + h) - f(c)}{h}$$

$$\text{or,} \quad f'(c) = \lim_{h \to 0} \frac{f(c - h) - f(c)}{-h}$$

Geometrical Meaning of $\frac{dy}{dx}$

Let $P(a, f(a))$ be any point on the curve $y = f(x)$.

Let $Q(a + h, f(a + h))$ be any neighbouring point on the curve. Let the secant PQ be inclined at an angle θ with, x-axis, as shown in the figure.

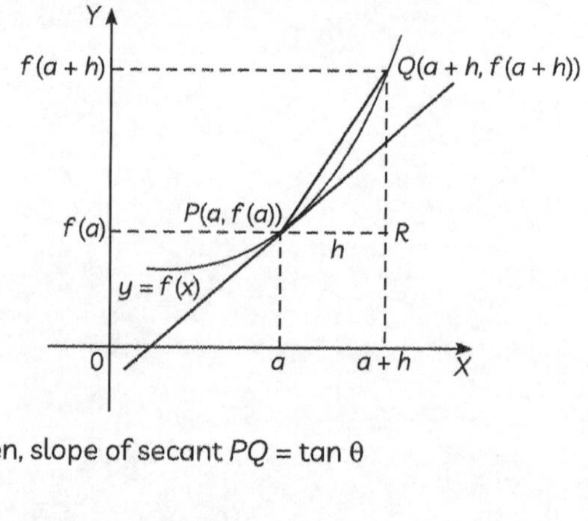

Then, slope of secant $PQ = \tan\theta$

$$= \frac{QR}{PR}$$

$$= \frac{f(a + h) - f(a)}{h}.$$

As $h \to 0$, we observe that $Q \to P$ and secant $PQ \to$ tangent at point P.

So, slope of tangent at $P = \lim_{Q \to P}$ [slope of secant PQ]

$$\lim_{h \to 0}\left[\frac{f(a + h) - f(a)}{h}\right] = \left(\frac{dy}{dx}\right)_{x = a}$$

Conclusion: $\left(\frac{dy}{dx}\right)_{x = a}$ represent slope of tangent to the curve $y = f(x)$ at the point $(a, f(a))$.

In general, $\frac{dy}{dx}$ represents the slope of the tangent to the curve $y = f(x)$ at the point (x, y).

Basic Rules of Differentiation

In the previous section, we have discussed the method of finding the derivative using the first principle. In this section, we shall learn how to find the derivation without using the first principle directly.

Let us now summarize the results from the previous section.

1. $\frac{d}{dx}(a) = 0$, where a is a constant.
2. $\frac{d}{dx}(x^n) = nx^{n-1}$.
3. $\frac{d}{dx}(\sin x) = \cos x$.
4. $\frac{d}{dx}(\cos x) = -\sin x$.
5. $\frac{d}{dx}(\tan x) = \sec^2 x$.
6. $\frac{d}{dx}(\cot x) = -\text{cosec}^2\, x$.
7. $\frac{d}{dx}(\sec x) = \sec x . \tan x$.
8. $\frac{d}{dx}(\text{cosec}\, x) = -\text{cosec}x . \cot x$.

Let us now state a very important theorem. This theorem tells us the method of finding the derivatives of sum, difference, product and quotient of functions.

Theorem

Let f and g be two real functions such that their derivatives are defined in domain D.

Let c be any real number. Then

(1) Derivative of the scalar multiple of a function is given by

$$\frac{d}{dx}[cf(x)] = c\frac{d}{dx}[f(x)]$$

(2) Derivative of the power of a function is given by

$$\frac{d}{dx}[\{f(x)\}^n] = n\{f(x)\}^{n-1}\frac{d}{dx}[f(x)].$$

(3) Derivative of sum of function is given by

$$\frac{d}{dx}[f(x)+g(x)] = \frac{d}{dx}[f(x)] + \frac{d}{dx}[g(x)].$$

(4) Derivative of difference of function is given by

$$\frac{d}{dx}[f(x)-g(x)] = \frac{d}{dx}[f(x)] - \frac{d}{dx}[g(x)].$$

(5) Derivation of product of function is given by

$$\frac{d}{dx}[f(x)g(x)] = f(x)\frac{d}{dx}[g(x)] + g(x)\frac{d}{dx}[f(x)].$$

(6) Derivation of quotient of functions is given by

$$\frac{d}{dx}\left[\frac{f(x)}{g(x)}\right] = \frac{g(x)\frac{d}{dx}[f(x)] - f(x)\frac{d}{dx}[g(x)]}{[g(x)]^2}$$

Whenever $g(x) \neq 0$.

Example 2.1: Find the derivative of the following functions w.r.t. x:

(A) $\frac{a}{x^4} - \frac{b}{x^2} + \cos x$

(B) x^4 **(5 sin x – 3 cos x)**

Ans. (A) Let $f(x) = \frac{a}{x^4} - \frac{b}{x^2} + \cos x$

Then, $f'(x) = \frac{d}{dx}\left(\frac{a}{x^4} - \frac{b}{x^2} + \cos x\right)$

$= \frac{d}{dx}\left(\frac{a}{x^4}\right) - \frac{d}{dx}\left(\frac{b}{x^2}\right) + \frac{d}{dx}(\cos x)$

$= a\frac{d}{dx}(x^{-4}) - b\frac{d}{dx}(x^{-2}) + \frac{d}{dx}(\cos x)$

$= a(-4x^{-5}) - b.(-2x^{-3}) - \sin x$

$= -\frac{4a}{x^5} + \frac{2b}{x^3} - \sin x.$

(B) Let $f(x) = x^4 (5 \sin x - 3 \cos x)$.

Then, $f'(x) = \frac{d}{dx}[x^4 (5 \sin x - 3 \cos x)]$

$= x^4 \frac{d}{dx}(5 \sin x - 3 \cos x) + (5 \sin x - 3 \cos x)\frac{d}{dx}(x^4)$

$= x^4\left[\frac{d}{dx}(5 \sin x) - \frac{d}{dx}(3 \cos x)\right] + (5 \sin x - 3 \cos x)(4x^3)$

$= x^4 (5 \cos x + 3 \sin x) + (5 \sin x - 3 \cos x)(4x^3)$

Example 2.2: Find the derivation of the following functions w.r.t x:

(A) **5 sin x – 6 cos x + 7**

(B) **2 tan x – 7 sec x**

Ans. (A) Let $f(x) = 5 \sin x - 6 \cos x + 7$

Then, $f'(x) = \frac{d}{dx}(5 \sin x - 6 \cos x + 7)$

$= \frac{d}{dx}(5 \sin x) - \frac{d}{dx}(6 \cos x) + \frac{d}{dx}(7)$

$= 5\frac{d}{dx}(\sin x) - 6\frac{d}{dx}(\cos x) + 0$

$= 5 \cos x + 6 \sin x$

(B) Let $f(x) = 2 \tan x - 7 \sec x$

Then, $f'(x) = \frac{d}{dx}(2 \tan x - 7 \sec x)$

$= \frac{d}{dx}(2 \tan x) - \frac{d}{dx}(7 \sec x)$

$= 2\frac{d}{dx}(\tan x) - 7\frac{d}{dx}(\sec x)$

$= 2 \sec^2 x - 7 \sec x \tan x.$

Example 2.3: Differentiate the following functions with respect to x:

(A) **sin (x + a)**

(B) $\frac{\sin(x+a)}{\cos x}$

Ans. (A) Clearly, $\frac{d}{dx}[\sin(x+a)]$

$= \frac{d}{dx}[\sin x \cos a + \cos x \sin a]$

$= \frac{d}{dx}(\sin x \cos a) + \frac{d}{dx}(\cos x \sin a)$

$= \cos a\frac{d}{dx}(\sin x) + \sin a\frac{d}{dx}(\cos x)$

$= \cos a \cos x + \sin a (-\sin x)$

$= \cos x \cos a - \sin x \sin a = \cos (x + a)$

(B) Clearly, $\frac{d}{dx}\left\{\frac{\sin(x+a)}{\cos x}\right\}$

$$= \frac{d}{dx}\left\{\frac{\sin x \cos a + \cos x \sin a}{\cos x}\right\}$$

$$= \frac{d}{dx}\{\tan x \cos a + \sin a\}$$

$$= \frac{d}{dx}(\tan x \cos a) + \frac{d}{dx}(\sin a)$$

$$= \cos a \frac{d}{dx}(\tan x) + \frac{d}{dx}(\sin a)$$

$$= \cos a \times \sec^2 x + 0 = \sec^2 x \cos a$$

Example 2.4: Find the derivatives of the $x^3 - 27$ function from first principles.

Ans. Let $f(x) = x^3 - 27$.

Then, $f(x + h) = (x + h)^3 - 27$

$$\therefore \quad \frac{d}{dx}(f(x)) = \lim_{h\to 0}\frac{f(x+h)-f(x)}{h}$$

$$\Rightarrow \quad \frac{d}{dx}(f(x)) = \lim_{h\to 0}\frac{\{(x+h)^3 - 27\} - (x^3 - 27)}{h}$$

$$\Rightarrow \quad \frac{d}{dx}(f(x))$$

$$= \lim_{h\to 0}\frac{(x^3 + 3x^2h + 3xh^2 + h^3 - 27) - (x^3 - 27)}{h}$$

$$\Rightarrow \quad \frac{d}{dx}(f(x)) = \lim_{h\to 0}\frac{3x^2h + 3xh^2 + h^3}{h}$$

$$\Rightarrow \quad \frac{d}{dx}(f(x)) = \lim_{h\to 0}(3x^2 + 3xh + h^2)$$

$$= 3x^2 + 3x \times 0 \div 0 = 3x^2$$

Example 2.5: Find the derivative of the following functions (it is to be understood that *a, b, c, d, p, q, r* and *s* are fixed non-zero constant *m* and *n* are integers).

(A) $\dfrac{4x + 5\sin x}{3x + 7\cos x}$ **(B)** $(ax + b)^n$

(C) $\dfrac{px^2 + qx + r}{ax + b}$ **(D)** $\dfrac{a}{x^4} - \dfrac{b}{x^2} + \cos x$

Ans. (A) Let $(x) = \dfrac{4x + 5\sin x}{3x + 7\cos x}$

By quotient rule,

$$f'(x) = \frac{(3x+7\cos x)\frac{d}{dx}(4x+5\sin x) - (4x+5\sin x)\frac{d}{dx}(3x+7\cos x)}{(3x+7\cos x)^2}$$

$$= \frac{(3x+7\cos x)\left[4\frac{d}{dx}(x) + 5\frac{d}{dx}(\sin x)\right] - (4x+5\sin x)\left[3\frac{d}{dx}(x) + 7\frac{d}{dx}(\cos x)\right]}{(3x+7\cos x)^2}$$

$$= \frac{(3x+7\cos x)[4+5\cos x] - (4x+5\sin x)[3-7\sin x]}{(3x+7\cos x)^2}$$

$$= \frac{12x + 15x\cos x + 28\cos x + 35\cos^2 x - 12x + 28x\sin x - 15\sin x + 35\sin^2 x}{(3x+7\cos x)^2}$$

$$= \frac{15x\cos x + 28\cos x + 28x\sin x - 15\sin x + 35(\cos^2 x + \sin^2 x)}{(3x+7\cos x)^2}$$

$$= \frac{35 + 15x\cos x + 28\cos x + 28x\sin x - 15\sin x}{(3x+7\cos x)^2}$$

(B) Let $f(x) = (ax + b)^n$.

Accordingly, $f(x + h) = \{a(x + h) + b\}^n$

$= (ax + ah + b)^n$

By first principle,

$$f'(x) = \lim_{h\to 0}\frac{f(x+h)-f(x)}{h}$$

$$= \lim_{h\to 0}\frac{(ax+ah+b)^n - (ax+b)^n}{h}$$

$$= \lim_{h\to 0}\frac{(ax+b)^n\left(1+\frac{ah}{ax+b}\right)^n - (ax+b)^n}{h}$$

$$= (ax+b)^n \lim_{h\to 0}\frac{1}{h}\left[\left\{1 + \left(\frac{ah}{ax+b}\right) + \frac{n(n-1)}{2}\left(\frac{ab}{ax+b}\right)^2 + \ldots\right\} - 1\right]$$

(using binomial theorem)

$$= (ax+b)^n \lim_{h\to 0}\frac{1}{h}\left[n\left(\frac{ah}{ax+b}\right) + \frac{n(n-1)a^2h^2}{2(ax+b)^2} + \ldots \text{ (terms containing higher degree of } h)\right]$$

$$= (ax+b)^n \lim_{h\to 0}\left[\frac{na}{(ax+b)} + \frac{n(n-a)a^2h^2}{2(ax+b)^2} + \ldots\right]$$

$$= (ax+b)^n\left[\frac{na}{(ax+b)} + 0\right]$$

$$= na\frac{(ax+b)^n}{ax+b}$$

$$= na(ax+b)^{(n-1)}$$

(C) Let $f(x)=\dfrac{px^2+qx+r}{ax+b}$

By quotient rule.

$$f(x)=\frac{(ax+b)\frac{d}{dx}(px^2+qx+r)-(px^2+qx+r)\frac{d}{dx}(ax+b)}{(ax+b)^2}$$

$$=\frac{(ax+b)(2px+q)-(px^2+qx+r)(a)}{(ax+b)^2}$$

$$=\frac{2apx^2+aqx+2bpx+bq-apx^2-aqx-ar}{(ax+b)^2}$$

$$=\frac{apx^2+2bpx+bq-ar}{(ax+b)^2}$$

(D) Let $f(x)=\dfrac{a}{x^4}-\dfrac{b}{x^2}+\cos x$

$$f'(x)=\frac{d}{dx}\left(\frac{a}{x^4}\right)-\frac{d}{dx}\left(\frac{b}{x^2}\right)+\frac{d}{dx}(\cos x)$$

$$= a\frac{d}{dx}(x^{-4})-b\frac{d}{dx}(x^{-2})+\frac{d}{dx}(\cos x)$$

$$= a(-4x^{-5}) - b(-2x^{-3}) + (-\sin x)$$

$$\left[\frac{d}{dx}(x^n)=nx^{n-1} \text{ and } \frac{d}{dx}(\cos x)=-\sin x\right]$$

$$=\frac{-4a}{x^5}+\frac{2b}{x^3}-\sin x$$

OBJECTIVE Type Questions

[1 mark]

Multiple Choice Questions

1. Find the deviation of e^{-9x}.

(a) e^{-9x} **(b) $9e^{-9x}$**

(c) $-9e^{-9x}$ **(d) None**

Ans. *(c) $-9e^{-9x}$*

Explanation: $\dfrac{d(e^{-9x})}{dx}=e^{-9x}\times\dfrac{d(-9x)}{dx}$

$= -9e^{-9x}$

Hence, option (c) is the correct answer

2. Derivation of $5e^{\log x}$ is:

(a) $5x^4$ **(b) x^5**

(c) $4x^4$ **(d) None**

Ans. *(a) $5x^4$*

Explanation: $\dfrac{d(5e^{\log x})}{dx}=e^{\log_x 5}$

$= x^5$

$= 5x^4$

Hence, option (a) is the correct answer.

3. Derivation of $\sin^3 x$ is:

(a) $\cos^3 x$ **(b) $3\sin^3 x$**

(c) $3\sin^2 x\cos x$ **(d) 0**

Ans. *(c) $3\sin^2 x\cos x$*

Explanation: $\dfrac{d(\sin^3 x)}{dx}=(\sin x)^3$

$= 3\sin^2 x\times\dfrac{d(\sin x)}{dx}$

$= 3\sin^2 x\cos x$

Hence, option (c) is the correct answer.

4. $f(x) = x^2 - 5x + 7$

$f'(3)$ = ... :

(a) 11 **(b) 1**

(c) 4 **(d) 0** **[DIKSHA]**

Ans. *(b) 1*

Explanation: $f(x) = x^2 - 5x + 7$

$f'(x) = 2x - 5$

$f'(3) = 2 \times 3 - 5$

$= 6 - 5$

$= 1$

Hence, option (b) is the correct answer.

5. Derivation of log *b* is:

(a) 1/*b* **(b) 0**

(c) Not define **(d) 1**

Ans. *(b) 0*

Explanation: $\dfrac{d(\log b)}{dx}$

Here, log *b* is constant so derivative of constant is 0.

Hence, option (b) is the correct answer.

6. Derivation of cos 0° is:

(a) 0 **(b) 1**

(c) 2 **(d) 3**

Ans. *(a) 0*

Explanation: $\dfrac{d(\cos 0°)}{dx}$

Value of $\cos 0° = 1$, which is a constant

So, the derivative of constant is 0.

Hence, option (a) is the correct answer.

7. **Derivation of $\log_x x$ is:**

(a) 1 (b) 0

(c) 2 (d) 3

Ans. *(b) 0*

Explanation: $\dfrac{d(\log_x x)}{dx}$

Here, value of base and numerator are same that means

$\log_x x = 1$ so differentiation of $\log_x x = 0$

Hence, option (b) is the correct answer.

8. **Differentiate $\left(\dfrac{x}{2}+\dfrac{2}{x}\right)$.**

(a) $\dfrac{1}{2}+\dfrac{2}{x^2}$ (b) $\dfrac{1}{2}-\dfrac{2}{x^2}$

(c) $\dfrac{x}{2}-\dfrac{2}{x^2}$ (d) $\dfrac{1}{2}-\dfrac{2}{x}$ **[DIKSHA]**

Ans. *(b) $\dfrac{1}{2}-\dfrac{2}{x^2}$*

Explanation: $\dfrac{d}{dx}\left(\dfrac{x}{2}+\dfrac{2}{x}\right)$

$$= \frac{d\left(\frac{x}{2}\right)}{dx}+\frac{d\left(\frac{2}{x}\right)}{dx}$$

$$= \frac{1}{2}-\frac{2}{x^2}$$

Hence, option (b) is the correct answer.

9. **Derivation of $\tan^2 x$ is:**

(a) $2 \tan x \cdot \sec^2 x$ (b) $\cot^2 x$

(c) 0 (d) None

Ans. *(a) $2 \tan x \cdot \sec^2 x$*

Explanation: $\dfrac{d(\tan^2 x)}{dx}=\dfrac{d(\tan x)^2}{dx}2$

$$= 2\tan x\frac{d(\tan x)}{dx}$$

$$= 2 \tan x \sec^2 x$$

Hence, option (a) is the correct answer.

10. **Derivation of $ax^3 + 2x$ is:**

(a) 0 (b) $3ax^2 + 2$

(c) $3x^2 + 2$ (d) None

Ans. *(b) $3ax^2 + 2$*

Explanation: $\dfrac{d(ax^3+2x)}{dx}=\dfrac{adx^3}{dx}+\dfrac{2dx}{dx}$

$$= 3ax^2 + 2$$

Hence, option (b) is the correct answer.

11. **If $y = (\sin x + \tan x)$, find $\dfrac{dy}{dx}$ at $x=\dfrac{\pi}{3}$.**

(a) $\dfrac{\sqrt{3}}{2}+\sqrt{3}$ (b) $\sqrt{\dfrac{3}{2}+\dfrac{4}{3}}$

(c) $\dfrac{\sqrt{3}}{2}+4$ (d) $\dfrac{9}{2}$ **[DIKSHA]**

Ans. *(d) $\dfrac{9}{2}$*

Explanation: Given: $y = (\sin x + \tan x)$

To find: $\dfrac{dy}{dx}$ at $x=\dfrac{\pi}{3}$

$y = (\sin x + \tan x)$

Differentiation w.r.t. 'x'

$$\frac{dy}{dx} = (\cos x + \sec^2 x)$$

$$\left[\text{As}\ \frac{d}{dx}(\tan x)=\sec^2 x;\quad \frac{d}{dx}(\sin x)=\cos x\right]$$

$$\therefore\quad \left.\frac{dy}{dx}\right|_{x=\frac{\pi}{3}}=\left(\cos\frac{\pi}{3}+\sec^2\frac{\pi}{3}\right)$$

$$= \frac{1}{2}+(2)^2=\frac{1}{2}+4=\frac{9}{2}$$

Hence, option (d) is the correct answer.

Assertion-Reason (A-R)

DIRECTION: In the following questions, a statement of assertion (A) is followed by a statement of the reason (R). Mark the correct choice as:

(a) Both assertion (A) and reason (R) are true and reason (R) is the correct explanation of assertion (A).

(b) Both assertion (A) and reason (R) are true but reason (R) is not the correct explanation of assertion (A).

(c) Assertion (A) is true but reason (R) is false.

(d) Assertion (A) is false but reason (R) is true.

12. **Let $u = f(x)$ and $v = g(x)$. Then,**

Assertion: **$(uv)' = u'v + uv'$ is a Leibnitz rule or product rule.**

Reason: $\left(\dfrac{u}{v}\right)'=\dfrac{u'v-uv'}{v'}$ **is a Leibnitz rule or quotient rule.**

Ans. *(c) Assertion (A) is true but reason (R) is false.*

Explanation: Let $u = f(x)$ and $v = g(x)$.

Then, $(uv)' = u'v + uv'$

This is referred as Leibnitz rule or the product rule for differentiating product of functions. Similarly, the quotient rule is $\left(\frac{u}{v}\right)' = \frac{u'v - uv'}{v^2}$.

Hence, option (c) is the correct answer.

13. Assertion: The derivation of $f(x) = x^3$ is x^2.

Reason: The derivation of $f(x) = x^n$ is nx^{n-1}.

Ans. *(d) Assertion (A) is false but reason (R) is true.*

Explanation: We have, $f(x) = x^3$

$\Rightarrow f'(x) = 3x^2 \neq x^2$

$\therefore$ Assertion is false but reason is true.

Hence, option (d) is the correct answer.

14. Assertion: The derivation of $y = 2x - \frac{3}{4}$ is 2.

Reason: The derivation of $y = cx$ is c.

Ans. *(a) Both assertion (A) and reason (R) are true and reason (R) is the correct explanation of assertion (A).*

Explanation: We have, $y = 2x - \frac{3}{4}$

$$\Rightarrow \frac{dy}{dx} = (2 \times 1) - 0 = 2$$

Hence, option (a) is the correct answer.

15. Assertion: The derivation of $h(x) = \frac{x + \cos x}{\tan x}$ is $\frac{(1-\sin x)\tan x - (x + \cos x)\sec^2 x}{(\tan x)^2}$.

Reason: $\left(\frac{u}{v}\right)' = \frac{u'v - uv'}{(v)^2}$.

Ans. *(a) Both assertion (A) and reason (R) are true and reason (R) is the correct explanation of assertion (A).*

Explanation: We have, $h(x) = \frac{x + \cos x}{\tan x}$ ...(i)

Differentiating both sides of (i) w.r.t. 'x', we get

$$h'(x) = \frac{(x + \cos x)' \tan x - (x + \cos x)(\tan x)'}{(\tan x)^2}$$

$$= \frac{(1 - \sin x)\tan x - (x + \cos x)\sec^2 x}{(\tan x)^2}$$

Hence, option(a) is the correct answer.

CASE BASED Questions (CBQs)

[4 & 5 marks]

Read the following passages and answer the questions that follow:

16. *Let f be a real valued function, the function defined by $f'(x) = \lim_{h \to 0} \frac{f(x+h) - f(x)}{h}$ whenever the limit exists is defined to be the derivative of f at x.*

For a function, f(x) = tan x, answer the following questions.

(A) Find the value of $f(x + h) - f(x)$.

(B) Find the value of $\lim_{h \to 0} \frac{f(x+h) - f(x)}{h}$.

Ans. (A) $f(x + h) - f(x) = \tan (x + h) - \tan x$

$$= \frac{\sin(x+h)}{\cos(x+h)} - \frac{\sin x}{\cos x}$$

$$= \frac{\sin(x+h)\cos x - \sin x \cos(x+h)}{\cos x . \cos(x+h)}$$

$$= \frac{\sin(x + h - x)}{\cos x . \cos(x+h)} = \frac{\sin h}{\cos x \cos(x+h)}$$

(B) $\lim_{h \to 0} \frac{f(x+h) - f(x)}{h}$

$$= \lim_{h \to 0} \frac{\sin h}{h} \cdot \lim_{h \to 0} \frac{1}{\cos x \cdot \cos(x+h)}$$

$$= \lim_{h \to 0} \frac{1}{\cos x \cdot \cos(x+h)} \qquad \left[\because \lim_{x \to 0} \frac{\sin x}{x} = 1\right]$$

$$= \frac{1}{\cos^2 x}$$

17. *Let f be a real valued function, the function defined by $f'(x) = \lim_{h \to 0} \frac{f(x+h) - f(x)}{h}$*

For a function f(x) = sin x + cos x, answer the following questions.

(A) The derivative of f(x) w.r.t x is:

(a) cos x + sin x **(b) cos x – sin x**

(c) 0 **(d) None of these**

(B) The value of f'(0) is:

(a) 2 **(b) 0**

(c) 1 **(d) –1**

(C) The value of $f'(90°)$ is:

(a) 2 (b) 0

(c) 1 (d) –1

(D) The value of $f'(60°)$ is:

(a) 2 (b) 0

(c) 1 (d) –1

Ans: (A) *(b) cos x – sin x*

Explanation: Since $f(x) = \sin x + \cos x$

Hence derivative, $f'(x) = \cos x - \sin x$

Hence, option(b) is the correct answer.

(B) *(c) 1*

Explanation: $f'(x) = \cos x - \sin x$

$$f'(0) = \cos 0° - \sin 0° = 1 - 0 = 1$$

Hence, option(c) is the correct answer.

(C) *(d) –1*

Explanation: $f'(x) = \cos x - \sin x$

$$f'(90) = \cos 90° - \sin 90° = 0 - 1 = -1$$

Hence, option(d) is the correct answer.

(D) *(d) –1*

Explanation: $f'(x) = \cos x - \sin x$

$$f'(60) = \cos 60 - \sin 60 = \frac{1}{2} - \frac{3}{2} = -1$$

Hence, option(d) is the correct answer.

VERY SHORT ANSWER Type Questions (VSA)

[1 mark]

18. **Evaluate** $\dfrac{x^3 + x^2 + x + 1}{x^2}$.

Ans. $\dfrac{d}{dx}\left(\dfrac{x^3+x^2+x+1}{x^2}\right) = \dfrac{d}{dx}\left(x+1+\dfrac{1}{x}+\dfrac{1}{x^2}\right)$

$$= \frac{d}{dx}x + \frac{d}{dx}\cdot 1 + \frac{d}{dx}\frac{1}{x} + \frac{d}{dx}\left(\frac{1}{x^2}\right)$$

$$= 1 + 0 - \frac{1}{x^2} + \left(-\frac{2}{x^3}\right)$$

$$= 1 - \frac{1}{x^2} - \frac{2}{x^3}$$

19. **Find (3x + 5)(1 + tan x).** **[NCERT Exemplar]**

Ans. Let $y = (3x + 5)(1 + \tan x)$

Applying product rule of differentiation that is

$$\Rightarrow \frac{dy}{dx} = (1+\tan x)\frac{d}{dx}(3x+5) + (3x+5)\frac{d}{dx}(1+\tan x)$$

$$\Rightarrow \frac{dy}{dx} = 3(1 + \tan x) + (3x + 5)\sec^2 x$$

$$= 3x\sec^2 x + 5\sec^2 x + 3 + 3\tan x.$$

(by using product rule)

Hence, the required answer is

$3x\sec^2 x + 5\sec^2 x + 3\tan x + 3$.

20. **Differentiate (3x – 5)(1 + cot x).**

Ans. Let $y = (3x - 5)(1 + \cot x)$

$$\therefore \frac{dy}{dx} = \frac{d}{dx}[(3x - 5)(1 + \cot x)]$$

$$= (3x - 5)\frac{d}{dx}(1 + \cot x) + (1 + \cot x)\frac{d}{dx}(3x - 5)$$

$$= (3x - 5)(-\operatorname{cosec}^2 x) + (1 + \cot x).3$$

$$= -(3x - 5)\operatorname{cosec}^2 x + 3(1 + \cot x)$$

$$= -3x\operatorname{cosec}^2 x + 5\operatorname{cosec}^2 x + 3\cot x + 3$$

21. **Evaluate** $\dfrac{x^5 - \cos x}{\sin x}$. **[NCERT Exemplar]**

Ans. Given $y = \dfrac{x^5 - \cos x}{\sin x}$

$\dfrac{d}{dx}(x^5 - \cos x)/\sin x = [\sin x.d/dx(x^5 - \cos x) - (x^5 - \cos x).d/dx(\sin x)]/\sin^2 x$

By using quotient rule,

$$= \frac{[\sin x(5x^4 + \sin x) - (x^5 - \cos x)(\cos x)]}{\sin^2 x}$$

$$= \frac{[5x^4.\sin x + \sin^2 x - x^5\cos x + \cos^2 x]}{\sin^2 x}$$

$$= \frac{[5x^4\sin x - x^5\cos x + (\sin^2 + \cos^2 x)]}{\sin^2 x}$$

$$= \frac{[5x^4\sin x - x^5\cos x + 1]}{\sin^2 x}$$

Hence, the required answer is

$$\frac{[5x^4\sin x - x^5\cos x + 1]}{\sin^2 x}.$$

SHORT ANSWER Type-I Questions (SA-I)

[2 marks]

22. If $y = x.e^{\sin x^2}$ then find $\frac{dy}{dx}$.

Ans. $y = x.e^{\sin x^2}$

using product rule.

$$= x\frac{d}{dx}\left(e^{\sin x^2}\right)+\left(e^{\sin x^2}\right)\frac{d}{dx}(x)$$

$$\frac{dy}{dx} = x.e^{\sin x^2}\cdot\cos x^2\cdot 2x + e^{\sin x^2}\cdot 1$$

$$= 2x^2\cdot e^{\sin x^2}\cdot\cos x^2 + e^{\sin x^2}.$$

So required solution is

$$\frac{dy}{dx} = e^{\sin x^2}(2x^2\cos x^2 + 1)$$

23. Find the derivation of a^{x+3}.

Ans. As we know that:

$$\frac{d(a^x)}{dx} = a^x \log a$$

So, $\frac{d(a^{x+3})}{dx} = a^{x+3}\log a$

24. Differentiate the functions with respect to x:

$\frac{x^4 + x^3 + x^2 + 1}{x}$ **[NCERT Exampler]**

Ans. Let $y = \frac{x^4 + x^3 + x^2 + 1}{x}$

$$\Rightarrow y = \frac{x^4 + x^3 + x^2 + 1}{x}$$

Dividing by x we get

$$\Rightarrow y = x^3 + x^2 + x + \frac{1}{x}$$

Differentiating a given equation with respect to x

$$\Rightarrow \frac{dy}{dx} = \frac{d}{dx}\left(x^3 + x^2 + x + \frac{1}{x}\right)$$

On differentiation, we get

$$= 3x^2 + 2x + 1 - \frac{1}{x^2}$$

Hence, the required answer is

$$3x^2 + 2x + 1 - \frac{1}{x^2}.$$

25. Find the derivative of tan x°.

Ans. Let $y = \tan x°$

Converting it into radian

$$y = \tan\frac{\pi x}{180}$$

So,

$$\frac{dy}{dx} = \sec^2\frac{\pi x}{180}\times\left(\frac{\pi}{180}\right)$$

SHORT ANSWER Type-II Questions (SA-II)

[3 marks]

26. Find the derivative of $\frac{3x+4}{5x^2 - 7x + 9}$. **[NCERT Exemplar]**

Ans. Given $\frac{3x+4}{5x^2 - 7x + 9}$

Applying quotient rule of differentiation that is

$$\Rightarrow \frac{d}{dx}\left(\frac{t}{s}\right) = \frac{s\cdot\frac{dt}{dx} - t\cdot\frac{ds}{dx}}{s^2}$$

$$\Rightarrow y = \frac{3x+4}{5x^2 - 7x + 9}$$

Applying the rule

$$\Rightarrow \frac{dy}{dx} = \frac{(5x^2 - 7x + 9)\frac{d}{dx}(3x+4) - (3x+4)\frac{d}{dx}(5x^2 - 7x + 9)}{(5x^2 - 7x + 9)^2}$$

$$\Rightarrow \frac{dy}{dx} = \frac{3(5x^2 - 7x + 9) - (3x+4)(10x - 7)}{(5x^2 - 7x + 9)^2}$$

On differentiation, we get

$$= \frac{(15x^2 - 21x + 27 - 30x^2 + 21x - 40x + 28)}{(5x^2 - 7x + 9)^2}$$

$$= \frac{(-15x^2 - 40x + 55)}{(5x^2 - 7x + 9)^2}$$

$$= \frac{(55-40x-15x^2)}{(5x^2-7x+9)^2}$$

Hence, the required answer is $\frac{(55-40x-15x^2)}{(5x^2-7x+9)^2}$.

27. Find the derivation of $\sqrt{\frac{1-\cos x}{1+\cos x}}$.

Ans. Let $\sqrt{\frac{1-\cos x}{1+\cos x}}$

$$y = \sqrt{\frac{2\sin^2\frac{x}{2}}{2\cos^2\frac{x}{2}}}$$

Here, $1 - \cos x = 2\sin^2\frac{x}{2}$

$1 + \cos x = 2\cos^2\frac{x}{2}$

So, $y = \sqrt{\tan^2\frac{x}{2}}$

$y = \tan\frac{x}{2}$

$$\frac{dy}{dx} = \sec^2\frac{x}{2}\cdot\left(\frac{1}{2}\right).$$

28. Find the derivative of $\frac{a+b\sin x}{c+d\cos x}$.

[NCERT Exemplar]

Ans. Given $y = \frac{a+b\sin x}{c+d\cos x}$

Applying quotient rule of differentiation that is

$$\Rightarrow \frac{d}{dx}\left(\frac{t}{sy}\right) = \frac{sy\cdot\frac{dt}{dx} - t\cdot\frac{dsy}{dx}}{sy^2}$$

$$\Rightarrow y = \frac{a+b\sin x}{c+d\cos x}$$

$$\Rightarrow \frac{dy}{dx} = \frac{(c+d\cos x)\frac{d}{dx}(a+b\sin x) - (a+b\sin x)\frac{d}{dx}(c+d\cos x)}{(c+d\cos x)^2}$$

On differentiating we get

$$\Rightarrow \frac{dy}{dx} = \frac{(c+d\cos x)(b\cos x) - (a+b\sin x)(-d\sin x)}{(c+d\cos x)^2}$$

$$\Rightarrow \frac{dy}{dx} = \frac{b\cos x(c+d\cos x) + d\sin x(a+b\sin x)}{(c+d\cos x)^2}$$

$$= \frac{[cb\cos x + bd\cos^2 x + ad\sin x + bd\sin^2 x]}{(c+d\cos x)^2}$$

$$= \frac{[cb\cos x + ad\sin x + bd(\cos^2 x + \sin^2 x)]}{(c+d\cos x)^2}$$

$$= \frac{cb\cos x + ad\sin x + bd}{(c+d\cos x)^2}$$

29. If $y = \cos x \cdot e^{\sin x^2}$ then find $\frac{dy}{dx}$.

Ans. $y = \cos x \,.\, e^{\sin x^2}$

using product rule.

$$= \cos x\frac{d}{dx}(e^{\sin x^2}) + (e^{\sin x^2})\frac{d}{dx}(\cos x)$$

$$\frac{dy}{dx} = \cos x\cdot e^{\sin x^2}\cdot\cos x^2\cdot 2x - e^{\sin x^2}\cdot\sin x$$

$$= 2x\cdot\cos x e^{\sin x^2}\cdot\cos x^2 - e^{\sin x^2}\cdot\sin x$$

So required solution is

$$\frac{dy}{dx} = e^{\sin x^2}(2x\cos x\cdot\cos x^2 - \sin x)$$

LONG ANSWER Type Questions (LA)

[**4** & **5** marks]

30. Find derivative of $(2x - 7)^2\ (3x + 5)^3$ with respect to x. **[NCERT Exemplar]**

Ans. Given $y = (2x - 7)^2 (3x + 5)^3$

Applying product rule of differentiation that is

$$\Rightarrow \frac{d}{dx}(t.y) = y\cdot\frac{dt}{dx} + t\cdot\frac{dy}{dx}$$

$$\Rightarrow y = (2x - 7)^2 (3x + 5)^3$$

$$\Rightarrow \frac{dy}{dx} = (3x+5)^3\frac{d}{dx}(2x-7)^2 + (2x-7)^2\frac{d}{dx}(3x+5)^3$$

On differentiating we get

$$\Rightarrow \frac{dy}{dx} = (2)(3x+5)^3 2(2x-7)^1 + (3)(2x-7)^2 3(3x+5)^2$$

$$\Rightarrow \frac{dy}{dx} = 4(3x+5)^3(2x-7) + 9(2x-7)^2(3x+5)^2$$

On Simplification, we get

$$\Rightarrow \frac{dy}{dx} = (2x-7)(3x+5)^2[4(3x+5) + 9(2x-7)]$$

$$\Rightarrow \frac{dy}{dx} = (2x-7)(3x+5)^2(30x-43)$$

31. Find derivative of $\sin^2 x.\cos x$ with respect to $e^{\sin(e^x)}$.

Ans. Let $u = \sin^2 x \cdot \cos x$

And $v = e^{\sin(e^x)}$

Now we have to find $\frac{du}{dv}$.

So, $\frac{du}{dx} = d(\sin^2 x \cdot \cos x)$

$$= \sin^2 x \frac{d(\cos x)}{dx} + \cos x \frac{d(\sin^2 x)}{dx}$$

$= \sin^2 x.(-\sin x) + \cos x.2 \sin x \cos x$

$= -\sin^3 x + 2 \sin x \cos^2 x$

$= \sin x (2 \cos^2 x - \sin^2 x)$

$= \sin x (\cos^2 x + \cos^2 x - \sin^2 x)$

$= \sin x (\cos^2 x + \cos 2x)$

and $\frac{dv}{dx} = \frac{d}{dx}(e^{\sin(e^x)})$

$$= e^{\sin(e^x)} \cdot \cos(e^x) \cdot e^x$$

Now, $\frac{du}{dv} = \frac{\sin x (\cos^2 x + \cos 2x)}{e^{\sin(e^x)} \cdot \cos e^x \cdot e^x}$

32. Differentiate with respect to x using the first principle $x^2 \cos x$. **[DIKSHA]**

Ans. Given, $f(x) = x^2 \cos x$

First principle, $f'(x) = \lim_{h \to 0} \frac{f(x+h) - f(x)}{h}$

$$f'(x) = \lim_{h \to 0} \frac{(x+h)^2 \cos(x+h) - x^2 \cos x}{h}$$

Using L-Hospital's rule, we have,

$$f'(x) = \lim_{h \to 0} \frac{2(x+h)\cos(x+h) + (x+h)^2 [-\sin(x+h)] - 0}{1}$$

$$f'(x) = \lim_{h \to 0} 2(x+h)\cos(x+h) + (x+h)^2 [-\sin(x+h)]$$

$f'(x) = 2(x + 0) \cos (x + 0) + (x + 0)^2 [-\sin(x + 0)]$

$f'(x) = 2x \cos x + x^2 [-\sin x]$

$\therefore \; f'(x) = 2x \cos x - x^2 \sin x$

13 Statistics

Traffic engineers regularly use statistics to monitor total traffic in different areas of a city, which allows them to decide whether or not they should add or remove roads to optimize traffic flow.

Topic Notes

- *Measures of Dispersion*
- *Variance and Standard Deviation*

MEASURES OF DISPERSION 1

TOPIC 1

MEASURE OF CENTRAL TENDENCY

These are three measures of central tendency.

1. Arithmetic Mean
2. Median
3. Mode

Range

The measure of dispersion which is easiest to understand and easiest to calculate is the range.

Range is defined as the difference between two extreme observations of the distribution.

Range of distribution = Largest observation – Smallest observation.

Mean of Ungrouped Data

Ungrouped data is the data you first gather from an experiment or study. The data is raw — that is, it's not sorted into categories, classified, or otherwise grouped. An ungrouped set of data is basically a list of numbers.

Consider the ungrouped data $x_1, x_2, ..., x_n$ consisting of n values. There are two methods for computing the mean (denoted by $\underset{\sim}{x}$) of the given data.

Direct Method

The mean of the given data is

$$\underset{\sim}{x} = \frac{x_1 + x_2 + ... + x_n}{n}$$

Deviation Method (or Short-cut Method)

This method involves the following steps:

Step I: Take an assumed mean a. (Any value can be taken as assumed mean, but for simpler calculations, a central value is chosen.)

Step II: Compute $d_i = x_i - a$, i.e., the deviations of the values of data from assumed mean.

Step III: The mean of the given data is

$$\underset{\sim}{x} = a + \frac{\Sigma d_i}{n}.$$

Example 1.1: Find the median of the following data:

36, 72, 46, 42, 60, 45, 53, 416, 51, 49 [NCERT]

Ans. Given data in ascending order is 36, 42, 45, 46, 46, 49, 51, 53, 60, 72.

Here, number of terms, $n = 10$, which is even.

Hence, median = $\dfrac{\left(\frac{n}{2}\right)^{th} \text{term} + \left(\frac{n}{2}+1\right)^{th} \text{term}}{2}$

$$\frac{5^{th}\text{term} + 6^{th}\text{term}}{2} = \frac{46+49}{2} = 47.5$$

Mean of Discrete Distribution

The mean of a discrete random variable X is a weighted average of the possible values that the random variable can take. Unlike the sample mean of a group of observations, which gives each observation equal weight, the mean of a random variable weights each outcome x_i.

Consider discrete frequency distribution consisting of m distinct values $x_1, x_2 ... x_m$ with frequencies $f_1, f_2, ...,$ f_m respectively. There are two methods for computing the mean (denoted by $\bar{x}$) of the given data.

Direct Method

The mean of the given data is

$$\bar{x} = \frac{\Sigma f_i x_i}{\Sigma f_i}$$

Deviation Method (or Short-cut Method)

This method involves the following steps:

Step I: Take an assumed mean a.

Step II: Compute, $d_i = x_i - a$, i.e., the deviations of the values of data from assumed mean.

Step III: The mean of the given data is

$$\bar{x} = a + \frac{\Sigma f_i d_i}{\Sigma f_i}$$

Mean of Continuous Distribution

Consider a continuous frequency distribution consisting of class intervals with their corresponding frequencies as f_i. We compute the mid-point of the class intervals and denoted them by x_i. There are three methods for computing the mean (denoted by $\bar{x}$) of the given data.

Direct Method

The mean of the given data is

$$\bar{x} = \frac{\sum f_i x_i}{\sum f_i}$$

Deviation method

This method involves the following steps:

Step I: take an assumed mean a and class-width h.

Step II: Compute $u_i = \frac{x_i - a}{h}$, i.e., the step - deviations of the mid-points of class-intervals from assumed mean.

Step III: The mean of the given data is

$$\bar{x} = a + \frac{h\sum f_i u_i}{\sum f_i}$$

Median of Ungrouped Data

Consider the ungrouped data $x_1, x_2, \ldots, x_n$ consisting of n values. In order to find the median, we have the following working rule:

Step I: Arrange the given up grounded data in ascending order.

Step II: Calculate median of the given data using the formula

(i) Median $= \left(\frac{n+1}{2}\right)^{th}$ term, if n is odd.

(ii) Median $= \frac{\left(\frac{n}{2}\right)^{th} \text{term} + \left(\frac{n}{2}+1\right)^{th} \text{term}}{2}$, if n is even.

Median of Discrete Distribution

Consider a discrete frequency distribution consisting of m distinct values $x_1, x_2, \ldots, x_3$ with frequencies, $f_1, f_2, \ldots, f_3$ respectively. In order to find the median, we have the following working rule.

Step I: Arrange the given data (i.e., values of x_i) in ascending order.

Step II: Find the cumulative frequency. Where cumulative frequency represents the sum of all previous frequencies up to the current values.

Step III: Denote $n = \mp\sum f_i$

Step IV: Calculate median of the given data using the formula.

(i) Median $= \left(\frac{n+1}{2}\right)^{th}$ term, if n is odd.

(ii) Median $= \left(\frac{n}{2}\right)^{th} + \left(\frac{n}{2}+1\right)^{th}$ term, if n is even.

Median of Continuous Frequency Distributions

Median of grouped data is the data that is continuous and is in the form of frequency distribution. Median is the middle most value of the given data that separates the higher half of the data from the lower half.

Step I: Find the mid-points of the class intervals and denote them by x_i.

Step II: Find the cumulative frequency, where cumulative frequency represents the sum of all previous frequencies up to the current value.

Step III: Denote $n = \sum f_i$.

Step IV: Identify median class, i.e., the class containing the cumulative frequency $\frac{n}{2}$.

Step V: Calculate median of the given data using the formula

$$\text{Median} = l + \frac{\frac{n}{2} - C}{f} \times h$$

Where l = lower limit of median class

h = width of median class

f = frequency of median class

C = cumulative frequency just preceding median class.

TOPIC 2

MEAN DEVIATION ABOUT MEAN AND MEDIAN

Mean Deviation

Mean deviation about a number represents the mean of the deviations from that number. In this section, we shall learn the methods of calculator mean deviation about mean and mean deviation about median for various types of data.

Mean Deviation About Mean of Ungrounded Data

Consider the up grouped data $x_1, x_2, \ldots, x_n$ consisting of n values. In order to find the mean of deviation about mean, we have the following working rule:

Step I: Calculate mean of the given data using the formula

Mean $\bar{x} = \frac{x_1 + x_2 + \ldots + x_n}{n}$.

Step II: Compute the deviation d_i of values of x_i from mean, ignoring the ± signs.

i.e., $|d_i| = |x_i - \bar{x}|$. Then

Mean deviation about mean $= \frac{\sum |d_i|}{n}$

Example 1.2: **Find the mean deviation about the mean for the data**
38, 70, 48, 40, 42, 55, 63, 46, 54, 44 [NCERT]

Ans. Mean of the given data = $\frac{\text{Sum of all terms}}{\text{Total number of terms}}$

$$\bar{x} = \frac{38+70+48+40+42+55+63+46+54+44}{10}$$

$$= \frac{500}{10}$$

$$= 50$$

x_i	$x_i - \bar{x}$	$\lvert x_i - \bar{x}\rvert$
38	38 – 50 = –12	|–12| = 12
70	70 – 50 = 20	|20| = 20
48	48 – 50 = – 2	|–2| = 2
40	40 – 50 = –10	|–10| = 10
42	42 – 50 = –8	|–8| = 8
55	55 – 50 = 5	|5| = 5
63	63 – 50 = 13	|13| = 13
46	46 – 50 = –4	|–4| = 4
54	54 – 50 = 4	|4| = 4
44	44 – 50 = –6	|–6| = 6
		$\sum_{1}^{10}\lvert x_i - \bar{x}\rvert = 84$

Mean deviation about mean

$$= \frac{\Sigma\lvert x_i - \bar{x}\rvert}{10}$$

$$= \frac{84}{10} = 8.4$$

Example 1.3: **Find the mean deviation about the mean for the data**

x_i	10	30	50	70	90
f_i	4	24	28	16	8

[NCERT]

Ans. First, we will calculate mean

x_i	f_i	f_ix_i	$\lvert x_i - \bar{x}\rvert$	$f_i\lvert x_i - \bar{x}\rvert$
10	4	4 × 10 = 40	|10 – 50| = |–40| = 40	4 × 40 = 160
30	24	24 × 30 = 720	|30 – 50| = |–20| = 20	24 × 20 = 480
50	28	28 × 50 = 1440	|50 – 50| = |0| = 0	28 × 0 = 0
70	16	16 × 70 = 1120	|70 – 50| = |20| = 20	16 × 20 = 320
90	8	8 × 90 = 720	|90 – 50| = |40| = 40	8 × 40 = 320
$\sum f_i$	= 80	$\sum f_ix_i = 4000$		$\sum f_i\lvert x_i - \bar{x}\rvert$ = 1280

$$\text{Mean } (\bar{x}) = \frac{\Sigma f_ix_i}{\Sigma f_i}$$

$$\bar{x} = \frac{4000}{80}$$

$$\bar{x} = 50$$

$$\text{Mean deviation about mean} = \frac{\Sigma f_i\lvert x_i - \bar{x}\rvert}{\Sigma f_i}$$

Putting $\Sigma f_i\lvert x_i - \bar{x}\rvert = 1280$, $\Sigma f_i = 80$

$$\text{M.D. } (\bar{x}) = \frac{1}{80} \times 1280 = 16$$

Example 1.4 **Find the mean deviation about the mean for the data 4, 7, 8, 9, 10, 12, 13, 17. [NCERT]**

Ans. The given data is

4, 7, 8, 9, 10, 12, 13, 17

Mean of the data,

$$\bar{x} = \frac{4+7+8+9+10+12+13+17}{8}$$

$$= \frac{80}{8} = 10$$

The deviation of the respective observations from the mean $\bar{x}$, i.e., $x_i - \bar{x}$, i.e. $x_i - 10$ are –6, –3, –2, –1, 0, 2, 3, 7

The absolute values of the deviations, i.e., $\lvert x_i - \bar{x}\rvert$, are

6, 3, 2, 1, 0, 2, 3, 7

The required mean deviation about the mean is

$$\text{M.D. } (\bar{x}) = \frac{\sum_{i=1}^{8}\lvert x_1 - \bar{x}\rvert}{8}$$

$$= \frac{6+3+2+1+0+2+3+7}{8} = \frac{24}{8} = 3$$

Mean Deviation About Mean of Discrete Distribution

Consider a discrete frequency distribution consisting of m distinct values $x_1, x_2, \ldots. x_m$ with frequencies $f_1, f_2, \ldots. f_m$ respectively. In order to find the mean deviation about mean, we have the following working rule:

Step I: Calculate mean of the given data using the formula

$$\text{Mean, } \bar{x} = \frac{\sum f_ix_i}{\sum fi}$$

Step II: Compute the deviations d_i of values x_i from mean, ignoring the ± signs, i.e., $|d_i| = |x_i - \bar{x}|$. Then

Mean deviation about mean = $\frac{\sum f_i |d_i|}{\sum f_i}$

Mean Deviation About Mean of Continuous Distribution

Consider a continuous frequency distribution consisting of class intervals with their corresponding frequencies as f_i. In order to find the mean deviation about mean, we have the following working rule.

Step I: Find the mid-points of the class intervals and denote the by x_i.

Step II: Calculate mean of the given data using the formula

$$\text{Mean, } \bar{x} = \frac{\sum f_i x_i}{\sum f_i}$$

Step III: Compute the deviations d_i of values x_i from mean, ignoring the ± signs,

i.e., $|d_i| = |x_i - \bar{x}|$.

Then, mean deviation about mean

$$= \frac{\sum f_i |d_i|}{\sum f_i}.$$

Example 1.5: Find the mean deviation about the mean of the data [NCERT]

Height in cms	95-105	105-115	115-125	125-135	135-145	145-155
Number of boys	9	13	26	30	12	10

Ans.

Height (in cms)	Number of boys	Mid-point x_i	$f_i x_i$	$\lvert x_i - \bar{x}\rvert$	$f_i \lvert x_i - \bar{x}\rvert$
95 – 105	9	100	900	$\lvert 100 - 125.3\rvert = 25.3$	227.7
105 – 115	13	110	1430	$\lvert 110 - 125.3\rvert = 15.3$	198.9
115 – 125	26	120	3120	$\lvert 120 - 125.3\rvert = 5.3$	137.8
125 – 135	30	130	3900	$\lvert 130 - 125.3\rvert = 4.7$	141
135 – 145	12	140	1680	$\lvert 140 - 125.3\rvert = 14.7$	176.4
145 – 155	10	150	1500	$\lvert 150 - 125.3\rvert = 24.7$	247
	$\Sigma f_i = 100$		12530		$\sum f_i \lvert x_i - \bar{x}\rvert = 1128.8$

$\Sigma f_i = 100$ and $\Sigma f_i x_i = 12530$

$$\therefore \quad \text{Mean } \bar{x} = \frac{\sum f_i x_i}{\sum f_i}$$

$$= \frac{12530}{100} = 125.3$$

Now,

$\Sigma f_i = 100$

$\Sigma f_i |x_i - \bar{x}| = 1128.8$

$$\text{Mean deviation about mean} = \frac{\sum f_i |x_i - \underline{x}|}{f_i}$$

$$= \frac{1128.8}{100}$$

$$= 11.288$$

Mean Deviation about Median of Discrete Distribution

Consider a discrete frequency distribution consisting of m distinct values $x_1, x_2, \ldots, x_m$ with frequencies, $f_1, f_2, \ldots\ldots f_m$ respectively. In order to find the mean deviation about median. We have the following working rule:

Step I: Arrange the given data (i.e., values of x_i) in ascending order.

Step II: Find the cumulative frequency, when cumulative frequency represents the sum of all previous frequencies up to the current value.

Step III: Calculate median of the given data using the formula given below:

(i) Median = $\left(\frac{n+1}{2}\right)^{th}$ term, if n is odd.

(ii) Median = $\frac{\left(\frac{n}{2}\right)^{th} \text{term} + \left(\frac{n}{2}+1\right)^{th} \text{term}}{2}$ if, n is even.

Step IV: Compute the deviations d_i of values x_i from median (M). Ignoring the ± signs.

i.e., $|d_i| = |x_i - M|$. Then

Mean deviation about median = $\frac{\sum f_i |d_i|}{\sum f_i}$

Example 1.6: Find the mean deviation about the median for the data.

13, 17, 16, 14, 11, 13, 10, 16, 11, 18, 12, 17 [NCERT]

Ans. The given data is

13, 17, 16, 14, 11, 13, 10, 16, 11, 18, 12, 17.

Here, the number of observations are 12, which is even.

Arranging the data in ascending order, we obtain

10, 11, 11, 12, 13, 13, 14, 16, 16, 17, 17, 18

$$\text{Median} = \frac{6^{th}\text{ observation} + 7^{th}\text{ observation}}{2}$$

$$= \frac{13+14}{2} = \frac{27}{2} = 13.5$$

The deviations of the respective observation from the median, i.e., $x_i - M$, i.e. $x_i - 13.5$ are −3.5, −2.5, −2.5, −1.5, −0.5, −0.5, 0.5, 2.5, 2.5, 3.5, 3.5, 4.5.

The absolute values of the deviations, $|x_i - M|$, are

3.5, 2.5, 2.5, 1.5, 0.5, 0.5, 0.5, 2.5, 2.5, 3.5, 3.5, 4.5.

The required mean deviation about the median is

$$M.D.(M) = \frac{\sum_{i=1}^{12} |x_i - M|}{12}$$

$$= \frac{3.5+2.5+2.5+1.5+0.5+0.5+0.5+2.5+2.5+3.5+3.5+4.5}{12}$$

$$= \frac{28}{12} = 2.33$$

Mean Deviation About Median of Continuous Distribution

Consider a continuous frequency distribution consisting of class interval with their corresponding frequencies, as f_i. To find the mean deviation about median. We have the following working rule.

Step I: Find the mid-points of the class intervals and denote them by x_i.

Step II: Find the cumulative frequency, where cumulative frequency represents the sum of all previous frequencies up to the current value.

Step III: Denote $n = \Sigma f_i$.

Step IV: Identify median class, i.e., the class containing the cumulative frequency $\frac{n}{2}$.

Step V: Calculate median of the given data using the formula given below:

$$\text{Median} = l + \frac{\frac{n}{2} - C}{f} \times h$$

Where, l = lower limit of median class

H = width of median class

f = frequency of median class

C = Cumulative frequency just preceding median class

Step VI: Compute the deviations d_i of values x_i from median (M), ignoring the ± signs, i.e., $|d_i| = |x_i - M|$. Then, mean deviation about median

$$\frac{\sum f_i |d_i|}{\sum f_i}$$

Example 1.7: **Calculate the mean deviation about median age for the age distribution of 100 persons given below:**

Age (in years)	16-20	21-25	26-30	31-35	36-40	41-45	46-50	51-55
Number	5	6	12	14	26	12	16	9

Converting the given data in continuous frequency by subtracting 0.5 in upper limit. **[NCERT]**

Ans.

Age	Number	Cumulative Frequency (c.f.)	Mid Point (x_i)	$\|x - M\|$	$f_i \|x_i - M\|$
15.5 – 20.5	5	5	18	|18 − 38| = 20	5 × 20 = 100
20.5 – 25.5	6	5 + 6 = 11	23	|23 − 38| = 20	6 × 15 = 90
25.5 – 30.5	12	11 + 12 = 23	28	|28 − 38| = 20	12 × 10 = 120
30.5 – 35.5	14	23 + 14 = 37	33	|33 − 38| = 20	14 × 5 = 70
35.5 – 40.5	26	37 + 26 = 63	38	|38 − 38| = 20	26 × 0 = 0
40.5 – 45.5	12	63 + 12 = 75	43	|43 − 38| = 20	12 × 5 = 60
45.5 – 50.5	16	75 + 16 = 91	48	|48 − 38| = 20	16 × 10 = 160
50.5 – 55.5	9	91 + 9 = 100	53	|53 − 38| = 20	9 × 15 = 135
Σf_i = 100					$\Sigma f_i \|x_i - M\|$ = 735

$N = \Sigma f_i = 100$

$$\text{Median class} = \left(\frac{N}{2}\right)^{th} \text{term}$$

$$= \left(\frac{100}{2}\right)^{th} \text{term}$$

$= 50^{th}$ term

In the above data, cumulative frequency of class 35.5 – 40.5 is 63 which is greater than 50.

∴ Median class = 35.5 – 40.5

$$\text{Median} = l + \frac{\frac{N}{2} - C}{f} \times h$$

Where,

l = lower limits of median class

N = sum of frequencies

f = frequency of median class

C = cumulative frequency of class before median class.

Here, $l = 35.5$, $N = 100$, $h = 5$, $f = 26$

$$\text{Median} = 35.5 + \frac{\frac{100}{2} - 37}{26} \times 5$$

$$= 35.5 + \frac{50 - 37}{26} \times 5$$

$$= 35.5 + \frac{13}{26} \times 5$$

$$= 35.5 + 2.5 = 38$$

Now,

$$\Sigma f_i = 100$$

$$\Sigma f_i |x_i - M| = 735$$

$$\therefore \quad \text{Mean deviation (M)} = \frac{\sum f_i |x_i - M|}{f_i}$$

$$= \frac{735}{100}$$

$$= 7.35$$

Example 1.8: Find the mean deviation about the median for the data **[NCERT]**

x_i	15	21	27	30	35
f_i	3	5	6	7	8

Ans. The given observation is already in ascending order. Adding a column corresponding to cumulative frequencies of the given data, we obtain the following table.

x_i	f_i	c.f.
15	3	3
21	5	8
27	6	14
30	7	21
35	8	29

$N = 29$ (odd)

c.f = cumulative frequency

$$\therefore \quad \text{Median} = \left(\frac{N+1}{2}\right)^{th} \text{ term}$$

$$= \left(\frac{29+1}{2}\right)^{th} \text{ term}$$

$$= \left(\frac{30}{2}\right)^{th} \text{ term}$$

$$= 15^{th} \text{ term}$$

As, 15th term lies in c.f of 21.

x_i	f_i	$\|x_i - M\|$	$f_i\|x_i - M\|$
15	3	$\|15 - 30\| = 15$	$3 \times 15 = 45$
21	5	$\|21 - 30\| = 9$	$5 \times 9 = 45$
27	6	$\|27 - 30\| = 3$	$6 \times 3 = 18$
30	7	$\|30 - 30\| = 0$	$7 \times 0 = 0$
35	8	$\|35 - 30\| = 5$	$8 \times 5 = 40$
$\Sigma f_i = 29$			$\Sigma f_i\|x_i - M\| = 148$

$$\Sigma f_i = 29$$

$$\Sigma f_i |x_i - M| = 148$$

$$\therefore \quad \text{Mean Deviation} = \frac{\Sigma f_i |x_i - M|}{f_i}$$

$$= \frac{148}{29}$$

$$= 5.1$$

Example 1.9 **Find the mean deviation about median for the following data:**

Class	0 – 10	10 – 20	20 – 30	30 – 40	40 – 50	50 – 60
Frequency	6	8	14	16	4	2

[NCERT]

Ans.

Class	Frequency	Cumulative Frequency	Mid point (x_i)
0 – 10	6	6	5
10 – 20	8	6 + 8 = 14	15
20 – 30	14	14 + 14 = 28	25
30 – 40	16	28 + 16 = 44	35
40 – 50	4	44 + 4 = 48	45
50 – 60	2	48 + 2 = 50	55
	$\Sigma f_i = 50$		

$N = \Sigma f_i = 50$

$$\text{Median class} = \left(\frac{N}{2}\right)^{th} \text{ term}$$

$$= \left(\frac{50}{2}\right)^{th} \text{ term}$$

$$= 25^{th} \text{ term}$$

In above data, cumulative frequency of class 20 – 30 is 28 which is slightly greater than 25.

$\therefore$ Median class = 20 – 30

$$\text{Median} = l + \frac{\frac{N}{2} - c}{f} \times h$$

Where,

l = lower limits of median class

N = sum of frequencies

f = frequency of median class

C = Cumulative frequency of class before median class

Here, $l = 20, N = 50, C = 14, h = 10, f = 14$

$$\text{Median} = l + \frac{\frac{N}{2} - c}{f} \times h$$

$$= 20 + \frac{\frac{50}{2} - 14}{14} \times 20 = 20 + \frac{25 - 14}{14} \times 10$$

$$= 20 + \frac{11}{14} \times 10$$

$$= 20 + 7.8 = 27.8$$

Finding mean deviation about median

$$= \frac{\sum f_i |x_i - M|}{\sum f_i}$$

Class	Frequency	Cumulative frequency	Mid point (x_i)	$\lvert x_i - M \rvert$	$f_i \lvert x_i - M \rvert$
0 – 10	6	6	5	$\lvert 5 - 27.8 \rvert = 22.8$	$6 \times 22.8 = 136.8$
10 – 20	8	$6 + 8 = 14$	15	$\lvert 15 - 27.8 \rvert = 12.8$	$8 \times 12.8 = 102.4$
20 – 30	14	$14 + 14 = 28$	25	$\lvert 25 - 27.8 \rvert = 2.8$	$14 \times 2.8 = 39.2$
30 – 40	16	$28 + 16 = 44$	35	$\lvert 35 - 27.8 \rvert = 7.2$	$16 \times 7.2 = 115.2$
40 – 50	4	$44 + 4 = 48$	45	$\lvert 45 - 27.8 \rvert = 17.2$	$4 \times 17.2 = 68.8$
50 – 60	2	$48 + 2 = 50$	55	$\lvert 55 - 27.8 \rvert = 27.2$	$2 \times 27.2 = 54.5$
	$\Sigma f_i = 50$				$\Sigma f_i \lvert x_i - M \rvert = 516.8$

$$\Sigma f_i = 50$$

$$\Sigma f_i |x_i - \bar{x}| = 516.8$$

$$\therefore \quad \text{Mean deviation } (M) = \frac{\sum f_i |x_i - M|}{f_i}$$

$$= \frac{516.8}{50}$$

$$= 10.336$$

$$= 10.34$$

OBJECTIVE Type Questions

[**1** mark]

Multiple Choice Questions

1. The mean of the first three prime number is:

(a) 3 **(b) 3.3**

(c) 4 **(d) None**

Ans. *(b) 3.3*

Explanation: Here first 3 number which are prime also 2, 3, 5.

So, mean $\bar{x} = \frac{2+3+5}{3} = \frac{10}{3} = 3.3$

Hence, option (b) is the correct answer

2. The mean deviation from the mean of the set observation –1, 0 and 4 is:

(a) 3 **(b) 1**

(c) –2 **(d) 2**

Ans. *(d) 2*

Explanation: $\bar{x} = -\frac{-1+0+4}{3} = 1$

$$\text{M.D } (\bar{x}) = \frac{\sum |x_i - \bar{x}|}{n}$$

$$= \frac{|-1-1| + |0-1| + |4-1|}{3} = 2$$

Hence, option (d) is the correct answer.

3. Calculate mean deviation about the median from the following data.

21, 30, 24, 32, 31

(a) 5.28 **(b) 5.18**

(c) 3.38 **(d) 3.6** **[DIKSHA]**

Ans. *(d) 3.6*

Explanation: x_i = 21, 24, 30, 31, 32

Number of observation = n = 5 (odd)

Since x is an odd

$$\text{Median} = \left(\frac{5+1}{2}\right)^{th} \text{ term}$$

$$= 3^{rd} \text{ term}$$

$$M = 30$$

$$\text{M.D} = \frac{9+6+0+1+2}{5}$$

$= \frac{18}{5}$

$= 3.6$

Hence, option (d) is the correct answer.

4. Mean deviation about median for 3, 4, 9, 5, 3, 12, 10, 18, 7, 19, 21.

(a) 4.27 **(b) 5.24**

(c) 5.27 **(d) 4.24**

Ans. *(c) 5.27*

Explanation: The data is

3, 3, 4, 5, 7, 9, 10, 12, 18, 19, 21

Now median $= \left(\frac{11+1}{2}\right)^{th}$ term = 9

Now $|r_n - M|$ are

6, 6, 5, 4, 2, 0, 1, 3, 9, 10, 12

Therefore, $MD(M) = \frac{1}{11}\sum |r_n - M|$

$= \frac{1}{11} \times 58$

$= 5.27$

Hence, option (c) is the correct answer.

5. Consider the following data, The mean deviation about median for the data is:

r_n	15	21	27	30	35
f_i	3	5	6	7	8

(a) 5 **(b) 5.3**

(c) 5.1 **(d) 5.2**

Ans. *(c) 5.1*

Explanation:

x_i	f_i	c.f	$\|x_i - M\|$	$f_i\|x_i - M\|$
15	3	3	$\|15 - 30\| = 15$	45
21	5	8	$\|21 - 30\| = 9$	45
27	6	14	$\|27 - 30\| = 3$	18
30	7	21	$\|30 - 30\| = 0$	0
35	8	29	$\|35 - 30\| = 5$	40
	29			148

$N = 29$ (odd)

c.f = cumulative frequency

$\therefore$ Median $= \left(\frac{N+1}{2}\right)^{th}$ term

$= \left(\frac{29+1}{2}\right)^{th}$ term

$= \left(\frac{30}{2}\right)^{th}$ term

$= 15^{th}$ term

As, 15th term lies in c.f of 21, so Median = 30.

$$M.D\ (M) = \frac{\sum f_i(x_i - M)}{\sum f_i}$$

$$= \frac{148}{29} = 5.1$$

Hence, option (c) is the correct answer.

6. Find the mean deviation about the mean of the distribution is:

Size	20	21	22	23	24
Frequency	6	4	5	1	4

(a) 1.25 **(b) 1**

(c) 1.50 **(d) 2**

Ans. *(a) 1.25*

Explanation: Given data distribution

Now we have to find the mean deviation about the mean of the distribution construct a table of the given data

Size (x_i)	Frequency (f_i)	f_ix_i
20	6	20 × 6 = 120
21	4	21 × 4 = 84
22	5	22 × 5 = 110
23	1	23 × 1 = 23
24	4	24 × 4 = 96
Total	20	433

We know that mean, $\bar{x} = \frac{\Sigma f_i x_i}{\Sigma f_i} = \frac{433}{20} = 21.65$

To find mean deviation, we have to construct another table

Size (x_i)	Frequency (f_i)	f_ix_i	$d_i = \|x_i - \text{mean}\|$	f_id_i
20	6	120	1.65	9.90
21	4	84	0.65	2.60
22	5	110	0.35	1.75
23	1	23	1.35	1.35
24	4	96	2.35	9.40
Total	20	433		25.00

Hence, Mean Deviation becomes,

$$M.D = \frac{\Sigma f_i d_i}{\Sigma f_i} = \frac{25}{20} = 1.25$$

Therefore, the mean deviation about the mean of the distribution is 1.25.

Hence, option (a) is the correct answer

7. The mean deviation from the median of the first three natural number is:

(a) 0.667 **(b) 0.253**

(c) 0.456 **(d) None**

Ans. *(a) 0.667*

Explanation: First 3 natural numbers are 1, 2, 3.

Then median $= \left(\frac{n+1}{2}\right)^{th}$ term

$= \left(\frac{3+1}{2}\right)^{th}$ item

$= 2^{nd}$ item

Hence, median = 2

So $\Sigma|x_i - Med| = 1 + 0 + 1 = 2$

$$\text{M.D.} = \frac{2}{3} = 0.667$$

Hence, option (a) is the correct answer.

8. Median is calculated by using the formula

(a) $M = l + \dfrac{\frac{N}{2} - cf}{f} \times h$

(b) $M = l + \dfrac{\frac{N}{2} + cf}{f} \times h$

(c) $M = l - \dfrac{\frac{N}{2} - cf}{f} \times h$

(d) None

Ans. *(a)* $M = l + \dfrac{\frac{N}{2} - cf}{f} \times h$

Explanation: Correct formula for finding median for a given data is $l + \dfrac{\frac{N}{2} - cf}{f} \times h$.

Hence, option (a) is the correct answer.

9. Mean deviation about median is calculated by using the formula

(a) $M.D = \dfrac{\Sigma f_i |x_i + M|}{N}$

(b) $M.D = \dfrac{\sum f_i |x_i - M|}{N}$

(c) $M.D = \dfrac{\Sigma |x_i - M|}{N}$

(d) None

Ans. *(b)* $M.D = \dfrac{\sum f_i |x_i - M|}{N}$

Explanation: The correct formula to finding mean deviation about median is $\dfrac{\Sigma f_i |x_i - M|}{N}$.

Hence, option (b) is the correct answer.

Assertion-Reason (A-R)

DIRECTION: In the following questions, a statement of assertion (A) is followed by a statement of the reason (R). Mark the correct choice as:

(a) Both assertion (A) and reason (R) are true and reason (R) is the correct explanation of assertion (A).

(b) Both assertion (A) and reason (R) are true but reason (R) is not the correct explanation of assertion (A).

(c) Assertion (A) is true but reason (R) is false.

(d) Assertion (A) is false but reason (R) is true.

10. Assertion: The mean deviation about the mean to find a measure of dispersion has certain limitations.

Reason: The sum of deviations from the mean is more than the sum of deviations from the median. Therefore, the mean deviation about the mean is not very scientific, where degree of variability is very high.

Ans. *(a) Both assertion (A) and reason (R) are true and reason (R) is the correct explanation of assertion (A)*

Explanation: The sum of the deviations from the mean (minus signs ignored) is more than the sum of the deviations from median.

Therefore, the mean deviation about the mean is not very scientific. Thus, in many cases, mean deviation may give unsatisfactory results. Also mean deviation is calculated on the basis of absolute values of the deviations and therefore, cannot be subjected to further algebraic treatment. This implied that we must have some other measure of dispersion. Standard deviation is such a measure of dispersion.

Hence, option (a) is the correct answer.

11. Assertion: The average marks of boys in a class is 52 and that of girls is 42. The average marks of boy and girls combined is 50. The percentage of boys in the class is 80%.

Reason: Mean marks scored by the students of a class is 53 and the mean marks of the boys is 50 and the mean marks of the girls is 55. The percentage of girls in the class is 64%.

Ans. *(c) Assertion (A) is true but reason (R) is false.*

Explanation: Let the number of boys and girls be x and y.

$\therefore \quad 52x + 42y = 50(x + y)$

$\Rightarrow \quad 2x = 8y$

$\Rightarrow \quad x = 4y$

$\therefore$ Total number of students in the class

$= x + y = 5y$

$\therefore$ Required percentage of boys

$= \frac{4y}{5y} \times 100\%$

$= 80\%$

Let the number of boys be x and number of girls be y.

$\therefore \quad 53(x + y) = 55y + 50x$

$\Rightarrow \quad 3x = 2y$

$\Rightarrow \quad x = \frac{2y}{3}$

$\therefore$ Total number of students

$= x + y = \frac{2y}{3} + y = \frac{5}{3}y$

Hence, required percentage

$= \frac{y}{5y/3} \times 100\%$

$= \frac{3}{5} \times 100\% = 60\%$

Hence, option (c) is the correct answer.

12. Assertion: The weights (in kg) of 5 students are as follows

31, 35, 27, 29, 32, 43, 37, 41, 34, 28, 36, 44, 45, 42, 30.

If the weight 44 kg is replaced by 46 kg and 27 kg is by 25 kg, then the new median is 35.

Reason: The mean deviation from the median of the weights (in kg) 54, 50, 40, 42, 51, 45, 455, 57 is 4.78.

Ans. *(b) Both assertion (A) and reason (R) are true but reason (R) is not the correct explanation of assertion (A).*

Explanation: Since, 44 kg is replaced by 46 kg and 27 kg is replaced by 25 kg, then the given series becomes 31, 35, 25, 29, 32, 43, 37, 41, 34, 28, 36, 46, 45, 42, 30.

On arranging this series in ascending order, we get 25, 28, 29, 30, 31, 32, 34, 35, 36, 37, 41, 42, 43, 45, 46.

Total number of students are 15, therefore the middle term is 8th term whose corresponding value is 35.

On arranging the terms in increasing order of magnitude

40, 42, 45, 47, 50, 51, 54, 55, 57

Number of terms, $N = 9$

$\therefore$ Median $= \left(\frac{9+1}{2}\right)th$ term = 5th terms = 50 kg

Weight (in kg)	Deviation from Median (d)	$\lvert d \rvert$
40	−10	10
42	−8	8
45	−5	5
47	−3	3
50	0	0
51	1	1
54	4	4
55	5	5
57	7	7
		$\lvert d \rvert = 43$

MD from median $= \frac{43}{9} = 4.78kg$

Hence, option (b) is the correct answer.

13. Assertion: The proper measure of dispersion about the mean of a set of observations, i.e. standard deviation, is expressed as the positive square root of the variance.

Reason: The units of individual observations x_i and the unit of their mean are different,then that of variance. Since, variance involves sum of square of $(x - \bar{x})$.

Ans. *(a) Both assertion (A) and reason (R) are true and reason (R) is the correct explanation of assertion (A)*

Explanation: In the calculations of variance, we find that the units of individual observations x_i and the unit of their mean $\bar{x}$ are different from that of variance, since variance involves the sum of squares of $(x_i - \bar{x})$.

For this reason, the proper measure of dispersion about the mean of a set of observations is expressed as the positive square root of the variance and is called standard deviation.

Hence, option (a) is the correct answer.

CASE BASED Questions (CBQs)

[4 & 5 marks]

Read the following passages and answer the questions that follow:

14. *A stopwatch was used to find the time that it took a group of students to run 100 m.*

Time (in Seconds)	0–20	20–40	40–60	60–80	80–100
No. of students	8	10	13	6	3

(A) The mean time taken by a student to finish the race is:

(a) 54 (b) 63
(c) 43 (d) 50

(B) The construction of cumulative frequency table is useful in determining the

(a) Mean (b) Median
(c) Mode (d) All of the above

(C) The lower limit of the median class is

(a) 20 (b) 40
(c) 60 (d) 80

(D) The algebraic sum of absolute values of deviations from the mean is:

(a) 0 (b) 788
(c) 1720 (d) None of these

(E) The value of mean deviation from mean is:

(a) 19.7 (b) 20.7
(c) 18.7 (d) 17.7

Ans. Calculation of Mean, Mean deviation and cumulative

C.I.	Mid-Valcue x_i	Fre-quency fi	fx_i	$\|x_i - \bar{x}\|$ =	$\Sigma f_i\|x_i - \bar{x}\|$
0–20	10	8	80	33	264
20–40	30	10	300	13	130
40–60	50	13	650	7	91
60–80	70	6	420	27	162
80–100	90	3	270	47	141
		N = 40	$\Sigma f_i x_i$ = 1720		$\Sigma f_i\|x_i - \bar{x}\|$ = 788

$\therefore$ Mean is given by $\bar{x} = \frac{\Sigma f_i x_i}{N} = \frac{1720}{40} = 43$

And Mean deviation from mean

$= \frac{\Sigma f_i |x_i - \bar{x}|}{N} = \frac{788}{40} = 19.7$

And $\frac{N}{2} = \frac{40}{2} = 20$, which lies in the class 40-60

$\therefore$ Median class is 40 – 60.

(A) *(c) 43*

Explanation: mean time = 43

Hence, option (c) is the correct answer.

(B) *(b) Median*

Explanation: The construction of the cumulative frequency table is useful in determining the median.

Hence, option (b) is the correct answer.

(C) *(b) 40*

Explanation: The median class is 40–60. So, the lower limit = 40.

Hence, option (b) is the correct answer.

(D) *(b) 788*

Explanation: The absolute value of algebraic sum of deviation from the mean is 788.

Hence, option (b) is the correct answer.

(E) *(a) 19.7*

Explanation: From the calculation above, mean deviation from mean is 19.7.

Hence, option (a) is the correct answer.

15. *A seminar on prime numbers was organized in a college to motivate students.*

(A) Find the mean deviation of the first three primes from their median.

(B) Find the median of first three primes and find the algebraic sum of deviations of first three prime numbers from the mean.

Ans. (A) The first three prime numbers in ascending order are 2, 3 and 5.

Median of these three prime numbers = Value of 2nd item = 3.

The sum of absolute values of deviations from the median

$= |2-3| + |3-3| + |5-3| = 1 + 0 + 2 = 3$

Mean deviations of first three prime numbers from median $= \frac{3}{3} = 1$

(B) Median is 3.

He algebraic sum of deviations from the mean is always zero.

VERY SHORT ANSWER Type Questions (VSA)

[1 mark]

16. Find the range of the following data

x	10–20	20–30	30–40	40–50
f	4	5	6	5

[DIKSHA]

Ans.

x	10–20	20–30	30–40	40–50
f	4	5	6	5

The highest class is 40–50

And the lowest class is 10–20

Hence, range = upper limit of highest class – lower limit of lowest class

= 50 – 10

= 40

17. Find the mean deviation from the mean for the data: 6, 7, 10, 12, 13, 4, 8, 20.

Ans. Let $\bar{x}$ be the mean of the given data. Then,

$$\bar{x} = \frac{6+7+10+12+13+4+8+20}{8} = 10$$

x_i	$\lvert d_i \rvert = \lvert x_i - \bar{X} \rvert = \lvert x_i - 10 \rvert$
6	4
7	3
10	0
12	2
13	3
4	6
8	2
20	10
Total	$\Sigma d_i = 30$

Now, $\quad \Sigma \lvert d_i \rvert = 30$ and $n = 8$

$$\text{M.D.} = \frac{1}{n}\sum \lvert d_i \rvert = \frac{30}{8} = 3.75$$

Thus, the mean deviation from the mean for the given data is 3.75.

18. Find the mean deviation about median for the following information. [DIKSHA]

x	15	21	27	30
f	3	5	6	7

Ans.

x_i	f_i	c.f	$d_i = \lvert x_i - 27 \rvert$	$f_i d_i$
15	3	3	12	36
21	5	8	6	30
27	6	14	0	0
30	7	21	3	21
	21		21	87

$$\text{Median} = \left(\frac{21+1}{2}\right)^{th}$$

$= 11^{th}$ term i.e. 27

$$\text{M.D} = \frac{\Sigma f_i d_i}{\Sigma f_i}$$

$$= \frac{87}{21} = = 4.14$$

19. Find the mean of the following data:

x_i	2	5	6	8	10	12
f_i	2	8	10	7	8	5

Ans. we have the following table:

x_i	f_i	$f_i x_i$
2	2	4
5	8	40
6	10	60
8	7	56
10	8	80
12	5	60
	$\Sigma f_i = 40$	$\Sigma f_i x_i = 300$

Hence, mean $\bar{x} = \dfrac{\sum f_i x_i}{\sum f_i} = \dfrac{300}{40} = 7.5$

SHORT ANSWER Type-I Questions (SA-I)

[2 marks]

20. Find the mean deviation about the median of the data: 36, 46, 42, 45, 55, 46, 51, 49.

Ans. Calculation of Median

Arranging the given data in ascending order : 36, 42, 45, 46, 46, 49, 51, 55.

Here, number of terms, $n = 8$, which is even.

So, median = $\dfrac{\left(\frac{n}{2}\right)^{th} term + \left(\frac{n}{2}+1\right)^{th} term}{2}$

$= \dfrac{4^{th} term + 5^{th} term}{2} = \dfrac{46+46}{2} = 46$

Calculation of Mean Deviation About Median

x_i	$\lvert d_i \rvert = \lvert x_i - 46 \rvert$
36	10
42	4
45	1
46	0
46	0
49	3
51	5
55	9
	$\Sigma \lvert d_i \rvert = 32$

Hence, mean deviation about median

$= \dfrac{\sum \lvert d_i \rvert}{n} = \dfrac{32}{8} = 4.$

21. The following data given the monthly income (in Rs) of 10 families in a city:

4600, 5560, 6440, 4530, 7670, 6850, 6750, 7910, 5490, 6800.

Find the mean using direct method.

Ans. Given data is 4600 5560, 6440, 4530, 7670, 6850, 6750, 7910, 5490, 6800.

Here, number of terms $n = 10$.

Hence, mean

$$\bar{x} = \frac{4600+5560+6440+4530+7670+6850+6750+7910+5490+6800}{10}$$

$= \dfrac{62600}{10} = 6260.$

22. Calculate mean deviation about mean from the following data:

x_i	3	9	17	23	27
f_i	8	10	12	9	5

[DIKSHA]

Ans. Calculation of mean deviation about mean

x_i	f_i	$f_i x_i$	$\lvert x_i - 15 \rvert$	$f_i \lvert x_i - 15 \rvert$
3	8	24	12	96
9	10	90	6	60
17	12	204	2	24
23	9	207	8	72
27	5	135	12	60
	$N = \Sigma f_i = 44$	$\Sigma f_i x_i = 660$		$\Sigma f_i \lvert x_i - 15 \rvert = 312$

Mean $= X = \dfrac{1}{N}(\sum f_i x_i) = \dfrac{660}{44} = 15$

Mean deviation = M.D.

$= \dfrac{1}{N}\sum f_i \lvert x_i - 15 \rvert = \dfrac{312}{44} = 7.09$

23. Calculate the mean deviation about the mean for the following frequency distribution:

Class Interval	0–4	4–8	8–12	12–16	16–20
Frequency	4	6	8	5	2

[NCERT Exemplar]

Ans. Given the frequency distribution

Now we have to find the mean deviation about the mean.

Let us make a table of the given data and append other columns after calculations

Class Interval	Mid-Value (x_i)	Frequency (f_i)	$f_i x_i$
0–4	2	4	8
4–8	6	6	36
8–12	10	8	80
12–16	14	5	70
16–20	18	2	36
		Total = 25	230

Here mean, $\bar{x} = \dfrac{\Sigma f_i x_i}{\Sigma f_i} = \dfrac{230}{25} = 9.2$

Now we have to find mean deviation

Class Interval	Mid-Value (x_i)	Frequency (f_i)	$f_i x_i$	$d_i = \lvert x_i - \text{mean} \rvert$	$f_i d_i$
0–4	2	4	8	7.2	28.8
4–8	6	6	36	3.2	19.2
8–12	10	8	80	0.8	6.4
12–16	14	5	70	4.8	24
16–20	18	2	36	8.8	17.6
		Total = 25	230		96

Hence, Mean Deviation becomes,

$M.D = \dfrac{\Sigma f_i d_i}{\Sigma f_i} = \dfrac{96}{25} = 3.84$

Therefore, the mean deviation about the mean of the distribution is 3.84.

24. Find the median age of the distribution of 100 persons given below:

Age	16 – 20	21 – 25	26 – 30	31 – 35	36 – 40	41 – 45	46 – 50	51 – 55
Number	5	6	12	14	26	12	16	9

Ans. Given data in inclusive form is

Age	16 – 20	21 – 25	26 – 30	31 – 35	36 – 40	41 – 45	46 – 50	51 – 55
Number	5	6	12	14	26	12	16	9

Which can be written in exclusive form as

Age	15.5–20.5	20.5–25.5	25.5–30.5	30.5–35.5	35.5–40.5	40.5–45.5	45.5–50.5	50.5–55.5
Number	5	6	12	14	26	12	16	9

We have the following table:

Class	Frequency (f_i)	Cumulative Frequency
15.5-20.5	5	5
20.5-25.5	6	11
25.5-30.5	12	23
30.5-35.5	14	37
35.5-40.5	26	63
40.5-45.5	12	75
45.5-50.5	16	91
50.5-55.5	9	100
	$n = \Sigma f_i = 100$	

Here, $n = 100$. So, $\frac{n}{2} = 50$.

The cumulative frequency just greater than 50 is 63, which belongs to the class 35.5 - 40.5.

So, 35.5-40.5 is the median class.

Lower limit of median class, $l = 35.5$

Width of median class, $h = 5$

Frequency of median class, $f = 26$.

Cumulative frequency of class just preceding median class, $C = 37$.

Hence, median

$$= l + \frac{\frac{n}{2} - C}{f} \times h = 35.5 + \frac{50-37}{26} \times 5 = 38$$

SHORT ANSWER Type-II Questions (SA-II)

[**3** marks]

25. Find the mean deviation about the median for the following data. [DIKSHA]

Class	0 – 6	6 – 12	12 – 18	18 – 24	24 – 30
Frequency	8	10	12	9	5

Ans. Calculation of mean deviation about the Median

Class	Mid-Values (x)	Frequency (f_i)	Cumulative Fequency (C. f)	$\|x_i - 14\|$	$f_i \|x_i - 14\|$
0–6	3	8	8	11	88
6–12	9	10	18	5	50
12–18	15	12	30	1	12
18–24	21	9	39	7	63
24–30	27	5	44	13	65
		$N = 44$			$\Sigma f_i \|x_i - 14\| = 278$

$N = 44$, so $N/2 = 22$ and the cumulative frequency just greater than $\frac{N}{2}$ is 30. Thus, 12– 18 is the median class.

$\therefore$ Median $= l + \frac{N/2 - F}{f} \times h$,

where $l = 12$, $h = 6$, $f = 12$, $F = 18$.

$\Rightarrow$ Median $= 12 + \frac{22-18}{12} \times 6 = 12 + \frac{4 \times 6}{12} = 14.$

Clearly, $\sum f_i |x_i - 14| = 278$

$\therefore$ Mean deviation about median

$$= \frac{1}{N} \sum f_i |x_i - 14| = \frac{278}{44} = 6.318$$

26. Calculate the mean deviation from the median for the following distribution:

x_i	10	15	20	25	30	35	40	45
f_i	7	3	8	5	6	8	4	9

Ans. We have to calculate mean deviation about median. So, first, we calculate median.

x_i	f_i	Cumulative fequency	$\lvert d_i\rvert = \lvert x_i - 30\rvert$	$f_i \lvert d_i\rvert$
10	7	7	20	140
15	3	10	15	45
20	8	18	10	80
25	5	23	5	25
30	6	29	0	0
35	8	37	5	40
40	4	41	10	40
45	9	50	15	135
	$N = \Sigma f_i$			$\Sigma f_i \lvert d_i\rvert = 505$

Clearly, $N = 50 \Rightarrow N/2 = 25$

The cumulative frequency just greater than 25 is 29 and the corresponding value of x is 30.

Therefore, median = 30

Clearly, $\Sigma f_i \lvert x_i - 30\rvert = \Sigma f_i d_i = 505$ and $N = 50$.

$$\therefore \text{ Mean deviation} = \frac{1}{N} \Sigma f_i \lvert d_i \rvert = \frac{505}{50} = 10.1$$

27. Calculate the mean deviation from the median of the distribution

Class Interval	0–6	6–12	12–18	18–24	24–30
Frequency	4	5	3	6	2

[NCERT Exemplar]

Ans. Given the frequency distribution

Now we have to find the mean deviation from the median

Let us make a table of the given data and append other columns after calculations.

Class Interval	Mid-Value (x_i)	Frequency (f_i)	c.f.	$d_i = \lvert x_i - \text{Median } M\rvert$	$f_i d_i$
0–6	3	4	4	11	44
6–12	9	5	9	5	25
12–18	15	3	12	1	3
18–24	21	6	18	7	42
24–30	27	2	20	13	26
	Total	**20**			**140**

Now, here $N = 20$, which is even.

Here median class $= \frac{N}{2} = 10^{th}$ term,

This observation lie in the class interval 12–18, so median can be written as,

$$M = l + \frac{\frac{N}{2} - cf}{f} \times h$$

Here $l = 12$, $cf = 9$, $f = 3$, $h = 6$ and $N = 20$, substituting these values, the above equation becomes,

$$M = 12 + \frac{\frac{20}{2} - 9}{3} \times 6$$

$$\Rightarrow M = 12 + \frac{10 - 9}{3} \times 6$$

$$\Rightarrow M = 12 + \frac{1 \times 6}{3}$$

$$\Rightarrow M = 12 + 2 = 14$$

Hence Mean Deviation becomes,

$$M.D. = \frac{\sum f_i d_i}{\sum f_i} = \frac{140}{20} = 7$$

Therefore, the mean deviation about the median of the distribution is 7.

28. Find the mean deviation about the median of the following distribution:

Marks Obtained	10	11	12	14	15
No. of students	2	3	8	3	4

[NCERT Exemplar]

Ans. Given data distribution

Now we have to find the mean deviation about the median

Let us make a table of the given data and append other columns after calculations

Now, here $N = 20$, which is even.

Here median,

$$M = \frac{1}{2}\left[\left(\frac{N}{2}\right)^{th} \text{observation} + \left(\frac{N}{2} + 1\right)^{th} \text{observation}\right]$$

$$M = \frac{1}{2}\left[\left(\frac{20}{2}\right)^{th} \text{observation} + \left(\frac{20}{2} + 1\right)^{th} \text{observation}\right]$$

$$M = \frac{1}{2}[10^{th} \text{observation} + 11^{th} \text{observation}]$$

Both these observations lie in cumulative frequency 13, for which the corresponding observation is 12.

$$M = \frac{1}{2}[12 + 12] = 12$$

So the above table with more columns is as shown below,

Marks Obtained x_i	Number of Students (f_i)	Cumulative frequency (cf)	$d_i = \|x_i - M\|$	$f_i d_i$
10	2	2	2	4
11	3	2 + 3 = 5	1	3
12	8	5 + 8 = 13	0	0
14	3	13 + 3 = 16	2	6
15	4	16 + 4 = 20	3	12
Total	**20**			**25**

Hence Mean Deviation becomes,

$$M.D = \frac{\sum f_i d_i}{\sum f_i} = \frac{25}{20} = 1.25$$

Therefore, the mean deviation about the median of the distribution is 1.25.

LONG ANSWER Type Questions (LA)

[**4** & **5** marks]

29. Calculate the mean deviation about the mean of the set of first n natural numbers when n is an even number. [NCERT Exemplar]

Ans. Given set of first n natural numbers when n is an even number.

Now we have to find the mean deviation about the mean.

We know first n natural numbers are 1, 2, 3,...,n and given n is an even number.

So mean is,

$$\bar{x} = \frac{1+2+3+...+n}{n} = \frac{\frac{n(n+1)}{2}}{n} = \frac{(n+1)}{2}$$

The deviation of numbers from the mean are as shown below,

$$1-\frac{(n+1)}{2}, 2-\frac{(n+1)}{2}, 3-\frac{(n+1)}{2}, ..., \frac{(n-2)}{2} - \frac{(n+1)}{2}, \frac{(n)}{2} - \frac{(n+1)}{2}, \frac{(n+2)}{2} - \frac{(n+1)}{2}, ..., n - \frac{(n+1)}{2}$$

Or,

$$\frac{2-(n+1)}{2}, \frac{4-(n+1)}{2}, \frac{6-(n+1)}{2}, ..., \frac{n-2-(n+1)}{2}, \frac{n-(n+1)}{2}, \frac{(n+2)-(n+1)}{2}, ..., \frac{2n-(n+1)}{2}$$

The above equation can be written as

$$\frac{2-(n+1)}{2}, \frac{4-(n+1)}{2}, \frac{6-(n+1)}{2}, ..., \frac{-3}{2}, \frac{-1}{2}, \frac{1}{2}, ..., \frac{2n-(n+1)}{2}$$

Or

$$\frac{1-n}{2}, \frac{3-n}{2}, \frac{5-n}{2}, ..., \frac{-3}{2}, \frac{-1}{2}, \frac{1}{2}, ..., \frac{n-1}{2}.$$

So the absolute values of deviation from the mean is

$$|x_i - \bar{x}| = \frac{(n-1)}{2}, \frac{(n-3)}{2}, \frac{(n-5)}{2}, ..., \frac{3}{2}, \frac{1}{2}, \frac{1}{2}, ..., \frac{n-1}{2}.$$

The sum of absolute values of deviations from the mean, is

$$\Sigma|x_i - \bar{x}| = \frac{(n-1)}{2} + \frac{(n-3)}{2} + \frac{(n-5)}{2} + ... + \frac{3}{2} + \frac{1}{2} + \frac{1}{2} + ... + \frac{n-1}{2}$$

We can write as

$$\Sigma|x_i - \bar{x}| = \left(\frac{1}{2} + \frac{3}{2} + ... + \frac{(n-1)}{2}\right)\left(\frac{n}{2}\right)$$

Now we know sum of first n odd natural numbers = n^2

Therefore, mean deviation about the mean is

$$M.D = \frac{\Sigma|x_i - \bar{x}|}{n} = \frac{\left(\frac{1}{2} + \frac{3}{2} + ... + \frac{(n-1)}{2}\right)\left(\frac{n}{2}\right)}{n} = \frac{\left(\frac{n^2}{2}\right)\left(\frac{n}{2}\right)}{n}$$

$$M.D = \frac{\Sigma|x_i - \bar{x}|}{n} = \frac{\left(\frac{n}{2}\right)^2}{n}$$

$$M.D = \frac{\Sigma|x_i - \bar{x}|}{n} = \frac{n^2}{4n} = \frac{n}{4}$$

Hence, the mean deviation about the mean of the set of first n natural numbers when n is an even number is $\frac{n}{4}$.

30. Calculate mean and mean deviation about median for the following data:

Class	0–10	10–20	20–30	30–40	40–50	50–60
Frequency	6	7	15	16	4	2

Ans. Calculation of mean deviation from median:

C.I.	Mid-values x_i	Frequency f_i	Cumulative Frequency	$\|x_i - \text{median}\| = \|x_i - 28\|$	$f_i\|x_i - \text{median}\|$
0–10	5	6	6	23	138
10–20	15	7	13	13	91
20–30	25	15	28	3	45
30–40	35	16	44	7	112
40–50	45	4	48	17	68
50–60	55	2	50	27	54
		$N = 50$			$\Sigma f_i\|x_i - \text{median}\| = 508$

Here, $N = 50$

$\therefore \quad \frac{N}{2} = \frac{50}{2} = 25$, so median class is 20 – 30.

From the table: $l = 20$, h = 10, $f = 15$, $cf = 13$

Using the formula:

$$\text{Median} = l + \frac{h}{f}\left(\frac{N}{2} - cf\right)$$

$$= 20 + \frac{10}{15}\left(\frac{50}{2} - 13\right) = 20 + \frac{2}{3}(25 - 13)$$

$$= 20 + \frac{2}{3} \times 12 = 20 + 8 = 28$$

Thus, mean deviation about median

= M.D. (Median)

$$= \frac{\Sigma f_i |x_i - Median|}{N} = \frac{508}{50} = 10.16$$

Calculation of Mean:

C.I.	Mid-values x_i	Frequency f_i	$\mu_i = \frac{x_i - a}{h} = \frac{x_i - 35}{10}$	$f_i\mu_i$
0–10	5	6	-3	-18
10–20	15	7	-2	-14
20–30	25	15	-1	0
30–40	35	16	0	0
40–50	45	4	1	4
50–60	55	2	2	4
		$N = \Sigma f_i = 50$		$\Sigma f_i \mu_i = -39$

Let the assume mean $a = 35$

$\therefore$ Mean is given by

$$\bar{x} = a + h\frac{\Sigma f_i\mu_i}{N} = 35 + 10 \times \frac{(-39)}{50} = 35 - 7.8 = 27.2$$

31. Calculate the mean deviation about the mean of the set of first *n* natural numbers when n is an odd natural number.

[NCERT Exemplar]

Ans. Since n is an odd natural number. Therefore, $n = 2m + 1$ for some natural number m.

$$\text{Let } \bar{X} = \frac{1 + 2 + 3 + \ldots + (n-1) + n}{n}$$

$$= \frac{n(n+1)}{2n} = \frac{n+1}{2}$$

$$\Rightarrow \bar{X} = \frac{2m+1+1}{2} = m+1$$

The mean deviation (*M. D.*) about mean is given by

$$M.D. = \frac{1}{n}\sum_{r=1}^{n}|r - \bar{X}|$$

$$\Rightarrow M.D = \frac{1}{2m+1}\sum_{r=1}^{2m+1}|r - (m+1)|$$

$$\Rightarrow M.D = \frac{1}{2m+1}\left\{\begin{matrix}\sum_{r=1}^{2m+1}|r - (m+1)| \\ + \sum_{r=1}^{2m+1}|r - (m+1)|\end{matrix}\right\}$$

$$\Rightarrow M.D = \frac{1}{2m+1}\left\{\begin{matrix}\sum_{r=1}^{m}|r + (m+1)| \\ + \sum_{r=1}^{m}\{r - (m+1)\}\end{matrix}\right\}$$

$$\Rightarrow M.D = \frac{1}{2m+1}\left\{\begin{matrix}-\sum_{r=1}^{m} r + (m+1)\sum_{r=1}^{m} 1 + \\ \sum_{r=m+1}^{2m+1} r - (m+1)\sum_{r=m+1}^{2m+1} 1\end{matrix}\right\}$$

$\Rightarrow$ M.D

$$= \frac{1}{2m+1}\left\{\begin{array}{l}-\frac{m(m+1)}{2}+m(m+1)+\left(\frac{m+1}{2}\right)\\ \{(m+1)+(2m+1)-(m+1)(m+1)\}\end{array}\right\}$$

$\Rightarrow$ M.D =

$$\frac{1}{2m+1}\left\{\begin{array}{l}-\frac{m(m+1)}{2}+m(m+1)+\\ \frac{1}{2}(m+1)(3m+2)-(m+1)^2\end{array}\right\}$$

$$\Rightarrow M.D = \frac{1}{2m+1}\left\{\begin{array}{l}\frac{m(m+1)}{2}+\frac{1}{2}(m+1)\\ (3m+2)-(m+1)^2\end{array}\right\}$$

$$\Rightarrow M.D = \frac{m+1}{2(2m+1)}\{m+(3m+2)-2(m+1)\}$$

$$\Rightarrow M.D = \frac{m+1}{2(2m+1)}(2m) = \frac{m(m+1)}{2m+1}$$

$$= \frac{\left(\frac{n-1}{2}\right)\left(\frac{n-1}{2}+1\right)}{n}$$

[$\because$ $n = 2m + 1$]

$$\Rightarrow M.D = \frac{1}{n}\left(\frac{n-1}{2}\right)\left(\frac{n+1}{2}\right) = \frac{n^2-1}{4n}$$

VARIANCE AND STANDARD DEVIATION 2

TOPIC 1

STANDARD DEVIATION

Standard Deviation of Ungrouped Data

Consider the ungrouped data $x_1, x_2, \ldots x_n$ consisting of n values. In order to find the variance and standard deviation. We have the following working rule:

Step I: Calculate mean of the given data using the formula

$$\text{Mean } \bar{x} = \frac{x_1 + x_2 + \ldots + x_n}{n}$$

Step II: Compute the variance and standard deviation of the formula

$$\text{Variance, } \sigma^2 = \frac{\sum (x_i - x)^2}{n}$$

$$\text{And standard Deviation, } \sigma = \sqrt{\frac{\sum (x_i - x)^2}{n}}$$

Example 2.1: Find the mean and variance for the first 10 multiples of 3. [NCERT]

Ans The first 10 multiplies of 3 are

3, 6, 9, 12, 15, 18, 21, 24, 27, 30

$$\text{Mean} = \frac{\text{sum of observations}}{\text{Number of observations}}$$

$$= \frac{3+6+9+12+15+18+21+24+27+30}{10}$$

$$= \frac{165}{10}$$

$$= 16.5$$

Finding variance

x_i	$x_i - \bar{x}$	$(x_i - \bar{x})^2$
3	3 – 16.5 = –13.5	$(-13.5)^2 = 182.25$
6	6 – 16.5 = –10.5	$(-10.5)^2 = 110.25$
9	9 – 16.5 = –4.5	$(-7.5)^2 = 56.25$
12	12 – 16.5 = –4.5	$(-4.5)^2 = 20.25$
15	15 – 16.5 = –1.5	$(-1.5)^2 = 2.25$
18	18 – 16.5 = 1.5	$(1.5)^2 = 2.25$
21	12 – 16.5 = 4.5	$(4.5)^2 = 20.25$
24	24 – 16.5 = 7.5	$(7.5)^2 = 56.25$
27	27 – 16.5 = 10.5	$(10.5)^2 = 110.25$
30	30 – 16.5 = 13.5	$(13.5)^2 = 182.25$
		$\Sigma(x_i - \bar{x})^2 = 742.5$

$\therefore \quad \Sigma(x_i - \bar{x})^2 = 742.5$

$$\text{Variance } (\sigma)^2 = \frac{\sum (x_i - \bar{x})^2}{n} = \frac{742.5}{10} = 74.25$$

Standard Deviation of Discrete Frequency Distribution

Consider a discrete frequency distribution consisting of m distinct values $x_1, x_2, \ldots x_m$ with frequencies, $f_1, f_2, \ldots f_m$ respectively. In order to find the variance and standard deviation, we have the following working rule:

Step I: Calculate mean of the given data using the formula

$$\text{Mean, } \bar{x} = \frac{\sum f_i x_i}{\sum f_i}$$

Step II: Compute the variance and standard deviation using the formula

$$\text{Variance, } \sigma^2 = \frac{\sum f_i (x_i - \bar{x})^2}{\sum f_i}$$

$$\text{And standard deviation, } \sigma = \sqrt{\frac{\sum f_i (x_i - \bar{x})^2}{\sum f_i}}$$

Standard Deviation Of Continuous Distribution

Consider a continuous frequency distribution consisting of class intervals with their corresponding frequencies as, f_i. In order to find the variance and standard deviation. We have the following working rule:

Step I: Find the mid-points of the class intervals and denote them by x_i.

Step II: Calculate mean of the given data using the formula

$$\text{Mean} = \frac{\sum f_i x_i}{\sum f_i}$$

Step III: Compute the variance and standard deviation using the formula

$$\text{Variance, } \sigma^2 = \frac{\sum f_i (x_i - \bar{x})^2}{\sum f_i}$$

And standard deviation, $\sigma = \sqrt{\dfrac{\sum f_i(x_i - \bar{x})^2}{\sum f_i}}$

Example 2.2: Find the mean and variance for the following frequency distribution. **[NCERT]**

Class	0-30	30-60	60-90	90-120	120-150	150-180	180-210
Frequency	2	3	5	10	3	5	2

Ans.

Class	Frequency f_i	Mid-point x_i	$f_i x_i$
0–30	2	15	30
30–60	3	45	135
60–90	5	75	375
90–120	10	105	1050
120–150	3	135	405
150–180	5	165	825
180–210	2	195	390
	$\Sigma f_i = 30$		$\Sigma f_i x_i = 3210$

$\therefore \quad \Sigma f_i x_i = 3210$

$\Sigma f_i = 30$

Mean $\quad (\bar{x}) = \dfrac{\sum f_i x_i}{\sum f_i} = \dfrac{3210}{30} = 107$

Class	(f_i)	(x_i)	$u_i = \dfrac{x_i - A}{h}$	u_i^2	$f_i u_i$	$f_i u_i^2$
0–30	2	15	–3	9	–6	18
30 –60	3	45	–2	4	–6	12
60–90	5	75	–1	1	–5	5
90–120	10	105	0	0	0	0
120–150	3	135	1	1	3	3
150–180	5	165	2	4	10	20
180–210	2	195	3	9	6	18
Total	30				2	76

Here, $N = 30$, $h = 30$

$$\text{Variance } (\sigma^2) = \frac{h^2}{N^2}\left[N\sum_{i=1}^{7} f_i u_i^2 - \left(\sum_{i=1}^{7} f_i u_i\right)^2\right]$$

$$= \frac{(30)^2}{(30)^2}\,[30 \times 76 - (2)^2]$$

$$= 2280 - 4$$

$$= 2276$$

Short-Cut Method For S.D. of Continuous Distribution

Consider a continuous frequency distribution consisting of class intervals with their corresponding frequencies as f_i. Let x_i be the mid-points of the class intervals.

$$\text{Variance,} \quad \sigma^2 = \frac{\sum f_i (x_i - \bar{x})^2}{\sum f_i}$$

$$= \frac{\sum f_i x_i^2}{\sum f_i} - \left(\frac{\sum f_i x_i}{\sum f_i}\right)^2$$

$$\text{Hence, variance,} \quad \sigma^2 = \frac{\sum f_i x_i^2}{\sum f_i} - \left(\frac{\sum f_i x_i}{\sum f_i}\right)^2$$

And standard deviation,

$$\sigma = \sqrt{\frac{\sum f_i x_i^2}{\sum f_i} - \left(\frac{\sum f_i x_i}{\sum f_i}\right)^2}$$

Short-Cut Method of S.D. of Discrete Distribution

Consider a discrete frequency distribution consisting of m distinct values $x_1, x_2, \ldots x_m$ with frequencies, $f_1, f_2, \ldots, f_m$ respectively.

$$\text{Then, variance, } \sigma^2 = \frac{\sum (x_i - \bar{x})^2}{\sum f_i}$$

$$= \frac{\sum \left(x^2{}_i - \bar{x}^2 - 2x_i x\right)}{\sum f_i}$$

$$= \frac{\sum f_i x^2{}_i}{\sum f_i} + \frac{\sum \bar{x}^2 f_i}{\sum f_i} - \frac{\sum 2x f_i \bar{x}_i}{\sum f_i}$$

$$= \frac{\sum f_i x_i^2}{\sum f_i} + \frac{x^2 \sum f_i}{\sum f_i} - \frac{2x \sum f_i x_i}{\sum f_i}$$

$$= \frac{\sum f_i x_i^2}{\sum f_i} + x^2 - 2x^2$$

$$= \frac{\sum f_i x_i^2}{\sum f_i} - x^2 = \frac{\sum f_i x_i^2}{\sum f_i} = \left(\frac{\sum f_i x_i}{\sum f_i}\right)^2$$

$$\text{Hence, variance, } \sigma^2 = \frac{\sum f_i x^2{}_i}{\sum f_i} - \left(\frac{\sum f_i x_i}{\sum f_i}\right)^2$$

And standard deviation,

$$\sigma = \sqrt{\frac{\sum f_i x^2{}_i}{\sum f_i} - \left(\frac{\sum f_i x_i}{\sum f_i}\right)^2}$$

The coefficient of variation is defined as

$$C.V. = \frac{\sigma}{\bar{x}} \times 100,$$

Where σ and $\bar{x}$ are the standard deviation and mean of the data, respectively and $\bar{x} \neq 0$.

For comparing the variability or dispersion of two series, we calculate the coefficient of variation for each series. We make the following conclusions:

(i) The series having greater C.V. is said to be more variable than the other.

(ii) The series having lesser C.V. is said to be more consistent than the other.

Example 2.3: Find the mean and standard deviation using the short-cut method. [NCERT]

Ans.

x_i	f_i	$y_i = x_i - A$	y_i^2	$f_i y_i$	$f_i y_i^2$
60	2	60 – 64= –3	16	–4 × 2 = –8	16 × 2 = 32
61	1	61 – 64= –3	9	–3 × 1 = –3	9 × 1 = 9
62	12	62 – 64= –3	4	–2 × 12 = –24	12 × 4 = 48
63	29	63 – 64= –3	1	–1 × 29 = –29	29 × 1 = 29
64	25	64 – 64= –3	0	0 × 25 = 0	25 × 0 = 0
65	12	65 – 64= –3	1	1 × 12 = 12	12 × 1 = 12
66	10	66 – 64= –3	4	2 × 10 = 20	10 × 4 = 40
67	4	67 – 64= –3	9	3 × 4 = 12	4 × 9 = 36
68	5	68 – 64= –3	16	4 × 5 = 20	5 × 16 = 80
	100	200		0	286

Let A = assumed mean = 64

h = width = 61 – 60 = 1

$$\text{Mean} = a + \frac{\sum f_i y_i}{\sum f_i} \times h$$

$$= 64 + \frac{0}{100} \times 1$$

$$= 64$$

$$\text{Standard Deviation} = \frac{h}{N}\sqrt{N\sum f_i y_i^2 - (\sum f_i y_i)^2}$$

$$= \frac{1}{100}\sqrt{100 \times 286 - (0)^2}$$

$$= \frac{1}{100}\sqrt{28600}$$

$$= \frac{169.1}{100}$$

$$= 1.691$$

	169.1
1	28600.00
	1
26	186
	156
329	3000
	2961
3381	3900
	3381
	519

OBJECTIVE Type Questions

[**1** mark]

Multiple Choice Questions

1. Mean and standard deviation of 100 items are 50 and 4, respectively. Find the sum of the squares of the items.

(a) 25000 **(b) 251600**

(c) 26000 **(a) None of these**

[NCERT Exemplar]

Ans. *(b) 251600*

Explanation: Given mean and standard deviation of 100 items are 50 and 4, respectively

Now we have to find the sum of the squares of the items.

As per given criteria,

Number of items, $n = 100$

Mean of the given items, $\bar{x} = 50$

But we know,

$$\bar{x} = \frac{\Sigma x_i}{n}$$

Substituting the corresponding values, we get

$$50 = \frac{\Sigma x_i}{100}$$

$\Rightarrow \Sigma x_i = 50 \times 100 = 5000$

Hence the sum of all the 100 items = 5000.

Also, given the standard deviation of the 100 items is 4.

i.e., $\sigma = 4$

But we know

$$\sigma = \sqrt{\frac{\Sigma x_i^2}{n} - \left(\frac{\Sigma x_i}{n}\right)^2}$$

Substituting the corresponding values, we get

$$4 = \sqrt{\frac{\Sigma x_i^2}{100} - \left(\frac{5000}{100}\right)^2}$$

Now taking square on both sides, we get

$$4^2 = \frac{\Sigma x_i^2}{100} - (50)^2$$

$$\Rightarrow \quad 16 = \frac{\Sigma x_i^2}{100} - 2500$$

$$\Rightarrow \quad 16 + 2500 = \frac{\Sigma x_i^2}{100}$$

On rearranging we get,

$$\Rightarrow \quad \frac{\Sigma x_i^2}{100} = 2516$$

$$\Rightarrow \quad \Sigma x_i^2 = 2516 \times 100$$

$$\Rightarrow \quad \Sigma x_i^2 = 251600$$

The sum of the squares of all the 100 items is 251600.

Hence, option (*b*) is the correct answer.

2. If for a distribution $\Sigma(x - 5) = 3$, $\Sigma(x - 5)^2 = 43$ and the total number of item is 18, find the standard deviation.

(a) 5.17 and 1.54 **(b) 4.27 and 4.81**

(c) 5.23 and 4.81 **(d) 4.03 and 4.81**

[NCERT Exemplar]

Ans. *(a) 5.17 and 1.54*

Explanation: Given for a distribution $\Sigma(x - 5) = 3$, $\Sigma(x - 5)^2 = 43$ and the total number of items is 18.

Now, we have to find the mean and standard deviation.

As per given criteria,

Number of items, $n = 18$

And given $\Sigma(x - 5) = 3,$

And also given, $\Sigma(x - 5)^2 = 43$

But, we know mean can be written as,

$$\bar{x} = A + \frac{\Sigma(x-5)}{n}$$

Here assumed mean is 5, so substituting the corresponding values in above equation, we get

$$\bar{x} = 5 + \frac{3}{18} = \frac{18 \times 5 + 3}{18} = \frac{93}{18} = 5.17$$

And we know the standard deviation can be written as,

$$\sigma = \sqrt{\frac{\Sigma(x-5)^2}{n} - \left(\frac{\Sigma(x-5)}{n}\right)^2}$$

Substituting the corresponding values, we get

$$\sigma = \sqrt{\frac{43}{18} - \left(\frac{3}{18}\right)^2}$$

$$\sigma = \sqrt{2.39 - (0.166)^2}$$

$$\sigma = \sqrt{2.39 - 0.027} = \sqrt{2.363}$$

Hence, $\sigma = 1.54$

So, the mean and standard deviation of given items is 5.17 and 1.54 respectively.

Hence, option (*a*) is the correct answer.

3. Mean and standard deviation of 100 observation were found to be 40 and 10, respectively. If at the time of calculation two observation were wrongly taken as 30 and 70 in place of 3 and 27 respectively, find the correct standard deviation.

(a) 14.24 **(b) 10.24**

(c) 19.23 **(d) 20**

[NCERT Exemplar]

Ans. *(b) 10.24*

Explanation: Given mean and standard deviation of 100 observations were found to be 40 and 10, respectively. If at the time of calculation, two observations were wrongly taken as 30 and 70 in place of 3 and 27 respectively.

Now we have to find the correct standard deviation.

As per given criteria,

Number of observations, $n = 100$

Mena of the given observations before correction, $\bar{x} = 40$

But we know,

$$\bar{x} = \frac{\Sigma x_i}{100}$$

$$\Rightarrow \quad \Sigma x_i = 40 \times 100 = 4000$$

It is said two observations were wrongly taken as 30 and 70 in place of 3 and 27 respectively,

So $\Sigma x_i = 4000 - 30 - 70 + 3 + 27 = 3930$

So, the correction mean after correction is

$$\bar{x} = \frac{\Sigma x_i}{n} = \frac{3930}{100} = 39.3$$

Also given the standard deviation of the 100 observations is 10 before correction i.e., $\sigma = 10$

But we know

$$\sigma = \sqrt{\frac{\Sigma x_i^2}{n} - \left(\frac{\Sigma x_i}{n}\right)^2}$$

Substituting the corresponding values, we get

$$10 = \sqrt{\frac{\Sigma x_i^2}{100} - \left(\frac{4000}{100}\right)^2}$$

Now taking square on both sides, we get

$$10^2 = \frac{\Sigma x_i^2}{100} - (40)^2$$

$$\Rightarrow \quad 100 = \frac{\Sigma x_i^2}{100} - 1600$$

$$\Rightarrow \quad 100 + 1600 = \frac{\Sigma x_i^2}{100}$$

$$\Rightarrow \quad \frac{\Sigma x_i^2}{100} = 1700$$

$$\Rightarrow \quad \Sigma x_i^2 = 170000$$

It is said two observation were wrongly taken as 30 and 70 in place of 3 and 27 respectively, so correction is

$\Rightarrow \Sigma x_i^2 = 170000 - (30)^2 - (70)^2 + 3^2 + (27)^2$

$\Rightarrow \Sigma x_i^2 = 170000 - 900 - 4900 + 9 + 729$

$= 164938$

$\Rightarrow \Sigma x_i^2 = 164938$

So the correct standard deviation after correction is

$$\sigma = \sqrt{\frac{164938}{100} - \left(\frac{3930}{100}\right)^2}$$

$$\sigma = \sqrt{1649.38 - (39.3)^2}$$

$$\sigma = \sqrt{1649.38 - 1544.49} = \sqrt{104.89}$$

$$\sigma = 10.24$$

Thus, the correct standard deviation is 10.24.

Hence, option (*b*) is the correct answer.

4. While calculating the mean and variance of 10 readings, a student wrongly used the reading 52 for the correct reading 25. He obtained the mean and variance as 45 and 16 respectively. Find the correct mean and the variance.

(a) 42.3 and 43.81 (b) 43.3 and 43.81

(c) 42.3 and 42.81 (d) 40.3 and 43.81

[NCERT Exemplar]

Ans. *(a) 42.3 and 43.81*

Explanation: Given while calculating the mean and variance of 10 readings, a student wrongly used the reading 52 for the correct reading 25. He obtained the mean and variance as 45 and 16 respectively

Now we have to find the correct mean and the variance.

As per given criteria,

Number of reading, $n = 10$

Mean of the given reading before correction,

$$\bar{x} = 45$$

But we know,

$$\bar{x} = \frac{\Sigma x_i}{n}$$

Substituting the corresponding values, we get

$$45 = \frac{\Sigma x_i}{n}$$

$$\Rightarrow \quad \Sigma x_i = 45 \times 10 = 450$$

It is said one reading 25 was wrongly taken as 52,

So, $\quad \bar{x}_i = 45 \times 10 = 450$

It is said one reading 25 was wrongly taken as 52,

So, $\quad \bar{x}_i = 450 - 52 + 25 = 423$

So the correct mean after correction is

$$\bar{x} = \frac{\Sigma x_i}{n} = \frac{423}{10} = 42.3$$

Also given the variance of the 10 reading is 16 before correction,

i.e. $\sigma^2 = 16$

But we know

$$\sigma^2 = \frac{\Sigma x_i^2}{n} - \left(\frac{\Sigma x_i}{n}\right)^2$$

Substituting the corresponding values, we get

$$16 = \frac{\Sigma x_i^2}{10} - (45)^2$$

$$\Rightarrow \quad 16 = \frac{\Sigma x_i^2}{10} - 2025$$

$$\Rightarrow \quad 16 + 2025 = \frac{\Sigma x_i^2}{10}$$

$$\Rightarrow \quad \frac{\Sigma x_i^2}{10} = 2041$$

$$\Rightarrow \quad \Sigma x_i^2 = 20410$$

It is said one reading 25 wrongly taken as 52, so

$\Rightarrow \Sigma x_i^2 = 20410 - (52)^2 + (25)^2$

$\Rightarrow \Sigma x_i^2 = 20410 - 2704 + 625$

$\Rightarrow \Sigma x_i^2 = 18331$

So the correct variance after correction is

$$\sigma^2 = \frac{18331}{10} - \left(\frac{423}{10}\right)^2$$

$$\sigma^2 = 1833.1 - (42.3)^2 = 1833.1 - 1789.29$$

$$\sigma^2 = 43.81$$

Thus, the corrected mean and variance is 42.3 and 43.81 respectively.

Hence, option (*a*) is the correct answer.

5. **The variance of the following data is:**

Intervals	4–8	8–12	12–16	16–20
Frequency	3	6	4	7

(a) 13 (b) 18

(c) 19 (d) 20

Ans. *(c) 19*

Explanation:

Class	x_i	f_i
4 – 8	6	3
8 – 12	10	6
12 – 16	14	4
16 – 20	18	7

$$\Sigma f_i x_i = 18 + 60 + 56 + 126 = 260$$

$$\Sigma f_i = 20$$

$$\bar{x} = \frac{\sum f_i x_i}{\sum f_i} = 13$$

$$\text{Variance} = \frac{\sum f_i (x_i - \bar{x})^2}{\sum f_i} = \frac{380}{20}$$

$$= 19$$

Hence, option (c) is the correct answer.

6. **Calculate standard deviation for the data 10, 20, 30, 40, 50.**

(a) $5\sqrt{2}$ (b) $8\sqrt{2}$

(c) $10\sqrt{2}$ (d) $15\sqrt{2}$ [DIKSHA]

Ans. *(c) $10\sqrt{2}$*

Explanation:

$$\bar{x} = \frac{10+20+30+40+50}{5} = \frac{150}{5} = 30$$

x	$d = x - \underline{x}$	d^2
10	10 – 30 = –20	400
20	20 – 30 = –10	100
30	30 – 30 = 0	0.
40	40 – 30 = 10	100
50	50 – 30 = 20	400
	Σd^2	1000

$$\text{Variance} = \frac{\sum d^2}{n} = \frac{1000}{5}$$

Standard deviation

$$= \sqrt{\text{variance}} = \sqrt{200} = 10\sqrt{2}$$

Hence, option (c) is the correct answer.

7. **The standard deviation of data 7, 6, 10, 14, 13, 9 and 11 is:**

(a) $\sqrt{\frac{52}{7}}$ (b) $\frac{52}{7}$

(c) $\sqrt{6}$ (d) 6

Ans. *(a) $\sqrt{\frac{52}{7}}$*

Explanation:

x_i	x_i^2
7	49
6	36
10	100
14	196
13	169
9	81
11	121
70	752

$$S.D. = \sqrt{\frac{\sum x_i^2}{N} - \left(\frac{\sum x_i}{N}\right)^2}$$

$$= \sqrt{\frac{752}{7} + \left(\frac{70}{7}\right)^2}$$

$$= \sqrt{\frac{5264 - 4900}{49}}$$

$$= \sqrt{\frac{364}{49}}$$

$$= \sqrt{\frac{52}{7}}$$

Hence, option (c) is the correct answer.

8. **Find the mean and the variance of the 8, 9, 12, 14, 15, 6, 10, 14.**

(a) 8.25 (b) 9.25

(c) 65.2 (d) 55

Ans. *(b) 9.25*

Explanation Given data is 8, 9, 12, 14, 15, 6, 10, 14

$$\text{Mean } \bar{x} = \frac{\sum_{i=1}^{8} x_i}{n}$$

$$= \frac{8+9+12+14+15+6+10+14}{8}$$

$$= \frac{88}{8} = 11$$

x_i	$(x_i - \bar{x})$	$(x_i - \bar{x})^2$
8	-3	9
9	-2	4
12	1	1
14	3	9
15	4	16
6	-5	25
10	-1	1
14	3	9
		74

$\therefore$ Variance $(\sigma^2) = \frac{1}{n}\sum_{i=1}^{8}(x_i - \bar{x})^2 = \frac{1}{8} \times 74 = 9.25$

Hence, option (b) is the correct answer.

9.

x_i	10	15	18	20	25
f_i	3	2	6	7	2

The variance for the data is:

(a) 22.5 **(b) 22.159**

(c) 21.159 **(d) 16.79**

Ans. *(d) 16.79*

Explanation:

x_i	f_i	$f_i x_i$	$x_i - \bar{x}$	$(x_i - \bar{x})^2$	$f_i(x_i - \bar{x})^2$
10	3	30	-7.9	62.41	187.23
15	2	30	-2.9	8.41	16.82
18	6	108	0.1	0.01	0.06
20	7	140	2.1	4.41	30.87
25	2	50	7.1	50.41	100.82
Total	**20**	**358**			**335.8**

$\bar{x} = \frac{\sum f_i x_i}{\sum f_i} = \frac{358}{20} = 17.9$

$\sigma^2 = \frac{1}{N}\sum f_i (x_i - \bar{x})^2$

$= \frac{335.8}{20} = 16.79$

Hence, option (d) is the correct answer.

10. The mean and variance for the data 6, 8, 9, 12, 13, 5, 7, 12 respectively are:

(a) 9 **(b) 10**

(c) 8 **(d) 5**

Ans *(c) 8*

Explanation:

x_i	x_i^2
6	36
8	64
9	81
12	144
13	169
5	25
7	49
12	144
Total = 72	712

Mean $= \frac{72}{8} = 9$

Variance $= \frac{712}{8} - \left(\frac{72}{8}\right)^2$

$= 89 - 81$

$= 8$

Hence, option (c) is the correct answer.

11. The standard deviation of the first ten natural numbers is:

(a) 5.5 **(b) 2.97**

(c) 3.87 **(d) 2.87** **[DIKSHA]**

Ans. *(d) 2.87*

Explanation: We know that the standard deviation of first *n* natural number is $\sqrt{\frac{n^2 - 1}{12}}$.

$\therefore$ Standard deviation of first 10 natural numbers

$= \sqrt{\frac{10^2 - 1}{12}}$

$= \sqrt{\frac{99}{12}}$

$= \sqrt{8.25}$

$= 2.87$

Hence, option (d) is the correct answer.

12. Let *x* is the variance and *y* is the standard deviation then which of the following is correct.

(a) $x = y^2$ **(b) $xy = 1$**

(c) $x^2 = y$ **(d) $x^2 y^2 = 1$**

Ans. *(a) $x = y^2$*

Explanation: The standard deviation is the square root of the variance.

$\therefore$ If x is the variance and y is the standard deviation, then $y = = \sqrt{x}$, or $y^2 = x$

Hence, option (a) is the correct answer.

CASE BASED Questions (CBQs)

[**4** & **5** marks]

Read the following passages and answer the questions that follow:

13. *For a group of 200 candidates, the mean and the standard deviation of scores were found to be 40 and 15, respectively. Later on, it was discovered that the scores of 43 and 35 were misread as 34 and 53, respectively:*

(A) Find the sum of correct scores.

(a) 7991 **(b) 8000**

(c) 8550 **(d) 6572**

(B) Find the correct mean.

(a) 42.924 **(b) 39.955**

(c) 38.423 **(d) 41.621**

(C) Find the correct variance.

(a) 280.3 **(b) 235.6**

(c) 224.143 **(d) 226.521**

(D) Find the correct standard deviation.

(a) 14.971 **(b) 11.321**

(c) 16.441 **(d) 12.824**

Ans. (A) *(a) 7991*

Explanation: We have, n = 200, incorrect mean = 40 and incorrect deviation = 15

Now, incorrect mean = 40

$$\Rightarrow \frac{\text{Incorrect} \sum x_i}{200} = 40$$

$$\text{Incorrect } \Sigma x_i = 8000$$

$$\Rightarrow \text{correct } \Sigma x_i = 8000 - (34 + 53) + (43 + 35)$$
$$= 8000 - 87 + 78 = 7991$$

Hence, option *(a)* is the correct answer.

(B) *(b) 39.955*

Explanation: Correct mean $= \frac{7991}{200}$

$$= 39.955$$

Hence, option *(b)* is the correct answer.

(C) *(c) 224.143*

Explanation: Incorrect *SD* = 15

$\Rightarrow$ incorrect variance = $(15)^2$ = 225

$$\Rightarrow \frac{\text{Incorrect} \sum x_i^2}{200} - (\text{incorrect mean})^2 = 225$$

$$\Rightarrow \frac{\text{Incorrect} \sum x_i^2}{200} - (40)^2 = 225$$

$$\Rightarrow \text{Incorrect } \Sigma x_i^2 = 200(1600 + 225)$$
$$= 200 \times 1825 = 365000$$

$$\Rightarrow \text{correct } \Sigma x_i^2 = \text{Incorrect } x_i^2 - (34^2 + 53^2) + (43^2 + 35^2)$$
$$= 365000 - 3965 + 3074$$
$$= 364109$$

So, correct variance

$$= \frac{1}{200}(\text{correct} \sum x_i^2) - (\text{correct mean})^2$$

$$= \frac{1}{200}(364109) - \left(\frac{7991}{200}\right)^2$$

$$= 1820.545 - 1596.402$$
$$= 224.143$$

Hence, option *(c)* is the correct answer.

(D) *(a) 14.971*

Explanation: correct standard deviation

$$= \sqrt{\textit{correct variance}}$$

$$= \sqrt{224.143} \quad \text{(using part (C)}$$

$$= 14.971$$

Hence, option (a) is the correct answer.

14. *The following values are calculated in respect of length and mass of the students of class XII*

	Length	*Mass*
Mean	*164cm*	*64kg*
Variance	*125cm²*	*25kg²*

(A) Find the coefficient of variation of length.

(B) Find the coefficient of variation of mass and standard deviation of length.

Ans. (A) *S.D.* of length = $\sqrt{25}$ = 11.18

The coefficient of variation of length

$$= \frac{S.D.}{Mean} \times 100$$

$$= \frac{11.18}{164} \times 100$$

$$= 6.81$$

(B) *S.D.* of mass = $\sqrt{25} = 5$

$$C.V. \text{ of mass} = \frac{S.D}{Mean} \times 100$$

$$= \frac{5}{64} \times 100$$

$$= 7.81$$

$$S.D. = \sqrt{\text{variance}} = \sqrt{125} = 11.18$$

VERY SHORT ANSWER Type Questions (VSA)

[1 mark]

15. Find the coefficient of variation when particular data will have a variance 4 and mean 5. **[DIKSHA]**

Ans. Coefficient of variation = $\frac{S.D}{Mean} \times 100$

Here variance = 4

So

$$S.D = \sqrt{4} = 2$$

Mean = 5

So,

$$C.V = \frac{2}{5} \times 100$$

$$C.V = 40$$

16. Find the variance of the following data 5, 4, 8, 11, 7

Ans. Given series is 5, 8, 11, 14, 17

$$\text{Mean} = \frac{5+8+11+14+17}{5} = \frac{55}{5}$$

Mean = μ = 11

Variance = $\Sigma(x_i - \mu)^{2/n}$

$$= \frac{1}{5}[(5-11)^2 + (8-11)^2 + (11-11)^2 + (14-11)^2 + (17-11)^2]$$

$$= \frac{1}{5}[36+9+0+9+36]$$

$$= \frac{90}{5}$$

$$= 18$$

17. Find the variance for the data 7, 6, 10, 12, 13, 4, 8, 12.

Ans.

x_i	x_i^2
6	36
7	49
10	100
12	144
13	169
4	64
8	64
12	144
Total = 72	722

$n = 8$

$$\text{Variance} = \frac{\Sigma x_i^2}{n} - \left(\frac{\Sigma x_i}{n}\right)^2$$

$$= \frac{722}{8} - \left(\frac{72}{8}\right)^2$$

$$= 9.25$$

18. If the Coefficient of variation is 45% and the mean is 12, then find its standard deviation.

Ans. Since, coeffcient of variance

$$= \frac{\text{standard deviation}}{\text{Mean}} \times 100$$

$$45 = \frac{\sigma}{12} \times 100$$

$$\sigma = \frac{45 \times 12}{100}$$

$$\sigma = 5.4$$

19. Variance of the data 2, 4, 5, 6, 8, 17 is 23.33. Then, find the variance of 4, 8, 10, 12, 16 34.

Ans. When each observation is multiplied by 2. Then variance is also multiplied by 2.

Variance new series = 2× variance of given data

= 2 × 23.33

= 46.66

SHORT ANSWER Type-I Questions (SA-I)

[2 marks]

20. If the mean and standard deviation of 100 observations are 50 and 4 respectively. Find the sum of all observations and the sum of their squares. **[NCERT Exemplar]**

Ans. Let $x_1, x_2, \ldots x_{100}$ be 100 observations and their mean and standard deviations be $\bar{X}$ and, σ respectively. Then,

$$\bar{X} = \frac{1}{100}\sum_{i=1}^{100} x_i \text{ and, } \sigma^2 = \frac{1}{100}\sum_{i=1}^{100} x_i^2 - \bar{x}$$

$$\Rightarrow \quad 50=\frac{1}{100}\sum_{i=1}^{100} x_i \text{ and, } 16=\frac{1}{100}\sum_{i=1}^{100} x_i^2-50^2$$

$$[\because \quad \bar{X}=50 \text{ and } \sigma=4]$$

$$\Rightarrow \quad 5000=\sum_{i=1}^{100} x_i \text{ and, } 1600=\sum_{i=1}^{100} x_i^2-250000$$

$$\Rightarrow \quad \sum_{i=1}^{100} x_i=5000 \text{ and } \sum_{i=1}^{100} x_i^2-251600$$

$$\Rightarrow \quad \sum_{i=1}^{100} x_i=5000 \text{ and } \sum_{i=1}^{100} x_i^2=251600$$

21. Consider the following data

Marks obtained	10 – 20	20 – 30	30 – 40	40 – 50	50 – 60	60 – 70	70 – 80
Number of students	4	6	16	28	16	6	4

Then, find the mean deviation about the mean.

Ans. Take the assumed mean $a = 45$ and $h = 10$, and form the following table:

Marks Obtained	No. of students (f_i)	Mid value (xi)	$d_i = \frac{x_i - 45}{10}$	$f_i d_i$	$\lvert x_i - \bar{x}\rvert$	$f_i \lvert x_i - \bar{x}\rvert$
10 – 20	4	15	–3	–12	30	120
20 – 30	6	25	–2	–12	20	120
30 – 40	16	35	–1	–16	10	160
40 – 50	28	45	0	0	0	0
50 – 60	16	55	1	16	10	160
60 – 70	6	65	2	12	20	120
70 – 80	4	75	3	12	30	120
	40			0		800

$$\text{Therefore, } \bar{x} = a+\frac{\sum_{i=1}^{7} f_i d_i}{N}\times h$$

$$= 45+\frac{0}{40}\times 10$$

$$= 45$$

$$\text{And M.D. } (\bar{x}) = \frac{1}{N}\sum_{i=1}^{7} f_i\lvert x_i-\bar{x}\rvert$$

$$= \frac{800}{40} = 20$$

22. Calculate the mean deviation from the median of the below data:

44, 48, 52, 54, 56, 73, 80, 58, 64, 65.

Ans. Arranging the data in ascending order, we have

44, 48, 52, 54, 56, 58, 64, 65, 73, 80

Here, $n = 10$

So, median is the mean of 5th and 6th terms

$$\therefore \quad \text{Median } (M)=\left(\frac{56+58}{2}\right)=57$$

We make the table from the given data

Scores (x_i)	Deviation form Median ($x_i - M$)	$\lvert x_i - M\rvert$
44	44 – 57 = –13	13
48	78 – 57 = –9	9
52	52 – 57 = –5	5
54	54 – 57 = –3	3
56	56 – 57 = –1	1
58	58 – 57 = 1	1
64	64 – 57 = 7	7
65	65 – 57 = 8	8
73	73 – 57 = 16	16
80	80 – 57 = 23	23
Total		86

$$\therefore \quad \text{Mean deviation} = \frac{\Sigma\lvert x_i - M\rvert}{n}=\frac{86}{10}=8.6$$

Hence, the mean deviation from the median is 8.6.

23. The frequency distribution:

x	A	2A	3A	4A	5A	6A
F	2	1	1	1	1	1

Where A is a positive integer, has a variance of 160. Determine the value of A.

[NCERT Exemplar]

Ans. Given frequency distribution table, where variance = 160

Now we have to find the value of A, where A is a positive number.

Now, we have to construct a table of the given data

Size (x_i)	Frequency (f_i)	$f_i x_i$	$f_i x_i^2$
A	2	$2A$	$2A^2$
$2A$	1	$2A$	$4A^2$
$3A$	1	$3A$	$9A^2$
$4A$	1	$4A$	$16A^2$
$5A$	1	$5A$	$25A^2$
$6A$	1	$6A$	$36A^2$
Total	7	$22A$	$92A^2$

And we know variance is

$$\sigma = \frac{\Sigma f_i x_i^2}{n} - \left(\frac{\Sigma f_i x_i}{n}\right)^2$$

Substituting values from above table and also given variance = 160, we get

$$160 = \frac{92A^2}{7} - \left(\frac{22A}{7}\right)^2$$

$$160 = \frac{92A^2}{7} - \frac{484A^2}{49}$$

$$160 = \frac{7 \times 92A^2 - 484A^2}{49}$$

$$160 = \frac{644A^2 - 484A^2}{49}$$

$$160 = \frac{160A^2}{49}$$

$\Rightarrow \quad A^2 = 49$

$\Rightarrow \quad A = 7$

Hence, the value of A is 7.

24. Find the mean and variance of the frequency distribution given below:

x	$1 \le x < 3$	$3 \le x < 5$	$5 \le x < 7$	$7 \le x < 10$
f	6	4	5	1

Ans. Given the frequency distribution.

Now we have to find the mean and variance.

Converting the ranges of x to groups, the given table can be rewritten as shown below,

X (class)	f_i	x_i	$f_i x_i$	$f_i x_i^2$
1 – 3	6	2	12	24
3 – 5	4	4	16	64
5 – 7	5	6	30	180
7–10	1	8.5	8.5	72.25
Total	**16**		**66.5**	**340.25**

And we know variance can be written as

$$\sigma = \frac{\Sigma f_i x_i^2}{n} - \left(\frac{\Sigma f_i x_i^2}{n}\right)$$

Substituting values from above table, we get

$$\sigma^2 = \frac{340.25}{16} - \left(\frac{66.5}{16}\right)^2$$

On simplifying we get

$$\sigma^2 = 21.265 - (4.16)^2$$

$$\sigma^2 = 21.265 - 17.305 = 3.96$$

We also know that mean can be written as

$$\bar{x} = \frac{\Sigma f_i x_i}{n}$$

Substituting values from above table, we get

$$\bar{x} = \frac{66.5}{16} = 4.16$$

Hence, the mean and variance of the given frequency distribution are 4.16 and 3.96 respectively.

SHORT ANSWER Type-II Questions (SA-II)

[3 marks]

25. For the frequency distribution:

x	2	3	4	5	6	7
f	4	9	16	14	11	6

Find the standard distribution.

[NCERT Exemplar]

Ans. Now, we have to find the standard deviation.

Let us make a table of the given data and append other columns after calculations

Size (x_i)	Frequency (f_i)	$f_i x_i$	$f_i x_i^2$
2	4	8	16
3	9	27	81
4	16	64	256
5	14	70	350
6	11	66	396
7	6	42	294
Total	**60**	**277**	**1393**

And we know standard deviation is

$$\sigma = \sqrt{\frac{\Sigma f_i x_i^2}{n} - \left(\frac{\Sigma f_i x_i^2}{n}\right)}$$

Substituting values from above table, we get

$$\sigma = \sqrt{\frac{1393}{60} - \left(\frac{277}{60}\right)^2}$$

$$\sigma = \sqrt{23.23 - (4.62)^2}$$

$$\sigma = \sqrt{23.23 - 21.34}$$

$$\Rightarrow \quad \sigma = 1.37$$

Hence, the standard deviation is 1.37.

26. Find the variance and standard deviation for the following distribution:

X:	4.5	14.5	24.5	34.5	44.5	54.5	64.5
f:	1	5	12	22	17	9	4

Ans. Calculation of variance and standard Deviation

x_i	f_i	$d_i = xi - 34.5$	$u_i = \frac{x_i - 345}{10}$	$f_i u_i$	u_i^2	$f_i u_i^2$
4.5	1	-30	-3	-3	9	9
14.5	5	-20	-2	-10	4	20
24.5	12	-10	-1	-12	1	12
34.5	22	0	0	0	0	0
44.5	17	10	1	17	1	17
54.5	9	20	2	18	4	36
64.5	4	30	3	12	9	36
	$N = \Sigma f_i = 70$			$\Sigma f_i u_i = 22$		$\Sigma f_i u_i^2 = 130$

Here $N = 70, \Sigma f_i u_i = 22, \Sigma f_i u_i^2 = 130$ and $h = 10$

$$\therefore \quad \text{var}(X) = h^2 [(\frac{1}{N}\sum f_i u_i^2) - (\frac{1}{N}\sum f_i u_i)^2]$$

$$\Rightarrow \quad \text{Var}(X) = 100\left[\frac{130}{70} - \left(\frac{22}{70}\right)^2\right]$$

$$= 100\left[\frac{13}{7} - \left(\frac{11}{35}\right)^2\right]$$

$$= 100\,[1.857 - 0.098] = 175.822$$

Hence, $S.D. = \sqrt{Var(X)} = \sqrt{175.822} = 13.259$

27. The following table gives the distribution of income of 100 families in a village. Calculate the standard deviation:

Income (₹)	0-1000	1000–2000	2000–3000	3000–4000	4000–5000	5000–6000
No. of Families	18	26	30	12	10	4

Ans. Calculation of standard deviation

Income (₹)	Mid-values x_i	No. of families (frequencies) f_i	$u_i = \frac{x_i - 2500}{1000}$	$f_i u_i$	u_i^2	$f_i u_i^2$
0–1000	500	18	-2	-36	4	72
1000–2000	1500	26	-1	-26	1	26
2000–3000	2500	30	0	0	0	0
3000–4000	3500	12	1	12	1	12
4000–5000	4500	10	2	20	4	40
5000–6000	5500	4	3	12	9	36
		$\Sigma f_i = 100$		$\Sigma f_i u_i = -18$		$\Sigma f_i u_i^2 = 186$

Here, $N = 100$, $\Sigma f_i u_i = -18$, $\Sigma f_i u_i^2 = 186$ and, $h = 1000$

$$\therefore \quad Var(X) = h^2\left\{\frac{1}{N}\left(\Sigma f_i ui^2\right) - \left(\frac{1}{N}\Sigma f_i ui\right)^2\right\}$$

$$= (1000)^2\left\{\frac{186}{100} - \left(\frac{-18}{100}\right)^2\right\}$$

$$= 1827600$$

Hence, $S.D. = \sqrt{Var(X)} = \sqrt{1827600} = 1351.88$

28. If for a distribution of 18 observations, $\Sigma(x_i - 5) = 10$ and $\Sigma(x_i - 5)^2 = 50$, find the mean and standard deviation.

Ans. We have $\sum_{i=1}^{18}(x_i - 5) = 10$ *and* $\sum_{i=1}^{18}(x_i - 5)^2 = 50$

$$\Rightarrow \quad \sum_{i=1}^{18} x_i - \sum_{i=1}^{18} 5 = 10 \text{ and}$$

$$\sum_{i=1}^{18} x_i^2 - 10\sum_{i=1}^{18} x_i + \sum_{i=1}^{18} 25 = 50$$

$$\Rightarrow \quad \sum_{i=1}^{18} x_i - 18 \times 5 = 10 \text{ and,}$$

$$\sum_{i=1}^{18} x_i^2 - 10\sum_{i=1}^{18} x_i - 18 \times 25 = 50$$

$$\Rightarrow \quad \sum_{i=1}^{18} x_i = 100 \text{ and, } \sum_{i=1}^{18} x_i^2 - 10$$

$$\times 100 - 18 \times 25 = 50$$

$$\Rightarrow \quad \sum_{i=1}^{18} x_i = 100 \text{ and, } \sum_{i=1}^{18} x_i^2 = 600$$

$$\therefore \quad \text{Mean} = \frac{1}{18}\sum_{i=1}^{18} x_i = \frac{100}{18} = 5.55$$

$$S.D. = \sqrt{\frac{1}{18}\sum_{i=1}^{18} x_i^2 - (\frac{1}{18}\sum_{i=1}^{18} x_i)^2} = \sqrt{\frac{600}{18} - \left(\frac{100}{18}\right)^2}$$

$$= \sqrt{\frac{10800 - 10000}{324}} = \sqrt{\frac{800}{324}}$$

$$= \sqrt{2.46} = 1.56$$

29. Find the variance and standard deviation of the following frequency distribution:

Variable (x_i)	2	4	6	8	10	12	14	16
Frequency (f_i)	4	4	5	15	8	5	4	5

Ans. Calculation of variance and Standard Deviation

Variable x_i	Frequency f_i	f_ix_i	$x_i - \bar{x} = x_i - 9$	$(x_i - \bar{x})^2$	$f_i(x_i - \bar{x})^2$
2	4	8	–7	49	196
4	4	16	–5	25	100
6	5	30	–3	9	45
8	15	120	–1	1	15
10	8	80	1	1	8
12	5	60	3	9	45
14	4	56	5	25	100
16	5	80	7	49	245
	$N = \Sigma f_i = 50$	$\Sigma f_i x_i = 450$			$\Sigma f_i (x_i - \bar{x})^2 = 754$

Here, $N = 50$, $\Sigma f_i x_i = 450$ and, $\Sigma f_i (x_i - \bar{X})^2 = 754$

$$\therefore \quad \bar{X} = \frac{1}{N}\Sigma f_i x_i = \frac{450}{50} = 9$$

And, $$Var(X) = \frac{1}{N}\left\{\Sigma f_i (x_i - \bar{X})^2\right\} = \frac{754}{50} = 15.08$$

Hence, $$S.D. = \sqrt{Var(X)} = \sqrt{15.08} = 3.88$$

LONG ANSWER Type Questions (LA)

[**4** & **5** marks]

30. There are 60 students in a class. The following is the frequency distribution of the marks obtained by the students in a test:

Marks	0	1	2	3	4	5
Frequency	$x - 2$	x	x^2	$(x + 1)^2$	$2x$	$x + 1$

Where x is a positive integer. Determine the mean and standard deviation of the marks.

[NCERT Exemplar]

Ans. Given there are 60 students in a class. The frequency distribution of the marks obtained by the students in a test is also given.

Now, we have to find the mean and standard deviation of the marks.

It is given there are 60 students in the class, so

$$\Sigma f_i = 60$$

$\Rightarrow$ $(x - 2) + x + x^2 + (x + 1)^2 + 2x + x + 1 = 60$

$\Rightarrow$ $5x - 1 + x^2 + x^2 + 2x + 1 = 60$

$\Rightarrow$ $2x^2 + 7x = 60$

$\Rightarrow$ $2x^2 + 7x - 60 = 0$

Splitting the middle term, we get

$\Rightarrow$ $2x^2 + 15x - 8x - 60 = 0$

$\Rightarrow$ $x(2x + 15) - 4(2x + 15) = 0$

$\Rightarrow$ $(2x + 15)(x - 4) = 0$

$\Rightarrow$ $2x + 15 = 0$ or $x - 4 = 0$

$\Rightarrow$ $2x = -15$ or $x = 4$

Given x is a positive number, so x can take 4 as the only value.

And let assumed mean, $a = 3$

Now put $x = 4$ and $a = 3$ in the frequency distribution table and add other columns after calculation, we get

Marks (x_i)	Frequency (f_i)	$d_i = x_i - a$	$f_i d_i$	$f_i d_i^2$
0	$x - 2 = 4 - 2$	–3	–6	18
1	$x = 4$	–2	–8	16
2	$x^2 = 4^2 = 16$	–1	–16	16
3	$(x + 1)^2 = 25$	0	0	0
4	$2x = 8$	1	8	8
5	$x + 1 = 5$	2	10	20
Total	**60**		**–16**	**78**

And we know standard deviation is

$$\sigma = \sqrt{\frac{\Sigma f_i d_i^2}{n} - \left(\frac{\Sigma f_i d_i}{n}\right)^2}$$

Substituting values from the above table, we get

$$\sigma = \sqrt{\frac{78}{60} - \left(\frac{-16}{60}\right)^2}$$

$$\sigma = \sqrt{1.3 - 0.07}$$

$\Rightarrow$ $\sigma = 1.10$

Hence the standard deviation is 1.10.

Now mean is

$$\bar{x} = A + \frac{\Sigma f_i d_i}{N} = 3 + \left(-\frac{12}{60}\right)$$

$$= 3 - \frac{1}{5} = \frac{14}{5} = 2.8$$

Hence, the mean and standard deviation of the marks are 2.8 and 1.10 respectively.

31. Determine mean and standard deviation of first *n* terms of an *A.P.* whose first term is *a* and common difference is *d*. **[NCERT Exemplar]**

Ans. Given first n term of an *A.P.* whose first term is *a* and common difference is *d*.

Now, we have to find mean and standard deviation.

The given *A.P.* in tabular form is as shown below,

x_i	$d_i = x_i - a$	d_i^2
a	0	0
$a + b$	d	d^2
$a + 2d$	$2d$	$4d^2$
$a + 3b$	$3d$	$9d^2$
—	—	—
$a + (n - 1)$	$(n - 1)d$	$(n - 1)^2 d^2$

Here we have assumed *a* as mean.

Given the *A.P.* have *n* terms, and we know the sum of all the terms of *AP* can be written as

$$\Sigma x_i = \frac{n}{2}[2a + (n-1)d]$$

Now we will calculate the actual mean,

$$\bar{x} = \frac{\Sigma x_i}{n}$$

Substituting the corresponding values, we get

$$\bar{x} = \frac{\frac{n}{2}[2a + (n-1)d]}{n}$$

The above equation can be written as

$$\bar{x} = \frac{[2a + (n-1)d]}{2}$$

$$\bar{x} = a + \frac{[(n-1)d]}{2}$$

$$\bar{x} = a + \frac{(n-1)}{2}d$$

We also have,

$$\Sigma d_i = \Sigma(x_i - a) = d[1 + 2 + 3 + ... + (n - 1)]$$

$$= d\left(\frac{n(n-1)}{2}\right)$$

$$\Sigma d_i^2 = \Sigma(x_i - a)^2 = d^2 [1^2 + 2^2 + 3^2 + ... + (n - 1)^2]$$

$$= d^2\left(\frac{n(n-1)(2n-1)}{6}\right)$$

Now we know standard deviation is given by

$$\sigma = \sqrt{\frac{\Sigma(x_i - a)^2}{n} - \left(\frac{\Sigma(x_i - a)^2}{n}\right)}$$

Substituting the corresponding values, we get

$$\sigma = \sqrt{\frac{d^2\left(\frac{n(n-1)(2n-1)}{6}\right)}{n} - \left(\frac{d\left(\frac{n(n-1)}{2}\right)}{n}\right)^2}$$

$$\sigma = \sqrt{d^2\left(\frac{n(n-1)(2n-1)}{6n}\right) - d^2\left(\frac{n^2(n-1)^2}{4n^2}\right)}$$

Cancelling the like terms, we get

$$\sigma = \sqrt{d^2\left(\frac{(n-1)(2n-1)}{6}\right) - d^2\left(\frac{(n-1)^2}{4}\right)}$$

Taking out common terms we get

$$\sigma = \sqrt{\left(\frac{d^2(n-1)}{2}\right)\left(\frac{(2n-1)}{3} - \frac{n-1}{2}\right)}$$

By taking the LCM, we get

$$\sigma = \sqrt{\left(\frac{d^2(n-1)}{2}\right)\left(\frac{2(2n-1) - 3(n-1)}{6}\right)}$$

$$\sigma = \sqrt{\left(\frac{d^2(n-1)}{2}\right)\left(\frac{2(2n-1) - 3(n-1)}{6}\right)}$$

$$\sigma = \sqrt{\left(\frac{d^2(n-1)}{2}\right)\left(\frac{n+1}{6}\right)}$$

$$\sigma = d\sqrt{\frac{(n^2 - 1)}{12}}$$

Hence, the mean and standard deviation of the given *A.P.* is

$$a + \frac{(n-1)}{2}d \text{ and } d\sqrt{\frac{(n^2-1)}{12}} \text{ respectively.}$$

32. Find the standard deviation of the first *n* natural numbers. **[NCERT Exemplar]**

Ans. Given set of first n natural numbers:

Now, we have to find the standard deviation.

Given first *n* natural numbers, we can write in table as shown below

So, the sums of these are

$$\Sigma x_i = 1 + 2 + 3 + ... + n = \frac{n(n+1)}{2}$$

And

$$\Sigma x_i^2 = 1^2 + 2^2 + 3^3 + ... + n^2 = \frac{n(n+1)(2n+1)}{6}$$

Therefore, the standard deviation can be written as,

$$\sigma = \sqrt{\frac{\Sigma x_i^2}{n} - \left(\frac{\Sigma x_i}{n}\right)^2}$$

Substituting the values we get

$$\sigma = \sqrt{\frac{\frac{n(n+1)(2n+1)}{6}}{n} - \left(\frac{\frac{n(n+1)}{2}}{n}\right)^2}$$

On simplifying

$$\sigma = \sqrt{\frac{n(n+1)(2n+1)}{6n} - \frac{n^2(n+1)^2}{4n^2}}$$

$$\sigma = \sqrt{\frac{n(2n+1)+1(2n+1)}{6} - \frac{(n^2+2n+1)}{4}}$$

Multiplying the numerator we get

$$\sigma = \sqrt{\frac{2n^2+n+2n+1}{6} - \frac{n^2+2n+1}{4}}$$

Taking *LCM* and simplifying we get

$$\sigma = \sqrt{\frac{2(2n^2+3n+1)-3(n^2+2n+1)}{12}}$$

$$\sigma = \sqrt{\frac{4n^2+6n+2-3n^2-6n-3}{12}}$$

$$\sigma = \sqrt{\frac{n^2-1}{12}}$$

Hence, the standard deviation of the first n natural numbers is $\sqrt{\frac{n^2-1}{12}}$.

33. The mean and standard deviation of some data for the time taken to complete a test are calculated with the following results: Number of observation = 25, mean = 18.2 seconds, standard deviation =3.25 seconds. Further, another set of 15 observation $x_1, x_2, ..., x_{15}$ also in seconds, is now available and we have

$$\sum_{i=1}^{15} x_i = 279 \quad \text{and} \quad \sum_{i=1}^{15} x_i^2 = 5524$$

Calculate the standard derivation based on all 40 observations. [NCERT Exemplar]

Ans. Given Number of observation = 25, mean = 18.2 seconds, standard deviation = 3.25 seconds. Another set of 15 observation $x_1, x_2, ..., x_{15}$ also in seconds, is $\sum_{i=1}^{15} x_i = 279$ and $\sum_{i=1}^{15} x_i^2 = 5524$

Now, we have to find the standard derivation based on all 40 observation.

As per the given criteria,

In first set,

Number of observation, $n_1 = 25$

Mean, $\bar{x}_1 = 18.2$

And standard deviation, $\sigma_1 = 3.25$

And

In second set,

Number of observation, $n_2 = 15$

$$\sum_{i=1}^{15} x_i = 279 \text{ αvδ } \sum_{i=1}^{15} x_i^2 = 5524$$

For the first set we have

$$\bar{x}_1 = 18.2 = \frac{\Sigma x_i}{25}$$

$$\Sigma x_i = 25 \times 18.2 = 455$$

Therefore the standard deviation becomes,

$$\sigma_1^2 = \frac{\Sigma x_i^2}{25} - (18.2)^2$$

Substituting the values, we get

$$(3.25)^2 = \frac{\Sigma x_1^2}{25} - 331.24$$

$$\Rightarrow \; 10.5625 + 331.24 = \frac{\Sigma x_i^2}{25}$$

Rearranging we get

$$\Rightarrow \; \frac{\Sigma x_i^2}{25} = 341.8025$$

On cross multiplication we get

$\Rightarrow \; \Sigma x_1^2 = 25 \times 341.8025 = 8545.06$

For the combined standard deviation of the 40 observation, $n = 40$

And

$\Rightarrow \; \Sigma x_i^2 = 8545.06 + 5524 = 14069.06$

$\Rightarrow \; \Sigma x_i = 455 + 279 = 734$

Therefore the standard deviation can be written as,

$$\sigma = \sqrt{\frac{\Sigma x_i^2}{n} - \left(\frac{\Sigma x_i}{n}\right)^2}$$

Substituting the values, we get

Therefore the standard deviation can be written as,

$$\sigma = \sqrt{\frac{14069.06}{40} - \left(\frac{734}{40}\right)^2}$$

On simplifying we get

$$\sigma = \sqrt{351.7265 - (18.35)^2}$$

$$\sigma = \sqrt{351.7265 - 336.7225}$$

$$\sigma = \sqrt{15.004}$$

$$\sigma = 3.87$$

Hence, the mean standard deviation based on all 40 observations is 3.87.

34. The mean and standard deviation of a set of n_1 observation are $\bar{x}_1$ and s_1, respectively while the mean and standard deviation of another set of n_2 observations are x_2 and s_2, respectively. Show that the standard deviation of the combined set of $(n_1 + n_2)$ observation is given by

$$\sqrt{\frac{n_1(s_1)^2 + n_2(s_2)^2}{n_1 + n_2} + \frac{n_1 n_2(\bar{x}_1 - \bar{x}_2)^2}{(n_1 + n_2)}}$$

Ans. Given the mean and standard deviation of a set of n_1 observations are $\bar{x}_1$ and s_1, respectively while the mean and standard deviation of another set of n_2 observations are $\bar{x}_2$ and s_2, respectively.

To show that the standard deviation of the combined set of $(n_1 + n_2)$ observations is given by

$$\sqrt{\frac{n_1(s_1)^2 + n_2(s_2)^2}{n_1 + n_2} + \frac{n_1 n_2(\bar{x}_1 - \bar{x}_2)^2}{(n_1 + n_2)^2}}$$

As per given criteria,

For first set

Let x_i where $i = 1, 2, 3, 4, ..., n_1$

For second set

And y_i where $j = 1, 2, 3, 4, ..., n_2$

And the means are

$$\bar{x}_1 = \frac{1}{n_1}\sum_{i=1}^{n} x_i, \bar{x}_2 = \frac{1}{n_2}\sum_{j=1}^{n} y_j$$

Now mean of the combined series is given by

$$\bar{x} = \frac{1}{n_1 + n_2} = \left[\sum_{i=1}^{n} x_i = \sum_{j=1}^{n} y_j\right] = \frac{n_1\bar{x}_1 + n_2\bar{x}_2}{n_1 + n_2} \quad ...(i)$$

And the corresponding square of standard deviation is

$$\sigma_1^2 = \frac{1}{n_1}\sum_{i=1}^{n}(x_i - \bar{x}), \sigma_2^2 = \frac{1}{n_2}\sum_{j=1}^{n}(y_j - \bar{x})^2$$

Therefore, square of standard deviation becomes,

$$\sigma^2 = \sigma_1^2 + \sigma_2^2$$

$$= \frac{1}{n_1 + n_2}\left[\sum_{i=1}^{n}(x_i - \bar{x})^2 \sum_{j=1}^{n}(y_j - \bar{x})^2\right] \quad ...(ii)$$

Now,

$$\sum_{i=1}^{n}(x_i - \bar{x})^2 = \sum_{i=1}^{n}(x_i - \bar{x}_j + \bar{x}_j - \bar{x})^2$$

$$\sum_{i=1}^{n}(x_i - \bar{x})^2 = \sum_{i=1}^{n}(x_i - \bar{x}_j)^2 + n_1(\bar{x}_j - \bar{x})^2 + 2(\bar{x}_j - \bar{x})^2 \sum_{i=1}^{n}(x_i - \bar{x}_j)^2$$

But the algebraic sum of the deviation of values of first series from their mean is zero.

$$\sum_{i=1}^{n}(x_i - x_j)^2 = 0$$

Also,

$$\sum_{i=1}^{n}(x_i - \bar{x})^2 = n_1 s_1^2 + n_1\left(\bar{x}_1 - \bar{x}\right)^2 \quad ...(iii)$$

But

$$d_1 = \bar{x}_1 - \bar{x}$$

Substituting value from equation (i), we get

$$\bar{x}_1 - \bar{x} = \bar{x}_1 - \frac{n_1\bar{x}_1 + n_2\bar{x}_2}{n_1 + n_2}$$

$$\bar{x}_1 - \bar{x} = \frac{(\bar{x}_1)(n_1 + n_2) - (n_1\bar{x}_1 + n_2\bar{x}_2)}{n_1 + n_2}$$

$$\bar{x}_1 - \bar{x} = \frac{(n_1\bar{x}_1 + n_2\bar{x}_1) - (n_1\bar{x}_1 + n_2\bar{x}_2)}{n_1 + n_2}$$

$$\bar{x}_1 - \bar{x} = \frac{(n_2\bar{x}_1) - (n_2\bar{x}_2)}{n_1 + n_2}$$

Substituting this value in equation (iii), we get

$$\sum_{i=1}^{n}(x_i - \bar{x})^2 = n_1 s_1^2 + n_1\left(\frac{n_1(\bar{x}_1 - \bar{x}_2)}{n_1 + n_2}\right)^2$$

$$\sum_{i=1}^{n}(x_i - \bar{x})^2 = n_1 s_1^2 + \frac{n_1 n_2^2(\bar{x}_1 - \bar{x}_2)^2}{(n_1 + n_2)^2} \quad ...(iv)$$

Similarly, we have

$$\sum_{j=1}^{n}(y_i - \bar{x})^2 = \sum_{j=1}^{n}(y_j - \bar{x}i + \bar{x}_i - \bar{x})^2$$

$$\sum_{j=1}^{n}(y_j - \bar{x})^2 = \sum_{j=1}^{n}(y_j - \bar{x}_j)^2 + n_2(\bar{x}_j - \bar{x})^2 + 2(\bar{x}_j - \bar{x})\sum_{j=1}^{n}(y_j - \bar{x}_j)^2$$

But the algebraic sum of the deviation of values of the second series from their mean is zero.

$$\sum_{j=1}^{n}(y_j - \bar{x}_i)^2 = 0$$

Also,

$$\sum_{j=1}^{n}(y_j-\bar{x})^2=n_2 s_2^2+n_2\left(\bar{x}_2-\bar{x}\right)^2 \quad ...(v)$$

But $d_2=\bar{x}_2-\bar{x}$

Substituting value from equation (i), we get

$$x_2-\bar{x}=\bar{x}_2-\frac{n_1\bar{x}_1+n_2\bar{x}_2}{n_1+n_2}$$

$$x_2-\bar{x}=\frac{(\bar{x}_2)(n_1+n_2)-(n_1\bar{x}_1+n_2\bar{x}_2)}{n_1+n_2}$$

$$\bar{x}_2-\bar{x}=\frac{(n_1\bar{x}_2+n_2\bar{x}_2)-(n_1\bar{x}_1+n_2\bar{x}_2)}{n_1+n_2}$$

$$\bar{x}_2-\bar{x}=\frac{(n_1\bar{x}_2)-(n_1\bar{x}_2)}{n_1+n_2}$$

$$\bar{x}_2-\bar{x}=\frac{n_1(\bar{x}_2-\bar{x}_1)}{n_1+n_2}$$

Substituting this value in equation (v), we get

$$\sum_{j=1}^{n}(y_j-\bar{x})^2=n_2s_2^2+n_2\left(\frac{n_1(\bar{x}_2-\bar{x}_1)}{n_1+n_2}\right)^2$$

$$\sum_{j=1}^{n}(y_j-\bar{x})^2=n_2s_2^2+\frac{n_2n_1^2(\bar{x}_2-\bar{x}_1)^2}{(n_1+n_2)^2} \quad ...(vi)$$

Substituting equation (iv) and (vi) i nequation (ii), we get

$$\sigma^2=\sigma_1^2+\sigma_2^2$$

$$=\frac{1}{n_1+n_2}\left[\sum_{i=1}^{n}(x_i-\bar{x})^2+\sum_{j=1}^{n}(y_j-\bar{x})^2\right]$$

$$\sigma^2=\frac{1}{n_1+n_2}\left[n_1s_1^2+\frac{n_1n_2^2(\bar{x}_1-\bar{x}_2)^2}{(n_1+n_2)^2}+n_2s_2^2+\frac{n_2n_1^2(\bar{x}_2-\bar{x}_1)^2}{(n_1+n_2)^2}\right]$$

$$\sigma^2=\frac{1}{n_1+n_2}\left[n_1s_1^2+n_2s_2^2+\frac{n_1n_2^2(\bar{x}_1-\bar{x}_2)^2}{(n_1+n_2)^2}+\frac{n_2n_1^2(-(\bar{x}_1-\bar{x}_2))^2}{(n_1+n_2)^2}\right]$$

$$\sigma^2=\frac{1}{n_1+n_2}\left[n_1s_1^2+n_2s_2^2+\frac{n_1n_2^2(\bar{x}_1-\bar{x}_2)^2}{(n_1+n_2)^2}+\frac{n_2n_1^2(\bar{x}_1-\bar{x}_2)^2}{(n_1+n_2)^2}\right]$$

$$\sigma^2=\frac{1}{n_1+n_2}\left[n_1s_1^2+n_2s_2^2+\frac{n_1n_2(\bar{x}_1-\bar{x}_2)^2}{(n_1+n_2)^2}(n_2+n_1)\right]$$

$$\sigma^2=\left[\frac{n_1s_1^2+n_2s_2^2}{n_1+n_2}+\frac{\frac{n_1n_2(\bar{x}_1-\bar{x}_2)^2}{(n_1+n_2)^2}(n_2+n_1)}{n_1+n_2}\right]$$

$$\sigma^2=\left[\frac{n_1s_1^2+n_2s_2^2}{n_1+n_2}+\frac{n_1n_2(\bar{x}_1-\bar{x}_2)^2}{(n_1+n_2)^2}\right]$$

So the combined standard deviation

$$S.D.(\sigma)=\sqrt{\frac{n_1s_1^2+n_2s_2^2}{n_1+n_2}+\frac{n_1n_2(\bar{x}_1-\bar{x}_2)^2}{(n_1+n_2)^2}}$$

Hence proved.

14 Probability

A probability forecast is a percentage-based evaluation of the likelihood of an occurrence occurring, as well as a record of the hazards connected with weather. Meteorologists utilize a variety of devices and technologies to forecast weather changes throughout the world. They compile a global weather prediction database to anticipate temperature changes and likely weather conditions for a certain hour, day, week, and month.

Topic Notes

- *Event and Algebra of Events*

EVENT AND ALGEBRA OF EVENTS

TOPIC 1

EVENT

Event

A subset of the sample space associated with a random experiment is called an event, generally denoted by 'E'.

An event associated with a random experiment is said to occur, if any one of the elementary events associated to it is an outcome of the experiment.

For eg: Suppose a die is thrown, the sample space

$S = \{1,2,3,4,5,6\}$. Then,

$E = \{2,3,4\}$ is an event.

Also, if the outcome of the experiment is, 4. Then we say that event E has occurred.

Occurrence of an Event

An event associated with a random experiment is said to occur, if any one of the elementary events associated to it is an outcome of the experiment.

e.g. suppose a die is thrown and let A be an event of getting an even number.

Then,

$$A = \{2,4,6\}$$

Types of Events

On the basis of the element in an event, events are classified into the following types:

Simple Event

If an event has only one sample point of the sample space, it is called a simple (element) event.

E.g., Let a die is thrown, then sample space,

$S = \{1,2,3,4,5,6\}$

Then, $A = \{4\}$ and $B = \{6\}$ are simple events.

Compound Event

If an event has more than one sample point of the sample space, then it is called a compound event.

E.g., on rolling a die, we have the sample space,

$S = \{1,2,3,4,5,6\}$

Then, $E = \{2,4,6\}$, F = the event of getting an odd number are compound events.

Sure Event

The event which is certain to occur is said to be the sure event. The whole sample 'S' is a sure or certain event, since it is a subset of itself.

E.g., on throwing a die, we have sample space,

$S = \{1,2,3,4,5,6\}$

Then, E = Event of getting a natural number less than 7, is a sure event, since $E = \{1,2,3,4,5,6\} = S$

Impossible Event

The event which has no element is called an impossible event or null event. The empty set 'ϕ' is an impossible event, since it is a subset of sample space S.

E.g., on throwing a die, we have the sample space,

$S = \{1, 2, 3, 4, 5, 6\}$

Then E = event of getting a number less than 1, is an impossible event, since $E = \phi$.

Equally Likely Events

Events are called equally likely when we do expect the happening of one event in preference to the other.

In general, events $E_1, E_2, ..., E_n$ be n subsets of a sample space S. Then, events $E_1, E_2, ..., E_n$ are exhaustive events, if $E_1 \cup E_2 \cup E_3 \cup ... \cup E_n = S$

E.g., consider the experiment of throwing a die. Then, S = {1, 2, 3, 4, 5, 6}

Let E_1 = event of getting a number less than 3.

E_2 = event of getting an odd number.

E_3 = event of getting a number greater than 3.

Then, $E_1 = \{1, 2\}$, $E_2 = \{1, 3, 5\}$, $E_3 = \{4, 5, 6\}$

Thus, $E_1 \cup E_2 \cup E_3 = S$. Hence, E_1, E_2, E_3 are exhaustive events.

Example 1: A die is thrown. Describe the following events:

(A) A : a number less than 7

(B) B : a number greater than 7

(C) C : a multiple of 3

(D) D : a number less than 4

(E) E : an even number greater than 4

(F) F : a number not less than 3

Ans. (A) If the die is thrown,

Possible outcomes are 1,2,3,4,5,6

$S = \{1,2,3,4,5,6\}$

A : a number less than 7

A = {1,2,3,4,5,6}

(B) $S = \{1,2,3,4,5,6\}$

There is no number greater than 7

Hence, $B = \phi$

(C) Possible multiple of 3 are 3, 6

Hence, C = {3,6}

(D) $S = \{1,2,3,4,5,6\}$

D : a number less than 4.

Numbers less than 4 are 1,2,3.

Hence, $D = \{1,2,3\}$

(E) $S = \{1,2,3,4,5,6\}$

E : an even number greater than 4

Even number greater than 4 is 6 only

Hence, $E = \{6\}$

(F) $S = \{1,2,3,4,5,6\}$

F : a number not less than 3

Number not less than 3 are 3, 4, 5 and 6

Hence, $F = \{3,4,5,6\}$

Example 2: Using the value of example 1; find

(A) $A \cup B$	**(B) $B \cup C$**	**(C) $A \cap B$**
(D) $E \cap F$	**(E) $D \cap E$**	**(F) $D - E$**
(G) $A - C$	**(H) F'**	**(I) $E \cap F'$**

(A) $A \cup B$ $A = \{1,2,3,4,5,6\}$ $B = \phi$ $A \cup B = \{1,2,3,4,5,6\} \cup \phi$ $= \{1,2,3,4,5,6\}$	(B) $B \cup C$ $B = \phi$ $C = \{3, 6\}$ $B \cup C = \phi \cup \{3,6\}$ $= \{3, 6\}$
(C) $A \cap B$ $A = \{1, 2, 3, 4, 5, 6\}$ $B = \phi$ $A \cap B = \{1,2,3,4,5,6\} \cup \phi$ $= \phi$	(D) $E \cap F$ $E = \{6\}$ $F = \{3,4,5,6\}$ $E \cap F = \{6\} \cap \{3,4,5,6\}$ $=\{6\}$
(E) $D \cap E$ $D = \{1,2,3\}$ $E = \{6\}$ $D \cap E = \{1,2,3\} \cap \{6\}$ $= \phi$	(F) $D - E$ $D = \{1,2,3\}$ $E = \{6\}$ $D - E = \{1,2,3\} - \{6\}$ $= \{1,2,3\}$
(G) $A - C$ $A = \{1,2,3,4,5,6\}$ $C = \{3,6\}$ $A - C = \{1,2,3,4,5,6\} - \{3,6\}$ $=\{1,2,4,5\}$	(H) F' $F = \{3,4,5,6\}$ $S = \{1,2,3,4,5,6\}$ $F' = S - F$ $= \{1,2,3,4,5,6\} - \{3,4,5,6\}$ $=\{1,2\}$
(I) $E \cap F'$ $E = \{6\}$ $F' = \{1,2\}$ $E \cap F' = \{6\} \cap \{1,2\}$ $= \phi$	

Algebra of Events

Let A and B be two events associated with a sample space S, then:

Complementary Event

For every E, there corresponds another event E' called the complementary event of E, which consists of those outcomes that do not correspond to the occurrence of E. E' is also called the event 'not E'.

E.g., In tossing three coins, the sample space is

$S = \{HHH, HHT, HTH, HTT, THH, THT, TTH, TTT\}$

Let $E = \{THT, TTH, HTT\}$ = the event of getting only one head.

Then, $E' = \{HHT, HTH, THH, TTT, HHH\}$.

The Event A or B

The event 'A or B' is same as the event $A \cup B$ and it contains all those elements which are either in event A or in B or in both. Thus,

A or $B = A \cup B = \{x : x \in A \text{ or } x \in B\}$

The Event A and B

The event 'A and B' is same as the event '$A \cap B$' and it contains all those elements which are both in A and B. Thus,

A and $B = A \cup B \{x : x \in A \text{ and } x \in B\}$

The Event A but not B

The event A but not B is the same as the event $A - B = (A \cap B')$ and it contains all those elements which are in A but not in B.

Then, A but not in $B = A - B = \{x : x \in A \text{ or } x \notin B\}$.

Events Equivalent Sets

The following are some events and their corresponding equivalent sets.

(1) Neither A nor B

$\underline{A} \cap \underline{B}$ or $U - (A \cap B)$ [U – universal set]

(2) Exactly one of A and B

$(A \cap \underline{B}) \cup (\underline{A} \cap B)$ or $(A \cap B) - (A \cap B)$

(3) At least one of A, B or C

$A \cup B \cup C$

(4) All three of A, B and C

$A \cap B \cap C$

(5) Exactly two of A, B and C

$(A \cap B \cap \underline{C}) \cup (A \cap \underline{B} \cap C) \cup (\underline{A} \cap B \cap C)$

Mutually Exclusive Events

Two events are said to be mutually exclusive, if the occurrence of any one of them excludes the occurrence of the other event, i.e., they cannot occur simultaneously.

Thus, two events N_1 and N_2 are said to be mutually exclusive, If $N_1 \cap N_2 = \phi$.

e.g., on throwing a die, we have the sample space $S = \{1,2,3,4,5,6\}$

Let N_1 = Event of getting even numbers = $\{2,4,6\}$

And N_2 = Event of getting odd number = $\{1,3,5\}$

Then, $N_1 \cap N_2 = \phi$.

So, N_1 and N_2 are mutually exclusive events.

Exhaustive Events

For a random experiment, a set of events is said to be exhaustive, if one of them necessarily occurs whenever the experiment is performed. Let $N_1, N_2, N_3, ..., N_n$ be n subsets of a sample space S. Then, events $N_1, N_2, N_3, ..., N_n$ are called exhaustive events, if $N_1 \cup N_2 \cup E_3 \cup ... \cup N_n = S$

e.g., Consider the experiment of throwing a die. We have,

$S = \{1,2,3,4,5,6\}$. Let us define the following events

N_1 : A number less than 4 appears.

N_2 : A number greater than 2 but less than 5 appears.

N_3 : A number greater than 4 appears.

Then, $E_1 = \{1,2,3\}$, $E_2 = \{3, 4\}$, $E_3 = \{5,6\}$

We observe that

$E_1 \cup E_2 \cup E_3 = \{1,2,3\} \cup \{3,4\} \cup \{5,6\} = S$

Thus, the events E_1, E_2 and E_3 are exhaustive events.

Important

- *A sample spaces is called a discrete sample space, if S is a finite set.*
- *We can define as many events as these are subsets of a sample space. Thus, the number of events of a sample space S is 2^n, where 'n' is the number of elements in S.*
- *Elementary events associated with a random experiments are also known as in decomposable events.*
- *All events other than elementary events and impossible events associated with a random experiment are called compound events.*
- *For any event E, associated with a sample space S, E' = not $E = S - E = \{\omega : \omega \in S \text{ and } \omega \notin E\}$.*
- *Simple events of a sample space are always mutually exclusive.*
- *If $E \cap E_j = \in$ for, $i \neq j$ i.e., events E_i and E_j are pair wise disjoint and $E_i \cup E_2 \cup ... \cup E_n = S$., then events $E_1, E_2, ..., E_n$ are called mutually exclusive and exhaustive events.*

TOPIC 2

AXIOMATIC APPROACH TO PROBABILITY

Probabilities of Equally Likely Outcomes

All the outcomes are said to be equal if the chances of occurrence of each simple event is the same.

Let S be the sample space of an experiment

$S = \{e_1, e_2, e_3, e_4, ..., e_n\}$

i.e., $P(e_1) = \phi$ for all $e_1 \in S$ where $O \leq PS$.

Since, $\sum_i^n = 1\ P(e_1) = 1$

i.e., $p + p + p ... p$ (ntimes) = 1

Or $np = 1$ i.e., $-p = \frac{1}{n}$

Example 3: A coin is tossed twice, what is the probability that at least one tail occurs?

Ans. When 2 coins are tossed,

Sample Space = $S = \{HH, HT, TH, HT\}$

$n(S) = 4$

Let A be the event that at least 1 tail occurs

Hence $A = \{HT, TH, TT\}$

$n(A) = 3$

$$P(A) = \frac{\text{Number of outcomes favourable to A}}{\text{Total number of possible outcomes}}$$

$$= \frac{n(A)}{n(S)}$$

$$= \frac{3}{4}$$

Probability of the Event 'A' or B' / Addition Rule of Probability

If N and M are two events associated with a random experiment, then

$P(N \cup M) = P(N) + P(M) - P(N \cap M)$

i.e., $P(N \text{ or } M) = P(N) + P(M) - P(N \text{ and } M)$

It is known as the additional law of probability for two events.

Also,

(i) when events N and M are mutually exclusive, then $P(N \cup M) = P(N) + P(M)$

(ii) when events N and M are mutually exclusive and exhaustive, then $P(N \cup M) = P(N) + P(M) = 1$

e.g., If $P(N) = \frac{4}{5}$ and $P(M) = \frac{7}{15}$

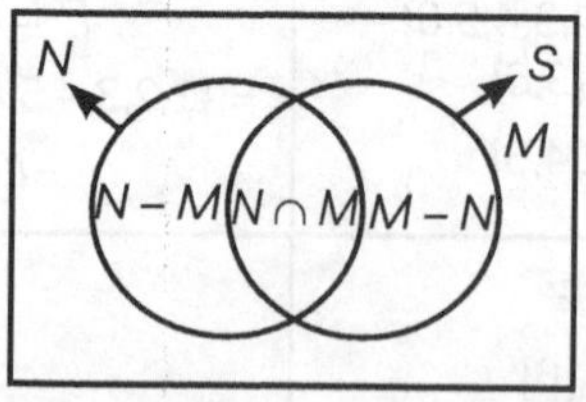

Example 4: If E and F are events such that $P(E) = \frac{7}{15}$, $P(F) = \frac{1}{2}$ and $P(E \text{ and } F) = \frac{1}{8}$, find:

(A) *P(E or F)*　　**(B) *P(not E and not F)***

Ans. (A) $P(E \text{ and } F) = P(E \cap F) = \frac{1}{8}$

We need to find

$P(E \text{ or } F) = P(E \cup F)$

We know that

$P(E \cup F) = P(E) + P(F) - P(E \cap F)$

Putting values

$$P(E \cup F) = \frac{1}{4} + \frac{1}{2} - \frac{1}{8}$$

$$= \frac{2+4-1}{8}$$

$$= \frac{6-1}{8}$$

$$= \frac{5}{8}$$

(B) $P(\text{not } E \text{ and not } F)$

$= P(E' \cap F')$

$= P(E \cup F)'$

$= 1 - P(E \cup F)$

Demorgan's law
If $(A' \cap B') = (A \cup B)'$
or $(A' \cup B') = (A \cap B)'$

(By Demorgan law)

$$= 1 - \frac{5}{8}$$

$$= \frac{8-5}{8}$$

$$= \frac{3}{8}$$

Probability of Event 'not A'

N is the event of drawing card from a deck of ten cards numbered from 1 to 10.

Let *S* be the sample space, $S = \{1, 2, 3, ..., 10\}$

If all the outcomes 1, 2, ..., 10 are considered to be equally likely, then the probability of each outcome is $\frac{1}{10}$.

Now, $P(N) = P(2) + P(4) + P(6) + P(8)$

$$= \frac{1}{10} + \frac{1}{10} + \frac{1}{10} + \frac{1}{10}$$

$$= \frac{4}{10} = \frac{2}{5}$$

Also event 'not *N*' $= N' = \{1, 3, 5, 7, 9, 10\}$

Now, $P(N') = P(1) + P(3) + P(5) + P(7) + P(9) + P(10)$

$$= \frac{6}{10} = \frac{3}{5}$$

Thus, $P(N') = \frac{3}{5}$

$P(N') = 1 - P(A) = \frac{2}{5}$

Important

N and N' are mutually exclusive and exhaustive events.

i.e., $N \cap N' = \phi$ *and* $N \cup N' = S$

or $P(N \cup N') = P(S)$

$P(N) + P(N') = 1$

$P(N') = P(\text{not } N) = 1 - P(N)$

Example 5: Three coins are tossed once. Find the probability of getting

(A) 3 tails **(B) exactly two tails**

(C) no tails **(D) at most two tails**

Ans. (A) 3 tails

Let F be the event of getting 3 tails.

$F = \{TTT\}$

$n(F) = 1$

Probability of getting 3 tails = $P(F)$

$$= \frac{n(F)}{n(S)}$$

$$= \frac{1}{8}$$

(B) Exactly two tails

Let *G* be the event of getting exactly 2 tails

$G = \{HTT, THT, TTH\}$

$n(G) = 3$

Probability of getting exactly two tails = $P(G)$

$$= \frac{n(G)}{n(S)}$$

$$= \frac{3}{8}$$

(C) *no tail*

Let *H* be the event of getting no tail

$H = \{HHH\}$

$n(H) = 1$

Probability of getting no tails = $P(H)$

$$= \frac{n(H)}{n(S)}$$

$$= \frac{1}{8}$$

(D) At most two tails

Let *I* be the event of getting at most 2 tails.

i.e., getting 0 tails, 1 tail or 2 tail

$I = \{HHH, HHT, HTH, THH, HTT, THT, TTH\}$

$n(I) = 7$

Probability of getting at most tails = $P(I)$

$$= \frac{n(I)}{n(S)}$$

$$= \frac{7}{8}$$

Example 6: **From the employees of a company, 5 persons are selected to represent them in the managing committee of the company. Particulars of five persons are as follows:**

S. No	Name	Sex	Age in years
1.	Harish	M	30
2.	Rohan	M	33
3.	Sheetal	F	46
4.	Alis	F	28
5.	Salim	M	41

A person is selected at random from this group to act as a spokesperson. What is the probability that the spokesperson will be either male or over 35 years?

Ans. Total number of persons =5

So, $n(S) = 5$

Probability spokesperson is male

There are 3 males

So, $n(A) = 5$

Probability spokesperson is male = $P(A)$

$$= \frac{n(A)}{n(S)}$$

$$= \frac{3}{5}$$

Probability spokesperson is over 35 years old

Let B be the event that person selected is over 35

There are 2 person over 35 years old.

So, $n(B) = 2$

Probability that the spokesperson is over 35 years old = $P(B)$

$$= \frac{n(B)}{n(S)}$$

$$= \frac{2}{5}$$

We need to find Probability that the spokesperson will be either male or over 35 years = $P(A \cup B)$

We know that

$$P(A \cup B) = P(A) + P(B) - P(A \cap B)$$

To find $P(A \cup B)$,

we must find $P(A \cap B)$ first.

Probability that spokesperson is male and over 35 years old

Here, 1 person is both male and over 35 years old.

So, $n(A \cap B) = 1$

$$P(A \cap B) = \frac{n(A \cap B)}{n(S)}$$

$$= \frac{1}{5}$$

Now,

$$P(A \cup B) = P(A) + P(B) - P(A \cap B)$$

$$= \frac{3}{5} + \frac{2}{5} - \frac{1}{5}$$

$$= \frac{3+2-1}{5}$$

$$= \frac{4}{5}$$

Hence, Probability that the spokesperson will be either male or over 35 years

$$= P(A \cup B)$$

$$= \frac{4}{5}$$

Example 7: **Check whether the following probabilities are consistently defined.**

(A) $P(A) = 0.5, P(B) = 0.7, P(A \cap B) = 0.6$

(B) $P(A) = 0.5, P(B) = 0.4, P(A \cup B) = 0.8$

Ans. (A) To be consistently defined $P(A \cap B)$ should be less than or equal to $P(A)$ and also P(B) but here $P(A \cap B) > P(A)$ {Here, 0.6 > 0.5}. Hence, not consistent.

(B) Using, $P(A \cup B) = P(A) + P(B) - P(A \cap B)$

$$P(A \cap B) = P(A) + P(B) - P(A \cup B)$$

$\Rightarrow$ $P(A \cap B) = 0.5 + 0.4 - 0.8$

$= 0.1$, which is true since it is less than $P(A)$ and $P(B)$

$\therefore$ The given probabilities are consistently defined.

Example 8: **Fill in the blanks in following table:**

	$P(A)$	$P(B)$	$P(A \cap B)$	$P(A \cup B)$
(A)	$\frac{1}{3}$	$\frac{1}{5}$	$\frac{1}{15}$	?
(B)	0.35	?	0.25	0.6
(C)	0.5	0.35	?	0.7

Ans. (A) Here, $P(A) = \frac{1}{3}$, $P(B) = \frac{1}{5}$, $P(A \cap B) = \frac{1}{15}$,

$P(A \cup B) = ?$

We know,

$$P(A \cup B) = P(A) + P(B) - P(A \cap B)$$

$$= \frac{1}{3} + \frac{1}{5} - \frac{1}{15}$$

$$= \frac{8}{15} - \frac{1}{15}$$

$$= \frac{7}{15}$$

(B) Here, $P(A) = 0.35$, $P(B) = ?$, $P(A \cap B) = 0.25$, $P(A \cup B) = 0.6$

We know,

$$P(A \cup B) = P(A) + P(B) - P(A \cap B)$$

$$\Rightarrow P(B) = P(A \cup B) + P(A \cap B) - P(A)$$

$$= 0.6 + 0.25 - 0.35$$

$$= 0.85 - 0.35$$

$$= 0.5$$

(C) Here, $P(A) = 0.5$, $P(B) = 0.35$, $P(A \cup B) = 0.7$, $P(A \cap B) = ?$

We know,

$$P(A) + P(B) - P(A \cap B) = P(A \cup B)$$

$$\Rightarrow P(A \cap B) = P(A) + P(B) - P(A \cup B)$$

$$= 0.5 + 0.35 - 0.7 = 0.15$$

Example 9: If E and F are events such that $p(E') = \frac{1}{4}$, $p(F') = \frac{1}{2}$ and $P(E \text{ and } F) = \frac{1}{8}$, find

(A) $P(E \text{ or } F)$ **(B) $P(\text{not } E \text{ and not } F)$.**

Ans. Given, $P(E') = \frac{1}{4}$, $p(F') = \frac{1}{2}$, $p(E \cap F) = \frac{1}{8}$

(A) We know: $P(E \text{ or } F) = P(E \cup F)$

Thus, using, $P(E \cup F) = P(E) + P(F) - P(E \cap F)$

$$= \frac{1}{4} + \frac{1}{2} - \frac{1}{8}$$

$$= \frac{3}{4} - \frac{1}{8}$$

$$= \frac{5}{8}$$

(B) $P(\text{not } E \text{ and not } F) = P(E' \cap F')$

Also, $P(E' \cap F') = P(E \cup F)'$

[From Demorgan law]

$$= 1 - P(E \cup F)$$

$$= 1 - \frac{5}{8}$$

$$= \frac{3}{8}$$

OBJECTIVE Type Questions

[**1** mark]

Multiple Choice Questions

1. A box contains 1 red and 3 identical blue balls. Two balls are drawn at random in succession without replacement. Then, the sample space for this experiment is:

(a) {RB,BR,BB} (b) {R, B, B}
(c) {RB} (d) {RB, BR}

Ans. *(a) {RB, BR, BB}*

Explanation:

Let red ball is denoted by R and blue ball is denoted by B. Now, two balls drawn at random in succession without replacement.

Then, the sample space is S = {RB, BR, BB}

Hence, option (a) is the correct answer.

2. Find the probability that when a hand of 7 cards are drawn from the well-shuffled deck of 52 cards, it contains all kings.

(a) $\frac{2}{7735}$ (b) $\frac{1}{7735}$
(c) $\frac{3}{7753}$ (d) $\frac{1}{7753}$ [DIKSHA]

Ans. *(b)* $\frac{1}{7735}$

Explanation: Total cards to be drawn = 7

So sample space contains = $^{52}C_7$

$$P(S) = \frac{52!}{7! \times 45!}$$

There are only 4 kings, so 3 cards come from remaining ones.

So, $P(A) = {^{48}C_3}$

$$= \frac{48!}{3! \times 45!}$$

Hence probability = $\frac{P(A)}{P(S)}$

$$= \frac{48!}{3! \times 45!} \times \frac{7! \times 45!}{52!}$$

$$= \frac{1}{7735}$$

Hence, option (b) is the correct answer.

3. A coin is tossed repeatedly until a head comes up for the first time. Then, the sample space for this experiment is:

(a) {H, TH, TTH}

(b) {HH, HHH, TTH, HTT}

(c) {H, TH, TTH, TTTH, TTTTH, ...}

(d) None of these

Ans. *(c) {H, TH, TTH, TTTH, TTTTH, ...}*

Explanation:

The sample space is

S = {*H, TH, TTH, TTTH, TTTTH*, ...}

Hence, option (c) is the correct answer.

4. A pair of dice is rolled, if the outcome is sum 12, a coin is tossed. Then, the total number of outcomes for this experiment is:

(a) 40 **(b) 38**

(c) 41 **(d) 43**

Ans. *(b) 38*

Explanation:

The sample space associated with the given random experiment is

S = {(1,1), (1,2), (1,3), (1,4), (1,5), (1,6), (2,1), (2,2), (2,3), (2,4), (2,5), (2,6),

(3,1), (3,2), (3,3), (3,4), (3,5), (3,6), (4,1), (4,2), (4,3), (4,4), (4,5), (4,6), (5,1)

(5,2), (5,3), (5,4), (5,5), (5,6), (6,1), (6,2), (6,3), (6,4), (6,5), (6,6), (6,6,*H*), (6,6,T)}

Hence, total number of sample points =38

Hence, option (b) is the correct answer.

5. A bag contains 4 identical red balls and 3 identical black balls. The experiment consists of drawing one ball, then putting it into the bag and again drawing a ball. Then, the possible outcomes of this experiment is:

(a) {RR, BB} **(b) {RR, B, B, RR}**

(c) {BB, R} **(d) {RR, RB, BR, BB}**

Ans. *(d) {RR, RB, BR, BB}*

Explanation: The sample space for this experiment is

S = {*RR, RB, BR, BB*}, where *R* denotes the red balls and *B* denotes the black ball.

Hence, option (d) is the correct answer.

6. A fair coin with 1 marked on one face and 6 on the other and a fair die are both tossed. Find the probability that the sum of numbers that turn up is 3.

(a) 1/6 **(b) 1/12**

(c) 2/3 **(d) 1/4** **[DIKSHA]**

Ans. *(b) 1/12*

Explanation: *S* = {(1,1) (1,2) (1,3) (1,4) (1,5) (1,6) (6,1) (6,2) (6,3) (6,4) (6,5) (6,6)}

Total events in sample space is 12

Now probability to come sum as 3 is (1,2) = $\frac{1}{12}$

Hence, option (b) is the correct answer.

7. Three coins (a Rs 2 coin, a Rs 10 coin and a Rs 5 coin) are tossed once. The total number of elements in sample space is:

(a) 4 **(b) 8**

(c) 3 **(d) 11**

Ans. *(b) 8*

Explanation:

The sample space is

S = {*HHH, HHT, HTH, HTT, THH, THT, TTH, TTT*}

i.e 8

Hence, option (b) is the correct answer.

8. A couple has two children, find the probability that both children are males, if it is known that at least one of the children is male.

(a) 2/3 **(b) 1/3**

(c) 4/5 **(d) 5/3** **[DIKSHA]**

Ans. *(b) 1/3*

Explanation: *S* = {*MM, MF, FM, FF*}

Total sample space is 4.

E : Both children are males.

F : atleast one child is male

E = {(*M, M*)}

F = {(*M, F*) (*F, M*) (*M, M*)}

$$P(E) = \frac{1}{4}$$

$$P(F') = \frac{3}{4}$$

$$P(E \cap F) = \frac{1}{4}$$

$$P(E/F) = \frac{\frac{1}{4}}{\frac{3}{4}} = \frac{1}{3}$$

Hence, option (*b*) is the correct answer.

Assertion-Reason (A-R)

DIRECTION: In the following questions, a statement of assertion (A) is followed by a statement of the reason (R). Mark the correct choice as:

(a) Both assertion (A) and reason (R) are true and reason (R) is the correct explanation of assertion (A).

(b) Both assertion (A) and reason (R) are true but reason (R) is not the correct explanation of assertion (A).

(c) Assertion (A) is true but reason (R) is false.

(d) Assertion (A) is false but reason (R) is true.

9. Assertion (A): A coin is tossed. If it shows head, we draw a ball from a bag consisting of 3 brown and 4 red balls; if it shows tail we throw a die, then the sample space of this experiment is *S* = {HB_1, HB_2, HB_3, HR_1, HR_2, HR_3, HR_4, *T1, T2, T3, T4, T5, T6*}.

Reason (R): **Consider the experiment in which a coin is tossed repeatedly until a head comes up, then the sample space is S = {H, TH, TTH, TTTH, ...}.**

Ans. *(b) Both assertion (A) and reason (R) are true but reason (R) is not the correct explanation of assertion (A).*

Explanation: Let us denote brown balls by B_1, B_2, B_3 and the red balls by R_1, R_2, R_3, R_4. Then, a sample space of the experiment is $S = \{HB_1, HB_2, HB_3, HR_1, HR_2, HR_3, HR_4, T1, T2, T3, T4, T5, T6\}$.

In the experiment, head may come up on the 1st toss, or the 2nd toss, or the 3rd toss and so on till head is obtained. Hence, the desired sample space is

$S = \{H, TH, TTH, TTTH, TTTTH, ...\}$.

10. Assertion (A): **A coin is tossed and then a die is rolled only in case a head is shown on the coin. The sample space for the experiment is**

$S = \{H1, H2, H3, H4, H5, H6, T\}$.

Reason (R): **2 boys and 2 girls are in room X, and 1 boy and 3 girls are in room Y. Then, the sample space for the experiment in which a room is selected and then a person, is**

$S = \{XB_1, XB_2, XG_1, XG_2, YB_3, YG_3, YG_4, YG_5\}$.

where B_i, denote the boys and Gj, denote the girls.

Ans. *(b) Both assertion (A) and reason (R) are true but reason (R) is not the correct explanation of assertion (A).*

Explanation: The sample space is

$S = \{H_1, H_2, H_3, H_4, H_5, H_6, T\}$

Where, H and T represents head and tail respectively of a coin.

When the room x is selected, then

X	Y
B_1, B_2 G_1, G_2	B_3 G_3, G_4, G_5

There are four possibilities for selection of a person which are B_1, B_2, G_1, G_2, similarly, there will be four possibilities for room Y.

So, the sample space is

$S = \{XB_1, XB_2, XG_1, XG_2, YB_3, YG_3, YG_4, YG_5\}$

11. Consider the experiment of rolling a die. Then, sample space is S = {1, 2, 3, 4, 5, 6}.

Assertion (A): **The event E :" the number appears on the die is a multiple of 7", is an impossible event.**

Reason (R): **The event F :" the number turns up is odd or even", is a sure event.**

Ans. *(b) Both assertion (A) and reason (R) are true but reason (R) is not the correct explanation of assertion (A).*

Explanation: Given, E be the event "the number appears on the die is a multiple of 7". It is impossible to have a multiple of 7 on the upper face of the die. Thus, the event $E = \phi$ is an impossible event.

The another event F is "the number turns up is odd or even". Clearly, $F = \{1,2,3,4,5,6\} = S$, i.e., all possible outcomes of the experiment ensure the occurrence of the event F. Thus, the event F is a sure event.

12. Assertion (A): **If sample space of an experiment is S = {1,2,3,4,5,6} and the events A and B are defined as**

A: "a number less than or equal to 3 appears"

B: "a number greater than or equal to 3 appears"

Then A and B are exhaustive events.

Reason (R): **Events are exhaustive if atleast one of them necessarily occurs whenever the experiment is performed.**

Ans. *(a) Both assertion (A) and reason (R) are true and reason (R) is the correct explanation of assertion (A).*

Explanation: We have A = {1, 2, 3} and B = {3, 4, 5, 6}

Since $A \cup B = S$, so, A and B are exhaustive events.

13. Assertion (A): **The probability of drawing either an ace or a king from a pack of cards in a single draw is $\frac{2}{13}$.**

Reason (R): **For two events A and B which are not mutually exclusive, $P(A \cup B) = P(A) + P(B) - P(A \cap B)$.**

Ans. *(b) Both assertion (A) and reason (R) are true but reason (R) is not the correct explanation of assertion (A).*

Explanation: *P* (Drawing either an ace or a king) = $\frac{4}{52}+\frac{4}{52}$

$= \frac{2}{13}$

($\because$ Both events are mutually exclusive)

If two events *A* and *B* are not mutually exclusive, then $P(A \cup B) = P(A) + P(B) - P(A \cap B)$.

CASE BASED Questions (CBQs)

[**4** & **5** marks]

Read the following passages and answer the questions that follow:

14. *One card is drawn from a well shuffled deck of 52 cards. Each outcome is equally likely.*

(A) The probability that the card will be a heart is:

(a) $\frac{1}{4}$ (b) $\frac{1}{2}$

(c) $\frac{3}{4}$ (d) $\frac{1}{52}$

(B) The probability that the card will be a black card is:

(a) $\frac{1}{4}$ (b) $\frac{1}{2}$

(c) $\frac{3}{4}$ (d) $\frac{1}{52}$

(C) The probability that the card will be an ace of spade is:

(a) $\frac{1}{4}$ (b) $\frac{1}{2}$

(c) $\frac{3}{4}$ (d) $\frac{1}{52}$

(D) The probability that the card will be a king of red color is:

(a) $\frac{1}{52}$ (b) $\frac{1}{26}$

(c) $\frac{1}{13}$ (d) $\frac{1}{39}$

(E) The probability that the card will be a face card is:

(a) $\frac{3}{13}$ (b) $\frac{4}{13}$

(c) $\frac{2}{13}$ (d) None of these

Ans. (A) *(a)* $\frac{1}{4}$

Explanation: Total number of possible outcomes = 52

Probability of drawing a heart card = $\frac{13}{52}=\frac{1}{4}$

Hence, option (a) is the correct answer.

(B) *(b)* $\frac{1}{2}$

Explanation: Probability of drawing a black card = $\frac{26}{52}=\frac{1}{2}$

Hence, option *(b)* is the correct answer.

(C) *(d)* $\frac{1}{52}$

Explanation: Probability of drawing an ace of spade = $\frac{1}{52}$.

Hence, option *(d)* is the correct answer.

(D) *(b)* $\frac{1}{26}$

Explanation: Probability of drawing a king of red color = $\frac{2}{52}=\frac{1}{26}$

Hence, option *(b)* is the correct answer.

(E) *(a)* $\frac{3}{13}$

Explanation: Cards of king, queen and jack are called face cards and there are four suits, namely, heart, diamond, club and spade.

Probability of drawing a face card = $\frac{12}{52}=\frac{3}{13}$

Hence, option (a) is the correct answer.

15. *On a Diwali's night, four members of a family plan to play a Ludo game. Head of the family is act as an initiator of the game. He throws a coin and a die.*

(A) Find the number of sample points and probability of getting a head.

(B) Find the probability of getting and odd number and also find the probability of getting a head and an even number.

Ans. (A) When a coin and a die are thrown, the sample space, *S*, is given by

S = {*H*1,*H*2,*H*3,*H*4,*H*5,*H*6,*T*1,*T*2,*T*3,*T*4,*T*5,*T*6}

The number of sample pointsis 12.

Probability of getting a head = $\frac{6}{12}=\frac{1}{2}$

(B) Probability of getting an odd number $= \frac{6}{12} = \frac{1}{2}$

Probability of getting a head and an even number $= \frac{3}{12} = \frac{1}{4}$

VERY SHORT ANSWER Type Questions (VSA)

[1 mark]

16. Brother, Sister and Father are lined up for a family picture. Find the sample space.

Ans. $S = \{BSF, SBF, FBS, BFS, FSB, SFB\}$

17. Events E and F are such that $P($ not E or not $F) = 0.25$, state whether E and F are mutually exclusive. [DIKSHA]

Ans. From the question it is given that, $P($not E and not $F) = 0.25$

So, $P(\underline{E} \cup \underline{F}) = 0.25$

Then we have,

$\Rightarrow \quad P(\underline{E} \cap \underline{F}) = 0.25$

$\Rightarrow \quad 1 - P(E \cap F) = 0.25$

$\Rightarrow \quad P(E \cap F) = 1 - 0.25$

$= 0.75$

$P(E \cap F) \neq 0$

Hence, E and F are not mutually exclusive events.

18. A biased coin with both side head and a fair dice is rolled, find the sample space.

Ans. $S = \{H1, H2, H3, H4, H5, H6\}$

19. 2 Boys and 2 Girls are in room A and 1 Boy and 2 Girls are in room B. Find the sample space in which room is selected and then a person.

Ans. Let B_1, B_2, G_1, G_2 are in room A and B_3, G_3, G_4 are in room B, then

$S = \{AB_1, AB_2, AG_1, AG_2, BB_3, BG_3, BG_4\}$ are the sample space.

20. A coin is tossed four times. Find the sample space. [DIKSHA]

Ans. Since either coin can turn up Head (H) or Tail (T), are the possible outcomes.

So, when 1 coin is tossed once the sample space = 2

Then,

Coin is tossed 4 times the sample space = 2^4 = 16

Thus, the sample space is $S = \{HHHH, THHH, HTHH, HHTH, HHHT, TTTT, HTTTT, THTT, TTHT, TTTH, TTHH, HHTT, THTH, HTHT, THHT, HTTH\}$

21. If the letters of the word 'ALGORITHM' are arranged at random in a row, what is the probability the letter 'GOR' must remain together as a unit? [NCERT Exemplar]

Ans. Number of letters in the word 'ALGORITHM' are 9 if 'GOR' remain together, then considered it as 1 number.

$\therefore$ Number of letters = 6 + 1 = 7

Number of word, if 'GOR' remain together = 7!

Total number of words from the letters of the word 'ALGORITHM' = 9!

$\therefore$ Required probability

$$= \frac{7!}{9!} = \frac{7!}{9 \times 8 \times 7!} = \frac{1}{9 \times 8} = \frac{1}{72}$$

SHORT ANSWER Type-I Questions (SA-I)

[2 marks]

22. A die is loaded in such a way that each odd number is twice as likely to occur as each even number. Find $P(G)$, where G is the event that a number greater than 3 occurs on a single roll of the die. [NCERT Exemplar]

Ans. It is given that, 2× Probability of even number = Probability of odd number

$\Rightarrow \quad P(A) = 2P(B)$

Let (A odd number, B even number)

$\Rightarrow \quad P(A) : P(B) = 2 : 1$

$\therefore$ Probability of occuring, odd number,

$$P(A) = \frac{2}{2+1} = \frac{2}{3}$$

And probability of occurring even number,

$$P(B) = \frac{2}{2+1} = \frac{1}{3}$$

Now, G be the even that a number greater than 3 occur in a single roll of die.

So, the possible outcomes are 4, 5 and 6 out of which two are even and one odd.

$\therefore$ Required probability = $P(G) = 2 \times P(A) \times P(B)$

$$= 2 \times \frac{2}{3} \times \frac{1}{3} = \frac{4}{9}$$

23. If E and F are events such that $P(E) = \frac{1}{4}$, $P(F) = \frac{1}{2}$ and $P(E \text{ and } F) = \frac{1}{8}$, find

(A) P(E or F), (B) P(not E and not F)

[DIKSHA]

Ans. From the question, we have $P(E) = \frac{1}{4}, P(F) = \frac{1}{2}$ and $P(E \cap F) = \frac{1}{8}$ and

(A) P(E or F)

i.e., $P(E \cup F) = P(E) + P(F) - P(E \cap F)$

$$= \frac{1}{4} + \frac{1}{2} - \left(\frac{1}{8}\right)$$

$$= \frac{5}{8}$$

(B) $P(\text{not } E \text{ and not } F) = P(\bar{E} \cap \bar{F}) = 1 - P(E \cup F)$

$$= 1 - \left(\frac{5}{8}\right)$$

$$= \frac{(8-5)}{8}$$

$$= \frac{3}{8}$$

24. Find P (not A and not B), If A and B are two events such that $P(A) = \frac{1}{6}$, $P(B) = \frac{1}{2}$ and $P(A \cap B) = \frac{1}{12}$.

Ans. $P(\text{not } A \text{ and not } B) = P(\bar{A} \cap \bar{B})$

$= 1 - P(A \cup B)'$

$= 1 - P(A) - P(B) + P(A \cap B)$

$$= 1 - \frac{1}{6} - \frac{1}{2} + \frac{1}{12}$$

$$= \frac{5}{12}$$

25. In a large metropolitan area, the probabilities are 0.87,0.36,0.30 that a family (randomly chosen for a sample survey) owns a colour television set, a black and white television set or both kinds of sets. What is the probability that a family owns either anyone or both kinds of sets? [NCERT Exemplar]

Ans. Let E_1 be the event that family own colour television set and E_2 be the event that family own Black and White television.

It is given that

$$P(E_1) = 0.87$$
$$P(E_2) = 0.36$$

And $P(E_1 \cap E_2) = 0.30$

We have to find probability that a family owns either anyone or both kind of sets i.e., $p(E_1 \cup E_2)$.

Now, $P(E_1 \cup E_2) = P(E_1) + P(E_2) - P(E_1 \cap E_2)$

[by addition theorem]

$= 0.87 + 0.36 - 0.30$

$= 0.93$

26. A coin is tossed and then a die is rolled only in case a head is shown on the coin. Find the total sample space when tail is encountered. [DIKSHA]

Ans. Since either coin can turn up Head (H) or Tail (T), are the possible outcomes.

Let us assume that 1,2,3,4,5 and 6 are the possible numbers that come when the die is thrown.

When head in encountered,

Then, number of space = (1 × 6) = 6

Sample space S_H = {H1, H2, H3, H4, H5, H6}

Now, tail is encountered, sample space S_T = {T}

Therefore the total sample space S = {H1, H2, H3, H4, H5, H6, T}

SHORT ANSWER Type-II Questions (SA-II)

[3 marks]

27. Six new employees, two to whom are married to each other, are to be assigned six desks that are lined up in a row. If the assignment of employees to desks is made randomly, what is the probability that the married couple will have non-adjacent desks? [NCERT Exemplar]

Ans. Let the couple occupied adjacent desks, consider those two as 1.

There are, (4 + 1) i.e., 5 persons to be assigned.

∴ Number of ways of assigning these five persons = 5! × 2!

Total number of ways of assigning 6 persons =6!

∴ Probability that the couple has adjacent desk $= \frac{5! \times 2!}{6!} = \frac{1}{3}$

Probability that the married couple will have non-adjacent desks $= 1 - \frac{1}{3} = \frac{2}{3}$

28. One card is drawn from a pack of 52 cards. Find the probability that the card is:

(A) a face cards. (B) not a diamond.

(C) an ace.

Ans. Total number of cards =52.

Number of cards drawn = 1.

(A) Number of favourable cases that the card is a face card =12.

Hence, required probability = $\frac{12}{52}=\frac{3}{13}$.

(B) Number of favourable cases that the card is not a diamond = 39.

Hence, required probability = $\frac{39}{52}=\frac{3}{4}$.

(C) Number of favourable cases that the card is an ace =4.

Hence, required probability = $\frac{4}{52}=\frac{1}{13}$.

29. There are four men and six women on the city council. If one council member is selected for a committee at random, how likely is it that she is a woman? [DIKSHA]

Ans. From the question, it is given that there are four men and six women on the city council.

Here, the total members in the council = 4 + 6 = 10

Hence, the sample space has 10 points

$\therefore$ $n(S) = 10$

Number of women are 6. ... (given)

Let us assume 'A' be the event of selecting a woman.

Then $n(A) = 6$

P(Event) = Number of outcomes favourable to event/Total number of possible outcomes

$\therefore$ $P(A) = \frac{n(A)}{n(S)}$

$= \frac{6}{10}$

[divide both numerator and denominator by 2]

$= \frac{3}{5}$

30. An experiment consists of a rolling a die until a 2 appears.

(A) How many elements of the sample space correspond to the event that the 2 appears on the kth roll of the die?

(B) How many elements of the sample space correspond to the event that the 2 appears not later than the kth roll of the die? [NCERT Exemplar]

Ans. In a throw of a die there are 6 sample points.

(A) If 2 appears on the kth roll of the die.

So, first (k – 1) roll have 5 outcomes each and k^{th} roll results 2 i.e., 1 outcomes.

$\therefore$ Number of element of sample space correspond to the die, then 2 appears on the kth roll of the die = 5^{k-1}.

$k-1$

(B) If we consider that 2 appears not later than k^{th} roll of the die, then it is possible that 2 comes in first throw, i.e., 1 outcome.

31. A bag contains 8 red and 5 white balls. Three balls are drawn at random. Find the probability that

(A) all the three balls are white

(B) all the three balls are red

(C) one ball is red and two balls are white [NCERT Exemplar]

Ans. $\because$ Number of red balls =8

And number of white balls =5

(A) P (all the three balls are white)

$$= \frac{^5C_3}{^{13}C_3} = \left(\frac{\frac{5\times4}{2}}{\frac{13\times12\times11}{3\times2}}\right)$$

$$= \frac{5\times4\times3}{13\times12\times11} = \frac{5}{143}$$

(B) P (all the three balls are red)

$$= \frac{^8C_3}{^{13}C_3} = \left(\frac{\frac{8\times7\times6}{3\times2\times1}}{\frac{13\times12\times11}{3\times2\times1}}\right)$$

$$= \frac{8\times7\times6}{13\times12\times11} = \frac{28}{143}$$

(C) P (one ball is red and two balls are white)

$$= \frac{^8C_1\times{^5C_2}}{^{13}C_3} = \frac{8\times10}{13\times2\times11} = \frac{40}{143}$$

LONG ANSWER Type Questions (LA)

[**4** & **5** marks]

32. Two dice are rolled, A is the event that the sum of the numbers on the two dice is 6 and B is the event that at least one of the dice shows 4. Are the two events A and B (A) mutually exclusive? (B) exhaustive?

Ans. When two dice are rolled, sample space is

$S = \{(1,1), (1,2), (1,3), (1,4), (1,5), (1,6), (2,1), (2,2), (2,3), (2,4), (2,5), (2,6), (3,1), (3,2), (3,3), (3,4), (3,5), (3,6), (4,1), (4,2), (4,3), (4,4), (4,5), (4,6), (5,1), (5,2), (5,3), (5,4), (5,5), (5,6), (6,1), (6,2), (6,3), (6,4), (6,5), (6,6)\}$.

$A = \{(2,4), (3,3), (4,2), (5,1), (1,5)\}$

$B = \{(1,4), (2,4), (4,1), (4,2), (4,4), (3,4), (4,5), (4,6), (4,3), (5,4), (6,4)\}$

$A \cap B = \{(2,4), (4,2)\}$ and $A \cup B \neq S$.

(A) A and B are not mutually exclusive.

(B) A and B are not exhaustive.

33. If an integer from 1 through 1000 is chosen at random, then find the probability that the integer is a multiple of 2 or a multiple of 9.

Ans. Multiple of 2 from 1 to 1000 are 2, 4, 6, 8, ..., 1000.

Let n be the number of terms of above series 1 to 1000.

$\therefore \quad l = 1000$

$\Rightarrow \quad 2 + (n-1)2 = 1000$

$\{l = a + (n-1)d, a = 2, d = 2\}$

$\Rightarrow \quad 2(n-1) = 998$

$\Rightarrow \quad n - 1 = 499$

$\Rightarrow \quad n = 500$

$$p(A) = \frac{500}{1000}$$

$l = 999$

$a = 9, d = 9$

These are m numbers.

Since, the number of multiples of 2 are 500.

So, the multiple of 9 are 9,18,27, ..., 999

$\therefore \quad 9 + (m-1) = 999$

$\Rightarrow \quad 9(m-1) = 990$

$\Rightarrow \quad m - 1 = 110$

$\therefore \quad m = 111$

$$P(B) = \frac{111}{1000}$$

Since, the number of multiple of 9 are 111, now the multiple of 2 and 9 both are 18,36, ..., 990

Let p be the number of terms in the above series.

$\therefore \quad p^{th}$ term $= 990$

$\Rightarrow \quad 18 + (p-1)\,18 = 990$

$\Rightarrow \quad (p-1)\,18 = 972$

$\Rightarrow \quad p - 1 = 54$

$\Rightarrow \quad p = 55$

and $p(A \cap B) = \dfrac{55}{1000}$

Required probability

$= p(A) + p(B) - p(A \cap B)$

$$\frac{500+111-55}{1000} = \frac{556}{1000}$$

34. Three coins are tossed once. Find the probability of getting

(A) 3 heads (B) 2 heads

(C) at least 2 heads (D) at most 2 heads

(E) no head [DIKSHA]

Ans. Since either coin can turn up Head (H) or Tail (T), are the possible outcomes.

But, now three coin is tossed so the possible sample space contains,

$S = \{HHH, HHT, HTH, THH, TTH, HTT, TTT, THT\}$

Where s is sample space and here $n(S) = 8$

(A) 3 heads

Let us assume 'A' be the event of getting 3 heads

$n(A) = 1$

$$\therefore \quad P(A) = \frac{n(A)}{n(S)} = \frac{1}{8}$$

(B) 2 heads

Let us assume 'B' be the event of getting 2 heads

$n(A) = 3$

$$\therefore \quad P(B) = \frac{n(B)}{n(S)} = \frac{3}{8}$$

(C) at least 2 heads

Let us assume 'C' be the event of getting at least 2 head

$n(C) = 4$

$$\therefore \quad P(B) = \frac{n(C)}{n(S)} = \frac{4}{8} = \frac{1}{2}$$

(D) at most 2 heads

Let us assume 'D' be the event of getting at most 2 heads

$N(D) = 7$

$$\therefore \quad P(D) = \frac{n(D)}{n(S)} = \frac{7}{8}$$

(E) no head

Let us assume 'E' be the event of getting no heads

$$n(E) = 1$$

$$\therefore \quad P(E) = \frac{n(E)}{n(S)}$$

$$= \frac{1}{8}$$

35. If the length of the 'ASSASSINATION' are arranged at random. Find the probability that

(A) four S's come consecutively in the word.

(B) two I's and two N's come together.

(C) all A's are not coming together.

(D) no two A's are coming together.

[NCERT Exemplar]

Ans. Total number of letters in the word 'ASSASSINATION' are 13.

Out of which $3A'$S, $4S's$, $2I's$, $1T's$ and 10.

(A) If four S's come consecutively in the word, then we considered these $4S's$ as 1 group Now, the number of letters is 10.

S	S	S	S	A	A	A	I	I	N	N	T	0
1				9								

Number of words all $S's$ are together

$$= \frac{10!}{3!2!2!}$$

Total number of words using letters of the word 'ASSASSINATION'

$$= \frac{13!}{3!4!2!2!}$$

$$\therefore \text{ Required probability} = \frac{10!}{3!2!2!} \times \frac{3!4!2!2!}{13!}$$

$$= \frac{10! \times 4!}{13!} = \frac{4!}{13 \times 12 \times 11}$$

$$= \frac{24}{1716} = \frac{2}{143}$$

(B) If $2I's$ and $2N's$ come together, then there as 10 alphabets.

Number of word when $2I's$ and $2N's$ are come together.

$$= \frac{10!}{3!4!} \times \frac{4!}{2!2!}$$

$$\therefore \text{ Required probability} = \frac{\frac{10!4!}{3!4!2!2!}}{\frac{13!}{3!4!2!2!}}$$

$$= \frac{4!10!}{2!2!3!4!} \times \frac{3!4!2!2!}{13!}$$

$$= \frac{4!10!}{13!} = \frac{4!}{13 \times 12 \times 11}$$

$$= \frac{24}{13 \times 12 \times 11} = \frac{2}{143}$$

(C) If all A's are coming together, then there are 11 alphabets Number of words when all A's come together $= \frac{11!}{4!2!2!}$

Probability when all A's come together

$$= \frac{\frac{11!}{4!2!2!}}{\frac{13!}{4!3!2!2!}} = \frac{11!}{4!2!2!} \times \frac{4!3!2!2!}{13!}$$

$$= \frac{11! \times 3!}{13!} = \frac{6}{13 \times 12} = \frac{1}{26}$$

Required probability when all A's does not come together

$$= 1 - \frac{1}{26} = \frac{25}{26}$$

(D) If no two A's are together, then first we arrange the alphabets except A's.

	S		S		S		S		I		N		T		I		O		N	

All the alphabets except A's are arranged in $\frac{10!}{4!2!2!}$.

There are 11 vacant places between these alphabets.

So, $3A's$ can be place in 11 places in ${}^{11}C_3$ ways $= \frac{11!}{3!8!}$

$\therefore$ Total number of words when no two A's together

$$= \frac{11!}{3!8!} \times \frac{10!}{4!2!2!}$$

$$\text{Required probability} = \frac{11! \times 10!}{3!8!4!2!} \times \frac{4!3!2!2!}{13!}$$

$$= \frac{10!}{8! \times 13 \times 12}$$

$$= \frac{10 \times 9}{13 \times 12} = \frac{90}{156} = \frac{15}{26}$$